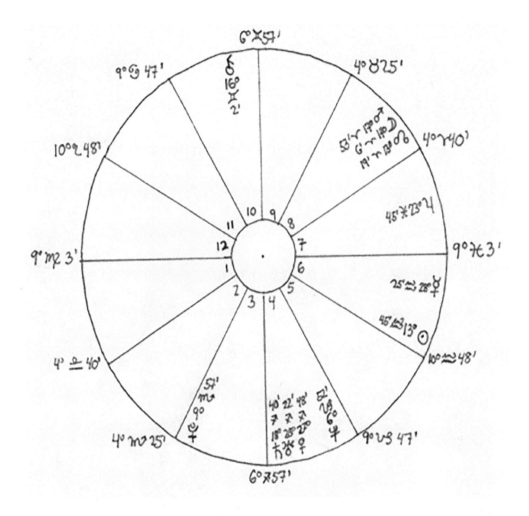

BIRTH CHART OF DOSAJNA

February 2nd, 1987

Anaheim, California

Longitude: 117° W 55'

Latitude: 33° N 50'

19:21 LOCAL TIME

03:21 (Feb 3rd) UNIVERSAL TIME

4:20:27 SIDERIAL TIME

Astrology For The New Century

DOSAJNA

PERMISSIONS

All images within this book are either created by the author or used commercially with permission via Creative Commons licenses. Respective licenses are notated with corresponding image when needed.

All charts and ephemerids were compiled using software designed and owned by Astrodienst AG at the website ASTRO.COM. Written permission has been granted for commercial use.

COVER IMAGE
File:After Jacques Callot, Frontispiece for the Sacred Cosmologia (Title With Astrologers), NGA 52062.jpg"
by after Jacques Callot is marked with CC0 1.0

Bolder-Atlas by Brockhaus, printed in 1849, an antique drawing of vintage astrological spheres and charts and diagrams. Digitally enhanced from our own original lithograph. by Free Public Domain Illustrations by rawpixel is licensed with CC BY 2.0. To view a copy of this license, visit https://creativecommons.org/licenses/by/2.0/"

ANEWPRESS

CHEAT SHEET

PLANETS

PLANET	GLYPH	FULL CYCLE
SUN	☉	360 DAYS
MOON	☽	27-28 DAYS
MERCURY	☿	0.24 YRS
VENUS	♀	0.67 YRS
MARS	♂	1.88 YRS
JUPITER	♃	12 YRS
SATURN	♄	29.5 YRS
URANUS	♅	84 YRS
NEPTUNE	♆	165 YRS
PLUTO	♇	248 YRS

SIGNS OF THE ZODIAC

SIGN	GLYPH	RULER	EXALTATION	DETTRIMENT	FALL
ARIES	♈	♂	☉	♀	♄
TAURUS	♉	♀	☽	♂	NONE
GEMINI	♊	☿	NONE	♃	NONE
CANCER	♋	☽	♃	♄	♂
LEO	♌	☉	NONE	♄	NONE
VIRGO	♍	☿	☿	♃	♀
LIBRA	♎	♀	♄	♂	☉
SCORPIO	♏	♂ & ♇	NONE	♀	☽
SAGITTARIUS	♐	♃	NONE	☿	NONE
CAPRICORN	♑	♄	♂	☽	♃
AQUARIUS	♒	♄ & ♅	NONE	☉	NONE
PISCES	♓	♃ & ♆	♀	☿	☿

MAJOR ASPECTS

DIVISION	NAME	GLYPH
0°	CONJUNCTION	☌
60°	SEXTILE	⚹
90°	SQUARE	□
120°	TRINE	△
180°	OPPOSITION	☍

NORTH AMERICAN TIME CONVERSIONS FROM UT

TIME ZONE	STANDARD TIME (ST)	DAYLIGHT SAVING TIME (DST)
PACIFIC	-08:00 PT	-07:00 PDT
MOUNTAIN	-07:00 MT	-06:00 MDT
CENTRAL	-06:00 CT	-05:00 CDT
EASTERN	-05:00 ET	-04:00 EDT

ASPECT COMBINATIONS

SIGN	☌	⚹	□	△	☍
♈	♈	♒ ♎	♑ ♋	♐ ♌	♎
♉	♉	♓ ♏	♒ ♌	♑ ♍	♏
♊	♊	♈ ♐	♓ ♍	♒ ♎	♐
♋	♋	♉ ♑	♈ ♎	♓ ♏	♑
♌	♌	♊ ♒	♉ ♏	♈ ♐	♒
♍	♍	♋ ♓	♊ ♐	♉ ♑	♓
♎	♎	♌ ♈	♋ ♑	♊ ♒	♈
♏	♏	♍ ♉	♌ ♒	♋ ♓	♉
♐	♐	♎ ♊	♍ ♓	♌ ♈	♊
♑	♑	♏ ♋	♎ ♈	♍ ♉	♋
♒	♒	♐ ♌	♏ ♉	♎ ♊	♌
♓	♓	♑ ♍	♐ ♊	♏ ♋	♍

INTERPOLATION EQUATIONS

$$\text{Transit Constant} = \frac{(C - A)}{(B - A)}$$

$$\text{Rx Transit Constant} = \frac{(A - C)}{(A - B)}$$

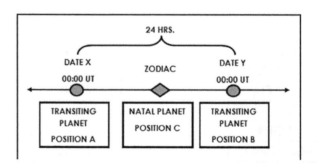

TABLE OF CONTENTS

INTRODUCTION

"The heavens themselves, the planets, and this center
Observe degree, priority, and place,
Insisture, course, proportion, season, form,
Office, and custom, in all line of order."
>—William Shakespeare from Troilus and Cressida, Act I, Scene 3

On February 2nd, 1987 03:22 Universal Time (UT), international soccer player Gerard Piqué was born in Barcelona, Spain. Eight hours later, at 11:04 UT, American actor Martin Spangjers was born in Tucson, Arizona. Finally, at 16:20 UT, thirteen hours after Gerard and five hours after Martin, professional motorcyclist Johnathon Rea was born in Ballymena, Ireland.

Three complete strangers from three different parts of the world all born within the first half of February 2nd, 1987 starting with the subtle breaking of twilight from the night before with Mr. Piqué, and ending with Mr. Rea right when the sun was just about to begin its descent into the horizon. Theoretically speaking, if astrology had no legitimate basis as a functioning system or study, then the lives of these three individuals, along with their personalities and life events, would possess no commonality whatsoever. For the past two-thousand years, this postulation has been the Achilles' heel of astrology which has single handedly curtailed any further exploration and development of the field to a point of near extinction.

The source of astrology's biggest woe comes from the 1st century Roman skeptic Marcus Cicero. His critique, which I have dubbed "Cicero's Paradigm," goes as such:

"...[individuals] who were born at the very same instant are unlike in character, career, and destiny. [Therefore,] the time of birth has nothing to do in determining [an individual's] course in life."[1]

Before astrology and this book can proceed any further, this lasting condemnation needs to be addressed once and for all. In order to do so, we need to dissect and scrutinize Cicero's Paradigm one line at a time using empirical evidence, the scientific method, and statistical probability.

It is true that the three men mentioned above were not born "at the very same instant," so let us begin with a few thought experiments based upon actual data that confronts this issue. Although it is difficult to determine the exact number of births at any given time, UNICEF gives an average estimate of 255 births per minute globally.[2] Although we cannot assume that every one of these births occurred within a hospital, let us assume that all 255 took place in a traditional hospital setting. According to a study in 2015, there are around 164,500 hospitals worldwide[3] indicating that the probability of two strangers being born at the same moment and location is approximately 0.00024%.

Why does this matter? It matters because, in astrology, it is perfectly fine if individuals are born at the same moment; if their births occur at different locations, their birth charts will look and manifest in distinctly unique ways. This is due to the fact that astrological computations not only include one's birth time and date, but also the global longitude and latitude in which it took place.

Take these four charts below as an example. All four of these individuals were born at the same exact moment, but at different parts of the world (Fig. INT-1).

Without knowing anything about astrology, it is still easy to see how each of these individual charts are oriented differently with their own distinct character.

When we consider this observation, along with the astronomically low probability of two strangers being born at the same moment and place, we can definitively rule out Cicero's first quibble about astrology for two main reasons:

---

1   Cicero: De Senectute De Amicita De Divinatinoe. Book 2, Section 95. With an English Translation. William Armistead Falconer. Cambridge. Harvard University Press; Cambridge, Mass., London England. 1923.
2   The World Counts: How Many Babies are Born Each Day? www.theworldcounts.com. 2018.
3   Cybermetricls Lab: Ranking Web of World Hospitals. Hospitals.webometrics.info. 2015.

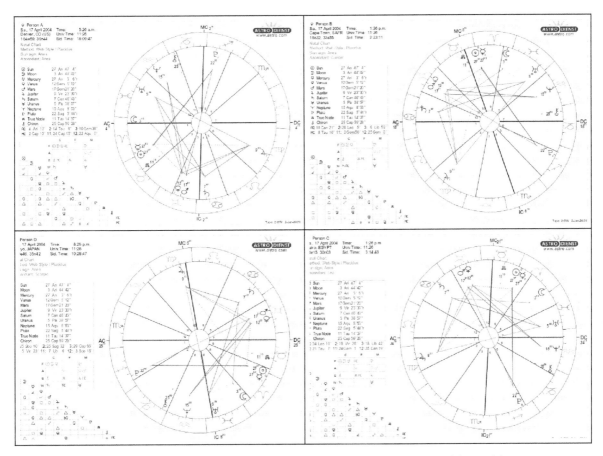

FIGURE INT-1. Four individuals born April 17, 2004 11:26 UT at various locations around the world.

(1) Two strangers being born "at the very same instant" in astrology is inconsequential because the parameters that determine a chart's appearance are mathematically determined by a person's birth date, time, <u>and</u> location.

(2) With the low likelihood of two strangers being born at the same time and location, it is safe to say that this occurrence is essentially nil.

Still, before we can move on to Cicero's next point, we need to also address what happens when two individuals are born at the same place and time as twins.

According to a statistical study, twins have a 61% chance of being born within 15 minutes or less and a 39% chance of being born at an interval longer than 15 minutes with a mean time of 21 minutes.[4] Due to this 60/40 split, we can assume that the distribution is more or less bell-shaped, indicating that the probability of two individuals being born at the exact minute to be substantially low. This is because those types of probable occurrences would happen at the lower percentile of the bell-shaped curve. Additionally, with a mean time of 21 minutes, this is still enough of a range to produce two distinct charts.

As the Earth rotates on its axis during its daily rotation, the entire length of the ecliptic traverses around our sky. The ecliptic is a circular band in which every planet, along with the sun and moon, travel around. Another term for the ecliptic is the zodiac which is composed of a 360° wheel divided into 12 equal parts of 30° each.

If there are 1440 minutes in a day, this means our view of the ecliptic changes approximately 0.25° per minute of time. Referring to our thought experiment, if twins were born at the mean time of 21 minutes, this indicates that the ecliptic in the sky would have shifted approximately 5° from birth to birth. This might not seem like a lot, but 5° is all it takes to derive a completely different chart. Below are four theoretical cases studies of two pairs of twins who were born at the same location, but within a time difference of 20 minutes (Fig. INT-2).

Although the changes within these charts are subtle, once they are spotted they show a drastically different picture. Chart interpretation will be explained further in this book, but for now, understand that the location of the planets within the various subdivisions of the sky map, which are called houses, cause planets to manifest in different ways.

For example, Person A's Venus is in the 11th house, while their twin's Venus (Person B) is located in the 10th house. This means that Venus will be expressed within different avenues of their life experience along with any other planet that is located in a different house. Furthermore, it is important to note that the cardinal points, the thicker black lines within the chart, also emphasize different manifestations unique to the individual. For example, Person C is a Virgo Rising which means their Mercury is a heavily emphasized planet within their chart. Conversely, their twin, Person D, is a Leo rising which means the Sun in their chart is weighed just as heavily as their twin's Mercury. This subtle difference emphasizes two radically unique manifestations of the planets whose locations around the zodiac, or ecliptic, are nevertheless shared by both twins.

---

4   W.F. Rayburn. *Multiple Gestation: Time Interval Between Delivery of the First and Second Twins.* Obstet Gynecol. 1984 Apr; 63 (4): 502-6.

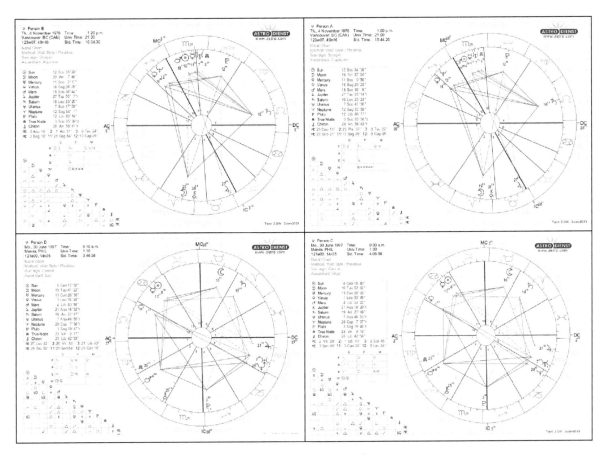

FIGURE INT-2. Two Sets of twins born 20 minutes apart from one another.

Once again, we can rule out Cicero's initial criticism of astrology even with the birth of twins for the following reasons:

(1) The mean time of 20 minutes between the birth of twins is still substantial enough to produce two uniquely individualized charts.

(2) The probability of two twins being born at the exact same minute is also substantially low.

Cicero's next objection is that people born at the same time are unlike the other in "character, career, and destiny." Taking from the first part of our argument, it should be noted that Cicero's statement is already no longer based within probable reality because we have now demonstrated that two people meeting Cicero's standards of being born at the "very same instant" is both statistically improbable and astrologically immaterial. Nevertheless, let us put the next segment of Cicero's Paradigm to the test with Mr. Piqué, Spanjers, and Rea using correlative evidence and methodical precision.

We will start with career. On the surface, Cicero's parameter holds true as all three of these men work within three completely different fields. However, I would argue that one's cultural influences, which are based upon one's nationality, make available certain professions for some, and a different list of potential paths for another.

For example, soccer is more heavily emphasized within Mr. Piqué's culture having hailed from Spain. Mr. Spanjers, being American, would simply not have had that career path as readily available as it was for Mr. Piqué. Similarly, Mr. Spanjers' proximity to Hollywood gave him the opportunity to become a film actor which, again, is heavily based upon his culture's emphasis toward the film industry along with his physical proximity to Los Angeles. I would further argue that cultural norms, interests, and opportunities are too diverse to allow for two individuals in question to possess specifically identical jobs. Again, we see a standard from Cicero that seems unreasonable when comparing people from different nationalities.

Still, it is true that there are similar professions that exists within the diverse spectrum of cultures, such as chefs, construction workers, and doctors, but I would once again reiterate that all three of these men are not born "at the exact moment" and cannot possibly be born within the same culture (location) based upon our statistical thought experiments that have been previously mentioned. Even so, if we remove the cultural layers of these three individuals' professions, numerous similarities are observed when comparing a soccer player, an actor, and a motorcycle racer:

(1) All involve performing in front of a crowd.

(2) Individual patronage, support, and representation is required.

(3) Each have a fan base.

(4) Fast-paced environments with high-pressure situations.

(5) Different forms of athleticism/physicality.

(6) Working as a team/ensemble but still receives individual glory.

(7) Requires charisma and working with the public/media.

(8) Highly competitive and specialized professions.

(9) Unpredictable stability with job security.

(10) Performance based upon physical ability.

(11) Requires international traveling.

The commonalities between all three of these professions cannot be ignored and fully satisfies Cicero's objection through these commonalities even though these men were born hours apart from one another albeit on the same day.

The next stipulation Cicero points out is destiny. Indeed, the discussion of destiny and astrology's ability to predict future events breaches the realm of sorcery instead of empirical science. However, scientists create mathematical models which can predict certain outcomes such as earthquakes along with other chemical, biological, and physical reactions all the time. When scientists predict statistically probable events such as these, do we burn them at the stake as heretics? No, because these realms of scientific speculation and exploration are accepted as legitimate within our culture; astrology is not. However, I would argue that an astrologer's ability to use mathematical data in order to predict future events is no different than a physicist who can predict the force of an impact, a chemist who can predict what happens when hydrochloric acid is added to an organic compound, or when a biologist can predict how a cell will respond to a certain hormone. In this same light, using astrological methodologies, I will now correlate specifically fated (or destined) events of these three individuals and demonstrate that they not only occurred at the same time, but they manifested very similar circumstances:

(1) **2002-2005. All three individuals were "learning the ropes" of their professions which climaxed in 2005/2006.**

    a. Mr. Piqué debuted with Manchester United in 2004, FA Cup Debut in 2005, and his first league start in 2006.

b. Mr. Spanjers was performing his most notable adolescent role in the show *Eight Simple Rules* from 2002-2005 while guest staring in other shows during this time. After 2005, Mr. Spanjers transitioned into more serious adult roles in shows like the substantially popular *Grey's Anatomy* and *True Blood*.

c. Mr. Rea began on the British circuit in 2003 demonstrating his potential as a legitimate contender finishing 16th in 2005.

(2) **During this time, all three individuals received a major shift in their career from other people's misfortune or death.**

a. Mr. Piqué's first league start in 2006 only occurred because starting right-back Gary Neville was injured.

b. Three episodes into filming *Eight Simple Rules*, main character John Ritter suddenly died in 2003, drastically altering the overarching plot for the rest of the season.

c. In 2005, a junior teammate of Mr. Rea died in a crash.

(3) **2011-2012. Two individuals experienced serious romances and marriages.**

a. In 2011, Mr. Piqué began dating singer-songwriter Shakira.

b. (Mr. Spanjers' only publicly known romance involves Ally Gasparian in 2016.)

c. Mr. Rea married his wife Tatia in 2012.

(4) **2017. All three individuals received national attention and recognition.**

a. In 2017 Mr. Piqué became heavily involved in the Catalan Independence Referendum and was known as a public face for the movement.

b. Mr. Spanjers received 8 film awards in 2017; the most he has ever received in a single year.

c. In 2017, Mr. Rea was appointed a Member of the Order of the British Empire.

(5) **2019. All three individuals experienced substantial public exposure for better or for worse relating to their countries of birth.**

a. In 2019, Mr. Piqué had to pay 2.1 million after being exposed for tax fraud in Spain.

b. In 2019, Mr. Spanjers became a prominent supporter and activist for political movements such as Medicare for All and the Dakota Access Pipeline.

c. In 2019, Mr. Rea was conferred an honorary doctorate from Queen's University Belfast.

These correlative similarities contain evidence to suggest that although these individuals were born hours apart on different parts of the globe, all three of them experienced similar events during the same time, proving that astrology not only possess the utility to correctly predict "fated" events, but that these events are shared by people who possess similar potentialities based upon their proximity in birth time and date. The statistical probability that all three of these individuals experienced similar events at similar times goes beyond the realm of coincidence, and the scientific approach was used to reach this conclusion.

If astrology did not work as a system or as a science, then this point alone would be the crux of Cicero's Paradigm and astrology would therefore be proven to be a falsehood and dismissed outright. However, as was just demonstrated, this is not the case, which means we can proceed further and address Cicero's final parameter: character.

This caveat is the hardest to prove empirically even though analyzing one's character and psychology is a major component of astrology's main utility. As such, one's character can only be confirmed by one's closest confidants, therapists, and/or the individual themself. We are therefore now entering the world of inference and for this reason, I will be using my own psychoanalysis because I myself was born just 7 hours after Mr. Rea, 16 hours after Mr. Spanjers, and exactly 24 hours after Mr. Piqué.

Before I address the psychological aspects of these individuals using my own birth chart as the goalpost, I would like to add my own life story to the events listed above to once again note the similarities in both theming and timing:

(1) **2002-2005. Learning the Ropes.** I was in high school during this length of time and while I was also obtaining grades to qualify for college, I also began exploration into music composition which eventually became my major. After graduation in 2005, I was admitted into a specialized program based upon my high school portfolio during these years.

(2) **Death/Misfortune of Another that Shifted Career.** While in high school, I was also heavily involved in theatre. In 2005, the Thespian play my senior year was a Shakespearean play where I had one of the most important roles of my high school career. Shortly after the start of rehearsals, our teacher sadly had a miscarriage and could no longer direct the play. The school decided to bring in the old drama teacher who was my teacher freshmen year, and even taught my father back in the 1970s. For me, this tragedy turned into a very memorable and impactful experience because I was reunited with my old teacher, and my entire high school theatre experience came around full circle from that reunion.

(3) **2011-2012. Serious Romance.** During this time, I was not only in the longest relationship of my life, but it was also the most "adult" relationship where I lived with my partner in the same apartment.

(4) **2017. National Attention and Recognition.** In 2017, I was awarded an artist in residence to one of the most competitive residencies in the United States. Also, my astrological writings culminated in 2017 with various articles along with the publishing of my first astrology book.

(5) **2019. Public exposure for better or for worse.** Like many people during this time, my life plans shifted dramatically due to the COVID pandemic. My public life disintegrated into nothing and I had to start from square one, including my life direction. This is when the inspiration to write this book began.

Again, although I, myself, was born 24 hours apart from Mr. Piqué, all four of our lives have some semblance of similarity. Therefore, having already done extensive psychoanalysis of my own chart over the past ten years, and having already demonstrated legitimate parallels among our various life paths, I would say it is safe to infer that these three individuals, like myself, possess similar qualities in our character and psychology.

Just as the previously mentioned life events were indicated by astrological markers, these character traits were similarly obtained using different astrological indicators. The difference is, instead of identifying and correlating specific events to a certain point in time, individualized character traits were interpreted using theories of Jungian Psychology. This will be explored further in Part I-Section 6.

In regards to the four of us that were born on the same day, if we were to survey any one of our friends, partners, or therapists, they would probably tell you that all four of us contain the following character traits (Note: This is not an extensive list):

(1) We are all willing and determined to slowly reach our long-term goals, but our motivation must be 100% intrinsic. We will not consider achieving something unless we feel completely motivated and behind what it is we want to accomplish.

(2) Effortless opportunities rarely come out of the blue and instead only come our way based upon individual input and effort. Therefore, there is a tendency to get swept away into pessimistic thinking if we are not too careful and lose our own perspective.

(3) Romantically speaking, we can have issues with martyrdom and victimhood, where we attract partners that either require saving, or we expect them to save us.

(4) Power struggles are common and are usually due to ego clashes with people or institutions of power.

(5) We are very open-minded individuals and have no problem with the unconventional.

(6) We feel our emotions strongly and quickly but sometimes not as deeply or permanently.

(7) It is very easy for us to be physically active and fit, but at the same time motivation into these matters can be difficult where we can have bouts of laziness. Typically, this is because gaining muscle and our overall health comes a little too easy for us.

Again, it is hard to prove if these characteristics are similar without interviewing all four of us in confidence. Nevertheless, we have already observed correlative accuracy when it comes to life-events and career, so it is not a far stretch to say that commonalities also exist between us four in terms of our personality and psychology. To understand how this is possible, let us observe all four of our birth charts side by side and note the commonalities between them (Fig. INT-3).

Just as we have observed in our theoretical case studies in Figure INT-1, all four of our charts have completely different orientations due to our various locations around the globe even though we were all born on the same day. Even so, there are similarities between all four charts that cannot be ignored. Namely, every single one of our planets is oriented at the same location within the zodiac.

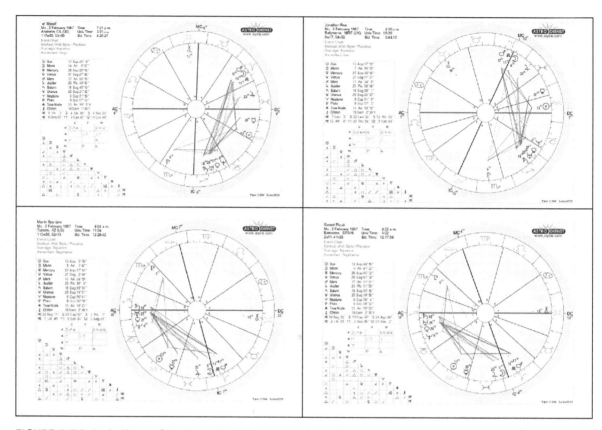

FIGURE INT-3. Birth Charts of Mr. Piqué, Spanjers, Rea, and myself all born February 2nd 1987 UT.

We each have a Sun in Aquarius (☉♒), a Moon in Aries (☽♈), a Mercury in Aquarius (☿♒), a Venus, Uranus, and Saturn in Sagittarius (♀♐, ♅♐, ♄♐), a Mars in Aries (♂♈), a Neptune in Capricorn (♆♑), and a Pluto in Scorpio (♇♏). Due to this similarity, the angles that these planets make to one another, which are called aspects, are also the same. This is observed by the grid on the lower left-hand corner of each chart called the aspectarian. If you compare all four of our aspectarians to one another, you will find that we possess practically the same exact planetary angles (aspects) which accounts for our similarities both in terms of personality and the timing of events. The difference, as seen in the case studies with the twins in Figure INT-2, comes with how these planets are oriented within the sky map subdivisions, the houses, and the darker lines within the chart, the cardinal points.

For example, Mr. Piqué and Spanjers have their Sun in the 2nd house, but Mr. Rea has his Sun in the 7th house, and I have the Sun in the 6th house. Just as it is with twins, although we possess the same Sun placement relative to the zodiac, these different house placements will cause the Sun's energy to manifest within different realms of our life experiences. Similarly, Mr. Piqué and Spanjers have a Sagittarius rising, Mr. Rea is a Leo rising, and I am a Virgo rising. Just as it was with the twins, this emphasizes certain planets over others which marks some of the differences in our personalities, physical appearance, and the realms of our lives that are emphasized or deemphasized. Nevertheless, the core foundation as to who we are as individuals, along with the timing of our life events, are similar and accurate due to all of us being born on the same day.

Before we continue further with our discussion, let us reiterate the major points within Cicero's Paradigm and explain how we have now fully satisfied every quarrel using the evidence that has been presented.

(1) *Individuals born "at the very same instant."*

    a. Astrological computations consider geographical latitude and longitude in addition to one's birth date and time. Therefore, it is inconsequential if the two individuals in question are born at the very same instant.

    b. Even so, using statistical data, it was demonstrated that the probability of two strangers being born at the same exact time and location to be 0.00024%. or nil.

    c. In the case of twins, the mean time between births, 20 minutes, is substantial enough to alter the chart's shape and character where two individual personalities are expressed even though similar life events can nevertheless occur.

(2) **Dissimilar in Career.**

    a. Due to the nil probability of two strangers being born at the same place and location, it is safe to assume that individuals are raised within different cultures and nationalities. Due to this fact, there are some professions that are readily available in some countries that might not be available in others. Therefore, we cannot expect a high probability of two strangers from two different nationalities to possess similar careers even if they were born at the same moment.

b. Even though there are professions that do cross national barriers, national and cultural influences cannot be ignored. This is therefore an unrealistic parameter set by Cicero.

c. Still, when comparing individuals who were born on the same day, similarities are observed and correlated when the literal title of the job is removed, and the overall themes of the professions are observed. When this is performed, similarities and consistencies do exist.

(3) **Dissimilar in Destiny.**

a. Observing four individuals who were born within a 24-hour time span showed that all four had similarly fated events at the same point in time.

b. The accuracy of the case study regarding four individuals born February 2nd, 1987 UT rules out the chances of pure coincidence. The empirical scientific method was used and therefore constitutes as legitimate evidence against Cicero's argument.

c. Furthermore, astrology's ability or inability to predict future events in this manner would immediately falsify astrology outright. This was not the case which only reinforces astrology's legitimacy.

(4) **Dissimilar in Character.**

a. Although this is the hardest to prove empirically, anecdotal evidence from my own experience was used to infer similar characteristics and psychological makeup of the other three individuals born on February 2nd, 1987 UT.

b. The only way to confirm these inferences is to survey the other individuals within the case study. However, given that similarities have already been demonstrated empirically through destined events and similarities in vocation, it is safe to assume that similarities can also translate through astrology's other utility as a form of psychoanalysis via Jungian psychological theory.

c. This was further demonstrated when all four birth charts were compared and similarities in planetary placements along the zodiac and aspect patterns we observed. Additionally, noting the differences in terms of rising signs and house placements still adds individuality to these four similar charts.

(5) **"[Therefore,] the time of birth has nothing to do in determining [an individual's] course in life."**

    a. We have now presented statistically based thought experiments, real case studies, theoretical case studies, empirical correlative evidence, and anecdotal evidence to suggest that one's individual character, destiny, and life goals are indeed heavily influenced not only by one's time and date of birth, but by their location as well.

    b. Individuals who are born within similar time spans have shown to possess strikingly accurate similarities in their personalities, careers, and destiny.

    c. Therefore, the planetary, solar, and lunar energies that exist during one's moment of birth, and their relative locations along the zodiac, firmly binds the individual into an accurately destined timetable along with a pre-determined psychological makeup. Both of these influences are just as profound as they are real, and are just as existential as they are internal.

    d. Therefore, 2000 years after the fact, it is finally scientifically safe to say that the time of birth has everything to do in determining an individual's course in life, effectively nullifying Cicero's Paradigm once and for all.

The inherent and assumed skepticism and cynicism that has been focused towards astrology has plagued this science for far too long. In my opinion, this outright dismissal stems from a fear of control and a fear of the unknown. Generally speaking, individuals do not like to be told they are sometimes not the masters of their own destinies. We will discuss free will and fate later in this book, but it is important to understand that just because an event appears to be fated does not necessarily mean that the individual did not possess any agency that led them to that event. In other words, an event can seem fated, but it only seems to be so because the individual was motivated and acted upon their unconscious mind, which constantly begs to be unearthed and understood. This is a core ideal of Jungian psychology.

Additionally, even when an individual experiences fated events such as the death of a loved one, an accident, or a severe medical illness, one always has the free will to react as they so desire to these external forces. Therefore, the issue is not about having any free will or autonomy, but how the individual has not been flexible or introspective enough to surrender to the things they cannot control along with their inability to analyze why they were not able to do so. But then again, how many times has a death, an illness, or hitting rock bottom caused an individual to "wake-up" and start to reevaluate their life's priorities and outlook? According to astrological theory, and as we have seen in the case study of four individuals born on the same day, yes, certain life events are inevitable and will be felt at specific moments in a person's life. However, the individual's own preparation and understanding can make difficult life experiences easier to comprehend and overcome. With astrology, it pays to be proactive.

In my opinion, one of the most significant reasons astrology has been ignored and feared is because it is very difficult for an individual to let go of their control over their own personality, life path, and goals. The study of astrology insists that the practitioner be open, flexible, and understanding to the natural ebb and flow of life while constantly striving to improve and understand their unconscious self. That way, fated events are not as severe because the true self, warts and all, is slowly being realized by the individual. It is only the fear of the unknown self and fear of control that immediately deters someone from the healing potential that is latent within astrology.

The other reason individuals shun astrology outright is due to fear of the unknown, both in literal and metaphysical terms. With the literal unknown, the actual glyphs of astrology, the aspects, the shape of the chart, etc., are incredibly overwhelming to understand at first. It is as though a person was given a Russian copy of *War and Peace* and was expected to translate it into English without knowing any Russian. That kind of fear is understandable and only takes patience and practice to eliminate this fear of astrology.

The second unknown fear, the metaphysical, is more prevalent within the minds of individuals who reject astrology. Astrology is a science, but it a science of self-discovery. Therefore, one cannot explore astrology without also probing into their own personal philosophy when it comes to topics such as the existence of a soul, god, karma, reincarnation, and even the meaning of life itself. This is not to say that you need to believe in these sorts of things; astrology is not a belief system. Still, inquiries and exploration into these incorporeal realms are, nevertheless, unavoidable. In my opinion, it is difficult for individuals to investigate these topics whether or not they believe in their existence. Inevitably, astrology will cause an individual to reevaluate their outlook on life in this way. Instead of taking the dive into these more ethereal topics, people outright shun what they do not fully understand without looking into it firsthand.

When I was growing up, like most children, new foods scared me, and I was naturally hesitant to try anything. My mom had one simple rule: you have to try it first before you can say you did not like it. This axiom has followed me my entire life, and I would say the same thing to any skeptic of astrology that has never tried to explore the study themself. You cannot say it does not work, you cannot say it does not provide any advantages, and you cannot say it is illegitimate without first attempting to explore astrology firsthand. Until that time, any stringent opinion you have about astrology is, in my eyes, invalid until you have put in the objective work yourself.

This is very easy to do without having any knowledge of astrology. Just as I was able to find certain individuals that share the same birthday as me, you also can look up your own "astro-twins" by using the website astro.com (Table INT-1).

TABLE INT-1. How to find your Astro-twins on astro.com

(1)	Obtain your birth certificate and make sure it displays the time of birth [NOTE: It is vitally important you do not use any other birth time other than the time on your birth certificate. It does not matter what time your Mom or Dad said you were born. The time that is only important is when the Doctor that delivered you officially declared you alive on this planet.]
(2)	Go to astro.com and make an account
(3)	Click on the HOROSCOPES tab and under DRAWINGS, CALCULATIONS, DATA select CHART DRAWING, ASCENDANT
(4)	Click on + ADD NEW PERSON
(5)	Input your Name, gender, birth date, month, year, time, and location
(6)	Click CONTINUE which will then show you your computed birth chart
(7)	On the upper left-hand corner, confirm that your birth data is correct
(8)	Once again, go to the HOROSCOPES tab and under DRAWINGS, CALCULATIONS, DATA select YOUR VIP ASTRO-TWINS
(9)	You will then find an extensive list of individuals that share the same birth data as you with the closest matches on top.

Once you have determined your astro-twins, look up their Wikipedia pages, and see if you can find any correlations around their life events and personality to your own. This is a sure and quick way you can witness and observe astrology in action. If doing this little experiment piqued your interest, the next step is to use the tools and information inside this book to obtain an even deeper understanding into the wonderful world of the astrological sciences.

This book is a culmination of the previous decade of my life. During this time, I became certified in astrology, taught classes, wrote articles, gave lectures, helped clients, read countless books, and studied with some of the best in the profession. You will learn methods that I have personally created and perfected over the years that I use on a daily basis. It is my hope that by the time you have finished this book, you will understand and possess a core foundational knowledge of astrology that you can use not only on in your own life, but in the lives of others if you decide to become an astrological practitioner.

All you need to possess is a willingness to learn, honesty to see your true colors, tenacity to learn from your mistakes, and an open mind to finally see the true essence and potentiality of astrology, which has mostly been dormant for the past two-thousand years and only understood by the select few who have dared to explore the vast workings of this universe and our place within.

In **Part I** we will establish a core understanding of the astrological sciences by exploring fundamental history, theory, and methodology. We will discuss the main objectives within astrology along with its connection to fate, free will, karma, and the soul. We will also explore the main themes of Jungian psychology and how they are applied in addition to common pitfalls, tips, and tools.

Part II covers the main astrological symbols and archetypes. Specifically, the signs, planets, houses, aspects, and cardinal points. Traditional rulerships and rules that are still relevant in modern-day astrology will also be discussed.

Part III covers the use of astrology as a calendar and will cover daily, monthly, and annual astrological phenomena. This includes the moon cycle, void of course moons, retrogrades, eclipses, and planetary hours.

Part IV covers how to observe present-day astrological bodies and how they interact with our birth chart planets and cardinal points. This study is called planetary transits, and basic astrological mathematics are required. Yes, you will need to understand and use math, but if you are able to utilize the methods within this section, you will be able to calculate your own transits up to the minute. This reward alone is worth the time and effort, and you will only need to go as far as algebraic interpolation and working in a base-60 system to get there. Both of which are simple and easy to use once you become accustomed. Nevertheless, if the math is too difficult, you will still learn how to read and use an ephemeris which will be a helpful tool that you can still use.

In **Part V**, we will begin to put everything you have learned all together and work on chart interpretation. We will discuss the ethics of astrology and how to approach a chart using my own methodologies with actual case studies.

Part VI will be the last piece of main chart interpretation where we discuss the progressed chart, why it is important, and how to utilize it in readings and within your own chart. There are still very few books written about the progressed horoscope making this knowledge even more occult than most of the astrological knowledge you will find elsewhere. We will learn how to compute your progressions and how to interpret them. Just like in Part V, we will conclude with various case studies of actual clients to see the progressed chart in action.

Finally, **Part VII** will cover miscellaneous topics and methodologies you will need to explore to become a well-versed astrologer. Although the Natal, Transit, and Progressed chart (Parts V, IV, and VI respectively) act as the core foundation for all astrological analysis, you will encounter clients that will want you to analyze other important topics such as relationships, moving to different parts of the world, and birthday charts. This section covers each of these techniques so that you can leave no stone unturned and provide for yourself and your clients a fully comprehensive counseling session with clarity and confidence.

Before we take the deep dive into this world, I would like you to take a moment and ponder a few things. We are practically one-quarter of the way into the 21st century. As a human race, where are we headed? As an individual, where are you headed? What kind of future are we co-creating? What kind of future do we want to create? What kind of future do you want to create?

Before we can answer any of these questions, before we can right any of the wrongs of this world and, as we say in the United States, strive for "a more perfect union" between ourselves and each other, we need first to remember what the 13th century Persian philosopher Rumi once said all those years ago: "Yesterday I was so clever, so I wanted to change the world. Today, I am wise, so I am changing myself."

This is the same sentiment we find in the *Bhagavad-Gita* and the same philosophy that was explained by the Klingon warrior Lieutenant Worf from *Star Trek: The Next Generation:* "You look for the battles in the wrong places. The true test of a warrior is not without; it is within. Here, here is where we meet the challenge. It is the weaknesses in here a warrior must overcome."

Before we can expect the world to change, we first need to change ourselves. Before we can purge the world of evil and wrongdoing, we must first purge out our own grosser tendencies and habits and admit the wrongdoings we have done ourselves. Before we have any right to tell anyone how to live their lives, we first need to look at our own life and make sure we are completely conscious and steadfast in our own journey first.

This is the true test of the 21st century and the test of any true warrior. Pick up your shield, enter the darkness of your unconscious mind, and find the light within yourself. Then, and only then, can you call yourself an astrologer and a true agent of change. I am with you on that battlefield. I have been fighting that fight for a decade now and still have not figured it out completely. But it is the work that must be done. This is your birthright. Now go and light the way with truth, forgiveness, and understanding. Once you do this, others will surely follow. This book is simply the torch of knowledge and wisdom that was passed down to me from the lineage of astrologers that came before me. I now humbly pass that torch onto you to do with as you will. All I ask is that you strive every day to know thyself and if you do, the knowledge within this book will be worth its weight in gold.

To the future, which has yet to be written,

—*Dosajna*
Tacoma, Washington September 9th, 2021.

30

PART I: FUNDAMENTAL HISTORY, THEORY, AND METHODOLOGY

"I know that I am mortal by nature and ephemeral, but when I trace at my pleasure the windings to and from of the heavenly bodies, I no longer touch earth with my feet. I stand in the presence of Zeus himself and take my fill of ambrosia." -Ptolemy from his treatise Almagest

As the old saying goes: every journey begins with a single step. This goes double for us because we have a lot of fundamental ground to cover. When it comes to the other sciences that exist, you were most likely being exposed to their methodologies, various realms of study, history, and main dogma as early as elementary school. The same, however, cannot be said for the astrology. Therefore, we must make up for lost time and cover the essential theories, objectives, approach, and history of the astrological sciences.

This is important because before you can even begin to analyze a birth chart, you first need to possess a strong adoration and comprehension of the science itself. Just as you cannot enter a chemistry lab without first understanding the dangers of working with strong acids and bases, we cannot expect anyone to approach astrology with confidence and safety without first learning about the various principles and astrologers that have made their mark on the oldest of human sciences.

We will start with a brief survey of astrology's history, but before we begin that discussion, let us first examine various sub-disciplines that exist within the astrological umbrella. Just how genetics, physiology, and evolution all fall under the study of biology, there are many sub-disciplines that exist within astrology (Table I-1).

When it comes to the traditions taught within this book, it is mostly based upon the fundamental rules of natal astrology with the philosophical backing of archetypal and evolutionary theories. Mainly, that the natal chart does indicate a pre-determined psychology based upon Jungian archetypes and that one's individual psychology encounters specifically timed events. Additionally, my astrological

TABLE I-1. Various Astrological Sub-Disciplines with Description [NOTE: Not an extensive list.]

SUB-DISCIPLINE	PRIMARY FOCUS
NATAL	The most common study. Natal astrology focuses on one's psychology and life events by examining the natal chart, the transiting chart, and the progressed chart. This study is the primary focus of this book.
HORARY	Derived for the Latin word meaning "hour", horary is a technique where a question is queried, and the astrologer then erects a chart at that precise moment the question was asked. From the information within that chart, one can discover the answer to their question. Astrologer William Lilly from the 15th century was paramount in distilling this ancient tradition into a newer framework. There are stories where he would have his friends hide certain items and would then erect a horary chart to find their location.
MEDICAL	The study of predicting and healing physical ailments by observing the natal and transit chart through an interpretive lens of the various parts of the body and their respective planetary and sign rulerships.
ELECTIONAL	Deriving for the Latin word "to pick out", electional astrology consists of determining specific times, dates, and locations for significant events such as weddings, the starting of a business, and filing a lawsuit.
ASTROECONOMICS	This branch observes correlations to the stock market along with the birth chart of businesses in order to predict when the market will become bearish or bullish, or when a business is about to enter a time of financial success or failure. If you think big business does not use this to their advantage, remember it was J.P. Morgan who once famously said, "Millionaires do not use astrologers; billionaires do."
ASTROCARTOGRAPHY	As the planets travel around the planet, they make certain path lines all around the globe. These specific lines can indicate places where an individual could find more success, difficulty, a community, or just a place for a good vacation.
JYOTISH	3,000 years older than the Western tradition, Jyotish is an astrological system that was developed in India about 5,000 years ago by conservative estimates.[5] The main difference between Jyotish and Western is that Jyotish works with sidereal planetary placements and Western works with tropical planetary placements. This will be covered more in Part I-Section 8.

---

5   Shyamasudara Dasa. *A Brief History of Jyotish.* https://shyamasundaradasa.com/jyotish/what_is_jyotish/jyotish_history.html. 2021.

TABLE I-1. Continued

SUB-DISCIPLINE	PRIMARY FOCUS
ASTROGEOGRAPHY	More recently, astrological scientists have been trying to create predictive models of astrology that can determine the timing of geographical phenomena such as earthquakes, tsunamis, and tornadoes.
RELATIONSHIP	This field focuses on the strengths, weaknesses, and longevity of individuals that are in a relationship whether it be romantic, business, or familial. This Is mostly done by working with the composite and bi-wheel charts.
ARCHETYPAL	This tradition sprang out of the 1970s with astrological authors like Liz Greene, Robert Hand, Steven Arroyo, and academic Joseph Campbell. This branch is heavily focused on Jungian psychological theory in that planetary archetypes and mythologies are echoed in both the individual and global psychology.
EVOLUTIONARY	According to evolutionary astrology founders Steven Forrest and Jeffery Wolf Green, this branch is less of a technical methodology and more of a philosophical framework that assumes some metaphysical rules such as reincarnation, a soul's evolutionary journey from one lifetime to the next, and that the individual possess a high degree of external and internal autonomy.[6]

approach also considers the idea that one's psychology is meant to be understood and improved upon from these events to be the primary objective for the individual during this lifetime.

My methods also incorporate realms of traditional astrology where we will be considering traditional rulerships and rules when necessary. Furthermore, in order to give a more comprehensive analysis for my clients, I use methods incorporating astrocartography, relationship charts, and solar return charts which will be examined in this book through various case studies (Part VII).

As you can see, the astrologer has a multitude of tools within their toolbox to choose from when it comes to approaching a natal chart. This book is simply my own method that I have derived by mixing and matching what works for me, and I would encourage you to do the same over time. In the meantime, it is my hope that this book simply acts as a foundational cornerstone before you begin any further exploration into this vast and vibrant study. So, without further ado, let us get into our first topic: the history of astrology.

---

6   Steven Forrest. *What is Evolutionary Astrology?* https://www.forrestastrology.com/pages/what-is-evolutionary-astrology. 2021

SECTION 1- A BRIEF HISTORICAL SURVEY OF THE WESTERN TRADITION

❧

PRE-CIVILIZATION: 32,000BC-3000BC

The earliest archeological evidence of the human race tracking celestial bodies in a form of a calendar is derived from the lunar trackers of the European Aurignacian culture c. 32,000BC. Due to the lack of a formal writing system during this period, there is only so much scientists can deduce in regards to the mindset of this early human society. Nevertheless, the discovery of these lunar trackers, which have been etched into stone and animal rib bones, have allowed scientist to recognize

> "…that there are phases of the moon and seasons of the year that can be counted – that should be counted because they are important – is profound…What [archeologists] uncovered is the intuitive discovery of mathematical sets and the application of those sets to the construction of a calendar."[7]

For the longest time, scientists have assumed that the earliest of humans were nothing more than an evolved animal with no real capacity for advanced mental processes. These archeological findings have now made it safe to say that early humans not only had the ability for such processes, they were using them to correlate human activity with some form of a working celestial calendar. This initiated a tradition of creating celestial calendars and using the information in order to correlate events here on Earth. Correlating data to natural phenomena is not only a

---

7   Soderman/NLSI Staff. *The Oldest Lunar Colanders*. Solar System Exploration Research. https://sservi.nasa.gov/articles/oldest-lunar-calendars/. 2021.

foundational principle of empirical scientific observation, it also indicates that astrology is a science that is as old as humanity itself.

Our ancient ancestors recorded these events because they inherently understood their importance. There was no logic or reasoning required that led them to these conclusions but an intuitive knowing along with empirical observation that led them to conclude that these celestial patterns were indeed relevant to their lives here on Earth. With these archeological discoveries, it has now become scientific and archeological fact that our earliest ancestors have been working with celestial time systems for tens of thousands of years.

Sadly, our modern mindset and perception on human history has decided to flatly reject and deny this historical truth due the explicit bias the scientific community has towards astrology. When we deny this past, we are not only ignoring historical and scientific fact, we are also cutting ourselves off from some of our oldest human heritage.

We must also recall that ancient temples were being constructed during this time that were aligned to significant celestial events forming our oldest examples of solar (annual) calendars like that of Stonehenge. Construction on Stonehenge started in 31,00BC approximately, and was aligned to the sunset of the winter solstice and the opposing sunrise of the summer solstice. These two points during the year were significant to early humans because it was essential for them to know when the days would get shorter and colder, or when the days would get longer and warmer so that they could survive and plan accordingly.

In addition to this practical use, monuments like Stonehenge allowed for humanity to create a mythology around the Sun and other celestial bodies. Attributing spiritual energies to objects such as these is the beginning of one of the oldest religious and philosophical ideals: animism. This ideology involves the universal concept that every living and nonliving thing, from the birds in the sky to a grain of sand on the beach, is alive and connected through one gigantic web of life.

This cosmic bond between humanity and nature was so strong and universally understood that practically all early developing cultures possessed this concept as one of their primary foundations within their society. As these cultures evolved over time, these bonds only became stronger and more complex in tandem with astrology, which similarly developed in complexity and scientific accuracy.

Babylon: 2300BC-141AD

Ancient Babylon developed one of the first working astrological systems (c. 1800BC-1200BC) because to them, understanding and predicting earthly events was essential to their king's ability to rule. This paved the way for astrology to become a fundamental pillar within Babylonian society and governance. Babylonian priests were responsible for the documentation and interpretation of celestial phenomena which was then communicated to the king so that his people could live happier lives.

These priests developed a scientifically sound record system that objectively observed and correlated celestial events to earthly events through a series of tablets called the *Enuma Anu Enlil*. These tablets contained celestial correlations to Babylonian life such as floods, deaths, poor crops, and so forth. According to academics, the *Enuma Anu Enlil*

> "...shares some of the defining traits of modern science: it is objective and value-free, it operates according to known rules, and its data are considered universally valid and can be looked up in written tabulations".[8]

Astrology, even in its earliest form, was deeply rooted in the collection, observation, and analysis of celestial data. Here is an example of an entry:

> "If the moon becomes visible on the first day: reliable speech; the land will be happy. If the day reaches its normal length: a reign of long days. If the moon at its appearance wears a crown: the king will reach the highest rank."[9]

The Babylonians also created mythologies around the seven traditional planets in astrology, giving humanity one of our initial understandings into the nature of the planets and their influences within the Western tradition. As Babylonian culture progressed, so did their mathematical measurements. By 400BC they were creating the first versions of ephemerides, which catalogued future planetary placements with astounding accuracy.[10] The Babylonians also created a vast

---

8   Ulla Koch-Westenholz. *Mesopotamian astrology*. Volume 19. CNI publications. Museum Tusculanum Press. p. 1, 1995.

9   Hermann Hunger, ed., State Archives of Assyria, *Astrological reports to Assyrian kings*, Volume 8, 1992.

10   K.P. Moesgaard. *Ancient Ephemeris Time in Babylonian Astronomy*. Journal for the History of Astronomy. Volume 14, 1983.

star map where we observe the primary outline of the zodiac along with other surrounding constellations. However, during this time, there was no Libra constellation. Instead, Libra was considered to be an extension of the claws of the scorpion associated with the sign Scorpio.

Unlike the Jyotish tradition, which was hermetically preserved within the culture of ancient India, the Western tradition is an amalgam of various ancient cultures (both Eastern and Western) beginning with the Babylonians and ending with present-day Western philosophy and psychology. Nevertheless, through advancements in technology and culture, the Babylonians took the biggest steps into creating a scientific, mythological, and cohesive approach to what we now call western astrology. All subsequent ancient civilizations took this foundation and merely expanded on its ideas and established a more refined and specialized approach. Consequently, more branches of astrological interpretation and application were developed and created over the course of time.

Ancient Greece: 1250BC-30BC

The conquests of Alexander the Great exposed the Greeks to the cultures and traditions of central Asia, Babylon, Persia, and Syria, which allowed for astrology to migrate from the east to the west, where it was further developed in ancient Greece and Hellenistic Egypt.

The most significant event that led to this melting pot occurred c. 280BC when the Babylonian priest Berossus moved to the Greek island of Kos and taught astrology along with Babylonian culture to the Greeks. Over time in ancient Greece, a form of astrology known as Theurgic Astrology was devised. This type of astrology paralleled with the Hermetic philosophy, which involved personal transformation and forming an intimate dialogue with the divine. Simultaneously, further development into astrology occurred within Hellenistic Egypt.

Hellenistic Egypt: 300BC-200BC

During this time in history, we begin to observe the merging of five great ancient cultures: Egypt, Babylon, the Middle East, India, and Greece, which occurred from the death of Alexander the Great (323BC) to the emergence of the Roman Empire (31BC). At the conquest of Egypt by Alexander the Great, the scholarly city Alexandria was founded and became the source of this melting pot. Prior to this event, ancient Egypt had its own working form of a celestial calendar known as the Dendera zodiac.

The Dendera zodiac includes all twelve zodiacal constellations, including Libra, and also includes a division system of 36 decans of ten days each. This is the first time we see the astrological year which contains 360 days instead of 365. The number 360 to form one year is more in-tune with the annual rotation of the Earth around the Sun. Furthermore, 360 is the number of degrees in a perfect circle thereby creating a more synchronistic calendar that not only parallels Earth's true annual orbit, but also the natural flow of the Sun around the ecliptic, which is essentially a wheel consisting of 360 degrees.

During this time, mostly in the city of Alexandria, the mixture of Babylonian, Egyptian, and Greek systems convalesced into what we call Horoscopic (Natal) Astrology. In this system, rules of Horoscopic Astrology mixed with the philosophical approach of Greek Theurgic Astrology. We can declare this hybrid approach to be the first generation of Western Natal Astrology, the most common astrology studied in today's Western world and the tradition explained within this book.

The meshing of these systems and their diverse applications were compiled within the book *Tetrabiblos* written by the Alexandrian astrologer and astronomer Claudius Ptolemy. At this point in our story, we sadly see a severe divergence in the modern telling and conceptualization of ancient history. Astronomers today will attribute a lot of their history to that of Ptolemy but will refuse to recognize his contributions to the astrological world as well. This is not only inappropriate, it is historically inaccurate. Once again, we see the explicit bias towards astrology causing academics to rewrite history to their own terms instead of relying on the objective truths which have already been historically documented and analyzed. For lack of a better term, this is academic malpractice.

From ancient history up to the European Renaissance, astronomy and astrology were not only interchangeable terms, they were taught to students simultaneously.[11] If you were to read the history lessons provided in a college astronomy textbook today, you would find that authors

---

11   Kenneth Bartlett. *Education in the Renaissance*. The Great Courses Daily, 2016. https://www.thegreatcoursesdaily.com/education-in-the-renaissance/.

deliberately attempt to deny and distance this association by discrediting astrology as nothing more than a mere carnival trick. This kind of inaccurate propaganda has contributed to the severe discrediting of astrology as a serious scientific study. Which, as you have been discovering during this survey of history, could not be further from the truth.

Ptolemy's book *Tetrabilos* was the first time western astrology was catalogued and categorized onto a physical record. This work also provided a sound philosophical case for the study of astrology which was used many times over to justify astrology as a study during the less-enlightened times of the Dark Ages in Medieval Europe. Up until then, the ancient and profound connection between astrology and society was unquestioned as it was always a part of ancient culture throughout many ancient civilizations.

The damaging schism and criticism towards astrology began when the Roman Empire took its seat as the Western world's superpower. This is when we witness the first among many attempts to disprove astrology with figures like Cicero in addition to the waning of astrology's place within philosophical thought and governmental decisions.

ANCIENT ROME: 753BC-57AD

Rome was exposed to astrology through the Greeks and at the start of the Roman Empire, astrology had a good relationship within the Roman aristocracy. Emperor Tiberius used his birth astrology as a propaganda tool along with surrounding himself with astrologers as rulers have been doing for centuries past.[12]

Toward the start of Roman rule, astrology was coupled with the concept of "Chaldean wisdom," which was the Roman vernacular for all things foreign and mystic. At one point in time, astrology was so popular that Roman satirist Juvenal once said, "there are people who cannot appear in public, dine, or bathe, without having first consulted an ephemeris." Sadly, this developing interest and cultivation began to diminish through a campaign whose primary goal was to eliminate astrology and astrologers at all cost.

---

12   Pauline Ripat. *Expelling Misconceptions: Astrologers at Rome*. Journal of Classical Philosophy. Vol. 106, No.2: April 2011.

During the rule of Emperor Claudius, philosophers vigorously attempted to debunk astrology by proposing the theoretical twin scenario as a way to prove astrology as invalid. In fact, there is historical proof that astrology was banned up to eight times.[13]

This is the moment in history where Cicero's Paradigm went into full effect because his arguments seemed like a logical conclusion for astrology's supposed ineffectiveness. However, as we have demonstrated in the introduction, even in the rare case of twins being born right after one another, it is still possible that both charts possess different qualities.

Another way Roman propaganda tried to squash astrology within its culture was by creating a stereotype around astrology as an insignificant and childish hobby of housewives, and nothing a true Roman man would dare bother to consider.[14] (A stereotype that is sadly and amazingly still prevalent within today's society.) Eventually, it became so severe that astrologers were downright hunted down and killed sending a clear message that astrologers and astrology were not welcomed within Roman society.

THE DARK AGES: 300AD-1000AD

Europe during this time was in complete disarray as old knowledge and wisdom became obliterated due to the traumatic fall of the once encompassing Roman Empire. It would seem that during this time, the art of western astrology could have been completely lost to the sands of time but thankfully this is not the case. Indeed, western astrology owes a big debt of gratitude to the cultures of Islam and India during the dark ages as western astrology was not only preserved by these two cultures, it was further developed and explored.[15]

We are sometimes taught to believe that the Western world developed in some sort of isolated bubble with no real influences from other cultures of the time. However, with the vast trade routes of the first century AD, commonly known as the Silk Road, knowledge was transported

---

13   Frederick Cramer. *Astrology in Roman Law and Politics*. American Philosophical Society. 1954, pp. 232-48.

14   Pauline Ripat. *Expelling Misconceptions: Astrologers at Rome*. Journal of Classical Philosophy. Vol. 106, No.2: April 2011.

15   Nicholas Campion. *A History of Wetern Astrology, Volume 1: The Ancient Word*. Continuum International Publishing Group. London, New York: 2008. p. 291.

and preserved throughout all of Europe, Eurasia, and Asia. It is not hyperbolic to say if it were not for the Eastern cultures' preservation of western astrology, it is very safe to assume that the previous centuries of development into this science could have been lost forever. Vedic scholars would have no quarrels with preserving this knowledge as they themselves already had a working astrological system approximately 3,000 years older before western astrology even came into existence with the Babylonians.

Likewise, in Islamic culture, western astrology's ability to deal with the future stirred up much debate within Islamic philosophy, causing two camps of thought to emerge.[16] The more traditional philosophy dealt with the concept that God is the only one that is aware of the future, and man is not able to predict or comprehend God's will. The other camp, with the aid of using western astrology as proof, debated this long-standing belief in Islamic thought by stating that it is possible to understand God's will and doing so was not blasphemy, but an adoration of this higher knowledge. Just how western astrology obtained the nodes from Vedic Astrology, certain Islamic points like the point of fortune were also added into western astrology.

MEDIEVAL EUROPE: 500AD-1500AD

In Medieval Europe, the Roman Catholic Church became the all-encompassing superpower along with their stringent religious philosophy which did not permit astrology's existence. The Catholic Church needed to maintain absolutism with all things spiritual for the sake of their power and therefore, the church considered themselves to be the one and only vessel that possessed any truth or divine understanding towards God and personal salvation. Any system or person that claimed they could comprehend God outside of the church was considered blasphemous and incredibly dangerous. Regardless, astrology was able to adapt during this time within these constrictions and a new branch of astrology developed and emerged: medical astrology.

Medical understanding of the human body and diseases were severely limited at this time in history due to the outlawing of human dissection. Astrology was used as a reliable system

---

16   George Saliba. *A History of Arabic Astronomy: Planetary Theories During the Golden Age of Islam.* New York University Press: 1994. p. 67-69.

where doctors carried around special almanacs allowing them to check the positions of the stars before making a diagnosis. Ancient studies of astrology were translated from Arabic to Latin in the 12th and 13th centuries and soon became a part of everyday medical practice in Europe. These astrological theories incorporated Galenic medicine which was inherited from the Greek physiologist Galen (129-216 AD).[17] The use of astrology within medieval medicine became so prominent that by the end of the 1500s, physicians across Europe were required by law to calculate the position of the moon before carrying out complicated medical procedures such as surgery or bloodletting. It could be deduced that because this form of astrology does not address questions regarding spirituality or the soul's salvation, it was permissible, if not tolerated, by the Roman Catholic Church.

Still, one of the biggest ironies during the medieval era is that although those in power highly condemned astrology, they themselves were using astrology on a daily basis just as ancient rulers have done for centuries before them. The most influential astrologer (and astronomer) during this time was Guido Bonatti who was the personal advisor to Holy Roman Emperor Frederick II and other monarchs of that time who were in direct conflict with the Pope in Rome.[18] In fact, Bonatti was specifically targeted in Dante's *Divine Comedy* where he is depicted as residing in hell as punishment for using astrology.

Bonatti's famous book *Liber Astronomiae* (The Book of Astronomy) was written in 1277AD and remained a classic astrology textbook for the next two centuries.[19] Thanks to Bonatti, Astrology was not only preserved and expanded upon during medieval Europe, the astrological philosophy and argument that was contained within its pages was strongly defended by Bonatti himself in public arenas. Bonatti is famously known for winning formal public debates against members of the priesthood on the validity of astrology as a serious academic study along with its utility towards understanding the workings of the universe and the creator. Astrologers like Bonatti kept a firm ground within European culture during this darker period. Thankfully, with the advent of the Renaissance 200 years later, astrology's popularity once again reached an all-time high.

---

17   Lois Magner. *Astrology and Medicine*. Encyclopedia.Com: Science. https://www.encyclopedia.com/
       science/encyclopedias-almanacs-transcripts-and-maps/astrology-and-medicine. 2020.
18   Science Source. *Guido Bonatti: Italian Astronomer and Astrologer*. Science Source Images.
19   Nicholas Campion. *An Introduction to the History of Astrology*. ISCWA: 1982. P. 46.

European Renaissance: 1400AD-1650AD

The European Renaissance (literally meaning "rebirth") created an upheaval within social and individual priorities and philosophies of the past 500 years from that of the church and salvation to that of humanitarianism, self-awareness, and the arts. In academia during this time, students were taught seven liberal arts (correlating to the seven traditional planets) which included astrology.

Classical Greek mythology became an important subject within the arts during this time cementing the importance of these stories and archetypes into our culture whose influences and inspirations are still observed within the stories we tell in today's world. To this point, a new genre emerged during this era called opera. This new genre initiated a tradition of retelling traditional Greek myths for the stage and continues to this day. According to scholars like Carl Jung and Joseph Campbell, the reason why these stories are still preserved within our culture today is because their morals, characters, and themes are just as relevant to our life experiences now as they were for our Western ancestors for centuries prior.

The most famous (and some during his time would say infamous) astrologer of this era was William Lilly. William Lilly was highly influential and even played a great part in the English Civil War of 1644. He was either admired or hated by many members of English parliament, and correctly predicted the 1666 Great Fire of London so accurately, that an investigation committee was established to see if it was Mr. Lilly that started the fire in the first place.[20]

Mr. Lilly composed an annual almanac that sold thousands of copies a year and wrote a renowned staple within the astrological repertoire: *Christian Astrology*. In this work, Mr. Lilly explores the study of horary astrology, the study of asking a question, erecting a chart at the time of questioning, and discovering an answer based upon that chart. In fact, just for the fun of it, Mr. Lilly would challenge his fellow colleagues by having them hide something of his, and he would then find the item using horary techniques.

Although horary is an ancient study, many ideas from horary continue to be utilized within natal astrology today. Concepts like planetary strengths and weaknesses (dignities and debilities), the

---

20   Maurice McCann. *William Lilly's Prediction of the Fire of London*. Astrological Journal: Vol. XXXII, No. 1: 1990.

natural temperaments of the planets, and the importance of the cardinal points, are all subjects that are helpful to the study of natal astrology and will be covered later in this book.

As astrology continued to advance and develop, so did other scientific studies such as astronomy, along with technologies like the telescope, and methodologies like the scientific method. For the first time, humanity was introduced to the heliocentric (sun-centered) model of the solar system demonstrated by Copernicus ca.1543. Due to the more enlightened viewpoint of this time, it was becoming more widely accepted that the Earth was not the center of the universe, but the Sun.

Although this scientific fact is indeed the true format of our solar system and humanity is better off for understanding this truism, it unfortunately became a major focal argument towards the invalidity of astrology during this time. Scientists began to conclude that because the Earth was not the center of the universe (the geocentric model), then astrology is therefore not true nor accurate. Just like Cicero thousands of years prior, scientists during this time yet again missed the point due to their lack of understanding when it comes to astrological theory.

Yes, it is true that the solar system does revolve around the Sun and there is not one astrologer even today that would disagree with this statement. Just how every astrologer today knows that the Sun and the Moon are not true "planets" in the astronomical sense even though we refer to them as planets within our vernacular. Nevertheless, we should be reminded that astrology is not the study of the solar system's journey around the Sun, it is the study of the human experience here on Earth. It is here on this planet that humanity is indeed the center of the universe because the entire human story exists and persists on this planet alone. Therefore, it makes sense why astrology is calculated on a geocentric model.

Another scientific discovery during this time that downplayed astrology as a study was the realization of the fading intensity of stars. Due to advancements in technology, scientists were able to observe that the intensity of a star's light faded over time. From this observation, scientists began to deduce that if stars were not permanent in state, then humanity is therefore not tied down to the destiny of the stars which are portrayed within astrology because they themselves are not perfect or static in state.[21] Just how it is with other anti-astrology arguments, there contains

---

21   Anna Herlihy. *Renaissance Star Charts*. History of Cartography. University of Chicago. Vol. 3, Part 1, Chapter 4. 1998.

an imperfect logic and misunderstanding towards how astrology operates. When it comes to astrological studies, star placement and intensity are not factors that are considered within analysis.

In actuality, astronomical entities like the planets are observed, not the stars. Planetary bodies, along with solar and lunar movements, follow along stable and predictable paths and brightness. These movements, since the time of the Babylonians, have proven to be steady and mathematically predictable via ephemerides. Furthermore, even though the brightness of a star does decay over time, their location within the sky stays unwavering with a very slow perception of movement over long periods of time. We will discuss this more in Part I-Section 8 with the procession of the equinox. Nonetheless, scientific advancement and thought began to superimpose their conclusions onto the study of astrology, which operates on completely different theories and methodologies. This trend only continued for centuries thereafter when scientific advancement became the hallmark of human prestige and competition for the next 300 years.

THE INDUSTRIAL REVOLUTION: 1712AD-1900AD

This time in history, which includes the discovery of the planet Uranus in 1781, became the age of revolutions. Although the outer planets Uranus, Neptune, and Pluto are common to modern astrologers, it is important to remember that these outer planets were not discovered until the 18th century AD and onward. For millennia prior, astrological systems used the seven traditional planets that ended with Saturn. Again, this is why throughout the course of this book we will consider traditional rules and concepts as needed simply because they have been part of the western astrological tradition for numerous generations.

The discovery of Uranus brought a time of change and upheaval both political (French and American revolutions) and societal (industrial revolution, scientific, labor movement, and women's suffrage). These events removed age-long boundaries of status and wealth by not only acknowledging the equality of humanity in theory but also in practice; as the middle class grew, the "rights of man" became law, and entrepreneurial commoners were finding themselves alongside "old money."

Uranus also brought the scientific age of enlightenment where superstition and religious rhetoric were replaced with objectivity, deductive logic, and Darwinism. As important as these scientific advancements were and still are, astrology was becoming even more distant from its roots as a respectable study because science seemed to be separating itself even further from their own history and heritage.

Consequently, humanity's priorities began to shift from self-reflection and understanding to profits and industry. Your self-worth was becoming more defined by your income and social status. Spirituality, along with astrology, was becoming less of a priority. However, exploring these types of realms slowly began to make a comeback with the discovery of Neptune in the 19th century.

THE METAPHYSICAL MOVEMENT: 1800AD-1960AD

Neptune, discovered in 1846, brought with it the age of mysticism, hypnotherapy, and Eastern thought. This was the era of Pamela Colman Smith, the artist of the Rider-Waite tarot deck, occultists such as Helena Blavatsky who co-founded the Theosophical Society in 1875, along with the scientific genius Nikola Tesla.

In addition, during this time, séances, psychics, and examining the unknown and hidden world through new psychological and metaphysical means were at the forefront of entertainment and healing. This is also the era of academics such as Sigmund Freud, Carl Jung, and James Braid. These three figures were interested in the subconscious and hidden psychological forces that motivate our ego expression, external perceptions, and internal motivations, all of which are part the core theory of the natal astrology taught within this book.

The Western world also engaged further into Eastern concepts such as reincarnation, yoga, karma, and universal oneness which was brought to their shores through Indian gurus such as Swami Vivekananda, Paramahansa Yogananda, and spiritualist Alice A. Bailey. In a way, religion underwent a transformation from creed (Medieval era) to critical thinking (Industrial area), and then back to spiritualism (1800s). It is as though Uranus first introduced the illogical inconsistencies within religious doctrine, and Neptune then picked up the pieces offering new answers to age-old questions.

However, it would seem that during these two centuries (1700s-1800s) astrology nevertheless fell into the background further as it was no longer considered legitimate enough to be a science and simultaneously not ethereal enough to be part of the mysticism movement. Be that as it may, the spiritual and psychological concepts that were being explored during this time have made a firm impression within astrology and the Western consciousness of today. Jung's psychological theories, Yogananda's ideas of self-realization, and Helena Blavatsky's exposure of occultism were paving the way for a completely new psychological and spiritual approach to astrology which emerged during the latter half of the 20th century AD.

The Astrology Renaissance: 1960AD-2000AD

The previous explorations into the otherworldly and psychological during the first half of the 20th century culminated during the latter half of the 20th century when astrology seemed to experience an immense rebirth. As such, a new branch made its way towards the foreground: Psychological/Archetypal Astrology. This movement was mostly spearheaded by the writings of Robert Hand, Liz Greene, and Steven Arroyo who to this day are noted as legitimate academic researchers, authors, and psychological counselors.

Within their writings, they combined old concepts of mythological archetypes with the ideas of Jungian psychology, which demonstrated how these archetypes are a reflection of one's personal perception of our outer world via one's inner psychological makeup. Ever since the ancient Greeks with Theurgic Astrology, astrology has been a tool for self-discovery. During this time, these authors and countless others took these newer psychological and archetypal concepts and adapted them within our modern-day thinking, cultural context, and complexities.

Consequently, an explosion of astrological literature, organizations, and even academic study emerged as some colleges would offer astrology once again as a legitimate discipline.[22] Sadly, this rebirth did not last for very long as it slowly became saturated and discredited as part of the "new age movement" which only dissipated astrology's legitimacy further. The scientific community also became even more absolute, cynical, and skeptical with their own opinions towards astrology, placing the study into the point of near extinction it is now currently facing. As the Western world proceeded into the 21st century, the skeptics only grew louder, and astrology became more of "that which it hates." Namely, over time, astrology began to commercialize

---

22   Kepler College. *Kepler's History*. https://www.keplercollege.org/index.php/about/history. 2021.

and delegitimatize itself into nothing more than obscure daily horoscopes one would find on the back of a newspaper.

The Present: 2000AD-Present

After observing the further dilution of astrology both in terms of legitimacy and understanding, it is no surprise to find that the majority of astrology that exists out there today is frivolous and inaccurate. Although respectable astrological organizations, journals, practitioners, and authors do exist and have been trying their hardest to maintain some form of legitimacy to the astrological sciences, these efforts are quickly quashed by the overwhelming saturation of daily horoscopes, blogs, and YouTube videos by individuals whose understanding of the subject matter is superficial and really more of an ends to a mean in order to obtain celebrity status. Countless times have I encountered astrologers whose names are recognizable and whose followings are just as grand, but they themselves do not even track their own transits, follow the void moons, or even know how to calculate a chart by hand.

As hard as organizations have been trying, this cannot be helped because there are no requirements or academic thresholds that an individual must demonstrate in order to be considered qualified to dispense astrological knowledge. Before a surgeon can put a scalpel to your body, or before a lawyer can defend someone in court, they need to be educated, tested, and certified. This kind of institutional confidence is simply not observed in astrology even though it does exist. How can you tell the legitimate astrologers from the soothsayers? I have composed a list of some common red flags that can easily demonstrate if an astrologer is legitimate or not (Table I-2).

The purpose of pointing out these red flags is to not condemn anyone for their way of making a living. However, I think it is important that the astrological community begin to point out the fraud and illegitimacies of our own profession not only for our own sake but for the sake of individuals who are sincerely seeking advice and wisdom and pay good money to do so. Before we can expect the world to take astrology seriously, we need to expect astrologers to be just as serious. If people are truly interested in learning and becoming an astrologer, there are certification tests along with legitimate academic journals and organizations that they can

48

TABLE I-2. Common Red-Flags of Astrologers who have a superficial understanding of the science.

- They possess no certification of any kind. This shows that the astrologer has not been tested on specific and required astrological techniques. It also demonstrates that the astrologer is not tied to any sort of ethical regulation that most professional astrologers who are certified obey.

- Astrologers that do not follow astrology. This is more common than you think. I cannot count the number of times I have sat on board meetings for astrological organizations and watch leaders plan meetings and events during inauspicious moments. Any astrologer that tells you to do or not do something but does not follow their own advice is a hypocrite and a fraud.

- The astrologer has not been published in any form of legitimate peer-reviewed astrological journal, book, or organization. If all they have to their name is their own website or channel, you should be skeptical of their opinions because they have never been countered by other astrologers in the field. I have had to defend my position many times at conferences and through journal writings. If the astrologer has never encountered any counterarguments to their own thinking, it means that they work in a bubble of their own ideas that have never been contested and therefore they assume that they are always right.

- Any astrologer who always tells you now is a good time or that this year is a good year without providing any warnings or pitfalls is misleading you. Even if you do have great things happening to you, there will also be pitfalls and down points to be mindful of. There is no such thing as a perfect year.

- Any astrologer who says an eclipse period is a good time to do anything is a big red flag. Or, if they provide any advice that goes against common astrological knowledge like saying signing a contract is OK during a Mercury retrograde when it most certainly is not. The eclipse is never a good time to do anything. Period. This shows you right away that the astrologer has no idea what they are talking about.

- If the astrologer uses flowery language like "watery Pisces" or "earthy Taurus" or only uses key words or phrases like "Neptune is all about the unknown" or "Chiron is known as the wounded healer." They are merely recycling shallow talking points that have been repeated *ad nauseum*.

- Any astrologer that mentions absolutes within your chart with no solution only serves to increase your anxiety without helping you to solve real problems you may be facing.

- If an astrologer cannot provide specific dates by consulting an ephemeris, or if they do not even possess an ephemeris they are not worth your time or money.

- Any astrologer that promotes pseudo new age talking points like "all you need to do is be more positive and you will attract positivity" or "Your soulmate is right around the corner if you believe hard enough" have no real understanding of the metaphysical makeup of this universe. They are using emotional manipulation to swindle you.

- The astrologer should possess a library of sorts, should be constantly reading astrology books to a point where they are able to list at least 10 books they have read from cover to cover

contribute to in order to demonstrate their abilities, in addition to possessing the appropriate credentials to back it up. To this point, one of the founders of the astrological movement of the 20th century, Robert Hand, has this to say about modern astrology:

"My only criticism of it is that in the hands of some of its less competent practitioners it has been an extremely mushy sort of astrology where anything can be made to mean anything, depending on the emotional frame of mind of the client and the astrologer. The language of 20th century astrology as a language tends to be imprecise, vague, inarticulate, and unclear. But the goals of 20th century astrology are absolutely commendable."[23]

My analysis is simply a reflection of this same criticism. It is time the astrological community begin to legitimize itself. Personally, I have been published in peer-reviewed journals three times, I am certified through NCGR-PAA, I have a library of countless astrological books, I have sat on the boards of astrological institutions, participated in astrological conferences, and am now writing a book to demonstrate my skills and abilities. My hope is that this book helps to once again legitimize this amazing and wonderful study as we are now well into the 21st century.

* * *

Now that you have received a thorough understanding of astrology's history, you are equipped with some ammunition in your pocket the next time you encounter a nay-sayer. The next time someone begins to criticize astrology's legitimacy, mention the prehistoric calendars of ancient cave dwellers, or the scientifically accurate books of the Babylonians, or the various other

---

23   Robert Hand. *Towards a Post-Modern Astrology.* Speech at the Astrological Conference of the British Astrological Organization. York, UK: 2005.

treatises written by prominent astronomers that contain legitimate defenses for astrology like those of Bonatti, Ptolemy, and Lilly. Remember, everything I have just mentioned in this survey is founded upon historical, archeological, and anthropological fact, which has been appropriately sourced. It is okay to see astrology within this more serious academic context. It is not okay to deny historical fact for scientific propaganda, and anyone who is passionate about astrology has a part to play in setting the record straight. Now, we will address the five primary objectives within astrology.

SECTION 2-THE FIVE PRIMARY OBJECTIVES

❧

Astrology is a tool that can be utilized in various ways. It can serve as a calendar, a map of the individual psyche, and as a gateway towards larger metaphysical principles just to name a few. If we are to use astrology to its fullest capacity, we need to understand the primary objectives that one should strive towards while working with astrology through these multiple facets. Surprisingly, however, very little effort is required because I have come to find that these objectives organically blossom as a consequence of simply working with astrology.

In other words, the following primary objectives seem to represent what the astrologer is naturally aspiring towards due to the nature of the science itself. This is indeed true for all sciences. For example, in a general chemistry course typically taken by all science majors in the United States, one quickly encounters the quantum-mechanical model of the atom with the famous thought experiment of "Schrödinger's Cat" and the experiments of Davisson-Germer. These experiments and mathematical formulas demonstrate that electrons, the smallest form of matter that constitutes an atom, simultaneously operate in an immaterial state as a wavelength. More specifically, a wavelength of possibilities.

These quantum experiments and mathematical theorems establish that these waves of possible outcomes do not manifest into fixed matter until an observer perceives the electron to behave as such.[24] Another way of putting it is: if a tree falls in the forest and nobody is around to hear it, does it make a sound? According to the quantum model of the atom, unless an observer is preserving the forest at all, then the forest does not even exist in its fully physical form. Until that time, it only exists as a waveform of possible outcomes until an observer expects it to operate as matter which begs the question: is there consciousness behind even the smallest form of matter? How does the electron know and understand when it is being perceived and when it

---

24   Nivaldo Tro. *Chemsitry: A Molecular Approach 4th Ed*. Pearson, England: 2017. p.349-351.

is not? Any individual that comes across these observations of the universe cannot help but to ask themselves bigger life questions such as these.

Ironically, however, those that have been lucky enough to become educated in these workings of the universe turn a blind eye to the philosophical questions they naturally procure. In a Pew Research Center survey, only 33% of scientists believe in God, 18% believe in a universal spirit or higher power, and 41% have atheistic views stating that they do not believe in either.[25] This practically splits scientists into a 50/50 split on the subject, which is far from the norm when the study compared the results to the general public, of which 91% claimed that they either believe in God or in a higher consciousness. One would think that when one is exposed to quantum mechanical models of matter, it would invigorate internal philosophical debates into the workings of nature, but sadly, it appears to have the reverse effect.

Astrology, being a science as well, will also inevitably present to the practitioner similar questions about the workings of nature, but with astrology, they are more difficult to ignore because astrology is indeed the study of how the universe operates within the microcosm of our consciousness and through the macrocosm of our place within the human race. This is not to say that these objectives are easy to understand or do not come without internal struggle. No, you will be facing these objectives head-on as an inevitability. It will be difficult at first. That is why it is helpful to understand what to expect as you begin along your astrological journey.

OBJECTIVE #1: KNOW THYSELF

Astrology is one of most effective tools the Western world has for what the Eastern world calls "self-realization". This entails the understanding of who we truly are and getting rid of the parts of our personality that are not really us. (More on this topic in Part I-Section 3.) The closer we get to this goal, the closer we become the embodiment of our fullest and true individual expression within this lifetime.

Many of us do not accomplish the true lifegoals we were set out to complete in this world due to of our lack of self-understanding. This causes ignorance and an inability to reach our

25   Pew Research Center. *Religion and Science in the United States: Scientists and Belief*. 2009. https://www.pewforum.org/2009/11/05/scientists-and-belief/.

fullest potential because we are allowing our unconscious self to run the show. (More on this in Part I-Section 6.) This is further echoed in Chapter 18, Verse 47 of the Bhagavad-Gita which states,

"It is better to engage in one's own occupation, even though one may perform it imperfectly, than to accept another's occupation and perform it perfectly. Prescribed duties, according to one's nature, are never affected by sinful reactions."[26]

With astrology, we begin to pick away at our unconscious self which, while being unearthed, exposes our self-destructive tendencies that have prevented us from achieving our highest life path. Studying one's natal chart and experiencing the life events that surround one's personal story will help to comprehend and detect these unconscious forces. Astrology is a great system that can bring you towards the goal of self-understanding in a very matter of fact and objective way.

OBJECTIVE #2: EASE ALONG THROUGH LINEAR TIME

Humanity lives in a world of completely artificial time. Our days are not in tune with the real daily rotation of our planet. Similarly, the Gregorian calendar is highly cumbersome, especially when it is compared to a calendar based on the ecliptic.[27,28] Although this dyssynchronization is provable by scientific observation, the biggest irony is that the entire civilized world is nevertheless permanently set and fixed into this artificial paradigm with most of humanity having no idea of the real cosmic calendar that governs our daily lives.

Becoming aware of such phenomena (Part III) allows for the practitioner to no longer erroneously go against the current, but to flow with it instead. When you start to align your life to the true nature and timing of our planet you remove a lot of unnecessary obstacles and frustrations. This is because you are synchronizing your body and life to the true nature of our planet's journey around the Sun. In essence, you are riding the cosmic wave of life.

26   A.C. Bhaktivedanta Swami Prabhupada. *Bhagavad-Gita As It Is*. Macmillan Company. New York: 1972. pp. 815-816.
27   Brad Plumer. *We've Been Using the Gregorian Calendar for 434 Years. It is Still Bizarre.* Vox News. 2016. https://www.vox.com/2016/10/4/13147306/434th-gregorian-calendar-anniversary-google-doogle.
28   Bob Enyart. *An Original 360 Day Year*. 2018. http://360dayyear.com/.

OBJECTIVE #3: FORGIVENESS OF YOURSELF AND OTHERS

This objective is a substantial and crucial goal within astrology. Some people want to continue to blame their parents for the way their lives have turned out. For others, they can never let go of that one time that one elementary school teacher really hurt them and their feelings. It is crucial to remember that the natal chart shows us not only the karma and experiences that must occur in this life, but it also shows us the ways in which this karma is received and can be addressed (more on this in Part I-Section 4).

In other words, you were meant to have those experiences because you were meant to have those experiences. It may seem like there is no rhyme or reason, but rest assured, there exists profound reasoning for our less-favored life events. An individual cannot go on their entire life without forgiving those that have hurt them in the past. They were going to experience those specific life lessons in any case, so it is of no importance how they came about. Astrology teaches us about the patterns of karma and with this understanding comes immense forgiveness. With this forgiveness comes untold healing from the release of psychological and emotional baggage.

OBJECTIVE #4: RESPECT AND ADORATION FOR THE WORKINGS OF NATURE

When I was preparing for an astrology certification test, I had to learn how to compute astrological birth charts by hand like the ancients have done for thousands of years before the computer age. When I was teaching myself how to accomplish this, I came to an amazing revelation: natal charts are incredibly mathematically precise and so unique that there is no other explanation other than an overarching influence of a higher consciousness, or energy, involved in the making of one's life. Again, astrology is not a belief system so even if you do not believe in a higher power, you still cannot not deny that there is some all-encompassing cosmic force at play. This is the same force that binds the entire universe; what some scientists call the "cosmic web."[29]

---

29   Matt Davis. *What is the Cosmic Web?*. Big Think: 2019. https://bigthink.com/surprising-science/cosmic-web?rebelltitem=5#rebelltitem5.

Every life is special, and every life journey is just as special as it is unique. Coming to this realization, there grew inside of me a deep and profound adoration for the cosmic web of life, the workings of nature, and the life-plan that has been mapped out for every individual as evidenced within their unique birth chart. The more you work with astrology, the more you will also witness these complexities of the natural world and your place within.

OBJECTIVE #5: Understanding of Personal, Parental, Familial, Generational, National, and Human Karma

This goal ties back to objective number three. The more you study astrology, the more you start to understand the patterns that govern the karma of your parents, your family, and indeed all of humanity.

People are not aware of this because they do not usually look back on their life experiences, those of their parents, their parents' parents, etc., etc. There will always be issues that we have inherited from the ones that have lived before us. Indeed, it is their own unconsciousness that has caused them to pass these issues onto their children in the first place allowing for the cycles of karma to continue. Astrology helps us to break these cycles and heal them instead. As a natural consequence, you not only heal yourself but your family, your children, your nation, and truly, the entire world. If humanity understood this, we would create a reality of complete and total unconditional love for everyone and as a further consequence, suffering would cease to exist (See Part 1-Section 8).

* * *

In her famous book *Time to Remember*, astrologer Nancy Anne Hastings famously says, "You can't blame your mother." Trust me, as someone with Saturn in the 4th house, I would know. In her statement, Ms. Hastings points to one of the biggest remedies that astrology can provide for an individual. Astrology removes blame, shame, guilt, and even vengefulness because it demonstrates that we all need to grow; we are all constantly evolving and struggling to evolve.

There cannot be growth without struggle. The butterfly cannot escape the chrysalis without force and will. The snake cannot shed its skin without first feeling uncomfortable. In this same light, we should not and cannot cower in the past and within our own misery. Instead, we should be thankful for our sufferings because it is through that misery which brings us closer to our true self. If life were simple, easy, and worry free then what would be the point? The good news is: if you allow yourself to fight through the inner friction and conflict and arise out of studying astrology, you not only grow and evolve as an individual, but the entire world benefits from your hard work. As I have mentioned in the introduction, for the 21st century, this is the work that must be done.

SECTION 3-ASTROLOGY AND THE ARCHETYPAL "IDEAL HUMAN"

Astrology is the science of self-realization. Who we think we are is not who we truly are. This is due to false impressions based upon our past experiences and future desires. When one reads this sentence, they probably think, "That is preposterous! I already know myself! I have a name, likes and dislikes, a family, a past, future goals, friends, a partner, hobbies, possessions, etc., etc. Are these things not expressions of my own identity? Of whom I am?"

The astrologer would argue, "Not really. This is because all your likes and dislikes, your associations, your interests, your hates and desires, are all derived from who you perceive yourself to be, not necessarily who you truly are. You might say, 'I hate the dark,' but why do you hate the dark? It could be due to your attachment of a negative past experience that gave you that opinion of the dark which you then internalized into part of your character. But the fact remains that the dark is objectively darkness no matter what. It was you that attached the emotional stigma of hate towards the dark; to another the dark could be comforting and pleasant. Even then, this is erroneous because it is still an opinionated attachment to an objective state of nature. The dark is simply darkness, and its character is in no way changed by your perception. This is what the Eastern philosophers mean when they say, 'attachment leads to suffering.'"

So, who are we truly? That is for you to discover with the help of astrology. As you begin to slowly peel away the layers of trauma, judgment, opinions, and faulty character traits, you will soon find a person of unconditional love and beauty. When you let go of your preconceived notions of the world and of yourself, you will begin to see the dark as darkness and nothing more. You will begin to see your enemies as yourself, and your hard life-lessons as the catalyst which awakens your true nature from within.

58

One of the oldest metaphors humanity has used in this regard is the idea that we all possess both a bestial and angelic nature constantly at war within ourselves. To this point, the old Cherokee proverb comes to mind:

> "The is a battle of two wolves inside us all. One is evil. It is anger, jealousy, greed, resentment, lies, inferiority, and ego. The other is good. It is joy, peace, love, hope, humility, kindness, empathy, and truth. Who wins the battle? The one you feed."

Again, an individual might object, "You Sir, are a dolt, a simpleton, a nincompoop! Why, just the other day I gave money to a homeless person and that was with full awareness of who I am. By that action alone, am I not showing that I already am a good person and have chosen good actions over evil ones?" Yet again, the astrologer would counter, "How often do we say, 'The road to hell is paved with good intentions?' Sure, you may have given the homeless person some money, but when was the last time you told your Mom or Dad that you loved them? When was the last time you looked at those who have intentionally wronged you and told them you forgave them with an open heart? How many words filled with venom did you spray onto social media today, yesterday, and the day after that?"

"One good action that is easy to perform does not compensate for the harder actions that require you to swallow your pride. The homeless person never wronged you, so you feel no animosity towards them. You did not have to swallow your pride to give the homeless person money and in fact, the sense of conceit and self-righteousness you have given yourself through that action negates any good that might have come out of that action. Until you can treat everyone you encounter with the same love you have given that homeless person, you cannot claim to be working on the side of unconditional love."

You are not your thoughts. Again, I repeat, you are not your thoughts. Ignorance towards this statement alone has been the ultimate downfall for all of humanity. Not only do we attach our own personality to our thoughts, we act upon these thoughts within the external world. Our opinions, even if we perceive them to be inherently good, are nonetheless subjective and based upon our attachments towards our thoughts which stem from our past experiences and future desires. The ancient Chinese philosopher Laozi understood this universal truth in his incredibly succinct quote:

"Watch your thoughts, for they become your words; watch your words, for they become your actions; watch your actions, for they become your habits; watch your habits, for they become your character; watch your character, for it becomes your destiny."

Astrology is a window to the soul. It exposes to you the dust that covers this window which is preventing the light from shining through. Slowly, one step at a time, with astrology, you begin to wipe away the dust of ignorance, allowing for your true nature to finally shine through. Nobody is perfect. Please understand I am not writing this from a place of "holier than thou." I am fully aware that I have my own shortcomings and imperfections. Just like you, I am only human, and to err is to be human. I am simply echoing what sages and wise people have understood about human nature for millennia. Sages like the Himalayan guru *Babaij* who once said, "There is no saint without a past, there is no sinner without a future."[30]

We all have within ourselves the capacity to let go of our own preconceived and artificial ideas as to who we are for the higher ideal of the archetypal supreme human being. Astrology is the gateway to this understanding, and if we put in the effort, we begin to truly evolve into our true self. Then and only then will the world around us begin to change, but this can only start from within through our own conscious desire to right our wrongs so that we may grow into our ideal self.

---

30   James Braha. *How to Be a Great Astrologer*. Hermetician Press, Florida: 1992. p. 10.

SECTION 4-ASTROLOGY AND KARMA

When I use the word karma in this setting, I am defining it in the simplest of terms: karma equals action. This is the same truism that is defined in Newton's Third Law of Motion: For every action, there is an equal and opposite reaction. Just as it is with the laws of motion with regards to matter, every action we perform has intended and unintended consequences. That is why we should seek to perform action with neutral intentions and attachments towards the outcome. This is because, as mentioned in the previous section, our intentions are typically based within the biased opinions of our ego attachments. Therefore, these desires, along with the actions the procure, are by their very nature besmirched.

Enter the skeptic, "So what you are saying is we should be incredibly passive in life? That we should not have goals or ambitions, and simply do nothing for anything we do is naturally going to possess consequences that could be detrimental?" To which the astrologer replies, "Even doing nothing is doing something. By the very act of breathing, even if you are completely immobile in doing so, it is still an action nonetheless."

"It is not about losing the will or desire to do action; it is about letting go of the expectations of said action. Let us say I am an artist that is trying to apply for a competition. I decide to make this wonderful, inspiring piece of art for the competition but the entire time I'm thinking 'I hope I win. I hope this beats all the other contestants. I hope I get all the glory from my piece of art.' By those thoughts alone, the artist has tarnished their own creation by attaching expectations and desires towards the end product. Naturally, if said artist does not get their way, there is suffering because they have placed all of that expectation onto their action."

"How many times have we done this in our own lives? Countless! If instead the artist thought, 'I am finding joy in the act of creating and this alone is my reward.' Then the artist would have succeeded in right action and thought because they are acting without expectation of the outcome simply by enjoying the work itself in the present moment." When we operate with this neutral lens of surrendering to the will of the universe instead of imposing our own, we negate any positive or negative karma that could come our way as a result.

We have just covered an example of karma in action through the microcosm of daily life, but what about the macrocosm when it comes to substantially fated life events that might have come from the actions of past lives? Indeed, the very nature of our birth chart shows us the karma, both good and bad, that we have inherited in this lifetime and must be understood and surmounted. Again, even if you do not believe in past lives or reincarnation, the birth chart can still be viewed as an impression of one's limitations, strengths, and the consequential availability of various possibilities that are based therein.

For example, some individuals could have good fortune and ease when it comes to their career, and others must deal with a harder struggle in life in order to achieve success within their own career. As a natural consequence, the individual with better fortune has available certain opportunities that the individual with a harder time might not be able to experience. These predetermined situations are fixed within the birth chart, and one could argue that they stem from the actions of past lives, which leads an individual to their specific life journey that they must presently experience.

In this same light, the individual that has a hard time with career could inversely possess a sound and peaceful domestic life while the other individual with an easy time with career could be perpetually single and struggling to find a decent partner. According to astrological theory, both individuals have unique lessons to learn so that they can evolve in their own way. The good news is, according to the wisdom of the past, both individuals are nevertheless headed towards the same goal: self-realization. It is simply up to the individual, by their own autonomous actions, how quickly or slowly will it take them to get there.

Think of astrology like a fast-track lane on a freeway during rush hour. True, you might have to sacrifice some money in order to use the lane, but you arrive towards your destination faster than the rest even though everyone else is headed towards the same destination: home. Everyone is on the same journey of self-discovery. Astrology simply accelerates this process by removing all of the guess work and allowing for the individual to become aware of their unconscious tendencies. Until the individual is able to bring these tendencies to light, they will continue to dictate our actions which could end up slowing down our progress. Regardless, every individual is still aiming towards the same goal of self-understanding, whether or not the individual is aware of this fact.

SECTION 5-ASTROLOGY, FATE, AND FREE WILL

∽

One hundred and twenty years after Albert Einstein postulated the Theory of Relativity, scientists have been attempting to further understand the mysterious principles that govern the fabric of time and space. One of the biggest unsolved mysteries in this regard includes the "Grandfather Paradox" when it comes to theoretical time travel. The paradox goes as such: if I were to travel back in time and murder my grandfather, would I no longer cease to exist? This similar quandary was the main basis for the timeless movie classic *Back to the Future*, along with other great films and stories in our culture.

As recently as 2020, new mathematical models have allowed scientists to further understand inconsistencies such as these which sheds new light on the true workings of time and space. In a new revolutionary study, scientists have now deduced that time actually has the ability to re-adjust itself in order to avoid theoretical paradoxes like the Grandfather Paradox from even occurring.[31] In an online interview, astrophysicist Dr. Joe Pesce explains further:

"Let's give an example here: I travel back in time to stop COVID-19 and I want to keep Patient Zero from being infected. So, I travel back in time and if I stop Patient Zero from being infected, then I stop the pandemic, then that eliminates my motivation for going into the past. That is the crux of the [Grandfather] Paradox. What researchers have now found within the mathematics is that the events would re-calibrate themselves. So maybe I go and I stop Patient Zero, but I then become Patient Zero and I start the infection. Or someone else becomes Patient Zero that is outside the realm of mine being able to manipulate. So, ultimately, the end point is still the same. There is still going to be a

---

31   Germain Tobar and Fabio Costa. *Reversible dynamics with closed time-like curves and freedom of Choice*. Classical and Quantum Gravity, 37: 205011, 2020.

pandemic, but the particular events…change…The end point will be the same, we just might get to it in a different way."[32]

Could it be, just as it is with electrons as evidenced by the double-slit experiment, that there is some consciousness behind the fabric of time and space which is not only aware, but simultaneously co-creating and reacting to our autonomous decisions? Science has already proven the existence of implicit bias and how observations influence outcomes many times over.[33] Now, there are mathematical models to prove that these same rules function within time itself.

As Dr. Pesce described, it seems that there are some events that are indeed inevitable and unavoidable. However, if fate was the all-pervading force, then one could argue that people who perform evil works like murder had no real autonomy in doing so and could therefore not really be blamed for their actions. This is not the case either because it seems everyone still has the free will to behave and act as they wish within the logical confines of their experience.

Instead, astrological theory would argue that both fate and free will exist as a hybrid of sorts. We might not have the ability to prevent certain fated events, but we always have the free will to react to them as we see fit. Within the astrological context, the individual is going to have a certain life-event occur at a specific point in time no matter what. How prepared they are and how healthy their psychology is at the time of the event will determine their ability to handle the event, which, in turn, influences the outcome. Similarly, if the individual was being proactive and working on the themes that the life-event was going to bring about, then it is also possible that the event "readjusts" and manifests in a less-impactful way.

For example, Pluto transits in astrology usually accompany a death or a severe ending of some kind like a marriage or a career. Let us say that the individual always had deeply seeded issues with their father throughout their entire life and never attempted to resolve them. Then, at the time of the Pluto transit, their father passes away and all the sudden, the pile of unconscious agony that they have been repressing finally emerges and reveals itself as a result. However, if the individual was in therapy for years prior to the event, they would have been more

32   The Hill: Rising with Krystal and Saagar. *Dr. Joe Pesce: Researchers PROVE that Time Travel Mathematically Possible.* Nov. 26, 2020. https://www.youtube.com/watch?v=2G886HiSgWk&t=15s.
33   Weizmann Institute of Science. "Quantum Theory Demonstrated: Observation Affects Reality." ScienceDaily. ScienceDaily, 27 February 1998. www.sciencedaily.com/releases/1998/02/980227055013.htm.

psychologically grounded and able to handle the event more maturely. The death of the father was inevitable, but the individual's freewill to tackle the issue prior to the event allowed for the event (and time) to re-adjust appropriately. As was mentioned in the introduction, it pays to be proactive in astrology.

Another example: let us say the individual has always had issues with eating unhealthily. They do nothing to fix the problem, and then Saturn conjoins their Sun which causes them to have a severe heart-attack. They survive, but the experience makes them realize they need to fix their diet once and for all. Had they have gone to an astrologer prior to the event, they could have seen the Saturn conjunction ahead of time and could have warned the individual that they needed to be more mindful of their diet now before it is too late. If they take the astrologer's advice, then time, along with the event, would readjust to where the heart-attack is no longer needed for that individual to learn that lesson. Keep in mind, they will still have an intense and unavoidable life event, but it will be less drastic and intense. Perhaps this time, instead of a heart attack, they experience an event which emotionally triggers them back into their bad eating habits. In other words, instead of life throwing them a hard life lesson like a heart-attack, life instead tests their dedication toward a healthy lifestyle allowing them to further understand why their bad eating habits existed in the first place. As these newer developments in physics have demonstrated, science now confirms that time does indeed operate in this fashion.

Another thing to keep in mind involves the perception of fated events. As mentioned in the introduction, fated events may only appear fated because the individual is operating within their unconscious motivations. In other words, a person could experience an intense life-event and go "Wow, God must really hate me. This came out of the blue and I do not understand why life had to throw a wrench in my life which was working out so perfectly for me beforehand." The astrologer would counter, "Was your life really working perfectly, or were you just giving yourself a false sense of security while unknowingly manifesting events that led you to this outcome?" This philosophical quandary is part of our next topic where we observe the workings of the individual and global psychology through the lens of renowned psychologist Carl Jung.

SECTION 6-JUNGIAN PSYCHOLOGICAL THEORY

Every time I encounter a psychologist at a party or a gathering of friends, the first question I always ask is, "What are your thoughts on Carl Jung?", and every time I am always surprised by their answers. Either the psychologist will have no idea who I am talking about, or they will brush him off dismissively. I remember one time a psychologist told me, "You learn about him early on in your studies, but then professors typically state that his theories are outdated and irrelevant." I could not believe what I was hearing! If Carl Jung's ideas were irrelevant in today's world, then why is Shakespeare still relevant? Or Greek myths? Are not the countless superhero movies we see today only reflections of the Greek myth and of the archetypal war hero like that of Achilles or Hercules or Odysseus? What about *Star Wars*? Even creator George Lucas admits that his biggest inspiration towards the Star Wars films were the writings of Joseph Campbell, whose studies in comparative mythology and religion echo the same sentiments of Carl Jung.

If Jungian psychology truly had no place in our world, then these timeless stories and characters would similarly have no relevancy in today's world. We would therefore witness an emergence of new archetypes out of every new generation of humanity. However, this is not the case. Shakespeare is still performed today, and even six hundred years later, audiences are still able to relate, laugh, and weep. Fifty years after its debut, multiple generations still watch *Star Wars* and identify with "the Hero's Journey." *The Odyssey* is a staple in literature and every teenager is expected to read it in high school. If Carl Jung's psychological theories were truly irrelevant, then no human alive would be able to establish any personal connection to these works of art because they would be considered outdated and intangible.

Suffice to say, Jungian psychological theory is a foundational cornerstone within modern astrological theory. When astrologers observe a planet like Mars, they are attributing the same character traits that the ancient Greeks placed upon the god of war thousands of years ago. Similarly, the signs of the zodiac correspond to very specific times in our nature's calendar. The themes of spring are seen within Taurus, the Winter solstice within Capricorn, etc., etc. When astrologers make these parallels, they are often criticized and indeed, this is one of the main talking points skeptics use towards astrology. They argue that because astrologers make these connections to mythology, they should not be taken seriously because it seems to be a cheesy pseudo-New Age way of thinking. However, I would argue that the connections astrologers make from myth to the human story is no different from what artists do in taking up inspiration from old stories and adapting their themes to accommodate their modern audiences.

Within the astrological context, there are four main theories of Jungian psychology that the astrological practitioner needs to be aware of so that they can properly approach a natal chart:

THEORY #1: Our subconscious mind heavily influences our conscious actions. Therefore, it is vital to understand our unconscious motivations in order to obtain greater autonomy within our own lives.

As mentioned above, our unconscious mind is the primary driving force for our actions. One of the greatest gifts astrology gives the practitioner is that it lays out these unconscious motivations with great transparency. If an individual is to understand these motivations, they can stop them in their tracks, which causes them to work less on autopilot even though they may be thinking they are operating with complete lucidity.

For example, let us say an individual is highly introverted and abhors all types of confrontation, good and bad. Maybe this was due to a childhood experience where they always witnessed their parents fighting and therefore assimilated conflict with feelings of anxiety and stress. However, these memories are so distant in the past that they do not realize their influence. They therefore go on through life assuming that their introverted nature is just a part of who they are.

Now, that individual needs to find a job. Naturally, they consciously chose jobs that do not involve working with the public. They think this is a willful act but in reality, their unconscious fears are driving them to find a career of this nature. However, as we will discover, the unconscious constantly strives to be unearthed, exposed, and understood. Therefore, the unconscious mind will manifest situations where these various phases can occur.

Back to our example, the individual works in a highly isolated job and has been doing well in this regard but suddenly, the business goes belly up and they no longer have that safety net. When the individual tries to find a new job, they have no choice but to work with the public and face their fear of confrontation. Or, their job may be isolated, but they experience confrontation with their superior on a daily basis. In other words, your unconscious problems will always seek to find you so that you can address them. You then have the choice to either repress it further or confront the issues at hand. With astrology, you are shown where these unconscious motivations exist so that you can address them and become aware of their existence.

THEORY #2: PSYCHOLOGICAL PROJECTION IS THE PRIMARY AGENT FOR UNCONSCIOUS MOTIVATIONS TO BE EXPRESSED.

One evening, an individual decides to go to a nightclub to listen to their favorite band play. At the club, there is a dance floor where a group of individuals are enjoying the music and dancing their hearts out. Out of the crowd, the individual spots a certain person who is dancing wildly and thinks to themself, "Wow, look at how embarrassing that person is acting! I cannot believe they are dancing around so provocatively with no common decency." As an objective third party, the astrologer would look at that and go, "Is that person really acting differently than the other people on the dance floor, or are you projecting your own insecurities onto that person? In other words, you yourself are embarrassed to dance and express yourself honestly and freely that you have to project that insecurity onto another person by putting them down."

We experience psychological projection like this all the time within our lives either as the person who is projecting our insecurities onto an individual or vice versa. In essence, everyone we encounter becomes a mirror where we are placing judgement onto that person but really, we are judging ourselves through that individual because they possess a quality which we lack and therefore envy.

The good news is, if we are able to catch ourselves in the act, we obtain amazing insight into our own psychology. The next time you have an intense thought like this stop yourself and ask, "Well, what does that say about me?" This ties back to Theory #1 because it is vitally important to understand where these "voices in our head" come from. They usually come from the unconscious self expressing itself through psychological projection. Instead of placing judgements, anger, hate, and the like onto others, ask yourself if they are just reflecting the anger, hate, and judgement you just feel about yourself. With this kind of introspection comes immense healing and a greater awareness of your individual psychology.

THEORY #3: GLOBAL CONSCIOUSNESS AND UNCONSCIOUSNESS IS DIRECTLY RELATED AND PROPORTIONAL TO THE INDIVIDUAL CONSCIOUSNESS AND UNCONSCIOUSNESS.

In 2006, researchers at Texas A&M University performed an experiment to see if universal symbols could be matched to their respective word description even if the individual never saw the symbol prior to the experiment. For example, the subject would be shown a picture of a heart which is associated with the word "charity." The participant would then have to choose if the symbol matched with the proper word association. Some pictures and word associations were logical while others were more abstract like an image of the number seven representing "completion." Furthermore, the study included bilingual Spanish-English speaking individuals in order to determine if the symbols were understood over linguistic and cultural barriers. From their data, they concluded that participants identified the correct image/word associations more often than an incorrect matching. They therefore deduced that the results "...provide further support for the Jungian concept of collective (archetypal) unconscious memory aid in recalling words that are matched with archetypal symbols."[34]

Similarly, when observing the character traits of serial killers, a pattern begins to emerge that reflects global and individual consciousness. When correlating upbringings of serial killers, there seem to be incidents of severe sexual abuse as a child, witnessing of drug abuse by their family, and intense bullying and social isolation during the same time.[35,36] When a serial killer is discovered along with their accompanying history of domestic abuse, it is easy to put the blame

---

34 Jeffery M. Brown and Terence P. Hannigan. *An Empirical Test of Carl Jung's Collective Unconscious (Archetypal) Memory.* Journal of Border Educational Research, Volume 5: Fall 2006, p. 119.
35 Shirley L. Scott. *"What Makes Serial Killers Tick?"* truTV. Aired July 28, 2010.
36 Eric W. Hickey, *Serial Murderers and their Victims.* Wadsworth, Cengage Learning, 2010.

onto the parents. However, drug addiction, school bullying, and sexual abuse are not isolated familial issues but societal issues that remain unaddressed.

As a society, we are well aware of these less desired qualities of our culture. However, just how we treat our own unconsciousness with contempt, society likewise tends to sweep these issues under the rug and ignore their influences instead of seeking to address them. As a consequence, people like serial killers emerge out of the woodwork and when they do, they serve as a message to the general public that these issues not only have fatal consequences, they have yet to be addressed. However, society tends to place the blame completely onto the family or towards the individual instead of observing how our own culture has led to these manifestations.

If we attempted to fix drug addiction, sexual abuse, or school outcasting as a collective group of peoples, then environments that breed harmful murderers would theoretically no longer exist. Carl Jung would go one step further and argue that the reason why these darker sides of our culture are prevalent is that we, as individuals, are similarly not addressing the darker parts of our psyche within ourselves. Until the majority of individuals work through and purge their darker tendencies, they will continue to be expressed through the society at-large through multiple mechanisms. As an astrologer, we have to be aware of this symbiotic relationship and remember the truth of Rumi's quote when he says we need to change ourselves first before we expect society to change. The good news is, if we take the time to work through our unconscious self, then society's unconscious self will likely follow and become equally healed.

THEORY #4: MYTHOLOGICAL ARCHETYPES, BOTH ANCIENT AND MODERN, SERVE TO COMPREHEND AND EXPRESS THE PERSONAL PSYCHOLOGICAL CONDITION.

According to Carl Jung, "An archetype is like an old watercourse along which the water of life has flowed for centuries, digging a deep channel for itself. The longer it has flowed in this channel the more likely it is that sooner or later the water will return to its old bed."[37] Looking back on our discussion, this is why timeless classics are still relevant and experienced in today's world either through the original source material or through a reinterpretation of the story and its morals using modern characters and themes. Either way, these stories reflect universal truths

---

37   C.G. Jung. *Civilization in Transition, 2nd Edition.* Princeton University Press, New Jersey. 1970.

of the human experience, which is why we identify so strongly with them, and why their place within the global society is just as prevalent as is it permanent.

This key concept explains why astrology's use of ancient archetypes works so effectively when it comes to an individual's psychological analysis. The only difference is the astrologer observes the individual as an actor living within the reality of their existence as opposed to a fictional character. Even so, the strengths and weaknesses of fictional characters are still observed and relatable to a real-life individual.

Furthermore, when we consider Jung's analysis as quoted above, ancient archetypes are firmly grounded within the personal and global psyche simply because they have existed for thousands of years through multiple generations and societies. In this way, the natal chart becomes a functioning metaphor of these timeless archetypes. This makes it easy for the astrologer to explain to the individual their unique psychology because they can relate to these archetypes effortlessly because these fictional stories and characters are literally embedded within our global society. It is simply up to the astrologer to put A and B together into a workable equation so that the individual can understand their personal story.

* * *

Jungian psychological theory provides multiple advantages for the modern astrologer. For one, it gives us greater context into how psychologies are manifested, how they operate, and how they are similar amongst individuals. Another advantage is that it takes away a lot of the guesswork around how these psychological energies manifest for the individual. With contemporary psychology, it could take years for the psychologist to get to the core issues surrounding the individual; astrologers typically only have one session.

Similarly, the psychologist must eliminate their own implicit bias and judgments and try to understand the more hidden motivations of the individual. What makes this difficult for the psychologist is that they have to interpret what their patient is subjectively telling them through the questions they ask. That is, assuming they are even looking for the unconscious motivations at all considering how Jung's theories are not prevalent in today's modern psychological thinking. Astrological authors like Steven Arroyo are in fact psychologists themselves and astrologers like him understand astrology's utility when it came to his own practice. In fact, even Jung himself tipped his hat towards astrology in this regard having said, "Astrology, like the collective unconscious with which psychology is concerned, consists of symbolic configurations: The "planets" are the gods, symbols of the powers of the unconscious."[38] The natal chart is incredibly objective with no biases or hidden answers. The entire psychology of the individual is exposed for the world to see. All it takes is a trained eye to understand how to properly analyze its content.

Hopefully, by now you are starting to understand that astrology is indeed deeply rooted within legitimate psychological and scientific theories which have been confirmed by academic and scientific experimentation and exploration. Now that we have a firm fundamental understanding of these various theories, we are now ready to learn more about astrology itself but before we get there, we need to go over common pitfalls, rules, and strategies.

---

38   Exploring Your Mind. *Carl Jung and Astrology in Psychoanalysis*. 2018. https://exploringyourmind. com/carl-jung-astrology-psychoanalysis/.

SECTION 7-APPROACH, TIPS, TOOLS, AND RESOURCES

∾

What does it mean when we say someone blazes a trial for others? We mean that the individual has gone into the thick brush of the forest, carved out a walkable path, and has returned safely to share the experience so that the expedition is easier for those that will subsequently follow. This section is my version of astrological trailblazing by looking back at my personal studies over the past decade.

Astrology requires a lot of self-study and because of this, you are discovering and setting your own guideposts which require constant readjustment the further along you travel down the path. I am most certain these insights will help to make your time with astrology less difficult and more efficient because you will have a better idea as to what to expect and how to appropriately react. To begin, I want to discuss eight basic tips that will help you along your astrological journey.

* * *

EIGHT TIPS FOR STUDYING ASTROLOGY

TIP #1: Do Not Panic!

The entirety of the astrological sciences is incredibly overwhelming at first. You are not only trying to understand various archetypes and how they interact with one another, you are also trying to apply these energies towards your own psychology and the psychology of others. Always remember to take it easy, take your time, and if it gets to be too overbearing, take a step back and regroup.

TIP #2: It is Okay to Take Breaks

Astrology requires a good amount of mental capacity, fortitude, and honesty. When I began to study astrology, sometimes I would overwhelm my mind with too much information and analysis. I found that if I closed the book and stepped away for a few days, this gave my mind ample time to process and integrate the new information. After these break periods, my mind was able to reset and continue. If you need to take a break, by all means, take a break.

TIP #3: It is Okay to Be Wrong

When it comes to the skeptics of astrology, they always expect you to be 100% right all of the time. If you are not, then they see that as an excuse for the invalidity of the science altogether, but I challenge anyone to find me a scientist who never made a mistake in their life. It is only due to the obsessive desire to prove astrology wrong that astrologers always feel pressured to be completely accurate and right all of the time, but this expectation is absurd. If a doctor misdiagnoses a patient, do they deserve to have their license to practice revoked? No, instead they learn heavily from their mistakes and improve. Hence why it is called a "practice" in the first place. Remember, it is not about being right, it is about trial and error. If you interpret a chart and you are completely off, at least you are trying. See what works, see what does not work, and give yourself permission to be wrong.

TIP #4: Allow Time for Daily Introspection

When you begin to observe your personal transits (Part IV), you will inevitably begin to perform introspective analysis on a daily basis. This means you are utilizing astrology to the fullest. As a practitioner, take time every day to really dig deep inside yourself with openness and honesty. Slowly over time, you begin to peel away the layers of your unconscious mind which brings you closer to astrology's end goal of self-realization.

TIP #5: Be Patient and Forgiving of Yourself and Others

As we discussed in Part I-Section 2, letting go and learning to forgive your past is a substantial boon astrology provides for the individual. The more you forgive and forget, the more you release unwanted baggage. If you begin to study astrology without a willingness to be forgiving, you are closing yourself off to one of the greater healing potentials of astrology.

It takes substantial courage and awareness to release the ego in this way, but you are showing a great level of maturity by pardoning your less-favored life choices, your upbringing, and the various people that have shaped your world perspective for the worse. Remember, you were meant to have those experiences because it was pre-determined within your natal chart. It is up to you to learn the lessons they provide so that you can properly move on with your life.

TIP #6: Be Prepared for Changes in Your Life

Studying astrology advances your character due to the vast amount of introspection you perform. Consequently, your true personality begins to shine forth because you begin to discern what aspects of your personality are not really a reflection of your true self. Therefore, you can expect to witness changes not only inside yourself, but with your friends, associations, hobbies, interests, and perhaps even changes in profession, living situation, and life direction. You are shedding the skin of the false ego and begin to arise as your authentic self. You should trust that the changes that occur as a consequence are for the betterment of your own existence because you are becoming more aligned with your authentic nature. That which no longer serves you will naturally slip away.

TIP #7: Pay Attention to Astrology's Influence on Others

When we explore the topics in Part III, you will begin to understand that everyone is influenced by the celestial calendar whether they know it or not. Paying attention to how other individuals work with or against the tide gives you daily case studies that demonstrate astrology's validity. Furthermore, if you are finding that people around you are planning events during inauspicious moments, you are then able to better circumnavigate because you are paying attention to the actual forces at play.

TIP #8: Astrology is Filled with Paradoxes

How can a planet like Saturn, which represents themes like tradition, obligation, and limitation rule the free-spirited sign of Aquarius? Look at Mars as another example. How can a planet that we associate with action, drive, and assertiveness rule the strategically introverted sign of Scorpio? Contradictions such as these are merely a reflection of the countless paradoxes that exist within human nature.

We are all filled with opposing forces that cancel and contradict one another, so it makes sense that astrology is similarly filled with contradicting data here and there. It is good to be aware of this fact so as to not accidentally conclude that astrology itself is a made-up system with no logic involved. The good news is, I have found that the more you work through these inconsistencies, the greater your understanding of the science becomes. All you are really doing is understanding the dual nature that planets and people represent.

* * *

FIVE QUALITIES OF THE WELL-TO-DO ASTROLOGER

Before you begin your studies into astrology, there are five distinct character traits that would be best to cultivate within yourself in preparation. These qualities put you in the correct mindset.

QUALITY #1: Trust

Sometimes you must take a leap of faith with astrology. At moments when you want to act, astrology could be telling you to wait a day, a month, or even years which begs the question: would you rather have your aspirations happen quickly, or to their fullest potential when the time is right? Timing is incredibly important in astrology. Indeed, one of astrology's primary functions is to track time. Using the celestial calendar requires trust because you must go on the assumption that astrology knows what is best for you, even more so than you do. This can be difficult because when it comes to your own life, it is hard to take a backseat. Nevertheless, once you learn the important lesson of releasing control and surrendering when it is needed, you will find astrology to be accurate and most helpful.

QUALITY #2: Introspection

In the Western world, introspection is not favored nor is it supported. Instead, we are encouraged to conquer others; not ourselves. We are pushed to achieve and to attain material possessions and status instead of comprehending who we truly are on the inside. Needless to say, the goals and ambitions of Western society are not the same goals and ambitions of self-realization and self-exploration. Looking deep into your faults and weaknesses raises your awareness into these matters.

QUALITY #3: Strength

Astrology requires perseverance and fortitude. Given the amount of objective truth you are receiving, it can become a challenge to continue. Therefore, maintaining a strong foundation into your personal character is essential to your success. Take whatever changes come your way and allow for yourself to understand the truth. The rewards are worth the struggle.

QUALITY #4: Ethics

We will discuss this further in Part V-Section 1 but for now, there are a few ethical rules to understand. For one, do not provide astrological information to anyone unless you have been given explicit approval to do so. When using astrology, it is important not to interfere with other people's problems or predicaments unless you have been personally asked to intercede. You do not want to cheat anyone out of any karmic lessons and take on their karma for yourself, which was not meant to be yours in the first place. Similarly, do not use astrology to trigger other people's pitfalls for your own personal gain. Having a high ethical standard leaves everyone, especially yourself, in a better predicament overall. Manipulating individuals, or attempting to help them without their permission, are sure ways to receive more complications and struggles in your own life, so do not even bother trying.

QUALITY #5: Patience

This is a big one when it comes to astrology. Life events can take years to experience, understand, and overcome, but knowing what to expect and when to expect it can allow for you to prepare your life for the storm that lies ahead. If we are about to experience a purge of unwanted and unneeded circumstances, then it is better to have your life uncluttered with unnecessary activities, jobs, and people. The more time and space we allow for these bigger life events, the better the outcome can be because we are listening to the higher energies that are at work.

The modern world is incredibly goal-oriented, which pressures the individual to constantly strive towards something external and material. However, astrology will sometimes tell you that there is simply no energy behind your motivations which means it is better to regroup and retreat than it is to push onwards. This is a very hard lesson for people in today's world to understand, but if you can surrender when astrology tells you to, you will be flowing through life with greater ease while working towards your higher purpose.

* * *

REQUIRED TOOLS

This section is a checklist of required tools and supplies you will need before you can apply astrology, and this book, to the fullest capacity. It is advisable to make sure you have these necessary items before you continue.

TOOL #1: Your Personal Birth Chart with Accurate Birth Data

Start by obtaining your birth certificate and make sure it has the time of birth. Do not go by the time your parents think you were born even if they have tremendously reliable memories. The only time that matters is when the Doctor that delivered you declared you alive as an autonomous individual on this planet. This is the only time that matters and should be located on your birth certificate. Refer back to Table INT-1 in order to obtain a free natal chart though astro.com.

TOOL #2: An Ephemeris for the 21st Century Set to Midnight GMT/UT or Your Current Time Zone

In Part IV-Section 1 we will explain further how to obtain an ephemeris online for free with your current time zone, but it is still advisable you purchase a 21st century ephemeris set to Midnight GMT/UT (more on the details are found below in the annotated bibliography section.)

TOOL #3: Basic Calculator

You will need to use a calculator for Part IV and VI of this book. Any standard calculator will do.

TOOL #4: Regular and Colored Pencils

It would be a good idea to have colored and regular pencils to help you better map out your thoughts and ideas on astrology.

TOOL #5: Graph Paper, Index Cards, and a Ruler

These items will become necessary in Part IV, so it is better to purchase them ahead of time in order to be prepared.

TOOL #6: An Astrologer's Calendar/Datebook

There will be more details on this below in the annotated bibliography section. In order to properly use the skills learned in Part III, you will need to purchase an astrologer's calendar that provides the void of course moon periods, daily transits, moon phases, eclipses, and retrogrades. You will find my recommendation below.

TOOL #7: A Journal

It helps to have a journal where you can write notes, ideas, and insights you have gathered along your journey. Have a journal handy and try to write in it daily.

* * *

ANNOTATED BIBLIOGRAPHY

The study of astrology does require an investment into a mini library of sorts. The books I have listed below are, in my opinion, a great place to start because they contain some of the most comprehensive, accurate, and easy to read information. I have also ranked them in order of difficulty so you can progressively work upwards towards more advanced topics and books.

LEVEL: BEGINNER

Llewellyn's Daily Planetary Guide (for current year), by Llewellyn Publications. As mentioned above, an astrological calendar is essential to study astrology. Llewellyn's Planetary Guide provides accurate and readable information with a good amount of blank space for you to add your own notes and personal calendar.

American Ephemeris Trans-Century Edition 1950-2050 Midnight, by Niel F. Miechelsen and Rique Pottenger. This is the recommended Ephemeris for every beginning astrologer. It provides the latter half of the 20th century and the first half of the 21st century, giving you a wide range of data from the recent past to the near future. Be sure to get midnight and not noon!

Alan Oken's Complete Astrology, by Alan Oken. Astronomy, mythology, and spiritualism are beautifully intertwined in order to explain the various planets, signs, and houses found in astrology. This book is a good starting point in order to understand the stories, mythologies, and energies surrounding the various archetypes in astrology.

The Contemporary Astrologer's Handbook, by Sue Tompkins. Similar to Mr. Oken's book, this book provides insightful paragraphs into aspects, planets, houses, and signs in astrology. Ms. Tompkins also delves into interpretation techniques with interesting case studies.

The Rulership Book, by Rex E. Bills. You can take this book anywhere you go. The author has taken countless records from antiquity to modern times and has aligned planetary, sign, and house rulerships to all things animal, plant, and mineral. This is a good book to observe which astrological archetypes rule which objects. It is also a good tool if you want to quiz yourself by guessing what rules what before you look it up.

The Only Astrology Book You'll Ever Need, by Joanna Martine Woolfolk. This book has become a modern-day classic. Similar to Mr. Oken and Ms. Tompkins, this book provides explanations of the planets, signs and houses involved in astrology. Ms. Woolfolk pays close attention to ascendants and sun signs and does so in a language that is witty and light-hearted.

LEVEL: INTERMEDIATE

Relating: An Astrological Guide to Living with Others on a Small Planet, by Liz Greene. Every starting astrologer should have this book. Although psychological in its approach, this book is easily understandable as astrologer Liz Greene explains the various elemental, planetary, and zodiacal archetypes, and how they interact with one another. Ms. Greene also discusses how one addresses the relationships inside oneself, and how this inner exchange between the personal feminine and masculine is reflected through the people that we attract into our lives.

The Gods of Change: Pain, Crises and the Transits of Uranus, Neptune and Pluto, by Howard Sasportas. Outer planetary transits, which will be explained further in Parts IV and V, represent the big life events that we experience within our lifetimes. This book helps you to understand the energies and themes involved with the three most outer planets Uranus, Neptune, and Pluto. This is important because these planets (in addition to Saturn) create intense energies and situations within our lives.

How to be a Great Astrologer, by James Braha. In all of his books, James Braha perfectly combines the knowledge and wisdom of western astrology and Jyotish (Indian) astrology. His book goes over natal planetary aspects as well as nodal house and sign placements. Throughout the book, there are profound quotes to live by along with angelic and inspirational pictures.

Astrology for the Soul, by Jan Spiller. This is a very insightful book into the moon's nodes in astrology. By looking up your north node by sign and house, you are presented with common pitfalls and weakness associated with that placement. Ms. Spiller provides amazing diagnoses and remedies for such ailments, which help you align your life to the appropriate karmic path of this lifetime.

Planets in Youth, by Robert Hand. This is the first book of what I like to call "The Robert Hand Collection." *Planets in Youth* provides an insightful look into your natal aspects and is written as if he was talking to your parents about you. This makes it easy to form a connection between your current psychological predicament and your childhood. There is also a great section where Mr. Hand discusses the astrological mother and father in the birth chart and their connection to one's life.

LEVEL: ADVANCED

Horoscope Symbols, by Robert Hand. This is Mr. Hand's thesis on all symbols found in astrology (aspects, signs, planets, and houses). The reason why this book is advanced is because it is highly psychological and requires a firm understanding in Jungian astrological theory.

Planets in Composite, by Robert Hand. *Planets in Composite* is a great resource for when you are looking at composite charts (charts about relationships) in astrology. This is the best resource on the topic, and if you are interested in doing a lot of relationship/comparison charts within your studies, this is the book to get.

Planets in Transit, by Robert Hand. Once you learn the techniques in Part IV of this book, this resource will become your bible. This book provides every combination of planetary transits and ingresses from the Sun to Pluto. Every time you experience a personal transit, this book gives you several paragraphs that explain what to expect and how to approach the given situation.

Astrology, Karma and Transformation, by Steven Arroyo. Being a psychologist himself, Mr. Arroyo's insights are heavily grounded within Jungian theories as he covers themes that you have found in the books in the beginning section. Mr. Arroyo's book simply adds a layer toward your understanding of astrological archetypes.

How to Predict Your Future: The Secrets of Eastern and Western Astrology, by James Braha. This book has two parts. The first part of this book goes over the planetary transits and ingresses of the outer planets (Jupiter-Pluto) in a very fatalistic, yet accurate, way. Using this book in parallel with *The Gods of Change* and *Planets in Transit* is highly recommended. The second half of this book touches on the same life events but through the Jyotish system. Even if you only use this book for the first half, it is worth the purchase.

<u>A History of Western Astrology Vol. 1 and 2, by Nick Campion</u>. Mr. Campion provides academic evidence in order to demonstrate the history of astrology within a historical context from antiquity to modern times. This two-volume series establishes a credible connection for astrology within the context of human history using academic integrity.

* * *

The trail has now been blazed, your supplies have been gathered, and you are now in the proper mindset to begin your astrological studies. Finally, it is time to begin discussing the various components of astrology which we will apply towards our daily lives along with our personal psychological analysis. The first topic I want to discuss is the bigger picture: the great ages of astrology.

SECTION 8-THE AGES AND LARGER CYCLES OF TIME

~

Right now, within the 21st century, we are facing a precipice of sorts where worn out institutions, philosophies, and societal structures that no longer serve our phase in human evolution starting to fade away along with the sands of time. To those who perceive time in a linear context, these changes appear disruptive, chaotic, and finite. However, if time is viewed within a cyclical framework, these changes are then observed to represent a turning point as humanity travels from one phase of existence into another. Naturally, the older, worn out phase must end before the new phase can begin.

Political historians William Strauss and Neil Howe have come to this metaphysical truism of cyclical time scientifically by examining the patterns and cycles that exist within United States' history. In their book *The Fourth Turning*, they describe these cycles to last approximately 80 years, which are then further subdivided into four uniquely individualized generations lasting 20 years each.[39] Strangely enough, this time frame echoes the same amount of time it take for the planet Uranus to make a full rotation around the Sun, which is 84 years.

When it comes to the larger cycles within astrology, these timetables can last for tens of thousands of years. Furthermore, both the Western and Jyotish traditions have their own versions of these larger time cycles, and both echo the sentiment that we are currently not firmly grounded within any stage of the cycle, but are instead in a time of conversion and flux which will take hundreds of years to complete. This explains the perceived turmoil and confusion we are currently facing. It is as though all of humanity has one foot in the old paradigm, and the other foot into the new

---

39   William Strauss and Neil Howe, *The Fourth Turning*. Three Rivers Press: New York, 1997. p. 61.

paradigm. As such, people living in the present moment, the 21st century to be exact, all have a part to play as the harbingers of the monumental change that will bring us into the new era.

We will begin our study with the Jyotish larger cycles of time which are called the *yugas*. These *yugas* are subdivided into two major sections: ascending and descending. In 2012, there was a moment of confusion and misinformation where people were associating this ascension with the Sun's position in space relative to the plane of the Milky Way Galaxy. Although it is true that the Sun, and therefore our entire solar system, is currently on the upper part of this plane, this cycle of ascension and descension takes 60 million years which is far too long of a time period to have any practical use.[40]

Instead, Jyotish astrologers associate this ascension with the Sun's journey towards its proposed star-twin which astronomers have dubbed Nemesis. This is our Sun's hypothetical binary star partner which has stirred up furious debate among astronomers. To this point, NASA claims that 90% of stars in our universe are part of a binary star system, but in that same breath, they will claim that "there has never been any evidence to suggest such a comparison [with our star]."[41,42]

According to Jyotish astrologers like Sri Yukteswar, when our Sun is ascending, it is not only approaching its binary star partner, it is also traveling closer to the grand galactic center which is called *Vishnunbadhi*. In Sanskrit it means "the seat of all creative power, *Brahama*, the universal magnetism."[43] When the human race reaches this point, all of humanity is able to fully develop into full mental comprehension. In other words, enlightenment becomes achievable for every human being on this planet because we are at the closest proximity towards the ultimate creator of this universe. However, we still have a very long way before we arrive; 10,500 more years to be exact.

"The great year" within Jyotish astrology is divided into four *yugas*: *Satya*, *Treta*, *Dwapara*, and *Kali*. These four *yugas* are observed twice within one great cycle, first descending, then ascending. The following table details the length of each *yuga* along with the dates of recent history that have spanned through each (Table I-3).

---

40   Alison Klesman. *In which direction does the Sun move through the Milky Way?* Astronomy. 2020. https://astronomy.com/magazine/ask-astro/2020/07/in-which-direction-does-the-sun-move-through-the-milky-way.

41   The Human Origin Project. *The Binary Star Model.* The Human Origin Project, 2018. https://humanoriginproject.com/two-suns-binary-star-model/.

42   Space.com. Nemesis Star Theory: The Sun's 'Death Star' Companion'. Space.com, 2017. https://www.space.com/22538-nemesis-star.html.

43   Sri Yuketeswar Giri. *The Holy Science.* Public Domain, 1894: p. 6.

TABLE I-3. Timespan of Each Yuga with Corresponding Historical Time Frame[44]

YUGA	EARTH YEARS				HUMAN HISTORY DATES	
	PRE-TRANSITION	YUGA PROPER	POST-TRANSITION	TOTAL	START	END
↓ SATYA	400	4000	400	4800	11500 BC	6700 BC
↓ TRETA	300	3000	300	3600	6700 BC	3100 BC
↓ DWAPARA	200	2000	200	2400	3100 BC	700 BC
↓ KALI	100	1000	100	1200	700 BC	500 AD
↑ KALI	100	1000	100	1200	500 AD	1700 AD
↑ DWAPARA	200	2000	200	2400	1700 AD	4100 AD
↑ TRETA	300	3000	300	3600	4100 AD	7700 AD
↑ SATYA	400	4000	400	4800	7700 AD	12500 AD
FULL CYCLE GRAND TOTAL				24000		

Before we continue into our discussion about what each *yuga* represents in terms of themes and energies, we need to first explain the divergence in thinking between the Vedic viewpoint of human history in comparison to the timeframe given to us by Western academia.

According to the later, around the time when humanity was supposedly at its peak of awareness, 11500BC, ancient humans were barely beginning their mass migrations into Europe, Eurasia, Asia, and Siberia. Prior to that, approximately 23,000 years even further into the past, the earliest *Homo sapiens* were beginning to emerge as a species.[45] How can it be that the time when humanity was supposedly at its highest form of evolutionary consciousness, according to the Jyotish tradition, could have simultaneously coincided with the emergence of the human race after having survived the Ice Age according to Western academia?

Again, tying back to the beginning of this discussion, this contradiction is due to the fact that academic time is perceived linearly, and astrological time is perceived cyclically. According to Vedic theory, humanity goes through these large cycles of time repeatedly. Simply put, the Earth and the human race have existed on this planet for millions of years. Swamis like *A.C.*

---

44   Sri Yuketes War Giri. *The Holy Science*. Public Domain, 1894: pp. 7-11.
45   Peter Stearns. *The Encyclopedia of World History, 6th Edition*. Houghton Mifflin, New York: 2001. pp.8-10.

Bhaktivedanta state that humanity has existed for as long as 2,000,000 years.[46] Within a cyclical frame of thinking, humanity and this planet go through various generations of large-scale evolutions and devolutions that span even further than known recorded history.

It should be noted that both the Vedic and academic viewpoints are evidenced based; they are just founded within two different forms of evidence. On the Vedic side, they consider the cyclical viewpoint of time along with measurements of the Earth's equatorial procession. (This procession is also used for calculating western astrology's larger time scales which will be further explained below.) Therefore, this evidence is based within calculatable astronomical time frames. For the academic perception of history, the framework is linear and mostly based upon archeological evidence whose timetable changes and adjusts as needed when newer evidence presents itself.

In other words, both systems have their strengths being based within empirical observation, Vedic being astronomical and academic being archeological, but at the same time, both also have their weaknesses. For the Vedic weakness, there is simply no Earth-based empirical evidence to back their claim. Instead, it is based within their philosophical outlook along with astronomical calculations. For the academia's weakness, their claims are solely based upon archeological evidence whose discoveries depend upon funding availability along with technologies that have demonstrated to possess errors such as carbon dating.[47] However, when we observe the date ranges shown within Table I-3, we nevertheless observe a correlative convergence of time and history when we compare the cyclical nature of Vedic time towards the linear timeframe of academic timekeeping.

DESCENDING SATYA YUGA 11500BC - 6700BC

Satya Yuga is considered "The Golden Age." During this time, all of humanity can comprehend all things. This includes all mysteries of the universe along with the subtle and gross forces that govern our existence. This is the longest of the *yugas* lasting 4800 years for a half cycle and 9600 years for the full *yuga* cycle. This is our starting point, which began in 11500BC, and as the saying goes, "It's all downhill from here." As time progressed, humanity lost this sacred knowledge as the descending half of the *yuga* cycle began. Slowly over time, the shroud of

---

46   A.C. Bhaktivedanta Swami Prabhupada. *Bhagavad-Gita As It Is*. Macmillan Company. New York: 1972. p. 215.

47   Cornell University. *"Inaccuracies in radiocarbon dating."* ScienceDaily. ScienceDaily, 5 June 2018. <www.sciencedaily.com/releases/2018/06/180605112057.htm>.

ignorance began to take form while the Sun simultaneously initiated a trajectory away from the grand galactic center and its binary star partner.

DESCENDING TETRA YUGA 6700BC - 3100BC

Tetra Yuga, also referred to as "The Silver Age" indicates a time when the human intellect was still able to understand the principles of divine magnetism. That is, the electrical forces of nature which all of creation depends upon for existence. The ultimate glue that binds the entire cosmic web some refer to as *prana*, *chi*, or electromagnetism. The only difference is that humanity has forgotten how to apply this knowledge into their own self-awareness. During this time in human history, state-organized societies were established, food production technologies were introduced, and the origins of the first civilizations began to emerge. Monuments like Stonehenge were developed along with the first concepts of animism. Within this context, it shows that humans during this time intuitively understood their connection to all things living and nonliving on this planet, along with the celestial calendar. According to Vedic theory, this knowledge was a remaining byproduct of the previous age, but humanity was not aware enough to understand how to utilize this knowledge for self-realization and liberation.

DESCENDING DWAPARA YUGA 3100BC - 700BC

Dwapara Yuga, "The Bronze Age," also echoes the same Bronze Age from the Western timetable (3000BC-1200BC). During this time, human intellect lost most of its power when it comes to understanding the finer qualities of our universe. Human societies grew and expanded substantially during this time which included organized religion and the genesis of ancient Egyptian, Middle Eastern, and Asian cultures. However, due to the decreasing nature of humanity's overall awareness, we also begin to witness the superseding of institutionalized priorities (religious, governmental, and economical) over spiritual pursuits.

DESCENDING KALI YUGA 700BC - 500AD

Kali Yuga, "The Iron Age," again parallels western's Iron Age which lasted from 500BC- 300AD. Human intellect is now reaching its lowest point where only gross material comprehension is the furthest the human mind can attain. During this era, human history experienced the classical Greeks and Romans along with the various wars that accompanied this time period. It is no surprise that the lowest point of this era, 500AD, represents the heart of the Dark Ages in Europe. During this time, superstition, religious rhetoric, disease, and archaic technologies were at the forefront. After this low point, the *yuga* cycle began its upward journey where human society slowly but surely started to comprehend once again the secrets of the universe.

ASCENDING KALI YUGA 500AD - 1700AD

The Renaissance, Newtonian Physics, and Western Europe's journey into the "New World" slowly came about along with newer technologies and scientific and philosophical discoveries. Humanity began its slow upward path towards enlightenment as individuals started to question the meaning of life once again. The arts were revived in glorious ways, and most of the known classics in literature, visual art, and music were created during this time. It is as though the human connection to their inner soul and the external world were becoming more of a conscious pursuit once again even though they did not have all the answers just yet.

ASCENDING DWAPARA YUGA 1700AD- 4100AD

This *yuga* stage began with the scientific age of enlightenment where new discoveries in electricity, magnetism, and radiation were discovered and utilized to help society progress into the industrial age. According to the time frame in Table I-3, 1700AD – 1900AD, marked the precursor period of this *yuga*. Although we are now in the 2000-year fixed period of this *yuga*, we are only 100 years into this 2000-year period, which is not set to end until 4100AD.

Now that our human culture is becoming more grounded within this *yuga* with each passing year, the archaic and worn-out ideals are starting to lose their authority. Humanity is ready to evolve and proceed forward into enlightenment according to this destined ascension. Therefore, we must be open and willing to let go of whatever is preventing us from reaching our higher ideals whether it be inner personal obstacles or grander societal ones. Either way, all of humanity is set into this *yuga* for the next 2000 years. Remember, although it seems like the world is ending, all that is ending are the things that no longer serve our purpose for our evolving individualized and collective consciousness.

* * *

Now that we have observed the *yugas* of the Jyotish tradition, let us dive into the great ages of the western astrological tradition: The Procession of the Equinox.

If you have a toy spinning top handy, go ahead and give it a good spin counterclockwise. As you watch the top spin, you will notice two forms of rotations occurring. The spinning of the top around itself represents the daily rotation of the Earth where we get our days and nights. Additionally, you will notice that the top simultaneously rotates on a swivel. This is because the spinning top cannot stay perfectly perpendicular to the ground and instead, it swivels around causing the top to have a sort of wobble in its movement.

Our planet operates in this same way. The best way to visualize this is to observe the top upper of the toy and visualize it as the north pole of Earth. As the Earth wobbles, the position of the north pole similarly shifts from one point to the other. Unlike the top, however, this wobble takes thousands of years to be noticed. Either way, throughout history, the North Star has changed from epoch to epoch as a result (Fig. I-1).

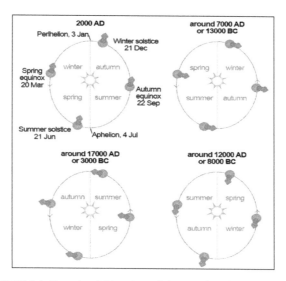

FIGURE I-1. Perceived Direction of the North Pole Over Time[48]

---

48   "File: Earth axial precession.svg" by Cmglee is licensed with CC BY-SA 3.0. To view a copy of this license, visit https://creativecommons.org/licenses/by-sa/3.0.

When the Earth proceeds down this procession, the ecliptic picture also changes and shifts. Astrologers have used the fall equinox to act as the time marker in this regard because it is the start of the astrological calendar. Over time, when the fall equinox occurs, a new position in our sky map would also shift just how a new north star also shifts over time. This has caused two sky maps to come about: Tropical and Sidereal. The Sidereal map takes this shift into consideration which has now shifted approximately 21° over the past 12,000 years.

For example, if you were to locate the Sun's placement at the exact time of the fall equinox, the Sun would not be located at 0° Aries (0°♈), but 9° Pisces (9°♓) which is a 21° shift backwards. This is why it is called the Procession of the Equinox and not the Precession. The Sidereal calendar takes the actual position of the Sun's location, the shifted position, 9° Pisces, and is used by the Jyotish tradition. The tropical position, 0° Aries, is used by the Western tradition.

This explains why if you were to look at your Jyotish chart and compare it to your western astrology chart, you will notice that your planetary positions have all shifted approximately 21° backwards from your western positions. This is because the Western tradition utilizes the Tropical framework. The way it works is that whenever the Fall Equinox takes place in the tropical framework, the sky map "resets" to 0° Aries no matter what. To put it another way, the Jyotish tradition (Sidereal) tells you where the planets are located along the ecliptic in real-time, but the Western tradition (Tropical) does not take the shift into consideration, and therefore assumes where the planets would be theoretically located if the shift were to never take place.

However, this shift is still considered within the Western tradition when we observe the procession of the equinoxes within the larger time scale of The Great Ages. Each age is evenly divided into 2000 years each and began in 10000BC with the age of Leo (TABLE I-4). Notice how the ages are proceeding backwards instead of forwards. Also notice how our current age, the Age of Aquarius, will end at around the same time as our current ascending *Dwapara yuga* (4000AD and 4100AD respectively).

Just as we have done with the Jyotish *yugas*, we will now observe these various eras and examine correlating themes between the signs that rule the respective age along with the human development that occurred therein.

TABLE I-4. Western Astrology's Great Ages with Corresponding Timetable

GREAT AGE	GLYPH	TIME START	TIME END
LEO	♌	10000 BC	8000 BC
CANCER	♋	8000 BC	6000 BC
GEMINI	♊	6000 BC	4000 BC
TAURUS	♉	4000 BC	2000 BC
ARIES	♈	2000 BC	0 AD
PISCES	♓	0 AD	2000 AD
AQUARIUS	♒	2000 AD	4000 AD

THE AGE OF LEO 10000BC – 8000BC

Leo is ruled by the Sun in astrology. During this time in human history, the final remnants of the last ice age were melted away from the rising Earth temperatures, along with the extinction of ice age animals like the mammoth.[49] The disappearance of large ice sheets additionally introduced new lands in Europe, and ancient cultures from every major continent survived within hunter-gatherer communities. Egyptian mythology possessed concepts of solar deities as early as the Neolithic era which eventually evolved into a full pantheon of Sun and sky deities. Many ancient cultures similarly referred to Sun worship as some of their earliest forms of religious philosophy.

THE AGE OF CANCER 8000BC – 6000BC

Cancer, being ruled by the Moon, is typically associated with food, nourishment, and protection. It is therefore of no surprise that during this time, cultures in the Middle East, Africa, the Jordan Valley, Europe, and Asia all began to develop farming techniques, farming communities, and the domestication of farm animals.[50] Cancer is also associated with the home and family. Consequently, archeological evidence demonstrates that these farming communities also developed various

---

49   Peter Stearns. *The Encyclopedia of World History, 6th Edition*. Houghton Mifflin, New York: 2001. p. 11.
50   Peter Stearns. *The Encyclopedia of World History, 6th Edition*. Houghton Mifflin, New York: 2001. pp. 13-14.

housing techniques transforming our hunter-gather ancestors into more stable, secure, and tightly knit groups. As a result, human societies slowly began to flourish under these new agricultural and architectural technologies.

THE AGE OF GEMINI 6000BC – 4000BC

Gemini is ruled by Mercury which is why we connect Gemini with ideas of communication, language, and short-distance traveling. Now that these farming cultures were becoming more established, a "web of relations" began where trading of exotic and raw materials were beginning to cause these communities to mingle more with one another. As a further consequence, societies also grew into more complex and organized state-run societies primarily in the Near East, Asia, and China.[51] Naturally, the need for transportation and translators were in more demand and similarly advanced.

THE AGE OF TAURUS 4000BC – 2000BC

Taurus is ruled by Venus and one of the first themes that comes to mind are the arts. This era marks the beginning of dynastic rule where early Greek, Egyptian, and Mesopotamian art and architecture were beginning to further establish cultural tastes and influences that continued into the well-known Classical era of the Mediterranean.[52] Similarly, in Mesopotamia and the Middle East, sophisticated musical instruments like the lute and harp were designed and utilized to further establish the arts within these cultures.[53]

THE AGE OF ARIES 2000BC – 0AD

Aries is ruled by the planet Mars and is associated with individuality, drive, ambition, and warfare. This period is the time of the Empires who began to expand their influences by military force.

---

51 Peter Stearns. *The Encyclopedia of World History, 6th Edition*. Houghton Mifflin, New York: 2001. pp. 15-16.

52 Shelley Esaak. *Outline of Art History- Visual Art Movements from 30000 BC-400 AD*. ThoughtCo. https://www.thoughtco.com/early-art-history-visual-arts-movements-4070855. 2020.

53 Encyclopedia Britannica. *Arched Harp*. https://www.britannica.com/art/harp-musical-instrument. 1999.

Military technologies and strategies simultaneously advanced such as the development of the sword in Europe ca. 1000BC and *Sun Tzu's* famous classic "The Art of War" ca. 500BC.[54] The way of the warrior was becoming an honored and noble pursuit while militaries were becoming embedded within society like the Roman Legions in ancient Rome and the *Samurai* in ancient Japan. Mythologies that glorified war and warriors like *The Iliad* and *The Odyssey* were both composed during this era.

The Age of Pisces 0AD – 2000AD

Pisces is ruled by Neptune in contemporary astrology and by Jupiter in traditional astrology. The sign represents ideas surrounding faith, surrender, religion, and mysticism. The most obvious expression of these energies has to do with Christendom that ruled over the European continent during this time along with the various holy wars that were fought in the Middle East for the sake of religion. A symbol for Christianity is the fish, and it is of no coincidence that the symbol for Pisces are two fish that are tied together. During the height of Roman Catholic rule, individuals were expected to obey religious and church doctrine without question, typically on pain of death. Consequently, this is also the era of the great inquisition and of the religious migrations from Europe to the New World where individuals were either escaping religious prosecution or trying to indoctrinate Christianity to the native peoples of the Americas.

The Age of Aquarius 2000AD – 4000AD

It should be noted that the Age of Aquarius only began approximately twenty years ago and is comprised of a two-thousand-year cycle just like the other ages that came before. In other words, because we are only 1% of the way through the Age of Aquarius, this means it is very possible that we may not witness the full expression of this age in our lifetimes. Nevertheless, this time in our history is incredibly important because we all have our own individual part in ushering in this new age. Aquarius is ruled by Uranus within contemporary astrology and by Saturn within ancient astrology. Aquarius possesses themes of humanitarianism, equality,

---

54   Michael Marshall. *Timeline: Weapons Technology.* New Scientist. https://www.newscientist.com/article/dn17423-timeline-weapons-technology/. 2009.

technological advancements, and intuition. When you observe today's societal chaos, however, it might seem like we are a far cry from these ideals. The reason for the turmoil we are now witnessing during the 21st century is because the older and unnecessary structures of the Piscean age are struggling to let go of their power.

One thing to notice with these various ages is that each one tends to build on top of the other even though the structures of our societies changed over time. For example, religion will still exist during the Age of Aquarius, but it will no longer be based on faith and dogma alone but by direct human and spiritual experience. To achieve this, humanity should cultivate the ideas of oneness and goodwill towards all of humanity that all religions tend to portray without the unnecessary clutter of religious judgement and hypocrisy. Similarly, large global structures that have connected the world like the internet, which is currently being used with more nefarious and toxic intentions, will hopefully be used to bring us closer together instead of dividing us more. Needless to say, it is hard to predict what and how the future will develop while we continue to progress into the Age of Aquarius. However, I believe the best prediction we have is found in John Lennon's timeless song "Imagine":

"Imagine there's no heaven
It's easy if you try
No hell below us
Above us only sky
Imagine all the people
Living for today

Imagine there's no countries
It isn't hard to do
Nothing to kill or die for
And no religion, too
Imagine all the people
Living life in peace

Imagine no possessions
I wonder if you can
No need for greed or hunger
A brotherhood of man
Imagine all the people
Sharing all the world

You may say I'm a dreamer
But I'm not the only one
I hope someday you'll join us
And the world will live as one"

Aquarius is the ultimate day dreamer. Indeed, it seems that these utopian principles are so incredibly out of reach and unrealistic that the only place they belong is within the head of a dreamer. This might have been true a thousand years ago, maybe even one hundred years ago, but now is the time of cultivation and to integrate these Aquarian structures into reality however we can.

Astrology, being ruled by Aquarius, is part of the solution as to how we will get there. With the help of astrology, we can slowly determine the psychological barriers and walls that we have placed within ourselves that forbid us to see one another with equanimity and unconditional love.

Greed, pride, hatred, and selfishness have no place within the Aquarian age. This is a time to build bridges between our fellow human beings. The division we see today is merely an outward projection of what needs to be purged within all of us in order to make the Aquarian dream a reality. When we can accomplish this goal, then the world will truly and unequivocally "live as one." Know that your astrological journey towards self-discovery is precisely the work you should be doing right now. With that in mind, let us begin the universal voyage towards our most ideal future that we can co-create, and learn all the ins and outs of the astrological sciences.

PART II: ASTROLOGICAL SYMBOLS AND ARCHETYPES

"Astrology is the study of man's response to planetary stimuli. The stars have no conscious benevolence or animosity; they merely send forth positive and negative radiations. Of themselves, these do not help or harm humanity, but offer a lawful channel for the outward operation of cause-effect equilibriums which each man has set into motion in the past.

A child is born on that day and at that hour when the celestial rays are in mathematical harmony with his individual karma. His horoscope is a challenging portrait, revealing his unalterable past and its probable future results. But the natal chart can be rightly interpreted only by men of intuitive wisdom: these are few.

The message boldly blazoned across the heavens at the moment of birth is not meant to emphasize fate—the result of past good and evil—but to arouse man's will to escape from his universal thralldom. What he has done, he can undo. None other than himself was the instigator of the causes of whatever effects are now prevalent in his life. He can overcome any limitation, because he created it by his own actions in the first place, and because he has spiritual resources which are not subject to planetary pressure."- Swami Sri Yukteswar from Autobiography of a Yogi, Chapter 16.

In Part I-Section 6, we lightly touched upon the definition of archetypes and their relevancy within human culture. Let us begin this section by further detailing the nature of an archetype and its use within astrology. The best way to think of an archetype is to picture the numerous Greek statues of their mythological pantheon which have existed and remained emulated for thousands of years (Figure II-1).

Greek archetypal statues such as these all contain three vital qualities: fixed, idealistic, and universal. Fixed in that their attributes and mythologies never change. Apollo will always be the god of

FIGURE II-1. Statue of the Greek Sun God Apollo.[55]

light and truth, Athena, the goddess of war, etc., etc. Over time, the stories that surround these characters are simply a retranslation through the contextual lens of the culture and time that the interpretation took place. However, their core characteristics, themes, and story never change.

Archetypes are idealistic because they represent qualities that we as humans strive to embody within our own lives. Christians, for example, try to imitate the values of Jesus, Hindus of *Krishna*, etc., etc. Archetypes are perceived to be god-like because they do not possess the imperfections that we as humans possess (recall the timeless axiom, "to err is to be human"). Due to this fact, humans constantly idolize archetypes that they consider to be personal heroes, which in turn motivate and drive them to achieve their goals.

Lastly, archetypes are universal because they cross cultural, linguistic, and religious barriers. To this point, it should be noted that the ancient sages of the Jyotish tradition attributed the same exact planetary archetypes as their ancient Babylonian, Egyptian, and Greek counterparts within their own respective astrological traditions. Similarly, in today's world, movies and novels can be enjoyed by individuals from all walks of life because every culture has a hero's story, the story of a broken heart, and the story of the prodigal son. These tales are universal human experiences that are felt and understood by all. Therefore, because astrology is similarly a universally understood human science, it can be utilized by any individual who attempts to try.

According to astrological theory, these various archetypes are either expressed in healthy or unhealthy ways. How they are manifested within the individual depends on the coordination and condition of the various planets within the birth chart which is the bulk of Part V of this book. To this point, the birth chart shows us the personal hero and enemy archetypes that individuals embody, idolize, and strive towards, or cower away from, fear, and shun.

In Part II, we will establish a firm understanding of all the various archetypes that are found within astrology and how they are expressed in both a positive and negative light. Think of this section as a hermetically sealed version of astrology where every archetype will be individually explained. It is vital to have this strong foundation now because when we get to Parts V-VII, all of these archetypes blend together, forming an individualized psychology, which is where a lot of confusion begins to arise. For now, we will take it one step and one archetypal symbol at a time, starting with the elements and modalities, and furthering our discussion into the signs, planets, houses, and cardinal points. To crystalize our understanding of these archetypes even further, we will also discuss traditional rulerships and rules which will help you to obtain an even greater understanding of the energies at play.

SECTION 1-ELEMENTS AND MODALITIES

❧

The elements and modalities are a quick way to get an easy snapshot of the birth chart and determine if there are deficiencies or an overabundance of energies within the chart. Although it will not provide you with the entire picture, you can learn a lot from this analysis. Typically, with a surplus of a modality or element, that person tends to overexpress said quality, and if they are lacking they tend to overcompensate.

For example, let us look at the birth chart of Joe Exotic, the famous imprisoned zoo owner from the Netflix documentary *Tiger King* (Fig. II-2A).

This birth chart has a Rodden Rating of "A" (More on this in Part V) which means the birth time is fairly reliable. For now, all we are only concerned with the element and modality grid located in the lower right-hand corner above the aspactarian. For the sake of convenience, let us zoom in to get a better look (Fig. II-2B).

On the left side of the grid, we see the four elements Fire, Air, Earth, and Water and on the top, we find the three modes Cardinal, Fixed, and Mutable. Without even knowing the astrology glyphs, it is easy to see which elements Joe Exotic has in abundance, and which ones he is lacking. In his case, he has an overabundance of water (Moon, Midheaven, Neptune, Sun, and Jupiter) and is lacking Fire (Mars).

At first, I was very surprised to discover this arrangement. Mr. Exotic is known for acting as though the entire world is a stage and is as a pyromaniac who enjoys shooting guns and explosives. He also enjoys being in front of a camera and working with dangerous, exotic animals. All these things lead to a Fire personality and when I discovered that he was mostly Water, at first it seemed confusing and contradictory, but remember, if someone is lacking an element they tend to overcompensate.

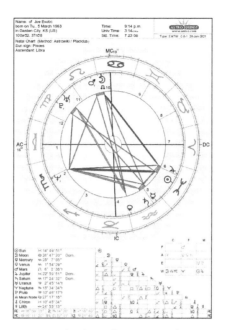

FIGURE II-2A. Birth Chart of Joe Exotic from Tiger King

FIGURE II-2B. Elemental and Modality Grid of Joe Exotic

Mr. Exotic's insatiable need for heat, attention, and firepower is him attempting to manifest the element that he is lacking within himself. Instead of trying to feed the fire within, he projects it outwardly though his various pyrotechnic antics and heavily ego-driven decision making. As you can see, without even looking at the birth chart, I already have an idea into Mr. Exotic's temperament and weaknesses.

When it comes to Mr. Exotic's modal placements, they are relatively balanced as he has three objects in Cardinal, five in Fixed, and four in Mutable. To get a better idea of an imbalanced modal arrangement, we now must look at Joe Exotic's sworn nemesis Carole Baskin.

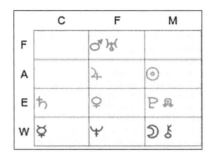

FIGURE II-3. Elemental and Modality Grid for Carole Baskin

Her chart has a Rodden rating of "X" which means the birth time is unknown, but we do know that she was born June 6, 1961 in San Antonio, TX. This is enough to get a picture of her modality and elemental grid. For the sake of convenience, let us simply look at her grid instead of the entire birth chart (Fig. II-3)

Ms. Baskin has two planets in Cardinal, five in Fixed and three in Mutable. [Note: The Nodes (☊) and Chiron are not counted.] This means that she is lacking in Cardinal energy and has an overabundance in Fixed energy. One character trait Ms. Baskin is known for is her tenacity. She is a person who wants things to go her way and will even pay millions and wait years to do so.

This is shown by her surplus of Fixed energy which makes her stubborn, opinionated, and unyielding. What is interesting is that she portrays herself to be a "go with the flow," flower-power kind of person who can sacrifice her own ego for the sake of something bigger. However, I would disagree with her self-assessment, and say this is her overcompensating for her lack of Cardinal energy which can give someone a low self-esteem and self-image. Instead of working on her lack of self-esteem, she must put other people's egos in check by stating that it is the world that is the problem and never her. Ms. Baskin also has issues with initiation due to her lack of Cardinal energy and tends to react more than act.

As you can see, we can gain significant information by observing very little. The more you keep it simple, the easier it will be when you have to combine all of the smaller pieces into a larger, more complex picture. Let us now look at the elements and modalities further and get a better idea as to what they entail.

104

THE FOUR ELEMENTS

AIR-OUR INTELLECT

Air is the element of our mental capacities. Gemini represents our basic mental functions. It tells us how we take in information, how we store this information, and how we communicate this information to others. Libra is the exchange of these ideas to another person. It shows us how our ideas need compromise in order to provide harmony with one another, and how learning other people's viewpoints is important for us to understand our own. Aquarius represents global consciousness. It shows us how thinking outside of the box and having an open mind can uplift and expand society so that we can evolve our personal outlook and create a brighter future.

When Air is balanced in the chart, there is a good mental outlook, an ability to learn things well, and an openness towards other people's ideas, perspectives, and thoughts. When Air is lacking in the chart, there could be learning disabilities, a lack of objectivism, narrow-mindedness, and an unwillingness to push oneself intellectually. If there is too much Air in the chart, there can be elitism, ungroundedness, use of the intellect to demean others, and a tendency to live in a sort of bubble where they do not consider other viewpoints because they consider theirs to be superior.

WATER-OUR EMOTIONS

Water is our inner emotional self. Cancer represents our actual feelings. It shows us how we feel, how we process our feelings, how we attach to others, and how connected we are to our own inner self. Scorpio represents how our emotions evolve over time. It shows us how we create strong bonds with others by becoming intimate, how our inner psychology changes through life experiences, and how we care for others and protect them. Pisces represents universal and unconditional love. It is our understanding of spirit, the concept of universal oneness, and our connectivity towards all living things, non-living things, and the creator of the universe.

When Water is balanced, they are well connected to their emotions and can express them properly, are able to harness unconditional love by being welcoming of others and of oneself, and do not feel the need to sacrifice the self for the sake of others. If Water is lacking, they can be cold and emotionally inept, unable to process their feelings and repress them instead. There is an inability to relax around others and an inflexibility towards individuals and situations that befall them. If they have too much Water, they can be unreasonable, emotionally volatile, too subjective, possess too much guilt or put guilt onto others, and use emotional manipulation.

FIRE-OUR INTUTIION

Fire is the element of action and going with our gut. Aries represents doing what we want to do when we want to do it. Aries goes without fear and with full confidence that the first choice is always the right choice. Leo represents the spark of our creativity. If we have an original idea, it comes from our own creative intuition, and Leo encourages us to go with that intuition and explore our ideas further. Sagittarius is the flame of righteousness and justice that maintains a well-ordered society. It shows us the higher truth of what is right and wrong so that our society can stay civilized and in harmony with one another.

If Fire is balanced, they are courageous, confident, non-judgmental, and fair. If Fire is lacking, they have a hard time believing in themself and getting things off the ground. They can second-guess themself and think that their self-expression is not important or worthy. They lack self-confidence and are introverted. If they have too much Fire, they are egotistical, judgmental, "shoot first, ask questions later," too energetic, and have a hard time being focused due to impatience.

EARTH-OUR FIVE SENSES

Earth is how we view the world by using our five senses (touch, taste, smell, vision, and hearing). Taurus represents our ability to be grounded and relaxed so that we may enjoy the moment and our surroundings. Virgo improves upon our five senses and shows us how we can make things even better and more enjoyable for ourselves. Capricorn works with the physical resources it has so that it can manifest what it wants by using discipline and concentration.

When Earth is balanced in the chart, they are frugal, practical, grounded, and focused. If Earth is lacking, they have a hard time with consistency, issues with money, unable to think logically, and have trouble with discipline and obtaining goals. If they have too much Earth, they are lazy, unmotivated, unambitious, expect things to come to them, closed-minded, and too self-critical.

THE THREE MODALITIES

CARDINAL-START OF THE SEASON

The cardinal signs Aries, Cancer, Libra, and Capricorn bring forth the start of each season. This is the time of our solstices and equinoxes which indicate important changes in our weather, the amount of daylight, and the overall temperament of the coming months.

Positive attributes of Cardinal energy are initiation, getting things off the ground, general optimism, strong self-identity, and confidence. Negative attributes are lack in follow-through, selfishness, and being overly ambitious.

FIXED-SEASON PROPER

Fixed signs Taurus, Leo, Scorpio, and Aquarius occur when the season reaches its fullest expression and thus, all attributes related to that season are in full bloom. The fixed signs act as anchors and allow for permanence in state so that the seasons can reach their purest embodiment.

Positive attributes of fixed energy are seeing things through, sticking up for causes and beliefs, lasting impressions, and permanence. Negative attributes are stubbornness, elitism, selfishness, and being unable to let go/surrender.

MUTABLE-END OF THE SEASON

The Mutable signs Gemini, Virgo, Sagittarius, and Pisces occur when the season begins to dissolve and reach their conclusions before entering the next season. Mutable signs remind us of the everchanging state of things, and how the blending of one season into the next is all part of the organic process of life, death, and rebirth.

Positive attributes for mutable energy are the ability to compromise, consider different opinions and ideas fairly, and the ability to work as a group.

Negative attributes are a lack of autonomy, indecisiveness, constant changes in opinion, and low energy.

* * *

The elements and modes may not give you the entire picture, but they are a good place to start. If right off the bat you observe an imbalance in an element or modality, you can immediately give remedies. Or, when you start to learn more about who they are, it can remind you why they keep winding up in the same pitfalls. However, the elements and modalities are only the place to start, not the place to end. With that in mind, let us now dive even deeper into our exploration with the twelve signs of the zodiac.

SECTION 2-SIGNS OF THE ZODIAC

If you were to lay out the entire sky map that surrounds our planet onto a two-dimensional sheet of paper, you will find this map to be cut into 88 different pieces or constellations. To further the argument that mythological archetypes are universal, it should be noted that ancient Greek, Middle Eastern, Jyotish, and Egyptian civilizations came up with very similar mythologies and pictures for the same corresponding constellations.

Out of the 88 constellations that create our entire sky map, all the planets in our Solar System, including the Sun and the Moon, run along the same band of 12 constellations which we call the zodiac. This circular band of 12 constellations is also called the ecliptic when referring to the Sun's yearly pathway from Earth's perspective (Fig. II-4).

FIGURE II-4. The Ecliptic/Zodiacal Band with the Earth in the Center.[56]

These 12 constellations perfectly fit into a 360° circular wheel, which is divided into 12 equal parts of 30° each with the Sun traveling approximately 1° per day on this pathway (1 celestial year=360 days every time with no leap years). Due to the easily divisible nature of 12 (/2,/3,/4,/6), the signs and planets therein interact with one another through various connections which we call aspects. This will be covered more in Part II-Section 5.

Each sign contains a specific modality, element, planetary ruler(s), time of the year, key phrase, and visual symbolism based upon the constellation itself. We will now discuss these various qualities along with three positive and three negative attributes for each sign.

ARIES ♈

"Be. Here. Now." -Ram Dass, Aries

THE RAM

Sheep have been an essential part of human history and tradition for thousands of years. For generations, we have used their wool for clothes, their grazing abilities to clear land, ate their meat, and drank their milk. In ancient Hebrew culture, *rabbis* would blow the ram's horn, or *shofar*, during important religious services such as *Rosh Hashanah* and *Yom Kippur*. The Celtic god Cernunnos was always depicted with a ram by his side, and the Egyptian god Khnum has the head of a ram. Even Jesus is considered to be "the good shepherd" by his followers.

Throughout many cultures, rams have been a symbol for power, drive, energy, virility, and fearlessness. Rams have no problem defending themselves by head-butting their opponents or by stomping their hooves into the ground as a warning. Goats also make the best mountain climbers and can scale a mountain with much ease. This parallels Aries' ability to push forth and reach the top regardless of the obstacles before them. Aries always love a good challenge.

"I AM"

The key phrase for Aries is "I am," the ultimate statement of being present and accounted for. Aries individuals are not ashamed to feel important nor do they feel unworthy when it comes to being noticed. It is the sign of personal identity and not being afraid to share that identity with the rest of the world. Aries people make themselves known and are the first ones to try anything.

They very much live in the moment and only worry about things if they need to be worried about presently. They do not bother themselves with hypotheticals or second-hand experiences. Instead, they would rather experience it personally and be the ones to share their experiences with others as they tend to take pride in being the trailblazers of our society.

CARDINAL FIRE

Aries energy can be thought of as a match. That first ignition of the flame that sets the entire firepit ablaze. It is that initial spark of inspiration, that intrinsic motivation inside of us that convinces us to get things accomplished. However, much like the match that represents them, eventually that once explosive flame will die out quickly if it is not tended to properly.

Aries people need to learn to continue with their inspirations and see things to the end. They do a great job of going with their gut, but sometimes, they do not follow their gut in order to reach the end-goal. They usually get bored or interested in something else along the way instead. Regardless, cardinal fire is the inspiration that has initiated many changes both globally and personally. It is when we finally decide to go on a diet, or when revolutionaries finally decide it is time to take up arms. When we experience cardinal fire, we feel motivated and ignited to get things done and to do things our way.

PLANETARY RULER: MARS ♂

Mars is the planet of action and assertion. It tells us how we are driven, how well we stand up for ourselves, and the quality of our temperament. Aries embodies these qualities by always seeming to be the confident go-getter of the group. Aries waits for no one and does not feel the need to explain themselves to anyone. Just like a rocket being launched into space, Mars is the planet of focused direction and using our own personal will to steer in that direction towards whatever ends we desire.

Mars does not tend to consider the thoughts and opinions of others because he sees himself as his highest priority. Because Mars is aware of the self in this way, he can defend himself and knows the difference between the self and others. This provides a strong sense of self-identity which Aries people tend to embody.

Spring Equinox

The start of Aries is a very important time for astrologers because it is the beginning of our astrological calendar. The spring equinox is the moment when the sunlight during the daytime on the Earth is equal (hence the term equinox) to the lack of light during the nighttime. From this moment onward, the amount of sunlight will slowly grow in duration, causing the climate to become warmer and the days longer.

During this time, the snow from winter slowly melts away, preparing the Earth for spring and life to flourish once again. It is a time of great celebration, as ancient cultures knew it was the time to no longer be afraid because life was coming back to earth, which meant the soil will once again be able to harvest crops. In fact, usually before crops were planted in the spring, some farmers would conduct a controlled burn of the soil to eliminate the weeds and prepare the land for seeding. Here, again, we observe the fire motif of the Aries cardinal fire as farmers prepare their lands for the planting.

Positive Attribute #1-Heroic

Heroes tend to have a quality that goes beyond the self. They seem to be above their own human limitations, which allows them to easily strive for the unthinkable and obtain it with ease and fearlessness. In *The Odyssey*, for example, we witness Odysseus' determination to reunite with his wife after the Trojan War. Even when he is faced with every kind of obstacle imaginable, he pushes himself for the sake of love and honor. This sort of unyielding passion is what we look for within our own personal heroes. People that have pushed themselves in order to become something bigger than themself whether it is for glory, fame, personal dignity, or righteousness inspire us to accomplish the unthinkable in our own lives.

Aries people always endeavor to be great in whatever they do. This drive motivates others around them to achieve their own goals because it makes others feel that if an Aries can do it, so can they. This is why Aries people make good personal trainers and motivational coaches. They lead by their own example, sending the message that you do not have to be special in order to achieve. You just have to possess the courage and drive to be yourself, and to believe that you are worth obtaining your own personal aims.

Positive Attribute #2- Defender

You can always count on an Aries person to stick up for themself and for the ideas and people they care about because they view these things as an extension of who they are. This is why one cannot help but feel protected around an Aries. Aries is the front line of a battle. The group of people that are sacrificing their lives for the sake of defending whatever they feel deserves defending. You can guarantee that an Aries will stand up for their own ideas and opinions of the world because they come from direct experiences.

Aries knows what is best for them because they have experienced it firsthand and therefore does not need to consider your own opinion. However, because Aries is not fixed, it is possible to change their perspective if it is brought to them through a path of self-discovery. For example, if an Aries is unable to tap into their feelings, show them a movie that you know would evoke emotions within them. This helps the Aries to relate to themself through their own identification. Or, if you are in an argument with an Aries, it is important to put them inside your own shoes. Once they understand your perspective through their own experience, they are then able to empathize and relate.

Positive Attribute #3- Pushes Limits

Aries individuals are highly self-motivated. They seek to improve and test their own plateaus frequently by seeing if they can just tip the scale a little bit more before giving up. This is why follow-through is very important for an Aries person to harness. If they are able to make their goals more long-term, they are able to improve over time quite well due to their endless supply of determination. Aries people love a challenge, and they love to challenge themselves even more.

This is why they have to make sure they pay attention to their actual limits as they can physically hurt themselves on accident. Still, Aries people are keen to go one step further than what is expected not to show others that they can, but to show themselves that they can, and then have others be impressed by their ability to endure.

Negative Attribute #1 - Forceful

Aries can sometimes become intimidating and too forceful when it comes to dealing with others. When this happens, it is usually the Mars energy that gets ignited and becomes out of control. This can put others into a corner where they are left to either fly or fight. Either way, the Aries wins.

The best way to handle this situation is to diffuse the energy immediately. When the Aries fire becomes too hot to handle, you do not want to feed it with more energy, but sizzle it out by breaking the fourth wall, and bringing their behavior to their direct attention. Sometimes Aries people are simply not aware that they are being too forceful on an issue and bringing that to their attention helps them to take a step back and evaluate a bit more.

Negative Attribute #2 - Shoot Now, Ask Questions Later

Aries people are risk takers, but they are not calculated risk takers as this is more of a Capricorn trait. This is because they can become so enthralled in the present moment, that they do not think too far enough ahead in order to consider the consequences of their actions. Similarly, Aries people can become obsessed with the need for instant movement and gratification that they rarely question their actions beforehand.

Aries people need to think about the pros and cons before making important and risky decisions. This will safeguard them for the better and will get them out of sticky situations preventatively. Not that the Aries should doubt their choices or hesitate on their choices; they simply need to ponder to see if their choice is the best option at that moment. This will also help Aries individuals with a better sense of strategy and planning.

Negative Attribute #3 - Bully/Bossy

When Aries energy is out of control, it becomes that of the bully. Ruled by Mars, Aries can create a world full of power struggles. Aries people can sometimes feel that they should be the boss without question. They achieve this by asserting fear, dominance, and power over the other and when this occurs, they need to seriously consider therapy because it is usually a projection of them not feeling secure inside their own body. Consequently, they feel that they need to make others feel inferior. When Aries children are showing these traits, parents should take care to nurture their feelings better and figure out where these frustrations are stemming from.

TAURUS ♉

"You are unique, and if that is not fulfilled, then something has been lost." -Martha Graham, Taurus

THE BULL

The cow has been a staple part of the human experience for millennia. Not only do we consume the cow's milk and meat, but bulls have also been used to plow the land in preparation for the seeding of crops. In countries like India, cows are heavily revered and honored for their service to humanity.

Cows are also highly intelligent animals that can remember things for a long time. In fact, animal behaviorists have found that cows interact in socially complex ways developing friendships over time, and even holding grudges against other cows that have treated them badly; very Taurian indeed. Although their stature is robust, cows can be surprisingly agile and playful. However, they can be just as stubborn, not wanting to leave a spot and moving only if they so desire.

"I Own"

The key phrase for Taurus is "I own" which makes these individuals attribute their personal qualities to the things that surround them. A Taurus feels the clothes they wear, the decorations in their house, and even the cars they drive make a statement towards their own personality and as an extension of themself.

This is why Tauruses can have trouble sharing their valuables with others because they are afraid that if they do not get the item back, a part of themself is also lost. You will rarely see a Taurus disheveled or looking drab. In fact, if you see a Taurus looking this way, this is a sign that they are not feeling in tip-top shape. Wanting better valuables and surrounding themselves with nicer things are big motivators for Tauruses. Similarly, as their personality evolves and changes, so does their wardrobe and valuables.

FIXED EARTH

Although our own planet is not considered in astrology, Taurus is the sign that best represents Mother Earth. Fixed earth is how we are able to create a foundation, support ourselves, and beautify our spaces. Just like the bull, fixed earth is not going anywhere and in doing so, creates a secure space for us to plant our goals, our things, and our relationships.

Being fixed earth, Taurus people are literally the physical anchors of this planet. They maintain stability, keep situations pleasant, and allow for others to simply relax and enjoy comforts. Fixed earth reminds us to stop and smell the roses. According to a Taurus, we are put on this earth to enjoy life and need to remember to take breaks from the rat race so that we can recharge our batteries and admire the fruits of our labors.

PLANETARY RULER: VENUS ♀

As mentioned above, the element earth functions through the five senses. Venus, as the ruler of Taurus, is a literal manifestation of our five senses and the enjoyment of using these senses to understand and experience the world around us. Venus is the planet of luxury, aesthetics, pleasure, and enjoyment; all of which are embodied within Taurus. For a visual example, the empress card within the tarot deck is an archetypal representation of Taurus and Venus. Here, we see the empress reclining on her couch, surrounded by a forest and wheat with her symmetrical crown and heart shield with the Venus symbol engraved on the front. Venus and Taurus remind

116

us of the beautiful works of art that humanity has created over the years, and Taurus certainly knows how to enjoy these pleasures.

Spring Proper

During the month of Taurus, the flowers are in full bloom, the birds are singing their songs, and the weather is perfectly mild and pleasant for a nice picnic and other outdoor activities. Once the frost of winter is finally gone thanks to the onset of spring brought on by Aries, it is now time to seed the harvest into the fertile soil. This explains why the astrological calendar was important to our ancestors because it told them when the timing was right to plant the crops for a year's harvest. Indeed, much of our vegetation is planted during this time.

POSITIVE ATRIBUTE #1 - Arts Curator

Tauruses appreciate all of the arts and tend to become patrons by purchasing works of art, attending concerts, and visiting museums. The arts are a vital part of human history, and thanks to Tauruses, the arts are preserved, honored, and valued. Tauruses act as a great litmus test to see if certain styles are going to catch on or not (famous *Vogue* editor Anna Wintour is a Taurus). They usually surround themselves with paintings, statues, and even their clothing is an art piece in itself. Thanks to their admiration for the creative, the arts are able to continue within our culture.

POSITIVE ATRIBUTE #2 - Femininity

Tauruses, both male and female, carry with them the positive attributes that society usually associates with femininity. Qualities like grace, poise, culture, and being well presented with a lightness to their movements, speech, and attitude. However, this is not to say that Tauruses should be expected to act inferior to masculinity.

Over the course of Western history, there has been a firm definition as to which character traits constitute femininity and which ones are more masculine. Today, we live in a world where these qualities are no longer divided by the sexes. Nor is a woman expected to act feminine, or a man masculine. Furthermore, we live in a society that encourages, and should encourage, a lack of labels and categorizations.

However, the fact that Tauruses contain these positive feminine characteristics is meant to be a compliment because they possess all of the favorable qualities society tends to associate with femininity. If a Taurus is invited to a gala, you can guarantee that they will be the best dressed, elegantly received, properly groomed, and thoroughly admired for their social graces.

POSITIVE ATRIBUTE #3 – Connection to Mother Earth

As previously mentioned, Tauruses are strongly connected to Mother Earth. Taurus people, if they so desired, can create an easy link to the spirit of Earth and communicate with her along with fairies, nature devas, and gnomes. Tauruses have a natural green thumb and can create robust and lush gardens. They also have big hearts when it comes to environmentalism, animal cruelty, and conservationism. The Venus quality of Taurus makes them lovers of peace, and Tauruses wish for world peace between humanity and nature.

NEGATIVE ATRIBUTE #1 - Vanilla

Taurus people know what they like and tend to not push themselves outside of their comfort zones making them predictable and unadventurous. It is very hard to convince a Taurus to try a new food or a new activity that is unfamiliar. Nor do they appreciate spontaneity and not having a plan.

Taurus people need to learn to push themselves out of routines and monotony so that they can experience more of what this world has to offer. The issue is, when it comes to the fixed signs, stubbornness tends to be the biggest downfall in most cases. The Taurus needs to be more flexible when it comes to trying new things, meeting new people, and just going with the flow.

NEGATIVE ATRIBUTE #2 - Unmotivated

Tauruses can have a very hard time getting motivated from working out, to diets, to personal projects. The fixed earth quality hinders their ability to become inspired and stay inspired as they usually tend to enjoy the inspiration of others. Taurus people need to find whatever it is that encourages them to become a better person and to pursue their vision.

Sometimes it is easy for the Taurus to become too complacent and not really care about grand schemes or big dreams. This is where the Taurus is doing a discredit to their own self because they are, in fact, immensely talented if they can focus their energy towards a goal. Having some sort of thought-out plan prior by laying out their goals into smaller pieces will help them to stay motivated and realize that they can accomplish anything.

NEGATIVE ATRIBUTE #3 - Fairy Tale Expectations

Due to the pleasant nature of "Happily Ever After," it is easy for Taurus people to fall into the trap of unreal expectations when it comes to love. This is complicated by the fact that Tauruses tend to be more of the romantic type of the zodiac, preferring candle-lit dinners and massages to more risqué activities. If you are dating a Taurus and forget your anniversary or Valentine's day, it is probably better you do not show up to home at all.

Taurus people need to release expectations of these fictional ideas of romance when it comes to their own relationships by remembering that people are not perfect, and that there will always be some discord when it comes to their partner. It is also important to remember that although they may be a romantic, sometimes their partner may not be as mushy as they would like, but this does not mean they love them less.

GEMINI ♊

"We must never forget that the highest appreciation is not to utter words, but to live by them."- John F. Kennedy, Gemini

THE TWINS

Twins are two people that have identical experiences but view these experiences differently due to their differences in personality. They have the same mother, father, and upbringing, but somehow, their psychology is incredibly unique and special.

For Geminis, there are two sides to every story. Like their fellow air sign Libra, they are concerned with weighing options and the variances of opinions. The difference is: Libra tries to take both sides of the argument and come to a compromise, where Gemini literally experiences both sides of the argument at the same time.

This ties into Gemini's mutability. Sometimes, it can be very hard for them to make a decision because they see both decisions as valid inside their own head. Either way, the twins represent an exchange of information from two different sides of the argument at hand.

Another theme that we see in twins is the sibling association. Even if the Gemini does not have any siblings, they associate with their friends and the like as if they were their own brothers and sisters. This creates a very informal, yet intimate, connection with the ones they care about. Geminis are always looking for their other twin, a person whom they can experience the same events together, and then share their differences in opinion. However, we must also remember that the term "sibling rivalry" exists for a reason, and that Geminis can become unreasonably argumentative and hostile towards those close to them.

"I Communicate"

For Geminis, communication is key as they are very curious individuals, wanting to ask other people their thoughts, opinions, and knowledge. Not only do they enjoy the exchange of communicating, they are very good at adjusting their own speech in order to keep conversations going.

Geminis are always asking the "what and how" of things. Just like Scorpios, they are inquisitive people. The difference is: Scorpios ask questions to get to the bottom of the situation, and Geminis are simply curious, and want to ask people what they think just for the sake of asking and understanding.

Mutable Air

When it comes to mutable air, one just needs to think about the air in which we inhale and exhale. One moment, we are inhaling oxygen, which travels into our bodies though our lungs, and then, we exhale carbon dioxide back out into the world. Indeed, it is breathing that allows for us to communicate in the first place because we use this air to vibrate our vocal cords.

Mutable air literally goes where the wind takes it. They are free flowing and unconcerned with where things are going. It is more about the journey than the destination. Because mutable air is this adaptable, Geminis can talk about anything because they are interested in learning about anything with anyone. They enjoy going with the flow of the people and the situations around them.

When it comes to participating in various activities, Geminis are not as concerned with the activity itself as long as they can participate in the activity with their intellect and speech. For example, a trip to an art museum might not be as fun to a Gemini as it would be for a Taurus, but if the Gemini is able to discuss the artwork and read up on the descriptions, they will have a fun time. However, if it is a strictly no talking affair, they will not have much fun, and may in fact become a little mischievous in the process in order to protest.

Planetary Ruler: Mercury ☿

Mercury (or Hermes) was the messenger of the gods in Roman and Greek mythology. Not only was he a fast traveler, he was also a fast thinker, able to come up with workable schemes at the quickest moment. In the natal chart, Mercury not only tells us how we communicate, but also how we think and process information.

Geminis, being ruled by Mercury, are quick on their feet, quick in their thoughts, and quick with their ideas. They have a pace about them that makes it hard to catch up sometimes. They can take in information rapidly and exchange ideas just as quickly. This is why Geminis are naturals when it comes to anything related to technology and the internet.

Mercury, although a god himself, seems to be more subservient to the other gods and tends to do their bidding. Geminis, in this same respect, like to be helpful and assist others with their goals and plans.

End of Spring

Towards the end of spring, we are wrapping up the academic school year with students graduating, saying their good-byes, and tying up friendships that they would like to continue throughout summer and beyond. Many pictures are taken, many speeches are given, and many yearbooks are signed.

This is a very active time when people are starting to conclude their work calendars and prepare for their summer vacations. Similarly in nature, now that the warmth of the Sun is in full swing, animals and people tend to be more relaxed as the fear of winter is no longer apparent and the intense heat of summer is on the way. Thus, people tend to be in lighter moods and are able to enjoy their friendships and families once again because not only is the weather more agreeable, but children are now on their vacations.

Positive Attribute #1- Social Chameleon

If you put a Gemini into any social setting, they will be able to get along with anyone regardless of how different they are. Gemini people know what to say and how to say it depending on the social circumstances in which they find themselves. This makes them very relatable people as anyone can feel as though they can talk to them.

This comes in handy when a situation needs to be diffused. Mutable signs have a talent for calming down heated arguments or tensions, and Geminis do this best by simply knowing what to say and when to say it. They usually do not have to think about it beforehand as they have a natural talent to have the most appropriate phrase simply roll off the tongue.

Positive Attribute #2- Brotherly Love

If you are living with a Gemini or have a Gemini friend or partner, they try to make you feel as though you are one of their siblings. This makes the environment intimate yet lighthearted. Even if you are meeting a Gemini for the first time, they try to create this association up front, making you feel at ease, as if they have known you their entire life.

Geminis are fun, loving, playful, and enjoy good humor and a carefree attitude. Geminis want you to feel as though you can trust them, and the casual feeling they bring to their relationships make it easy for others to approach them. Not only for comfort, but also for fun and enjoyment. You can guarantee that the Gemini is up for anything and enjoys outings and get-togethers.

Positive Attribute #3 - Good with Technology

When it comes to anything involving technology or the internet, Geminis are the masters in this department. Highly skilled in social networking and internet searching, they make great media experts. Their speed, matched with their ability to understand the technological process, allows for them to compute, create, and find whatever they need on the internet with ease and speed.

This also makes them talented in creating spreadsheets, computing data, working with digital financial books, word documents, and fast responses when it comes to emails and texting. Geminis are also great at troubleshooting technology as well as buying the latest technological products such as smart phones, laptops, and smart cars.

Negative Attribute #1- Instigator

Sometimes for a Gemini, any communication is good communication. It can be very hard for a Gemini to be still and silent which causes them to demand a perpetual dialogue even though the other person does not want to engage with them. The Gemini frankly does not care. In order to keep the conversation going, they encourage conflict so that the other person will talk to them even though it is argumentative.

Geminis really know how to push buttons. They tend to do this by riling up the other person, getting them flustered, and when the other person voices their frustrations, the Gemini makes it seem as if it was you that caused yourself to feel that way instead of the Gemini.

When Geminis are acting in this way, they need to learn the art of silence. Sometimes we need to rest, and not converse. This is not a bad thing, nor does it indicate that something is wrong. Simply, if everyone were to spend every moment in conversation, eventually we would run out of things to talk about, and the quality of the dialogue would dwindle with each passing moment.

Negative Attribute #2- Compulsive Liars

As mentioned above, Geminis have the ability to keep others engaged without thinking twice. That, mixed with their ability to say things in the right tone, allows for them to easily lie and have the other person believe them with much ease.

Unlike water signs, who can use emotional manipulation to get what they want, Geminis get what they want by having you foolishly believe that they are right because they sound so sure. If you come across this issue and something does not register within your own deductive logic, counter the Gemini by having them explain what they mean by asking for further details. Even Geminis have a hard time building up lies on top of lies.

Negative Attribute #3- Short-Term Focus

Just like Aries, Geminis tend to live in the moment and can have trouble seeing the bigger picture and working towards long-term objectives as their critical thinking can sometimes be a little too much on the surface.

They need to do as Virgos do and ask themselves, "What is the function of the thing I am trying to understand?" This allows for them to go more in depth because they are attempting to comprehend the why and how in addition to what.

CANCER ♋

"Could a greater miracle take place than for us to look through each other's eyes for an instant?" -Henry David Thoreau, Cancer

The Crab

Crabs are in tune with the tides of the ocean because they live under the sand where the land and water meet. Not only do they need to know when the water is approaching for breathing purposes, the low and high tides tell them when it is safe to emerge.

When crabs have gotten too big for their shell, they need to leave their outer casing in order to search for a bigger one, making them incredibly vulnerable until they have found a new shell that properly fits. However, when they do come across their new shell, they once again become impenetrable and protected from predators.

Crabs are known as bottom feeders because they feed on the smaller sea creatures and organisms that live on the seabed. The crab's pincers are used primarily for finding food, but if a crab feels threatened they quickly become a dangerous tool for defense.

Cancers similarly possess identical attributes to the animal that represents their sign. Being ruled by the Moon, they are very much in synch with the ebb and flow of life just as crabs are in tune with the ebb and flow of the ocean. They also contain a strong intuition that tells them if the circumstance is a safe one or a dangerous one.

Cancers have a hard time coming out of their shell because they do not like to feel threatened or vulnerable. Still, if they take the leap of faith and put themselves out there, they find that they grow and indeed, become stronger.

Cancers know what they need in order to be nourished, usually going about their lives peacefully, but are very much able to stand their ground if they feel threatened and confident enough.

"I Feel"

The keyword for Cancer is "I feel." Cancers are connected to their feeling function. They approach everything in life with how they are inwardly affected. All water signs approach life through the emotions but in Cancer's case, they are emotions incarnate because they are ruled by the Moon.

When you talk to a Cancer, they understand the meaning behind what it is you are saying. They are able to tell if you are sincere or artificial not by what you are saying, but by the emotional content underneath what it is you are saying.

They are gentle, delicate, and very loving towards the ones they care about.

CARDINAL WATER

With Aries, which was cardinal fire, we saw the initial intuitive reaction of going with our gut. With Cancer, which is cardinal water, we see the primary responses of our emotions. Our feelings sometimes have no logic. We can be angry, sad, or happy with no real rhyme or reason. If we are in touch with our inner feelings, like Cancer, we experience our first emotional response fully, immediately, and genuinely just as Aries is when it comes to their desire to act.

A lot of people tend to repress their emotions or negate their existence altogether. This is seen in the more traditional way men are brought up in this world by being taught to "suck it up" and that "crying is for babies." With Cancer, there is no hiding what it is they are feeling because, just like Aries, their responses are instantaneous.

PLANETARY RULER: THE MOON ☽

Put simply, the Moon represents our inner self. It shows us our capacity for emotions, how we handle our emotions, and whether we take our emotions seriously or not. If we are emotionally self-sufficient, we experience a kind of confidence where no matter what we do, we feel secure because we are grounded in who we are as a person on the inside. If we are not in touch with our inner self, we can become volatile or dependent on others because we do not feel that sense of inner security. Cancers should take care in paying attention to the moon phases because, although we are all effected by the moon's monthly nature, this is even more true for Cancers.

SUMMER SOLSTICE

The summer solstice is the halfway point between the spring and fall. From now until the fall equinox, the days will get slightly shorter, but the temperature will stay warmer. It is hard to understand why a water sign ushers in the hot season of summer, but we must remember that during this time, the air is very humid and sticky which is thanks to the added moisture and heat in the air.

Now that children are out of school during this time, families get together and celebrate traditional holidays like Independence Day in the United States, and Canada Day in Canada. Also, now that it is officially summer, people begin to visit the beach in addition to other tropical destinations. Watery fruits like oranges, watermelons, mangos, and coconuts are enjoyed during this time to cool ourselves off from the humid climate.

Positive Attribute #1 - Good Listener

Cancers are very caring individuals who sincerely want to listen to your problems because they enjoy being there for the ones they care about. They can detect how you are feeling and are able to cool down frustrations quite easily if they are not angered themselves. Cancers have this unique ability to transmute your emotions while you are speaking to them because you are both cooperatively processing them with their help without you even realizing.

Positive Attribute #2 - Builder

Like their opposition Capricorn, Cancers know how to work from the ground up. Not only are Cancers good at nurturing feelings, they are also sufficient in nurturing projects and relationships. They understand the value of baby steps and building something significant slowly over time. This is why Cancers take relationships very seriously. They invest their entire being towards whomever it is they care about and are thus willing to stick it out through thick and thin. This ability gives Cancers a great threshold for patience because they know that Rome was not built in a day, and that taking great care creates some of the most majestic, secure, and profitable outcomes.

Positive Attribute #3 - Intimate

Cancers can create an environment that makes you feel secure and loved. It is very easy to become personable and close to them because you do not feel threatened. Cancers are non-judgmental people and are very connected to their empathy. Indeed, all elements have the capability to demonstrate some facet of unconditional love in their own unique ways.

With fire, you experience the love of experiencing life. Air is the love of conversing ideas and thoughts with others. Earth is the love of enjoyment. Water, however, is literally the purest essence of what we mean when we say love as the polar opposite to fear.

Cancers, without saying anything, send out a message that says, "It is okay to feel whatever it is that is inside of you. It is okay to cry, and it is okay to be scared. I am here for you." Because of this, Cancers create a bubble of emotional security where people can let their guard down and express whatever it is on the inside that needs to be expressed.

Negative Attribute #1 - Irritable

When people are feeling moody or touchy, it is no wonder we call them crabby! Cancers can easily be at the mercy of daily moon energies which makes it very easy for them to feel uncomfortable and irritable. They need to make sure to use objective reasoning when their emotions become irrational, so they do not lash out towards others. The best way to handle illogical outbursts is by thinking through the situation. Cancers should ask themselves if they have just cause for feeling the way they do, or if is it due to waking up on the wrong side of the bed. If it is the latter, they can put themselves in a better mood by engaging in activities that always make them calm and happy.

Negative Attribute #2 – Dependent

Cancers have a reputation for being clingy. Similar to Libra, they become so focused on the other person that they can lose themselves in the process. Both signs love and desire to feel needed. The difference is: Libra is concerned about maintaining the relationship in the literal sense, and Cancer is concerned about maintaining their sense of security.

This comes from Cancer's love for memories and past experiences. If a relationship was positive and loving at first, the Cancer wants to keep these memories alive, even if it is no longer the case. Cancers need to make sure they can release relationships and situations when they have passed their expiration date, and to have the confidence to stand on their own two feet.

Negative Attribute #3 - Irrational

Water, as our emotional function, does not use reasoning or logic in their processes like Air. Therefore, Cancers can have a reputation for coming up with bizarre conclusions that have no real findings within reality. This is especially true when they are riled up and allow for their emotions and mood get the better of them.

Although they make good listeners, Cancers need to be able to do some of the talking themselves. If they discuss their conclusions with others who are more objective, this will help them to realize the holes within their reasoning. However, if Cancers decide to bottle it up and create actions based upon their irrationalities, they find themselves unconsciously manifesting their paranoia.

For example, if a Cancer thinks that their partner is cheating on them with no real evidence, they might start to treat the relationship as if their partner was cheating on them, which causes unneeded tension and disharmony. Eventually, that partner will leave due to the unjustified anger Cancer is emanating towards them. But instead of understanding that this was due to the Cancer's own self-undoing, they might instead say "See?! I knew you were going to leave me," further perpetuating the irrationality that got them there in the first place. Cancers should strive to balance emotions with rationality to alleviate this common pitfall.

LEO ♌

"Love yourself first and everything else falls into line. You really have to love yourself to get anything done in this world." – Lucille Ball, Leo

The Lion

The power, majesty, and glory surrounding Leo is paralleled to the multitude of stories and regal representations of the lion that we observe within Western history and mythology. For example, King Richard I of England was known as "The Lionheart" due to his military prowess and bravery. Strangely enough, the heart is the body part that is ruled by Leo.

A Leo does not require a literal kingdom because whomever they are and wherever they are, they will build up a monarch-like following where they are constantly admired. Similar to the Sun that rules their sign, Leos have a natural gravitational pull about them where others cannot help but be tugged into their orbit. This is because Leos, without even realizing it, project an aura of confidence, poise, and an all-encompassing ability to be present. If you have the Leo's attention, you will have all of their attention, which is one of the reasons why people are so attracted to their energy. The catch is, of course, that you need to be able to keep the Leo's attention else they slip away looking for their next form of entertainment.

The allure that Lions have is almost indescribable. People tend to respect and admire their beauty along with their ability to harm if they so choose. Just like lions, people are incredibly curious around Leos. They possess within them the ability to exist so well in the moment, that people are amazed by their ability to possess that spark of originality which comes from a purely genuine individual. What you see is what you get with Leos and if you do not like it, the Leo does not consider it to be their problem but yours. The lesson people learn from a Leo is to be yourself and to not care about what the world thinks.

Leos walk the fine line between mercy and tyranny. They can either understand the value of paying it forward and that good deeds come back to you, much like the fable of the Lion and the Mouse. Or, they can act like King John of England, who was cruel and vindictive just because he simply could. When Leos balance power with perspective, in other words, if they can put themselves in other people's shoes while in their positions of authority, then their truly regal nature shines forth because they are balancing personal agency with control and restraint.

"I Create"

Leos are immensely talented within the arts. This is because the act of creating involves imprinting your own self and your own expression onto a medium. Leos, like their fellow fire sign Aries, do not question their motives and simply do. Leos do not need nor ask for approval, nor do they question or second-guess their creative output. This intuitive approach mixed with Leo's confidence allows for them to blossom wonderfully artistic expressions out of nothing and be honored for their work.

Furthermore, Leos are able to create just for the sake of creating. There does not have to be a message or some sort of pervasive theme. The simple fact that it came from within is itself a genuine enough reason for their creation to exist. Even if the Leo does not work in the arts, they are imaginative, inspirational, and are able to think up original ideas in whatever profession they chose.

Fixed Fire

Fixed fire is that of the eternal flame. The all-pervasive, unceasing, omnipresent light of the soul that exists within all of us. Leos stand as a reminder of this fire, which is simply spirit shining forth as a unique expression of the creator that manifested this universe. This is why people are so attracted to Leos: they see their souls on full display and people crave that ability to be as true and genuine to themselves just like a Leo.

Fixed fire burns away and purges all of the sorrows on Earth. It reminds us of the happiness and light-heartedness of our experience that makes life worth living in the first place. Within our souls, there is no suffering, agony, or duality, but only light and love. Leos take away our pain with their cheerful and carefree attitude, and we thank and honor them as kings and queens for keeping this flame alive within our tumultuous world.

Planetary Ruler: The Sun ☉

The Sun is unceasing in its light and warmth. It loves us so much and has so much love to give that not only is our planet pulled in by its gravitational force, but all other planets in our solar system are as well. Indeed, without the Sun, there would be practically no life on this planet.

Stars within our universe are born out of nebulas which contain the chemicals needed for life, like hydrogen. It is scientific fact that all organic life, including ourselves, are composed of this star-stuff. Naturally, the Sun represents all parts of us that we have in common. The difference is Leos act more individualistically because they appreciate that their unique life was meant to be lived. Leos, being ruled by the Sun, emanate light and joy.

Just how ancient cultures honored the Moon as the mother and provider, the Sun was also worshiped and indeed, our entire celestial calendar's primary function was to tell ancient cultures when the seasons would change due to the Sun's apparent path around the ecliptic (or zodiac).

Just like the Sun, Leos tend to give off a warmth that helps others burn away their own darkness and fears. The Sun does not fear. On the contrary, it sizzles out fear and darkness as the giver of light. Light from the Sun makes the crops grow, gives us warmth, and keeps the earth in orbit. If a comet, which could destroy our planet, gets pulled into the Sun's gravity, it dissolves into nothingness as it approaches the Sun's rays and surface.

All planets in our solar system are loyal to our Sun and the Sun is similarly loyal to its planetary subjects. As such, Leos are very loyal creatures. If you have been swept into their sphere of influence, it is because they truly care about you and want to provide for you just how our own Sun provides for every living thing on this planet.

SUMMER PROPER

Leo occurs during the heart of summer when people have the most freedom from their obligations. This is the time for enjoyment and doing what it is you want to do because of the agreeable weather and open schedule. This is also the time where "summer bodies" are shown off and admired, as people tend to wear less layers. Themes involving children are also observed because this is a time when children tend to go to summer camp, theme parks, and zoos so that they may enjoy their carefree existence.

POSITIVE ATTRIBUTE #1 - THE CHILD OUTLOOK

In Eastern philosophy, the goal of having a "child's eye" is one many people aspire towards. This Buddhist concept means you approach everything in life with innocence, non-judgment, curiosity, and unconditional love just as a child would, with no comprehension of fear or dread. As children, we start off life without care and worry; it is only the world of adults that slowly corrupt the mind to think a certain way which causes the child to eventually lose touch with their once carefree mentality.

Leos very much embody the child outlook by approaching life with gusto and confidence by not being concerned with the opinions of others and being excited about life. They are naturally curious individuals who simply observe more than they analyze. Instead, Leos are present in the moment and are open to whatever experiences come their way.

Positive Attribute #2 – Loyalty

Leos are very loyal creatures not only in relationships and friendships, but also towards their ideals and objectives because they are very true to themselves. You can expect a Leo to defend what they believe in, protect who they care about, and finish their endeavors to the end.

This is because Leos have an innate understanding of the self. To them, there is no question or doubt towards who they are as a person. It is their fixed fire quality, their lack of second-guessing that allows for them to stand up for their opinions. Leos are very good at expressing themselves through action. What you see is what you get because they are so sure of their understanding and therefore see it as truth.

Positive Attribute #3 - Social

Leos are very much social butterflies. They make great hosts and hostesses and guests at parties. Their liveliness mixed with their interesting personality makes them a great addition to any social gathering. Leos are able to create large social circles around them along with admirers and professional associations.

Leos always feel that they are on a stage performing for those who are watching (and not watching). This makes them entertaining and energetic creatures in whatever social situation they are placed. Their curiosity makes them interested in other people even though they tend to always turn it around back towards their own knowledge and experiences. For example, if you are conversing with a Leo and you mention astrology, the Leo will then take that opportunity to dive into everything they know about astrology and might even neglect to ask you about your opinion. Still, people find Leos fascinating and interesting because they seem to have an opinion on any topic.

Negative Attribute #1 - Self-Absorbed

Leos can sometimes forget that there are other people in a room. They can become obsessed with their self-importance that they assume everyone around them is simply an audience member for their own one-woman or one-man show. Leos need to remember that, although they have strong opinions, they are not the only person with opinions and thoughts.

Leos need to make sure that they do not become too self-centered to a point where they flat out ignore other people in their lives. This ties back to their dedication towards their own objectives and ideas. They can sometimes forget the need for collaboration for the sake of the group. This is where Leo stubbornness can become their worst enemy because not only are they unwilling to budge in their opinions, they have this attitude that their opinion is the only one that matters, which can put them in a bad light.

Negative Attribute #2 - Gets Away with It

When you are trying to discipline a child, sometimes they can become so endearing, so adorable, that you cannot even fathom punishing them. Leos can captivate this charm readily to where they easily slip out of consequences. This is particularly dangerous if you are in a relationship with a Leo, or if they are your employee within a professional setting.

Even when Leos are 100% in the wrong, giving them a free pass only encourages their bad behavior and keeps others in toxic environments. The Leo then has the free range to do as they please while the others have to suffer and obey the rules. Leos are not unintelligent and know when they are in the wrong. Meaning, they should be more honest with themselves and own up to their wrong doings instead of manipulating those around them with their smile and charisma.

Positive Attribute #3 - Tyrannical

If a Leo is in a position of authority, they need to make sure that they lead by example and not by "do as I say, not as I do." When they are the ones with the power, they then have the approval to boss others around due to the power structure that is in place.

134

Although the Leo can get what they want, they are leaving space for feelings of bitterness, anger, and resentment towards them if the only thing that is forcing others do as they command is solely due to the division of power. Consequently, when that division of power disappears and the Leo is then put on the same level as the ones they once terrorized, this can make them prone to feeling alone, isolated, and in their eyes, disrespected. Leos should remember that throughout history, there are many examples of dethroned kings and queens who took their power a little too far. To this point, a great example is King Charles I of England who was so obstinate with parliament's decisions, he eventually decided to dissolve the parliament, which subsequently led to a civil war and his execution for high treason. The Leo must never forget that their crown is only as secure as the people's trust that put them there in the first place.

VIRGO ♍

"Talent is cheaper than table salt. What separates the talented individual from the successful one is a lot of hard work." – Stephen King, Virgo

THE VIRGIN

The archetype of the Virgin is one that has been honored for thousands of generations. In Rome, Vestal Virgins were keepers of the temple of the goddess Vesta and were revered as the maintainers of Roman society. In Christian mythology, the Virgin Mary is likewise honored as a symbol of temperance, good deeds, duty, and morality.

In many religions, leaders are asked to take vows of chastity. In the Hindu faith, for example, the reasoning behind this is to preserve their sexual energy stored in the lower chakras so that it may be used to awaken the kundalini.

Being chaste not only requires discipline, it requires the sacrifice of one's animal instincts of procreation for the sake of something higher like that of spiritual evolution, the preservation of a culture, or simply our own goals and ambitions. However, in our society today, we do not honor the choice of abstaining. On the contrary, those that decide to save their more intimate encounters for either someone special or for a greater cause are chastised and criticized within our culture.

To this point, academia has noted a contemporary phenomenon known as "the Virgin/Whore dichotomy" which tends to effect women more than men. Put simply, if a woman decides to not be sexually active, they are thought of as a prude. However, if a woman is decisively sexually active, they are thought of as a whore. Men also experience this dichotomy because if they decide to be abstinent, they can be teased for not being a "real man." However, men are less likely to experience the whore label of this dichotomy because men are very much encouraged to be sexual creatures within our society.

Patience, discipline, and saving your most sacred part for the person or situation that you feel is worthy are some of the great gifts that Virgo offers. The problem is, because we are no longer a culture of the land where we cultivate crops and pay homage to our harvest gods and goddesses, Virgos can feel shunned, dishonored, and rejected. Indeed, Virgo, Scorpio, and Pisces (and sometimes Aquarius) seem to be the most misunderstood signs of our zodiac because their energies are not considered valuable within our modern-day culture.

Virgos teach us to be patient when we are taught to want things immediately. Virgos preserve their energy for the most sacred of experiences. Virgos improve because they have a higher standard and value quality over quantity.

"I Analyze"

Virgos seek to understand and attempt to comprehend everything from the ground up. This makes them incredibly good learners and teachers because they understand the function of things in addition to the thing itself. Where Gemini is the actual data, Virgo takes the data and looks for trends, patterns, and inconsistencies.

This gives Virgos a good critical eye and a talent to improve upon matters because they can easily discover flaws not for the sake of criticizing, but for the sake of improvement. Virgos like to ask, "What is the meaning?" behind circumstances. They feel as though there is always a lesson to be learned and that one can discover the truth if they simply analyze their observations.

MUTABLE EARTH

Mutable earth is the loose soil that we use to grow our corps. If the soil is rich enough and in the proper climate, it is able to grow just about anything we so desire. Once the crops have been harvested, the soil is then replaced, replenished, and the cycle starts again.

Moss, which is considered to be the earliest of plant life, is highly adaptable to its surroundings. It simply plants little roots into where it wants to grow, and its seeds then fly away and attach themselves to trees or stones. Moss does not require a lot to grow and is able to work with what it has in order to live.

Virgos, in this light, can stay planted within short-term situations and easily move their ideas and processes towards whatever the situation calls for.

PLANETARY RULER: MERCURY ☿

In our discussion, we have now come to the point where we find one planet ruling two signs. In this case, it is the planet Mercury ruling both Gemini and Virgo. When it comes to Mercury ruling Virgo, we see the furthering of data that Gemini has brought about. Mercury, in regards to Virgo, improves upon communication by having an extensive vocabulary, the ability to break things down into smaller pieces, and filter information to its most essential essence.

Mercury ruling Virgo also represents the health aspect of the planet. The staff held by Mercury, the caduceus, is used as our symbol for the health sciences in our society. Similarly, the image of the two snakes intertwining around a pole imitates the idea of kundalini energy rising up and down the spine which can be thought of as the purest form of spiritual health.

Mercury ruling Virgo is where we get puns, poetry, novels, editors, and critics. We simply see a more refined way of looking at communication as opposed to Gemini who communicates regardless of the situation. Virgos, on the other hand, choose their words carefully and understand that sometimes, less is more.

End of Summer

The time of Virgo is the time of the harvest where the seeds that were planted during Taurus are now ready for the picking. The harvest moon allows for bright light to occur even during the nighttime as our ancient cultures would work around the clock harvesting their crops in preparation for the upcoming fall and winter.

This is where we get the phrase "separating the chaff amongst the wheat," as the time during Virgo is all about trying to identify what part of the harvest was useable and which parts were not. Again, this emphasizes their sense of quality and having high tastes and standards. In our modern times, this is the conclusion of summer vacation as students mentally prepare for the start of school and the academics that lie ahead.

Positive Attribute #1 - Hard Worker

Regardless of their profession, Virgos take pride in their work and hold themselves to do the best job they can. Employers of Virgos do not need to tell them how they can be doing better because they are most likely doing the best job out of all of their employees.

Virgos understand the value of using discipline now in order to get the reward later. This makes them good at focusing on smaller steps with amazing precision. Just like Geminis, Virgos have a good amount of endurance and stamina and use it to work until the job gets done.

Positive Attribute #2 - High Attention to Details

Virgos make sure nothing gets passed them. They are very good at leaving no stone unturned, and they even constantly consider the stones that others might have missed. This makes them natural double-checkers, making them highly prepared for any situation. If you are working on a group project you want a Virgo on your team because they will make sure all parts of the project are completed and that everyone does what needs to get done.

This talent is also helpful when the Virgo needs to observe a lot of information all at once. They are able to correlate evidence well and detect patters in statistical and correlative analysis. This is also helpful in the health sciences because they are calculating, caring, and comprehensive. If you go to a Virgo doctor with issues involving your kidney, rest assured that they will also consider your liver, your stomach, and everything in-between.

POSITIVE ATTRIBUTE #3 - TEACHER

The art of teaching is the ability to understand a topic so comprehensively and thoroughly that you are not only able to grasp the information yourself, you are also able to relay this information to your student in an adaptable way. Virgos are able to explain the same topic in many different ways making them excellent teachers. They also have a good sense of patience and understanding, allowing for the student to learn at their own pace without pressure.

Teaching also involves taking a larger curriculum and breaking it down into smaller lessons and sections. Virgo's organizational skills make it easy for them to take larger plans and concepts into smaller and more modest chunks so that students do not become overwhelmed.

NEGATIVE ATTRIBUTE #1 - DEBBIE DOWNER

Virgos can fall into the habit of thinking that everything could be better. When this happens, they criticize everything just to belittle others which can make them unpleasant people to be around. If the atmosphere is happy and joyous, the Virgo could say something rather depressing or awkward causing the entire mood to shift.

They need to remember that although perfection is a noble pursuit, to err is to be human, and there is no such thing as a perfect anything. Everything simply is as it should be, and Virgos should admire whatever circumstances and people they encounter.

NEGATIVE ATTRIBUTE #2 - WORKAHOLIC

Virgos are hard workers, but they can become obsessed over their work to a point where it becomes their life's focus. Virgos need to make sure they listen to their bodies and take breaks from working or else they can become immensely run down and unhealthy. With any addiction, the person tends to sacrifice all other aspects of life for the thing that they are addicted to. To prevent this, when it comes to Virgos and their jobs, they need to balance their professional life with their personal life, and remind themselves that sometimes the overtime is not worth it.

Negative Attribute #3 - Uptight/Wound Up

Virgos can have a hard time relaxing and simply enjoying the situation. This makes them stiff and unable to relax because they are constantly seeing how things could change and improve. To safeguard this, Virgos should learn from Leos and understand that sometimes in life, you just have to let loose and enjoy yourself. Like Capricorns, Virgos can have a very somber and serious attitude and they need to remember that although there is a time and place for professionalism, there is also a time and place for fun, games, and enjoying the fruits of your labor.

LIBRA ♎

"The truth is rarely pure and never simple." - Oscar Wilde, Libra

The Scales

One of the greatest ancient stories around the scales of judgement has to do with "The Judgment of Osiris" in Egyptian mythology. According to ancient Egyptian lore, when a soul passed into the afterlife, they were met with the god of the dead Osiris who then tested the soul's purity to see if it was worthy enough to enter into the blissful field of reeds. If the soul was not pure and good, it was cast into the great void of nonexistence.

The measurement of the soul's purity was determined by Osiris placing the heart on one side of the scale, and the white feather of truth onto the other. If the heart was lighter than the feather, this meant they lived a pure and morally sound life. If it was heavier than the feather, the crocodile-faced god Amenti devoured the heart, and they were then cast into the void.

140

This idea of righteousness translates into the archetype Justice who appears on top of our courts, usually blindfolded and holding scales that are equally balanced.

To a Libra, each side of an argument is equally valid. The key is to have these two ideas coexist in harmony because all ideas are true depending on the person who perceives that truth. For example, creationism to one person is just as valid as atheism is to another. For the Libra, both are right because they are true for that individual and every person is entitled to an opinion and to seek their own truth.

"I Balance"

Moderation, equilibrium, and the middle road are all important to a Libra. In a world full of extremes and polarity, Libras strive to work and live in harmony by finding commonality. At the end of the day, we are all human, which is very much an Air message. Libras attempt to bridge this gap by having two sides come together and listen to one another for the sake of understanding, coexistence, and empathy. Moderation is so important to a Libra that they understand the crucial importance of spending an equal amount of time working, relaxing, eating, and so forth. They try to live life with a balanced agenda and divvy up their time appropriately.

Cardinal Air

When we find ourselves in a disagreement with another and have stopped talking, it takes cardinal air to break the silence in order to mend the gaps. This is why Libras are very talented with diplomacy and world affairs. They are able to let both sides know that they are being listened to equally.

Libras are the first to inquire about anything. They are interested in hearing other people's opinions, which encourages people to open up and share their own thoughts. Geminis tends to communicate about anything and everything, but Libras want to talk about your perspective on things. Another difference is with Geminis, conversations usually revolve around two people but for Libra, it usually involves three: the two people on opposite sides of the argument with the Libra standing in-between.

Planetary Ruler: Venus ♀

Once again, we see a planet ruling two signs as Venus rules both Taurus and Libra. Venus ruling Taurus represents the relaxation and enjoyment of the senses, but Venus ruling Libra represents the harmony between one another, humanity, and nature. Venus embodies peace and tranquility and both Taurus and Libra strive towards these goals. Taurus does this through means of luxury and the enjoyment of life, and Libra through personal relationships and through a balance within oneself.

Just like Taurus, Libras are a calming influence that tend to relax the atmosphere wherever they may be. They both have a talent for making you feel comfortable and at ease because Venus does not enjoy conflict like Mars. Instead, Venus strives for serenity on all fronts.

Fall Equinox

During the time of Libra, we have reached the fall equinox where the daytime and nighttime are again equal just as it was during the spring equinox. Only this time, the days will get shorter, and the weather will start to become colder.

It is no coincidence that the fall equinox happens during Libra because the daytime and nighttime are both 50/50 in duration. Now that the school year has started, relationships between teachers and students emerge along with interactions between employers and employees and politicians towards the public if it is an election year.

It is vital for humans to cozy up to one another during this time in preparation for the colder months ahead. Due to this fact, this is a time to find likeminded individuals and to also mend any conflicts from the past because pretty soon, everyone will be huddled up in a hut somewhere around a fire and will need to get along for the sake of survival.

Positive Attribute #1 - Diffuser

Libras have an amazing talent for neutralizing any conflict and tension within a situation. Their Venus influence allows for a calming demeanor, and their love for harmony superimposes any anger felt between two parties. Libras are amazing moderators in this way because they see what the other person cannot and therefore they do a great job at diagnosing where the misunderstandings are stemming from.

Positive Attribute #2 - Fair

If a Libra parent has two children, you can guarantee that both children will be treated with fairness and equality. Libras strive to make things right through fairness. If something does not sound fair, they will usually speak up to make sure that the punishment fits the crime.

Libras understand the sacrifice of the self for the sake of equality. Even if they were offered a bigger slice of the pie than someone else, they are more than willing to speak up and make sure everyone gets an equal share. Even if that means less for them. This explains why Libras are in harmony with their fellow air sign Aquarius as both strive for social justice of some kind.

Positive Attribute #3 - Pleasant

Libras have a calming and pleasant aurora about them. They are great to talk to and make excellent company. Again, we see the influence of Venus at work. This calming demeanor makes people trust them, which allows for Libras to be talented social workers, professional mediators, and counselors.

Similar to Taurus, Libras know how to enjoy themselves when others are in their presence. One cannot help but feel relaxed and cared for because the Libra's energy is naturally soothing.

Negative Attribute #1 - No Personal Opinions

Libras spend a lot of their time trying to understand the thoughts and opinions of others. The issue is, if you were to ask a Libra what they thought, they would probably draw a blank. Libras need to ask themselves the same question they ask others: what do they think?

This is where the Libra can learn a lot from its opposition, Aries, who is full of personal opinions and ideas. One of the reasons why Libras feel as though they cannot have any opinions is because they feel that it might interfere with their objectivity and neutrality. However, the truth is you can be both. There is simply a time to be opinionated, and a time to hear the opinions of others.

NEGATIVE ATTRIBUTE #2 - INDECISIVE

That old story of asking your partner where they want to go for dinner, and your partner replies with "I don't know, where do you want to go?" is the typical Libra response. It is very hard for a Libra to make a firm decision on anything because they try to weigh in all the options by simultaneously observing the pros and cons to each one within their head.

Sometimes, a Libra just needs to make a decision and go with it. It does not matter if it is the right one or the wrong one. All that matters is that the Libra decided on one direction over the other, automatically making it the right choice. By doing this, the Libra starts to learn the thrill of spontaneity and how going with your first thought is usually your best thought.

NEGATIVE ATTRIBUTE #3 - SELF-DOUBT

Because Libras are so concerned with the other, they sometimes forget to create a persona around themselves. Consequently, they are not able to make decisions because they genuinely do not know how they would respond in the first place, because they are not familiar with their own character.

It is important for Libras to ask themselves these questions and figure out what they like and dislike in addition to what they would do or not do within situations. Libras needs to remember that they themselves are also human beings with opinions and a life of their own.

SCORPIO ♏

"Nothing in life is to be feared, it is only to be understood. Now is the time to understand more, so that we may fear less."- Marie Curie, Scorpio

THE SCORPION

Scorpions representing Scorpios is a little misleading because there are in fact three animals that are associated with this sign: the scorpion, the eagle, and the phoenix. Each one of these animals represents the three stages of evolution and transformation.

With the scorpion, we see our most basic instinct of flight or fight. Just by their appearance alone, scorpions can seem very terrifying. However, their personality is a lot like the bee in that they only attack you for self-defense and not just for the sake of it.

Scorpions do not want to harm you unless you give them a reason. Similarly, Scorpios can seem very intimidating just by appearances alone as they tend to have very stern and dominating statures. But what you are experiencing is the same phenomenon one experiences when dealing the other water sign Pisces. Namely, you are simply looking at yourself through them and what you fear is really the exposure of the darker side of your own personality. Indeed, it can seem that Scorpios can see right through you at times.

You feel vulnerable around a Scorpio because you are not sound within your own self. This is where we find the stages of evolutionary transformation to be of importance. When we do not feel at ease within our own skin, it is because there are parts of our personality that are outdated and thus desire to be eliminated.

When the Scorpio sheds their skin of worn-out behaviors, they evolve onto the next stage and become the eagle. Eagles are very majestic and respected creatures. Chiefs of many Native American tribes wear eagle feathers as part of their regalia. Although eagles are predators, we honor them and admire them for their ability to use their sharp vision in order to attack their prey.

Transformation comes in three stages: the old, the limbo where the old is dying and the new is trying to obtain a solid footing, and the new. This explains why transformation is difficult for individuals because the middle stage, where you have one foot in the old and one foot in the new, can bring about a lot of chaos and frustration. Anyone with addictive tendencies can attest to the difficulty of rehabilitation and the upheaval of emotional suppression contained therein. Once the middle stage of limbo is surmounted, however, the next and final stage is that of the phoenix.

The phoenix is a mythological creature thought to possess the highest form of magic and majesty. Indeed, when we release our old self so that our true self can come about, it is quite a magical experience because we have struggled where many people have failed, usually because their vices eventually get the better of them.

Scorpios remind us that who we are is not who we really are, and that is why we sometimes feel uncomfortable around Scorpios. Their ability to pierce through the layers of B.S. and see the truth of the matter is very hard for artificial people to handle. In this light, Scorpios have a hard time being social because they feel that it is them who is making these people feel uncomfortable.

"I Desire"

Desire is usually a trait that is seen as a sin. Desire is having a want so intensely that you become blindly focused in achieving that desire. We are taught that desire is bad because it implies a lack of self-discipline and contempt for society and others.

But desire is one of the reasons why Mars traditionally rules Scorpio. Desire is a self-motivator that seems to have a vigilant bend. The Scorpio asks, "Why is pursuing our desires a bad thing?" Afterall, desire is not that far off from passion. The only difference seems to be that passion is more of an exterior feeling, something you are passionate about, and desire is an internal feeling, something you embody or become.

Desire shows you what your body and mind truly want even if it is bad for you. If we have desires that even in the long run would do us harm, we still feel the need to experience these desires because we have a need to learn from them. In fact, it was Carl Jung himself who once said, "A [person] who has not passed through the inferno of [their] passions has never overcome them." Scorpios are heavily driven individuals because of their desires. This makes them very honest in who they are because, like all fixed signs, they do not deny any part of themselves.

Whether we want to admit it or not we all have desires, and this ties back to the three layers of transformation. Desires are basic and animalistic, and before we can transform to higher states of being, we must first cave into our desires and learn how much they lead to our downfall. The biggest challenge is to not become swept up within our desires while we explore them, for it is too easy to get stuck into the abyss of our animal nature, and therefore become stagnant within that negativity, for a very long time.

Desire shows us what we unconsciously need to purge out from ourselves. If we do not acknowledge this, we experience repression which only exacerbates the issue. Conversely, the moment we address our desires, experience them, and learn from them, we evolve.

Fixed Water

Fixed water is that of the river. The contours of the river tell the water where to go and the flowing current continues until it reaches its destination: the ocean. In our culture, we talk about the metaphor of going with the current or fighting up stream. When we need to experience change, we can either fight or surrender. The power of Scorpio, and Pluto for that matter, is inevitable and beyond our control. That is why we must listen and adhere to what we are being told to change about ourselves.

Planetary Rulers: Mars ♂ (Traditional)/Pluto ♇ (Modern)

Ruled by Mars, Scorpio people are forceful and determined. Their fixed quality allows for them to maintain discipline and the courage that Mars gives them allows for them to be confident in who they are. Scorpios also have very potent sexual energies that can be channeled through intimacy or through spiritual and magical endeavors.

Pluto is the god of the underworld and with Scorpio, we see a lot of parallels to the unconscious underworld inside ourselves. Pluto exposes the hidden forces of our psyche and when they appear out into the open, we can experience chaos because we do not understand or acknowledge what we are feeling and why we are feeling it. Pluto is the awakening of the unseen shadow self that influences our decisions without us even knowing. Scorpios, by embodying Pluto, have a great ability to get to the bottom of situations and people. They have the gift of penetrating laser vision that directly addresses the heart of any matter.

Fall Proper

During this time of the fall season, we start to notice the death of our planet as leaves begin to change, animals prepare for winter hibernation, birds prepare to fly south towards warmer climates, and ancient cultures began to store their crops in order to prepare for the coming winter. One of the metaphysical lessons we learn during fall is that although it appears that the Earth is dying, it is only eliminating that which is not needed in order to survive the winter, until life inevitably returns to the planet in the springtime.

Positive Attribute #1 - Healer

Scorpio's ability to figure people out allows for them to be great healers because they can aid others through psychological transformations. Their connection to the unconscious mind allows them to see what people cannot see inside themselves. This makes Scorpios a guide of sorts towards an individual's journey of self-discovery. Not only do Scorpios possess psychological healing, they also embody magical healing, like that of the shaman.

Positive Attribute #2 - Guardian of the Strange

Scorpios love all things violent, bizarre, abnormal, and taboo. These topics are very much subjective, and what society considers strange is simply an opinion of the times and the society therein. Scorpios remind us that it is okay to be an outlier and not accepted by society. As long as you are true to yourself, that is all that matters.

Scorpios are fans of horror movies, gore, anti-social crowds, occult teachings, and anything else shunned by the mainstream. They keep these darker aspects of our culture alive to remind us that they are, yet again, the hidden part of our culture's personality. Remember in Part I-Section 6, the individual unconsciousness is directly proportional to society's unconsciousness. Scorpios are here to remind us of this universal truism.

Positive Attribute #3 - Protective

Scorpios are highly protective over the people they care about. They see them as their own kin and are willing to do whatever they can to make sure they are safe. Scorpio parents are not afraid to stick up for their kids if they are bullied in school by calling out the bully's parents on their poor parenting. Like their fellow water sign Cancer, Scorpios have a lot of love to give, and they express this love by showing that they can shield their loved ones from danger. This is the effect of Mars ruling Scorpio.

Negative Attribute #1 - Self-Destructive

When Scorpios are not in control of their energies, they can do more harm than good as they tend to push the limits of people or situations a little too far. If a Scorpio is just starting to get on their feet from a time of turmoil, they might purposely self-sabotage themself so that they can fall right back into misery. This is also due to the fact that Scorpios can sometime become too obsessed with negative emotions, situations, and people. They can become so comfortable around the darker side of life that they surround themselves with the wrong kind of people and circumstances. Instead of breaking free, a sort of self-masochism occurs where they love inflicting pain onto themselves. It is true that "misery loves company," but the Scorpio should learn not to thrive within this predicament.

Negative Attribute #2 - Vengeful

"All is fair in love and war" was most likely said by a Scorpio. To them, revenge and backstabbing is fair game if the ends justify the means. Scorpios need to watch out for questionable tendencies they can use to get their way or to make others feel pain. They need to remember that although they help others transmute their karma, they themselves are not the bringers of karma.

One of the reasons why Scorpios feel justified in being vengeful is because they want others to feel as much pain as they have felt. Instead, they should take their own advice and ask themselves to see what the pain they are feeling says about their own life choices.

Negative Attribute #3 - Complacent

Much like their opposition, Taurus, Scorpios can have a tendency to become stagnant. It takes a lot to motivate a Scorpio because they must become motivated with every fiber of their being. If not, they are more than likely to just stand around, wait for things to happen, or not happen. It is a balancing act where the Scorpio needs to be an agent of change within their own lives but not as an agent of self-destruction and implosion.

SAGITTARIUS ♐

"If you tell the truth, you don't have to remember anything." - Mark Twain, Sagittarius

THE CENTAUR ARCHER

Sagittarius contains a lot of symbols within its depiction. Sagittarius, as the archer, possesses focus, calmness, and an unwavering path towards their goals. The centaur is always depicted with a bow in the aim position as if he were ready to shoot the arrow at any given moment. All they need to do is to find their target and release.

In most cases, the archer is not aiming at a target in front of him, but behind, as if he were in motion, galloping away from someone or something. Shooting a target in this pose is not only harder, it requires some reliance on intuition because it is hard to keep your hands steady. In other words, it is not only the aim of the Sagittarian that gets them to their target; it is their trust that everything will work out as it should because that is the law of nature. They inherently feel that connection because that are ruled by the ultimate planet of manifestation: Jupiter.

In other words, Sagittarians are lucky because they are highly connected to the power of manifestation and have the mentality of, "Life is full of abundance and I am deserving of this abundance because, after all, I am one of God's creatures, and all God wants to do is provide for their children."

Sagittarians are inherently lucky in everything they do but it is not because luck is some sort of God-given blessing, it is because they believe in the power of abundance and manifestation

150

even on an unconscious level. Within our society, our main thesis of economics is that all supplies are in limitation, but if a Sagittarian oversaw our economy, there would be no limitation for one's basic needs.

We are all at the mercy of what we manifest, what we will into being. Referring to Part I-Section 2, this is why introspection is immensely important. Recall, the more we do not understand our unconscious side, the more the unconscious has control over our lives and over what we manifest. People are unlucky because they unconsciously think to themselves "I am unlucky," and that becomes their mantra in life.

The idea of the centaur (half man, half horse) represents the higher intellect of humanity having control over their more animal self. This explains why Sagittarius represents institutions, ethics, morality, and philosophy. They emanate a higher intelligence that demonstrates an elevated thinking that has been obtained from a command over the grosser self through the exploration of higher human academics.

"I Understand"

Sagittarians are able to comprehend ideas rather quickly. They usually do not have to rely on repetition or meaningless drills in order to grasp an idea. Instead, they have a natural ability to study just about anything with a strong appetite to learn.

Sagittarians also have high ethical standards. They understand in the innate rights of humanity that all are entitled to so that we may live in a civilized society. Sagittarians hope to maintain these principles so that our human institutions are functioning for the greater good of humanity.

Mutable Fire

The mutability of Sagittarius allows for their ideologies to adapt and change over time. If the courts still followed laws from the 16th century, people would still be burned at the stake for bogus crimes. Similar to Libra, Sagittarius allows for everyone to share their own ideals when it comes to creating some sort of doctrine or democracy. In this way, Sagittarius heavily relies on the morality of the current culture so that the rules can parallel the current step upon the human evolutionary ladder. They plainly accept humanity for what it is and therefore accept whatever institutional ideals arise out of their respective societies. In other words, they respect the process of societal evolution and understand that this is directly related to the contemporary views and ideals of the time in which they live. According to the Sagittarian, institutions of power should uphold these doctrines, whatever they may be, because the integrity of these institutions (ie. democratic, academic, and religious) is more important than the doctrine itself.

PLANETARY RULER: JUPITER ♃

In Roman mythology, Jupiter was the king of the gods. Similarly, Sagittarians receive a lot of their good fortune from Jupiter because he is revered as the god of gods. In traditional astrology, Jupiter is said to be the "great benefic" making Jupiter's influence, for the most part, highly favorable. Being ruled by the great benefic, Sagittarians have an overall jovial mentality and content demeanor. Like Leo, this brightness emanates outwardly, and others cannot help but feel great around them.

END OF FALL

It is a little strange that the bright, optimistic sign of Sagittarius occurs during the time of the year when fall is coming to a close and the colder season of winter quickly approaches. Even within this context, this is still a time of celebration and joy because it is the last hurrah before winter. The holiday Thanksgiving in the United States not only celebrates family, but also togetherness and brotherhood with the hopes that one day, all cultures will come together at the dinner table and feast as brothers and sisters. University applications become due and college students are similarly getting their first taste of freedom while continuing into their fall semesters. This is a time of looking back, observing where you have come from, and see where you are going. With the optimistic outlook of Sagittarius, to them, the only direction they are headed is up.

POSITIVE ATTRIBUTE #1 - GENEROUS

Sagittarians want to share their abundance with others. They are immensely generous with their resources and love. Even on an energetic plane, the Sagittarian loves to share their energy, and you cannot help but feel brighter in their presence. The idea behind this generosity is that when all people have what they require, people tend to be more civil as they do not see any reason to covet. Sagittarians tend to embody this ideal which is why they are always willing to pay it forward. They also find great joy in giving people chances and opportunities in life and will seek to open doors for others. For the Sagittarian, when anyone succeeds, everyone succeeds.

Positive Attribute #2 - High on Life

Sagittarians do not spend a moment of their time in self-pity or depression. They are genuinely happy to be alive, and this joy makes it so that sad and depressing energies cannot invade their personal bubble due to their higher vibrational thinking. When Sagittarians feel frustrated, it is mostly due to the negative people around them trying to bring them down. This is not because Sagittarians live in blissful ignorance or that they repress their sadness, it is because, like Aquarians, they seek to understand a more spiritually elevated way of living where the denser emotions tend to no longer exist.

Positive Attribute #3 - Believes in People and in Society

Sagittarians make the greatest utopians and motivators because they believe in the power of uplifting and encouraging others. Sagittarians never run out of their optimism and love to aid others in surmounting their negativity by encouraging them to find the brighter side to things. They have tremendous trust that people will eventually do the right thing.

These feelings of trust and hope translate into society at-large. Sagittarians believe that humanity is inherently good, and that genuine human nature is to be loving and caring, not evil and selfish. The Sagittarian philosophy on this subject can be found within the preamble of the American constitution where it promises to "…establish justice, ensure domestic tranquility…promote the general welfare, and secure the blessings of liberty to ourselves and our posterity…." These lofty goals, Sagittarius believes, are already understood by all of humanity, and they trust that one day every person will enact on these ideals for the betterment and evolution of society.

Negative Attribute #1 - Too Philosophical

Sometimes, Sagittarians can live in a hermetically sealed utopia without considering the reality of people or situations. They know how things should be handled and how people should act in theory, but do not realize that this is not how things truly operate in practice. This can make them quite naïve and too trusting of people that they should be more cautious around. They need to remember that although they treat others with respect and kindness, this does not mean that others have yet to learn those lessons. Therefore, they should not give their energy so freely towards people who would not return the favor.

Negative Attribute #2 - Overindulgent

Sagittarians can sometimes take the expansive quality of Jupiter a little too literally and neglect their health because they always feel protected by Jupiter. They can easily gain weight or perform other unhealthy habits because they do not think it will cause them harm. I once knew a Sagittarian who was diabetic and would still eat sugary desserts all the time. This is incredibly dangerous for a diabetic, but I surmised that he took the chance because he felt that the Jupitarian safety net was there and would always catch him. Sagittarians need to remember that bad habits are bad habits any way you slice it, and that they are never worth the risk because, even with Jupiter on your side, sometimes your luck does eventually run out.

Negative Attribute #3 - Blind Sighted

Sagittarians are such big thinkers that they can have a hard time with the details. They have difficulty pondering theocraticals and tend to base their decisions on their own personal outlook, sometimes neglecting their own two eyes when the truth of a person or a situation is right in front of them. Sagittarians need to think things through and figure out how they are actually going to get from Point A to Point B.

CAPRICORN vs

"Intelligence is the ability to adapt to change." -Stephen Hawking, Capricorn

154

THE SEA GOAT

The sea goat is quite an awkward animal to say the least. Half of the animal is supposed to live on land, and the other half is supposed to live in the water. Both cannot accommodate for the other which parallels Capricorn's attitude of working with what you have as there is no use in complaining about what you cannot change.

Similarly, the humorous idea of watching a goat with a fish's tail trying to scale a mountain or trying to breath under water matches Capricorn's capacity for humor and comedy. Capricorns are known for their gifts in comedy because they are very familiar with Murphy's law. However, instead of taking this as a negative, they tend to flip it around and laugh at their misfortunes. Remember, it was Paramahansa Yogananada, a Capricorn, who once said that the first stage in overcoming the world's sufferings is to learn how to laugh at the suffering outright.

"I Use"

Capricorns are the masters at building something out of nothing. They are calculating, resourceful, and follow the principle of "waste not, want not." Where Taurus represents actual resources, Capricorns know how to use their resources in order to achieve their goals. Unlike the ram of Aries, the sea goat is not able to climb the mountain on their own, which is why they heavily rely on teamwork and are very appreciative when others help them towards their objectives. However, the Capricorn will never explicitly ask for help because they abhor dependence almost to a fault. They will be the last to ask their friends for money or ask for help in school. Instead, they will use whatever tools they can first in order to accomplish their goals and almost always prefer to do it alone. From a young age, Capricorns learn to become self-reliant and find much pride in being able to say, "Back in my day...."

CARDINAL EARTH

Capricorns are highly motivated people even though they may not seem like the most exuberant. If Taurus is the earth and Virgo is the soil, Capricorn is the big oak tree that stands tall and proud so that others can marvel at its accomplishments. Just as a tree takes many years to become strong and sturdy, Capricorns consider patience to be one of their biggest virtues.

Their cardinal nature makes them stubborn up to a point in that the Capricorn usually feels that they know what is best for them until they are proven otherwise. It can take a long time for a Capricorn to change their strategy or opinion because they usually only trust themselves. Therefore, before a Capricorn will shift their perspective, they first need to be shown that their thinking needs adjustment. Until that time, like the mountains that represent them, they will continue to be steadfast and immobile until they are ready to move.

PLANETARY RULER: SATURN ♄

In the simplest of terms, Saturn is karma. Saturn represents limitations, discipline, obligations, structure, and dealing with the cards that were handed to you. Just how Sagittarians inherently possess Jupitarian qualities of abundance and joy, it is common for Capricorns to always face some sort of adversity in their lives because they are ruled by Saturn, the "great malefic."

Nothing comes easy for the Capricorn, and their struggles can sometimes outweigh the easier times. Again, it is their humor that sees their misfortunes as a satire to their own lives which keeps them from falling into a deep depression. Capricorns understand that there are circumstances that you simply cannot control so there is no use in focusing on these issues because it is rather pointless. If Capricorns continue to strive and surmount their obstacles, they are some of the most successful and wisest people of the zodiac.

WINTER SOLSTICE

Capricorn ushers in the cold season of winter which is where we witness Capricorn's sense of discipline. All of the resources that our agricultural ancestors saved up during the fall are now ready to be used in order to get them through the harsh winter. However, as abundant as their supplies may seem, and as tempting as it is to use a lot of their resources now that the days are getting colder and shorter, it is best to conserve during the time of Capricorn because colder months still lie ahead. Similarly, in our modern world, saving one's money is important because when the holidays approach during the time of Capricorn, we can use our savings to buy presents for the ones we care about.

Positive Attribute #1 - Fatherly Wisdom

Capricorns are great people to turn to if you need guidance and wisdom in your life as they understand the concepts of suffering and striving. They are very practical, realistic, and well in touch with reality, which diffuses other people's illusions within their own situations. It may be tough love, but it is love nonetheless. Even if you do not realize it in that moment, you eventually become thankful.

Positive Attribute #2 - Disciplined/Frugal

Capricorns know how to stay focused and concentrated on any goal they decide to achieve. They can save and conserve money and energy easily because they understand that not spending money now is worth the ambitions they have for their future. This all has to do with Capricorn's great ability to appreciate the art of sacrifice. Similarly, Capricorns will not spread themselves too thin and will only make promises they can keep.

Capricorns can become masters in whatever they choose. For example, if a Capricorn partakes in martial arts, they can easily become black belts over their long journey because they maintain the concentration and steadiness that is required in order to master anything. Indeed, this is why we call them "disciplines" in the first place.

Positive Attribute #3 - Calculating

When a Capricorn takes a risk, it usually works out in their favor because they are always calculated risks. Unlike Aries, Capricorns do not just jump into things headfirst. They consider the pros and cons and are great strategists. This gives them a sharp eye in observing how Move A effects Move Z down the road. This provides stability and success in whatever they do because they are able to positively manipulate events towards their goals without doing much of the manipulation themselves. It is interesting to see how, although Capricorn is concerned with creating and developing, which are active activities, they do it in a very passive way by having others make the first move. Then, they work with what they have and allow for the circumstance to unfold naturally without too much personal influence.

Negative Attribute #1 - Old-fashioned

Capricorns can sometimes be too conservative both in lifestyle and mentality. As we further our society into the progressive Age of Aquarius, some Capricorns can have trouble as they tend to enjoy traditional gender, familial, marital, and societal roles.

Similarly, Capricorns are not ones to be personally expressive or flamboyant. Like their fellow earth sign Virgo, they can be a little uptight and unwilling to let their hair down. This has to do with the pervasive seriousness that seems to always surround the Capricorn. They can have very somber and mundane attitudes which can make them, as my astrology teacher likes to say, "meat and potatoes" kind of people. In other words, they can sometimes be bland, boring, and not really motivated to try new things.

Negative Attribute #2 - Unimaginative

You would not want to go to a Capricorn for new ideas or creativity. Capricorns are funny, but their humor comes from their observations of the world, not necessarily from creating an imaginative world of whimsy. Capricorns can be quite predictable and not the best at thinking outside of the box. They rely more on the tested and true ways of doing things adhering to the saying, "if it ain't broke, don't fix it."

Negative Attribute #3 - Conceited

This character trait is a little bizarre as we tend to not think of Capricorns as egotistical. Nevertheless, sometimes they take their accomplishments and hard work as badges of honor and can develop a "I know better than you" mentality. This can make them very opinionated, holier-then-thou, and always giving you their advice even though you did not ask for it. This is a different kind of self-centeredness, where Capricorns feel they should be appreciated and honored by those around them not through their creativity or talents, but through their accomplishments and struggles. Capricorns should take their life experiences to help guide others, but not out of a sense of self-importance.

Aquarius ♒

"If there must be trouble, let it be in my day, that my child may have peace." - Thomas Paine, Aquarius

The Water Bearer

Aquarius is readily mistaken for a water sign, but one must remember that Aquarius is not the water inside the jar, they are the bearer of that water. Aquarius is the archetype of the angel who is depicted to be a conduit between humanity and god. Benevolent beings that have the job of aiding humanity towards goodness, oneness, and enlightenment as the water contained within the jar is the spiritual and unconditional love that Pisces represents and embodies.

Aquarius and Pisces are the only signs of the zodiac whose mythologies merge together in this way. It seems that Aquarian optimism and empathy comes from an underlining current or understanding that is surprisingly spiritual and Piscean in nature.

The problem is, a lot of Aquarians eventually lose this spiritual part of themselves and become immensely jaded due to their acute observations of humanity's sufferings and mistreatments, which parallels the way they have been treated within their own lives by being marked as bizarre, strange, and/or different according to others. We must remember that the Sun is in its fall in Aquarius (Part II-Section 4) and thus, Aquarians automatically become shunned by society, which makes it difficult for them to express themselves.

Aquarian minds are so open, and their empathy is so grand, that the grosser levels of human nature are incomprehensible to them. Aquarians do not understand why humans seek to destroy and as a consequence, they become orphans within this denser world of duality. Just how Scorpios have taken on the burden of reminding society of its darker side, Aquarians have taken on the burden of keeping society aware and awake of the injustices that exist within this world. Even if that means they themselves must suffer from this knowledge. Although ignorance is bliss, the Aquarian believes that the truth, as painful as it might be, does indeed set you free, and the embodiment of freedom is Aquarius.

The person who is bearing the water in the Aquarian constellation is actually a boy named Ganymede. According to Greek mythology, he was the Trojan prince who was deeply admired by Zeus. So much so, that Zeus transformed himself into an eagle and brought Ganymede back to Mount Olympus to make him the immortal cupbearer of the gods.

The bowl Ganymede carried contained ambrosia, the magical liquid that was said to keep the gods immortal. When it comes to humans living on Earth, our own version of ambrosia, the special elixir that makes us immortal, is the awakening of the omnipresent, unceasing, and unconditional archetypal ideal human (See Part I-Lecture 3).

This is where we see a parallel between Aquarius and their opposite sign Leo. They are both an unedited and unapologetic expression of the self with a proud and strong sense of personal identity. The difference is, Leo is usually expressing their individual human personality, and the Aquarian is expressing the spirit's personality emanating through their human façade.

Aquarians are friendly and likable because they look at their fellow humans without judgment. They believe that all humans are victims of circumstance brought on by society's rules, judgments, and autocracy. They want you to be just as true and free from your own insecurities and from these limitations brought on by societal structures as they are. They understand that it is our present day culture's expectations and presumptions that prevent our true individualistic nature from shining forth. This naturally makes others feel respected around an Aquarius simply because they are treated as a fellow human being with equanimity. Aquarians tend to put everyone on this equal plane regardless of who they are.

"I Know"

Aquarians have a sharp sense of intuition. They can gauge people and circumstances rather quickly, and most of their insights come through like a flash of lightning. The Aquarian brain works very fast, and they are able to process multiple layers of meaning within a single moment. This allows them to conceptualize reality through multiple dimensions and angles.

When Aquarians say, "I know," they truly do. The more negative side to this ability is that they can use this as a weapon to demean others. The more positive side, however, is that Aquarians have developed an inherent knowing of truth, empathy, and justice. Aquarians conceptualize their idea of society vividly and see it as an obtainable future within the pillars of egalitarianism, non-judgment, and the right to self-expression and freedom to be the cornerstones of a just society, which would create a world of peace and abundance (see Part I-Lecture 8). Clearly, this is why Aquarians can be thought of as a daydreamer with never having a solid footing within reality. They simply do not live in the harsher world of the present. Instead, they live in the reality of the future realm of what could be or, more importantly, what should be.

Fixed Air

Fixed air is a little bit of an oxymoron but if you think about breathing, fixed air is that zero point where the inhale and exhale are in flux. During that moment, you're placed in between the paradoxical realm of inhale and exhale, of non-existence and existence. Aquarius, in this respect, is the medium of two worlds: the spiritual and the human.

They want to introduce higher ideals into society and thankfully, Aquarians honor democracy and typically do not have a reputation for tyranny. However, a lot of Aquarians think that if they could be king or queen of the universe, a whole lot of good would get done rather quickly. Permanence is characteristic of the fixed signs and with Aquarians, their fixed nature says, "This is the way life ought to be, this is the way society should be, and my requisites are nonnegotiable."

Planetary Rulers: Saturn ♄ (Traditional) and Uranus ♅ (Modern)

It can be a little confusing to see that Saturn, the planet of authority and conservatism, rules the avant-garde and nonconforming sign of Aquarius. To remedy this, we must remember that in order to rebel (Uranus), we must first have something to rebel against (Saturn). Like Capricorns, Aquarians strive towards their goals and can be quite successful if they overcome their personal obstacles. Also, similar to Capricorns, the Aquarian life is simply a little more difficult than it would be for others.

Uranus is the aching need for rebellion against the old that lies within every one of us. When it comes to revolutions within history, the symptoms of revolution have typically been a group of people that have reached their personal threshold of mistreatment. In this respect, Uranus reminds us to constantly rebel against ourselves because the only true constant in this world is change, even towards our personality.

WINTER PROPER

During the dead of winter, hope for the future is all you have. Our ancient ancestors had to remind themselves that the world would eventually get warmer once again. All it will take is time and patience. During this time of the year, early human tribes were huddled up inside housing to escape from the cold and thus, strong bonds of brotherhood were formed.

The pagan holiday of Imbolc during the time of Aquarius marks the time when daylight is becoming noticeably longer, which parallels the Aquarian themes of optimism and hope. The worst is in the past, and the warmth of the spring, the future, and all of the prospects therein, lie ahead. This is why Aquarians can be very forgiving as they tend to not care about what happened in the past but are only concerned about where to go from here.

POSITIVE ATTRIBUTE #1 - FREE THINKERS

Aquarians are not susceptible to propaganda or towards other individual's baseless ideas. They are creators of their own mentality and view every argument with the discernment of Occam's razor. They are objective and not easily convinced. People admire their ability to not be held down by any sort of dogma or tradition. Aquarians tend to question the validity and truth in everything and if it proves to not pass their litmus test, they easily and quickly discard it. Either way, they are still willing to give everything a fair chance but will always come to their own conclusion.

162

Positive Attribute #2 - Genius

Aquarians truly are the geniuses of the zodiac. They can think outside of the box and are able to understand concepts through many layers of comprehension. The work that they produce in this world has been known to change and influence society and people's lives through invention, art, and ideas. FDR, Mozart, Darwin, Galileo, Rockwell, Lincoln, and Edison were all Aquarians. In fact, according to a statically study, there have been more Aquarian presidents in the United States than any other sign of the zodiac (20% or 1 in 5).[57]

Positive Attribute #3 - Empathy

Aquarians are thought to be emotionally detached and cold to a fault, but it is not that they are emotionally aloof, it is that being ruled by Saturn, they understand that karma is karma and do not enjoy it when people expect their sympathy. However, when it comes to empathy, the ability to put yourself into another person's shoes, Aquarians are the exemplar. This is why they make good and honest humanitarians. They truly feel and understand the pain and suffering of others. Indeed, it is this empathy that makes them rebel against society because they refuse to live a life through rose-tinted glasses just to become another peg in an unjust system.

Negative Attribute #1 – Anarchy

If the Aquarian feels shunned enough by society and/or if they feel powerless to face the injustice in the world, they can easily turn into an anarchist with a desire for chaos in order to seek change. Aquarians believe in the full independence of a person both internally and externally and anarchy parallels this message.

The problem is when it comes to anarchy, there is an assumption that people are civilized enough in order to maintain order. However, human nature does not operate this way as of yet, which would cause severe atrocities to occur for the sake of the apparent freedom given from the lack of social order. Aquarians with this mindset need to remember Ghandi's famous quote: "an eye for an eye makes the whole world blind."

---

57   Dr. Eric Ostermeier. *Presidents Day Special: The Astrological Signs of the Presidents.* Smart Politics. https://smartpolitics.lib.umn.edu/2010/02/15/presidents-day-special-the-ast/. 2010.

Negative Attribute #2 - Demeaning

Aquarians are always going to be five steps ahead of you when it comes to intellectual discussions and debates. Having this kind of power can make it tempting for the Aquarian to belittle the people around them by mocking their perspectives, proving their inconstancies for fun, or correcting people on facts and figures. This is one way for the Aquarian to lose a lot of friends and allies quickly. The irony here is that Aquarians need the people they are alienating because they are incredibly people-oriented individuals. Aquarians need to remember that not everyone thinks as openly and quickly as they do. This does not mean that they are intellectually inferior.

Negative Attribute #3 - Flighty

Aquarians are all about the new and fresh. If you cannot keep their attention, they will most likely leave without any remorse or regret. This is one of the keys to dating an Aquarius. The more freedom you give them, the better off the relationship will be. Aquarians can have such a carefree and *c'est la vie* attitude, that you will be quite surprised to see how easy it is for them to just drop everything and go. Aquarians should learn the value of investing in people, relationships, and projects, and should not back away from commitment in order to fulfill an artificial sense of autonomy and independence.

Pisces ♓

"Said I'm a Pisces, Zika deka del, Well well I'm raising hell, People always tryin' to find the world I'm in, I'm the envy of the women and I rule the men, Two fish, one swimmin' up stream, One swimmin' down livin' in a dream, But when she loves she tends to cling." - Erykah Badu, Pisces

Two Fish Tied Together

When it comes to the imagery of the two Piscean fish, we sometimes forget that they are both tied together at the fin. This is because if Pisceans were given free range, their spirits would probably float away from Earth as quickly as possible, never to return. The rope attached to the fin reminds Pisceans of their karma here on earth, which is hard to understand sometimes because Pisceans are the embodiment of spirit, or, spirit incarnate.

Fish have been essential to many people's diets, and there is no coincidence to why there contains fish symbolism within Christianity as Pisces is the sign of religion. The two fish represent the constant force of yin and yang, the continual cosmic motor that creates relentless change in our world, and therefore, Pisces rules realms such as yoga, surrender, and ego denial.

However, these two fish also have a downside. As with all mutable signs, there are two forces at work that are trying to cohabitate. In the case of Pisces, we see the ultimate feminine trying to blend and mix with the ultimate masculine, making Pisceans a vortex of high spiritual energy that people pick up on and want to consume psychically. Due to this fact, Pisceans are highly susceptible to psychic vampires and need to make sure they are not influenced by the emotions of those around them. It is vital they keep themselves psychically guarded.

"I Believe"

Faith and trust are important parts to the Piscean nature because this is what is required to connect to spirit. However, before you can connect to spirit, you need to have faith that spirit is on the other end to receive you. This is why Pisces squares Sagittarius because Sagittarius thinks that seeing is believing, and Pisces thinks that you must first believe so that you can truly see. Pisces effortlessly takes leaps of faith, trusting that it will all work itself out in the end. The Pisces individual might have a strange way of getting to where they want to go, but they still get there nonetheless.

Mutable Water

Mutable water is the vast ocean that covers most of our planet. Our entire rain cycle depends upon the evaporation of water. Similarly, countless life forms rely on the ocean for life and food. The ocean is all one body but at the same time, you can put your hand in it and separate a portion.

Similarly, Pisces is the sign of ultimate surrender and assimilation. They are able to go where their life path and spirit takes them. Pisces encourages you to listen to your heart, not your head, and to approach all peoples and circumstances in your life with non-judgment, non-attachment, and gratitude.

Planetary Rulers: Jupiter ♃ (Traditional) and Neptune ♆ (Modern)

The expansive nature of Jupiter is seen in the all-encompassing love of Pisces and their trust in the universe. Just like Sagittarius, which is also ruled by Jupiter, Pisces innately feel that the cosmos has their back and will always protect them. The difference is, Sagittarius is better able to focus this energy into tangible goals, and Pisces interprets this abundance to be the hand of God guiding them towards the goal of spiritual realization.

This mindset of trusting in the universe fully without question is simply amplified with the modern ruler of Neptune. Neptune is the god of the ocean and Pisces is likewise the sign of the cosmic ocean that combines all living and nonliving things on this planet and beyond. Neptune allows for Pisces to let go of ego drives and motivations so that they can quietly hear what the universe wants them to achieve. Neptune is also where Pisces get their big heart for unconditional love and non-judgement.

End of Winter

During the time of Pisces, it is the time of ultimate endings. Just how the spirit leaves this world at the time of death, so does the cycle of the yearly celestial calendar conclude as energies fade completely before starting once again. This is a time where the world has a strange quiet to it because there does not seem to be a lot of action externally. Instead, this is a time for mediation and contemplation.

One of the biggest morals of this story is that endings are never permanent but simply a necessary step for a new beginning. As such, after the end of winter, we enter the new fresh start of spring with the celestial calendar at the start of Aries. When this happens, the seasonal year simply starts anew and will ceaselessly continue with its cycle of birth, growth, death, repeat.

Positive Attribute #1 - Psychic

Because Pisceans are connected to the spiritual realm with much ease, they are highly psychic and can tap into the hidden angelic and spiritual worlds around us. They are very good at gauging what is going on with someone internally and can help them by communicating messages that their spirit needs to hear.

Positive Attribute #2 - Unconditional Love

Pisceans embody the idea of unconditional love and non-judgment. They have the ability to ignore the other person's ego and look straight into the soul. This makes them inherently realize that we are all the same. Thus, people around them feel supported and loved simply by the fact that the Piscean communicates these feelings of being welcomed on an unconscious level.

Positive Attribute #3 - Transparent

There is little guesswork when it comes to Pisceans. They are honest creatures, and this helps others to pick up on their frustrations in order to help them out. Like their fellow water sign Cancer, Pisceans are uncensored and embody their emotions fully. This helps others to see their problems more readily and gives the Piscean a flexible body and mentality due to the fluidity of their thoughts and emotions.

Negative Attribute #1 - Needy

Pisceans crave the merging of their soul with the soul of others. However, this can turn into emotional neediness, which can lead to drug addiction or staying in poor relationships for the sake of emotional security. Pisceans need to learn more independence and that their feelings of instability come from them not being grounded enough.

Positive Attribute #2 - Unfocused

Because Neptune is so ethereal and foggy, it is hard for the Piscean to buckle down and come up with a coherent plan. This is more of a talent of their opposition Virgo. Pisceans can live in the world of illusion and confusion. Thus, they sometimes have trouble remembering what is real. They need to keep both feet in this world before they can dive into the world of the unseen.

Positive Attribute #3 - Emotional Punching Bag

Pisceans can act like a mirror for others. When someone is being harsh or cruel to a Piscean, they are actually projecting the things about themself that they do not like onto the Pisces individual. Sadly, Pisceans are so open and forgiving that they usually take the abuse. Pisceans need to learn when to put their foot down, and when to tell others to stop. This is a very hard thing for a Piscean to do. Still, the healthier their boarders are around people, the better off their own health will be because they will be less prone to picking up the negativity of others.

* * *

The mythologies and symbolism within the 12 signs of the zodiac have been imprinted into the human psyche with each passing generation and society that has come before us. They tie us to the natural tug and pull of our yearly calendar and towards the other planets within our solar system due to planetary rulerships. As you will see in Part V, individuals can possess a multitude of signs all contained within themselves. Or, they can contain a few signs within their psychology very strongly. Either way, the signs of the zodiac reflect the human experience that is true for all of humanity whether it be in the past, present, or future. Now, we will observe the ten planets within astrology because without the planets, the signs have no way of expressing themselves within the natal chart. Indeed, it is the planets that bring out the signs' positive and negative traits within a birth chart; therefore, through the planets, the unique psychological makeup is born.

SECTION 3-PLANETS

The natural temperament of the planets is a good place to start when it comes to understanding the ten planets within astrology. Astrology has used a lot of linguistic combinations to explain this temperament: positive or negative, yin or yang, masculine or feminine, etc., etc. For the sake of simplicity and semantic impartiality, I will use the following terms: active, passive, and neutral.

When it comes to the traditional planets in astrology (Sun, Moon, and Mercury through Saturn) these temperaments have been determined by ancient astrological systems. The modern planets (Uranus, Neptune, and Pluto) are placed within their respective positions based upon my own personal experience (Table II-1).

Active planets are agents of doing. They cause events to happen and function as an outlet for our personal expression and motivations. Extroversion, movement, and manifestation are all due to the active planets.

Passive planets are receptive towards the actions of the active planets. They react rather than act, and demonstrate how we function internally. Introversion, receptivity, and emotional states are derived from the passive planets.

TABLE II-1. Natural Planetary Temperaments

ACTIVE		NEUTRAL		PASSIVE	
SUN	☉	MERCURY	☿	MOON	☽
MARS	♂			VENUS	♀
SATURN	♄	URANUS	♅	JUPITER	♃
PLUTO	♇			NEPTUNE	♆

Neutral planets derive their nature and motivations depending on how they are situated relative to the other planets within the birth chart. These planets react when they need to react and initiate when they need to initiate. However, because they are incredibly versatile, they can be easily influenced by the active and passive planets around them. This will be easier to comprehend when we cover aspects in Part II-Section 5, and chart analysis in Part V-Section 2.

For now, let us examine each planet individually and explore key concepts, major realms of rulership, and what happens if the planet is working harmoniously and inharmoniously.

SUN ☉

KEY CONCEPTS

The Sun represents our ego-expression and self-confidence. It is how we portray our personality out into the world, and how we individualize ourselves when compared to others around us. The Sun shows how we influence others by the impressions we make, and how we express our individuality by demonstrating our own uniqueness.

The Sun shows if we enjoy being chosen out of a crowd, and how much we desire or despise attention. It demonstrates our charisma and whether we are skillful at sacrificing our ego-drives for the sake of the group, or if we act more self-centeredly. The Sun shows how we tell the world who we are along with our comfortability as an individual within the world.

The Sun is like your fingerprint. There is only one individualized pattern throughout all of humanity. In this same light, the Sun manifests your own individualized mark on this world. Even within our own solar system, there are numerous planets but only one Sun. Similarly, there will only be one of you and anybody who came before or after you will not share your unique personalized individuality.

REALMS OF RULE

Creativity, charisma, ego-drive, self-esteem, leadership, self-awareness, ambition, extroversion, individuality, confidence, how we fit within social circles, the aura we project and how others are attracted to that aura, our interests and hobbies, and how we express our personal opinions, outlooks, and judgments.

IF FUNCTIONING HARMONIOUSLY

The individual is incredibly self-confident but not egotistical. They are creative and know when to stand in and out of the spotlight. They are bright and cheerful, and others gravitate to them because of this. They stand out in a crowd and are well liked with few enemies. They are great with children and their confidence is contagious and inspirational to others. They make effective leaders because not only do people look up to them, people are willing to work for them.

IF FUNCTIONING INHARMONIOUSLY

The individual can either be a narcissist or incredibly introverted to a point of anti-social. They only consider their own priorities and do not care about the feelings and opinions of others. They have too much pride and cannot admit when they are wrong, and either crave too much attention or will avoid any kind of attention. Their opinions can get them into trouble and their ego-drives can come into direct conflict with others.

MOON ☽

KEY CONCEPTS

The Moon represents our innermost emotional nature. It shows us how secure we are within our feelings and if we are good at nurturing the feelings of others. The Moon shows how we express our empathy and sympathy, and whether we are good at processing our feelings into healthy or unhealthy emotional responses.

The Moon demonstrates our inner comfortability and whether we are confident within our inner wellbeing, overly sensitive, or emotionally inept. It represents the meaning behind our words and actions and whether we are in tune enough to interpret these more subtle forces behind our own active tendencies and those of others. It shows if we are caring and supportive or if we are cold and callous.

The Moon signifies our unconscious side and where we hide our vulnerabilities. It determines if we are emotionally shallow or deep, and if we are consequently emotionally shut off or too open towards others. Our upbringing is reflected in the Moon and therefore demonstrates how we were comforted as children, and if we interpret the world around us as a scary or safe place.

REALMS OF RULE

Inner emotional wellbeing, comfortability within our own self and within the world at-large, our sympathy and empathy, our ability to comprehend the subtleties behind language and action, ability to nurture ourselves and others, dependencies, our unconscious and more vulnerable side, and the mother or the mother figure within our lives.

IF FUNCTIONING HARMONIOUSLY

The individual is emotionally strong and can be supportive in this strength for others. They are not offended easily and can take a joke rather well. They are able to be easily vulnerable due to their emotional confidence. They can quash down frustrations and they are slow to anger or any other intense emotion. They do not get jealous easily and do not rely on others for emotional support and guidance. Instead, others come to them for those things.

IF FUNCTIONING INHARMONIOUSLY

They are either too emotionally volatile or not in tune with their emotional functions making them cold towards the feelings of others. They can easily take offence, especially if they are teased over something that they are not confident about. They have a hard time putting themselves in new predicaments and do not enjoy going out of their routine or with meeting new people and going to new places.

MERCURY ☿

KEY CONCEPTS

Mercury represents our mental functions and capabilities along with how we communicate, conceptualize, analyze, and process ideas and information. It shows how well we can explain and develop intellectual concepts along with our own thoughts, and how receptive we are to the thoughts and opinions of others. It shows our desire for learning and our kinesthetic skills.

Mercury is where we get our discourse abilities, along with our talents in presenting in large crowds, and our skills in technology, typing, essays, and research. It shows how we can think outside of the box and how well we can teach others. Although Mercury is not where we get our sense of humor, Mercury shows us if we have any sense of comedic timing or any sort of linguistical emphasis in the way we speak along with the overall quality of our lexicon.

Mercury shows how persuasive and convincing we can be. It also displays our approach and philosophy towards health and exercise. Our individualized metabolism comes from Mercury along with various processes of the body such as digestion, nutritional absorption, circulation, and breathing.

REALMS OF RULE

Mental capacity, learning and conversational abilities, general health and our approach towards health and exercise, our skills as a conversationalist, teacher, researcher, and writing abilities. Various ways we can approach mental quandaries, our desire for intellectual expansion and education, our analytical capacities, our vocabularies, and speech patterns.

IF FUNCTIONING HARMONIOUSLY

The individual is able to converse well with others and express their ideas clearly. There is generally good health and a proactive mindset in these endeavors. The person can think logically and is effective at explaining. They can self-teach and enjoy reading and obtaining knowledge. They have a voice that is easy to listen to with an extensive vocabulary and knowledge base.

IF FUNCTIONING INHARMONIOUSLY

The individual can have learning disabilities and be socially awkward in the way they speak or with what they speak about. They can use their words to demean others and are prone to arguments and instigating unhealthy debates. They have a hard time saying what the mind is thinking and can have poor hand/eye coordination, which can make driving, writing, and sports difficult. There could be physical ailments and an overall poor outlook towards their health.

VENUS ♀

KEY CONCEPTS

Venus indicates our ability to get along with others so that we can work cooperatively and live harmoniously with other individuals. It shows how we listen to the opinions and thoughts of others, how we share our ideas back to them, and the appropriate understandings that come out of that discourse. Indeed, Venus is the ultimate planet for finding common ground and dissolving conflict.

Venus is also the planet of style, aesthetics, and tastes in art. Our living environment and the types of clothes we wear are all ruled by Venus. She rules our ability to make others feel comfortable and relaxed, and whether we can feel the same way in other people's spaces.

Venus is where we get our appreciation for the arts along with our various preferences in music, visual art, home décor, and design. This is because, in many ways, the arts are universal in that all cultures have their own styles of artistic expression, although people from different cultures can come together based within the collective language that the arts possess.

REALMS OF RULE

Our ability to compromise and hear differences of opinion, our sense of style and artistic preferences, how well we can relax and be grounded within the environments we are placed within, artistic talents along with the type of art we enjoy, and the ability to sacrifice our ego for the sake of collective coexistence.

IF FUNCTIONING HARMONIOUSLY

The individual has a pleasing and symmetrical face and body and an acute sense of style and tastes. They have artistic abilities and/or an aptitude for spotting that talent in others. They have very few enemies because they easily meet people halfway. Their home environments are calm

174

and grounded, and they can feel the same regardless of where they are located. They have a gentle, unthreatening demeanor. Their romantic relationships are typically healthy and fruitful.

IF FUNCTIONING INHARMONIOUSLY

The individual is prone to unresolved conflict typically due to their inability to let go of their points of view and pride. They can have issues with hygiene and overall appearances. They cannot find solace in artistic expression and enjoyment. They dislike house cleaning or any kind of required upkeep. They also withhold information and feelings in relationships so that other people do not have to compromise on their behalf, which leads to resentment.

MARS ♂

KEY CONCEPTS

Mars is where we get our drive, ambition, and tenacity. It shows how well we initiate our personal goals and projects along with our willingness to see them through to the end. It is where we find our courage and willingness to face potentially dangerous situations. To this point, Mars shows if we are risk seeking or more prone to risk aversion.

Our confidence is highly tied into Mars because if we do not feel confident in who we are and in what we are doing, then our drive is likewise hampered by our lack of personal determination. Mars acts without thinking or hesitation and therefore is tied to our "go with the gut" intuition we find within ourselves.

Mars is also the planet of desire and sexual virility. It shows our various ranges of aggressiveness, forcefulness, and how much our sense of longing drives our motivations. Similarly, our athletic abilities and physical prowess are also determined by the condition of Mars within the birth chart.

REALMS OF RULE

Our sense of self-confidence not only in who we are but in what we are doing. The ability to react on instinct but also know when it is strategic to hold back or to push forward, our passions and motivations which fuel our ambitions and personal goals. Our sexual libido and desires, muscle tone and growth, physical stamina, and overall physical attractiveness.

IF FUNCTIONING HARMONIOUSLY

The individual is admired for their poise as they find it easy to simply be who they are and act upon these personal impressions. They are courageous and others see them as inspirational. They are athletic, toned, and people find them sexually attractive. Additionally, these individuals also know when it is a good time to act, and when is a good time to react. This is especially true in terms of intimacy because although they are heavily ego-driven, they can still make themselves vulnerable because they do not judge themselves.

IF FUNCTIONING INHARMONIOUSLY

The individual has a hard time with initiation and finding motivation to accomplish their goals. They can therefore be lazy and not really committed so self-help and self-improvement. There can either be sexual dysfunction or they could be too aggressive with their sexual desires. They are too prideful and readily seek conflict because they are absorbed with their sense of self. This makes it hard for them to be well received by others due to this intensity.

JUPITER ♃

KEY CONCEPTS

Jupiter is the planet of mental and spiritual expansion. It shows our philosophical outlook and how our view of the world manifests due to this outlook. Therefore, Jupiter is also the planet that represents our judgments and opinions that are not necessarily based upon our actual experiences, but through our theoretical idealism found within our minds.

Fortune, speculation, and abundance all stem from Jupiter. Consequently, the powers of manifestation and optimism are determined by him. For example, if our personal outlook is consciously or subconsciously pessimistic, then we naturally shut off opportunities that could have come our way if we were only more open minded and trusting.

Jupiter shows how we as a society function and rule. All our higher institutions (academic, governmental, religious, and vocational) stem from Jupiter because these are realms where we can apply our intellectual and spiritual ideas into practice within the real world. Similarly, Jupiter represents the universality of human nature which either leads to acceptance or prejudice.

REALMS OF RULE

Our moral compass and ethical codes. Our opinions and thoughts towards individuals, cultures, and nations. Our ability to believe that the universe will provide everything we require. Our political and philosophical viewpoints and how these are reflected by the various organizations we associate with due to these preferences, and our sense of abundance and fortune.

IF FUNCTIONING HARMONIOUSLY

The individual easily obtains security and aid from the universe because they are open to such abundance. They are immensely positive individuals but not to a point of hopeless optimism. Due to this fact, others are attracted to their buoyant and generous nature which they gladly extend outwards because they inherently know that they are paying it forward. They are nonjudgmental and very understanding when it comes to the errors of human nature.

IF FUNCTIONING INHARMONIOUSLY

These individuals gamble and speculate incorrectly because they think that their big break is right around the corner. This can breed a jaded and cynical outlook which can consequently corrupt ethical principles. They have bad timing when it comes to obtaining their goals and typically need to work harder than those around them. They can have an overinflated sense of superiority which leads to bias and assumptions that get them into trouble.

SATURN ♄

KEY CONCEPTS

Saturn is the planet of discipline and sacrifice because he understands the need to give up pleasures for today for the sake of tomorrow's achievements. It is the planet of slow and steady progress, especially towards career goals. Saturn believes that nothing comes easy and that everything worth obtaining requires the pushing of our own weaknesses so that we can grow from them. In this light, he believes that it is our own internal flaws that forbid us from reaching our fullest potential in the first place.

Limitations and the struggles that emerge out of our weaknesses are also represented by Saturn. He teaches you to work with what you have, and that restrictions are a way to help you maintain focus. Indeed, Saturn is the ultimate life-teacher whose lessons we may not enjoy, but they nevertheless give us great transformative powers if we are able to learn from those lessons.

Obligations and dedication also stem from Saturn. There are some parts of our life that simply hold us down because we have promised ourselves to see it through such as a marriage, having children, or fulfilling contractual agreements. As such, Saturn is where we get our sense of integrity and reputation.

REALMS OF RULE

Our areas of personal weaknesses and restrictions. Areas in which we are inherently lacking and therefore need to overcome, not overcompensate. Our ability to be self-controlled and organized to see things to the end. Frugality and our sense of commitment. How truthful we are towards ourselves and towards others in this regard, and the father or the father figure.

IF FUNCTIONING HARMONIOUSLY

The individual is well grounded and highly successful due to their own output. They have a good sense of humor and can provide insights and wisdom into your personal dilemmas. They make great parents and partners (romantic and business) because they are people of their word and will see it through thick and thin. They have no problem seeing and admitting their own faults for the sake of improvement.

IF FUNCTIONING INHARMONIOUSLY

These individuals have issues with authority and hearing the advice of others. They have a hard time with sacrifice and therefore their addictive and less-favored tendencies can get the better of them. They blame the world for their problems instead of admitting fault when it is needed. They can cut corners and try to follow the easier path instead of the path that must be taken.

URANUS ♅

KEY CONCEPTS

Uranus is the planet of freedom and flexibility when it comes to our persona and personal outlook. He reminds us that the only constant in the universe is change and therefore, we need to be constantly ready to adapt and adjust our opinions and personality the more we, and society, grow and evolve. He reminds us that an open mind and heart are the best way to approach life.

Uranus is where we get unconventionality and trendsetting because he can see into the future by examining the present and past. This is because he has a keen sense of human nature and therefore can see where everything is going years ahead. Uranus knows that societal norms and taboos are only subjective and impermanent due to the inevitable sands of time.

Uranus is highly intelligent and inventive because he can observe the issues within the current society and desires to help improve upon the condition. His open mind allows for him to accept varying theories and outlooks that he then discerns within his own impartial filtration system. This allows for him to take the personal out of professional as he can simply see things as they truly are.

REALMS OF RULE

Scientific exploration, observation, and invention. Adaptability and open-mindedness with the ability to adjust based upon our observations. Fringe societal groups and unorthodox ways of thinking and lifestyles. Shocking and possibly disruptive events that take us out of our fixed mindsets. Unconventional wisdom, unpredictability, and going against the grain.

IF FUNCTIONING HARMONIOUSLY

The individual is highly intelligent and uses their intelligence to help humanity instead for selfish gains. They are open to all walks of life and lifestyles and do not judge individuals who follow a different path. They are not tied to familial or societal traditions and can therefore see how we can reform these realms for the better. They have a strong social net with deep and loyal friendships.

IF FUNCTIONING INHARMONIOUSLY

The individual is shocking and outrageous for its own sake. They are too extreme in their thinking to a point of being dogmatic. They are elitist and tend to demean others due to their overinflated sense of intellectual superiority. They will take unpopular views and opinions just to cause a stir. They can be antisocial or a social recluse because they perceive the world to be the problem instead of themselves. They therefore expect the world to change to their unreasonable standards.

NEPTUNE Ψ

KEY CONCEPTS

Neptune is the planet of human spiritualism that connects all religious ideals, but at the same time supersedes the ego-driven judgements found within religion. He understands that all souls come and go, and that everyone is on the same journey towards self-realization.

Therefore, Neptune is filled with immense acceptance and understanding of all types of individuals.

Surrender and ego-denial naturally come as a consequence to accepting these Neptunian ideals because we need to not only let go of our own prejudices and judgments in order to see others as equal, we need to let go of our sense of self so that we may experience these universal truths within the nonphysical and meditative planes of existence.

Neptune represents other worlds of reality other than our own along with the unexplainable. Faith and trust are needed in order to "cross over" to the other side of the spiritual world, and Neptune shows us how this is accomplished so that we can attain higher states of consciousness and understanding.

REALMS OF RULE

Religion and the universal standards of acceptance and forgiveness that are found within. Meditation, yoga, and other spiritual disciplines. The ability to release our personal identity for the sake of connecting to our souls. Personal sacrifice so that we can unconditionally give to others. Universal love and acceptance that only comes from seeing others and the world as one.

IF FUNCTIONING HARMONIOUSLY

The individual has good psychic abilities and possess faith in spirit and god. They approach others with ultimate unconditional love and forgiveness, and truly sees others from a lens of nonjudgement. They make great energy healers and therapists because they sympathize and understand the struggles of others. They can easily swallow their pride but at the same time stand their ground when it is required.

IF FUNCTIONING INHARMONIOUSLY

The individual can experience unhealthy victim/savior relationships where they are either too dependent or too giving towards their partners. They can have issues with drug addictions and can get swallowed up in the fog of confusion this creates within their personal outlook. They have a hard time connecting and believing in the existence of a soul or a universal creator. They also have a hard time relaxing due to their lack of trust in the universe.

PLUTO ♇

KEY CONCEPTS

Pluto is the agent of change. Individuals, societies, and even humanity itself are in a constant cycle of birth, stability, and then destruction. However, Pluto does not destroy just for the sake of chaos, he simply terminates the unwanted and unneeded for the sake of improvement. Pluto removes the superfluous parameters that are holding us down, but we have allowed to remain due to a false sense of security that these useless structures provide.

Pluto reminds us that there is no such thing as an ultimate ending for all endings always lead to a new beginning. As the axiom goes, "When a door closes, a window opens." Such is the nature of Pluto in that he simply concludes the current chapter so that you can move on to the next part of the story.

There comes immense wisdom with Pluto if we can understand and release our fear of change and fear itself. Pluto ensures that we never get stuck in a rut for too long so that we can always evolve and improve the way we were destined to in this lifetime.

REALMS OF RULE

Power structures and power dynamics such as institutions of law and justice in addition to boss/employee relationships. Conclusions and completions of cycles whether this be towards relationships, life paths, or the ultimate conclusion: physical death. Therefore, Pluto rules our deepest most unconscious fears and phobias that make us inflexible to the inevitabilities and universal truths of endings that Pluto represents.

IF FUNCTIONING HARMONIOUSLY

The individual has a healthy outlook on death and always seeks to improve the self. They are able to get to the bottom of situations which makes them great detectives, doctors, and psychologists. They have a keen awareness into their unconscious motivations and can easily access more occult knowledge. They are emotionally open and willing to divulge their secrets to those they trust, and those they trust find it incredibly easy to do the same.

IF FUNCTIONING INHARMONIOUSLY

The individual is riddled with irrational fears and phobias that prevent them from being open to what they cannot control. Therefore, they can obsessively attempt to control whatever they can however they can. They find themselves trapped within power struggles and can either abuse power or be the one that is abused. They can be vindictive and have shoddy morals when it comes to treating others equally or when it comes to obtaining their goals, which causes many enemies to emerge.

* * *

At this point, you are starting to get a better understanding into the similarities between planets and signs. The overlap between energies is due to the planets and the signs that they rule. For example, you might have noticed themes around Venus also involve themes around Taurus and Libra, the two signs that are ruled by Venus, and so on. Indeed, planetary sign placements within the birth chart can drastically alter the natural temperament of a planet because there are some signs that give planets more power, and other signs that give planets less power. This is the main topic of the next section, and another layer where you can begin to see how planets change and adjust from birth chart to birth chart.

SECTION 4-PLANETARY DIGNITIES AND DEBILITIES

Now that you have a firm understanding of the twelve signs and the ten planets within Astrology, the next step is to mold the two together. When you analyze a birth chart, you will not just see Saturn (♄) or Venus (♀), but you will witness these planets within a sign of the zodiac such as Saturn in Gemini (♄Ⅱ) or Venus in Pisces (♀♓). Due to this fact, it important to know how the signs effect the natural temperament of the planets (See Part II-Section 3). For example, a Mars in Aries (♂♈) functions a lot more differently than a Mars in Taurus (♂♉). Thankfully, ancient astrologers have devised a working table that helps to determine this adjustment which we call the table of planetary dignities and debilities. The table is named as such because some signs "dignify" a certain planet which makes it more harmonious in its function, or a sign can "debilitate" a planet and make it function inharmoniously.

This table stems from a collection of ancient knowledge that was first complied by the Greek astrologer and astronomer Ptolemy in his book, *Tetrabiblos*, Second Century C.E. As mentioned in Part I-Section 1, *Tetrabiblos* is thought to be the first astrological treatise to be written on the western astrological tradition. If you recall, western astrology is a cohesive mixture of Egyptian (rising signs), Babylonian (planetary exaltations/triplicates, and wisdom of eclipses), Greek (system of planetary gods and their archetypes, dividing the zodiacal into equal parts) and Jyotish (the lunar nodes) astrological systems. *Tetrabiblos* was the first successful attempt to combine and consolidate this information into one reliable source.

Later, in 17th century England, astrologer William Lilly finely tuned Ptolemy's initial findings and improved upon them in his books *An Introduction to Astrology* and *Christian Astrology*. Mr. Lilly demonstrated the practical application of planetary dignities and debilities within the context of horary astrology. This easy to understand and use system helps the astrologer to determine which planets are emphasized in a chart, if they are weakened or strengthened, and if they function to do us harm or good.

In other words, dignities and debilities shows us that in a natal chart, not all planets are created equal. Determining how each one is behaving helps to guide the astrologer into a better understanding into the person's psychology.

Put simply, there are signs where planets love to reside, and signs where planets hate to reside. When they are in an accommodating sign, the planets are strong, healthy, and exist to support the person. However, if the sign is not as welcoming, planets can feel irritable, malignant, and inefficient.

The table of dignities and debilities does not incorporate the modern planets Uranus, Neptune, and Pluto because these planets were yet to be discovered. Modern astrologers have attempted to fit these planets into the table. However, in my opinion, I do not consider these placements for two main reasons: (1) there is too much debate and not enough consensus as to where these planets go and (2) because these planets move so slowly, it is insignificant what sign they are in because people born years before and after the individual in question will possess the same sign placement regardless. With the outer planets, house placements and aspect configurations are significantly more important than sign placement. Therefore, in this section, we will only be observing the traditional rules and rulerships of the traditional planets which begins with the Sun and ends with Saturn (Table II-2).

TABLE II-2. Abridged Table of Planetary Dignities and Debilities according to Ptolemy

SIGN	GLYPH	RULER	EXALTATION	DETTRIMENT	FALL
ARIES	♈	♂	☉	♀	♄
TAURUS	♉	♀	☽	♂	NONE
GEMINI	♊	☿	NONE	♃	NONE
CANCER	♋	☽	♃	♄	♂
LEO	♌	☉	NONE	♄	NONE
VIRGO	♍	☿	☿	♃	♀
LIBRA	♎	♀	♄	♂	☉
SCORPIO	♏	♂ & ♇	NONE	♀	☽

SIGN	GLYPH	RULER	EXALTATION	DETTRIMENT	FALL
SAGITTARIUS	♐	♃	NONE	☿	NONE
CAPRICORN	♑	♄	♂	☽	♃
AQUARIUS	♒	♄ & ♅	NONE	☉	NONE
PISCES	♓	♃ & ♆	♀	☿	☿

As you read over this table, you will notice new terms have emerged: Exaltation, Detriment, and Fall. We will cover these new terms more specifically in this section but before we do, I want to review and reintegrate the dual nature of some of the planets found within the rulership column. This will ensure that we firmly understand planetary rulerships before we get into further specifics.

Planetary Paradoxes

If you recall from Part I-Section 7, the study of astrology is riddled with paradoxes. As you can see in the table above and in Part II-Section 2, there are some signs that are ruled by the same planet. This is typically not an issue, but in some cases the two signs that are ruled by the same planet make no sense because of the contradictory nature of the signs involved. I want to further discuss these apparent contradictions with the hope of clarifying and showing that in reality, there are more similarities than incongruities. After that, we will further discuss Exaltation, Detriment, and Fall, and how they add another layer of analysis.

Contradiction #1: Gemini and Virgo are Ruled by Mercury but Square Each Other

We have yet to discuss aspects, but for now know that squares are the most difficult placement that planets and signs can find themselves. How is it that these two signs, Gemini and Virgo, are ruled by Mercury even though these two signs square one another at a 90° angle? One of the biggest factors that causes Gemini and Virgo to not understand one another is the way they both process and handle information; a Mercurial function.

Gemini is the data gatherer. They know how to obtain the information they need, say what they need to say, and take in whatever information they wish to gather. In essence, Gemini becomes a big storage facility of facts, figures, and information. The issue is, unlike their Virgo counterparts, Geminis hardly ever process the information given to them. This frustrates Virgo because they are all about the function of things. Virgo asks the Gemini why they are not doing anything with the information provided, and Gemini cannot understand why Virgo cannot respect communicating and gathering information just for the sake of mental exploration and expression.

Virgo wants to take information one step further via application and analysis, thus creating the efficiency and attention to detail that Virgos are well known for. However, Virgo needs Gemini because they are the best at obtaining the raw data that Virgo uses. Virgos are not known for their social charm, unlike Gemini, so both are needed in order to fully express the abilities of Mercury.

Gathering information (Gemini) and processing information (Virgo) are both important qualities that create the planet Mercury. So, again, the question remains: why the square? It simply has to do with the two specific stages of childhood development that an individual encounters. The Gemini experience occurs around the toddler years, and this is when you get your first understandings of the world around you. When we approach our Virgo experience, we are now in elementary school where our formal education officially begins. Now that we are acquiring new knowledge, our past Gemini experiences are improved upon but first, a conflict occurs because you need to comprehend, blend, and adjust your previous thinking with your newly gathered information.

So, the conflict (square) occurs simply because of the stages of life that happen during the Gemini and Virgo phases within a person's life (this will be covered more in Part II-Section 6). Both experiences are required in order to understand the full extent of the planet Mercury. Virgo is in some ways the next evolutionary step to Gemini. Mercury "upgrades" into a more complex form of thinking and analyzing. This is not to say that Geminis are simpletons or less evolved, quite the opposite. Gemini is a required experience that needs to happen first before the Virgo experience can take place. However, when it is time for your Virgo stage in life (elementary school) you are adjusting your previous knowledge (toddler years) towards your growing and developing mental capacities.

Contradiction #2: Pisces and Sagittarius are Ruled by Jupiter but Square Each Other

Pisces and Sagittarius both involve ideas of expansion, but the difference comes from their respective elements. Sagittarius, a fire element, sees expansion through ideas, higher education, and institutions of truth and knowledge such as religion, government, and the university. Pisces, a water sign, is all about the expansiveness of the cosmos and of spirit. Pisces is the most unconditional of all the signs which makes people feel comfortable and at ease around them. Pisces subconsciously says, "I do not judge, I am a soul just like you," which causes Pisces to experience people and situations from all walks of life; a very Jupitarian theme.

Sagittarius also believes in spiritually expansive ideas such as human togetherness and equality but through the vessels of societal institutions and community. Sagittarius understands Pisces' ability to live within the spiritual abundance of life but cannot understand how they have no guidance or borders around themselves, their goals, or with others.

Sagittarius believes in the same principles as Pisces but believes that these ideas are obtainable through the society at-large. This is where the confusion with Pisces towards Sagittarius lies. Pisces, like their neighbor Aquarius, understands the imperfections of human error and thus believes that human connection is best done outside of corrupt institutions through a one-on-one, person-to-person basis or though spiritual techniques such as meditation and yoga.

Again, just as it was with Mercury, you can start to see how both signs are still aspects of the same planetary themes of their ruler, Jupiter. Jupiter is welcoming of all ideas and situations and wants to give all it can to its earthly children. The difference is: Sagittarius sees this abundance and love through the evolution of the human experience, and Pisces through spiritual evolution.

Similar to Gemini and Virgo, Pisces is the next evolved step to Sagittarius. Sagittarius is when we experience our college years and our minds expand even further to understand and accept human ideas, cultures, and perspectives that are different from our own, giving us our first examples of "we are all one." This realization first comes through the Sagittarian mechanism of institutional academics. With Sagittarius, these ideas are more philosophical, but with Pisces, these ideas are then put into practice as Pisces literally lives out the ideas of love, kindness, and non-judgment transforming the theoretical into the actual. Again, both are required for the individual to progress.

CONTRADICTION #3: THE PROGRESSIVE SIGN AQUARIUS IS RULED BY THE OBSTINATE PLANET SATURN

Aquarius ruled by Saturn is the last paradox to observe. This planetary/sign combination is very confusing indeed as Saturn is the ruler of Capricorn, a sign very much opposite to the ideals of Aquarius. Capricorn is about structure, stability, the status-quo, corporate ladders, and the tested, tried, and true. Aquarius, on the other hand, represents the tearing down of structures, antiestablishment, anti-societal norms, the avant-garde, and individualism.

Put another way, at its most extreme, Capricorn can be viewed as capitalism and Aquarius as communism.

If this is the case, then how can a planet like Saturn possibly rule a sign like Aquarius, which is basically everything that Capricorn stands against? The answer is strangely within this inherit contradiction. You cannot have the protester (Uranus) if you do not have the thing to protest (Saturn). Similarly, you cannot improve upon the human condition (Uranus) if there are no institutional structures in the first place (Saturn). Uranus is simply the reaction to Saturn, but Saturn is needed so that Uranian futuristic ideas can come out of the initial struggle brought on by Saturn.

A great example that demonstrates Saturn's rulership of Aquarius and Capricorn can be found in both signs' ability for humor. Capricorns and Aquarians are known for an acute sense of humor. Capricorn is a common sign for comedians and the court jester is an Aquarian archetype. The difference is: Capricorn humor is dry and sarcastic whereas Aquarian humor is witty and outlandish. Still, both signs are equipped with a sense of humor because both understand the realities of the human condition. Capricorn sees the humor behind life's concept of Murphy's law, and Aquarius sees humor in the absurdities of life. These two different types of humor come from the same source of understanding of what it means to be a human being living and experiencing life on planet Earth.

* * *

Now that we have covered more extensively these contradictions found within the Rulership column, we can now continue to discuss the other three columns: Exaltation, Detriment, and Fall.

189

Exaltation, Ruler, Detriment, Fall

According to Table II-2, there are four possible categories that will change the natural temperament of the various planets. These four categories differ in quality and strength and are described below:

EXALTATION: The planet revels in this sign and therefore their planetary energies are positively exemplified and powerful.

RULER: The planet is in the sign it rules and therefore it is comfortable, beneficial, and functions properly.

NEUTRAL: The planet is in a sign that does not affect it negatively or positively.

DETRIMENT: These are the signs in opposition to the planetary ruler and therefore, the planet's energies are thwarted and not well expressed.

FALL: The planet feels incredibly agitated in this sign and therefore their planetary energies are malignant and need to be addressed.

Now, let us go into further detail as we will take each dignity and debility and explain why the planets and signs work harmoniously or inharmoniously. Again, we will only be observing the seven traditional planets excluding Uranus, Neptune, and Pluto.

☉ Sun

EXALTATION-ARIES ♈, Action meets Drive

The Sun enjoys ego expression and Aries expresses themselves fully in the present. Here, the Sun is confident, engaged, and values the individual self.

DETRIMENT-AQUARIUS ♒, The Black Sheep

Aquarius is the sign of the all of humanity whereas the Sun wants to feel special and unique. Here, the Sun is shunned by society, does not think their uniqueness is worth exploring, and can be humble to a fault.

190

FALL-LIBRA ♎, The Need to Self-Sacrifice

The Sun hates having to compromise and only wants to do as it dictates regardless of those around them, and Libra is the sign of compromise. Here, the Sun is lacking in self-identity, experiences indecisiveness, and is conflicted as to how to express their individuality out into the world.

☽ Moon

EXALTATION-TAURUS ♉, The Healthy Garden

Similar to the Taurus/Cancer sextile, the Moon loves the conformability that Taurus provides. Here, the Moon is nurturing, emotionally secure, and joyous.

DETRIMENT-CAPRICORN ♑, Peter Pan Syndrome

The Moon does not want to grow up and Capricorn is all about growing up. Here, the Moon is a child in adult's clothing, emotionally callous, and unsympathetic.

FALL-SCORPIO ♏, Emotional Turmoil

The Moon wants to remain in one place while Scorpio is constantly in a state of change. Here, the Moon is self-destructive, unable to relax, and paranoid.

☿ Mercury

EXALTATION-VIRGO ♍, Double Power

Mercury is doubly powered in Virgo and works at its highest functionality in this sign. Here, Mercury is constantly moving and focused, possesses high energy and vitality, intelligent, and has a talent with words and writing.

DETRIMENT No. 1-SAGITTARIUS ♐, Blind-sighted

Mercury is about the day-to-day while Sagittarius is concerned with philosophy and the big picture. Here, Mercury is unable to see all angles, gets lost in the details, and can miss opportunities that are right in front of them.

DETRIMENT No. 2 and FALL-PISCES ♓, Making Sense out of Nonsense

Mercury wants to analyze and correlate while Pisces is nothing but ethereal and the unexplainable. Here, Mercury is confused, has trouble communicating, and cannot stay grounded.

♀ Venus

EXALTATION-PISCES ♓, Unconditional Love

Venus is about love and harmony and Pisces is the higher octave of universal love. Here, Venus is highly psychic, unconditional, and nonjudgmental towards others.

DETRIMENT No. 1-SCORPIO ♏, Bringer of Bad News

Scorpio wants to get to the darker points while Venus wants to keep things lighthearted and pleasant. Here, Venus is irritated, unable to be calm, and seeks to put others down.

DETRIMENT No. 2-ARIES ♈, Fast and Furious

Venus wants to take it easy while Aries wants to go, go, go. Here, Venus is angered easily, has trouble thinking of their partner in relationships, and can be shallow.

FALL-VIRGO ♍, Cannot Relax

Virgo is the sign of constant understanding and analyzing while Venus is about luxury and leisure. Here, Venus is too critical, doubtful of others, and only sees the glass half empty.

♂ Mars

EXALTATION-CAPRICORN vs. Productive Success

Mars' drive is geared towards the right direction thanks to the help of Capricorn. Here, Mars is successful, unafraid to take responsibilities, and enjoys physical challenges.

DETRIMENT No.1-LIBRA ♎, Lack of Self

Mars wants to do what it wants to do, and Libra is about sacrificing the self. Here, Mars is unable to act on instinct, puts himself too much into other people's shoes, and lacks identity.

DETRIMENT No.2-TAURUS ♉, Unmotivated

Taurus wants to relax and approach life in a calm and collected manner whereas Mars wants to bolt out the door running. Here, Mars is a sloth, has a hard time staying active, and requires extra effort to get things done.

FALL-CANCER ♋, The Wanderer

Cancer is feeling oriented and Mars rules on instinct, not intuition. Here, Mars is insecure, unable to find direction, and lacks virility.

♃ Jupiter

EXALTATION-CANCER ♋, Connected to Spiritual Love

Jupiter wants everything to be alright in the end and Cancer wants to make everything alright in the end. Here, Jupiter is caring, supportive, and a provider.

DETRIMENT No. 1-GEMINI ♊, Lack of Focus

Gemini is about quick information in small doses while Jupiter is too grand for those kinds of details. Here, Jupiter is unable to focus, has a hard time approaching conclusions, and cannot understand both large and small concepts simultaneously.

DETRIMENT No. 2-VIRGO ♍, Halted by the What-Ifs

Virgo is constantly criticizing while Jupiter hates thinking in terms of limitations. Here, Jupiter is cynical, bitter, and unable to trust in his own power of manifestation.

FALL-CAPRICORN ♑, The Land of Plenty vs. The Land of Drought

Jupiter is about abundance and Capricorn is about limitations. Here, Jupiter is unable to stay optimistic, does not believe in his own power, and cannot bring forth opportunities.

♄ Saturn

EXALTATION-LIBRA ♎, Let's Work Together

Libra is about teamwork and Saturn enjoys the help of others to achieve a goal. Here, Saturn is proud of their output, responsible, and collaborative.

DETRIMENT No. 1-LEO ♌, Son versus Dad

Leo wants to do what Leo wants to do and Saturn pushes Leo into a box. Here, Saturn hates to spoil itself, does not take things lightly, and does not like children.

DETRIMENT No. 2-CANCER ♋, Dad versus Mom

Cancer is loving while Saturn is about tough love. Here, Saturn is emotionally stunted, cannot open up to others, and can be irritable and grumpy.

194

FALL-ARIES ♈, OVER BEFORE IT BEGAN

Aries is about the here and now, and Saturn is about building up slowly over time. Here, Saturn is unable to see things through, easily angered, and can have patterns of ignorance and bigotry.

* * *

Although this is not an extensive list of how every planet interacts within every sign of the zodiac, this is a great first step into understanding how signs and planets operate with one other. Already, you are getting a better understanding towards how signs and planets operate, and the various dignities and debilities help to conceptualize these concepts. Remember, the table of dignities and debilities have been a part of astrology for centuries and their theories should not be ignored.

In addition to planets being located within various signs, they are also configured into various angles and patterns which are called aspects. The nature of aspects is heavily determined by the signs that make up the various patterns, which is why this section is a good stepping stone to help you transition from Planets and Signs into the aspects they can create. Let us now observe the next layer of astrological analysis, aspects, which will begin to further solidify everything we have already learned in Part II.

SECTION 5-ASPECTS

As previously mentioned, from our perspective here on Earth, the entire solar system, including the Sun and the Moon, travel along a circular band in the sky known as the zodiac. This circular band is made up of 360° which is then divided into 12 equal parts of 30° each. This is where we get the 12 signs of the zodiac.

The number 360 is very special in that it is heavily divisible. When two planets interact with one another through one of these divisions, we say they are in aspect to one another and when this occurs, their energies are engaged in either harmonious or inharmonious ways.

In terms of divisibility, the astrological circle of 360° is divided into eleven different combinations. This is where we get the major and minor aspects within astrology. This book will only cover and utilize the five major aspects: the conjunction (☌), sextile (✶), square (□), trine (△), and opposition (☍). However, in order to exhibit the fully divisible nature of 360, all eleven combinations are demonstrated below (Table II-3).

TABLE II-3. The Major and Minor Aspects within Astrology

EQUATION	DIVISION	NAME	GLYPH	MAJOR OR MINOR
360/1	**360° or 0°**	**Conjunction**	☌	**Major**
360/12	30°	Semi-Sextile	⌄	Minor
360/8	45°	Semi-Square	∠	Minor
360/6	**60°**	**Sextile**	✶	**Major**
360/5	72°	Quintile	Q	Minor
360/4	**90°**	**Square**	□	**Major**
360/3	**120°**	**Trine**	△	**Major**

EQUATION	DIVISION	NAME	GLYPH	MAJOR OR MINOR
360 x (3/8)	135°	Sesquiquadrate	⚼	Minor
360 x (2/5)	144°	Bi-Quintile	bQ	Minor
360 x (5/12)	150°	Inconjunct	⚻	Minor
360/2	**180°**	**Opposition**	☍	**Major**

How to Approach Aspects

In the past, astrologers have often used vague umbrella terms to define the difficulty or ease of an aspect. For example, easier aspects like the sextile and trine were considered "soft aspects," and the difficult aspects like the square and opposition were considered "hard aspects." This terminology is insufficient because not only should you take aspects on a case-by-case basis, but aspects are incredibly specified towards the overall picture of the birth chart and therefore should not be categorized as soft, hard, difficult, or easy. Instead, aspects simply are.

For example, squares are typically considered difficult, but if it is a square involving transiting Venus or Jupiter, then the effect of the square is weakened due to the fact that Venus and Jupiter are the two benefics within astrology. Similarly, if Venus is in a trine with Jupiter, which is usually considered an easy aspect and yes, there are a lot of benefits to this trine, the person could also be prone to laziness, weight gain, and overindulgence.

A person's psychological make-up is so complex and unique that when you are studying a natal chart, you should be focusing on the entire picture, not just one aspect here and there. The good news is there is a way to determine the importance of an aspect by prioritizing aspects from the most significant and impactful to the least using orbs of influence. This method will be discussed towards the end of this section.

We will now observe the nature of the five major aspects (conjunction, sextile, square, trine, and opposition), and the various combinations that the signs find themselves therein. Once you see how the signs interact to one another in this fashion, you will be able to get a better understanding of the nature of the aspects. Then, all you will have to do is take this understanding and apply it to the planets that are in aspect using the signs as secondary information (more on this in Parts V-VII).

We will be observing planetary combinations when it comes to the conjunctions, but keep in mind that the other various planetary combinations by aspect are beyond the scope of this book simply because there are already exemplar books out there on the subject. If you want to get a better idea of the planets' interactions by aspect, I would recommend the books *Planets in Youth* by Robert Hand and *How to Be a Great Astrologer* by James Braha for natal aspects, and *Planets in Transit* by Robert Hand for transit aspects. Now, let us cover each of the five major aspects within astrology, along with how the various signs interact with one another by aspect.

☌ Conjunction (0°)

Keyword: Blending

When two planets are in conjunction, their energies blend together and become inseparable in the way they function. For example, if Mars conjoins Saturn in a natal chart (♂☌♄), Mars operates with the characteristics of Saturn and vice versa in the same way two molecules in chemistry can combine together and create a new molecule altogether. The only difference is, with planets in a conjunction, they become inseparable and are therefore infinitely and permanently bound to one another. Therefore, the planetary interactions within these various connections are constantly manifested and observed throughout one's life.

If the planetary energies are complimentary, like the Sun and Mars (☉☌♂) or the Moon and Venus (☽☌♀), then the conjunction functions more soundly. However, if the planetary energies are less complimentary, like Mars and Neptune (♂☌♆), or Venus and Saturn (♀☌♄), then the conjunction will be a little more difficult to handle.

This is where Table II-1 comes in handy because you can tell if planetary combinations are more harmonious than others by simply observing their natural temperaments. Now, let us expand upon Table II-1 and view the various conjunction combinations and whether or not they behave harmoniously, inharmoniously, or neutrally (Table II-4). [NOTE: This table does not include the outer planetary conjunctions because they are generational and/or rarely happen due to the slow movement of the outer planets. For example, the last time Neptune conjoined Pluto (♆☌♇) was in the late 1800s and will not occur again until well into the 22nd century.]

TABLE II-4. Various Planetary Conjunction Combinations and Natural Temperaments

CONJ.	GLYPH	H/I/N	CONJ.	GLYPH	H/I/N	CONJ.	GLYPH	H/I/N
Sun/ Moon	☉☌☽	I	Moon/ Jupiter	☽☌♃	H	Venus/ Mars	♀☌♂	I
Sun/ Mercury	☉☌☿	N	Moon/ Saturn	☽☌♄	I	Venus/ Jupiter	♀☌♃	H
Sun/ Venus	☉☌♀	I	Moon/ Uranus	☽☌♅	I	Venus/ Saturn	♀☌♄	I
Sun/ Mars	☉☌♂	H	Moon/ Neptune	☽☌♆	H	Venus/ Uranus	♀☌♅	I
Sun/ Jupiter	☉☌♃	H	Moon/ Pluto	☽☌♇	I	Venus/ Neptune	♀☌♆	H
Sun/ Saturn	☉☌♄	N	Mercury/ Venus	☿☌♀	N	Venus/ Pluto	♀☌♇	N
Sun/ Uranus	☉☌♅	I	Mercury/ Mars	☿☌♂	N	Mars/ Jupiter	♂☌♃	H
Sun/ Neptune	☉☌♆	I	Mercury/ Jupiter	☿☌♃	N	Mars/ Saturn	♂☌♄	H
Sun/ Pluto	☉☌♇	I	Mercury/ Saturn	☿☌♄	N	Mars/ Uranus	♂☌♅	N
Moon/ Mercury	☽☌☿	N	Mercury/ Uranus	☿☌♅	H	Mars/ Neptune	♂☌♆	I
Moon/ Venus	☽☌♀	H	Mercury/ Neptune	☿☌♆	I	Mars/ Pluto	♂☌♇	H
Moon/ Mars	☽☌♂	I	Mercury/ Pluto	☿☌♇	N			

KEY: H=Harmonious, I=Inharmonious, N=Neutral

Do not take tables such as these to be completely set in stone. Remember, astrology is filled with paradoxes and caveats which cause some exceptions to occur. For example, although Jupiter is a passive planet, it still reacts harmoniously with the majority of active planets because Jupiter is the "great benefic," making his presence relatively beneficial for the individual regardless of the other planet involved.

Similarly, the majority of Mercury conjunctions are neutral, but Mercury conjoined Neptune is inharmonious because the innate nature of Mercury is uncomplimentary to that of Neptune.

199

Therefore, it is important to treat tables like these as starting points but remember to treat every birth chart with the individuality and minuteness they require. As we will examine in Part V, the birth chart is never cut and dry.

SIMILARITY: SAME SIGN

Conjunctions typically occur within one sign. Meaning, it is less about the signs in which they occur and more about the two planets involved. The way to observe how the sign influences the conjunction is to consider dignities and debilities (Part II-Section 4).

For example, with the Moon/Venus conjunction in Capricorn (☽♑︎☌♀♑︎), the harmony of Moon blending with Venus is slightly disrupted because the Moon is in detriment in Capricorn and is thus weakened, even though both of these planets are passive and therefore work harmoniously. Let us now get into the specifics of the various conjunctions observed in Table II-4 in order to get a better understanding.

☉ SUN CONJUNCTIONS

SUN CONJOINED MOON (☉☌☽)

At first, one would think this conjunction to be complimentary, but Robert Hand makes a very good point in his book *Planets in Youth* about this conjunction. He points out that fundamentally, the Sun represents our yang/outer functions and that the Moon represents our yin/inner functions. Therefore, the Sun/Moon conjunction becomes complicated because these two distinct ways of approaching life become inseparable and unable to function without the other.

For example, with a Sun/Moon conjunction, one might want to perform Action A, but then hesitates and doubts their choice due to Emotion B which begins to question Action A. The inner self is at odds with the outer self because these two modes of being function so differently. One through ego expression (Sun) and the other through emotional expression (Moon). Due to the conjunction, both are inseparable.

People with this conjunction should slow everything down as much as they can. Their motivations are ignited through a rapid cycle of mental and emotional conflict/resolution due to the nature of the Sun and Moon. Moderation and balance within all things in life is the key to success.

SUN CONJOINED MERCURY (☉☌☿)

This person says what they mean and means what they say. They can construct their personal stance with logic and deductive reasoning. When it comes to their thoughts and opinions, they are well grounded within the self and within the expression of the self. If they are creative, they do not have struggles with writer's block or coming up with ideas as the channels between what they want to communicate and the ability to do so comes easily. However, they could have a hard time listening to the viewpoints of others.

SUN CONJOINED VENUS (☉☌♀)

The Sun wants to express but Venus wants to relate. This individual has a hard time with autonomy because they are constantly sacrificing their ideas and personality for others.

SUN CONJOINED MARS (☉☌♂)

Although this placement gives the individual drive, passion, and power, ego clashes can get the better of them. It is a little too easy get their ego damaged, and they will not think twice to retaliate and cause conflict when it comes to others. They should attempt to avoid confrontational people and try to incorporate patience and understanding instead of flying off the handle.

SUN CONJOINED JUPITER (☉☌♃)

This conjunction makes it easy for the person to have it all, but they are sometimes stunted by this fact. They should try to not become complacent and strive to maintain direction and moderation in their lives. The problem is, because things come too easily, struggle is hardly an issue, which makes them indecisive and unmotivated.

SUN CONJOINED SATURN (☉♂♄)

These people have good skills in business deals and partnerships. Still, they should have a firm understanding of the other person on the other side of the deal as they are susceptible to ego stroking and can completely misjudge people's intentions. They value teamwork and are able to work well with others even at a young age. Not only does this conjunction give them the ability to work with their peers, they easily deal with people in authority and with elders. However, they can be immensely shy and introverted as Saturn can quash the ego-expression of the Sun.

SUN CONJOINED URANUS (☉♂♅)

These people can carry a lot of nervous tension and feel constantly ungrounded within themselves and their own opinions. This is due to their want for constant change, not only within their own attitudes, but within the situations that befall them. They should attempt to slow down their thinking, harness personal strength and self-esteem, and remember that whatever happens outside of themselves, it is important to stay firmly planted inside of the body and mind.

SUN CONJOINED NEPTUNE (☉♂♆)

The less these people try to control their predicaments, the better off they will be. Neptune gives them the ability to be placed at the right place at the right time if only they allow Neptune to work properly. The issue is people tend to think that they are masters of their own destiny which ironically causes them to miss opportunities and situations that are beneficial for them. Still, these people are easily relatable and empathize with anyone. Others find solace and healing through them, but they need to watch out for addictive tendencies.

SUN CONJOINED PLUTO (☉♂♇)

This conjunction can be rather difficult because their ego changes its personality constantly making it hard to figure out who they are and what they want. It seems that whatever they pursue, it becomes futile over time because as their personality changes, they find their interests shift into other things instead. For them, it is better to learn from their experiences and be receptive to what comes their way instead of planning everything out. Pluto is going to act however it wants, so it is of no use trying to go against his plan. Simply be reflective with his lessons, and the personality will grow and change the way it is supposed to.

☽ Moon Conjunctions

MOON CONJOINED MERCURY (☽☌☿)

This is very helpful in communicating their feelings. Emotions can be abstract and difficult to put into words, but this conjunction makes it easy for them to voice their inner self properly. The Moon's influence on Mercury means that there are feelings behind everything they say, but this can also be problematic as it will be hard for them to hide their feelings when they are conversing with others.

MOON CONJOINED VENUS (☽☌♀)

This is a very pleasant conjunction with the two inner feminine planets. Similar to the Taurus/Cancer sextile, the Moon/Venus conjunction gives a balanced, loving nature, an amazing sense of style, and a high appreciation for the arts.

MOON CONJOINED MARS (☽☌♂)

These two planets by their very nature function at cross-purposes. Similar to the Aries/Cancer square, this conjunction makes one emotionally volatile, impatient, and thin-skinned. However, this person believes in their feelings very strongly and can stick up for causes and ideas that they consider to be part of their personal identification.

MOON CONJOINED JUPITER (☽☌♃)

This makes an individual abundant in their feelings which they must remember to reel in at times. This conjunction is similar to the Pisces/Cancer trine in that it gives them a deep ocean of love and affection, but this could also make them needy and suffocating. The best way to channel this energy is through the arts and through personal passions.

MOON CONJOINED SATURN (☽☌♄)

Saturn provides stability for the Moon, but it also makes the moon stiff and closed off. This conjunction can make life seem serious all the time. Especially when it comes to expressing themselves. These people might not want to pour out their feelings and will therefore require security and trust before they will open up.

MOON CONJOINED URANUS (☽☌♅)

It is very hard for this person to stay still as they can constantly feel erratic internally. Uranus wants to continually seek the new, and the Moon wants to rest and enjoy the moment for as long as possible. They should take it easy and make sure to stay grounded through meditation and breathing techniques.

MOON CONJOINED NEPTUNE (☽☌♆)

Similar to the Moon/Jupiter conjunction, this blending creates a deep emotional capacity that the person can use for psychic ability, creativity, and intimate relationships. However, these individuals should be weary of addictions because if the Moon is not stable, it can easily fall into coping mechanisms.

MOON CONJOINED PLUTO (☽☌♇)

You can never pull the wool over this conjunction's eyes. They can see emotional manipulation coming a mile away. In fact, these people might be the ones to be doing the emotional manipulation. This conjunction gives intimate and sexual relationships immense meaning and virility but causes their emotions to constantly change from day to day.

☿ Mercury Conjunctions

MERCURY CONJOINED VENUS (☿☌♀)

This conjunction is rather special due to the orbital relationship between Mercury and Venus. From our perspective, Mercury and Venus only find themselves at maximum 72° apart. Meaning, the only major aspects Mercury and Venus can make to one another are the conjunction and the sextile making these combinations very special occurrences indeed. People with Mercury/Venus conjunctions have some sort of artistic talent and can express that talent very well. They are good humored and good company.

MERCURY CONJOINED MARS (☿☌♂)

This conjunction makes for a good team leader and someone that has courage to make decisions. They can approach people with authority so that others will listen, but not in way where others feel as though they are being belittled. However, this conjunction can make it hard to be a good listener.

MERCURY CONJOINED JUPITER (☿☌♃)

Mercury and Jupiter do not tend to get along because the signs that they rule are in opposition with one another (Gemini/Sagittarius, and Virgo/Pisces). Depending on the placement of this conjunction, the person can either have a hard time discerning larger concepts with smaller goals, or vice versa. On the more positive side, they are able to manifest their own ambitions through the use of their people skills.

MERCURY CONJOINED SATURN (☿☌♄)

This person is not one of many words. They can be very matter of fact and do not enjoy thinking about theocraticals or invisible realms like the imagination. They should seek others that are more carefree to help them loosen up and realize that it is okay to not talk shop all the time. This conjunction can also give the person learning or speech disabilities.

MERCURY CONJOINED URANUS (☿♂♅)

This Mercury and Uranus combination is quite harmonious due to the trine made by Aquarius and Gemini. Mercury enjoys Uranus' thinking and intelligence, and Uranus enjoys Mercury's platform to voice his thoughts. This conjunction gives people a high opinion and the ability to say profound insights sometimes out of nowhere. However, their mental capacities might work too fast for their own good.

MERCURY CONJOINED NEPTUNE (☿♂♆)

This conjunction can be tricky due to the Virgo/Pisces opposition. Mercury tries to sort out the details and Neptune is the world of the intangible and unexplainable. These people have issues communicating and learning but can have a great talent within metaphysical and psychic fields if they are able to quiet their minds.

MERCURY CONJOINED PLUTO (☿♂♇)

These people will tell it like it is and rarely censor themselves. They can be intrusive, and their curiosity for finding the answers make them great detectives and mystery writers. Like their Mercury/Saturn counterparts, they need to learn to lighten up a little and remember some conversations are meant to be whimsical and meaningless.

♀ Venus Conjunctions

VENUS CONJOINED MARS (♀♂♂)

This conjunction can work out harmoniously or inharmoniously. On the one hand, you have the feminine and the masculine working together with understanding, but on the other hand, this conjunction requires reaching an end point with some sort of compromise.

206

Essentially, you have Mars wanting to do what he wants, and Venus wanting to do what she feels they both should do. These opposing forces can be difficult to handle and give someone an indecisive yet aggressive nature. However, if they can compromise these two forces inside themselves, they can reach a state of calmness and harmony of a very high degree.

VENUS CONJOINED JUPITER (♀☌♃)

It does not get any better than the Venus/Jupiter conjunction. Having the two benefics in contact with one another gives the person a lively buoyancy and natural attraction. They are able to enjoy life and its pleasures thanks to the help of Jupiter, who is able to provide them with comforts. However, these people need to remember to watch out for overindulgence, weight gain, and not taking life seriously enough.

VENUS CONJOINED SATURN (♀☌♄)

On one hand, this person is able to have some sort of permanence in their love relationships, but on the other, they can be seen as conservative when it comes to their values and sexual nature. They should seek more vibrancy in their relationships and try to take more chances when it comes to their intimate encounters.

VENUS CONJOINED URANUS (♀☌♅)

This person seeks the unconventional in their relationships. They surround themselves with friends and partners that are not within the fold and can be seen as social outcasts. Still, these people value free thinkers and the less boundaries and obligations that are placed within their relationships, the better. This conjunction makes it hard for people to settle down and follow traditional gender, societal, marital, and parental roles. They can be notorious cheaters if they are not careful.

VENUS CONJOINED NEPTUNE (♀☌♆)

This conjunction is very powerful as Venus and Neptune tend to get along very well because Venus enjoys being in Pisces. These people have profound psychic encounters with others they meet no matter how mundane the situation may seem. They need to make sure they keep themselves grounded and psychically protected as they can be prone to gathering other people's energies and illnesses. Still, these people have a very acute sixth sense and when it comes to unconditional love they can experience this with their most intimate partners. However, they need to remember to not stay in toxic relationships for the sake of dependence.

VENUS CONJOINED PLUTO (♀☌♇)

Similar to The Venus/Neptune conjunction, these people are able to have very intimate and powerful sexual encounters. They have a presence about them that is strong and intimidating, yet calm and confident. If a woman has this conjunction, they can experience negative projection from men because they embody strong feminine energy, which could be off putting for more traditional men. If a man has this transit, they can likewise experience projection as having a lot of feminine power but in the body of a male. Due to this fact, males with this transit can experience an ongoing sexual identity crisis due to this psychological projection and need to cultivate courage and confidence in order to ignore society's judgments.

♂ MARS CONJUNCTIONS

MARS CONJOINED JUPITER (♂☌♃)

These people need to make sure their excitement does not get the better of them. These two planets can cause the individual to be passionate with their motivations, but they expect everything to occur as soon as possible. It is better for these people to tread slowly and to not always act on their first impulse.

MARS CONJOINED SATURN (♂☌♄)

This allows for the person to keep at their goals and maintain their drive. Males with this conjunction are highly attractive, and females with this conjunction have similar projection issues as males do with the Venus/Pluto conjunction. Meaning, women with this immense masculine energy can experience a type of sexual identity crises. This conjunction can make the person conservative, self-sufficient to a fault, and opinionated.

MARS CONJOINED URANUS (♂☌♅)

When it comes to their personal beliefs, they are not afraid to say what they feel, regardless of how bizarre it may seem. These people feel the need to stick up for adversity and injustice, but instead as someone who has "boots on the ground." These people are on the front lines as Doctors without Borders or members of the Peace Corps. In order to calm down the active nature of this combination, the person needs to remember that not every occasion calls for their opinion, and that the world will not be fixed overnight. It will also be beneficial to listen to other viewpoints as well.

MARS CONJOINED NEPTUNE (♂☌♆)

Mars becomes overwhelmed by the waves of Neptune as these two planets have a hard time with one another. Mars tends to seek initiation and self-identification where Neptune slows down and convolutes. This person can have a hard time figuring out what they want to do and need to really think things through with others in order to help them get out of their own fog. However, using the Mars towards spiritual pursuits activates a more positive use of this conjunction.

MARS CONJOINED PLUTO (♂☌♇)

This is a very powerful conjunction as Mars and Pluto are both the rulers of Scorpio. These people can obtain a lot of occult wisdom and use it for their own benefit. Therefore, it is very important that these individuals obtain some sort of high ethical moral standing and should also remember to not dive too deeply into the dark shadows of reality as Scorpios tend to do. This aspect is great in dealing with stock markets or any other investments that require courage and a lot of money.

♃-♇ JUPITER-PLUTO CONJUNCTIONS

Conjunctions with the outer planets Jupiter, Saturn, Uranus, Neptune, and Pluto, are generational due to their slower orbits and are beyond the scope of this book.

⚹ SEXTILE (60°)

KEYWORD: COOPERATION

It is all too easy to take for granted the amazing properties found within sextiles. Instead, we brush them off as minor windows of opportunity here and there, and nothing too serious or beneficial. However, with sextiles, we see a sort of alchemical process where two elements work together in harmony and therefore bring about the positive characteristics of the elements involved. Sextiles within the birth chart are inherent strengths that lay dormant within the individual. They can be very beneficial for the individual, but they require active and conscious utilization in order for the sextile to be properly expressed.

SIMILARITY: SAME POLARITY

Fire and Air (Masculine/Yang/Active) or Water and Earth (Feminine/Yin/Passive) are the two combinations of sextiles. Air encourages Fire and helps to breath more life into the flames. Fire encourages Air to keep going with their instincts. Water replenishes Earth and makes the garden grow. Earth feeds into Water, allowing for life to exist where it dwells. Sextiles embody these mutual and powerful relationships but again, they require the individual to actively use these forces to their advantage else their potential benefits lay dormant.

SEXTILE COMBINATIONS

ARIES SEXTILE GEMINI (♈⚹♊), ACTIVE PARTICIPATION

Aries encourages Gemini to continue with their findings and ponderings. Gemini loves to talk and Aries loves to be heard. This sextile gives one the ability to keep conversations going, let opinions be heard, and have courage when it comes to meeting new people and situations.

TAURUS SEXTILE CANCER (♉✶♋), FEMININE LOVING ENERGY

Taurus provides life for Cancer in her oceans, and Cancer provides life for Taurus through her rains. Both signs embody the ultimate loving feminine energy that exists on this planet. People with this sextile are caring, loving, and bountiful.

GEMINI SEXTILE LEO (♊✶♌), CREATIVE BRAINSTORMING

Gemini helps Leo brainstorm his creativity. Leo is able to write and create works that reach his audience. These signs greatly aid in the creative and artistic process. People with this sextile are creative, clever, and charismatic.

CANCER SEXTILE VIRGO (♋✶♍), SLOW AND STEADY IMPROVEMENT

Cancer tells Virgo that it is ok to be different and shy. Virgo tells Cancer that she does not mind Cancer's faults because she knows how much Cancer loves her in return. People with this sextile are gentle, hard workers that are invested in their output, and make great nannies/parents.

LEO SEXTILE LIBRA (♌✶♎), ARTIST WITH AN AUDIENCE

Leo exchanges and connects his ideas with the audience of Libra. Libra admires Leo's skills and also hopes to create a personal relationship due to Leo's laid-back and authentic nature. People with this sextile are great at politics, know what the audience wants, and feel confident in who they are when others are around.

VIRGO SEXTILE SCORPIO (♍✶♏), THE BEST OF THE BEST

Virgo does not feel afraid to tell Scorpio what they can be doing better, and Scorpio appreciates Virgo's honesty and bluntness. These two signs allow for no stone to be unturned, and people with this sextile are great with any detective work, occult knowledge, and finding beneficial master/apprentice relationships.

LIBRA SEXTILE SAGITTARIUS (♎✶♐), THE HIGHEST RULE OF LAW

Libra works with Sagittarius to make sure that people are working together towards a better society through the art of compromise. Sagittarius ensures that they are doing so for the betterment of human society. People with this aspect make excellent debaters, intelligent professors, and tend to see the best in people.

SCORPIO SEXTILE CAPRICORN (♏✶♑), EXECUTIVE POWERS

Scorpio's ability to handle other people's resources mixed with Capricorn's ability to be frugal and strategic makes this combination unstoppable in the corporate world. People with this aspect are great at calculating risks, obtaining wealth, and have strong abilities for self-analysis and self-improvement.

SAGITTARIUS SEXTILE AQUARIUS (♐✶♒), HUMAN PROGRESS

Sagittarius provides the institutions where humanity can create a world of elevated peace and cooperation. Aquarius ensures that these institutions and laws change with the times so that they are always adapting for the betterment of society. People with this aspect have a high faith in their fellow man, fight for minorities within the system, and have a finely tuned gauge of what is right and what is wrong.

CAPRICORN SEXTILE PISCES (♑✶♓), SPIRITUAL DISCIPLINE

Capricorn is the Guru that can lead you towards enlightenment. Pisces is the doorway to that spiritual knowledge. People with this aspect are highly psychic, can reach high states of consciousness, and can maintain equilibrium within entropy.

AQUARIUS SEXTILE ARIES (♒⚹♈), Revolutionary Courage

Aquarius is the injustice that sparks the revolution, and Aries is the brave patriot that has stood up against tyranny throughout the world's history. People with this aspect are true revolutionaries, not afraid to stand up for injustice, and are highly original.

PISCES SEXTILE TAURUS (♓⚹♉), Ultimate Healing

Pisces gives the person the connection to the spiritual and psychic realm, and Taurus allows for them to use their five senses in order to convey the messages that spirit wants to convey. These people have great talents in massage/reiki, energy work, and feng shui.

□ Square (90°)

Keyword: Unconscious

It should not be understated that squares are our most important karmic work in this lifetime. They are the self-destructive parts of our psychology that are so hidden, we are not even aware of their presence. With the square, you have two planets working with a lot of energy but at cross-purposes. Both planets want you to address their urges and demands, and their influences effect your ability to make lucid, coherent decisions in life.

By their very nature, squares require immense psychological introspection and observation because the first step is to simply put them on your radar. Once you have detected their sabotage, you can then begin to analyze, understand, and overcome. Squares require a lot of personal attention and perseverance, but the more you work on overcoming them, the more you take yourself out of the karma that was given to you in this lifetime. This helps you to evolve your consciousness to higher realms because you are simply peeling off layers of previous karma that you were meant to address and overcome. In other words, you are doing the work you were meant to be doing and as a result, you are rewarded with inner peace because you are calming down the erratic, shadow energies inside of you.

Similarity: Same Modality

The reason for the square's confusing and unaccommodating nature has to do with the fact that squares involve signs of the same modality. That is, they are both either cardinal, fixed, or mutable. When you have two signs of the same modality, you have two signs that see life the same way, but due to them being different elements, they approach that similar worldview differently and cannot understand why the other is approaching life in that way.

This is echoed by the fact that squares involve elements of different polarities as well. For example, Aries squares Cancer. Both are cardinal, but Aries is Fire (Yang) and Cancer is Water (Yin). Another example, Virgo squares Sagittarius. Both are mutable, but Virgo is Earth (Yin) and Sagittarius is Fire (Yang). Signs and planets in a square look at one another and go "No! You are doing it wrong! It needs to be done this way!" When it comes to your psychology, you have these two aggressive forces unconsciously motivating you to act on their behalf. The problem is, because you have two signs and two planets telling you this, and because they are at cross-purposes to one another, self-destructive tendencies begin to arise.

The trick to squares is to catch them when they flair up, put them on your radar, work through them, talk to both of them, and consciously put an effort to not rely on their energies. Instead, use the energies in your chart that are more beneficial and are there to help you, like your trines, sextiles, and beneficial conjunctions.

Square Combinations

Aries Square Cancer (♈□♋), The Emotionally Insecure

Aries wants to proceed how it wants to proceed. Cancer wants to evaluate the situation first and see if they feel comfortable before they act. Aries is aggressive and inconsiderate. Cancer is too considerate and sensitive. People with this square can have issues connecting with their emotions, can be emotionally volatile, and can take things too personally.

TAURUS SQUARE LEO (♉□♌), THE BATTLE OF THE WILLS

Taurus and Leo both want to do what they want to do. The problem is, Taurus wants to stay at home and watch a movie with popcorn, and Leo wants to go out clubbing. Due to their fixed nature, it is impossible for the other to sacrifice their wants for the other, especially because they cannot understand why the other person wants what they want. People with this square fight introversion with extroversion, excitement with predictability, and taking a risk with playing it safe.

GEMINI SQUARE VIRGO (♊□♍), THE WHIRLWIND

Gemini wants to talk and talk where Virgo wants to talk about something meaningful. Gemini relays fact after fact, and Virgo becomes overwhelmed with data. People with this square have a hyperactive brain, cannot stand still, and analyze before they get the entire picture.

CANCER SQUARE LIBRA (♋□♎), SAME RELATIONSHIP, DIFFERENT APPROACH

Cancers and Libras both desire relationships with another. The problem is, Cancer's relationship is based on emotions and with Libra, it is based on an intellectual connection. Cancer wants to cuddle and coddle; Libra wants to chat and go out on dates. People with this square cannot seem to find the right partner, push their emotional insecurities onto their partners, and have a hard time with personal identity and autonomy.

LEO SQUARE SCORPIO (♌□♏), LIGHT VERSUS DARK

Leo wants to approach life with vigor and brightness. Scorpio only sees the dark in everything and hates the spotlight. People with this aspect have issues with optimism and pessimism, background versus foreground, and are unable to enjoy the moment because they are always trying to downplay everything as happenstance.

VIRGO SQUARE SAGITTARIUS (♍□♐), INTENSE DEFLATION AND EXPANSION

Sagittarius wants to think of all possibilities and outcomes. Virgo reminds Sagittarius that there is a big difference between what is possible and what is practical. Sagittarius wants to expand

and reach out while Virgo wants to reel in and conserve. People with this square cut themselves down, dream big but have poor drive, and are not able to see the good times when they are to be had.

LIBRA SQUARE CAPRICORN (♎□♑), Daddy Issues

Libra wants to connect and relate. Capricorn does not believe in sharing one's feelings. Libra wants to learn from others while Capricorn believes in self-sufficiency. People with this square are too serious to be casual, experience conflict with authority figures, and lack professional skills and professionalism.

SCORPIO SQUARE AQUARIUS (♏□♒), Two Different Types of Transformation

For both signs, transformation and change are important, but for Scorpio, it is more on the emotional and psychological side and for Aquarius, it is on the societal side. Both signs value freedom, change, and, most importantly, seeing to it that all justice is served but both disagree on how to get there. For Scorpio, this change is internal and deep and for Aquarius, it is not emotionally deep but ideological instead. People with this square are social in the wrong crowds, see themselves as a victim of society, and have a hard time opening up emotionally.

SAGITTARIUS SQUARE PISCES (♐□♓), Both Sides of Jupiter

Sagittarius and Pisces have similarities because they are both ruled by Jupiter and are thus both signs of expansion and growth. With Sagittarius, this is expansion of knowledge, but with Pisces, it is expansion of consciousness. People with this square have a hard time releasing logic around spiritual endeavors, can be too in over their heads, idealize people and situations, can be hopelessly naïve and optimistic, and avoid confrontation at all cost.

CAPRICORN SQUARE ARIES (♑□♈), The Wonder Years

Capricorn tells the Aries that there are rules. Aries tells the Capricorn where he can stick it. Aries has no real prerogative except that of his own self-interest, and Capricorn is about being

216

a responsible and reliable provider. People with this square can be bigoted, have issues around what the self wants to do versus obligation, and can have a very hard time with empathy.

AQUARIUS SQUARE TAURUS (♒□♉), FLIGHT VERSUS IMMOBILITY

Aquarius wants to go out into the world and experience the adventures of life. Taurus wants to stay at home, watch a movie, and eat popcorn. Aquarius thinks outside the box and loves new ideas. Taurus is more interested in pursuits of the senses, not the mind. People with this square have a hard time with money, crave social gatherings but can be anti-social and secluded, and can lack motivation for their ideas which, if they were to pursue, would work out wonderfully for them.

PISCES SQUARE GEMINI (♓□♊), TOO MUCH CONFUSION

Gemini is all about words and communicating. Pisces is about the lack of meaning and the abstract. Gemini continually craves connections where Pisces is too psychically open to be around too many people. People with this square are highly influenced by others around them, have trouble processing factual information, and, on the other hand, cannot sit still to meditate. They need to relax the mind as much as possible and be sure to keep their surroundings as calm and clean as possible.

△ TRINE (120°)

KEYWORD: HARMONY

The trine is thought to be the strongest and most beneficial aspect within astrology. In a trine, the two planets in question are operating in highly agreeable ways, bringing about the most positive qualities of the planets and signs within the individual.

The trines in your chart are the skills, abilities, and attitudes that have positively shaped you into the person you are today. Unlike sextiles, trines act without provocation, and seem to always be present inside the person. It is here where we see the amazing benefits of the trine but also, the trine's biggest enemy: apathy. In other words, because trines are automatic and beneficial by their nature, one hardly notices their benefic influences and therefore, we can miss out on taking full advantage of the trine's power due to complacency.

For example, if you have Mars trine Saturn (♂△♄) it is very easy for you to gain muscle mass, maintain muscle mass, and to stay relatively healthy with a good amount of un-depleted energy. However, if you have Mars square Saturn (♂□♄), you can be prone to weight gain, have a lack of motivation, and become depressed about your lack of physical prowess or health.

The difference is that the person with the Mars/Saturn trine does not completely realize their full potential because the energy is automatic and effortless. Therefore, it is possible that they do not gain as much muscle or be as healthy as they can be. On the other hand, the person with the Mars/Saturn square has to consciously put an effort into maintaining good health and physique and therefore has a higher reverence for their struggle and for the rewards that it has bestowed onto them. It is important for us to not take for granted our trines and rest on their laurels. Instead, capitalize on their potential because they are the pillars of strength where our struggles fall upon. Without those pillars, our shadow side can, and will, get the better of us.

SIMILARITY: SAME ELEMENT

Planets in a trine share signs of the same element which is how they get their increased power and fortune. Like energy attracting like energy is a universal truth, and we see this manifested in birth charts via trines where energies are manifested and magnified due to their complimentary nature.

TRINE COMBINATIONS

ARIES TRINE LEO (♈△♌), THE MODEL

Aries is a risk taker and Leos are creative geniuses. These people are forces to be reckoned with and make great personal trainers, directors, and stunt men.

TAURUS TRINE VIRGO (♉△♍), The Finest Tastes

Taurus' keen eye for aesthetics with Virgo's eye for purity makes for immaculate tastes in the fine arts. These people are stunning, have talents in fashion and interior decorating along with any kind of craftsmanship.

GEMINI TRINE LIBRA (♊△♎), The Networker

Gemini knows what to say and Libra knows all the right people. This trine allows for the person to have impeccable communication skills with others along with talents in the media, mediation, and relationship counseling.

CANCER TRINE SCORPIO (♋△♏), The Gentle Psychologist

Cancer is caring and understanding while Scorpio knows what you need to do to make yourself more psychologically sound. These people have a gentle way of helping others get through tough times and have an infinite amount of emotional support and love. They make great drug addiction therapists, real estate agents, and guidance counselors.

LEO TRINE SAGITTARIUS (♌△♐), The Ethical Politian

Leo is the leader and Sagittarius is the platform for the leader. However, thanks to the trine, Leo's desire for tyranny is calmed down and focused into a more cooperative approach. These people are great at politics, judicial institutions, universities, are immensely fair and ethical, and pleasant to be around.

VIRGO TRINE CAPRICORN (♍△♑), The Decisive Strategist

Virgo does not let anything get past them and Capricorns are brilliant at taking it one small step at a time. These people are able to stick to a plan and see it through, make effective bosses/union leaders that listen and care about their workers, and are confident in every step they take.

LIBRA TRINE AQUARIUS (♎△♒), The Egalitarian

Libra creates positive relations with others and Aquarius wants to be friends with the world and share their thoughts with everyone they meet. These people make excellent activists, have great friendships, and very few enemies.

SCORPIO TRINE PISCES (♏△♓), The High Priestess

The occult magic of Scorpio mixed with the spiritualism of Pisces creates a potent vessel for bringing those realms onto this planet. These people are energy healers both for humans and for the Earth. They are highly psychic, gifted in occult knowledge, and have a strong connection to spirits, angels, and God.

SAGITTARIUS TRINE ARIES (♐△♈), The Ultimate Manifester

Sagittarius' optimism for seeing all things as possible mixes with Aries' drive and self-motivation. These people are highly motivated especially in academic pursuits, have great physical vigor, and inspire and influence others through their ideas and personal confidence.

CAPRICORN TRINE TAURUS (♑△♉), The Wise Parental Figure

Capricorn's ability to provide mixes with Taurus' appreciation and respect for what the Capricorn accomplishes. These people are immensely frugal, talented in woodwork, and are able to create legacies.

AQUARIUS TRINE GEMINI (♒△♊), The Profound Professor

The forward-thinking ideas of Aquarius mixes with Gemini's ability to share those ideas with others. These people are profound in thought and in word, make excellent writers and scientists, and are honest with themselves and with those that are around them.

220

PISCES TRINE CANCER (♓△♋), The Guru

Pisces' love for love mixed with Cancer's tenderness creates a well of feminine knowledge that is unparalleled. These people make caring parents and nurses, are able to channel higher realms, and allow for others to feel vulnerable around them.

☍ Opposition (180°)

Keyword: Midpoint

Oppositions may be complicated to control but are not complicated to understand. Unlike the square, where we have two opposing forces blind-sighted by the other, with the opposition, you are well aware of the two forces in play. The trick is to come to the middle of these two perspectives. This differs from the square because you are asked to listen to both sides and allow for both sides be expressed consciously. Oppositions require the art of compromise between two forces. Sometimes, you favor Side A, other times Side B. Either way, oppositions require you to sacrifice both sides in order to meet in the middle.

Similarity: Opposite Sign

It is true when we say, "opposites attract," and this truth is echoed within oppositions because opposite signs are surprisingly similar in many respects. Indeed, is it their commonalities that make them two sides of the same pole. The critical difference is that Sign A seems to have what Sign B is lacking and vice versa. Approaching oppositions this way makes them less intimidating and cryptic.

Opposition Combinations

ARIES OPPOSITION LIBRA (♈☍♎), Me vs. You

Aries thinks about his priorities while Libra thinks about the other. Both require the other person in order to function. Libras need to learn how to be self-motivated with their own ideas and thoughts, and Aries needs to learn compromise and meet others half-way.

TAURUS OPPOSITION SCORPIO (♉☍♏), MY NEEDS VS. YOUR NEEDS

Taurus wants things to stay the same while Scorpio wants things to change constantly. However, both involve the possessions and feelings of the other. Taurus need to learn to be more flexible and movable in their thoughts and perspectives, and Scorpios need to learn to relax and enjoy life.

GEMINI OPPOSITION SAGITTARIUS (♊☍♐), SIMPLE VS. COMPLEX

Gemini wants to look at the small picture while Sagittarius is looking at the larger picture. They both involve obtaining some sort of knowledge and applying that knowledge towards their interests and understanding. Geminis need to zoom out and think of larger concepts while the Sagittarius needs to zoom in and see what they are missing.

CANCER OPPOSITION CAPRICORN (♋☍♑), WHAT I FEEL VS. WHAT IS REAL

Cancer wants to live life solely based on their emotional perspective while Capricorn sees life as very matter-of-fact and does not let emotions get in the way of decision making. Both require stability and enjoy the idea of making a family and a legacy. Cancers need to learn to be motivated and take the personal out of business matters, and Capricorns need to open up to others, to themselves, and learn to enjoy the fruits of their labors.

LEO OPPOSITION AQUARIUS (♌☍♒), SINGULARITY VS. MULTIVERSE

Leos consider their personal expression to be the only one that matters, and Aquarius does not think that their individuality matters in the great sea of humanity. However, both involve social circles and creative outlets. Leos need to learn that they are not the only person on this planet, and Aquarians need to learn that their uniqueness is special and must be brought out into the world.

VIRGO OPPOSITION PISCES (♍☍♓), MEANING VS. ABSTRACT

Virgo wants to figure out the meaning behind everything and Pisces is the absence of meaning. They both involve improvement of the self. The Virgo needs to learn to let go of meaning and understand that sometimes, there is such a thing as the unexplainable, and Pisces need to learn how to focus, make goals, and plan things out in order to achieve.

* * *

Orbs of Influence and Aspect Hierarchy

When it comes to aspects, not all of them are precise hits. For example, if Venus is at 12°♒ and the Sun is at 14°♒ we still say that these two planets are in a conjunction but with an orb (gap) of 2° (14°-12°=2°). Similarly, if Mars is at 26°♈ with Saturn at 20°♑, we still say that these two planets are in a square, but with an orb of 6° (26°-20°=6°).

When the orb is smaller, we say the aspect is tighter. When the orb is wider, the aspect is looser. The tighter the aspect, the more significant and intense it is for a person. There are just as many orb ranges as there are astrologers. Every astrologer has their own viewpoint, and it is up you to find out what works. It appears on average, most astrologers give an orb range as wide as 10° to still be considered valid. Personally, I tend to be more conservative with my orbs and only accommodate aspects with an orb of 6° or less to be of the most importance with my biggest perimeter extending to 8° and here is why:

(1) Starting out, this gives you fewer aspects to analyze making it less overwhelming at first. Furthermore, any aspect that is 6° or less is a great place to start because those aspects are clearly the most important for that person.

(2) If you think about it, a 10° range is 1/3 of the 30° allotted to one sign, and in my opinion, if you were meant to have that aspect, you were meant to have that aspect.

(3) When you focus on the tightest orbs first, you get to the heart of the chart and address the more relevant points with greater ease as it tends to take out a lot of the guesswork.

My personal orb scale is as follows (Table II-5):

Table II-5. My Personal Orb Scale with Description

ORB RANGE	DESCRIPTION
0°-1°	These aspects are highly important for the individual and if it is a square, opposition, or a difficult conjunction, it is some of their most difficult hindrances in this lifetime. If it is a sextile, trine, or a beneficial conjunction, then those are the strongest resources the individual has in order to counter their more difficult aspects.
1°-2°	These aspects are just as important and powerful, but orbs between 0°-1° should get priority.
3°-6°	Again, these aspects are important and significant, but not as tightly bound as other tighter aspects. Nevertheless, these aspects are still felt and are relevant for natal chart analysis.
6°-8°	Not felt as heavily but can still have an influence for the individual.
8°-10°	Ignore any aspect that has this range.

Organizing your aspects from the tightest to the widest is a great way to approach a natal chart and is in fact one of the strategies we will cover in Parts V, VI, and VII of this book. Approaching aspects this way takes an overwhelming map of aspects and helps you to break it down from the most relevant to the least.

Aspect Patterns

When certain aspects are formed in a pattern, their energies become amplified and can become more difficult or beneficial depending on the circumstance. I will be discussing the three main aspect patterns, although there are more than these three:

The Grand Trine

When three planets are all in the same element and all trine one another, they are in a grand trine. The grand trine is what I like to call "the spiritual safety net." These people are never able to reach rock bottom and because of this, their lives are always secure, which gives them plenty of free will to do as they choose. The issue is, when you have that much free will and life hands you benefits that easily, it is very hard to come up with a life direction. However, once these people follow a path, there is no stopping them.

THE T-SQUARE

When two planets are in an opposition and another planet is squared to the two planets that are in an opposition, they are said to be in a T-square. T-squares involve three out of the four signs of the same modality and thus, these energies are very intense and highly psychological in nature. The issues that involve the planets, signs, and houses of the T-square are incredibly significant for that individual's lifepath because there is a crystallization that forms, which makes these planetary energies difficult to thaw and uncover.

THE YOD

The Yod is a little difficult to discover because it involves a minor aspect that was not covered: the inconjunct. The yod is when one planet is in inconjunct with two other planets, and those two planets are in sextile to one another. This creates a sort of arrow image on the natal chart. The yod is nicknamed "the finger of God" because these people are very much tied down to their life path. Unlike the grand trine, which is ultimate free will, people with the yod have a very clear life path that must be experienced due to the laws of karma. The key is to accept whatever comes their way.

* * *

Recall from the introduction, people that are born at the exact moment, regardless of location, will contain the same planetary locations within the zodiac. Consequently, these planets will make the same aspect combinations to one another for everyone born at that same moment as well.

The aspects within the natal chart provide the moral fiber for the individual that they carry for the rest of their lives. The information they provide for you as an astrological counselor allows you to better determine an individual's most unconscious motivations and struggles along with the realms of fortitude that they carry in order to approach their darker self. Indeed, aspect analysis, in my opinion, constitutes the highest emphases within the natal chart. All other components (ie. Signs, Houses, Cardinal Points, etc.) simply paint the picture with a finer brush. They help to explain how these energies are manifested, but the aspects tell you what these energies are in the first place.

Up to this point in the book, we have now examined the Signs, Planets, and Aspects within Astrology. There are two final major components to consider so that we have a full understanding of all the archetypal symbols found within the birth chart. The last two components of the birth chart are the most unique for the individual because they are both computed by incorporating the birth time and birth location. These two data points are the most personalized for the individual and therefore it is where the birth chart receives its uniqueness. Of course, I am referring to of the Houses and Cardinal Points of Astrology.

SECTION 6-HOUSES

❧

Think of the natal chart as two wheels on top of one another. The first wheel is the zodiac, the band of 12 signs around a 360° wheel. Remember, wherever the planets are located within this wheel, their location will be the same for everyone else that was born at that same exact moment in time. However, this wheel's orientation relative to the sky at the moment of birth depends on the birth time and birth location (latitude and longitude).

For example, let us say that Child A is born in Oregon and Child B is born in Florida at the same time. This means, both Child A and B's planets are located around the zodiac at the same location. However, if the parents of both Child A and B were to look East, towards the horizon where Sun rises, they would be looking at two different signs (orientations) of the zodiac (Fig. II-5).

On the birth chart, East is the dark horizontal line pointing left as indicated by the arrow. As you can see, for Child A's parents, they would be observing the constellation of Aries and for

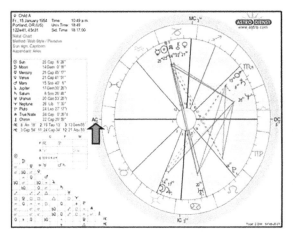
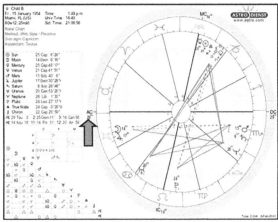

FIGURE II-5. Child A and B birth charts with East/Sunrise/Ascendant Indicated.

Child B's parents, they would see the Taurus/Gemini cusp of the zodiac. We call this point the Ascendant (Asc) and its opposite point, West, the place of Sunset, the Descendant (Dsc). In every birth chart, this line will be completely horizontal and therefore acts as the foundation for which all other calculations and divisions of the sky map are determined.

Although the natal chart will always appear as a perfect circle, it is important to remember that the zodiac functions in three-dimensional space. To this point, if the parents of either Child A or B were to face East and with their finger traced all the way up to the highest point in the sky (the zenith), we would expect the zodiac band to exist at that point, but that is not the case. In fact, the zodiacal band is tilted and angled depending on the latitude and longitude and time of year of the birth (Fig. II-6A-C).

By analyzing Figures II-6A-C, you can begin to notice that the highest point of the zodiac (Midheaven or MC) does not necessarily mean it is the highest point in the sky (zenith). Due to this fact, the perfectly circular band of the zodiac becomes slightly oval/parabolic.

The intensity of the parabola's compression or expansion, along with the location of the highest point of the zodiac (Midheaven/MC), is completely dependent upon the latitude and longitude of the birth location and birth time. Let us once again examine Child A and Child B's birth charts (Fig. II-7). Notice this time that the arrows are pointing towards the Midheavens.

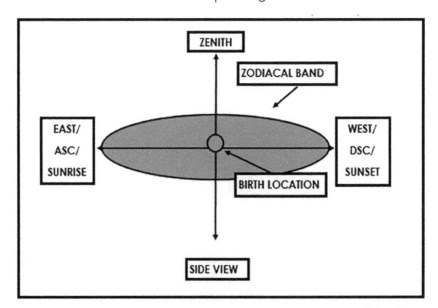

FIGURE II-6A. Zodiacal Band Relative to the Horizon and Zenith (Side View)

228

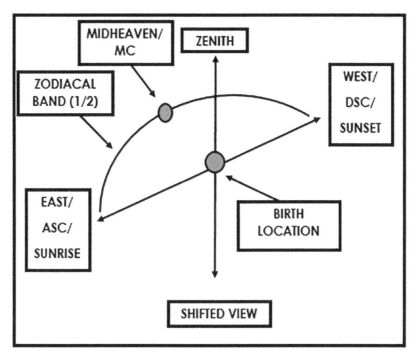

FIGURE II-6B. Zodiacal Band Relative to the Horizon and Zenith (Shifted View)

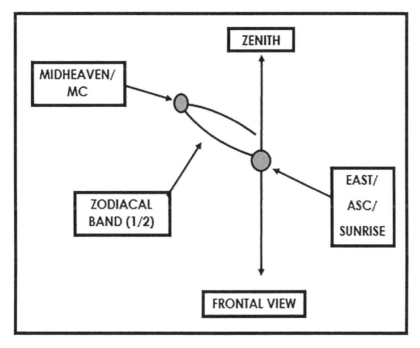

FIGURE II-6C. Zodiacal Band Relative to the Horizon and Zenith (Frontal View)

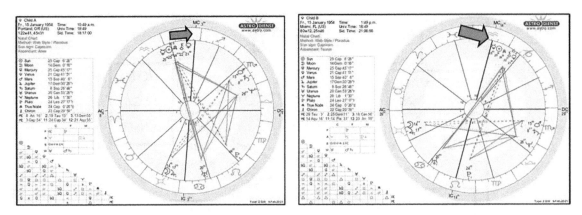

FIGURE II-7. Child A and Child B's Birth charts with Midheaven (MC) Indicated

For both children, the Midheaven (arrows in the image above) are different relative to the center point because the parabolic equations differ for each child. For Child A, their parabola is more "compressed" because they live further North on the globe where the sky's surface area is decreased, but for Child B, who lives closer to the equator, their parabola is more thinned out and therefore closer to a circular shape than an oval shape.

To this point, examine the charts once again, but this time notice the various subdivisions between the Ascendant line and the Midheaven line. All that is happening is the Astrologer is taking that surface area of the zodiac and splitting it into equal parts. However, notice that Child A's divisions are more lopsided and Child B's divisions are slightly more symmetrical, although not completely equal (Fig. II-8). This is how astrology transforms three-dimensional space onto a two-dimensional birth chart.

These subdivisions of the zodiacal band are called the Houses of Astrology. There are twelve Houses which correspond to the twelve Signs of the zodiac and therefore the Houses represent similar themes. The Houses also indicate when certain areas of our lives will be emphasized or not depending on when transiting planets enter and exit a certain House (See Part IV-Section 3 & 4, and Part V-Section 3). For now, we will examine each House individually in order to understand what themes are present in each House.

The Houses each represent a certain life stage along with qualities of the Sign that is originally associated with that House. Due to this fact, I always find it easier to remind myself which Sign has authentic rule over which house. For example, instead of saying "The 1st House" I tell myself

230

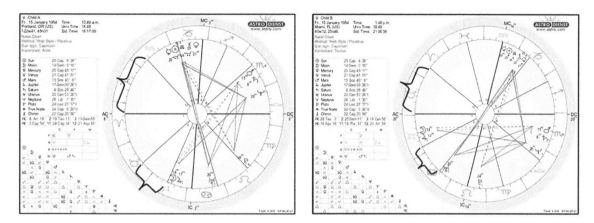

FIGURE II-8. Sub-Division Lengths of Child A and Child B.

"The House of Aries" so I know that this House is associated with Aries themes. Or, instead of saying "The 10th House" I will acknowledge it as "The House of Capricorn," and so on and so forth. This way, your brain instantly connects themes associated with each House. Let us now take it one House at a time and learn more about each one.

THE 1ST HOUSE/THE HOUSE OF ARIES

TIME OF DEVELOPMENT: BIRTH

The 1st House represents the exact moment we came into this world within this body. Once we have left our mother's womb, we are now autonomous, breathing entities whose life is now separate and independent from the mother's, even though both parents are involved with the conception and, often, the subsequent upbringing. Recall, the key phrase for Aries is "I am," and when we are birthed, it is the moment when we tell the world "Here I am! Ready to start my life on this planet."

VARIOUS REALMS OF CONTROL

The physical body and its appearance, our vitality, our sense of ego and self-identity, personal boundaries, how we initiate things within our life, physical abilities, and first impressions.

231

THE 2ᴺᴰ HOUSE/THE HOUSE OF TAURUS

Time of Development: Toddler (0-2yrs)

Once we are born and our brain begins to develop, we start to get a better sense as to where our body ends, and other things begin. This spatial awareness is a key component of this stage of child development. We begin to think "I am this, I am not this." It is also where we begin to utilize our five senses in order to map out our surroundings.

Various Realms of Control

Our possessions and outlook towards material objects, sense of style, the five senses (taste, touch, smell, sight, and hearing), artistic endeavors, our surroundings, overall temperament, and sense of self-worth.

THE 3ᴿᴰ HOUSE/THE HOUSE OF GEMINI

Time of Development: Pre-School (3-4yrs)

At this time in the story of life, the child is now beginning to communicate with their parents and others. They start to voice their preferences and opinions and are becoming quite fond of the word, "No!" The child is starting to get to an age where familial friendships, such as relating to siblings and cousins, begin. Additionally, this is the time where children are becoming skilled in locomotion through crawling and walking.

Various Realms of Control

Communication, mental capacities, short-distance traveling, mediums of communication and travel, language and writing abilities, siblings, and the press/journalism.

THE 4ᵀᴴ HOUSE/THE HOUSE OF CANCER

Time of Development: Early Childhood (5-7yrs)

The time of the 4th House is when we begin to separate from our parents and home for the first time by attending school. We are taught how to be more comfortable within our own skin and learn about our sensitivities towards others and ourselves. We also begin to be nurtured more by the community via teachers, babysitters, neighbors, and extended family.

Various Realms of Control

The mother or the mother figure, home, being nurtured, food, family, ancestry, unconscious self, emotions, sense of security, emotional self-reliance, memories, personal foundation, local neighborhood, real estate, and traditions.

THE 5ᵀᴴ HOUSE/THE HOUSE OF LEO

Time of Development: Middle Childhood (8-10 yrs.)

Now that the child is growing into their own, they are beginning to express themselves more freely and uniquely. They are beginning to show their likes, dislikes, hobbies, and interests. In general, individuals are simply enjoying the bliss of childhood. They begin to show their level of extroversion or introversion, and the personality of the child begins to shine through.

Various Realms of Control

Creative expression, theme parks and other places of recreation, vacations, hobbies. drama, innocence, leadership, children, desire for attention, courage, politics, figureheads, individuality, film industry, romance, and games.

THE 6ᵀᴴ HOUSE/THE HOUSE OF VIRGO

Time of Development: Late Childhood (11-13 yrs.)

At this time, the child is now getting into the routine of school along with their extracurricular activities. Life becomes a little more sobering as the carefree nature of early childhood is now replaced with the need to focus on learning and getting a decent education. This is a time when thinking processes adjust and improve as our learning styles begin to be fully utilized.

Various Realms of Control

Elementary education in general, teachers, routines, domesticated pets, daily work, service-oriented professions, health, nutrition, detailed and hard work, skillsets and specialized training, digestion, dexterity, and analytical abilities.

THE 7ᵀᴴ HOUSE/THE HOUSE OF LIBRA

Time of Development: Early Adolescence (14-17 yrs.)

Now that the child is reaching the age of puberty and leaving the elementary education system, they are beginning to relate with others on a more intimate basis. They begin to create closer bonds with their friends and start to branch out of their normal social circles. Their interests and preferences change as they start to accept their individualized nature because they now have more freedom to be who they are.

Various Realms of Control

Relationships, personal and professional partners, diplomacy, quality of married and romantic life, our social nature, debate, the law, resolutions, maintaining equilibrium, agreements, and mediation.

THE 8ᵀᴴ HOUSE/THE HOUSE OF SCORPIO

Time of Development: Middle Adolescence (18-21 yrs.)

With the individual now having experienced puberty with even more autonomy as a legal adult, boundaries are pushed even more, and individuals begin to have sexual encounters, along with trying drugs and alcohol for the first time. This is also when individuals need to consider how to make a living and therefore begin to rely on the resources of others to provide access to funds.

Various Realms of Control

Sexuality and the reproductive system, occult subjects, secrets, inheritance, death (more metaphorical as opposed to literal), cycles of transformation and rebirth, joint finances, resources and ventures, debt, regeneration, and intimacy.

THE 9ᵀᴴ HOUSE/THE HOUSE OF SAGITTARIUS

Time of Development: Late Adolescence (22-25 yrs.)

During this stage of life, the individual is expanding their mind by either attending college or by simply experiencing the world as a young adult. Their worldview, ideologies, and opinions are likewise adjusted due to this new exploration. They start to examine the diversity of various cultures, lifestyles, and upbringings.

Various Realms of Control

Institutions (academic, governmental, religious, and judicial), higher-education, long-distance traveling, philosophy, wisdom, good fortune, foreign affairs and cultures, belief systems, ethics, long-term goals and plans, ideologies, wisdom, and professors.

THE 10ᵀᴴ HOUSE/THE HOUSE OF CAPRICORN

Time of Development: Adulthood (25-40 yrs.)

This is the time when individuals begin to "settle down" into realms like marriages, careers, and having children. Roots are beginning to take hold due to hard work and past experiences as the individual begins to become a functioning member of society. Naturally, younger people begin to look towards them for guidance and wisdom.

Various Realms of Control

Career, achievements, ambitions, authority, father or the father figure, status, long-term investments and planning, limitations, restrictions, government, integrity, mastery, state officials, and aspirations.

THE 11ᵀᴴ HOUSE/THE HOUSE OF AQUARIUS

Time of Development: Late Adulthood (40-55 yrs.)

By now, the individual is reaping many fruits of their labors from their adulthood, which finalizes at the second Saturn return at around 60 years of age. At this point, Saturn (the traditional ruler of Aquarius) asks for us to take stock of our lives as awareness into one's inevitable passing from this Earth becomes an unavoidable topic. Hopefully, through introspection and understanding, a sort of optimism grows as the bigger picture of life begins to make more sense, having now lived for so many years.

Various Realms of Control

Civic organizations, friends and acquaintances, legislative branches of government, daydreams, communities, like-mindedness, non-profits, fruits from your labors, hopefulness, fraternities and sororities, and flashes of insight.

THE 12ᴛʜ HOUSE/THE HOUSE OF PISCES

Time of Development: Elder (55-80 yrs.)

We are now headed towards the twilight of an individual's life as they become that of the wise old hermit. They rely on the charity of humanity as they will now have to ask for those younger than them to take care of their ailments. The moment of ultimate surrender, death, begins to befall us. As the body approaches this inevitability, the beauty in it all is that it is merely a repetition of the oldest story ever told: the cycle of life.

Various Realms of Control

Psychic abilities, meditation, religion, refuge and where we seek seclusion, addictions, healing abilities, peace of mind, conclusions and endings, hospitals and clinics, retirement life, bluffing and thievery, and large animals.

* * *

Every individual has all the 12 houses within their birth chart. It is only a question of how activated or inactivated these houses are depending on the malefic or benefic statuses of the planets that rule them within the birth chart, and the planets that are placed or not placed within. For example, if the planet that rules the 9ᵗʰ House is powerful but also inharmonious, then realms related to the 9ᵗʰ House will similarly be affected. Or, if a planet is working harmoniously and resides in the 2ⁿᵈ House, even if it does not rule the 2ⁿᵈ House, 2ⁿᵈ House realms will still feel the beneficial nature of the planet in question. We will cover this more in greater detail in Part V-Section 2.

This same concept can also be applied to transiting planets when they enter and exit house after house. Similarly, the nature of the planet, along with the energy of the House they are about to enter, shifts the experience for the individual during the entire time that planet resides within that House. More on this in Part IV-Section 4 and Part V-Section 3.

If you recall at the start of this section, the various subdivisions of the parabola that constitutes your House sizes and placements is heavily determined by your birth time and location. In other words, your House placements and sizes are the most individualized part of your birth chart, even more than your Sun and Moon placements. You will certainly see this in action when you learn how to compute your transits in Part IV. Before we get there, let us dive deeper into our House divisions by examining the four most important points within: the cardinal points.

SECTION 7-THE CARDINAL POINTS

∽

If you recall from the previous section, we discussed how there are two main points along the zodiac that establish all of the other House locations: the Ascendant, the point located east at the horizon, and the Midheaven, the highest point of the zodiac. Remember, just because the Midheaven is the highest point along the zodiac does not necessarily mean that the Midheaven is also the zenith, the highest point in the sky located directly above you. It is this slanted feature that creates variations in House sizes and shapes. Indeed, the Ascendant and Midheaven anchors the birth chart and the various House subdivisions.

The four cardinal points are associated with the two solstices and equinoxes of the yearly astrological calendar. These are pivotal moments during the year that signify when the start of a new season is underway. The major shifts to the environmental climates during the solstices and equinoxes parallel shifts in individual priorities. As such, they indicate major vortexes within us that heavily dictate our character, both on an external and subconscious level.

The four cardinal points indicate how we portray ourselves out into the world (The Ascendant), how well that persona interacts with other individuals (The Descendant), our highest ambitions (The Midheaven), and the deeply hidden psychology that governs it all (The Imum Coeli (IC)). Suffice to say, the various planets and signs that rule the cardinal points within a birth chart are heavily emphasized within their respective realms. Furthermore, if natal planets are connected to the cardinal points via aspects, this also manifests specific details into their varying conditions and the ways in which they are expressed. Let us now examine each of the cardinal points in greater detail.

THE ASCENDANT (ASC): THE MASK WE WEAR

When we think of the Ascendant, it is easy to assume that it represents who we are as a person, but this is not entirely true. Instead, the Ascendant shows us the person we portray out into the world, not necessarily the person we truly are. Remember, within astrology, our unique individuality stems from our Sun and Moon, where the Sun represents our external character, and the Moon represents our internal wellbeing.

In other words, the Sun and Moon constitute our personal psychology, but the Ascendant is the persona that we project out into the world. For example, if I was a Cancer rising, I would come off as timid and shy at first, but if my Sun was in Leo, this would be slightly contrary because the Leo Sun indicates that I desire some form of sociability and individual expression. As such, it could be possible that the person is incredibly shy at first (Cancer Rising) but once someone becomes their friend, they in turn become comfortable, which allows for their extroversion to come forth (Leo Sun).

As is true for all cardinal points, the overall condition of the planet(s) that rule the signs involved are vitally important in demonstrating how these various energies manifest. With the Ascendant, it shows if the person's actual psychology is in harmony with the person they portray; the actor in the show of life. In fact, many astrologers emphasize the planetary ruler(s) of the Ascendant to be the "chart ruler(s)," which adds emphases towards the entirety of the birth chart.

The Ascendant demonstrates the qualities of the person we become when we are out there within society. How planets are aspected to the Ascendant line itself also indicate if the actual psychology and outward persona are working in harmony or at cross purposes. In this way, it can also show the difficulty or ease for an individual to let go their self-image for the sake of psychological evolution. The Ascendant is the mask we put on with the hopes that others will accept our mask, along with the individual behind its façade. How others react to this mask is determined by the Ascendant's opposite pole, the Descendant.

The Descendant (Dsc): How We Relate to Others and Vice Versa

Whenever we encounter anyone within the world, they see our Ascendant and we see theirs. How we both react to one another and towards any sort of personal interaction is indicated by the Descendant and its planetary ruler(s). The Descendant shows the second part of the Ascendant's story. For example, if we are too abrasive due to our Ascendant, others might be apprehensive to engage with us. Or, if we are charming with charisma due to our Ascendant, then this would naturally lead to pleasant personal interactions which again would be demonstrated by the Descendant.

Due to this fact, if planets aspect our Ascendant they also aspect our Descendant. For example, if a planet is sextile to the Ascendant, it is simultaneously in a trine to the Descendant and vice versa. Similarly, if a planet forms a conjunction to the Ascendant, then they also form an opposition to the Descendant and vice versa. Lastly, if a planet is in a square to the Ascendant, they are similarly in a square to the Descendant (Fig. II-9).

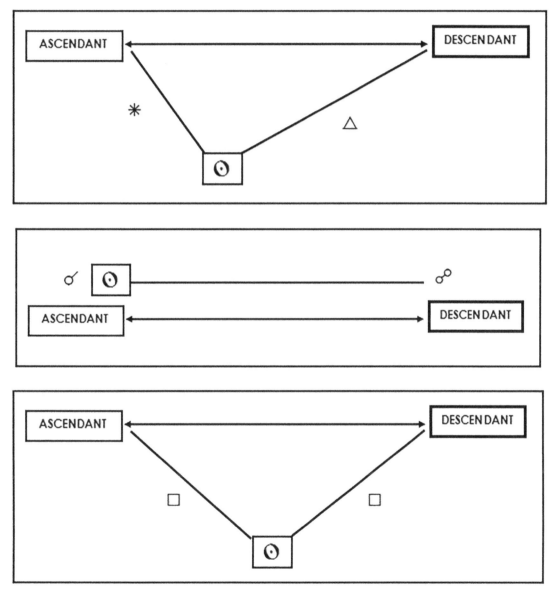

FIGURE II-9. How Planets interact with both Poles of the Cardinal Points

By this logic, it is easy to see how the person we portray (Ascendant) affects our interpersonal relationships (Descendant). The various aspects to both would logically affect both for better or worse.

Be that as it may, the Descendant line and its planetary ruler(s) show us how well we are received by others, how well we receive others, and if this is due to a personality that is true to the actual self or due to a front that was created to hide our true nature based on the condition of the Ascendant or Descendant. Therefore, if planets are in difficult connection to the Descendant or Ascendant, this can indicate possible areas of trauma that cause the individual to not be truthfully expressive.

The Midheaven (MC): Our Highest Goals and Ambitions

The Midheaven indicates our highest aspirations and our means of obtaining them. It indicates our sense of motivation, dedication, and overall approach towards success. It also represents our major purpose that we have been set out to do in this world. As the highest point of the zodiac during our moment of birth, the types of people and stories we look up to for inspiration are also indicated by the Midheaven.

Just how it was with the Ascendant/Descendant (Asc/Dsc) line, planets can make aspects to the Midheaven/IC line, which would subsequently alter their manifestations. Additionally, the planetary ruler(s) of the Midheaven and their condition demonstrates various manifestations of the Midheaven. Our vocations and personal dignity are also tied into these matters.

Just as psychological trauma towards the expression of our personality and its connection to our actual psychology is tied into the Asc/Dsc line, reasons for dysfunction into our sense of self-worth and ambitions can also be affected by poorly aspected planets to the MC/IC line. For example, we could be self-destructive or overly ruthless towards our personal objectives and this could be due to past trauma leading to a dysfunctional way of responding to our place within the professional world and adult society. Consequently, our integrity and place within society is also dictated by the Midheaven.

The Imum Coeli (IC): Our Unconsciousness

Imum Coeli is Latin for "bottom of the sky" and is the least known of the four cardinal points. This makes sense given that the IC is representative of our deepest, most unconscious parts of our being. Our ancestry and previous experiences (whether in this life or in previous lives) are tied down to the IC and essentially show us the psychological and karmic "baggage" of these previous experiences and that of our familial karma.

According to astrological theory, children are typically born at the expense of unprocessed karma of the parents involved. Therefore, parents tend to place a lot of their personal issues onto their children for better or for worse. This cycle is multi-generational, and psychologists along with doctors can attest to the genetic connection between mental and physical disease. In this same light, astrology, specifically the IC, shows us those various genetic connections that have now been placed onto us for us to transmute or further repress. Suffice to say, the quality of our upbringing, parents, and family life are all tied to the IC.

The pool of our unconscious can either be deep or shallow, understood or ignored. The IC demonstrates these varying degrees of our most hidden psychology. It also shows us the type of strengths and weaknesses that arose out of past action. In some ways, the entire birth chart can be seen as a story of the karma that we have obtained from past action, but the IC explains why and how we have obtained this karma and have yet to release its hold. Metaphysically speaking, even if the IC condition is a harmonious one, any sort of karmic ties, good or bad, still tie us down, nevertheless. In other words, if we come into this life with more fortunate karma than others, this does not necessarily mean we have an overall advantage because we are still being tied down to attachment through one form or the other.

* * *

As we will see in Part V, the condition of the cardinal points and their planetary ruler(s) provides a foundational core into the individual and how they express that personality into the person they truly are, along with the aims they strive to attain. Additionally, they indicate our deepest unknown aspects of ourselves, along with how other people interact with our persona. Indeed, many astrologers put great emphases into the cardinal points and state that our Sun, Moon, and cardinal point placements indicate the core structures of the individual.

* * *

Part II served as the bulk of the various astrological symbols and archetypes you will encounter during your studies. Now that you have a firm foundation into the various astrological energies, and the nature in which they react to one another, it is time to put all of that theory into actual practice through the various ways one can. We will start by observing the daily, weekly, and annual phenomena that affect all individuals on the planet regardless of their birth chart. This is because all events that occur in Part III engage with the entire human race repeatedly from day to day, month to month, and year to year simultaneously.

PART III: DAILY, MONTHLY, AND YEARLY PHENOMENA

"Astrology's roots lie in an ancient world-view which perceived the universe as a single living organism, animated by divine order and intelligence."-Liz Greene

Astrology has two primary functions: to be used as a celestial calendar that is perfectly in tune with the natural flow of life here on planet Earth, and as a map towards an individual's psychology. Although these two separate utilities are discussed individually in this book (Parts III/IV and V/ VI/VII respectively), the key is to become simultaneously engaged with both on a daily basis. Before we can understand how both work in perfect harmony, we need to first recalibrate our lives to the oldest and most universal calendar system on this planet: the astrological calendar.

Recalling from Part I-Section 1, annual sun-calendars became important for humanity as early as the farming communities c. 2500BC, and moon calendars were invented and functional even earlier than that with Aurignacian cultures c. 32,000BC.

The yearly astrological calendar consists of 360 days where the Sun travels along the 360° of the zodiac at an approximate rate of 1° per day. Each year begins a 0° Aries, also known as the Spring Equinox, and each month within that year is equally divided into 12 equal months of 30°/30 days each. In other words, each sign of the zodiac would incorporate one month during the astrological year which is heavily tied to the natural energies of the seasons that coincide with those respective months.

The Moon cycle is approximately 28 days and serves a multitude of roles during the monthly, yearly, and daily cycles. Daily cycles are primarily affected by Void of Course Moons which will be discussed in Part III-Section 2. Yearly influences involve the semiannual eclipse events which is the discussion of Part III-Section 3. Finally, the Moon's influence towards monthly energies and biorhythms will be discussed in Part III-Section 1.

Another daily phenomenon involves the planetary hours which was developed by ancient Greek astrologers. In Part III-Section 5, we will learn how they computed the hours of the day and how you can use their energies towards everything you do in life from appointments to parties to annulments.

In addition to the Moon and Sun primarily acting as the driving force for our celestial calendar, retrograde periods of the inner planets Mercury, Venus, and Mars are just as influential towards the energies that are felt by everyone, regardless of where they are located on planet Earth. These retrogrades are the topic of Part III-Section 4.

When you begin to align your life towards these various subtle forces of nature, you will begin to notice an immediate change. This is mostly due to the fact that you are no longer accidentally going against the natural current of time and space. Countless times, individuals plan events during inopportune moments which causes unnecessary stress and frustrations. When you work with astrology as a calendar, you eliminate these avoidable misfortunes.

Similarly, adhering to the Moon cycle is incredibly important because it indicates when it is a time for activation or a time for recuperation. Two weeks out of every month, we are asked to slow down and consolidate our energies and projects but instead, most individuals are constantly on the go or they are constantly listless and do not act when they should. The moon cycle is literally like trying to catch a wave on the ocean; all it takes is the right timing.

When you time your life this way and ride that wave, you are riding the cosmic wave of time and space which makes you incredibly present and conscious. I encourage you to experiment and try to see what happens to events that you have no control over, but you were able to observe using your astrological calendar. This is a game of trial and error, but when you get the hang of it, you will observe literal manifestations of the rules that are established in this part of the book. With that, let us begin with the Moon and all her facets as a working calendar.

SECTION 1-THE MOON CYCLE

The moon travels approximately 27-28 days during its monthly cycle. During this cycle, it makes one full rotation around the entire zodiac. This means the Moon resides in each sign for approximately 2.5 days per monthly period. At the start of every moon cycle, the Moon will begin its cycle within one different sign per month. For example, if the Sun is in Taurus, sometime during those 30 days, there will be a new moon in Taurus. During the next month, Gemini, there will be a new moon in Gemini and so on and so forth. By this logic, if we pay close attention to each new moon, we are able to make 12 distinct intentions every year as each sign of the zodiac tends to represent a certain facet of the human experience.

When the new moon is in Aries, this is a good time for intentions regarding the body and the year ahead. Taurus is for relaxation, enjoyment of the arts, and improving upon what we own. Gemini is a time to improve upon how we communicate, how we process, and how we interact. Cancer is a time to get in touch with our feelings and become introverted. Leo is a time for recreation, hobbies, and for taking pleasure in life. Virgo is for hard work, reassessing, taking care of your health, and organizing. Libra's intensions are ones involving relating with others, creating strong bonds, and resolving conflicts. Scorpio is a time for change, intimacy, and deep reflection. Sagittarius is for expanding your knowledge and awareness, travel, and creating abundance for yourself.

Capricorn is a time for achievement, discipline, and working towards long-term goals. Aquarius is a time for friends, social endeavors, and harnessing intuition and empathy. Pisces is a time for spiritual practices, meditation, and embracing unconditional love.

During every moon cycle, these new intensions go through a time of testing, reward, climax, integration, and rest, through what we call the eight stages of the lunar monthly cycle. If you

247

recall in Part II-Section 5, there are five major aspects within astrology. Now, it is time to learn that these aspects are in fact cyclical in nature.

Aspects involve a planet to planet connection. When we are comparing two planets in transit, the faster planet is revolving around the slower planet. In the case of the moon cycle, the faster planet (the Moon) is revolving around the slower planet (the Sun). This is how the Moon receives its various shading of light and darkness because of her rotation relative to the Sun (Fig. III-1). The eight primary moon phases parallel the eight stages of the aspect cycle (Table III-1).

FIGURE III-1. Various Moon Phases are due to the Aspect cycle.[58]

TABLE III-1. Aspect Cycle with Corresponding Moon Phase

#	STAGE NAME	GLYPH	MOON PHASE
1/8	Birth/Conjunction	☌	New Moon
2/8	Opening Sextile	✶	Waxing Crescent
3/8	Opening Square	□	Waxing Quarter
4/8	Opening Trine	Δ	Waxing Gibbous
5/8	Climax/Opposition	☍	Full Moon
6/8	Closing Trine	Δ	Waning Gibbous
7/8	Closing Square	□	Waning Quarter
8/8	Closing Sextile	✶	Waning Crescent
1/8	Birth/Conjunction	☌	New Moon

---

58 "moon phases all" by walberto30 is licensed with CC BY-ND 2.0. To view a copy of this license, visit https://creativecommons.org/licenses/by-nd/2.0/

The Aspect cycle found above will also be helpful when it comes to interpreting transits (Part IV-Section 4 and Part V-Section 3). Observing the parallels of the aspect cycle to the monthly cycle of the Moon is a logical way to begin your understanding towards the various components therein. Let us now observe each stage of the Moon and Aspect cycle one event at a time.

STAGE ONE: The New Moon/Conjunction

Every cycle begins at the conjunction with the new moon. This is the time to think about your intentions for that month based upon the sign of the new moon and the house where it is placed within your natal chart. Usually, new moon energy lasts up to three days after the new moon occurs.

For example, let us say it is the new moon in Aries (☽♈) and we decide to start an exercise routine to get back into shape. You begin to make a plan, gather the supplies you will need to accomplish this goal, like weights or gym clothes, and begin to start working out daily.

STAGE TWO: Waxing Crescent/Opening Sextile

This is a time to adjust your intentions slightly depending how it is unfolding. The sextile is cooperative and helpful which gives you a sense of optimism. Therefore, during this time you will most likely find an opportunity that will steer your intentions into the right direction. The catch is you have to put in the effort in order to obtain the benefits.

With our example, during this time you might find a nice discount for a gym membership during the waxing crescent while the Moon is in Gemini, the opening sextile. Or, you find a friend that wants to be your fitness partner and offers to join you on your daily runs. Again, we only reap the rewards of the sextile if we actively take what is offered to us.

STAGE THREE: Waxing Quarter/Opening Square

During this time of the moon cycle, the amount of light and dark seen on the moon is 50/50, which is reflected towards the square aspect within astrology. Recall from Part II-Section 5, squares involve two opposing forces that have the same amount of energy and drive but are working at cross purposes. Naturally, this is a time of conflict.

This is now the time where the universe tests you to see if you are keeping up with your end of the bargain. The moon cycle's manifesting powers do not come about without you demonstrating that you are willing to make the appropriate sacrifices.

Back to our example, with the new moon in Aries, this would occur when the moon ingressed (entered) into Cancer. This would be the time where you are starting to become more lax with your gym attendance. Or maybe you are starting to eat the wrong things again. In any case, your goals become more difficult during this time of testing.

The answer is to introspectively address your motivations and be willing to adjust. If you can admit that you should not be eating poor foods and instead should be going back to the gym, that takes a lot of admission of your own self-destructive actions. If we work through the dilemmas brought on by the square, we emerge stronger because we have a better understanding into why we were not progressing in the first place. This is the ultimate lesson found within squares, and one of the most important struggles within astrology.

STAGE FOUR: Waxing Gibbous/Opening Trine

After the time of conflict and tribulation, you are rewarded with the opening trine of the moon phase which, in the case of the Aries new moon, would occur when the moon ingressed into Leo. If you stuck with your goals and fought through the struggle of the first quarter moon, you are rewarded during this time. Maybe you begin to see results on your body from your hard work, or perhaps your workouts are getting easier to handle because you are becoming more fit. In either case, this is a time to look back and congratulate yourself on the hard work you have done.

STAGE FIVE: Full Moon/Opposition

The opposition is a time of climax and culmination. Your goals have now reached their peak, and you are experiencing the fullest expression of the fruits of your labors. The sign where the full moon occurs is relevant because it ties back to the sign of the new moon as its opposition.

So, if you had an intention of getting fit during the Aries new moon, during the full moon in Libra, you might find that our new self-confidence (Aries) has attracted the attention of others (Libra). Either way, this is a time of high energy.

STAGE SIX: WANING GIBBOUS/CLOSING TRINE

Once the full moon occurs, we then transition from the waxing (developing) period into the waning (disseminating) period. When we switch into the waning phase, energy starts to dwindle and slow down over time. This is critical to understand, as most people will have the hardest time with the waning period because we are constantly encouraged by our society to be active, go-getting, and yang oriented. However, there are two weeks out of every lunar month where we are asked to slow down, relax, and become tranquil and reflective instead.

During the waning gibbous, we experience the closing trine. In the case of the Aries new moon would be Sagittarius. Now that you have experienced the highest climax from the full moon, and assuming you were attentive and doing everything to the best of our abilities, everything becomes easier and more routine because you have been instilling good habits.

During the closing trine, going back to the workout analogy, this is not a time to push yourself too hard at the gym, and your diet also becomes manageable as everything has now fallen into a comfortable routine. Nevertheless, progress and results are still apparent because you have been going at it for almost three weeks now, and your body is now use to the regiment.

STAGE SEVEN: WANING QUARTER/CLOSING SQUARE

The closing square, which would occur in Capricorn during the Aries new moon, is a time for permanent integration and instillation of these better habits so that they may go beyond the current moon cycle and into the future. You are able to firmly cement your habits into permanency during this time. This could be difficult because out of all of the positive progress you have now seen, it might be hard to continue because you have now witnessed a good amount of success already. Still, one must keep in mind that continuing our good practices overtime yields even greater results because we are pursuing goals for longer periods.

To our analogy, your body and overall health are looking good but yet again, you can be tempted to eat poorly or skip a workout. However, this conflict is easier to handle because you have already experienced this conflict with the opening square. Only now you have more to show for it which makes the right decision easier to make.

STAGE EIGHT: WANING CRESCENT/CLOSING SEXTILE

During this time, the moon phase is winding down in preparation for the next one. This is a time for rest and relaxation as the entire energy surrounding the moon for that month is almost gone completely. With the Aries new moon, this is when the moon ingresses into Aquarius, making it a good time to be social and outgoing with your fresh, healthier body and vitality. It is important that during this time we take it easy because the overall energy is very low during this phase. Nevertheless, these are the ultimate "treat yourself" days because the only thing left to do with this lack of energy is to take it easy.

YOUR PERSONAL BIORHYTHMS

While the Moon travels along her monthly journey, she is simultaneously creating aspects to every one of your natal planets in the process. Therefore, it is easy to tell if your natal planets in your chart are working in harmony or disharmony with the Moon depending on the day. You can easily discover your monthly biorhythms for every single planet in your chart, but for the sake of simplicity and importance, I would only compare the transiting Moon to your natal Sun (☉), Moon (☽), Ascendant (ASC), and Midheaven (MC) because these are the four main important points within your birth chart. Simply determine their signs and follow the table below as the moon phase progresses through the zodiac from month to month (Table III-2).

Now, using your celestial calendar datebook, every time you see the moon in one of these signs, you can then understand how your own personal energies are being affected.

This is the first part of the puzzle when it comes to observing the Moon's influences on a monthly and daily basis. The next piece involves determining when the Moon is Void of Course (VOC) because, regardless of the waxing or waning periods, these are moments where we need to be mindful as they can occur during any part of the moon cycle.

TABLE III-2. Personal Bio-Rhythm Tracking Chart

Personal Planet/ Cardinal Point Location	Stage1: New Moon	Stage 2: Waxing Crescent	Stage3: Waxing Quarter	Stage 4: Waxing Gibbous	Stage 5: Full Moon	Stage 6: Waning Gibbous	Stage7: Waning Quarter	Stage 8: Waning Crescent
♈	♈	♊	♋	♌	♎	♐	♑	♒
♉	♉	♋	♌	♍	♏	♑	♒	♓
♊	♊	♌	♍	♎	♐	♒	♓	♈
♋	♋	♍	♎	♏	♑	♓	♈	♉
♌	♌	♎	♏	♐	♒	♈	♉	♊
♍	♍	♏	♐	♑	♓	♉	♊	♋
♎	♎	♐	♑	♒	♈	♊	♋	♌
♏	♏	♑	♒	♓	♉	♋	♌	♍
♐	♐	♒	♓	♈	♊	♌	♍	♎
♑	♑	♓	♈	♉	♋	♍	♎	♏
♒	♒	♈	♉	♊	♌	♎	♏	♐
♓	♓	♉	♊	♋	♍	♏	♐	♑

SECTION 2-VOID OF COURSE MOONS

The monthly Moon cycle last approximately 28 days with the Moon residing in each sign of the zodiac for approximately 2.5 days. While the Moon is traveling around the zodiac, she is making various aspects with the other planets in transit. However, when she ingresses (transitions) from one sign to the other, there is a moment when these aspect connections are no longer made with the other planets. When this occurs, the moon is said to be Void of Course (VOC).

Think of the VOC period like a light switch and the aspects the moon makes to the other planets as the electrical cord that give the light switch its power. When the Moon is VOC, the cord detaches, and the light switch turns off cutting out the power. Because aspects and planetary positions are mathematical in nature, these VOC periods are mathematically predictable and accurate. VOC periods can occur during the waxing or waning phase and can be as short as a few minutes or as long as 30 hours in some instances. In other words, VOC periods are arbitrary albeit predictable.

When the moon is void of course, the mantra is: "nothing will come of it." Starting new endeavors, making purchases, or plans during void moons simply do not end up working out. Observe the table below for a more comprehensive list as to what one should or should not do during a VOC moon (Table III-3).

The more you pay attention to void moons, the more you will realize that people who are out of synch with their own lives tend to unconsciously plan things against this natural flow of energy. Void moons are more common than we realize, and when you put them on your radar, you are able to align your body and your life to the natural flow of this planet. This greatly helps in your endeavors and your own wellbeing because you are eliminating unnecessary

TABLE III-3. Do/Do Not List for VOC Period

DO DURING VOC MOON	DO NOT DURING VOC MOON
• Meditate/Yoga	• Parties or planning of parties
• Clean house/cleaning in general	• Make plans or have plans
• Organize/Sort	• Purchases of any kind
• Review/Edit	• Meet new people
• Brainstorm	• Initiation of any project
• Cancel things/Endings	• Meetings (unless brainstorming)/ Presentations
• Exercise with no specific planning/routine	• Planning/Scheduling for the future
• Leisure	• Correspondence
• Sleep In/Take a nap	• Begin a new job/Interview/ Send out Resumes
• Things you do not want to develop into anything	• Judge people or situations too quickly as judgment is clouded
• Keep life as simple as possible. The more you plan, the more your plans get foiled	• Medical procedures or professional testing

chaos that can easily be avoided by simply waiting for the active time when the Moon is out of the void.

When you purchase an Astrological calendar, make sure it includes the VOC periods and mark them with a highlighter or a pen so you can easily see when they will occur. Now that we understand VOC periods and the monthly moon cycle, the last lunar observation involves the semiannual eclipse cycle with the Sun.

255

SECTION 3-ECLIPSES

Twice every year, we experience a complete moon cycle as an eclipse period. Eclipses occur when the orbital planes of the Earth, Moon, and Sun are parallel, lining up with one another. They always occur in pairs of two: Solar to Lunar or Lunar to Solar.

Solar eclipses occur on the new moon when the Moon is in front of the Sun blocking out the Sun while the Moon travels across. Normally, the Moon would be invisible because the Sun's light is covering up its surface. Only this time the opposite is true, and the Sun becomes engulfed by the moon. Lunar eclipses happen on the full moon when the Moon is opposite the Sun. This time, the Earth is sandwiched between them, blocking out the Sun's light onto the full moon. The shadow that you see on the Moon during a lunar eclipse is actually the shadow of the Earth as it travels between them.

Astrologically, there is a way to determine when an eclipse will occur by observing the North Node (☊) and South Node (☋). The nodes are there to tell us "if an eclipse were to happen, around here is where it would happen along the zodiac." Now, keep in mind that some eclipses do not occur on that precise spot. The range in which an eclipse can occur is very wide and sometimes, we only receive a penumbral eclipse, which are ones that occur but are not exact.

As a side note, I personally do not work with the nodes extensively for a few reasons: (1) They do not indicate any triggering of events other than the eclipses and (2) The nodes are taken from the Jyotish tradition and only make the most sense within that context. In my opinion, the Western tradition does not have a full enough consensus towards the nodal energies and because of this, I tend to passively acknowledge nodal placement within a birth chart. However, if a natal planet conjoins the North or South Node, or if an individual's North or South Node conjoin planets on a partner's chart, then these are times when I would consider the nodes to be of importance. Please refer to the annotated bibliography in Part I-Section 7 if you want to discover books written about the nodes.

Some astrologers believe that during eclipses, the Earth receives a sort of "karmic exchange" when the old souls and energies that have passed away are able to leave the Earth plane, and the new souls that are entering begin to integrate into their earthly bodies. To this point, some astrologers like to look at the "pre-natal eclipse" in natal charts as part of their studies. This is based on a theory that whichever eclipse occurred before your birthday is the time when your soul entered your body inside of your mother's womb.

During eclipses, we experience a time of testing. A time when there are two distinct roads to take: face whatever comes your way with a clear head in order to release anxiety, or get swept into the chaos and build up anxiety and undesirable situations around yourself. When eclipses occur, you need to be incredibly alert, sober, and cautious.

Try not to react to things suddenly, arrive to any conclusions, or make definitive plans that would drastically alter your life direction or circumstance. Any agitation or stress you feel during an eclipse is your unconsciousness showing you what needs to be worked out. Essentially, your inner fears are emerging and taking hold, which can cause you to act incorrectly because you become frightened. Instead of acting on these fears, the point is to understand and process.

Eclipses of the Sun and Moon are very much an Earthly phenomenon that have been going on since time immemorial. For millennia, humanity has been witnessing eclipses and the energies they bring. In order to better understand this global context, we need to put ourselves in the shoes of our ancient ancestors.

Picture a time when our concept of the universe was still primitive. No major cities or empires have yet to emerge, and humanity is mostly made up of small farming communities that worship the Sun as the eternal life-giver and the Moon as the nurturing mother.

Now, imagine you and your farming friends are out in the field one day, just like any other day, but then something strange begins to happen. You look up and you see the Sun, the god that you worship, the god that makes the crops grow and provides heat and light, becomes engulfed and swallowed up by who knows what! Imagine the confusion, chaos, and the lack of understanding that every member of the community must have felt. Although humanity now is more advanced in our ways of thinking, these inherent and anxious energies are still prevalent during eclipses even within our modern-day society because eclipses are a global and eternal phenomenon.

Regardless of the time in history, during eclipses, fear takes over. Fear takes over because we do not know which way is up. The Sun, the king of the solar system is being swallowed, engulfed, and we are now left alone with our unconscious anxieties. During eclipses, you are being asked to understand what fears you have been neglecting so that you can overcome them. Eclipses, in this way, are very positive and beautiful in that you are able to face what you fear head-on, but more often than not, individuals react to these stressors and make regrettable decisions.

Do not let these anxieties run the show. If you do, not only will you understand them less, you will build up unwanted situations by acting upon these impulses. Many times, I have witnessed friends make drastic life decisions like moving into another state, changing occupations, or selling property, only to find out that it was a huge mistake to do so after the fact. These apparently obvious mistakes only become apparent until after the eclipse cycle is over and the fog finally lifts.

An excellent example of the eclipse metaphor can be observed in the opera *Prince Igor,* written and composed by Alexander Borodin. The story takes place in medieval Russia with Prince Igor who is about to take arms to battle the Kahns. Before leaving his homeland, Prince Igor meets with the Russian peasants and army who are praising his name and glory as he prepares to take off for battle.

However, during these wishes of good fortune, an ominous event occurs right in front of everyone's eyes: an eclipse. As the event takes place, his wife begs and pleads with him not to go as the eclipse is a terrible omen. Ignoring her advice, he continues onward towards his enemy only to be obliterated on the battlefield.

If we consider these two characters, Prince Igor and his wife, we can see a parallel in universal archetypes of the masculine and feminine within ourselves and how they handle the eclipse energy differently. The masculine side, Prince Igor, is only listening to his ego. He does not care about what his wife (inner feminine/intuition) says. Instead, he is only fixated on his will as he feels invisible. His wife, on the other hand, is receptive, attentive, and aware of the energies that govern us.

The mantra during an Eclipses is: "Wait and see." Even when we want to act, and during an eclipse it is incredibly tempting to act, we are nevertheless doing so out of our unconscious ego drive. Therefore, during each eclipse cycle, all of us have a choice to either be the Prince Igor in our own story and follow our egos towards destruction, or to act as his wife and tap into our intuition instead and subdue the ego flair-ups that occur during eclipses.

Again, it is only after the eclipse cycle that the dysfunction behind our choices become incredibly obvious (TABLE III-4). During the eclipse, you literally think to yourself "how can this possibly go wrong?" Once the eclipse disappears, you are literally no longer eclipsed yourself, and all of the reasons as to why it would not work out becomes painstakingly clear. This is why it is better to simply "wait and see" instead of finding yourself in a hole that you need to now dig yourself out.

A few things to note about this table. If you look at the location column, you will notice that eclipses occur in the same location from time to time. This is because energies that arise

TABLE III-4. Upcoming Eclipses (NOTE: Date times are UT. Subtract 1 day for USA Dates.)

FIRST ECLIPSE (TYPE)	SECOND ECLIPSE (TYPE)	LOCATION	CLARITY DATE
MAY 26 2021 (L)	JUNE 10 2021 (S)	SAGITTARIUS/GEMINI	JUNE 24 2021
NOV 19 2021 (L)	DEC 4 2021 (S)	TAURUS/SAGITTARIUS	DEC 19 2021
APR 30 2022 (S)	MAY 16 2022 (L)	TAURUS/SCORPIO	MAY 30 2022
OCT 25 2022 (S)	NOV 8 2022 (L)	SCORPIO/TAURUS	NOV 23 2022
APR 20 2023 (S)	MAY 5 2023 (L)	ARIES/SCORPIO	MAY 19 2023
OCT 14 2023 (S)	OCT 28 2023 (L)	LIBRA/TAURUS	NOV 13 2023
MAR 25 2024 (L)	APR 8 2024 (S)	LIBRA/ARIES	APR 23 2024
SEP 18 2024 (L)	OCT 2 2024 (S)	PISCES/LIBRA	OCT 17 2024
MAR 14 2025 (L)	MAR 29 2025 (S)	VIRGO/ARIES	APR 13 2025
SEP 7 2025 (L)	SEP 21 2025 (S)	PISCES/VIRGO	OCT 7 2025
FRB 17 2026 (S)	MAR 3 2026 (L)	AQUARIUS/VIRGO	MAR 19 2026
AUG 12 2026 (S)	AUG 28 2026 (L)	LEO/PISCES	SEP 11 2026

KEY: L=Lunar Eclipse, S=Solar Eclipse

during eclipses are connected. In other words, any stressful situations or thought patters that emerge during an eclipse, but are repressed instead of addressed, will simply remerge at the next eclipse cycle. Secondly, it is important to notice the Clarity Date column. Eclipse energies are still present even after the second eclipse event. It is not until after the clarity date that everything becomes lucid and normalized. Until that time, yourself and the entire world are influenced by the eclipse energies.

* * *

Now that we have covered all factions of the Moon's utility as a daily, monthly, and yearly calendar, there are just two more astrological phenomena that influences our daily lives: inner planetary retrogrades and planetary hours.

SECTION 4-INNER PLANETARY RETROGRADES

With the exception of the Sun and the Moon, all planets within Astrology turn retrograde relatively frequently. The outer planets Jupiter, Saturn, Uranus, Neptune, and Pluto tend to change directions every five months or so, and the inner planets Mercury, Venus, and Mars have shorter episodes with more frequent intervals. A lot of this lecture can be applied towards all retrogrades, but we will be focusing mostly on retrogrades of the three inner planets: Mercury, Venus, and Mars (TABLE III-5).

Retrogrades are not a time where the energy seems to be completely shut off like during a void moon, but instead energies shift towards a different focus in that we are asked process instead of progress. An easy guide for any retrograde is to observe the themes in the domain column from the table above, and consider any word that has the re- prefix. For example, retrogrades are a time to reevaluate, revisit, reconnect, rekindle, rejuvenate, reassess, review, reorganize, etc., etc.

Certain individuals, emotions, and circumstances that have yet to be removed out of your psychic clutter seem to reappear during this time reminding you that you still have work to do. Just like eclipses, this is not a time for action or making plans as they will similarly fall through

TABLE III-5. Summary of Inner Planetary Retrogrades

PLANET	FREQUENCY AND LENGTH	DOMAINS
MERCURY ☿	3 Times Per Year for 30 Days	Communication Negotiations Travel
VENUS ♀	Every 20 Months for 40 Days	Romance Leisure Cooperation
MARS ♂	Every 2 Years for 80 Days	Drive Conflict Agitation/Aggression

or become thwarted. Instead, take this time to gear up for the future, when the planet will no longer be in retrograde, because that will be the time to act. During the retrograde, it is a time to clean up the excess junk that has been holding you back.

Anatomy of a Retrograde (℞)

Astronomically, retrogrades are a visual phenomenon where the planet appears to be moving backwards in our sky, when in fact, the Earth's orbit has either jumped ahead or behind the other planet's orbit giving it the optical illusion of going backwards from our perspective here on Earth.

Every retrograde consists of five phases: Shadow I, Stationary Retrograde, Retrograde, Stationary Direct, and Shadow II (Fig. III-2). The shadow periods are when the planet is going direct (the astrological word for "forward motion") through the zodiacal degrees that the planet is going to pass through during the retrograde. The stationary periods are when the planet slows down to a grinding halt so that it may switch directions. The retrograde period is when the planet is

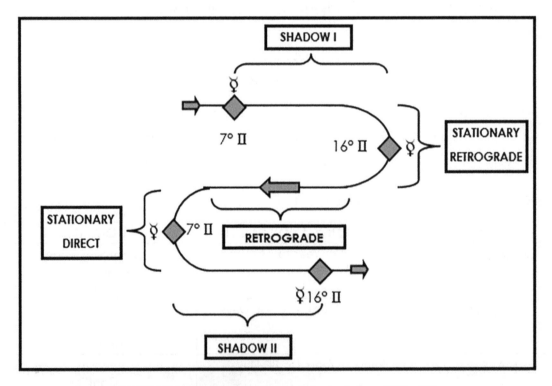

FIGURE III-2. Anatomy of a Mercury Retrograde from 16°Ⅱ – 7°Ⅱ

appearing to move backwards relative to our observations here on Earth, but it is traveling at the same speed as it normally would if it was going direct.

PHASE #1: SHADOW 1

During this time, you will start to experience the themes of the upcoming retrograde because the planet will revisit these degrees while it is traveling backwards. In our example, Mercury will be traveling in retrograde from 16°♊ – 7°♊ which means when the planet is traveling forward from 7°♊ – 16°♊ prior to the retrograde it indicates the Shadow 1 period.

PHASE #2: STATIONARY RETROGRADE

Think of stationary periods like changing directions in a car. Before you can go from forward to reverse, you first need to slow down, stop, change from forward to reverse, and then accelerate once again. This same concept applies to stationary periods because this is the time when the planet slows down, stops, and then speeds up only in the opposite direction.

Stationary periods are the most stressful and intense part of the retrograde period because any movement, even if it is backwards, is better than no movement at all. Therefore, it is important to be mindful of when they occur so you can be more prepared.

PHASE #3: RETROGRADE PERIOD

This is the more familiar phase of the retrograde, when the planet is traveling backwards for an extended amount of time. During the retrograde period, the energies of the retrograde are in full expression and you should respond accordingly, following the guidelines outlined in this section.

PHASE #4: STATIONARY DIRECT

Just as it was with the stationary retrograde, the planet slows down only to stop and then pivot towards the opposite direction. Again, these are intense moments when you should take care and wait until the stationary period is over before you react.

PHASE #5: SHADOW II PHASE

Once the planet has finished travelling in retrograde, it is time for it to change back into direct motion. It will cover the same ground that was covered during the Shadow I phase, only this time the planet will continue to proceed along the zodiac until the next retrograde period. This is the time when you should be wrapping up the retrograde themes and act upon what you have learned during the retrograde period in order to make the appropriate adjustments.

* * *

When it comes to the stationary periods, Mercury stations are felt for a week before it turns retrograde, a week after it turns retrograde, a week before it turns direct, and a week after it turns direct. Venus stations are felt 1.5 weeks before it turns retrograde, 1.5 weeks after it turns retrograde, 1.5 weeks before it turns direct, and 1.5 weeks after it turns direct. Mars stations are felt 2 weeks before it turns retrograde, 2 weeks after it turns retrograde, 2 weeks before it turns direct, and 2 weeks after it turns direct. These, of course, are approximations and once you learn how to read an Ephemeris (Part IV-Section 1), you will be able to obtain precise dates for these stationary periods. In the meantime, follow the table below in order to get a running start on this data (Table III-6A-C).

AFFECTED DOMAINS DURING THE RETROGRADE

Mercury retrogrades affect areas of communication, traveling, efficiency, and negotiations. It is hard to explain yourself during this time and can have cases of "it's on the tip of my tongue" along with misunderstandings. Messages, emails, and packages get lost or take longer to be delivered or answered. Commuting to work takes longer, and there are unexpected mishaps with traffic and public transportation. Take care if you are naturally accident prone or a poor car driver. This is a good time to edit, clear out junk, make processes more efficient, read contacts but do not sign them, review for exams, brainstorm, and turning off the mental functions through meditation.

Venus retrogrades affect romance, aesthetics, one-to-one relationships, and leisure. Old romances can reappear, or you can find that your feelings for an ex have changed. Break ups

TABLE III-6A. Upcoming Mercury Retrogrades and Stationary Periods

ZODIACAL RANGE	Stationary Rx Start	Stationary Rx End	Stationary Direct Start	Stationary Direct End
24°♊ - 16°♊	MAY 23 2021	JUNE 9 2021	JUNE 16 2021	JULY 1 2021
25°♎ - 10°♎	SEP 22 2021	OCT 2 2021	OCT 16 2021	OCT 24 2021
10°♒ - 24°♑	JAN 10 2022	JAN 19 2022	JAN 31 2022	FEB 10 2022
4°♊ - 26°♉	MAY 6 2022	MAY 17 2022	MAY 29 2022	JUNE 8 2022
8°♎ - 24°♍	SEP 5 2022	SEP 17 2022	SEP 29 2022	OCT 8 2022
24°♑ - 8°♑	DEC 27 2022	JAN 2 2023	JAN 14 2023	JAN 24 2023
15°♉ - 5°♉	APR 17 2023	APR 26 2023	MAY 12 2023	MAY 20 2023
21°♍ - 8°♍	AUG 19 2023	AUG 31 2023	SEP 13 2023	SEP 21 2023
8°♑ - 22°♐	DEC 8 2023	DEC 18 2023	DEC 30 2023	JAN 8 2024
27°♈ - 15°♈	MAR 31 2024	APR 7 2024	APR 20 2024	MAY 4 2024
4°♍ - 21°♌	AUG 1 2024	AUG 11 2024	AUG 25 2024	SEP 4 2024
22°♐ - 6°♐	NOV 22 2024	DEC 2 2024	DEC 13 2024	DEC 24 2024
9°♈ - 26°♓	MAR 11 2025	MAR 19 2025	APR 3 2025	APR 15 2025
15°♌ - 4°♌	JUL 14 2025	JUL 25 2025	AUG 8 2025	AUG 20 2025
6°♐ - 20°♏	NOV 6 2025	NOV 14 2025	NOV 27 2025	DEC 6 2025

TABLE III-6B. Upcoming Venus Retrogrades and Stationary Periods

ZODIACAL RANGE	Stationary Rx Start	Stationary Rx End	Stationary Direct Start	Stationary Direct End
26°♑ - 11°♑	DEC 11 2021	JAN 1 2022	JAN 22 2022	FEB 7 2022
28°♌ - 12°♌	JUL 16 2023	AUG 3 2023	AUG 28 2023	SEP 17 2023
10°♈ - 24°♓	FEB 23 2025	MAR 15 2025	APR 5 2025	APR 24 2025

TABLE III-6C. Upcoming Mars Retrogrades and Stationary Periods

ZODIACAL RANGE	Stationary Rx Start	Stationary Rx End	Stationary Direct Start	Stationary Direct End
25°♊ - 8°♊	OCT 19 2022	NOV 15 2022	DEC 30 2022	FEB 1 2022
6°♌ - 17°♋	NOV 24 2024	DEC 21 2024	FEB 12 2025	MAR 16 2025

and reevaluating current relationships are also possible. Individuals are more sensitive to *Feng Shui*. Therefore, your living environment can become more stressful. It is easier to disagree with coworkers, romantic partners, children, and bosses. It can also be difficult to simply relax. This is a good time to make amends, move around furniture, clean out your wardrobe but do not dedicate to a new style just yet, think about your tastes, and ponder if every acquaintance you have in your life is good for you in the long run.

Mars retrogrades affect action, movement, aggression, and conflict. In fact, Mars retrogrades are the most difficult because Mars is the planet of forward motion so when he is not allowed to move in the direction he wants, he becomes highly irritable. There can be shorter tempers and sudden acts of violence or personal injuries/accidents. It is hard to get anything off the ground and you have to contend with feelings of impatience. This is a good time for addressing anger, slow breathing techniques, outlets that allow you to release your pent-up physical energy, and to observe your sense of self-esteem and confidence.

* * *

The frequency of inner planetary retrogrades should not be ignored. You will find yourself having to balance between retrogrades along with eclipses and VOC moons all the time now that you know how to observe these various celestial forces that influence every human on the planet at the exact same time, regardless of their location. The final astrological calendar observation involves planetary hours which were created by the ancient Greeks.

SECTION 5-PLANETARY HOURS

❧

When the ancient Greeks, along with the various cultures that existed alongside them and before them, were working with Astrological systems, their understanding of the solar system only extended to Saturn because it is the last outer planet that can be viewed without the help of modern-day telescopes. These seven planets each ruled a day out of the seven-day week. These daily rulerships were so deeply ingrained within Greek and Latin culture, that it has influenced not only our modern use of the seven-day week, but the words that are used to signify which planet rules which day is still apparent (Table III-7).

TABLE III-7. Planetary Day Rulers in English and Spanish (A Latin-Based Language)

PLANET	GLYPH	NAME IN ENGLISH	NAME IN SPANISH
MOON	☽	**MON**DAY	**LUNE**S
MARS	♂	TUESDAY	**MART**ES
MERCURY	☿	WEDNESDAY	**MIÉRC**OLES
JUPITER	♃	THURSDAY	**JUEV**ES
VENUS	♀	FRIDAY	**VIERN**ES
SATURN	♄	**SATUR**DAY	**SÁBA**DO
SUN	☉	**SUN**DAY	DOMINGO

When considering the days of the week in this respect, certain energies are emphasized and become available for us depending on the day. On Monday, emotions are heightened, and it is a time to relax, get groceries, and stay home. No wonder people have "a case of the Mondays;" we are starting the work week on possibly the worst day! It would make more sense to have the week begin on Tuesday because this is the day of Mars, which makes it good for initiation and physical vigor. Wednesday, Mercury's day, is the best time to write correspondences, have meetings, run errands, and short-distance traveling. Thursday, Jupiter's day, is the day to take a chance and plan events that you want to work out favorably. Venus rules Friday and it is no wonder we call it "TGIF." This is the day to relax and save your hard work for the next day, Saturn's day, or, Saturday. Sunday should be "your day" where you plan and do whatever your heart desires.

When it comes to the planetary hours, these same energies still exist, only during a shorter window throughout the day. For example, if it is Monday, the day is ruled by the Moon, then anything you do that is Moon themed on the hour of the Moon doubles the power behind the intention. On the other hand, if you plan something during the Mercury hour and it is during a time when Mercury is in retrograde, then this could have the same powerful effect but in the opposite direction.

There are countless phone apps and websites that calculate planetary hours, but it is still important to understand how the hours are calculated. The 24-hour day we are familiar with is evenly divided into a 12-hour day period and a 12-hour night period. Planetary hours are similarly divided into a day period and night period as well, but the time allotted for each depends on the time between the sunrise and the sunset. In other words, daytime is from sunrise to sunset, and nighttime is from sunset to the sunrise of the next day. The time between these two events are calculated and divided into 12 "hours" using the table below (Table III-8).

According to this method, there will always be 12 hours of daytime and 12 hours of nighttime, but these hours could last approximately 54 minutes each to 63 minutes each depending on when the Sun would rise and set relative to the location of the individual. This means that every

TABLE III-8. Planetary Hour Rulers

DAY	DAY HOURS (SUNRISE TO SUNSET)												NIGHT HOURS (SUNSET TO SUNRISE)											
	1	2	3	4	5	6	7	8	9	10	11	12	1	2	3	4	5	6	7	8	9	10	11	12
SUN	☉	♀	☿	☽	♄	♃	♂	☉	♀	☿	☽	♄	♃	♂	☉	♀	☿	☽	♄	♃	♂	☉	♀	☿
MON	☽	♄	♃	♂	☉	♀	☿	☽	♄	♃	♂	☉	♀	☿	☽	♄	♃	♂	☉	♀	☿	☽	♄	♃
TUES	♂	☉	♀	☿	☽	♄	♃	♂	☉	♀	☿	☽	♄	♃	♂	☉	♀	☿	☽	♄	♃	♂	☉	♀
WED	☿	☽	♄	♃	♂	☉	♀	☿	☽	♄	♃	♂	☉	♀	☿	☽	♄	♃	♂	☉	♀	☿	☽	♄
THUR	♃	♂	☉	♀	☿	☽	♄	♃	♂	☉	♀	☿	☽	♄	♃	♂	☉	♀	☿	☽	♄	♃	♂	☉
FRI	♀	☿	☽	♄	♃	♂	☉	♀	☿	☽	♄	♃	♂	☉	♀	☿	☽	♄	♃	♂	☉	♀	☿	☽
SAT	♄	♃	♂	☉	♀	☿	☽	♄	♃	♂	☉	♀	☿	☽	♄	♃	♂	☉	♀	☿	☽	♄	♃	♂

TABLE III-9. Recommended Activities During a Planetary Hour

HOUR	GLYPH	RECOMMENDED ACTIVITIES
SUN	☉	Personal hobbies, Events with children, Presentations, Recreation, Brainstorming, Acting upon what you want to do in the moment
MOON	☽	Eat and make food, Counseling, Taking showers and baths, House cleaning, Events involving the mother
MERCURY	☿	Correspondence, Traveling and commuting, Breathing exercises, Mental puzzles and games, Making lists, Studying
VENUS	♀	Relaxation, Spa and skin treatments, Making amends, Going on a date, Mediation, Romance
MARS	♂	Exercise, Anything requiring expedience, Sexual encounters, Physical labor, Strategic moves
JUPITER	♃	Present and take up opportunities, Spiritual and academic pursuits, Taking chances, Any form of growth or expansion
SATURN	♄	Activities involving focus and tenacity, Events involving the Father, Career and Long-Term decisions, Dedicating to something or someone, Disciplined activities

latitude and longitude has varying planetary hour lengths throughout the year, but there will always be 12 hours per night and day, nevertheless. For example, individuals living in Alaska will have immensely short day hours during the winter because there is very little sunlight, but will have very long day hours during the summer because the time of daylight is very long.

Monitoring planetary hours gives you on an hourly and daily basis for auspicious timing to activate certain planetary energies (Table III-9). Try to experiment and observe how certain events unfold during certain hours.

* * *

During Part III, we have been working with planets that are currently moving in the present moment (in transit) and how we can utilize this information making daily, monthly, and yearly decisions. It is now time to take these observations one step further and observe how these moving planetary bodies interact with our fixed planetary bodies found within our birth chart. By doing this, we are able to determine specific and uniquely timed events that only affect us at the certain moment. This study within Astrology is called planetary transits and comprises the next part.

PART IV: PLANETARY TRANSITS

"The study of transits is one of the most fundamental techniques in Astrology. That transits indicate important trends and issues in your life is one of the few points upon which all Astrologers agree." - Robert Hand, Planets in Transit p. 3

The birth chart is essentially a snapshot of the planets along the zodiac at a specific point in time and space. However, after that snapshot is taken, the planets, zodiac, and even the Earth itself continue to move unceasingly. Therefore, wherever and whenever the planets are situated along their ongoing journey through the zodiac means that they are constantly and continually creating aspect connections to the fixed natal points within the birth chart. We call this "Planetary Transits" because it involves the aspects being made by the moving (transiting) planets with the fixed natal points inside the birth chart.

Determining when these aspects occur along with their nature gives you immensely personal and accurate data. This is because your transits signify moments when the planets in the present-day sky are interacting with your chart and your chart alone. However, everyone on the planet will always experience transits with the inner planets frequently because their cycles are no longer than 2 years (Table IV-1).

TABLE IV-1. Cycle Lengths for All Planets

PLANET	GLYPH	FULL CYCLE
SUN	☉	360 DAYS
MOON	☽	27-28 DAYS
MERCURY	☿	0.24 YRS
VENUS	♀	0.67 YRS
MARS	♂	1.88 YRS
JUPITER	♃	12 YRS
SATURN	♄	29.5 YRS
URANUS	♅	84 YRS
NEPTUNE	♆	165 YRS
PLUTO	♇	248 YRS

Although everyone will experience inner planetary transits frequently, they will nevertheless occur at different times and in different ways depending on the individual.

When it comes to the outer planets (Jupiter-Pluto) their transit interactions are less frequent and occur for longer periods of time. Therefore, when you experience an outer planetary transit, these are more pivotal moments in your life that I like to call, "Significant Life Events."

As an independent student of Astrology or as a practitioner, these significant life events are the crux of any reading and preparation for the year ahead. It indicates what the lessons will be for that year and how they will come about. They indicate when life is going to provide easier means of obtaining gains and psychological insight or if the opposite is true. In other words, the outer planetary transits are always significant and procure growth, but the intensity of the struggle or ease depends not only on the nature of the transit and aspect itself, but also upon your preparation and awareness during the event. This will be covered more in Part V-Section 3.

In this part of the book, we are going to precisely determine when transiting planets create an aspect to our natal chart by using simple mathematics and an astrologer's ephemeris. Once we are able to determine when these events occur, we will then look into how they will manifest by analyzing certain particulars surrounding the transiting events such as House, Sign, and Aspect placement.

As Robert Hand mentioned at the start of this segment, transits are a fundamental part of astrology and towards becoming a legitimate astrologer. Ethically speaking, it makes sense to practice what you preach, and therefore you cannot expect to tell others how to live if you yourself do not observe, experience, and calculate your own astrological circumstances. Furthermore, tracking your transits is the only legitimate way to put astrology to the empirical test.

You will now have hard, factual data to work with which mean you can then compare events and see if they line up in terms of timing and energy. The skills in this section take time to understand and utilize, but it is truly the first step to organically composing all of your astrological knowledge into a tangible and practical application. With that, the first skill we need to learn is how to read an ephemeris.

SECTION 1-HOW TO READ AN EPHEMERIS

Although the planets are constantly moving around the sky, we need to obtain some sort of "check point" we can use in order to calculate planetary positions at certain points in time. An ephemeris provides these check points by indicating where each planet will be located on the zodiac within a pre-determined 24-hour interval. Contemporary ephemerids set their 24-hour periods to Universal Time (UT). This is because all international measurements, including astronomical, are set to UT as this is the global standard. The two options are either UT Midnight (00:00) or UT Noon (12:00).

Typically, astrologers work with the Midnight intervals because it is simply easier to convert from 00:00 (Midnight) rather than 12:00 (Noon). Let us now observe an ephemeris for June 2021 (Fig. IV-1).

On the upper right-hand corner, we can determine this ephemeris is set to Midnight UT because it says 00:00 UT. This means that every one of these data points indicates where the planet is located at midnight UT for that date. For example, look at the Sun column for June 1st and 2nd. According to the ephemeris, the Sun is located at 10° ♊ 44' on the zodiac at midnight (00:00) June 1, 2021, and then 24-hours later at midnight (00:00) on June 2, 2021, the Sun moved to 11° ♊ 41'. Refer to the figure below for a visual representation (Fig. IV-2).

Take a moment to go up and down each column and observe how fast or slow the planets move. Within some columns, you will see a D or an R like how it is for Mercury on June 1 with an R and June 23 with a D. This indicates the exact moment planets are turning direct or retrograde (Part III-Section 4). If you go down the Mercury column, you can now watch the planet slowing down during the stationary periods. Refer back to Table III-4 and observe how the stationary dates now reflect these slower stationary events.

Day	Sid.t	☉	☽	☿	♀	♂	♃	♄	♅	♆	♇	☊	☋	⚷	δ	Day
T 1	16 38 47	10Ⅱ44'05	25≈ 0	24°R34	28Ⅱ 6	23♋30	1♓34	13°R27	12♉25	23♓ 2	26°R33	10°R45	10Ⅱ52	24♉45	12♈ 6	T 1
W 2	16 42 44	11°41'35	8♓ 2	24Ⅱ22	29°19	24° 7	1°38	13≈27	12°29	23° 3	26♋32	10°D45	10°49	24°52	12° 8	W 2
T 3	16 46 40	12°39'04	20°43	24° 7	0♋33	24°44	1°41	13°26	12°32	23° 4	26°31	10Ⅱ45	10°45	24°58	12°10	T 3
F 4	16 50 37	13°36'32	3♈ 5	23°48	1°46	25°21	1°45	13°25	12°35	23° 4	26°30	10°45	10°42	25° 5	12°12	F 4
S 5	16 54 34	14°33'59	15°12	23°26	2°59	25°58	1°48	13°23	12°38	23° 5	26°29	10°45	10°39	25°12	12°14	S 5
S 6	16 58 30	15°31'26	27° 9	23° 0	4°13	26°34	1°51	13°22	12°41	23° 6	26°28	10°45	10°36	25°18	12°16	S 6
M 7	17 2 27	16°28'52	8♉59	22°32	5°26	27°11	1°53	13°21	12°44	23° 6	26°27	10°46	10°33	25°25	12°18	M 7
T 8	17 6 23	17°26'17	20°46	22° 2	6°39	27°48	1°56	13°19	12°47	23° 7	26°26	10°47	10°29	25°32	12°20	T 8
W 9	17 10 20	18°23'42	2Ⅱ34	21°30	7°52	28°25	1°58	13°18	12°50	23° 7	26°25	10°47	10°26	25°38	12°22	W 9
T 10	17 14 16	19°21'06	14°24	20°57	9° 5	29° 2	2° 0	13°16	12°53	23° 8	26°24	10°R47	10°23	25°45	12°23	T 10
F 11	17 18 13	20°18'29	26°19	20°23	10°19	29°39	2° 2	13°14	12°56	23° 8	26°23	10°47	10°20	25°52	12°25	F 11
S 12	17 22 9	21°15'51	8♋21	19°50	11°32	0♌16	2° 4	13°13	12°59	23° 9	26°21	10°46	10°17	25°58	12°27	S 12
S 13	17 26 6	22°13'13	20°33	19°17	12°45	0°53	2° 5	13°11	13° 1	23° 9	26°20	10°45	10°14	26° 5	12°28	S 13
M14	17 30 3	23°10'33	2♌55	18°45	13°58	1°30	2° 7	13° 9	13° 4	23°10	26°19	10°43	10°10	26°12	12°30	M14
T 15	17 33 59	24° 7'53	15°31	18°15	15°11	2° 7	2° 8	13° 7	13° 7	23°10	26°18	10°41	10° 7	26°18	12°32	T 15
W16	17 37 56	25° 5'12	28°21	17°47	16°24	2°44	2° 9	13° 5	13°10	23°10	26°17	10°40	10° 4	26°25	12°33	W16
T 17	17 41 52	26° 2'30	11♍29	17°22	17°37	3°21	2°10	13° 2	13°13	23°11	26°16	10°38	10° 1	26°32	12°35	T 17
F 18	17 45 49	26°59'47	24°56	17° 0	18°50	3°58	2°10	13° 0	13°15	23°11	26°14	10°D38	9°58	26°38	12°36	F 18
S 19	17 49 45	27°57'04	8♎43	16°41	20° 3	4°35	2°11	12°58	13°18	23°11	26°13	10°38	9°55	26°45	12°37	S 19
S 20	17 53 42	28°54'19	22°50	16°27	21°16	5°12	2°11	12°55	13°21	23°11	26°12	10°39	9°51	26°52	12°39	S 20
M21	17 57 38	29°51'34	7♏17	16°16	22°29	5°49	2°R11	12°53	13°23	23°12	26°11	10°40	9°48	26°58	12°40	M21
T 22	18 1 35	0♋48'48	22° 0	16°10	23°42	6°26	2°11	12°50	13°26	23°12	26° 9	10°41	9°45	27° 5	12°41	T 22
W23	18 5 32	1°46'02	6♐53	16°D 8	24°55	7° 3	2°11	12°47	13°29	23°12	26° 8	10°R42	9°42	27°11	12°42	W23
T 24	18 9 28	2°43'15	21°52	16°10	26° 8	7°40	2°10	12°44	13°31	23°12	26° 7	10°42	9°39	27°18	12°44	T 24
F 25	18 13 25	3°40'28	6♑46	16°18	27°21	8°18	2° 9	12°41	13°34	23°12	26° 6	10°40	9°35	27°25	12°45	F 25
S 26	18 17 21	4°37'40	21°28	16°30	28°34	8°55	2° 8	12°39	13°36	23°R12	26° 4	10°38	9°32	27°31	12°46	S 26
S 27	18 21 18	5°34'52	5≈52	16°47	29°47	9°32	2° 7	12°35	13°38	23°12	26° 3	10°35	9°29	27°38	12°47	S 27
M28	18 25 14	6°32'04	19°52	17° 9	0♋59	10° 9	2° 6	12°32	13°41	23°12	26° 2	10°31	9°26	27°45	12°48	M28
T 29	18 29 11	7°29'16	3♓26	17°35	2°12	10°46	2° 4	12°29	13°43	23°12	26° 0	10°28	9°23	27°51	12°49	T 29
W30	18 33 8	8♋26'28	16♓34	18Ⅱ 6	3♌25	11♌23	2♓ 3	12≈26	13♉46	23♓12	25♋59	10Ⅱ25	9Ⅱ20	27♉58	12♈49	W30

FIGURE IV-1. Midnight UT Ephemeris for June 2021.

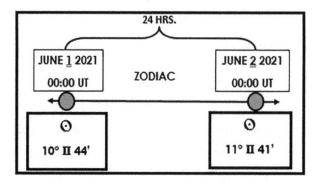

FIGURE IV-2. Visual Representation of Ephemeris Data

The sign location for each planet is implied until a new symbol emerges. For example, in the Mars column, June 1 shows the Cancer (♋) symbol and then the Leo (♌) symbol on June 12. This means all locations from June 1-11 are assumed to be in Cancer, and all locations from June 12-30 are assumed to occur in Leo.

274

Other than these two caveats, the ephemeris is incredibly simple to read and understand once you know the type of data it provides. You can ignore the Moon, Node, and asteroid data because these locations are not significant for transiting aspects. For the Moon, refer to Part III-Section 1 and use the biorhythm chart within Table III-2 to follow the motion of the Moon. Similarly, the column that reads SID. T. stands for "Sidereal Time" and is only relevant if you are planning to calculate a birth chart by hand, which goes beyond the scope of this book. Nevertheless, we will still be working with simple mathematics to compute transiting events. The first step in that process is to understand how to work in a Base-60 system because this is how the planetary positions are measured on the 360° wheel.

SECTION 2-THE SEXAGESIMAL (BASE 60) SYSTEM

Referring back to our example in the previous section, let us observe the Sun's placement on June 1, 2021 at 10° Ⅱ 44'. When you write down zodiacal points, the sign always goes in the middle. The number to the left indicates the degree within that sign and the number to the right indicates minutes, which is a subdivision of one degree (Table IV-2).

TABLE IV-2. Subdivisions of the Astrological Base-60 System

WHOLE PART	SUBDIVISON
1 ZODIAC	12 SIGNS (360°)
1 SIGN OF THE ZODIAC	30 DEGREES (30°)
1 DEGREE (1°)	60 MINUTES (60')

When you are performing an astrological math equation, you align degrees with degrees, sign with sign, and minutes with minutes. The next step is to add or subtract the minutes and degrees and then carry over if necessary. The only time you will be adding in astrology is if you are working with advanced chart calculations. Transiting math only requires subtraction so let us examine some examples you may encounter.

We will continue to use the example above and subtract the Sun's placement on June 2, 2021 from June 1, 2021. The first step is to align the two data points on top of one another with the higher value on top and the lower value on bottom. (The higher value is the point that is further along the zodiac).

	☉
JUNE 02	11° Ⅱ 41'
JUNE 01	- 10° Ⅱ 44'

Taking from our example, we have aligned the degrees, signs, and minutes appropriately, and we even included the Sun symbol and dates, so we are reminded of when this is occurring and with what planet.

With astrology, you will never encounter a negative number. If you end up with a negative number, it means you performed a step incorrectly. Due to this fact, if the subtraction would yield a negative number, we need to "carry over" just as you would in the normal Base-10 system. In our example, we have 41 minutes (41') subtracted into 44 minutes (44'). This would produce a negative number, which means we need to carry over and convert 1 degree (1°) into 60 minutes because 1 degree is equal to 60 minutes (1°=60').

	☉			
JUNE 02	11° ♊ 41' →	11° ♊ 41' →	10° ♊ 101'	
JUNE 01	- 10° ♊ 44'	-1° + 60'	- 10° ♊ 44'	
		10° ♊ 101'	**57'**	

What does the answer 57 minutes (57') tells us? It tells us that within a 24-hour period from June 1, 2021 to June 2, 2021, the Sun ☉ traveled an entire length of 57' of a 360° wheel from Point A (10° ♊ 44') to Point B (11° ♊ 41') (Refer to Fig. IV-2).

Let us do another example and examine Venus' movement from June 5, 2021 (2° ♋ 59') to June 6, 2021 (4° ♋ 13').

	♀			
JUNE 06	4° ♋ 13' →	4° ♋ 13' →	3° ♋ 73'	
JUNE 05	- 2° ♋ 59'	-1° + 60'	- 2° ♋ 59'	
		3° ♋ 73'	1° **14'**	

Again, this information tells us that from June 5, 2021 to June 6, 2021, Venus moved a total of 1 degree and 14 minutes (1° 14') along the zodiac from Point A (2° ♋ 59') to Point B (4° ♋ 13'). Although this answer is correct, there is one more step we need to perform. When working with zodiacal degrees and minutes, you need to work within one conversion or the other. In other words, you need to always convert you answers into minutes. We do this by simply converting the degrees from our answer back into minutes.

♀			
JUNE 06 4° ♋ 13′ →	4° ♋ 13′ →	3° ♋ 73′ →	1° 14′
JUNE 05 - 2° ♋ 59′	- 1° + 60′	- 2° ♋ 59′	-1° +60′
	3° ♋ 73′	1° 14′	0° 74′

You are essentially converting your answer from degrees and minutes into minutes only. In other words, 1 degree and 14 minutes is the same amount as 74 minutes (1° 14′ = 74′). For the sake of convenience, we need to always work in minutes.

Below, I have provided six practice problems. I have given you the planet and dates and would like you to refer to the ephemeris above to plug in the right data points and then subtract, telling me the amount of minutes each planet has traveled within that respective 24 hour period. You will find the answers on the next page.

☉
JUNE 20
JUNE 19

☉
JUNE 28
JUNE 27

♀
JUNE 19
JUNE 18

♀
JUNE 10
JUNE 09

♂
JUNE 20
JUNE 19

☉						
JUNE 20	28° ♊ 54'	→	28° ♊ 54'	→	27° ♊ 114'	
JUNE 19	- 27° ♊ 57'		- 1° + 60'		- 27° ♊ 57'	
			27° ♊ 114'		0° **57'**	

☉						
JUNE 28	6° ♋ 32'	→	6° ♋ 32'	→	5° ♋ 92'	
JUNE 27	- 5° ♋ 34'		- 1° + 60'		- 5° ♋ 34'	
			5° ♋ 92'		0° **58'**	

♀						
JUNE 19	20° ♋ 3'	→	20° ♋ 3'	→	19° ♋ 63'	→	**1° 13'**
JUNE 18	- 18° ♋ 50'		- 1° + 60'		- 18° ♋ 50'		- 1° +60'
			19° ♋ 63'		1° 13'		0° **73'**

♀						
JUNE 10	9° ♋ 5'	→	9° ♋ 5'	→	8° ♋ 65'	→	**1° 13'**
JUNE 09	- 7° ♋ 52'		- 1° + 60'		- 7° ♋ 52'		- 1° +60'
			8° ♋ 65'		1° 13'		0° **73'**

♂						
JUNE 20	5° ♌ 12'	→	5° ♌ 12'	→	4° ♌ 72'	
JUNE 19	- 4° ♌ 35'		- 1° + 60'		- 4° ♌ 35'	
			4° ♌ 72'		0° **37'**	

Now that you have a grasp of basic astrological subtraction and conversion, there are a few caveats that we must learn and address. The first has to do with planetary positions that are on the cusp, which means the planet is transitioning from one sign to the next. For example, let us look at the Sun's placement on June 22, 2021 and June 21, 2021.

☉	
JUNE 22	0° ♋ 48'
JUNE 21	- 29° ♊ 51'

Just as it was with our previous examples, you should never have a negative number when working with astrology. Same as before, the minutes will need to be converted so we can prevent a negative number, but the degrees as well need to be addressed because we cannot subtract 0 from 29. Just as before, we need to carry over and convert from the next higher value which would be 1 Sign (1 Sign = 30°). What that means is if we subtract one sign, we can add 30 degrees.

```
        ☉
JUNE 22     0° ♋ 48'   →   0° ♋ 48'   →   30° ♊ 48'
JUNE 21   - 29° ♊ 51'     +30° -1         - 29° ♊ 51'
                           30° ♊
```

Now, the degrees will subtract the correct way because we will now get a positive number. However, the minutes are still going to produce a negative number which means we must yet again convert and carry over 1 degree into 60 minutes as we have been doing in the previous examples.

```
        ☉
JUNE 22     0° ♋  48'   →   0° ♋ 48'   →   30° ♊ 48'   →   30° ♊    48'   →   29° ♊ 108'
JUNE 21   - 29° ♊ 51'     + 30° -1         - 29° ♊ 51'       - 1°   + 60'       - 29° ♊  51'
                           30° ♊                           29° ♊  108'              57'
```

I should note by now that at times, this can seem incredibly time consuming, but the more you work through this, the less you will have to set up each equation step by step by hand and will be able to visualize the conversion mentally and with a calculator. You will inevitably speed up the process when this happens. In the meantime, let us once again do some practice examples.

```
        ♀
JUNE 03
JUNE 02
```

```
        ♀
JUNE 28
JUNE 27
```

```
        ♂
JUNE 12
JUNE 11
```

♀						
JUNE 03 0° ♋ 33'	→	0° ♋ 33'	→	30° ♊ 33'	→	1° 14'
JUNE 02 - 29° ♊ 19'		+30° -1		- 29° ♊ 19'		- 1° + 60'
		30° ♊		**1° 14'**		0° **74'**

♀						
JUNE 28 0° ♌ 59'	→	0° ♌ 59'	→	30° ♋ 59'	→	1° 12'
JUNE 27 - 29° ♋ 47'		+30° -1		- 29° ♋ 47'		- 1° + 60'
		30° ♋		**1° 12'**		0° **72'**

♂								
JUNE 12 0° ♌ 16'	→	0° ♌ 16'	→	30° ♋ 16'	→	30° ♋ 16'	→	29° ♋ 76'
JUNE 11 29° ♋ 39'		+30° -1		- 29° ♋ 39'		- 1° + 60'		- 29° ♋ 39'
		30° ♋				29° ♋ 76'		0° **37'**

The final exception you will need to be aware of involves computing for retrograde planets. If you recall, when we set up astrological equations, we place the higher value on top of the lower value. The higher value is the planetary point that is located further along the zodiac. This is why equations are typically formatted with the later date on top of the earlier date because, logically, the planet travels further along the zodiac when the planet is in direct motion. However, when the planet is in retrograde motion, it is moving backwards through the zodiac instead of forward. This means that the earlier date will have the higher value rather than the later date. All this means is when we set up equations for planets in retrograde, we switch the date order to prevent a negative number from occurring.

For example, look at Mercury in the ephemeris above for June 2021. Let us set up the equation as we have been doing for June 6 and 7 with the later date on top and the earlier date on the bottom.

☿ (Rx)
JUNE 7   22° ♊ 32'
JUNE 6 - 23° ♊ 00'

If we were to solve this equation, we would end up with a negative number which means we cannot use this set up. Instead, we need to flip the order of the equation so that we may get a positive number. When the equation is set up this way, we can then solve the way we have been doing.

☿ (Rx)				
JUNE 6 23° ♊ 00'	→	23° ♊ 00'	→	22° ♊ 60'
JUNE 7 - 22° ♊ 32'		-1° + 60'		- 22° ♊ 32'
		22° ♊ 60'		**28'**

This is the last exception you will find within astrological math. For good measure, complete the problems below.

☉
JUNE 30
JUNE 29

♀
JUNE 15
JUNE 14

♂
JUNE 26
JUNE 25

☿ (Rx)
JUNE 17
JUNE 18

♀
0° ♈ 30'
- 29° ♓ 16'

☿
0° ♈ 5'
- 28° ♓ 46'

☿
16° ♓ 13'
- 14° ♓ 38'

CHALLANGE ☽

  13° ♎ 14'

- 29° ♍ 4'

☉

JUNE 30   8° ♋ 26'   →   8° ♋ 26'   →   7° ♋ 86'

JUNE 29 - 7° ♋ 29'   -1° +60'   - 7° ♋ 29'

                              7° ♋ 86'   **57'**

♀

JUNE 15   15° ♋ 11'   →   15° ♋ 11'   →   14° ♋ 71'   →   **1° 13'**

JUNE 14 - 13° ♋ 58'   -1° +60'   - 13° ♋ 58'   -1°+60'

                              14° ♋ 71'   **1° 13'**   **73'**

♂

JUNE 26   8° ♌ 55'

JUNE 25 - 8° ♌ 18'

            37'

☿ (Rx)

JUNE 17   17° ♌ 22'

JUNE 18 - 17° ♌ 00'

            22'

♀

   0° ♈ 30'   →   0° ♈ 30'   →   30° ♓ 30'   →   **1° 14'**

- 29° ♓ 16'   +30°-1   - 29° ♓ 16'   - 1° +60'

                    30° ♓   **1° 14'**   **74'**

☿

   0° ♈ 5'   →   0° ♈ 30'   →   30° ♓ 5'   →   30° ♓ 5'   →   29° ♓ 65'   →   **1° 19'**

- 28° ♓ 46'   +30°-1   - 28° ♓ 46'   - 1° +60'   - 28° ♓ 46'   - 1° +60'

                  30° ♓   29° ♓ 65'   **1° 19'**   **79'**

☿

  16° ♓ 13'   →   16° ♓ 13'   →   15° ♓ 73'   →   **1° 35'**

- 14° ♓ 38   -1° +60'   - 14° ♓ 38'   - 1° +60'

                    15° ♓ 73'   **1° 35'**   **95'**

CHALLANGE ☽

13° ♏ 14'	13° ♎ 14'	→	43° ♏ 14'	→	14° 10'
- 29° ♏ 4'	+30° -1		- 29° ♏ 4'		- 14° +840' (14x60=840)
	43° ♏		14° 10'		850'

By this point, you are now prepared to encounter any type of astrological computation that will occur while you are calculating transits. In the next section, we will put theory into practice and determine where our aspect points are located along the zodiac, and the subsequent conversion of zodiacal data into time data.

SECTION 3-CALCULATING TRANSITS

☙

If you have yet to obtain an ephemeris, you can get one for free at Astro.com (Table IV-3). For the sake of consistency, I will be assuming that you will be working with a Midnight UT (00:00) standard ephemeris. However, if you look at the table below, there is an extra step where you can obtain an ephemeris set to your exact location. This will eliminate a few steps along the way and when that occurs, I will notify you.

Another point to consider deals with the fact that astrology works within the 24-hour clock system (military time) as opposed to the 12-hour clock system (civilian time). Reference the table

TABLE IV-3. How to Obtain an Ephemeris on Astro.com

(1)	Go to astro.com and click on the HOROSCOPES tab and under DRAWINGS, CALCULATIONS, DATA select CREATE AN EPHEMERIS
(2)	Under PLEASE SELECT choose EPHEMERIS FOR A YEAR, PDF and type a year under START DATE.
(3)	Click CLICK HERE TO SHOW EPHEMERIS and confirm that 00:00 UT is located in the upper right-hand corner.
(4)	**TO GET A CUSTOMIZED EPHEMERIS** on the ephemeris settings page under DEFAULT SETTINGS click MODIFY DATA for reference place.
(5)	Type in your location and click CONTINUE.
(6)	It will send you back to the ephemeris settings page. Once again, click CLICK HERE TO SHOW EPHEMERIS.
(7)	You can confirm that the ephemeris has been adjusted by looking at the upper right-hand corner and observe the time conversion, and by also seeing the name of your city at the top of every page.

below if you need help working within the 24-clock system (Table IV-4). You also want to make sure you have a few other supplies such as a ruler, note cards, graph paper, pencils, and a calculator.

TABLE IV-4. Conversion from 12-Hr to 24-Hr Clock Systems

12-HR DAY	24-HR DAY	12-HR NIGHT	24-HR NIGHT
12:00 AM	00:00	12:00 PM	12:00
1:00 AM	01:00	1:00 PM	13:00
2:00 AM	02:00	2:00 PM	14:00
3:00 AM	03:00	3:00 PM	15:00
4:00 AM	04:00	4:00 PM	16:00
5:00 AM	05:00	5:00 PM	17:00
6:00 AM	06:00	6:00 PM	18:00
7:00 AM	07:00	7:00 PM	19:00
8:00 AM	08:00	8:00 PM	20:00
9:00 AM	09:00	9:00 PM	21:00
10:00 AM	10:00	10:00 PM	22:00
11:00 AM	11:00	11:00 PM	23:00

As we have been discussing, transits only occur when a planet currently in motion within the zodiac makes an aspect to one of your fixed natal points. These fixed natal points include the ten planets along with your Ascendant and Midheaven points equating to a total of twelve specific objects that a transiting planet can aspect while moving along the sky.

In addition to determining the various aspect locations for the twelve natal points, we also need to keep track of the moments when a transiting planet ingresses (or enters) into a house within our chart.

Every physical house has a door that must be crossed before one can enter. The same is true for the houses within the natal chart, and when a planet enters a certain house, they activate themes related to that house for their entire journey.

Keep in mind that because of the slower movement of the outer planets, when they ingress from house to house, these are just as significant as an outer planetary transit, which is why it is important to keep track of them because they indicate significant life events for the individual. We monitor ingresses by determining what location around the zodiac the various house "doorways" are located. That way, when a planet crosses that door, we know they have entered a new house and consequently activated new energies.

If you were to look at your natal chart from Astro.com, on the lower left-hand corner next to the aspectarian, you will notice a print out of all of your planetary locations along with house placements on the bottom (Fig IV-3).

Below, you will find a sheet titled "Transit Points Reference Sheet" with a table titled "Houses (Ingresses)" (Fig IV-4).

We are now going to use the information provided in the birth chart to fill out this table by imputing the data from FIG. IV-3. into FIG. IV-4 (FIG. IV-5A).

| AC: 9 Vir 2'38" | 2: 4 Lib 40' | 3: 4 Sco 25' |
| MC: 6 Gem 56'33" | 11: 9 Can 47' | 12: 10 Leo 48' |

FIGURE IV-3. House Data from a Natal Chart

HOUSES (INGRESSES)			
ASC/1		DSC/7	
2		8	
3		9	
IC/4		MC/10	
5		11	
6		12	

FIGURE IV-4. From Transit Points Reference Sheet

HOUSES (INGRESSES)			
ASC/1	9° ♍ 2'	DSC/7	
2	4° ♎ 40'	8	
3	4° ♏ 25'	9	
IC/4		MC/10	6° ♊ 56'
5		11	9° ♋ 47'
6		12	10° ♌ 48'

FIGURE IV-5A. Imputing of Data from Natal Chart into the Reference Sheet.

287

You will notice that we only have half of the information from the birth chart, but this is because house doorways for the opposite house are merely the same point but the opposite sign. In other words, opposite houses are exactly 180° apart from one another. This means in order to complete the rest of the table, simply copy the exact number and apply the opposite sign. If you do not know what the opposite sign is, refer to Table IV-5 or the Cheat Sheet at the start of the book (FIG. IV-5B).

Now that we have our twelve doorways that will indicate planetary ingresses for each of our twelve houses, we need to now figure out the various aspect points for each natal point.

Recall from Part II-Section 5, Planets can make five major aspects with one another. These are the conjunction, sextile, square, trine, and opposition. Similarly, from Part III-Section 1, we discussed that aspects form an eight-stage cycle with opening and closing aspects. Having said that, there are eight points along the zodiac where a transiting planet can make an aspect to a natal point (Fig. IV-6, p.290).

In the example shown in Fig. IV-6, we are observing transiting Sun interacting with the fixed natal Sun. Remember, transiting planets are constantly moving, and natal points are fixed and never move. Nevertheless, there are eight exact moments along the zodiac where aspects occur.

As you can see from this figure, there contains one conjunction, one opposition, two sextiles, two squares, and two trines equating to the eight points where a transiting planet can interact with a natal point. These eight points correspond to eight signs within the zodiac which depend on the sign in which the natal point is located.

HOUSES (INGRESSES)			
ASC/1	9° ♍ 2'	DSC/7	9° ♓ 2'
2	4° ♎ 40'	8	4° ♈ 40'
3	4° ♏ 25'	9	4° ♉ 25'
IC/4	6° ♐ 56'	MC/10	6° ♊ 56'
5	9° ♑ 47'	11	9° ♋ 47'
6	10° ♒ 48'	12	10° ♌ 48'

FIGURE IV-5B. Filling out Opposite Houses into Reference Sheet.

288

TABLE IV-5. Aspect Patterns by Sign Relative to the Fixed Natal Point

FIXED NATAL POINT	CONJUNCTION ♂	SEXTILE ✶	SQUARE □	TRINE △	OPPOSITION ☍
♈	♈	♒ ♎	♑ ♋	♐ ♌	♎
♉	♉	♓ ♏	♒ ♌	♑ ♍	♏
♊	♊	♈ ♐	♓ ♍	♒ ♎	♐
♋	♋	♉ ♑	♈ ♎	♓ ♏	♑
♌	♌	♊ ♒	♉ ♏	♈ ♐	♒
♍	♍	♋ ♓	♊ ♐	♉ ♑	♓
♎	♎	♌ ♈	♋ ♑	♊ ♒	♈
♏	♏	♍ ♉	♌ ♒	♋ ♓	♉
♐	♐	♎ ♊	♍ ♓	♌ ♈	♊
♑	♑	♏ ♋	♎ ♈	♍ ♉	♋
♒	♒	♐ ♌	♏ ♉	♎ ♊	♌
♓	♓	♑ ♍	♐ ♊	♏ ♋	♍

In order to determine where these aspects occur, we need to recall which signs create which aspects to other signs. The answer to this question is located within the cheat sheet at the start of this book and the table above (Table IV-5).

Now, all that is left to do is to apply our natal data to the table above in order to determine where transiting planets will make aspects to our natal points. To do this, refer back to your natal chart from Astro.com, and observe the planetary data located above your house placement data (Fig. IV-7, p.290).

Just as we have filled out the house information on our transit point reference sheet, we are now going to fill out the natal points using the planetary data in Fig. IV-7 using the various sign combinations from Table IV-5.

To start, let us look at Table IV-7 for the Sun and insert our fixed natal Sun position 13° ♒ 45'. Remember, transits are precise aspect hits which equate to precise moments in time. Due to this fact, regardless of the aspect being made, they will always occur at the same degree and minute value as the fixed natal point; the only thing that will change is the sign. Having said that, the first step is to simply copy the fixed natal point's degree and minute into each box.

289

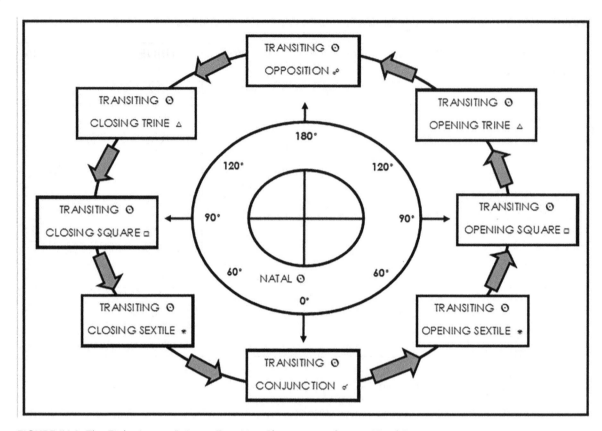

FIGURE IV-6. The Eight Aspect Points a Transiting Planet can make to a Natal Point

☉ Sun	13 Aqu 45' 9"
☽ Moon	14 Ari 5'57"
☿ Mercury	28 Aqu 25'18"
♀ Venus	27 Sag 47'46"
♂ Mars	17 Ari 53'16"
♃ Jupiter	23 Pis 44'40"
♄ Saturn	18 Sag 40'19"
♅ Uranus	25 Sag 21'42"
♆ Neptune	6 Cap 51'59"
♇ Pluto	9 Sco 57'12"

FIGURE IV-7. Planetary Data from a birth chart on Astro.Com

290

SUN ☉ = 13° ♒ 45'		
♂		
✶		
□		
△		
☍		

→

SUN ☉ = 13° ♒ 45'		
♂	13° 45'	
✶	13° 45'	13° 45'
□	13° 45'	13° 45'
△	13° 45'	13° 45'
☍	13° 45'	

Once that is complete, all that is left to do is to refer to the information in Table IV-5 and place in the appropriate corresponding sign(s) that will make the appropriate aspects to the natal position. In this example, I will be following the Aquarius (♒) row because the fixed natal Sun is located in Aquarius.

SUN ☉ = 13° ♒ 45'		
♂	13° ♒ 45'	
✶	13° ♈ 45'	13° ♐ 45'
□	13° ♉ 45'	13° ♏ 45'
△	13° ♊ 45'	13° ♎ 45'
☍	13° ♌ 45'	

On the next page, you will find blank tables for you to add your own personal house ingress points along with the aspect points for the twelve natal positions that we will monitor. For reference, the subsequent page is filled out using the data in Fig. IV-5B and IV-7 above so that you can observe what a complete reference sheet is supposed to look like.

Before you can proceed, take this time to determine all these data points within your personal natal chart. I would also recommend placing the data onto individual notecards because you can then use the notecard to go down the ephemeris one column at a time when you are trying to locate transits. This expediates the process.

TRANSIT POINTS REFERENCE SHEET

HOUSES (INGRESSES)			
ASC/1		DSC/7	
2		8	
3		9	
IC/4		MC/10	
5		11	
6		12	

SUN ☉ = _____

♂		
✱		
□		
△		
☍		

MOON ☽ = _____

♂		
✱		
□		
△		
☍		

MERCURY ☿ = _____

♂		
✱		
□		
△		
☍		

VENUS ♀ = _____

♂		
✱		
□		
△		
☍		

MARS ♂ = _____

♂		
✱		
□		
△		
☍		

JUPITER ♃ = _____

♂		
✱		
□		
△		
☍		

SATURN ♄ = _____

♂		
✱		
□		
△		
☍		

URANUS ♅ = _____

♂		
✱		
□		
△		
☍		

NEPTUNE ♆ = _____

♂		
✱		
□		
△		
☍		

PLUTO ♇ = _____

♂		
✱		
□		
△		
☍		

ASC= _____

♂		
✱		
□		
△		
☍		

MC= _____

♂		
✱		
□		
△		
☍		

TRANSIT POINTS REFERENCE SHEET

HOUSES (INGRESSES)			
ASC/1	9° ♍ 2′	**DSC/7**	9° ♓ 2′
2	4° ♎ 40′	**8**	4° ♈ 40′
3	4° ♏ 25′	**9**	4° ♉ 25′
IC/4	6° ♐ 56′	**MC/10**	6° ♊ 56′
5	9° ♑ 47′	**11**	9° ♋ 47′
6	10° ♒ 48′	**12**	10° ♌ 48′

SUN ☉ = 13° ♒ 45′		
☌	13° ♒ 45′	
⚹	13° ♈ 45′	13° ♐ 45′
□	13° ♉ 45′	13° ♏ 45′
△	13° ♊ 45′	13° ♎ 45′
☍	13° ♌ 45′	

MOON ☽ = 14° ♈ 5′		
☌	14° ♈ 5′	
⚹	14° ♊ 5′	14° ♒ 5′
□	14° ♋ 5′	14° ♑ 5′
△	14° ♌ 5′	14° ♐ 5′
☍	14° ♎ 5′	

MERCURY ☿ = 28° ♒ 25′		
☌	28° ♒ 25′	
⚹	28° ♈ 25′	28° ♐ 25′
□	28° ♉ 25′	28° ♏ 25′
△	28° ♊ 25′	28° ♎ 25′
☍	28° ♌ 25′	

VENUS ♀ = 27° ♐ 47′		
☌	27° ♐ 47′	
⚹	27° ♒ 47′	27° ♎ 47′
□	27° ♓ 47′	27° ♍ 47′
△	27° ♈ 47′	27° ♌ 47′
☍	27° ♊ 47′	

MARS ♂ = 17° ♈ 53′		
☌	17° ♈ 53′	
⚹	17° ♊ 53′	17° ♒ 53′
□	17° ♋ 53′	17° ♑ 53′
△	17° ♌ 53′	17° ♐ 53′
☍	17° ♎ 53′	

JUPITER ♃ = 23° ♓ 44′		
☌	23° ♓ 44′	
⚹	23° ♉ 44′	23° ♑ 44′
□	23° ♊ 44′	23° ♐ 44′
△	23° ♋ 44′	23° ♏ 44′
☍	23° ♍ 44′	

SATURN ♄ = 18° ♐ 40′		
☌	18° ♐ 40′	
⚹	18° ♒ 40′	18° ♎ 40′
□	18° ♓ 40′	18° ♍ 40′
△	18° ♈ 40′	18° ♌ 40′
☍	18° ♊ 40′	

URANUS ♅ = 25° ♐ 21′		
☌	25° ♐ 21′	
⚹	25° ♒ 21′	25° ♎ 21′
□	25° ♓ 21′	25° ♍ 21′
△	25° ♈ 21′	25° ♌ 21′
☍	25° ♊ 21′	

NEPTUNE ♆ = 6° ♑ 51′		
☌	6° ♑ 51′	
⚹	6° ♓ 51′	6° ♏ 51′
□	6° ♈ 51′	6° ♎ 51′
△	6° ♉ 51′	6° ♍ 51′
☍	6° ♋ 51′	

PLUTO ♇ = 9° ♏ 57′		
☌	9° ♏ 57′	
⚹	9° ♑ 57′	9° ♍ 57′
□	9° ♒ 57′	9° ♌ 57′
△	9° ♓ 57′	9° ♋ 57′
☍	9° ♉ 57′	

ASC = 9° ♍ 2′		
☌	9° ♍ 2′	
⚹	9° ♋ 2′	9° ♏ 2′
□	9° ♊ 2′	9° ♐ 2′
△	9° ♉ 2′	9° ♑ 2′
☍	9° ♓ 2′	

MC = 6° ♊ 56′		
☌	6° ♊ 56′	
⚹	6° ♌ 56′	6° ♈ 56′
□	6° ♍ 56′	6° ♓ 56′
△	6° ♎ 56′	6° ♒ 56′
☍	6° ♐ 56′	

It might be a bit daunting at first to realize that the reference sheet above indicates 108 various locations along the 360° wheel of the zodiac where transiting planets can interact with our natal chart. Indeed, this speaks volumes not only to the organically ceaseless interaction the planets create with our chart, but to the specialized moments at which these interactions occur because they are solely based upon the planetary and cardinal point locations during our specific moment and location of our birth.

To reiterate, determining these moments allows for you to empirically observe not only astrology as a science but astrology in action through your own individualized existence. With that, the final skill we need to learn is how to convert space into time. Namely, how to convert zodiacal locations into a precise moment in time.

Referring back to our example and the Ephemeris in Part IV-Section 1, let us once again review the Sun's journey along the zodiac from June 1 to June 2, 2021 (FIG. IV-8).

Now, let us say that my natal Sun is located at 11° Ⅱ 14′. This means that when the transiting Sun reaches 11° Ⅱ 14′, it will form a conjunction with my natal Sun. Observe the figure below for a visual representation (Fig. IV-9).

For a moment, I am going to take ourselves out of the example and point out the various data points we now have. (Fig. IV-10).

| _____ ☉_____ _____ |
| JUNE 02   11° Ⅱ 41′ |
| JUNE 01   - 10° Ⅱ 44′ |

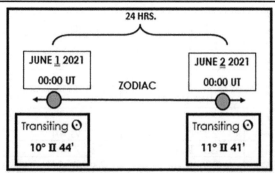

JUNE 2021		
Day	Sid.t	☉
T 1	16 38 47	10Ⅱ44'05
W 2	16 42 44	11°41'35

FIGURE IV-8. Summary of Previous Example from Part IV-Section 1

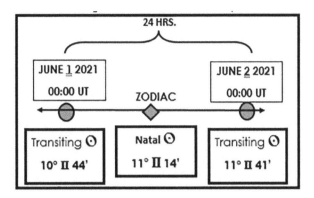

FIGURE IV-9. Natal Planet Added

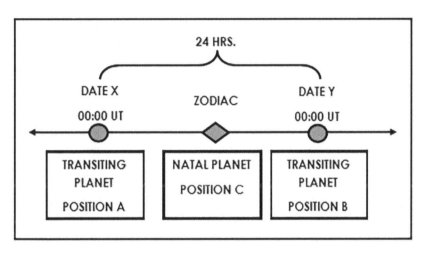

FIGURE IV-10. Mathematical Representation of the Transit Data Points

From this perspective, it appears that the transiting planet moves from Position A to Position B during a 24-hour period, from midnight to midnight. If we were to take the difference of these two positions (B-A) we would get the total distance that the planet has traveled for that 24-hour period. Recall from our example in Part IV-Section 2, we determined that the Sun moved a total of 57 minutes (57') form June 1 to June 2.

☉			
JUNE 02	11° ♊ 41' →	11° ♊ 41' →	10° ♊ 101'
JUNE 01	- <u>10° ♊ 44'</u>	<u>-1° +60'</u>	- <u>10° ♊ 44'</u>
		10° ♊ 101'	**57'**

Without even realizing it, you were essentially subtracting Point B from Point A (B-A) and in doing so, you calculated the Sun's total journey during that 24-hour period. In fact, in every math equation in Part IV-Section 2, you were practicing how to compute the total distance traveled (B-A) for each 24-hour period so by now you should feel very confident in figuring that part out.

However, knowing the total distance traveled by the transiting planet is literally only half of the equation. We need to also determine how much distance exists between the fixed natal point (Point C) to the starting point (Point A) (C-A). In other words, out of the entire length of travel during that 24-hour period (B-A), how much distance did the transiting planet travel before it made an exact connection to that natal planet along the way (C-A)?

I know this sounds a bit confusing so let us break it down a bit more. Let us pretend that my hypothetical fixed natal planet, located at Point C, is halfway between Point A and Point B. If Point C is halfway between Point A and Point B, then we can assume that the aspect occurred at noon (12:00) because 12:00 is the halfway point from midnight to midnight. This is because half, or 50% or 0.50 x 24 hours = 12:00 hours.

Another example, let us say that the hypothetical natal planet Point C is located one-quarter of the way through the total distance traveled during that 24-hour period. This means that the aspect occurred at 06:00 because 06:00 is one quarter of the way through a 24-hour period. This is because one-quarter, or 25%, or 0.25 x 24 hours = 06:00 hours.

By this logic, we can also assume when the aspect will take place if the natal planet Point C is located three-quarters (75% or 0.75) of the way through the 24-hour period. The answer would be 18:00 because 0.75 x 24 hours = 18:00 hours. Observe the figure below for a visual representation (Fig. IV-11).

This is all good in theory, but your natal planetary point (Point C) will rarely be conveniently located at exactly 1/2, 1/4, or 3/4 of the way through the 24-hour period. Nevertheless, Position C's location is still a fraction of the total distance traveled. That fraction can then tell us how much time has passed along the 24-hour period. This fraction is called the "Transit Constant" and the formula is as follows:

$$\text{Transit Constant} = \frac{\text{Distance Between Natal Point and Starting Point}}{\text{Total Distance Traveled}} = \frac{(C - A)}{(B - A)}$$

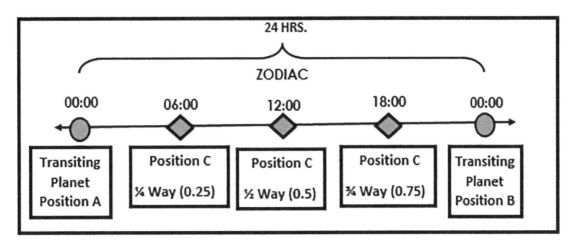

FIGURE IV-11. Visual Representation of Converting Distance into Time

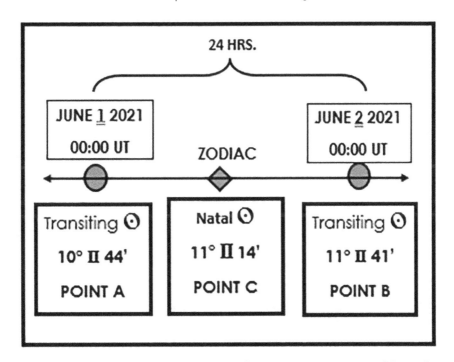

FIGURE IV-12. Determining the Transit Constant for Transiting Sun conj. Natal Sun in Gemini

To see this in action, let us once again revisit our example above with the transiting Sun in Gemini. All we need to do is simply plug in Points A, B, and C to the equation above (Fig. IV-12).

$$Transit\ Constant = \frac{(C-A)}{(B-A)} = \frac{(11°14' - 10°44')}{(11°41' - 10°44')} = \frac{(10°74' - 10°44')}{(10°101' - 10°44')} = \frac{30'}{57'} = 0.526$$

297

Before we explain how we utilize the transit constant, you will notice some shorthand techniques within the above equation that we must discuss. For one, the signs are now completely taken out of the equation for the sake of simplicity. Similarly, conversion equations are now assumed as you can see 11°14′ converted into 10°74′ and 11°41′ converted into 10°101′. Essentially I am still adding 60 minutes (60′) by removing 1 degree (1°) only the math for this step is now implied.

After we made all appropriate conversions so that we avoid a negative number, we determined that the Transit Constant = 0.526. What does this mean? It means that the transiting planet was 52.6% of the way through its entire journey during the 24-hour period at the moment it created an aspect with the natal planet.

By the same logic we have been using, this means we can expect to see the time of the aspect to occur roughly at 12:00 because 12:00 is halfway (50%/0.50) from midnight to midnight, and our natal Planet C is located at 52.6%/0.526 of the total distance traveled from midnight to midnight. In order to get the precise answer, we need to simply multiply the transit constant by 24-hours.

Time of Event = (Transit Constant x 24 hours) = (0.526 x 24 hours) = 12.624 hours.

As expected, when we multiply the Transit Constant of 0.526 by 24-hours, we get 12.624 hours where the whole number (12) indicates the hour during the day and the decimals (0.624) equates to the minutes within that hour which is the next step. In order to determine what the minutes are during that hour, simply multiply the decimal into 60 because there are 60 minutes in an hour:

0.624 x 60 minutes = 37 minutes.

Now, we can officially say that the event of transiting Sun in Gemini conjoining natal Sun in Gemini (t. ☉Ⅱ ☌ n. ☉Ⅱ) exactly occurs on June 1, 2021 at 12:37 UT. Do not get discouraged if you do not fully understand at this point. We will be performing numerous examples shortly to help solidify the methodology.

Before we get to those practice problems, there is one final step we need to perform: convert UT into our individual time zones (Table IV-6). If you have a personalized ephemeris, you can skip this step.

This table indicates how many hours you must subtract from the UT time depending on your time zone and whether or not it is Standard Time (SD) or Daylight-Saving Time (DST). For the sake of our example, let us say we are located in the Pacific time zone and it is currently standard time (PT). This means we need to subtract 8 hours (-08:00) from the UT time.

June 1, 2021 12:37 UT – 08:00 hours = June 1, 2021 04:37 PT

Now, this means that although the transit occurs at 12:37 UT, it will hit me at my current location at 04:37 Local Time (LT) because I reside within the Pacific time zone. Before we begin to engage with more practice, the entire process has been summarized in the table below (Table IV-7).

TABLE IV-6. Time Zone Conversions for Unites States.

TIME ZONE	STANDARD TIME (ST)	DAYLIGHT SAVING TIME (DST)
PACIFIC	-08:00 PT	-07:00 PDT
MOUNTAIN	-07:00 MT	-06:00 MDT
CENTRAL	-06:00 CT	-05:00 CDT
EASTERN	-05:00 ET	-04:00 EDT

TABLE IV-7. Steps to Calculate the Time of a Transit.

STEP #	DESCRIPTION	EQUATIONS/MATERIALS USED
1	Determine the event and which transit point will cause the event (Point C).	Compare the points on the Transit Point Reference Sheet (Point C) to the Planetary movements within the ephemeris (Points A and B).
2	Write down the dates and locations for the appropriate 24-hour window (Points A and B).	Ephemeris
3	Set up the Transit Constant Equation and solve being mindful of converting when necessary.	$Transit\ Constant = \dfrac{(C - A)}{(B - A)}$
4	Multiply the Transit Constant by 24 hours to determine the hour in which the event occurred.	Transit Constant x 24 hours = 00.00 where 00.= hours and .00=minutes
5	Take the decimals from the previous answer and times by 60 to determine the minutes in which the event occurred.	.00 x 60 minutes = minutes
6	Combine Steps 4 and 5 to get hour and minutes of the event in UT.	00:00 UT
7	Subtract the answer from Step 6 by your relative time zone. (Ignore this step if you have a personalized ephemeris set to your location.)	00:00 UT – Your Time Zone = Time event will occur where you live.

FIGURE IV-13. Midnight Ephemeris for October 2021

OCTOBER 2021

Day	Sid.t	☉	☽	☿	♀	♂	♃	♄	♅	♆	♇
F 1	0 39 47	8♎ 2'06	29♋32	24°R37	22♏51	10♎24	22°R49	6°R58	14°R 6	21°R20	24°R19
S 2	0 43 44	9° 1'06	12♌11	24♎ 6	23°58	11° 3	22≈46	6≈57	14♉ 4	21♓19	24♑19
S 3	0 47 40	10° 0'09	25°13	23°27	25° 4	11°42	22°43	6°56	14° 3	21°17	24°19
M 4	0 51 37	10°59'14	8♍40	22°40	26°11	12°22	22°40	6°55	14° 1	21°15	24°19
T 5	0 55 33	11°58'21	22°32	21°47	27°17	13° 1	22°37	6°55	13°59	21°14	24°19
W 6	0 59 30	12°57'31	6♎45	20°47	28°23	13°40	22°35	6°54	13°57	21°12	24°19
T 7	1 3 26	13°56'42	21°14	19°43	29°29	14°20	22°32	6°54	13°55	21°11	24°D19
F 8	1 7 23	14°55'56	5♏54	18°34	0♐35	14°59	22°30	6°53	13°53	21° 9	24°19
S 9	1 11 20	15°55'11	20°36	17°24	1°40	15°39	22°28	6°53	13°50	21° 8	24°19
S 10	1 15 16	16°54'28	5♐14	16°13	2°46	16°18	22°27	6°53	13°48	21° 7	24°19
M 11	1 19 13	17°53'47	19°43	15° 4	3°51	16°58	22°25	6°D53	13°46	21° 5	24°19
T 12	1 23 9	18°53'08	4♑ 0	13°58	4°56	17°37	22°24	6°53	13°44	21° 4	24°19
W 13	1 27 6	19°52'31	18° 2	12°58	6° 1	18°17	22°23	6°53	13°42	21° 2	24°19
T 14	1 31 2	20°51'55	1≈50	12° 5	7° 5	18°57	22°22	6°53	13°40	21° 1	24°20
F 15	1 34 59	21°51'22	15°23	11°21	8°10	19°36	22°21	6°53	13°37	20°59	24°20
S 16	1 38 55	22°50'49	28°42	10°46	9°14	20°16	22°20	6°54	13°35	20°58	24°20
S 17	1 42 52	23°50'19	11♓48	10°23	10°18	20°56	22°20	6°54	13°33	20°57	24°20
M 18	1 46 49	24°49'50	24°40	10°10	11°21	21°36	22°D20	6°55	13°31	20°55	24°21
T 19	1 50 45	25°49'23	7♈19	10°D 8	12°25	22°16	22°20	6°56	13°28	20°54	24°21
W 20	1 54 42	26°48'58	19°47	10°18	13°28	22°55	22°20	6°57	13°26	20°53	24°21
T 21	1 58 38	27°48'35	2♉ 2	10°38	14°31	23°35	22°21	6°58	13°24	20°52	24°22
F 22	2 2 35	28°48'14	14° 8	11° 8	15°33	24°15	22°21	6°59	13°21	20°50	24°22
S 23	2 6 31	29°47'56	26° 4	11°47	16°36	24°55	22°22	7° 0	13°19	20°49	24°23
S 24	2 10 28	0♏47'39	7♊54	12°35	17°38	25°35	22°23	7° 1	13°16	20°48	24°23
M 25	2 14 24	1°47'25	19°41	13°30	18°39	26°15	22°24	7° 2	13°14	20°47	24°24
T 26	2 18 21	2°47'12	1♋29	14°32	19°41	26°55	22°26	7° 4	13°12	20°46	24°24
W 27	2 22 18	3°47'02	13°21	15°40	20°42	27°35	22°27	7° 5	13° 9	20°45	24°25
T 28	2 26 14	4°46'54	25°22	16°53	21°43	28°16	22°29	7° 7	13° 7	20°44	24°26
F 29	2 30 11	5°46'48	7♌38	18°10	22°43	28°56	22°31	7° 9	13° 4	20°43	24°26
S 30	2 34 7	6°46'45	20°13	19°32	23°43	29°36	22°34	7°11	13° 2	20°41	24°27
S 31	2 38 4	7♏46'43	3♍12	20♎56	24♐42	0♏16	22≈36	7≈13	12♉59	20♓40	24♑28

Let us review these steps several times in order to make sure we have it down. For the sake of practice, we are going to use the completed Transit Point Reference Sheet above and determine planetary ingresses and transits for the natal Sun during October 2021 (Fig. IV-13).

PART I: DETERMINE INGRESSES

The first transiting events we want to obtain are the planetary ingresses. This will require our ingress chart located on our reference sheet (see below). Then, we will go down each planetary column within the ephemeris to determine if any planet ingresses into a house.

HOUSES (INGRESSES)			
ASC/1	9° ♍ 2′	DSC/7	9° ♓ 2′
2	4° ♎ 40′	8	4° ♈ 40′
3	4° ♏ 25′	9	4° ♉ 25′
IC/4	6° ♐ 56′	MC/10	6° ♊ 56′
5	9° ♑ 47′	11	9° ♋ 47′
6	10° ♒ 48′	12	10° ♌ 48′

Let us start by going down the Sun (☉) column. On October 1, the Sun is located at 8° ♎ 2′. This means the Sun is currently in the 2nd house because the doorway for the 2nd house is 4° ♎ 40′ which comes before the Sun's location of 8° ♎ 2′. This means that the Sun will continue to reside in the 2nd house until it passes the 3rd house doorway at 4° ♏ 25′.

This is my Point C. Continue to go down the Sun column and determine if the Sun intersects at 4° ♏ 25′, which means it would have entered the 3rd house.

Indeed, the Sun does pass this point between October 27 and 28 because the Sun travels from 3° ♏ 47′ to 4° ♏ 46′. Now we have our Points A and B. Let us take this time to transition into the various steps in Table IV-7 to make sure we are doing everything correctly.

STEP #	DESCRIPTION	STEP PERFORMED
1	Determine the event and which transit point will cause the event (Point C).	**EVENT:** Transiting Sun ingresses into the 3rd house (t. ☉ → 3rd) **POINT C:** 4° ♏ 25′ (3rd House Doorway)
2	Write down the dates and locations for the appropriate 24-hour window (Points A and B).	**POINT B:** OCT 28 4° ♏ 46′ **POINT A:** OCT 27 3° ♏ 47′
3	Set up the Transit Constant Equation and solve being mindful of converting when necessary.	$Transit\ Constant = \dfrac{(C-A)}{(B-A)} = \dfrac{(4°25' - 3°47')}{(4°46' - 3°47')}$ $= \dfrac{(3°85' - 3°47')}{(3°106' - 3°47')}$ $= \dfrac{38'}{59'} = 0.644$
4	Multiply the Transit Constant by 24 hours to determine the hour in which the event occurred.	0.644 x 24 hours = 15.46
5	Take the decimals from the previous answer and times by 60 to determine the minutes in which the event occurred.	.46 x 60 minutes = 28 minutes
6	Combine Steps 4 and 5 to get hour and minutes of event in UT.	Oct 27 15:28 UT
7	Subtract the answer from Step 6 by your relative time zone.	15:28 UT – 08:00 hours (PT) = **Oct 27, 2021 07:28 Local Time**

Excellent! We have computed our first transit event when the transiting Sun enters the 3rd house (t. ☉ → 3rd) on Oct 27, 2021 07:28 Local Time. All that is left to do is to put that event into a personal date planner so we are now aware of it.

Although we have examined the transiting Sun all the way down through October 2021, there are still nine more planets we need to observe. Next, we move on to Mercury (☿). Mercury starts the month in retrograde because there is an R on the Oct 1 point which reads 24° ♎ 37′. If we examine our ingress points back on the reference sheet, we see that Mercury is currently in the 2nd house because 24° ♎ 37′ comes after the 2nd house doorway (4° ♎ 40′) and before the 3rd doorway (4° ♏ 25′). Even if a planet is moving backwards, it can still reverse back into a house. If Mercury were to do this, it would have to cross 4° ♎ 40′ while in retrograde in order to regress back into the 1st house. However, as we go down the Mercury column, the furthest back he travels is 10° ♎ 8′ on Oct 19, which means Mercury stays in the 2nd house for the entire month and does not ingress or regress into another house.

We now repeat the process again by going down the Venus (♀) column. Venus starts the month at 22° ♏ 51′ which means she is currently in the 3rd house because 22° ♏ 51′ is located after the 3rd house doorway of 4° ♏ 25′ and before the 4th house doorway of 6° ♐ 56′. However, this means that if Venus intersects at 6° ♐ 56′, then she will have ingressed into the 4th house as this is the doorway for the 4th house. Going down the Venus column, look to see if Venus crosses that point.

Indeed, Venus does cross this point between Oct 13 and 14 because the 4th house doorway point (6° ♐ 56′) lies between Venus' location on Oct 13 (6° ♐ 1′) and Oct 14 (7° ♐ 5′). Again, let us use the step-by-step table to make sure we complete all of the steps correctly (see p. 303).

Let us continue onto Mars (♂) located at 10° ♎ 24′ at the start of October. Again, we have a planet currently located in the 2nd house because Mars' position at 10° ♎ 24′ comes after the 2nd house doorway at 4° ♎ 40′ and before the 3rd house doorway at 4° ♏ 25′. This would mean that if Mars were to ingress during this month, he would have to cross the 3rd house doorway at 4° ♏ 25′ and if he were to do so, this would be our Point C.

However, Mars ends October at 0° ♏ 16′ which means we can logically deduce that Mars will ingress into the 3rd house in early to mid-November because Mars will be starting November at 0° ♏ 16′ and the 3rd house doorway is close in proximity, being located at 4° ♏ 25′.

302

STEP #	DESCRIPTION	STEP PERFORMED
1	Determine the event and which transit point will cause the event (Point C).	**EVENT:** Transiting Venus ingresses into the 4th house (t. ♀ →4TH) **POINT C:** 6° ♐ 56'(4th House Doorway)
2	Write down the dates and locations for the appropriate 24-hour window (Points A and B).	**POINT B:** OCT 14 7° ♐ 5' **POINT A:** OCT 13 6° ♐ 1'
3	Set up the Transit Constant Equation and solve being mindful of converting when necessary.	$Transit\ Constant = \dfrac{(C-A)}{(B-A)} = \dfrac{(6°56' - 6°1')}{(7°5' - 6°1')}$ $= \dfrac{(6°56' - 6°1')}{(6°65' - 6°1')}$ $= \dfrac{55'}{64'} = 0.859$
4	Multiply the Transit Constant by 24 hours to determine the hour in which the event occurred.	0.859 x 24 hours = 20.616
5	Take the decimals from the previous answer and times by 60 to determine the minutes in which the event occurred.	.616 x 60 minutes = 37 minutes
6	Combine Steps 4 and 5 to get hour and minutes of event in UT.	Oct 13 20:37 UT
7	Subtract the answer from Step 6 by your relative time zone.	20:37 UT – 08:00 hours (PT) = **Oct 13, 2021 12:37 Local Time**

Jupiter (♃) is in retrograde at 22° ♒ 49' which means he is currently in the 6th house because the 6th house doorway is 10° ♒ 48'. If Jupiter were to regress back into the 5th house via the 6th house doorway, he would have to reach this point sometime during the month. Jupiter, being in a stationary period for the entire month, does not budge from his position and therefore does not ingress or regress.

Saturn (♄) is in Retrograde at 6° ♒ 58' meaning he is currently in the 5th house because the 6th house doorway is 10° ♒ 48' and the 5th house doorway is 9° ♑ 47'. Needless to say, Saturn is not moving from the 5th house anytime soon, so we move on.

Neptune (♆) is located at 21° ♓ 20' which means he is currently in the 7th house and does not move that far from his starting point which keeps him within the 7th house because the 7th house doorway is 9° ♓ 2' and the 8th house doorway is 4° ♈ 40'.

Finally, Pluto (♇) is in the 5th house at 24° ♑ 19' because the 5th house doorway is 9° ♑ 47' and the 6th house doorway is located at 10° ♒ 48'. Pluto, similarly, does not move substantially enough to ingress or regress into another house and stays in the 5th house for the entire month.

Now having gone through the column of each transiting Planet, I was able to determine that I would encounter two separate ingresses. Transiting Sun will ingress into the 3rd house (t. ☉ → 3rd) precisely on Oct 27, 2021 07:28 Local Time, and transiting Venus will ingress into the 4th house (t. ♀ →4TH) on Oct 13, 2021 12:37 Local Time. Remember, these are events that most people will encounter throughout a year, but these events will only happen to this individual at those precise moments.

Now, it is your turn to take your ingress doorways and determine what your ingresses are going to be for the current or the upcoming month. Once you have figured out your ingresses, you can then move on to transiting aspects, which we will cover next.

Part II: Determine Planetary Transits

Now that we have discovered the ingresses for October 2021, it is time to move on to the transit aspects. Just as we went down each column for each planet within the ephemeris for the ingress doorways, we will now repeat this process for the natal Sun. Normally, each twelve of the fixed natal points found on the Transit Point Reference Sheet would be observed, but we will only be observing the natal Sun within this book for the sake of brevity. For our examples, we will be continuing to use the October 2021 ephemeris and the data found on the completed reference sheet.

By looking at the natal Sun on the reference sheet, I know that if any transiting planet hits any of these points, then an aspect occurs at a precise moment that we need to compute.

SUN ☉ = 13° ♒ 45'		
♂	13° ♒ 45'	
✳	13° ♈ 45'	13° ♐ 45'
□	13° ♉ 45'	13° ♏ 45'
△	13° ♊ 45'	13° ♎ 45'
☍	13° ♌ 45'	

304

Again, starting with transiting Sun, I will begin to go down the column and see if any of these points are intersected. At the start of the month, I notice that the Sun starts at 8° ♎ 2′. When I look at my data, I see that the point 13° ♎ 45′ is valid as it produces a trine with the natal Sun (t. ☉♎ Δ n. ☉♒) which could happen during this month.

Continuing down the transiting Sun column, I see that transiting Sun does indeed intersect at this point between Oct 6 and Oct 7. All I need to do now is to plug in the information as before and I will have the time that this transit will occur.

STEP #	DESCRIPTION	STEP PERFORMED
1	Determine the event and which transit point will cause the event (Point C).	**EVENT:** Transiting Sun in Libra trines Natal Sun in Aquarius (t. ☉♎ Δ n. ☉♒) **POINT C:** 13° ♎ 45′ (Libra Trine Point)
2	Write down the dates and locations for the appropriate 24-hour window (Points A and B).	**POINT B:** OCT 7 13° ♎ 56′ **POINT A:** OCT 6 12° ♎ 57′
3	Set up the Transit Constant Equation and solve being mindful of converting when necessary.	$Transit\ Constant = \dfrac{(C-A)}{(B-A)} = \dfrac{(13°45' - 12°57')}{(13°56' - 12°57')}$ $= \dfrac{(12°105' - 12°57')}{(12°116' - 12°57')}$ $= \dfrac{(48')}{(59')} = 0.814$
4	Multiply the Transit Constant by 24 hours to determine the hour in which the event occurred.	0.814 x 24 hours = 19.54
5	Take the decimals from the previous answer and times by 60 to determine the minutes in which the event occurred.	.54 x 60 minutes = 32 minutes
6	Combine Steps 4 and 5 to get hour and minutes of event in UT.	Oct 6 19:32 UT
7	Subtract the answer from Step 6 by your relative time zone.	19:32 UT – 08:00 hours (PT) = **Oct 6, 2021 11:32 Local Time**

Let us now continue onto transiting Mercury with the Natal Sun. Mercury is in retrograde and is located at 24° ♎ 37′. Just like the transiting Sun, if transiting Mercury were to make an aspect to the natal Sun, it would be a trine at the same location, 13° ♎ 45′. What is interesting is that Mercury will intersect that point between Oct 12 and Oct 13, but because Mercury is in retrograde, there are a few caveats to consider.

Recall in Part IV-Section 2, if planets are in retrograde, you need to reverse the dates so that you do not end up with a negative number. Similarly, the Transiting Constant also changes to accommodate for this fact:

$$Rx\ Transit\ Constant = \frac{(A - C)}{(A - B)}$$

Other than that, the steps are completely the same. Let us now calculate the moment when transiting Mercury Retrograde in Libra will trine the natal Sun in Aquarius (t. ☿R ♎ △ n. ☉♒).

STEP #	DESCRIPTION	STEP PERFORMED
1	Determine the event and which transit point will cause the event (Point C).	**EVENT:** Transiting Mercury Retrograde in Libra trine Natal Sun in Aquarius (t. ☿R ♎ △ n. ☉♒). 2ND RX EVENT OUT OF 3. **POINT C:** 13° ♎ 45' (Libra Trine Point)
2	Write down the dates and locations for the appropriate 24-hour window (Points A and B).	**POINT A:** OCT 12 13° ♎ 58' **POINT B:** OCT 13 12° ♎ 58'
3	Set up the Transit Constant Equation and solve being mindful of converting when necessary.	$Rx\ Transit\ Constant = \frac{(A - C)}{(A - B)} = \frac{(13°58' - 13°45')}{(13°58' - 12°58')}$ $= \frac{13'}{(12°118' - 12°58')}$ $= \frac{13'}{60'} = 0.217$
4	Multiply the Transit Constant by 24 hours to determine the hour in which the event occurred.	0.217 x 24 hours = 5.21
5	Take the decimals from the previous answer and times by 60 to determine the minutes in which the event occurred.	.21 x 60 minutes = 13 minutes
6	Combine Steps 4 and 5 to get hour and minutes of event in UT.	Oct 6 05:12 UT
7	Subtract the answer from Step 6 by your relative time zone.	05:12 UT – 08:00 hours (PT) = Oct 12, 2021 -03:13 Local Time **Oct 11, 2021 21:13**

If you look at Step 7 in the equation above, you will notice that when we subtracted -08:00 from 05:13 in order to accommodate for the respective time zone, we got the answer of -03:13. Because we cannot have a negative number, we need to carry over from the next bigger value as we always have been doing. This means, we will need to subtract 1 day and add 24 hours (1 day = 24hrs). When we do this to the equation, the UT time of Oct 12 05:13 UT becomes Oct 11 21:13 Local Time because we took away 1 day and added 24 hours to remove the negative value of -03:13.

Continuing on down the Mercury column, we notice that Mercury goes direct on Oct 18 at 10° ♎ 10′. What is interesting here is that this means Mercury will once again hit the trine aspect point of 13° ♎ 45′ only this time in direct motion instead of retrograde motion.

Recall from Part III-Section 4, retrograde planets will intersect with zodiacal points three times during a retrograde. Similarly, if you have a transit that occurs during a retrograde, you will also experience it a total of three times. One time during the Shadow I phase, one time during the Retrograde phase, and one time during the Shadow II phase, equating to a total of three aspect hits during the entire retrograde period.

Going back to our example, as we follow Mercury's direct travel for the rest of the month, we notice that Mercury does intersect the trine aspect point 13° ♎ 45′ between Oct 25 and Oct 26. This would be the third and final aspect hit because it is occurring during the Shadow II phase.

STEP #	DESCRIPTION	STEP PERFORMED
1	Determine the event and which transit point will cause the event (Point C).	**EVENT:** Transiting Mercury Direct in Libra trine Natal Sun in Aquarius (t. ☿♎ △ n. ☉♒). **3ᴿᴰ RX EVENT OUT OF 3.** **POINT C:** 13° ♎ 45′ (Libra Trine Point)
2	Write down the dates and locations for the appropriate 24-hour window (Points A and B).	**POINT B:** OCT 26 14° ♎ 32′ **POINT A:** OCT 25 13° ♎ 30′
3	Set up the Transit Constant Equation and solve being mindful of converting when necessary.	$Transit\ Constant = \dfrac{(C - A)}{(B - A)} = \dfrac{(13°45' - 13°30')}{(14°32' - 13°30')}$ $= \dfrac{15'}{(13°92' - 13°30')}$ $= \dfrac{15'}{62'} = 0.242$

STEP #	DESCRIPTION	STEP PERFORMED
4	Multiply the Transit Constant by 24 hours to determine the hour in which the event occurred.	0.242 x 24 hours = 5.81
5	Take the decimals from the previous answer and times by 60 to determine the minutes in which the event occurred.	.81 x 60 minutes = 49 minutes
6	Combine Steps 4 and 5 to get hour and minutes of event in UT.	Oct 25 05:49 UT
7	Subtract the answer from Step 6 by your relative time zone.	05:49 UT – 08:00 hours (PT) = Oct 25, 2021 -03:49 Local Time = **Oct 24 21:49 Local Time**

Once again, during Step 7 we had to subtract 1 day and add 24 hours into the UT time in order to obtain a positive number when we converted into Local Time.

Moving on, we now look at the transiting Venus column and compare her values to the natal Sun aspect point values. Venus starts off the month at 22° ♏ 51'. If we look back at our aspect points for the natal Aquarius Sun, transiting planets do create a square when they are in Scorpio, but this intersection has to occur at 13° ♏ 45' and Venus has passed this point already.

Nevertheless, on Oct 8, Venus ingresses into Sagittarius and if we look at the aspect point reference sheet, transiting planets in Sagittarius create a sextile with the Aquarius Sun at 13° ♐ 45'. All we have to do now is to continue down the column and determine if transiting Venus intersects at this point at any time during the rest of the month. Sure enough, she intersects this point between Oct 20 and Oct 21.

STEP #	DESCRIPTION	STEP PERFORMED
1	Determine the event and which transit point will cause the event (Point C).	**EVENT:** Transiting Venus in Sagittarius sextiles Natal Sun in Aquarius (t. ♀♐ ✶ n. ☉♒). **POINT C:** 13° ♐ 45' (Sagittarius Sextile Point)
2	Write down the dates and locations for the appropriate 24-hour window (Points A and B).	**POINT B:** OCT 21 14° ♐ 31' **POINT A:** OCT 20 13° ♐ 28'

STEP #	DESCRIPTION	STEP PERFORMED
3	Set up the Transit Constant Equation and solve being mindful of converting when necessary.	$\text{Transit Constant} = \dfrac{(C-A)}{(B-A)} = \dfrac{(13°45' - 13°28')}{(14°31' - 13°28')}$ $= \dfrac{17'}{(13°91' - 13°28')}$ $= \dfrac{17'}{63'} = 0.270$
4	Multiply the Transit Constant by 24 hours to determine the hour in which the event occurred.	0.270 x 24 hours = 6.48
5	Take the decimals from the previous answer and times by 60 to determine the minutes in which the event occurred.	.48 x 60 minutes = 29 minutes
6	Combine Steps 4 and 5 to get hour and minutes of event in UT.	Oct 20 06:29 UT
7	Subtract the answer from Step 6 by your relative time zone.	06:29 UT – 08:00 hours (PT) = Oct 20, 2021 -02:29 Local Time = **Oct 19 22:29 Local Time**

Now we continue on to the Mars column which begins his journey at 10° ♎ 24'. Once again, we have a planet in Libra which means Mars can intersect at the trine aspect point at 13° ♎ 45'. Going down the Mars column, we notice that this intersection occurs between Oct 6 and Oct 7.

STEP #	DESCRIPTION	STEP PERFORMED
1	Determine the event and which transit point will cause the event (Point C).	**EVENT:** Transiting Mars in Libra trines Natal Sun in Aquarius (t. ♂♎ Δ n. ☉♒) **POINT C:** 13° ♎ 45'(Libra Trine Point)
2	Write down the dates and locations for the appropriate 24-hour window (Points A and B).	**POINT B:** OCT 7 14° ♎ 20' **POINT A:** OCT 6 13° ♎ 40'
3	Set up the Transit Constant Equation and solve being mindful of converting when necessary.	$\text{Transit Constant} = \dfrac{(C-A)}{(B-A)} = \dfrac{(13°45' - 13°40')}{(14°20' - 13°40')}$ $= \dfrac{5'}{(13°80' - 13°40')}$ $= \dfrac{5'}{40'} = 0.125$

STEP #	DESCRIPTION	STEP PERFORMED
4	Multiply the Transit Constant by 24 hours to determine the hour in which the event occurred.	0.125 x 24 hours = 3.00
5	Take the decimals from the previous answer and times by 60 to determine the minutes in which the event occurred.	.00 x 60 minutes = 00 minutes
6	Combine Steps 4 and 5 to get hour and minutes of event in UT.	Oct 6 03:00 UT
7	Subtract the answer from Step 6 by your relative time zone.	03:00 UT – 08:00 hours (PT) = Oct 6, 2021 -05:00 Local Time = **Oct 5 19:00 Local Time**

Let us continue to the next column

Jupiter starts at 22° ♒ 49'. According to our aspect reference sheet, transiting planets in Aquarius make conjunctions to the natal Sun in Aquarius at 13° ♒ 45'. However, Jupiter stays at 22° ♒ during the entire month of October which means he does not intersect at the conjunction point.

Moving to Saturn, he is also located in Aquarius at 6° ♒ 58' and only moves from 6° ♒ - 7° ♒ and therefore does not intersect at the conjunction point of 13° ♒ 45'.

The next planet, Uranus, is in retrograde and starts his journey in October at 14° ♉ 6'. According to our reference sheet, there is a square aspect point when a transiting planet is in Taurus and intersects at 13° ♉ 45'. Following Uranus down the column, we discover that Uranus does intersect this point between Oct 11 and Oct 12.

Before we calculate the occurrence of this transit, we have to take note of a few things. Firstly, just like it was with Mercury, Uranus is in retrograde which means we will have to switch the dates and incorporate the Rx Transit Constant. Additionally, because this transit is occurring with a retrograde planet, it means that we are experiencing the 2nd hit of this transit with the 3rd hit occurring later on during the Shadow II period. Furthermore, because this transit involves one of the outer planets, this transit is incredibly important because outer planetary transits involve significant life events. Knowing these caveats, we now know how to proceed ahead.

STEP #	DESCRIPTION	STEP PERFORMED
1	Determine the event and which transit point will cause the event (Point C).	**EVENT:** Transiting Uranus Retrograde in Taurus square Natal Sun in Aquarius (t. ♅ᴿ ♉ □ n. ☉♒). 2ND RX EVENT OUT OF 3. SIGNIFICANT LIFE EVENT. **POINT C:** 13° ♉ 45'(Taurus Square Point)
2	Write down the dates and locations for the appropriate 24-hour window (Points A and B).	**POINT A:** OCT 11 13° ♉ 46' **POINT B:** OCT 12 13° ♉ 44'
3	Set up the Transit Constant Equation and solve being mindful of converting when necessary.	$Rx\ Transit\ Constant = \dfrac{(A-C)}{(A-B)} = \dfrac{(13°46'-13°45')}{(13°46'-13°44')}$ $= \dfrac{1'}{2'} = 0.5$
4	Multiply the Transit Constant by 24 hours to determine the hour in which the event occurred.	0.5 x 24 hours = 12.0
5	Take the decimals from the previous answer and times by 60 to determine the minutes in which the event occurred.	.0 x 60 minutes = 00 minutes
6	Combine Steps 4 and 5 to get hour and minutes of event in UT.	Oct 11 12:00 UT
7	Subtract the answer from Step 6 by your relative time zone.	12:00 UT – 08:00 hours (PT) = **Oct 11, 2021 04:00 Local Time**

We can now continue on to Neptune which starts Oct at 21° ♓ 20'. According to the reference sheet, natal Sun makes no aspect points with any planets in Pisces, so we can ignore Neptune's travels because he will not be making a transit to the natal Sun while in Pisces. The same goes for Pluto who is located at 24° ♑ 19'. Again, we see that no transiting planets within Capricorn will make an aspect point to a natal planet in Aquarius. With that, we have now gone through every single planetary column with the natal Sun aspect points whose summary is in the table below (Table IV-8).

Just by observing one natal planet alone, we were able to determine six individualized transits that will occur during October 2021 for the individual. The next step would be to repeat the same process for every natal point that is found within the reference sheet. Take this time now to

TABLE IV-8. Summary of Transiting Aspects to Natal Sun in Aquarius for October 2021

TRANSIT	GLYPH	DATE	ADDITIONAL NOTES
Transiting Sun in Libra trine Natal Sun in Aquarius	t. ☉♎ △ n. ☉♒	Oct 6 11:32 Local Time	
Transiting Mercury Retrograde in Libra trine Natal Sun in Aquarius	t. ☿R♎ △ n. ☉♒	Oct 11 21:13 Local Time	2nd Retrograde hit out of 3.
Mercury in Libra trine Natal Sun in Aquarius	t. ☿♎ △ n. ☉♒	Oct 24 21:49 Local Time	3rd Retrograde hit out of 3.
Transiting Venus in Sagittarius sextile Natal Sun in Aquarius	t. ♀♐ ✶ n. ☉♒	Oct 19 22:29 Local Time	
Transiting Mars in Libra trine Natal Sun in Aquarius	t. ♂♎ △ n. ☉♒	Oct 5 19:00 Local Time	
Transiting Uranus Retrograde in Taurus square Natal Sun in Aquarius	t. ♅R♉ □ n. ☉♒	Oct 11 04:00 Local Time	2nd retrograde hit out of 3. Significant life event.

determine your own transits with your own reference sheet for the current month or the month ahead. Once you have completed this process with each twelve of the fixed natal points in your reference sheet, you will then have determined all of your transits and ingresses for that entire month. Next, we will take a closer look into how to properly analyze these transits.

SECTION 4-INTERPRETING PERSONAL TRANSITS

When it comes to anything involving transits, the ultimate reference book is Planets in Transit by Robert Hand. He provides information on every transit and ingress combination that exists and objectively explains the energies involved. I would also recommend the book How to Predict Your Future by James Braha. His book primarily observes the outer planetary transits, but it is still a great book to cross-reference with Mr. Hand's book.

Although these books do provide specific details into the energies involved with these transits, they will never be able to predict the unique manner in which these energies manifest for each individual. To this fact, three separate factors determine the outcome, which comprises the bulk of this section: house placement and rulership, the aspect cycle, and the overall psychological temperament of the individual.

FACTOR #1: HOUSE PLACEMENTS AND HOUSE RULERSHIP (THE TRANSIT FORMULA)

The first factor incorporates house placements and rulerships at the time of the transit. This shows us which areas of life are activated because, recall from Part II-Section 6, each house possesses individualized energies depending on the area of life they represent. In order to determine which houses are going to be activated, there is a formula you need to learn which we are going to discuss.

Recall from Part II, each sign of the zodiac has certain planetary ruler(s). For the sake of convenience, here is a reminder (Table IV-9). If every sign has a ruler, this means that every house within the natal chart also has a planetary ruler because every house doorway is located within a particular sign of the zodiac.

TABLE IV-9. Planetary Rulership by Sign

SIGN	GLYPH	RULER
ARIES	♈	♂
TAURUS	♉	♀
GEMINI	♊	☿
CANCER	♋	☽
LEO	♌	☉
VIRGO	♍	☿
LIBRA	♎	♀
SCORPIO	♏	♂ & ♇
SAGITTARIUS	♐	♃
CAPRICORN	♑	♄
AQUARIUS	♒	♄ & ♅
PISCES	♓	♃ & ♆

Using Table IV-9 above, all we have to do is replace the sign placements for each house doorway with the ruler(s) of each respective sign. This will tell us which planets rule which houses within the birth chart (Table IV-10A-B).

The next step is to determine which houses the natal planets are located within. This is where examining the birth chart itself comes in handy (Fig. IV-14). The natal chart makes it very easy to read. If I follow where the black lines are located and pay attention to the numbers located within each piece, I am able to quickly determine where each natal planet is located (Table IV-11).

TABLE IV-10A. House Positions from Reference Sheet

HOUSES (INGRESSES)			
ASC/1	9° ♍ 2′	DSC/7	9° ♓ 2′
2	4° ♎ 40′	8	4° ♈ 40′
3	4° ♏ 25′	9	4° ♉ 25′
IC/4	6° ♐ 56′	MC/10	6° ♊ 56′
5	9° ♑ 47′	11	9° ♋ 47′
6	10° ♒ 48′	12	10° ♌ 48′

TABLE IV-10B. House Rulerships Using Table IV-9

HOUSES RULERS			
ASC/1	☿	DSC/7	♃ & ♆
2	♀	8	♂
3	♂ & ♇	9	♀
IC/4	♃	MC/10	☿
5	♄	11	☽
6	♄ & ♅	12	☉

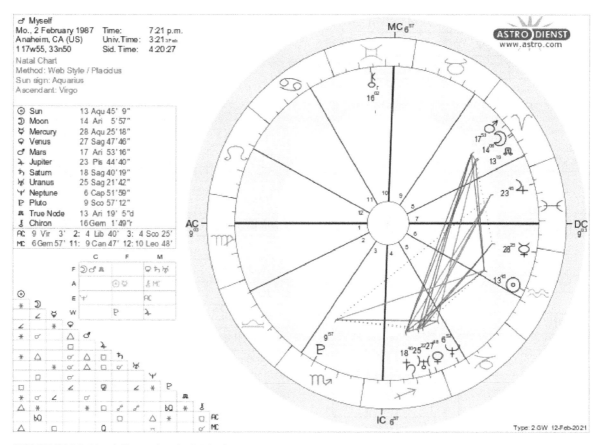

FIGURE IV-14. Natal Chart of an Individual

315

TABLE IV-11. Natal Planetary House Locations as Determined by Natal Chart

NATAL PLANET	GLYPH	HOUSE LOCATION
SUN	☉	6
MOON	☽	8
MERCURY	☿	6
VENUS	♀	4
MARS	♂	8
JUPITER	♃	7
SATURN	♄	4
URANUS	♅	4
NEPTUNE	♆	4
PLUTO	♇	3

Use the space below to fill out your own information.

HOUSES (INGRESSES)			
ASC/1		DSC/7	
2		8	
3		9	
IC/4		MC/10	
5		11	
6		12	

HOUSES RULERS			
ASC/1		DSC/7	
2		8	
3		9	
IC/4		MC/10	
5		11	
6		12	

NATAL PLANET	GLYPH	HOUSE LOCATION
SUN	☉	
MOON	☽	
MERCURY	☿	
VENUS	♀	
MARS	♂	
JUPITER	♃	
SATURN	♄	
URANUS	♅	
NEPTUNE	♆	
PLUTO	♇	

For convenience, here is the data we will be referencing for the examples below.

HOUSES (INGRESSES)			
ASC/1	9° ♍ 2'	DSC/7	9° ♓ 2'
2	4° ♎ 40'	8	4° ♈ 40'
3	4° ♏ 25'	9	4° ♉ 25'
IC/4	6° ♐ 56'	MC/10	6° ♊ 56'
5	9° ♑ 47'	11	9° ♋ 47'
6	10° ♒ 48'	12	10° ♌ 48'

NATAL PLANET	GLYPH	HOUSE LOCATION
SUN	☉	6
MOON	☽	8
MERCURY	☿	6
VENUS	♀	4
MARS	♂	8
JUPITER	♃	7
SATURN	♄	4
URANUS	♅	4
NEPTUNE	♆	4
PLUTO	♇	3

HOUSES RULERS			
ASC/1	☿	DSC/7	♃ & ♆
2	♀	8	♂
3	♂ & ♆	9	♀
IC/4	♃	MC/10	☿
5	♄	11	☽
6	♄ & ♅	12	☉

Now that we have the house ruler and natal house placement information that we require, we apply this information to the aspect data that we obtained from the previous section. For reference, here is a list of the eight transit events we uncovered for the Natal Sun in Aquarius along with ingresses for October 2021 (Table IV-12).

In order to determine which houses are activated, we need to apply the transit formula. However, Events 1 and 2 do not require the formula because those are ingresses and not transits. Still, we can gauge which areas of life might be activated because we see which new houses the planets are entering.

TABLE IV-12. October 2021 Ingresses and Transit Events for Natal Sun

EVENT #	TRANSIT	GLYPH
1	Transiting Sun ingresses into the 3rd House	t. ☉ → 3rd
2	Transiting Venus ingresses into the 4th House	t. ♀ → 4TH
3	Transiting Sun in Libra trine Natal Sun in Aquarius	t. ☉♎ △ n. ☉♒
4	Transiting Mercury Retrograde in Libra trine Natal Sun in Aquarius	t. ☿R♎ △ n. ☉♒
5	Mercury in Libra trine Natal Sun in Aquarius	t. ☿♎ △ n. ☉♒
6	Transiting Venus in Sagittarius sextile Natal Sun in Aquarius	t. ♀♐ ✶ n. ☉♒
7	Transiting Mars in Libra trine Natal Sun in Aquarius	t. ♂♎ △ n. ☉♒
8	Transiting Uranus Retrograde in Taurus square Natal Sun in Aquarius	t. ♅R ♉ □ n. ☉♒

EVENT #	TRANSIT	GLYPH	TRANSIT FORMULA	ACTIVATED AREAS
1	Transiting Sun ingresses into the 3rd House	t. ☉ → 3rd	N/A	3rd House= Communications, Short-distance travel, Negotiations and Siblings.
2	Transiting Venus ingresses into the 4th House	t. ♀ → 4TH	N/A	4th house= Family, Unconscious, Nurturing, The physical dwelling.

Remember, the activated areas are simply general themes that the house represents and is in no way absolute or extensive. Think of the activated areas as a hypothesis, in that these areas of life are reflected within the 3rd house so I am hypothesizing that these are the areas that will now be activated. It is up to my empirical observation to see if my hypothesis was correct or incorrect.

Now, with Events 3-8, we must incorporate the transit formula because they are transit events. Let us start with Event 3, transiting Sun in Libra trine Natal Sun in Aquarius (t. ☉♎ △ n. ☉♒). Referring back to the previous section, we determined that this event occurs at 13° ♎ 45'. If we were to look at our house doorway chart above, we see that transiting Sun is located in the 2nd house at this time. Now, we have to see what houses are ruled by the Sun because the transiting Sun is involved. According to our data, the Sun rules the 12th house.

In other words, we have just discovered is that transiting Sun in Libra is residing within the 2nd house and rules the 12th house. Or, if we're to put this into a shorthand, we would say, t. ☉♎ in 2nd (R. 12th).

Now we have to do the same thing for the natal planet involved. Remember, the natal planets are fixed and never move. According to the data above, the natal Sun is located in the 6th house and also rules the 12th house because it is also the Sun. In other words, Natal Sun in Aquarius resides in the 6th house and rules the 12th house. The shorthand of which would be n. ☉♒ in 6th (R. 12th). All we need to do now is connect the two together with the aspect that is being created in the middle:

t. ☉♎ in 2nd (R. 12th) Δ n. ☉♒ in 6th (R. 12th)

This is the transit formula for the event. What this formula is saying in English is, "The transiting Sun in Libra, which is currently in the 2nd house and rules the 12th house, is trining the Natal Sun in Aquarius which resides in the 6th house and rules the 12th house." Now that we have this formula, we can speculate which areas of life are going to be activated, and then observe how the transit occurred when it eventually arrives to determine if our hypothesis was correct.

EVENT #	TRANSIT	GLYPH	TRANSIT FORMULA	ACTIVATED AREAS
3	Transiting Sun in Libra trine Natal Sun in Aquarius	t. ☉♎ Δ n. ☉♒	t. ☉♎ in 2nd (R. 12th) Δn. ☉♒ in 6th (R. 12th)	2nd house= Possessions, ownership, relaxation, arts. 12th house=spiritualism, ego-denial, unconditional love 6th house=work, learning, education, revision

Let us do another example with Event 4, Transiting Mercury Retrograde in Libra trine Natal Sun in Aquarius (t. ☿℞♎ Δ n. ☉♒). At the time of this transit intersection, Mercury is located at 13° ♎ 45' just like the transiting Sun in the example above. This means Mercury is similarly in the 2nd house at the time of the aspect hit. Now, according to our data, Mercury rules the 1st and 10th houses which is the other information we need for the first part of the equation. The natal Sun, being fixed, is once again residing in the 6th house, and ruling the 12th. With that, we can construct the transit formula:

t. ☿R♎ in 2nd (R. 1st and 10th) △ n. ☉♒ in 6th (R. 12th)

EVENT #	TRANSIT	GLYPH	TRANSIT FORMULA	ACTIVATED AREAS
4	Transiting Mercury Retrograde in Libra trine Natal Sun in Aquarius	t. ☿R♎ △ n. ☉♒	t. ☿R♎ in 2nd (R. 1st and 10th) △ n. ☉♒ in 6th (R. 12th)	2nd house= Possessions, ownership, relaxation, arts. 6th house=work, learning, education, revision 12th house=spiritualism, ego-denial, unconditional love 1st house= physical body, reputation, drive 10th house=career, long-term goals, superiors/bosses

For good measure, let us do one more and examine Event 6, transiting Venus in Sagittarius sextile Natal Sun in Aquarius, (t. ♀♐ ✶ n. ☉♒). Transiting Venus would have to be located at 13° ♐ 45' at the time of the transit which places her in the 4th house. According to our data, Venus rules the 2nd and 9th houses. Again, the natal Sun data remains the same,

t. ♀♐ in 4th (R. 2nd and 9th) ✶ n. ☉♒ in 6TH (R. 12th)

EVENT #	TRANSIT	GLYPH	TRANSIT FORMULA	ACTIVATED AREAS
6	Transiting Venus in Sagittarius sextile Natal Sun in Aquarius	t. ♀♐ ✶ n. ☉♒	t. ♀♐ in 4th (R. 2nd and 9th) ✶ n. ☉♒ in 6TH (R. 12th)	2nd house= Possessions, ownership, relaxation, arts. 4th house= Family, unconscious, nurturing, the physical dwelling. 6th house=work, learning, education, revision 12th house=spiritualism, ego-denial, unconditional love 9th house=long distance travel, idealism, scholarly pursuits, mind expansion

By observing the time the event takes place, along with the reference books and transit formula, you can easily determine how astrological energies produce specific events in your life. Keep a

320

journal and record correlations because, as you will see in the next factor, events are connected through time in addition to being connected by house rulerships and placements.

FACTOR #2: THE ASPECT CYCLE

Recall in Part I-Section 8, astrological time is cyclical, not linear. Also, recall in the previous section and from Part III-Section 1, aspects follow the same eight-phase cycle that our moon experiences monthly. This means that all events and dates that occur on the aspect cycle are related both in terms of themes and experiences.

Take for example Fig. IV-6 which visually represents transiting Sun interacting with the natal Sun at all eight aspect points along the aspect cycle. If we were to use the natal point we have been using (n. ☉ = 13° ♒ 45′) the aspect cycle would look something as follows (Fig IV-6 and Table IV-13):

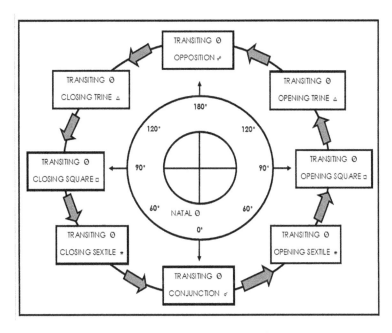

FIGRE IV-6. The Aspect Cycle

TABLE IV-13. Respective Dates and Aspect Points

#	STAGE NAME	GLYPH	ASPECT POINT	CORRESPONDING DATE
1/8	Conjunction	☌	13° ♒ 45′	FEB 2, 2021
2/8	Opening Sextile	✶	13° ♈ 45′	APR 3, 2021
3/8	Opening Square	□	13° ♉ 45′	MAY 5, 2021
4/8	Opening Trine	△	13° ♊ 45′	JUNE 4, 2021
5/8	Opposition	☍	13° ♌ 45′	AUG 3, 2021
6/8	Closing Trine	△	13° ♎ 45′	OCT 6, 2021
7/8	Closing Square	□	13° ♏ 45′	NOV 5, 2021
8/8	Closing Sextile	✶	13° ♐ 45′	DEC 5, 2021
1/8	Conjunction	☌	13° ♒ 45′	FEB 2, 2022

Without a doubt, the events and corresponding storyline that unfolds from date to date is intwined with one another. The more you journal and monitor your transits in this way, you can connect events from the past in order to see not only where the story is heading, but what part of the story you are currently facing.

When it comes to the nature of the various phases, I will refer you back to Part III-Section I where the eight phases were discussed in parallel to the moon cycle as the energies are similar to the same ones that the moon encounters every month. Regardless, remember that connecting events this way further explains an unfolding of a much larger, more complex story that you are co-creating with the universe in your present-day life.

FACTOR #3: NATAL CHART TEMPERAMENT AND TEMPERAMENT OF THE INDIVIDUAL

This next section will make more sense once you have completed the next part of this book. For now, I want to bring it up so that you are aware of this caveat when it comes to transit interpretation.

Soon, you will discover that planets within a natal chart are either expressing themselves in harmonious or inharmonious ways. Therefore, if a transiting planet were to aspect a natal planet that is in a poor condition, then we can expect the transit to be somewhat diluted with this energy, even if it is a beneficial aspect like a trine. Similarly, the opposite can be true when transiting aspects interact with natal planets that are properly expressed and beneficial for the individual.

Additionally, as we have discussed in Part I, the individual's overall psychological condition and awareness naturally will cause the events to manifest and unfold in certain ways depending on the respective journey that the individual is presently partaking. As was mentioned in Part I, the more proactive and aware you are, the more the transit will manifest differently than if you were within a more unconscious and ego-driven mindset. These are two factors to keep in mind and will become easier to notice the further along you work with your transits and natal chart interpretation.

* * *

Now having completed this part of the book, you are well equipped with immensely valuable astrological skills that very few people utilize and observe. Take this information and watch astrology in action by viewing yourself as an objective witness that is watching the story of life unfold before you. Astrological transits give you the essential astrological tools required in order to be more present and aware within your life by showing you when and what certain life events are going to unfold. Knowing this information, along with the openness to be present and aware during transit events, is a prominent step towards becoming a legitimate and skillful astrologer. In the next part of the book, we are going to apply everything we have learned, and put it into practice through comprehensive natal chart interpretation.

PART V: CHART INTERPRETATION

" I believe God rules all by [their] divine providence and that the stars, by [God's] permission, are instruments."- William Lilly

Up to this point in the book, you are now equipped with all of the required theory, knowledge, and skills you will need in order to fully and accurately interpret a birth chart. We are now going to put all of these skills into actual practice by observing various case studies of five unique individuals. We will be following the same five people for the next three parts, so it is a good idea to get familiar with their birth data and charts now (Table V-1 and Figures V-1A-E). Please note, we will be observing their various charts as needed. For now, we will only be observing their birth charts, which all other charts are essentially founded upon. In order to ensure a random sample, the following individuals were recruited using astrological Reddit servers, and were chosen on a first-come, first-serve basis.

In Table V-1 below, you will notice a column that reads "Rodden Rating". This is how astrologers categorize the accuracy of the birth data because, as you have been learning, the birth time is such a crucial and unique data point that if it is not from a reputable source, then there is only so much information the chart can tell us. In this same light, if we know under what pretense

TABLE V-1. Case Studies Birth Data

CLIENT	BRITH MONTH, DATE, AND YEAR	BIRTH TIME	BIRTH LOCATION	RODDEN RATING
A	JUL 21 1990	03:40	OMSK, RUSSIA	AA
B	APR 4 1993	12:17	GREENVILLE, PA, USA (MERCER COUNTY)	AA
C	DEC 29 1993	06:34	ASHEVILLE, NC, USA	AA
D	AUG 22 1986	09:39	HOUSTON, TX, USA	AA
E	JUL 16 1988	06:13	MORRISTOWN, NJ, USA	AA

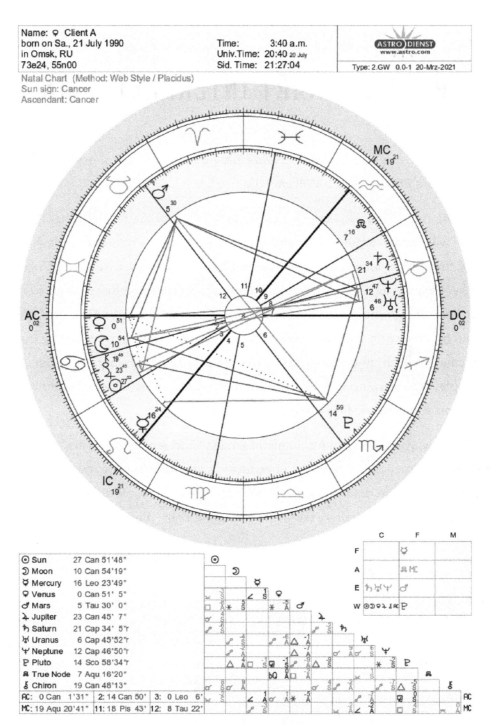

FIGURE V-1A. Birth Chart of Client A

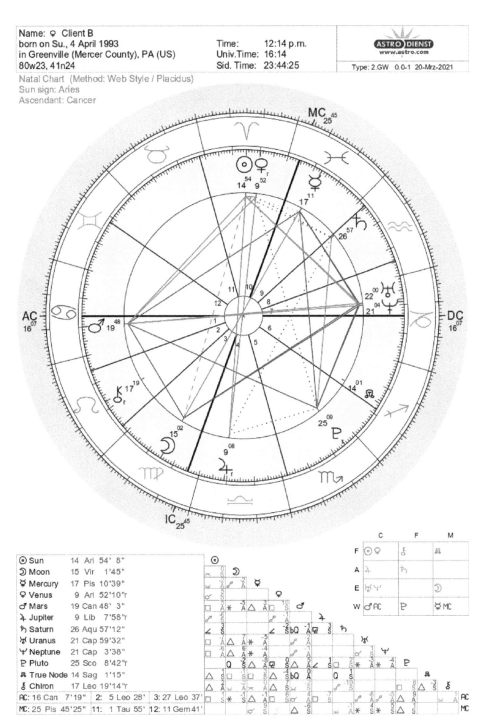

FIGURE V-1B. Birth Chart of Client B

327

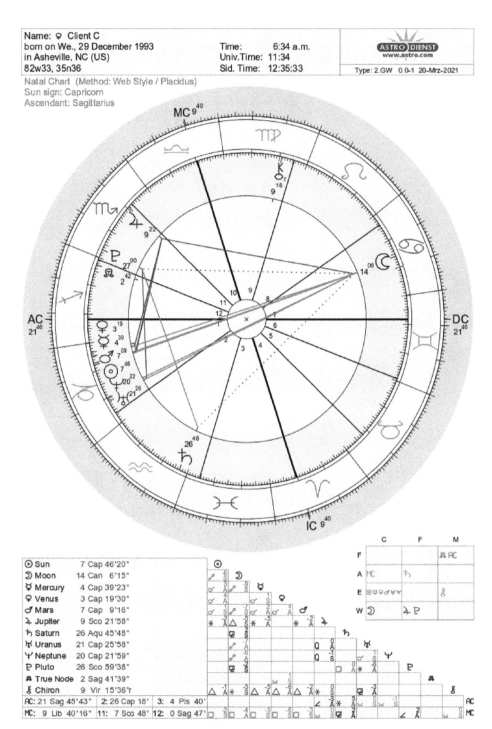

☉ Sun	7 Cap 46'20"	
☽ Moon	14 Can 6'15"	
☿ Mercury	4 Cap 39'23"	
♀ Venus	3 Cap 19'30"	
♂ Mars	7 Cap 9'16"	
♃ Jupiter	9 Sco 21'58"	
♄ Saturn	26 Aqu 45'48"	
♅ Uranus	21 Cap 25'58"	
♆ Neptune	20 Cap 21'59"	
♇ Pluto	26 Sco 59'38"	
☊ True Node	2 Sag 41'39"	
⚷ Chiron	9 Vir 15'36"r	

AC: 21 Sag 45'43"	2: 26 Cap 18'	3: 4 Pis 40'
MC: 9 Lib 40'16"	11: 7 Sco 48'	12: 0 Sag 47'

FIGURE V-1C. Birth Chart of Client C

328

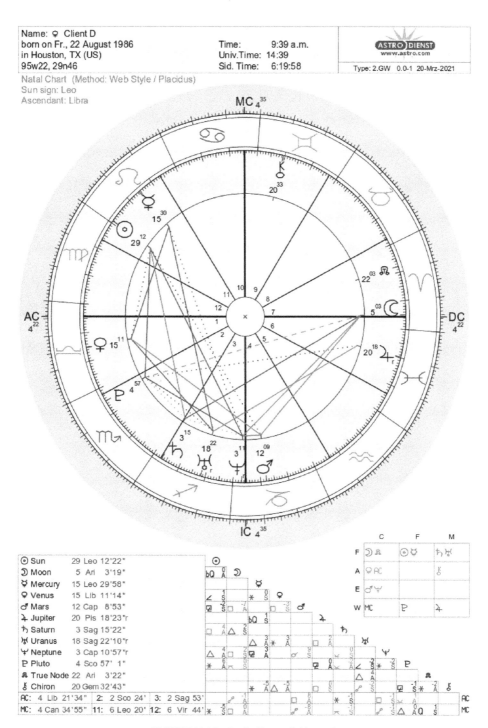

☉ Sun	29 Leo 12'22"	
☽ Moon	5 Ari 3'19"	
☿ Mercury	15 Leo 29'58"	
♀ Venus	15 Lib 11'14"	
♂ Mars	12 Cap 8'53"	
♃ Jupiter	20 Pis 18'23"r	
♄ Saturn	3 Sag 15'22"	
♅ Uranus	18 Sag 22'10"r	
♆ Neptune	3 Cap 10'57"r	
♇ Pluto	4 Sco 57' 1"	
♋ True Node	22 Ari 3'22"	
⚷ Chiron	20 Gem 32'43"	
AC: 4 Lib 21'34"	2: 2 Sco 24'	3: 2 Sag 53'
MC: 4 Can 34'55"	11: 6 Leo 20'	12: 6 Vir 44'

FIGURE V-1D. Birth Chart of Client D

329

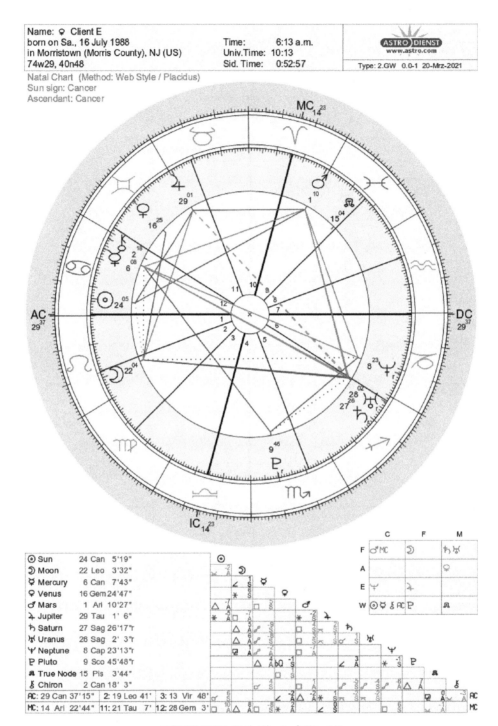

FIGURE V-1E. Birth Chart of Client E

the chart's data falls under, we can therefore conclude which information is valid and which information is shoddier due to the inaccuracies of the birth data. Below is the table of the various Rodden Ratings (Table V-2).

TABLE V-2. Rodden Rating with Corresponding Meaning

RATING	AA	A	B	C	DD	X
PRIMARY SOURCE	Birth Certificate	Secondary Source (Family/Friends)	From Biography	Caution	Dirty Data	Birth Time Unknown

When it comes to individual readings for your clients, you need to make sure and reiterate that their birth data has a "AA" rating. Always confirm that the birth time they give you comes directly from the birth certificate and is not an estimation given to them by a family member that was there. Remember, the time the doctor who delivered them and claimed they were alive and autonomous is the only time that matters.

In today's modern society, it is very rare for the birth time to not be on the birth certificate. Having said this, if you are working with a birth chart that has anything lower than a "AA" reading, you should automatically become suspect of the information because it is simply not accurate from the get-go. However, sometimes when you are researching events, businesses, or celebrities, the birth data can range from "X-AA" and you might simply have to work with what you have.

If you have a client that does not have their birth time from their birth certificate, then there is an advanced astrological skill where you can determine their birth time by basically reverse engineering the chart. This is called "Chart Rectification" where the astrologer correlates significant life events to the individual and works backwards to determine what time the birth must have taken place so that these events line up appropriately. This skill goes beyond the scope of this book but just know if you lack a birth time, there are ways to obtain this information from a skilled astrologer. Or, if you want to become knowledgeable in this skill yourself, there are resources available to learn how to rectify a chart.

When it comes to reading the chart itself, after any counseling session, your client should experience three major outcomes: empowerment, catharsis, and understanding. Empowerment in that your client should walk out of the session feeling that whatever is coming their way, they can face it head-on with their own skills and resources. Catharsis in that they should feel as though a huge weight has been lifted off their shoulders, and as though they are being listened to and supported. Finally, they should experience a sense of understanding in that they leave the session knowing more about themselves than when they began the session. To put it bluntly, if you are not able to provide these three major results, then you are not giving your client their money's worth.

This is why, when starting out as an astrological counselor, your fees need to reflect your experience and quality until you can comprehensively provide a strong and memorable session for your client. Furthermore, there are other boundaries and considerations you need to be mindful of while starting out as a counselor. This is where we will start this part of the book, with a discussion on ethics. After that, we will take an extensive look into how to properly analyze your client's birth chart and transit chart by using the five individuals listed above.

SECTION 1- ETHICS

Just as it is with any other major profession, practitioners are required to follow and abide by specific ethical boundaries for the safety and health of their clients and the practitioner. We should not take lightly the ability to pierce into one's psychological profile or to predict when certain life events are to occur. The way in which we offer this information along with other circumstances must always be considered before discussing confidential and fateful information.

Many astrological institutions require their practitioners to adhere to a certain ethical code, and the code I will be mostly commenting on is the NCGR Code of Ethics.[59] In this section, I am going to highlight and paraphrase certain topics within their Code of Ethics that I believe should be considered and observed in order to practice astrology to the highest of standards.

PART 1: GENERAL ETHICS

1. DO NO HARM

Just as it is with any profession that is based around a client/practitioner relationship, the astrologer needs to consider when doing something or nothing will ultimately lead to the best outcome. To this point, be very mindful of recommending significant life-altering decisions for the individual. For example, if you are discussing with your client to file for a divorce or leave a profession, discuss the pros and cons, listen to their concerns, and simply explain the astrological influences that are leading them to that crossroad in the first place. Do not explicitly make the decision for them.

Similarly, do not withhold information from the client unless they are mentally unprepared to hear what you have to say. For example, if your client's chart is signaling that they should separate

---

59   https://geocosmic.org/ncgr-code-of-ethics/

from their partner, but they are too emotionally committed to the relationship, instead of outright telling them they should divorce, help them to work through those emotional hesitations and frustrations so that they can derive their own self-directed decision. You are not there to direct their lives; you are there to help them navigate through their own life. As the old saying goes, you are leading the horse to water, but you cannot make the horse drink the water.

The good news is, you will find that clients deep down really know what the answer is and what should be done. Mostly, they are using you as a soundboard to bounce back ideas, thoughts, and emotions. It is simply your job to help them discern clarity among the fog that is making them hesitant, confused, and/or fearful. Always remember, their own unconsciousness is what brought them to you in the first place so that they can obtain some form of understanding and awareness. They already have all the answers deep within themselves; it is simply up to you to help them discover those answers.

2. RESPECT YOUR LIMITATIONS

As an astrologer, especially starting out, it is perfectly fine to say, "I do not know." No matter how prepared you are for a reading, there will always be questions that pop up where you will have to quickly determine the answer in real-time and this is hard to do at the beginning. Additionally, if your client is looking for a specialized reading, like a horary reading or an astrocartography reading, and you are not familiar with those disciplines, tell them so.

Do not put yourself on a higher pedestal than your skills can match. It is much more ethically sound to tell your client of your actual experience and abilities than it is to overpromise and underperform. This not only does you a disservice by tarnishing your reputation, it also tarnishes the reputation of the astrological profession in general by perpetuating the stereotype that there is no legitimacy behind the study and that all astrologers are frauds.

3. PROFESSIONAL BOUNDARIES BETWEEN CLIENT AND PRACTITIONER

Just as it is with any client/practitioner relationship, it is vital to keep the affiliation strictly professional and never personal. Do not date your clients or use astrology so that you can go on dates. If at any time your relationship becomes personal, then you need to refer them to another astrologer so that you both maintain objectivity within a reading. This is why it is a good idea to keep the personal out of your astrological practice. It not only ensures appropriate ethical boundaries, it allows for you to objectively tell your client truths that you might otherwise hide from people that are emotionally close to you.

4. Respect the Diversity of Human Individuals

As an astrological counselor, you are going to encounter people from all walks of life. This means it is inevitable that you will meet individuals that have backgrounds, political views, religious views, and life philosophies that could be the polar opposite to yours. If you cannot ignore these differences in opinions and lifestyles, then you need to express to the client that you cannot ethically analyze their chart due to your explicit biases.

After that, you then need to work through those biases because being prejudiced in this way is not only bad for business, it is bad for the metaphysical outlook that astrology portrays. Namely, that every human is imperfect but is nevertheless deserving of psychological understanding through their astrological charts. If you cannot come to terms with this, then you need to seriously consider if joining the astrological profession is the right choice for you.

Part II: Confidentiality

1. General Rules on Confidentiality

You should treat confidentiality similarly to the parameters that health professionals follow via HIPAA regulations. Mainly, do not disclose confidential information to anyone, such as your client's name, birth data, location, contact information, and/or personal information without explicit permission from your client.

2. Permissions and Discussions

If you want permission to share your client's data, you still need do to so under an alias if it is going to become a public publication. For example, for this book, every participant was notified as to how their information would be used along with their rights with complete transparency (See Fig. V-2).

I _____ am giving the author of the book "Astrology for the New Century" permission to use my astrological data in the following ways:

1. Disclose my birth data including birth time, date, location, and year under an alias.

2. Examine and display my birth chart, transit chart, progressed chart and any other astrological charts that are relevant to the case study.

3. Discuss personal insights and analysis found within said astrological charts within the book with the upmost sensitivity and respect.

4. Record the audio of our counseling session so that it can be referenced while the book is being written.

In exchange for participating in the above-mentioned book as a participant, the author promises to do the following:

1. Assign a letter to the case study such as "Client A" so as not to disclose your real name.

2. Will not disclose other personal information like location and contact information.

3. Provide for you an extensive astrological reading free of charge in exchange for participating as a case study.

By signing below, I agree to the following terms and allow the author to use my astrological findings and data for commercial use.

FIGURE V-2. Permissions Acknowledgement for all Participants of this Book

Notice how there is complete honesty with regards to who I am, what I am going to do with their information, and their rights to privacy throughout. I only included individuals within this book who gave me explicit permission to do so via a signature to the contract above. This is how I maintained integrity not only towards my practice and towards my book, but also towards the profession and science at-large.

Even if you are in a private setting, it is not best practice to share and discuss your client's personal information and circumstances. The only exception would be if you are brainstorming with another astrologer but even then, you need to keep their data private. Similarly, do not discuss private matters in a public space.

Part III: Astrological Practices

1. All Statements Must be Credible

Every statement you make should be backed up by astrological proof. Additionally, you need to properly source your materials if you are writing or presenting anything within astrology, focusing on primary sources if possible. You should not make claims that were not thought out in your head. Even though your client might not know enough astrology to ask you, "where in the chart do you see that?" you need to always ask yourself that question with every insight you discover.

2. Astrological Misuse

It is all too easy to use astrology for nefarious purposes such as sabotage, instigation, and exploiting people's faults. All of these should be avoided and if you have any desire to do so, you need to seriously consider your motivations and reasons for practicing astrology. Astrology is meant to help, heal, and progress the individual along with society. If you are using astrology immorally, this goes against this primary objective, and is therefore incredibly counterproductive and unethical.

Part IV: Business Ethics

1. Sensationalism

Do not tell someone shocking or over-the-top information just to get clientele. For example, do not tell a potential client that they need a reading from you or else something bad is going to happen to them. Similarly, do not inflate the individual's ego by saying great things about them just to butter them up without providing any substantial information for your client. Remember, it is better to under promise and overperform than it is to overpromise and underperform.

2. Fair and Honest Services and Fees

Countless times, I hear horror stories of clients paying a substantial amount of money for sub-par readings. Your fees should reflect your experience and quality of your work. If you are starting out, there are many individuals online that will gladly take a free reading from you so you can practice. After this, a $60-$80 introductory reading rate is a good place to start as a beginner. On average, the industry standard for a professional astrological reading is about $100-$250 for 60-90 minutes of counseling. You should never charge this much (or more) unless you can deliver on quality. Also, some astrologers provide a sliding scale for fees depending on income to allow for less financially sound individuals to still obtain a reading. Either way, be ready to put your money where your mouth is.

* * *

If you ever find yourself within an ethical conundrum, use the guideposts above, but also use decent common sense. The key is to always "do no harm," so if what you are doing hinders your client more than helps them, it is a logical conclusion to simply do nothing. Astrology is not a way to get a date, nor is it a way to get rich quick, or become a celebrity. Astrology is a legitimate and serious examination into one's psychology which should never be taken lightly.

Similarly, you should not even attempt to analyze an individual, let alone charge them, unless you feel secure in your own abilities and are likewise following your own astrological influences as pointed out in Part IV. The good news is the rest of Part V details exactly how to analyze a birth chart confidently and accurately so that you can appropriately and ethically begin an astrological practice with poise and professionalism.

SECTION 2-BIRTH CHART INTERPRETATION WITH CASE STUDIES

❧

The main reason that astrological chart analysis is overwhelming and daunting is simply due to the fact that there is so much information within a birth chart. The key is to prioritize the information and then slowly scrutinize this information one line at a time. In the table below, I have provided a step-by-step guide on how to analyze a birth chart (Table V-3B). In this table, you will also see a column that shows you where in the book you can obtain more information on the topic because we have already covered almost every strategy already found within the table.

Keep in mind that the table above is not the end all be all of analysis nor is it set in stone. This is simply a starting point for you to work with and I encourage you to mix and match and add and remove steps of your own when you become more comfortable within your own methodology. Every astrologer is different and although this table is a great place to start, I guarantee over time, you will adjust the various steps with your own preferences as you continue along your studies.

The other key item to point out is that this table does not make you a good astrologer; it simply helps you to prioritize and organize the information. The artistry comes with your own analysis

TABLE V-3A. How to obtain a Natal Chart through ASTRO.COM

> (1) On the ASTRO.COM main page, under the HOROSCOPES tab, chose EXTENDED CHART SELECTION under DRAWINGS, CALCULATIONS, DATA.
>
> (2) Confirm that the appropriate individual is selected under HOROSCOPE FOR.
>
> (3) Under CHART TYPE, select NATAL CHART WHEEL
>
> (4) Click CLICK HERE TO SHOW CHART.

TABLE V-3B. Steps on how to Comprehensively Analyze a Birth Chart

STEP #	SECTION IN BOOK	DESCRIPTION	INFORMATION IT PROVIDES
1	II-1	Determine any imbalances within the elements and modalities.	Gives you a quick picture of the individual with simple remedies.
2A	II-7 IV-4 II-5 II-6	Determine the Planetary ruler(s) of the Ascendant along with their house placement, sign placement, and any aspect(s) within an orb range of 0°-6°.	The Planet(s) that rule the ascendant show how the individual portrays themselves along with their sense of self-confidence.
2B	II-7 IV-4 II-5 II-6	Determine the Planetary ruler(s) of the Midheaven along with their house placement, sign placement, and any aspect(s) within an orb range of 0°-6°.	The Planet(s) that rule the midheaven signify the individual's main lifegoals, aspirations, and their approach towards these endeavors.
3A	II-4	Determine if any planet(s) are in a sign of exaltation, rulership, detriment, or fall.	This will adjust the natural temperament of the planet(s) for better or worse.
3B	IV-4	If any planet(s) exist in Step 3A, determine the houses these planets rule and are placed within.	Houses ruled and resided by effected planets from Step 3A will be influenced by their dignity or debility.
4	II-5	Determine the chart's aspects with an orb range of 0°-5°.	Indicates the individual's most rudimentary strengths and weaknesses.
5A		From the information gathered in Steps 3-4, determine the chart's most afflicted planet(s).	Shows which planet(s) are the most self-destructive and inharmonious.
5B		From the information gathered in Steps 3-4, determine the chart's most beneficial planet(s).	Shows which planet(s) are the most harmonious and helpful.
6	IV-4	Determine which houses are ruled and occupied by the planets in step 5A & 5B.	This will also show which areas of life are greatly hindered or aided.
7		Compose a summary of your findings from Steps 1-6.	An overall and comprehensive analysis of the individual based upon the most important factors within the birth chart.

of the information and like anything in life this takes time, devotion, and practice. In other words, do not expect to fill out this table and then all of the answers will automatically appear out of thin air. You will still need to take the information you have gathered and put the pieces together like one giant human puzzle.

The best way to demonstrate effective chart analysis in practice is by filling out these tables for each one of our case studies. If you feel confident in your skills, I urge you to first fill out each step by yourself on a separate piece of paper first and then compare your answers to mine to see how accurate you were. We will now observe each case study's birth chart with proper analyzes based upon the steps listed above.

CLIENT A: BIRTH CHART

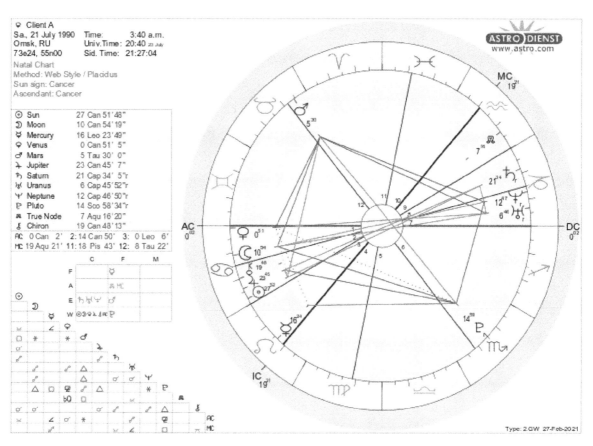

CLIENT A: BIRTH CHART ANALYSIS

1	II-1	Determine any imbalances within the elements and modalities.	Gives you a quick picture of the individual with simple remedies.

Client A has an overabundance of water and is lacking in fire and air. They are heavily emotionally driven with a very subjective outlook. Furthermore, their lack of air makes it hard for them to communicate their intense feelings, which can cause them to bottle it up more than express it outwardly in a healthy matter. It is also difficult for them to take the personal out of any kind of social interaction because they are incredibly emotionally invested with anything they do. This can make professional matters and associations problematic. The lack of fire makes it hard for them to initiate and to go on instinct. They second guess themselves and do not engage with an activity or individual unless they feel inwardly secure which makes them heavily risk adverse. I would recommend breathing techniques, high cardio exercises, and more spontaneity when it comes to social interactions and life in general.

Client A is also lacking in mutable energy with a fair balance of cardinal and fixed energy. They have a hard time following through even though they have great ease with initiation. If they feel inwardly confident they proceed forward, but the lack of fire and mutability makes it so the moment they no longer feel up to it, it is easy for them to give up. They should focus on completing their goals regardless of how their opinions have changed on the subject. They also need to watch their energy levels as they can have too much energy with not enough relaxation time. It would help to talk more with friends and other supportive individuals who can help them to keep on going when it gets rough.

[Step 2A] Client A's sense of security is highly tied within their physical body. If they feel physically ill, for example, it will also affect their personal self-esteem. Similarly, emotional conditions of Client A can create psychosomatic illnesses if they are not too careful. This need to feel secure on the physical and emotional front comes to head when they are expected to change their outlook (Moon oppose Uranus) or if they receive some insight that is not in tune with their personal metaphysical outlook (Moon oppose Neptune). In other words, Neptune and Uranus can force the individual to be taken out of their comfort zone by changing their mentality on more progressive and spiritual realms by the individuals they encounter (Uranus and Neptune in

342

2A	II-7 IV-4 II-5 II-6	Determine the Planetary ruler(s) of the Ascendant along with their house placement, sign placement, and any aspect(s) within an orb range of 0°-6°.	The Planet(s) that rule the ascendant show how the individual portrays themselves along with their sense of self-confidence.

ASCENDANT	RULER	SIGN	HOUSE	ASPECTS		
♋	☽	♋	1	**NAME**	**GLYPH**	**ORB**
				Natal Moon in Cancer opposes Natal Neptune in Capricorn	n. ☽♋ ☍ n. ♆♑	2
				Natal Moon in Cancer opposes Natal Uranus in Capricorn	n. ☽♋ ☍ n. ♅♑	4
				Natal Moon in Cancer trine Natal Pluto in Scorpio	n. ☽♋ △ n. ♇♏	4
				Natal Moon in Cancer sextile Natal Mars in Taurus	n. ☽♋ ✶ n. ♂♉	5

the 7th House). This usually happens when they meet people with different backgrounds and life experiences that contradict what they personally have experienced. As such, they naturally shy away from these types of interactions due to Cancer's natural introversion, which is exacerbated by the four planets that reside within Cancer.

However, if they are able to sacrifice their personal comfortability in these realms and acquiesce to what these planets are asking them to do, great personal change can occur, and they can find more like-minded individuals and friendships because they eventually realize that they are similarly as like-minded as these unconventional individuals. They only need the courage to inquire and put themself out there. The issue is, however, if there is one thing Client A hates the most, it is being forced to do anything. Thankfully, the sextile to Mars gives them the capacity to initiate those new perspectives and experiences with new people out in the world if they put in the initiative, although this is not their primary M.O.

2B	II-7 IV-4 II-5 II-6	Determine the Planetary ruler(s) of the Midheaven along with their house placement, sign placement, and any aspect(s)within an orb range of 0°-6°.		The Planet(s) that rule the midheaven signify the individual's main lifegoals, aspirations, and their approach towards these endeavors.	

MIDHEAVEN	RULER	SIGN	HOUSE	ASPECTS		
♒	♄	♑	8	**NAME**	**GLYPH**	**ORB**
	♅	♑	7	Natal Saturn in Capricorn opposes Natal Jupiter in Cancer	n. ♄♑ ☍ n. ♃♋	2
				Natal Uranus in Capricorn opposes Natal Moon in Cancer	n. ♅♑ ☍ n. ☽♋	4
				Natal Uranus in Capricorn opposes Natal Venus in Cancer	n. ♅♑ ☍ n. ♀♋	6
				Natal Uranus in Capricorn conjoin Natal Neptune in Capricorn	n. ♅♑ ☌ n. ♆♑	6
				Natal Uranus in Capricorn opposes natal Ascendant in Cancer	n. ♅♑ ☍ n. Asc♋	6
				Natal Saturn in Capricorn opposes Natal Sun in Cancer	n. ♄♑ ☍ n. ☉♋	6

Client A's Ascendant's story is directly related to their Midheaven story because the ruler of the Ascendant (Moon) is in opposition to the Midheaven ruler (Uranus). Therefore, we can conclude that the issues and strengths that were already mentioned in the Ascendant step are related to their career and personal goals. In other words, the inner conflict that arises from meeting different people and circumstances, and generally residing in their comfort zone, is experienced daily within their line of work regardless of what that may be. This is where they are forced to make a lot of those personal compromises but instead, they usually close up, which can create friction between coworkers and superiors. This is emphasized even more because both rulers of the Midheaven, Saturn and Uranus, oppose the personal points Sun, Venus, and Ascendant. This tells me that Client A's introversion truly forbids them at times to express themselves fully, which hinders professional relationships.

I would recommend that the client work on their lack of fire and air because, indeed, this is becoming the core problem that other issues stem from. Their lack of fire affects their perception of self-confidence and self-worth, and the lack of air makes it hard for them to get out of this subjective mindset because they do not open up well to others. They lack a sounding board to voice their frustrations. The more they try to work through these issues, the more they will realize that the world and the people within are not as scary as it all seems. Their career and romantic life will also be aided by their bump in self-confidence and the realization that they have more in common with others than they realize. However, as previously mentioned, it is up to Client A to initiate the desire to work on their self-esteem and to interact with others more.

3A	II-4	Determine if any planet(s) are in a sign of exaltation, rulership, detriment, or fall.		This will adjust the natural temperament of the planet(s) for better or worse.
3B	IV-4	If any planet(s) exist in Step 3A, determine the houses these planets rule and are placed within.		Houses ruled and resided by effected planets from Step 3A will be influenced by their dignity or debility.
PLANET	SIGN	E/R/D/F	HOUSE PLACEMENT	HOUSE RULERSHIPS
☽	♋	RULER	1	1 & 2
♂	♉	DETRIMENT	11	6
♃	♋	EXALTATION	2	11
♄	♑	RULER	8	7, 8, 9, & 10

The planetary dignities above tremendously help with the previously mentioned issues. For one, the chart ruler (Moon) is in the sign of their rulership (Cancer) which helps to strengthen the planet while it is experiencing those oppositions to Uranus and Neptune. In other words, although Client A has trouble with meeting new people, circumstances, and ideas, they are nevertheless strong and self-supportive within themself. If they come into uncomfortable situations, they are still able to remain stable and solid within themself and not experience an emotional breakdown of sorts.

Furthermore, Jupiter being it exaltation greatly helps out the chart and their Sun because Jupiter is conjoined with their Sun (see Step 4). To this point, if you recall from Step 2, the MC ruler (Saturn) is opposed the Sun similar to how Uranus is opposed their Moon. This means that just as the Moon is aided by being in its sign of rulership, the Sun is also greatly aided by being conjoined to the exalted Jupiter which is also opposed to the MC ruler of Saturn. This means that both the Sun and the Moon are protected by powerfully harmonious planets which gives Client A a strong buoyancy in dealing with the issues that those oppositions manifest. Namely, even though they do not enjoy and come into contact with uncomfortable people and circumstances often, they are nevertheless still very confident in their stance and personality because the Sun and Moon are strengthened for the better. The problem arises when the personality needs to evolve because that is when Client A digs in their heels.

If you recall from Step 2A, their chart ruler (Moon) sextiles Mars, which is where they have the ability to work through these conflicts if they seek out initiation. However, Mars being in the sign of its detriment makes the process of self-initiation even more difficult because Mars in the chart is naturally hindered and therefore slow to react. This is confirmed by the lack of fire and air we witnessed in Step 1 and by now, you are probably starting to notice how the data and evidence we have been gathering confirms itself in this way. In other words, the lack of fire from Step 1 is confirmed by Mars being in detriment. Both of these parameters equate to the same conclusion, and this is a good way to approach a chart because you are obtaining multiple forms of evidence that confirms the same analysis.

4	II-5	Determine the chart's aspects with an orb range of 0°-5°.	Indicates the individual's most rudimentary strengths and weaknesses.	
NAME			**GLYPH**	**ORB**
Natal Venus in Cancer conj. Natal Cancer Ascendant			n.♀♋ ☌ n.Asc♋	0
Natal Mars in Taurus trine Natal Uranus in Capricorn			n.♂♉ △ n.♅♑	1
Natal Jupiter in Cancer opposes Natal Saturn in Capricorn			n.♃♋ ☍ n.♄♑	1
Natal Moon in Cancer opposes Natal Neptune in Capricorn			n.☽♋ ☍ n.♆♑	2
Natal Mercury in Leo square Natal Pluto in Scorpio			n.☿♌ □ n.♇♏	2
Natal Neptune in Capricorn sextile Natal Pluto in Scorpio			n.♆♑ ✶ n.♇♏	2
Natal Mercury in Leo conj. Natal Leo IC			n.☿♌ ☌ n.IC♌	3

Natal Sun in Cancer conj. Natal Jupiter in Cancer	n.☉♋ ☌ n.♃♋	4
Natal Moon in Cancer trine Natal Pluto in Scorpio	n.☽♋ △ n.♇♏	4
Natal Sun in Cancer sextile Natal Mars in Taurus	n.☽♋ ✶ n.♂♉	5
Natal Venus in Cancer sextile Natal Mars in Taurus	n.♀♋ ✶ n.♂♉	5
Natal Mars in Taurus sextile Natal Cancer Ascendant	n.♂♉ ✶ n.Asc♋	5
Natal Pluto in Scorpio square Natal Aquarius Midheaven	n.♇♏ □ n.MC♒	5

Client A's strongest aspect is their natal Venus conjoined to their Ascendant. This makes them very easy to get along with and the fact that the Venus is also in sextile to Mars shows that men and women both feel comforted and pleasant around them. They utilize this Venus energy by making others feel secure, welcomed, and amicable. Remember, the problem is when they are placed out of their comfort zone by the oppositions of Uranus and Saturn, but when Client A is in their element within familiar surroundings, they come off as incredibly gentle, secure, confident, and inviting.

Although Mars is in its detriment and Uranus is in opposition to their Venus and Moon, Uranus is still in a trine with Mars which greatly helps the conflict that these oppositions create. Keep in mind that Mars is in the 11th house and Uranus is in the 7th and they are in a trine which tells me that their friends and social circles, in addition to those that they are close to by intimate relationships, also give them comfort and confidence that they require. The problem is that these friendships and romantic partners are probably few and far between due to the detriment nature of Mars and the oppositions of Uranus to Venus and the Moon. This ties back to the lack of air in the chart. If they can cast a wider net towards new friendships and intimate relationships, then the trine between Mars and Uranus will help them out greatly in being more comfortable outside of their comfort zone because friends and partners can give them that objective sounding board that they lack due to their lack of air.

To this point, Client A's Mercury is squared their Pluto and Pluto is also squared to their Midheaven. This simply confirms the above analysis because Client A's biggest issues stem from a lack of objective communication and not being able to put themselves outside of their comfort zone. Even more so, with Mercury in the 3rd house, the house of communication, and Pluto in the 6th house, the house of critical thinking, this tells me that Client A's subjective mindset goes through constant cycles of self-criticism because they are unable to work outside of these parameters. It is as though Client A has this internal feedback loop where they will have a thought, typically irrational due to Mercury, and then mull over that thought in a negative way due to Pluto's placement. Again, this ties back to the lack of air and the need for the client to seek out people who can take them out of their internal perspective more often. They need to start asking themselves, "Is this thought logical or emotional?", "Is this a good idea, or am I just being too harsh towards my idea where I tear it down instead of going with it?" Remember, squares are unconscious so the more we can catch them in the act, the more their power over us begins to wane.

The good news is that Pluto also trines the Moon which is their chart ruler. This again gives them a stronger backing into these harder placements because it gives them strength to handle ego death and rebirth. In other words, they may be hesitant to go and seek new perspectives about themself but once they understand who they are and how they need to improve, they do so gracefully without any conflict. It is only a matter of getting the ball rolling and then they have no problem in admitting what needs to be released and what needs to change.

5A		From the information gathered in Steps 3-4, determine the chart's most afflicted planet(s).		Shows which planet(s) are the most self-destructive and inharmonious.			
5B		From the information gathered in Steps 3-4, determine the chart's most beneficial planet(s).		Shows which planet(s) are the most harmonious and helpful.			
6	IV-4	Determine which houses are occupied and ruled by the planets in step 5A & 5B.		This will also show which areas of life are greatly hindered or aided.			
MOST BENEFICIAL				MOST AFFLICTED			
PLANET	SIGN	HOUSE PLACEMENT	HOUSE RULERSHIP	PLANET	SIGN	HOUSE PLACEMENT	HOUSE RULERSHIP
☽	♋	1	1 & 2	☉	♋	2	3 & 4
♃	♋	2	11	☿	♌	3	5

Although the Moon can have issues being in opposition to Uranus and Neptune, it is still nevertheless very strong being in the sign of rulership and in sextile to Mars and a trine to Pluto. This confirms what was already mentioned in that Client A is very strong within themselves and can therefore be a comforting force for others due to their inner emotional strength. With the aid of Pluto, they can admit when they are wrong and need to change when it comes about. The only issue is they are prone to settling into a rut instead of initiating that positive change.

Jupiter, being in the sign of exaltation and conjoining the Sun, also strengthens the chart, giving them circumstances where they might not have to experience the discomfort that the opposition to Saturn can provide. In other words, although they do not enjoy being taken out of their comfort zone, this might not occur often, and even when it does, it is done in a gentle way. Also, Jupiter being the greater benefic gives the client a lot of good fortune and luck when it comes to their life. This ease of life that Jupiter provides helps with their inner confidence and outward self-expression. Especially when they are in environments that they can control and feel relaxed within.

This helps with the fact that the Sun is not the best placed, being in Cancer and opposing Saturn. Again, although they do feel confident and are easy to get along with, they are still very shy, hesitant, and introverted especially when it comes to authority figures and possibly the father or father figure. Mercury is also not helping the client because the inability to get their emotional bent out into the open with objective reasoning is simply exacerbated by Mercury residing in the 3rd house and squaring Pluto in the 6th house. They get easily intimidated by others and, as already mentioned, encounter constant mental cycles of having ideas but then tearing them down before they even get a chance to be expressed outwardly. It would help the client if they would just go with it without thinking too much about the what ifs.

7		Compose a summary of your findings from Steps 1-6.	An overall and comprehensive analysis of the individual based upon the most important factors within the birth chart.

Client A is highly amicable, and others often enjoy their company (Venus conjunct Asc/Venus sextile Mars). Similarly, the friends and close relationships they do have do them much good because they provide for them the support and the sounding board that they require (Mars in 11th house trine Uranus in 7th house). When these friendlier forces give them advice, the client is able to take it well and change their personality and psychology for the better (Moon in sign of Rulership/Moon trine Pluto). The issue comes when the client is not able to control the environment and comes into contact with people in authority or those with different lifestyles and spiritual philosophies (Moon oppose Neptune and Uranus/Sun oppose Saturn). Nevertheless, they are very confident within themself and life does not tend to throw them into hard circumstances too often because they are typically fortunate in all matters of life, which helps with the overall ease of life along with their sense of self-worth (Jupiter in sign of exaltation/Jupiter conjoin Sun). The issues are usually mental in nature because the client lacks objectivity and is heavily self-critical (Mercury in 3rd house square Pluto in the 6th house/Lack of air). They should also take care of psychosomatic illnesses due to this fact (Cancer stellium in the 1st House). Additionally, they lack initiation and have a hard time as a self-starter (Mars in detriment/Lack of fire). If they can open up their social circles more and go with their gut more without being too self-critical, both of these actions will greatly help the client by addressing their weaknesses in ways that also ties into their strengths.

CLIENT B: BIRTH CHART

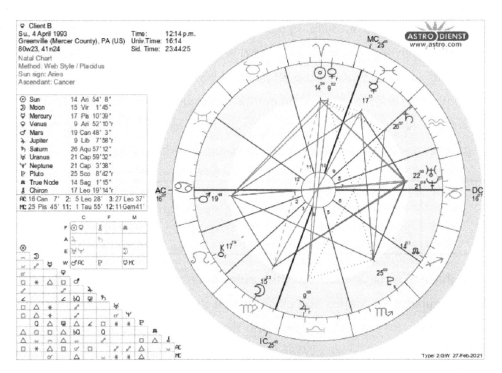

CLIENT B: BIRTH CHART ANALYSIS

1	II-1	Determine any imbalances within the elements and modalities.	Gives you a quick picture of the individual with simple remedies.

Client B's chart is relatively balanced elementally with a stronger emphasis within the water element. However, Client B has too much cardinal energy and not enough fixed energy. This tells me that Client B eagerly initiates thoughts, projects, and feelings but they can go away just as quickly as they came about. This is especially true within emotional realms due to their emphasized water. I would recommend holding their ground more in life to help with the lack of fixed energy and recommend they do not act upon their initial thoughts or reactions too quickly to help with their abundance of cardinal energy. Similar to Client A, Client B is lacking air which means they need to think things over more before they make any sort of conclusions on any matter.

2A	II-7 IV-4 II-5 II-6	Determine the Planetary ruler(s) of the Ascendant along with their house placement, sign placement, and any aspect(s) within an orb range of 0°-6°.	The Planet(s) that rule the ascendant show how the individual portrays themselves along with their sense of self-confidence.

ASCENDANT	RULER	SIGN	HOUSE	ASPECTS		
♋	☽	♍	3	**NAME**	**GLYPH**	**ORB**
				Natal Moon in Virgo sextile Cancer Ascendant	n. ☽♍ ✶ n.ASC♋	1
				Natal Moon in Virgo oppose Natal Mercury in Pisces	n. ☽♍ ☍ n. ☿♓	2
				Natal Moon in Virgo sextile Natal Mars in Cancer	n. ☽♍ ✶ n. ♂♋	4
				Natal Moon in Virgo trine Natal Neptune in Capricorn	n. ☽♍ △ n. ♆♑	6

For the most part, Client B's chart ruler (Moon) is well aspected and properly expressed. The sextile to the Ascendant tells me that they do a good job at portraying themselves honestly, especially when it comes to emotional matters. Unlike Client A, whose Moon oppositions to Neptune and Uranus cause conflict when they encounter individuals who are unlike them in life experiences and metaphysical philosophies, Client B relishes meeting people from different walks of life with unorthodox ways of thinking and believing because, instead of the Moon opposing these planets as it was with Client A, Client B's Moon trines both of these planets. Furthermore, their Moon is in the 3rd house of communication which trines Neptune and Uranus in the 7th house, the house of personal relationships. This tells me that Client B has a very open mind and enjoys individuals who also have an open mind and heart. Due to the Moon sextile the Ascendant, when Client B is around such individuals, they find it very easy to express themself.

However, the issue comes with Client B's inability to share their own thoughts and opinions on the matter outside of these closer relationships as evidenced by Mercury's opposition to the Moon and the Sun's square to the Ascendant (See Step 4). They might feel as though what they think and believe is a little too out there so they project that by finding individuals who will express their unconventionality openly. Client B will simply interact with those kinds of people and allow others to express these latent parts within themself instead. Client B should work on expressing their quirkiness just as much as they enjoy watching others express theirs. Nevertheless, the chart ruler is healthy and properly expressed, and if they feel comfortable to be themself, they find it very easy to do so.

[Step 2B] The Midheaven rulers tell an interesting story with one of the rulers, Jupiter, being in conflict with their Sun and Venus but on the other hand, Neptune is nicely aspected to the chart ruler (Moon) through trine and to Mercury trough sextile. With the Jupiter story, Jupiter is in the 4th house and it opposes the Sun and Venus in the 10th house. This tells me that they can have conflict with individuals from their family and/or the mother and father figures within their lives. Relating back to the chart ruler story, Client B enjoys the company of unconventional individuals because they agree with their outward thinking and metaphysical ideals. However, Client B could have come from a more conservative and closed-minded upbringing which makes it hard for them to express themself in this way, which consequently effects their outlook on achieving goals that are similarly unconventional.

2B	II-7	Determine the Planetary ruler(s) of the Midheaven along with their house placement, sign placement, and any aspect(s) within an orb range of 0°-6°.		The Planet(s) that rule the midheaven signify the individual's main lifegoals, aspirations, and their approach towards these endeavors.		
	IV-4					
	II-5					
	II-6					

MIDHEAVEN	RULER	SIGN	HOUSE	ASPECTS		
♓	♃	♎	4	NAME	GLYPH	ORB
	♆	♑	7	Natal Jupiter in Libra opposes Natal Venus in Aries	n. ♃♎ ☍ n. ♀♈	0
				Natal Neptune in Capricorn oppose Natal Mars in Cancer	n. ♆♑ ☍ n. ♂♋	2
				Natal Neptune in Capricorn sextile Pisces Midheaven	n. ♆♑ ✶ n. MC♓	4
				Natal Neptune in Capricorn sextile Natal Mercury in Pisces	n. ♆♑ ✶ n. ☿♓	4
				Natal Neptune in Capricorn sextile Natal Pluto in Scorpio	n. ♆♑ ✶ n. ♇♏	4
				Natal Neptune in Capricorn conjoin Capricorn Descendant	n. ♆♑ ☌ n. DSC♑	5
				Natal Jupiter in Libra opposes Natal Sun in Aries	n. ♃♎ ☍ n. ☉♈	5
				Natal Neptune in Capricorn trines Natal Moon in Virgo	n. ♆♑ △ n. ☽♑	6

For example, Client B might want to seek a profession that is not predictable or accepted by society, and they would do well in these professions due to the beneficial aspects made by Neptune. But the Jupiter oppositions tell me it is hard for them to tell their family of their life goals and/or their life goals are hindered because their family and parental units do not approve. This is further evidenced by Neptune in the 7th house opposition to Mars in the 1st house. This means that they can be too influenced by these familial forces that they go, "Ok, maybe this is not a good idea to peruse this profession," and they begin to doubt their motivations and skillset. Again, this is why they attract others who are more in tune to their unconventional nature. Client B needs to achieve and strive for whatever they personally have an interest in because they do in fact have skills in professions like psychic abilities, energy healing, and counseling as evidenced by Neptune. They simply need to ignore the nay-sayers in their life and find supportive people that will act as their "second family" who will support and approve of their decisions no matter what. The answer involves the numerous sextiles in that they have to be the one to take the first step and initiate those types of plans.

3A	II-4	Determine if any planet(s) are in a sign of exaltation, rulership, detriment, or fall.	This will adjust the natural temperament of the planet(s) for better or worse.	
3B	IV-4	If any planet(s) exist in Step 3A, determine the houses these planets rule and are placed within.	Houses ruled and resided by effected planets from Step 3A will be influenced by their dignity or debility.	
PLANET	SIGN	E/R/D/F	HOUSE PLACEMENT	HOUSE RULERSHIPS
☉	♈	EXALTATION	10	2 & 3
☿	♓	DETRIMENT & FALL	9	4 & 12
♀	♈	DETRIMENT	10	11
♂	♋	FALL	1	5
♄	♒	RULER	8	7, 8, & 9

The first thing that stands out is the flipped nature of Venus and Mars with Venus in the highly masculine sign of Aries and Mars in the highly feminine sign of Cancer. This causes both of these planets to work at cross purpose because the client on one hand comes off as too emotionally intense with the Venus in Aries, and the Mars in Cancer makes it so they have to be in control constantly because they can be a little too sensitive to the words and thoughts of others. This causes the ability to relate to others a little difficult, and Client B should focus on when to act verses when to react. This is confirmed by the abundance of cardinal energy and water energy, which means they sometimes react inappropriately due to unprocessed emotions and thoughts. Instead, they go off their gut reaction, which is sometimes not appropriate for the situation at hand.

Mercury's placement makes it hard for them to process and communicate their feelings and ideas because there is simply too much confusion. At times, Client B becomes frustrated because they feel stuck between a rock and a hard place, and when they feel cornered, they revert to flight or fight instead of processing it through. This is due to their Mercury placements which hinders their thinking abilities. The issue is that Client B is too psychically open and tends to soak up the psychic energies of those around them, which makes it hard for them to discern what is their thought and what are the thoughts that they have picked up from others. This effect is very subtle, but it is nevertheless impactful.

The Sun's placement allows for Client B to be true to themself. However, with the square to the Ascendant this can make it hard for them to express themself outwardly even though they are being true from within. Even if things may be confusing and difficult to portray at times, they nevertheless are able to be honest in their expression when it does occur. For example, if they are flustered, at least they will express being flustered as opposed to repressing those emotions. The issue is they might not tell anyone they are flustered but they nevertheless know what they are feeling and therefore feel it fully. The Sun rules the 2nd and 3rd houses which tells me that if they have siblings, they find it very easy to be themselves around them due to the 3rd house. With the 2nd house, their aesthetics are a great reflection of their personality, which gives them a good sense of style and attractiveness. They are also good at bargaining and finding good deals on quality items.

With Saturn, this gives the Client easy access to authority figures especially in realms of the occult and academia because Saturn rules the 8th and 9th houses. Saturn also rules the 7th which tells me they have great rapport with elders and wise individuals, and they similarly enjoy the company and insights of Client B.

[Step 4] Client B's Pluto trine to the Midheaven further confirms that they would be prosperous in any sort of counseling or metaphysical profession because they can help others with healthy ego death and therapy. Similarly, Mercury's trine to the Ascendant tells me that, although they have a hard time figuring out what to say or what they are thinking, they are nevertheless honest about it and do a good job with healthy expression as opposed to repression.

4	II-5	Determine the chart's aspects with an orb range of 0°-5°.	Indicates the individual's most rudimentary strengths and weaknesses.	
NAME			**GLYPH**	**ORB**
Natal Pluto in Scorpio trine Natal Pisces Midheaven			n.♇♏ △ n.MC♓	0
Natal Venus in Aries opposes Natal Jupiter in Libra			n.♀♈ ☍ n.♃♎	0
Natal Moon in Virgo sextile Natal Cancer Ascendant			n.☽♍ ✶ n.ASC♋	1
Natal Mercury in Pisces trine Natal Cancer Ascendant			n.☿♓ △ n.ASC♋	1
Natal Saturn in Aquarius square Natal Pluto in Scorpio			n.♄♒ □ n.♇♏	1
Natal Uranus in Capricorn conjoin Natal Neptune in Capricorn			n.♅♑ ☌ n.♆♑	1
Natal Moon in Virgo opposes Natal Mercury in Pisces			n.☽♍ ☍ n.☿♓	2
Natal Sun in Aries square Natal Cancer Ascendant			n.☉♈ □ n.ASC♋	2
Natal Mercury in Pisces trine Natal Mars in Cancer			n.☿♓ △ n.♂♋	2
Natal Mars in Cancer opposes Natal Neptune in Capricorn			n.♂♋ ☍ n.♆♑	2
Natal Mars in Cancer opposes Natal Uranus in Capricorn			n.♂♋ ☍ n.♅♑	3
Natal Uranus in Capricorn sextile Natal Pluto in Scorpio			n.♅♑ ✶ n.♇♏	3
Natal Mercury in Pisces sextile Natal Neptune in Capricorn			n.☿♓ ✶ n.♆♑	4
Natal Neptune in Capricorn sextile Natal Pluto in Scorpio			n.♆♑ ✶ n.♇♏	4
Natal Neptune in Capricorn sextile Natal Pisces Midheaven			n.♆♑ ✶ n.MC♓	4
Natal Sun in Aries conjoin Natal Venus in Aries			n.☉♈ ☌ n.♀♈	5
Natal Sun in Aries square Natal Mars in Cancer			n.☉♈ □ n.♂♋	5
Natal Sun in Aries opposes Natal Jupiter in Libra			n.☉♈ ☍ n.♃♎	5
Natal Mercury in Pisces sextile Natal Uranus in Capricorn			n.☿♓ ✶ n.♅♑	5
Natal Neptune in Capricorn conjoin Natal Capricorn Descendant			n.♆♑ ☌ n.DSC♑	5

Their Saturn squaring Pluto means that, although they have great access to wise and knowledgeable individuals, they still come into conflict and can end up in fights with people in authority and institutions of power. This is probably due to their honest expression as was previously mentioned. Although Client B is less likely to repress, others can still be taken aback by the intensity they project, which can cause others to naturally go on the defensive. What would help Client B in this regard is to work on their self-esteem and to not be so sensitive when others call out

356

their faults or shoddy performances. Unlike Client A, who has an easier time accepting fault and improving the self from those faults, Client B immediately takes it into a realm of conflict, even subconsciously, because they are not addressing their personal vulnerabilities. Again, they need to relax and calm down before they react and take what other people are saying to heart. If they do, they will realize that others are only being honest to help them and not to make them feel inferior.

Although their exalted Sun helps with proper self-expression and less repression, they may nevertheless have troubles being honest with others about who they are and what they want to do based on the Sun squaring the Ascendant. This means that even though they have a good idea of who and what they are, they might sometimes not fully express that with others and hide it more. This comes from the opposition between planets in the 4th and 10th houses. Perhaps when they were younger they were expected to act a certain way which went against their true nature. This explains why they project outwardly friction with authority because they relate those past experiences into adulthood, which causes frustrations and the inability to accept fault when it is required.

These frustrations are further provoked by the Sun in the 10th house squaring Mars in the 1st house. Again, authority figures and the father figure in their lives have greatly hindered their self-expression in the past, which causes Client B to be stuck within their own emotions at times. As previously mentioned, although they might be honest with those emotions, they nevertheless can affect the way they react to others along with their personal motivations. At their worst manifestation, Client B can essentially be swimming around in their own frustrations due to their faulty self-esteem, and instead of ignoring how others are putting them down, they project that frustration towards other individuals who are perceived to be authority figures and/or the parental figure within their adult life. Client B would do well to ignore and dismiss any and all negative people and opinions, and work on strengthening their own self-worth.

Although Mercury is in a tough predicament being in detriment and fall, it is greatly helped by the multitude of aspects that is has between other planets. Namely, the sextiles to Uranus and Neptune along with the trine to Mars and the loose trine to Pluto. These four planets greatly help in Mercury's dilemma by the way Client B seeks refuge with likeminded individuals who they can trust to speak their mind and emotions. This creates a safe bubble for them where they would otherwise feel threatened. Just as it is with Client A, the more Client B relies on these individuals who are a positive influence will overall help them to gain confidence and drive to not only improve upon themself, but the proper ambition to achieve what they truly want to achieve.

5A		From the information gathered in Steps 3-4, determine the chart's most afflicted planet(s).		Shows which planet(s) are the most self-destructive and inharmonious.			
5B		From the information gathered in Steps 3-4, determine the chart's most beneficial planet(s).		Shows which planet(s) are the most harmonious and helpful.			
6	IV-4	Determine which houses are occupied and ruled by the planets in step 5A & 5B.		This will also show which areas of life are greatly hindered or aided.			
MOST BENEFICIAL				MOST AFFLICTED			
PLANET	SIGN	HOUSE PLACEMENT	HOUSE RULERSHIP	PLANET	SIGN	HOUSE PLACEMENT	HOUSE RULERSHIP
☽	♋	3	1	☉	♈	10	2 & 3
☿	♓	9	4 & 12	♀	♈	10	11
♆	♏	5	5	♂	♋	1	5

The above information can seem contradictory at first because Mercury is in the sign of detriment and fall but is working beneficially and the Sun is in exaltation, but it is working with affliction. Remember, astrology is hardly ever cut and dried, and it can sometimes be filled with contradictions and paradoxes that need to be considered and worked over. The reason why these planets switch their temperaments so drastically is due to the aspects they experience. Mercury is greatly aided by the loose grand trine between Pluto and Mars and the sextiles between Neptune and Uranus. The Sun is hindered due to being conjoined to Venus, which is in detriment along with the loose T-square the Sun makes with Mars, Uranus, and Neptune along with an opposition to Jupiter. These cumulative aspects drastically alter the temperaments of these two planets so much so that they reverse in quality.

To put it succinctly, the afflicted planets of the Sun, Venus, and Mars makes it hard for Client B to relate well with others because they come off as too emotionally intense. However, the positive power of Mercury, Pluto, and the Moon make it so they have amazing transformative abilities within themself. The issue is that they normally project these skills onto the problems of others. All they need to do is simply reflect those healing abilities back onto their own person. In other words, they need to take the advice they give to others and support themself in the same way they support others. If they can do this, they will have an easier time in handling overly critical individuals and people that are perceived to be a threat.

7		Compose a summary of your findings from Steps 1-6.	An overall and comprehensive analysis of the individual based upon the most important factors within the birth chart.

Client B has amazing healing skills that are both physical and psychological in nature (Pluto trine Midheaven/Mars trine Mercury/Mercury trine Pluto/Mercury sextile Uranus and Neptune). This also gives them great psychic and empathic abilities. They are highly in tune with their feelings (Moon as chart ruler in good condition) and when they are around people that are likeminded and unconventional in nature, they feel incredibly confident (Moon in 3rd house trine Uranus and Neptune in the 7th house). Their intuition is usually spot on and they can tell others what needs to change, and others seek their astute advice in these realms (Pluto trine Mercury). However, when they are out of this comfort zone of likeminded individuals, they become vulnerable and are more prone to flight or fight responses (Mars square Sun/Mars square Venus). This is especially true when they are dealing with authority figures or institutions of power (Saturn square Pluto). This uneasiness stems from their upbringing that might have been more conservative and closed-minded than they are (Sun and Venus in the 10th house opposing Jupiter in the 4th house). This causes them to doubt themself and to not feel validated in their thoughts and goals (Sun square Ascendant). All Client B needs to do is take their immense healing abilities and revert them onto themself which will give them the confidence and healthy ego death they give others. What will also help is to start with people they already feel comfortable around (Moon trine Neptune and Uranus) and to ignore people that are bringing them down (Saturn square Pluto/Moon opposes Mercury).

CLIENT C: BIRTH CHART

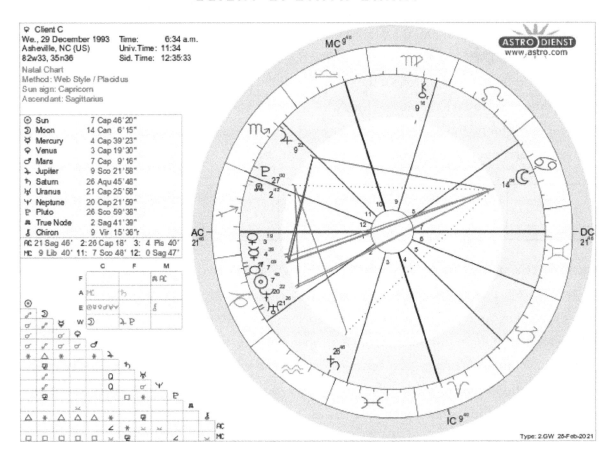

CLIENT C: BIRTH CHART ANALYSIS

1	II-1	Determine any imbalances within the elements and modalities.	Gives you a quick picture of the individual with simple remedies.

Client C is earth heavy with the other elements containing lower, yet similar, values. They are also cardinal heavy and lack mutable energy. This tells me that their motivation is completely intrinsic, but the issue is that they can be prone to inaction rather than action. In other words, they wait to see how other individuals and the situations around them unfold first, and then they decide whether or not to get involved. If they do decide to engage, they can nevertheless have issues with follow through similar to our other clients who lack fixed and mutable energy. I would recommend that the client take initiation more, participate in intense workout regiments, and expand their thinking by reading and meeting people whose ideas are new and different from theirs. The abundance of Capricorn energy means that they can be too conservative in thinking or in lifestyle. As such, they should take more chances and see more of what the world has to offer instead of staying with the tried, tested, and true.

2A	II-7 IV-4 II-5 II-6	Determine the Planetary ruler(s) of the Ascendant along with their house placement, sign placement, and any aspect(s) within an orb range of 0°-6°.		The Planet(s) that rule the ascendant show how the individual portrays themselves along with their sense of self-confidence.	
ASCENDANT	**RULER**	**SIGN**	**HOUSE**	**ASPECTS**	
♐	♃	♏	11		

NAME	GLYPH	ORB
Natal Jupiter in Scorpio sextile Natal Sun in Capricorn	n. ♃♏ ✶ n. ☉♑	2
Natal Jupiter in Scorpio sextile Natal Mars in Capricorn	n. ♃♏ ✶ n. ♂♑	2
Natal Jupiter in Scorpio sextile Natal Mercury in Capricorn	n. ♃♏ ✶ n. ☿♑	5
Natal Jupiter in Scorpio trine Natal Moon in Cancer	n. ♃♏ △ n. ☽♋	5

The chart ruler, Jupiter, is incredibly well aspected by other planets within the natal chart. Furthermore, the personal planets Sun and Moon are harmoniously aspected to Jupiter which indicates an amazing ability to be not only truthful to themself, but to be very much "what you see is what you get" when it comes to meeting other people. This is confirmed even more with Mercury and Mars in sextile with Jupiter. This means Client C is able to stand up and speak for themself when the time calls. The issue, as we will see later, is that due to the lack of aspect connections to the Ascendant itself, it is hard for them to share their truth with the world although, ironically, they are incredibly truthful and transparent as to who they are. Nevertheless, these harmonious aspects to the chart ruler indicate that Client C has a strong connection between their psychology and the persona that stems out of that psychology.

2B	II-7 IV-4 II-5 II-6	Determine the Planetary ruler of the Midheaven along with their house placement, sign placement, and any aspect(s) within an orb range of 0°-6°.			The Planet(s) that rule the midheaven signify the individual's main lifegoals, aspirations, and their approach towards these endeavors.		
MIDHEAVEN		**RULER**	**SIGN**	**HOUSE**	**ASPECTS**		
♎		♀	♑	1	**NAME**	**GLYPH**	**ORB**
					Natal Venus in Capricorn conjoin Natal Mercury in Capricorn	n. ♀♑ ☌ n. ☿♑	1
					Natal Venus in Capricorn conjoin Natal Sun in Capricorn	n. ♀♑ ☌ n. ☉♑	4
					Natal Venus in Capricorn conjoin Natal Mars in Capricorn	n. ♀♑ ☌ n. ♂♑	4
					Natal Venus in Capricorn square Libra Midheaven	n. ♀♑ □ n.MC♎	6

The Midheaven ruler, Venus, in in conjunction with Sun, Mercury and Mars. This means that their motivations, personality, and intellect are all heavily devoted to who they are, and what they want to accomplish. This is exemplified even more with Client C because of their multiple planets in Capricorn because this sign is known for always striving towards their goals and ambitions. These various aspects to the Midheaven ruler tell me that who they are is very much in tune with their drive and personal motivations. Again, as we will see below, the issue has to do with how the planets in the chart are aspected to the Midheaven itself. To this point, the Midheaven ruler, Venus, is squared to the Midheaven. This tells me that there is a disconnect between what Client C wants to accomplish, and the outside world where they aim to achieve their various inspirations. Still, as we have witnessed with the Ascendant, Client C is very much in tune with what they want to do and how they want to do it.

3A	II-4	Determine if any planet(s) are in a sign of exaltation, rulership, detriment, or fall.		This will adjust the natural temperament of the planet(s) for better or worse.
3B	IV-4	If any planet(s) exist in Step 3A, determine the houses these planets rule and are placed within.		Houses ruled and resided by effected planets from Step 3A will be influenced by their dignity or debility.
PLANET	SIGN	E/R/D/F	HOUSE PLACEMENT	HOUSE RULERSHIPS
☽	♋	RULER	7	8
♂	♑	EXALTATION	1	11 & 4
♄	♒	RULER	2	2

The Moon in Cancer in the 7th makes Client C an incredibly great listener and mediator with everyone they meet. This makes them unthreatening to others, which allows for others to trust Client C. Furthermore, Mars in the 1st house in Capricorn aids with their drive and self-identity. They are not one to be tested, and others can make this mistake due to their unthreatening nature. However, if they are instigated, their strong sense of self-worth allows for them to stand up and stick up for themself when it is needed. Although Saturn is in the sign of rulership, as we will see below, it is not in a good predicament because the only aspect that is made to it is a square to Pluto. However, Saturn being in the sign it rules dilutes the effects of this aspect connection somewhat.

[Step 4] One thing to mention right away is that although the multiple oppositions to the Moon did not make this orb range, we still need to consider them for a couple of reasons. For one, there are numerous oppositions that exist and the planets that are in opposition are all conjoined to one another. Secondly, these oppositions constitute the majority of the Moon's aspects with other planets. Remember, astrology is never cut and dried, and sometimes you will have to make exceptions in order to get the full picture. As mentioned, these steps are merely a starting point to help you obtain a firm grasp into the bulk of significant factors within the chart. Regardless, you will find yourself having to expand and adjust these steps as needed.

4	II-5	Determine the chart's aspects with an orb range of 0°-5°.	Indicates the individual's most rudimentary strengths and weaknesses.

NAME	GLYPH	ORB
Natal Sun in Capricorn conjoin Natal Mars in Capricorn	n.☉♑ ☌ n.♂♑	0
Natal Mercury in Capricorn conjoin Natal Venus in Capricorn	n.☿♑ ☌ n.♀♑	1
Natal Saturn in Aquarius square Natal Pluto in Scorpio	n♄♒ □ n.♇♏	1
Natal Uranus in Capricorn conjoin Natal Neptune in Capricorn	n.♅♒ ☌ n.♆♑	1
Natal Sun in Capricorn sextile Natal Jupiter in Scorpio	n.☉♑ ⚹ n.♃♏	2
Natal Sun in Capricorn square Natal Libra Midheaven	n.☉♑ □ n.MC♎	2
Natal Mars in Capricorn sextile Natal Jupiter in Scorpio	n.♂♑ ⚹ n.♃♏	2
Natal Mars in Capricorn square Natal Libra Midheaven	n.♂♑ □ n.MC♎	2
Natal Sun in Capricorn conjoin Natal Mercury in Capricorn	n.☉♑ ☌ n.☿♑	3
Natal Sun in Capricorn conjoin Natal Venus in Capricorn	n.☉♑ ☌ n.♀♑	4
Natal Mercury in Capricorn conjoin Natal Mars in Capricorn	n.☿♑ ☌ n.♂♑	4
Natal Venus in Capricorn conjoin Natal Mars in Capricorn	n.☿♑ ☌ n.♂♑	4
Natal Moon in Cancer trine Natal Jupiter in Scorpio	n.☽♋ △ n.♃♏	5
Natal Moon in Cancer square Natal Libra Midheaven	n.☽♋ □ n.MC♎	5
Natal Mercury in Capricorn sextile Natal Jupiter in Scorpio	n.☿♑ ⚹ n.♃♏	5
Natal Mercury in Capricorn square Natal Libra Midheaven	n.☿♑ □ n.MC♎	5

The multiple oppositions to the Moon in the 7th house to the planets in the 1st house tells me that Client C can find themself in conflicts with others easily; especially when emotional subjectivity is involved. Either Client C can take the issue personally which causes conflict, or the other individual projects conflict because they envy Client C's inner and outer strength.

Either way, when emotions are involved, they find that they are on one side of the issue and have a hard time meeting in the middle due to the sheer number of oppositions that are within the birth chart. Client C should work on objective thinking more and try to not let things get to them if they can. This is emphasized with the lack of air and fire. Meaning, Client C can have difficulty properly venting frustrations and taking the initiative to resolve conflict even though they, ironically, are good at relating to others when their personal emotions, or that of others, are not on the line.

Recall from Part II-Section 5 that the keyword for the conjunction is blending. By that we mean that when planets are in conjunction, their energies become inseparable and act as a cohesive unit. For Client C, their Sun, Venus, Mercury, and Mars are all combined together in this way which is a lot to handle. This explains why Client C has a hard time stepping out of their subjective self because they identify so strongly with their thoughts, opinions, and conceptualizations over how a situation or a person should be handled. This is why they encounter struggles with others because they are very much in tune with who they are in this way. Additionally, this Capricorn stellium in the 1st house tells me that they should be mindful of their physical body which could easily flair up or cause them distress if they are not in good physical health.

A very interesting and unique feature of Client C's chart has to do with how their planets are situated relative to their Ascendant and Midheaven. More specifically, every aspect to their Midheaven is a square and there is absolutely no planetary connection to the Ascendant by aspect. Again, this confirms that although Client C is very much in tune with who they are and what they want, there is a severe disconnect with the outside world, who either does not relate to who they are or hinders the goals they strive towards.

This makes Client C not only self-reliant by necessity, but also untrusting of others. Additionally, this causes Client C to possess extreme introversion at times because they can portray the outside world to be a threatening place. Client C should remember that what they are experiencing is simply projection from others who envy their ability to be true to themself. This makes others want to step on their toes because they wish they were just as transparent and honest as Client C can be. To this point, the Neptune opposition to the Moon means that Client C can sometimes rely on victimhood in this regard, and should ignore those that are always trying to put them down, but at the same time not feel sorry for themselves because they are stronger than they realize.

Another factor to mention is the square between Pluto and Saturn. If you recall, Client B also possesses this aspect because, although they were born eight months apart, due to the slow-moving nature of both planets, they both have the same square. This means they both can have issues with authority and powers of institutions, but for Client C, this energy is simply stronger because the orb is tighter. However, this is expected given that the other planetary combinations allude to Client C's constant clashing with others even though they are not even looking for a fight. Client C needs to make sure that these issues do not affect their mindset towards the world.

The good news is that the amazingly aspected chart ruler of Jupiter resides in the 11th house, which means that Client C's friendship and social circles are where they are able to recharge and reground themselves. Similarly, working in professions that aid the downtrodden or studying unconventional metaphysical topics like astrology also help them with their perspective. It is helpful for Client C to know that they can always rely on their friends for comfort and support.

5A		From the information gathered in Steps 3-4, determine the chart's most afflicted planet(s).		Shows which planet(s) are the most self-destructive and inharmonious.			
5B		From the information gathered in Steps 3-4, determine the chart's most beneficial planet(s).		Shows which planet(s) are the most harmonious and helpful.			
6	IV-4	Determine which houses are occupied and ruled by the planets in step 5A & 5B.		This will also show which areas of life are greatly hindered or aided.			
MOST BENEFICIAL				MOST AFFLICTED			
PLANET	SIGN	HOUSE PLACEMENT	HOUSE RULERSHIP	PLANET	SIGN	HOUSE PLACEMENT	HOUSE RULERSHIP
♃	♏	11	12, 1, & 3	♄	♒	2	2
♂	♑	1	4 & 11	♇	♏	11	11
☽	♋	7	8	ASC/MC	♐/♎	N/A	N/A

Although the Ascendant and Midheaven are not technically planets, the intense squares to the Midheaven and lack of aspects to the Ascendant cannot be ignored. Furthermore, the only aspects towards Pluto and Saturn is the square between them. These two considerations indicate the already mentioned struggle Client C has with interacting with the world around them, and the various individuals within.

However, their well aspected Mars and Jupiter along with Jupiter's trine to their Moon counterbalances this perspective with a great understanding of who they are as already mentioned. Essentially, Client C is a square peg trying to fit into a world filled with round holes. They nevertheless do not mind at all being an awkward square peg. In fact, they relish in their individuality, and see the outside world as the problem and not them. In some ways they are correct, but they also must remember that this is where the conflict arises. The best option is to be prideful of who they are, but at the same time try their hardest to accept that they live in a world that is sometimes not appreciative of this.

7		Compose a summary of your findings from Steps 1-6.	An overall and comprehensive analysis of the individual based upon the most important factors within the birth chart.

Client C needs to watch their health (Stellium in the 1st House in Capricorn) and be more open and detached when it comes to relating with others (Lack of air). They should also take initiation into different and new things and ideas and try to be more spontaneous and less afraid of the world around them (Lack of fire). They are incredibly secure and grounded within themselves (harmonious aspects to chart ruler Jupiter), but they can find that this comes into conflict with others, especially when emotions are involved (Moon in 7th opposes Capricorn stellium in the 1st). Nevertheless, they make great listeners and have very supportive friends (Moon in Cancer/ Jupiter in the 11th house). Any conflict that arises stems from others projecting their envy in Client C's ability to be confident and grounded in their own skin (Strong chart ruler), but they can misconstrue this projection into victimhood (Moon opposes Neptune). These conflicts can also branch out into positions and intuitions of power and authority (tight Saturn square Pluto) which can cause an uphill battle for Client C when it comes to their goals (Venus, the Midheaven ruler, squares the Midheaven). They need to work on taking emotions out of business (Lack of air) and remember that although people can rub them the wrong way, it does not mean that they should shy away from life and others altogether. Client C is incredibly resilient (Capricorn stellium) and has immense inner strength and self-confidence when it is not contested (Stellium in the 1st house). But when it is contested, they can easily go on the defensive and lose their footing (Multiple oppositions from stellium in the 1st house to the Moon in the 7th house). Still, with Jupiter as strong as it is within their birth chart, there is always a brighter side to things. The trick is for Client C to remember and utilize what is working for them and to remember how the universe really has their support and protection in mind, even though the world and other individuals can be difficult to handle.

CLIENT D: BIRTH CHART

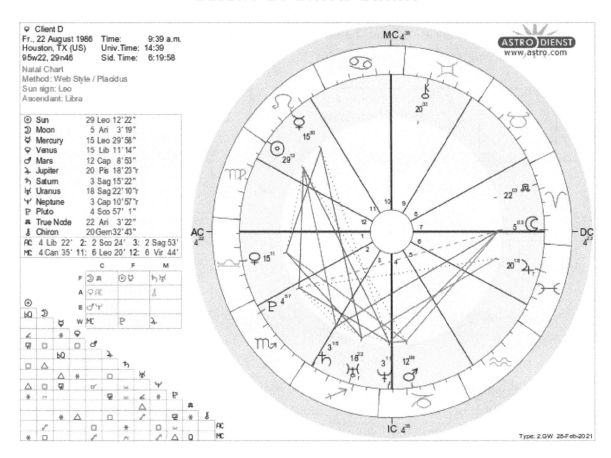

CLIENT D: BIRTH CHART ANALYSIS

1	II-1	Determine any imbalances within the elements and modalities.	Gives you a quick picture of the individual with simple remedies.

Client D is fire heavy with relatively equal values for the other three elements. They are also cardinal heavy with lower yet similar values for fixed and mutable. Overall, this gives Client D a balanced modality and elemental distribution, but they still need to be mindful of their cardinal and fire tendencies. This means that they can be prone to jumping to conclusions, action, and judgments without much forethought. Thankfully, the other elements and modalities still have strong values with the exception of the earth element. This tells me that these flair ups only occur when Client D is not grounded and secure. I would recommend that they seek recreation when they can, spend time in nature, and make their environments as calm, peaceful, and clean as possible.

2A	II-7 IV-4 II-5 II-6	Determine the Planetary ruler(s) of the Ascendant along with their house placement, sign placement, and any aspect(s) within an orb range of 0°-6°.			The Planet(s) that rule the ascendant show how the individual portrays themselves along with their sense of self-confidence.		
ASCENDANT	**RULER**	**SIGN**	**HOUSE**	**ASPECTS**			
♎	♀	♎	1	**NAME**		**GLYPH**	**ORB**
				Natal Venus in Libra sextile Natal Mercury in Leo		n. ♀♎ ✳ n. ☿♌	0
				Natal Venus in Libra square Natal Mars in Capricorn		n. ♀♎ □ n. ♂♑	2
				Natal Venus in Libra sextile Natal Uranus in Sagittarius		n. ♀♎ ✳ n. ♅♐	3

Interestingly, many of our case studies have had their chart rulers in the 1st house, or they have a lot of 1st house energy due to multiple planets being placed within. Due to this fact, we are starting to notice identical trends between them, so you will have to excuse the redundancy when it comes about. For Client D, their chart ruler, Venus, is in sextile to Uranus in the 3rd house and Mercury in the 11th house. This tells me that they are very much in their element when they associate with people who are unorthodox and untraditional in mindset and lifestyles. Client D feels very much at home with these individuals and finds it easy to express themselves fully. The more open minded the person is that encounters Client D, the more Client D is able to associate and relate to them on a personal level because they, too, have similar mindsets.

The issue, however, involves Mars in Capricorn in the 4th house squaring Venus. This tells me that Client D could have come from a more conservative family similar to Client B who also has issues with their family and parental dynamics due to their 4th house and 10th house oppositions. The difference is, for Client D, the aspect made is a square, which means that where Client B usually finds themselves in arguments and disagreements with their family ties, Client D harbors these disagreements within their own self due to the square nature of the aspect. In other words, Client D can be prone to self-censure and subduing their more progressive tendencies due to past unconscious events that could have occurred in childhood. The fact that Mars is involved tells me that this is probably due to the men in their family that expected Client D to act more subservient to men in general due to traditional values. Even though Client D does not agree at all with these outdated gender roles, they nevertheless find themselves restricting their own self-expression due to these past experiences. Client D should work on their confidence more, and also try not to project their resentment when they encounter more closed-minded individuals (particularly men) within society.

2B	II-7 IV-4 II-5 II-6	Determine the Planetary ruler(s) of the Midheaven along with their house placement, sign placement, and any aspect(s)within an orb range of 0°-6°.		The Planet(s) that rule the midheaven signify the individual's main lifegoals, aspirations, and their approach towards these endeavors.		
MIDHEAVEN	**RULER**	**SIGN**	**HOUSE**	**ASPECTS**		
♋	☽	♈	7	**NAME**	**GLYPH**	**ORB**
				Natal Moon in Aries conjoin Aries Descendant	n. ☽♈ ☌ n. DSC♈	1
				Natal Moon in Aries square Cancer Midheaven	n. ☽♈ □ n. MC♋	1
				Natal Moon in Aries trine Natal Saturn in Sagittarius	n. ☽♈ △ n. ♄♐	2
				Natal Moon in Aries square Natal Neptune in Capricorn	n. ☽♈ □ n. ♆♑	2

Tying back to what was previously being discussed with regards to the Ascendant, this is confirmed by the client's Moon being in Aries. This means that they possess very masculine qualities that society attributes to men like a competitive nature, a go-getting attitude, and blunt emotional expression. Again, Client D should not be ashamed of these qualities within themself and should honor their individuality and uniqueness which causes them to not fit into a mold that their family might have expected them to fit into.

Nevertheless, Client D's Saturn trine to their Moon tells me that this nature is very advantageous within their career because it gives them a thick skin, tenacity, and discipline that is respected by their superiors. With the Midheaven ruler conjoining the Descendant, this means that they can relate to others easily, and this is good for their goals because they know how to make the right connections and can properly network. However, similar to Client C, Client D also has their Midheaven ruler in a square to the Midheaven itself. This means that although sometimes people can admire their courage and abilities, there is still a constant struggle in obtaining their goals. This is mostly due to Neptune in the 3rd house square to the Moon. It could be easy for misunderstandings in communication with Client D either trying too hard to uplift others that are not worth uplifting, or they can play the victim card similar to Client C who also has issues with Neptune. Again, the fact that Neptune is in conjunction to the IC, tells me that these issues stem form deeply tied familial wounds that have been placed unto Client D, which they are now expected to overcome for the sake of their family's karma.

Client D needs to be mindful of get rich quick schemes and too good to be true situations with regards to their career as this is Neptune playing tricks on them. Similarly, the Neptune square can make it easy for Client D to be taken advantage of because when they try to play nice instead of putting their foot down, others perceive that to be a sign of weakness. Again, this comes from Client D's inner conflict of having to act the way they are expected to act verses who they truly are. Additionally, Client D should be mindful of drug addiction and other addictive tendencies which could also stem from familial karma due to Neptune's conjunction to the IC. To counter all of this, they should capitalize on their Saturn trine and remember that hard work and slow, steady progress is the surest way to obtain permanent success in whatever they strive to achieve. They should also remember that, similar to Client C who also has 11th house connections, Client D can easily seek refuge with friends and organizations that are more forward thinking that create a helpful and supportive space for Client D's unconventionality.

3A	II-4	Determine if any planet(s) are in a sign of exaltation, rulership, detriment, or fall.		This will adjust the natural temperament of the planet(s) for better or worse.
3B	IV-4	If any planet(s) exist in Step 3A, determine the houses these planets rule and are placed within.		Houses ruled and resided by effected planets from Step 3A will be influenced by their dignity or debility.
PLANET	**SIGN**	**E/R/D/F**	**HOUSE PLACEMENT**	**HOUSE RULERSHIPS**
☉	♌	RULER	11	11
♀	♎	RULER	1	1 & 8
♂	♑	EXALTATION	4	7 & 2
♃	♓	RULER	6	6 & 3

These planetary placements are incredibly beneficial for Client D and help to dilute the various issues we have been previously discussing. Although Client D can have issues with communicating their true self, the fact that Jupiter rules the 3rd house helps to ease these inherent problems. Similarly, although Mars is a trouble spot for them, the fact that Mars rules the 7th house means that they are nevertheless able to get along with others regardless of conflict. This is confirmed with the chart ruler, Venus, being in the sign of rulership. This means that even if Client D clashes with individuals, they are nevertheless able to dismantle any real conflict before it gets too out of hand due to the peaceful nature of their Venus and the fact that Mars rules the 7th house. This is also due to the fact that Venus rules the 8th house which means that others can feel emotionally susceptible around Client D in a positive way, and therefore find it easy to tell them deeper secrets and vulnerabilities that they might not share with others. The only issue is when Client D tries to save others from their trauma instead of helping them to be more self-sufficient instead.

Jupiter ruling the 6th house tells me that Client D is a hard worker with an incredible work ethic and can handle responsibility well. They have great leadership qualities and again, this is why others might subconsciously feel threatened around Client D because they possess traits that are typically not stereotypically expected of their gender. Nevertheless, Client D can be relied upon to complete any task with the highest of standards due to their organized mind and acute sense of planning.

[Step 4] At first, you will notice some strange aspect combinations with Client D. For example, their Sun in Leo squares their Saturn in Sagittarius when normally these two signs would create a trine. Or, when observing their Sun in Leo yet again, it makes a trine to their Neptune in Capricorn when normally an aspect would not be made between these two signs at all. This has to do with the fact that their Sun is on the cusp of Leo. Due to this fact, planets can still make the appropriate aspects to the Sun because they are still within the correct aspect range even if the signs do not line up. In other words, the reason why Neptune is making a trine to their Sun is because Neptune is approximately 120° away from their Sun even though Neptune is in a sign that does not traditionally make an aspect to Leo in the first place. This is something to be mindful of when you are dealing with planets that are on the cusp because you will encounter these types of scenarios.

4	II-5	Determine the chart's aspects with an orb range of 0°-5°.	Indicates the individual's most rudimentary strengths and weaknesses.		
		NAME		**GLYPH**	**ORB**
		Natal Mercury in Leo sextile Natal Venus in Libra		n.☿♌ ✶ n.♀♎	0
		Natal Pluto in Scorpio trine Natal Cancer Midheaven		n.♇♏ △ n.MC♋	0
		Natal Mars in Aries conjoin Natal Aries Descendant		n.♂♈ ☌ n.DSC♈	1
		Natal Mars in Aries square Natal Cancer Midheaven		n.♂♈ □ n.MC♋	1
		Natal Saturn in Sagittarius sextile Natal Libra Ascendant		n.♄♐ ✶ n.ASC♎	1
		Natal Neptune in Capricorn square Natal Libra Ascendant		n.♆♑ □ n.ASC♎	1
		Natal Moon in Aries trine Natal Saturn in Sagittarius		n.☽♈ △ n.♄♐	2
		Natal Moon in Aries square Natal Neptune in Capricorn		n.☽♈ □ n.♆♑	2
		Natal Jupiter in Pisces square Natal Saturn in Sagittarius		n.♃♓ □ n.♄♐	2
		Natal Sun in Leo square Natal Saturn in Sagittarius		n.☉♌ □ n.♄♐	3
		Natal Mercury in Leo trine Natal Uranus in Sagittarius		n.☿♌ △ n.♅♐	3
		Natal Venus in Libra square Natal Mars in Capricorn		n.♀♎ □ n.♂♑	3
		Natal Venus in Libra sextile Natal Uranus in Sagittarius		n.♀♎ ✶ n.♅♐	3
		Natal Sun in Leo trine Natal Neptune in Capricorn		n.☉♌ △ n.♆♑	4
		Natal Sun in Leo sextile Natal Pluto in Scorpio		n.☉♌ ✶ n.♇♏	5
		Natal Sun in Leo sextile Natal Cancer Midheaven		n.☉♌ ✶ n.MC♋	5

If you recall from Part II-Section 5, the only two aspects that can be made between Venus and Mercury are the conjunction and the sextile. This is because these two planets do not travel far away from one another to create any other aspects that goes beyond 60°. In the case of Client D, they have a very tight sextile between these two planets. This tells me that Client D has a natural artistic talent because the conjunction and sextile between these two planets are usually indicative of some artistic ability. This is also confirmed by the fact that Venus is in Libra which is visually stunning given the nature of Venus and that it rules the sign of Libra. Additionally, Mercury is in the sign of Leo, a sign that is naturally creative and self-expressive. Even if Client D is not involved in the arts, they nevertheless utilize this ability, which gives them a sort of Midas touch with everything they do, making it aesthetically pleasing as well as original. This includes their own fashion and sense of style.

Their major doubts in this regard come from the Saturn square to the Sun, and the Mars square to Venus as already previously mentioned along with Mars' loose square to the Moon. This all confirms the same story we have already been portraying with Client D's insecurities stemming from familial ties. Particularly with men within the family or considering that they possess stereotypically masculine traits within themself. The Saturn square to the Sun shows that they are not inherently expressive even though they have incredibly original expressive abilities latent within. With Saturn in the 3rd house, communication issues are already a problem. Client D should strive to unlock these latent abilities without any regard of judgment around them.

The good news is if they utilize their harmonious Pluto and Neptune aspects towards their Sun and Mercury, they will find that the only thing that is keeping them down is themself. However, they normally project these positive traits onto other people with their lack of self-esteem instead. In other words, Client D is really good at being the cheerleader for other people's talents, abilities, and struggles, but when it comes to themself, they sometimes do not channel that energy from within. The positive aspects to Pluto tell me that they are able to admit what needs to be adjusted, and that they can release the ego to do so. Similarly, the positive Neptune aspects tell me that they have a strong connection to the spiritual world which means they not only value their own uniqueness, but they respect the journey that they are on. They simply need to remember all of this when they have moments of low self-esteem and low confidence.

5A		From the information gathered in Steps 3-4, determine the chart's most afflicted planet(s).		Shows which planet(s) are the most self-destructive and inharmonious.			
5B		From the information gathered in Steps 3-4, determine the chart's most beneficial planet(s).		Shows which planet(s) are the most harmonious and helpful.			
6	IV-4	Determine which houses are occupied and ruled by the planets in step 5A & 5B.		This will also show which areas of life are greatly hindered or aided.			
MOST BENEFICIAL				MOST AFFLICTED			
PLANET	SIGN	HOUSE PLACEMENT	HOUSE RULERSHIP	PLANET	SIGN	HOUSE PLACEMENT	HOUSE RULERSHIP
☿	♌	11	9 & 12	☽	♈	7	10
♆	♏	2	2	♂	♑	4	7 & 2

The various aspects made towards Mercury tells me that Client D is incredibly open minded, original, creative, and has a great support network of friends. This allows for them to be a helpful friend, coworker, and partner. The issue comes with them being willing to share these abilities with the rest of the world outwardly but not inwardly within themselves due to the conflicts with Mars. Client D has no trouble being their original self when they are in familiar environments and are surrounded by people that are supportive. Also, Client D's astute and accurate insights and observations stem from an intuitive knowing that they need to trust more.

The harmonious aspects made with Pluto show us that Client D is good at nurturing, counseling, and supporting others, particularly when it comes to moments of crisis. They can help others determine what is preventing them from achieving their goals, and likewise help them to let go of what needs to be released. Due to this fact, they have an ability to channel that from within, and admit when they need to release the ego for the sake of spiritual and psychological evolution.

The combination of Client D being fire heavy, along with their Moon being in Aries, makes them a warrior of sorts. The issue is that others are typically threatened by this intensity which causes Client D to not shine as brightly as they potentially can due to the inharmonious aspects made by Mars. This quality is emphasized with the fact that the Moon is conjoined with the Descendant, which causes Client D to pick and choose which situations would be most ideal for them instead of going with the flow of life and giving themself permission to be fully expressive regardless of who and what comes their way. Again, all Client D needs to do is tap into their positive Pluto and Neptune energies that they readily provide for others and channel that from within.

7		Compose a summary of your findings from Steps 1-6.	An overall and comprehensive analysis of the individual based upon the most important factors within the birth chart.

Client D has great spontaneity, creativity, and intuitive knowing (fire heavy/ Sun and Mercury in Leo/Mercury sextile Venus). When they are around friends they can trust or around networks of open-minded individuals, they are able to fully blossom into the person they truly are (Mercury in 11th trine Uranus in 3rd). Furthermore, they are very open and honest with themself and know when to let go of pride when it is needed (Pluto sextile Sun). They are also potentially psychic and have a keen sense of empathy (Neptune trine Sun). These abilities make it so they can be supportive of friends when they are encountering moments of crises (strong chart ruler Venus in Libra/Pluto sextile Sun/Venus rules the 8th House). The issue is that due to familial trauma, they are not as expressive and honest with their true self as they should be when they are in environments and around people that are unfamiliar to them (Mars in 4th squares Venus in 1st/Lack of Earth). They should also watch out for addictive tendencies and falling into victim/savor relationships (Neptune conjoin the IC/Neptune square Moon). Sometimes, communications and misunderstandings can occur (Saturn in 3rd squares Sun) or others can project being threatened around Client D due to their intensity that is normally associated with masculine energy (Moon in Aries conjoin Descendant/Mars in Capricorn square Venus in Libra). All Client D needs to do is channel their therapeutic and counseling abilities towards themself and process how their upbringing has caused them to self-censure. Nevertheless, Client D is a hard worker (Saturn trine Moon, Midheaven Ruler) and is able to release unwanted and unneeded ego identification for the sake of personal evolution (Pluto sextile Sun). This stems from Client D's inherent trust in the universe that everything will work out as it should even though they may at times be hesitant to trust that inherent knowing (Neptune trine Sun). Again, they should rely on their friends and communities that allow for them to be their true self without any judgement and use that as a sort of home base where they can recharge and ground themself before dealing with the outer world (Mercury in 11th trine Uranus in the 3rd/Lack of earth).

CLIENT E: BIRTH CHART

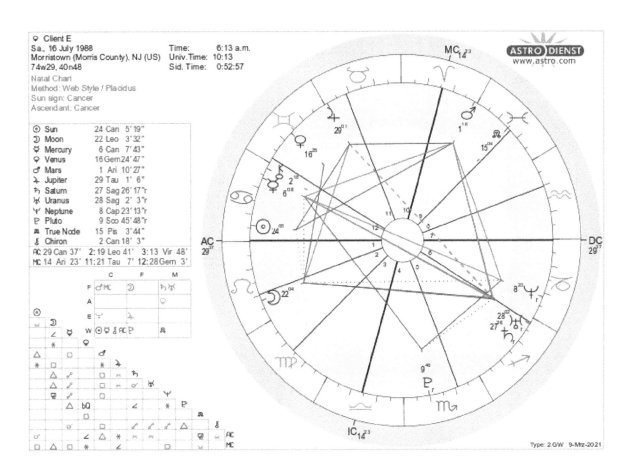

CLIENT E: BIRTH CHART ANALYIS

1	II-1	Determine any imbalances within the elements and modalities.	Gives you a quick picture of the individual with simple remedies.

Client E is lacking air but has a good amount of the other elements. When it comes to the modalities, they have a very balanced distribution. This means that Client E can lack objective observations similar to Client D. Moreover, they both can react too quickly before they take time to think things through. This is emphasized more with Client E because they have a high amount of water in addition to fire. If Client E is emotionally charged or feels deeply passionate about a certain situation, they will act upon these initial motivations and feelings instead of thinking it through. Client E should be mindful that their initial opinion or feeling might not be the same when they end up concluding on the issue as time passes. If they take the time to hold off and allow for these primary feelings to simmer down, it will make certain they do not accidently put themself into a hole that they have to dig out of later. To help with the lack of air, puzzles (like logic puzzles), discussing situations more with others, and breathing techniques will help to counter this deficiency.

2A	II-7 IV-4 II-5 II-6	Determine the Planetary ruler(s) of the Ascendant along with their house placement, sign placement, and any aspect(s) within an orb range of 0°-6°.			The Planet(s) that rule the ascendant show how the individual portrays themselves along with their sense of self-confidence.		
ASCENDANT	**RULER**	**SIGN**	**HOUSE**	**ASPECTS**			
♋	☽	♌	2	**NAME**	**GLYPH**	**ORB**	
				Natal Moon in Leo trine Natal Uranus in Sagittarius	n. ☽♌ △ n. ♅♐	5	
				Natal Moon in Leo trine Natal Saturn in Sagittarius	n. ☽♌ △ n. ♄♐	5	
				Natal Moon in Leo sextile Natal Venus in Gemini	n. ☽♌ ✶ n. ♀♊	6	

Client E shares their opinions and feelings outwardly without censure due to the Sun conjoining the Ascendant. This is exemplified with Mars in a trine with the Sun which indicates that there is no holding back with Client E. The good news is, with the Mars trine aspect along to the Sun with a sextile to Jupiter indicates that usually, their truthfulness works out in their favor.

When it comes to the Moon, the ruler of the Ascendant, Client E desires to stand up for justice in their life due to the trine to Saturn and Uranus. You can expect Client E to stand up for unfairness and possess a highly moral ethical code. The Moon in Leo also indicates a strong will with a friendly personality that makes it easy for others to relate to them and feel strengthened by their presence. The issue, as we will observe below, is that Client E, similar to Client D, has a hard time taking the values and support that they give to others back onto themself when they are the ones being treated unfairly. This is due to Jupiter's square to the Moon even though it is in an orb of seven degrees. With Jupiter in the 11th squaring the Moon in the 2nd, Client E desires to fit in and be part of a social network further emphasized with the Leo Moon. Due to this fact, they may not cause a stir if need be when it comes to their own conflicts with others. Client E does not have a good poker face because they are incredibly truthful as to what they are feeling and thinking towards the outside world at any given time due to the fact that the Ascendant is conjoined the Sun, and the Ascendant ruler, the Moon, is placed in Leo.

2B	II-7	Determine the Planetary ruler(s) of the Midheaven along with their house placement, sign placement, and any aspect(s) within an orb range of 0°-6°.	The Planet(s) that rule the midheaven signify the individual's main lifegoals, aspirations, and their approach towards these endeavors.
	IV-4		
	II-5		
	II-6		

MIDHEAVEN	RULER	SIGN	HOUSE	ASPECTS		
♈	♂	♈	9	**NAME**	**GLYPH**	**ORB**
				Natal Mars in Aries trine Leo Ascendant	n. ♂♈ △ n. ASC♌	1
				Natal Mars in Aries square Natal Uranus in Sagittarius	n. ♂♈ □ n. ♅♐	3
				Natal Mars in Aries sextile Natal Jupiter in Taurus	n. ♂♈ ✳ n. ♃♉	4
				Natal Mars in Aries square Natal Saturn in Sagittarius	n. ♂♈ □ n.♄♐	4
				Natal Mars in Aries trine Natal Sun in Cancer	n. ♂♈ △ n. ☉♋	6
				Natal Mars in Aries square Natal Mercury in Cancer	n. ♂♈ □ n. ☿♋	6

Client E is an individual that likes to do things their own way on their own time. Although this is admirable in many respects, it can cause Client E to come into conflict with others in a few ways. For one, Client E may not know exactly where these motivations come from because Mercury in Cancer in the 12th house tells me that there can be a lot of confusion and an emotionally driven thinking process that causes them to act or to react before they take the time to figure out the real truth to the matter. This is emphasized more with Mars in the 9th house because Client E has a certain personal philosophy that drives them to think and act in a certain way. If other individuals or situations come into conflict with those inner feelings and personal outlooks, they are more likely to take defense instead of slowing down and trying to think things through. This is due to the lack of air.

Furthermore, these issues cause Client E to come into direct conflict with superiors due to the Midheaven Ruler, Mars, squaring Saturn along with Uranus. This makes it hard for Client E to utilize objective thinking at times. However, with the good news is that due to Mars' trine to the Ascendant and the Sun, at least they are very forthcoming with their thoughts, feelings, and opinions. In other words, they are not trying to hide behind these things in order to overcompensate. Instead, they are trying to truly communicate to others how they are feeling and what they are thinking in any situation. Additionally, with the sextile to Jupiter, they are more likely to be in the right for the most part and others eventually come to their side of the issue over time. The problem is that because Client E relays their feelings and thoughts without holding back, they can sometimes rub people the wrong way. Client E should try to remember that although they are more than likely correct, and although it is admirable that there are transparent and truthful when it comes to these matters, they should try to hear where others are coming from in order to get people onto their side more readily and with less conflict.

3A	II-4	Determine if any planet(s) are in a sign of exaltation, rulership, detriment, or fall.		This will adjust the natural temperament of the planet(s) for better or worse.
3B	IV-4	If any planet(s) exist in Step 3A, determine the houses these planets rule and are placed within.		Houses ruled and resided by effected planets from Step 3A will be influenced by their dignity or debility.
PLANET	**SIGN**	**E/R/D/F**	**HOUSE PLACEMENT**	**HOUSE RULERSHIPS**
♂	♈	RULER	9	10 & 5

Mars being in the sign of rulership and ruling the 5th and 10th house tells me that Client E is brave and courageous when it comes to their originality. Whatever they do, they certainly have their own unique take on the issue at hand are not afraid to take chances if they feel comfortable in doing so. This is less due to calculated risk assessment and more due to a "gut feeling" that Client E can experience. If their gut feeling tells them that this is the solution or the way to go about It, then they will trust that instinct. However, as mentioned above, the issue as that others might be rubbed the wrong way with Client E's brashness and assuredness. Again, although

Client E has great talent for knowing what is right verses what is wrong, and has a good moral and spiritual backbone, they nevertheless need to learn that working well with others is the last key to this puzzle in order to get their prerogatives manifested into the physical world.

4	II-5	Determine the chart's aspects with an orb range of 0°-5°.	Indicates the individual's most rudimentary strengths and weaknesses.	
NAME			GLYPH	ORB
Natal Venus in Gemini sextile Natal Aries Midheaven			n.♀Ⅱ ✳ n.MC♈	1
Natal Mars in Aries trine Natal Leo Ascendant			n.♂♈ △ n.ASC♌	1
Natal Saturn in Sagittarius conjoin Natal Uranus in Sagittarius			n.♄♐ ♂ n.♅♐	1
Natal Neptune in Capricorn sextile Natal Pluto in Scorpio			n.♆♑ ✳ n.♇♏	1
Natal Mercury in Cancer oppose Natal Neptune in Capricorn			n.☿♋ ☍ n.♆♑	1
Natal Mercury in Cancer trine Natal Pluto in Scorpio			n. ☿♋ △ n. ♇♏	2
Natal Mars in Aries sextile Natal Jupiter in Taurus			n.♂♈ ✳ n.♃♉	2
Natal Sun in Cancer sextile Natal Jupiter in Taurus			n.☉♋ ✳ n. ♃♉	4
Natal Mars in Aries square Natal Saturn in Sagittarius			n.♂♈ □ n.♄♐	4
Natal Sun in Cancer conjoin Natal Leo Ascendant			n.☉♋ ♂ n.ASC♌	5
Natal Moon in Leo trine Natal Uranus in Sagittarius			n.☽♌ △ n.♅♐	5
Natal Mars in Aries square Natal Uranus in Sagittarius			n.♂♈ □ n.♅♐	5

The first thing that I notice when observing the various aspects has to do with the lack of aspects towards Client E's Venus, which makes no aspect connections to any of the planets with the exception of the sextile to the Midheaven. This explains how Client E can become one-sided when it comes to other people and predicaments. Venus is how we compromise and mediate, and Client E's Venus in Gemini in the 11th house would make this easier for Client E to do so if it were connected to other planets. However, tying back to the lack of air, this is why Client E finds themself on one side of the issue or the other. Client E should work on hearing other people out and to try to release some of their opinions on the matter at hand for the sake of compromise.

When it comes to personal and emotional topics, Client E is an incredible source of comfort and support for others. This is because their Mercury trines their Pluto and their Moon is the Ascendant ruler. With Mercury in the 12th and Pluto in the 4th, Client E is able to sympathize and empathize with others who are down on their luck, and others come to Client E to vent their frustrations. The good news is that Client E is incredibly non-judgmental and supportive with the 12th and 4th houses coming into play. Similarly, with the Sun and Mercury in the 12th house, they can act as a sort of conduit between an individual and the spiritual realm. Sometimes, Client E might not even know where their advice is coming from, but it causes them to say exactly what the other person needs to hear, and others find great comfort in this. The only issue is due to Jupiter in the 11th house squaring the Moon which can cause Client E to be either too dogmatic or nit-picky at other times when other people are just as self-assured and more on the defensive than offensive.

Client E's inherent critical lens does them a service sometimes, and other times a disservice. As mentioned above, with planets in the 12th house and Pluto trine Mercury, this is how it does them a service, because it allows for Client E to get to the bottom of things easily and almost instinctually. It does a disservice to Client E due to the Mercury opposition to Neptune in the 6th house and Jupiter square the Moon in the 11th house. This causes Client E to sometimes be too self-critical, either towards themself or towards others, to a point where they feel like they must get to the bottom of things no matter what. However, they have a hard time because Neptune in the 6th opposing Mercury in the 12th adds too much confusion where Client E is trying to hack away at getting towards a conclusion. Unfortunately, the fog of uncertainty paradoxically grows instead. What would help Client E is to be vulnerable when they do not have the answers and allow for others to comfort them when it is needed. That way, they can get out of their own head and clear the air a bit.

5A		From the information gathered in Steps 3-4, determine the chart's most afflicted planet(s).		Shows which planet(s) are the most self-destructive and inharmonious.			
5B		From the information gathered in Steps 3-4, determine the chart's most beneficial planet(s).		Shows which planet(s) are the most harmonious and helpful.			
6	IV-4	Determine which houses are occupied and ruled by the planets in step 5A & 5B.		This will also show which areas of life are greatly hindered or aided.			
MOST BENEFICIAL				MOST AFFLICTED			
PLANET	SIGN	HOUSE PLACEMENT	HOUSE RULERSHIP	PLANET	SIGN	HOUSE PLACEMENT	HOUSE RULERSHIP
☽	♌	2	1	♂	♈	9	10 & 5

Even with Jupiter squaring Client E's Moon, the Moon is still incredibly strong, providing for them a great sense of individual creativity, aesthetics, and a capacity to make solid financial and property investments. They know how to slowly build up towards something, and they can easily find financial and physical security through their home life. Additionally, with Uranus and Saturn in the 5th trine the Moon, they not only can harness personal discipline, they are forward thinking in their mindset and are therefore very open minded to new ideas. This causes them to not only be uniquely creative, but a leader of sorts where others admire their courage, inventiveness, and unconditional acceptance of others.

The issue comes with Mars which shows that Client E's ideas and mindsets can come into conflict with others who are not ready to handle Client E's perspective. This either causes Client E to lose their self-confidence or to react by going instinctually in fight or flight with others who disagree. Again, the positive aspects around their Midheaven and Ascendant mean that Client E is very truthful and honest about who they are and what they want. It is only when others get in their way that they can begin to internalize too much and as a result form anxiety which eats away at their utility because they begin to lose faith in themself. Again, all Client E needs to do is channel the faith they have in others into their own psychology and process, and trust that they usually are in the right. They just have to believe that they are, and that others are simply taken aback by Client E's inherent confidence and brashness which others try to quash because they are projecting their own insecurities onto Client E. Client E should not inherit other people's projections and mistake other individual's lack of confidence and self-criticalness as their own.

7		Compose a summary of your findings from Steps 1-6.	An overall and comprehensive analysis of the individual based upon the most important factors within the birth chart.

Client E has a great sense of originality that is portrayed in their sense of style and creativity. They can establish a secure financial situation and homelife. Client E possesses discipline and honesty it takes to reach these various goals (Moon, chart ruler, in the 2nd trine Uranus and Saturn in the 5th). They also have great instincts and intuition that they use to help others with their problems (Sun and Mercury in the 12th House/Mercury in the 12th sextile Moon). However, they can sometimes shy away from rocking the boat and causing a stir when it comes to their own concerns. Particularly within their friendships and social environments (Jupiter in the 11th squares Moon). This causes more confusion towards predicaments and within themself when they lean more on the negative side with their abilities of discernment. This also can cause conflict among others (Mercury oppose Neptune/Mars square Uranus and Saturn). Client E also has a hard time meeting other people in the middle and seeing other points of view that do not align with their personal philosophy (Mars in the 9th square Mercury and Neptune/Lack of aspects to Venus). Similarly, Client E can lack objectivity and can be too emotionally driven (Lack of air). Client E needs to rely on others as a sounding board where they can properly vent their frustrations in the same way they provide this for others. Regardless, Client E is incredibly truthful and does not hold back with a very honest and transparent portrayal of who they are, what they are thinking, and what they are feeling (Sun conjoin Ascendant/Mars, Midheaven ruler, trine Sun). Client E is usually on the right side of arguments and disagreements (Jupiter sextile Mars). They just need to be more accepting of the fact that others are not on their level and that different people require different approaches.

* * *

The birth chart is the essential cornerstone of astrological analysis. This is because all other events and relationships that are experienced as evidenced by other astrology charts all stem from the fundamental psychology and persona that is established within the individual's birth chart. Essentially, all other forms of astrological exploration tell you the "what," but the birth chart tells you the "why." Why does the individual act the way they do? Why do their strengths and insecurities exist in the first place? Why were they meant to have certain experiences and life lessons?

Now that we have a firm idea into these questions with our case studies and with yourself using the same techniques, it is time to go further into the "what" and "when." Namely, what will these individuals experience during their life, and when will they occur? We answer these questions by looking into their personal transits which is the next section of this book.

SECTION 3-TRANSIT CHART INTERPRETATION WITH CASE STUDIES

In addition to birth chart interpretation, transit chart interpretation will comprise the bulk of your astrological analysis. This is because the birth chart tells you who the induvial is as a person, and the transit chart tells you the most immediate life events in the present that the they are going to experience, along with events in the near future and recent past.

Unlike the personal transits that we have learned how to calculate in Part IV-Section 3, transit interpretation only involves the outer planets of Jupiter, Saturn, Uranus, Neptune, and Pluto. This is for a couple of reasons. For one, the inner planetary transits are indicative of daily energetic influences and secondly, there is simply too much information to gather which can make analysis too overwhelming. The reason why we only focus on the outer planets is because, if you recall, they indicate significant life events that will drastically alter the individual's life story for better or worse. Becoming aware of these outer planetary transits allows for you and your client to be proactive by preparing for the harder moments or by cultivating the more harmonious ones.

Due to the slow nature of the outer planets, their effects towards the birth chart, and subsequently the individual in question, can have a long-lasting effect that can take a while before the energy completely subsides. This is especially true if the event is encountered three times due to a retrograde planet (See Part III-Section 4). In fact, as you will soon observe, sometimes outer planetary transits can have up to five hits towards a natal planetary point if their stationary periods hit the natal point at the same degree.

It is also important to remember that although a planet has left the aspect point which causes the event, if it is part of a multiple stage event due to a retrograde, these events can occur over a longer time span and are subsequently felt more intensely at the time of the exact hit. For example, if you witness a Jupiter event three times due to a retrograde, you will experience the energy intensely for about one week three times over the course of approximately eight months which would be the approximate time it would take for all three events to occur (See Table V-4).

If this is confusing at first do not fret. We will experience multiple examples within our case studies below.

Another few caveats to point out before we proceed. First, I will not be providing a reference sheet for each planetary aspect point because at this point in the book, it is assumed that you can recognize the various aspect patterns that each sign makes. Furthermore, there is no need to mathematically determine the exact moment of each aspect due to the slow-moving nature of these planets. Instead, I will be simply estimating the date by determining when the point occurs as determined by the ephemeris.

Below are the steps required to obtain a transit chart and the various steps we will utilize in order to properly organize and interpret transiting events (Table VA-B). Next, we will take these steps with the same five case studies we have already analyzed in Part V-Section 2 and see how their current year and the year prior manifested for them with regards to their outer planetary transit events.

TABLE V-4. Length of Outer Planetary Transit Events and Range for Retrograde Hits

PLANET	GLYPH	EVENT DURATION*	EVENT RANGE IF A MULTIPLE HIT EVENT (Rx Event)*
Jupiter	♃	1 WEEK	8 MONTHS
Saturn	♄	1.5 WEEKS	10 MONTHS
Uranus	♅	4 WEEKS	11 MONTHS
Neptune	♆	5 WEEKS	12 MONTHS
Pluto	♇	6 WEEKS	13 MONTHS

*=Average Approximations

TABLE V-5A. How to obtain a Transit Chart through ASTRO.COM

> (1) On the ASTRO.COM main page, under the HOROSCOPES tab, chose EXTENDED CHART SELECTION under DRAWINGS, CALCULATIONS, DATA.
> (2) Confirm that the appropriate individual is selected under HOROSCOPE FOR.
> (3) Under CHART TYPE, select NATAL CHART AND TRANSITS
> (4) Under START DATE choose today's date.
> (5) Click CLICK HERE TO SHOW CHART.
> (6) This is the reference point you will use to trace outer transiting planets from year to year (See Table V-5B below).

TABLE V-5B. Steps on how to Comprehensively Analyze Significant Life Events via Transits

STEP #	SECTION IN BOOK	DESCRIPTION	INFORMATION IT PROVIDES
1	IV-3	Obtain a transit chart for the present day as a reference.	Preliminary data.
2A	IV-3	Trace the Ephemeris one year before and after from the day of the reading and observe if transiting Jupiter has ingresses or regressed into a house.	Preliminary data.
2B	IV-3	Repeat for transiting Saturn.	Preliminary data.
2C	IV-3	Repeat for transiting Uranus.	Preliminary data.
2D	IV-3	Repeat for transiting Neptune.	Preliminary data.
2E	IV-3	Repeat for transiting Pluto.	Preliminary data.
3A	IV-3	Trace the Ephemeris one year before and after from the day of the reading and observe if Jupiter makes an aspect to any of the 12 natal points.	Preliminary data.
3B	IV-3	Repeat for transiting Saturn.	Preliminary data.
3C	IV-3	Repeat for transiting Uranus.	Preliminary data.
3D	IV-3	Repeat for transiting Neptune.	Preliminary data.
3E	IV-3	Repeat for transiting Pluto.	Preliminary data.
4		Place all events from Steps 2A-3E in chronological order.	Information as to when these events will occur and if they occur simultaneously.
5		Determine the most inauspicious and auspicious months for the individual.	This will let the individual know when there are times of immense struggle or benefit which they can either prepare for the harder times and/or utilize the better times to their fullest potential.
6	IV-4	Create transit formulas for every event listed in steps 3A-3E.	Various realms within the person's life that will be influenced by the event.
7		Compose a summary of your findings from step 4-6.	Summary of Analysis.

1	IV-3	Obtain a transit chart for the present day as a reference.	Preliminary data.

CLIENT A: TRANSIT CHART

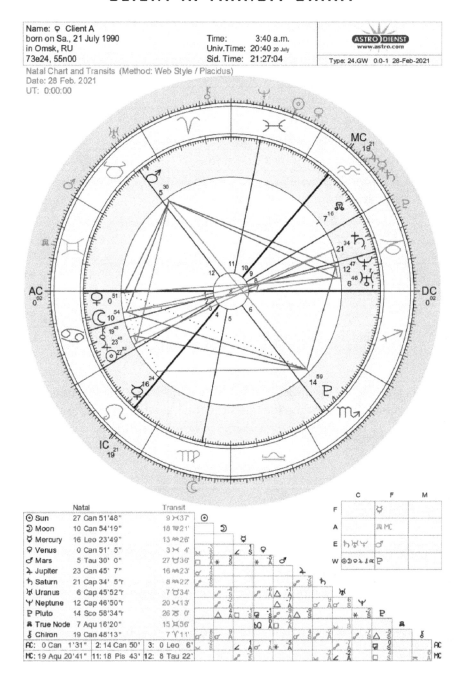

	Natal	Transit
☉ Sun	27 Can 51'48"	9 ♓ 37'
☽ Moon	10 Can 54'19"	18 ♍ 21'
☿ Mercury	16 Leo 23'49"	13 ♒ 26'
♀ Venus	0 Can 51' 5"	3 ♓ 4'
♂ Mars	5 Tau 30' 0"	27 ♉ 36'
♃ Jupiter	23 Can 45' 7"	16 ♒ 23'
♄ Saturn	21 Cap 34' 5"r	8 ♒ 22'
♅ Uranus	6 Cap 45'52"r	7 ♉ 34'
♆ Neptune	12 Cap 46'50"r	20 ♓ 13'
♇ Pluto	14 Sco 58'34"r	26 ♉ 0'
☊ True Node	7 Aqu 16'20"	15 ♓ 56'
⚷ Chiron	19 Can 48'13"	7 ♈ 11'
AC: 0 Can 1'31"	2: 14 Can 50'	3: 0 Leo 6'
MC: 19 Aqu 20'41"	11: 18 Pis 43'	12: 8 Tau 22'

Name: ♀ Client A
born on Sa., 21 July 1990
in Omsk, RU
73e24, 55n00

Time: 3:40 a.m.
Univ.Time: 20:40 20 July
Sid. Time: 21:27:04

ASTRO DIENST
www.astro.com

Type: 24.GW 0.0-1 28-Feb-2021

Natal Chart and Transits (Method: Web Style / Placidus)
Date: 28 Feb. 2021
UT: 0:00:00

2A	IV-3	Trace the Ephemeris one year before and after from the day of the reading and observe if transiting Jupiter has ingresses or regressed into a house.	Preliminary data.
2B	IV-3	Repeat for transiting Saturn.	Preliminary data.
2C	IV-3	Repeat for transiting Uranus.	Preliminary data.
2D	IV-3	Repeat for transiting Neptune.	Preliminary data.
2E	IV-3	Repeat for transiting Pluto.	Preliminary data.

♃

EVENT	GLYPH	DATE
Transiting Jupiter ingresses into the 9th House	t. ♃ → 9th	DEC 20, 2020
Transiting Jupiter ingresses into the 10th house	t. ♃ → 10th	MAR 13, 2021

♄

EVENT	GLYPH	DATE
Transiting Saturn ingresses into the 9th House (1/3)	t. ♄ → 9th (1/3)	MAR 23, 2020
Transiting Saturn regresses into the 8th House (2/3)	t. ♄ → 8th (2/3)	JUL 1, 2020
Transiting Saturn ingresses into the 9th House (3/3)	t. ♄ → 9th (3/3)	DEC 17, 2020

♅

EVENT	GLYPH	DATE
Transiting Uranus ingresses into the 12th House (1/3)	t. ♅ → 12th (1/3)	MAY 28, 2020
Transiting Uranus regresses into the 11th House (2/3)	t. ♅ → 11th (2/3)	NOV 8, 2020
Transiting Uranus ingresses into the 12th House (3/3)	t. ♅ → 12th (3/3)	MAR 19, 2021

♆

EVENT	GLYPH	DATE
Transiting Neptune ingresses into the 11th House (1/3)	t. ♆ → 11th (1/3)	MAR 17, 2020
Transiting Neptune regresses into the 10th House (2/3)	t. ♆ → 10th (2/3)	OCT 14, 2020
Transiting Neptune ingresses into the 11th House (3/3)	t. ♆ → 11th (3/3)	JAN 14, 2021

♇

EVENT	GLYPH	DATE
NONE		

3A	IV-3	Trace the Ephemeris one year before and after from the day of the reading and observe if Jupiter makes an aspect to any of the 12 natal points.	Preliminary data.

3B	IV-3	Repeat for transiting Saturn.	Preliminary data.
3C	IV-3	Repeat for transiting Uranus.	Preliminary data.
3D	IV-3	Repeat for transiting Neptune.	Preliminary data.
3E	IV-3	Repeat for transiting Pluto.	Preliminary data.

♃		
EVENT	**GLYPH**	**DATE**
Transiting Jupiter Station Retrograde in Capricorn opposes Natal Sun in Cancer (1/2) Transiting Jupiter in Capricorn opposes Sun in Cancer (2/2)	t.♃♑ SR ☍ n.☉♋ (1/2) t.♃♑ ☍ n.☉♋ (2/2)	MAY 14, 2020 MAR 13, 2021
Transiting Jupiter in Aquarius opposes Natal Mercury in Leo	t.♃♒ ☍ n.☿♌	FEB 28, 2021
Transiting Jupiter in Pisces trine Natal Venus in Cancer	t.♃♓ △ n.♀♋	JAN 3, 2021
Transiting Jupiter in Aquarius square Natal Mars in Taurus	t.♃♒ □ n.♂♉	JAN 12, 2021
Transiting Jupiter in Pisces sextile Natal Mars in Taurus	t.♃♓ ✳ n.♂♉	JAN 24, 2022
Transiting Jupiter in Capricorn opposes Natal Jupiter in Cancer (1/3) Transiting Jupiter Retrograde in Capricorn opposes Natal Jupiter in Cancer (2/3) Transiting Jupiter in Capricorn opposes Natal Jupiter in Cancer (3/3)	t.♃♑ ☍ n.♃♋ (1/3) t.♃♑ Rx ☍ n.♃♋ (2/3) t.♃♑ ☍ n.♃♋ (3/3)	MAR 27, 2020 JUL 4, 2020 NOV 19, 2020
Transiting Jupiter in Capricorn conjoin Natal Saturn in Capricorn (1/3) Transiting Jupiter Retrograde in Capricorn opposes Natal Saturn in Capricorn (2/3) Transiting Jupiter in Capricorn conjoin Natal Saturn in Capricorn (3/3)	t.♃♑ ☌ n.♄♑ (1/3) t.♃♑ Rx ☌ n.♄♑ (2/3) t.♃♑ ☌ n.♄♑ (3/3)	MAR 12, 2020 JUL 21, 2020 NOV 4, 2020
Transiting Jupiter in Pisces sextile Natal Uranus in Capricorn	t.♃♓ ✳ n.♅♑	JAN 30, 2021
Transiting Jupiter in Pisces sextile Natal Neptune in Capricorn	t.♃♓ ✳ n.♆♑	FEB 24, 2022
Transiting Jupiter in Capricorn sextile Natal Pluto in Scorpio	t.♃♑ ✳ n.♇♏	FEB 6, 2020
Transiting Jupiter in Aquarius square Natal Pluto in Scorpio	t.♃♒ □ n.♇♏	FEB 21, 2021

EVENT	GLYPH	DATE
Transiting Jupiter in Pisces trine Cancer Ascendant (1/3) Transiting Jupiter Retrograde in Pisces trine Cancer Ascendant (2/3) Transiting Jupiter in Pisces trine Cancer Ascendant (1/3)	t.♃♓ △ n.ASC♋ (1/3) t.♃♓Rx △ n.ASC♋ (2/3) t.♃♓ △ n.ASC♋ (3/3)	MAY 14, 2021 JUL 28, 2021 DEC 29, 2021
Transiting Jupiter in Aquarius conjoin Aquarius Midheaven	t.♃♒ ☌ n.MC♒	MAR 19, 2021

♄

EVENT	GLYPH	DATE
Transiting Saturn in Capricorn oppose Natal Sun in Cancer (1/3) Transiting Saturn Retrograde in Capricorn oppose Natal Sun in Cancer (2/3) Transiting Saturn in Capricorn oppose Natal Sun in Cancer (3/3)	t.♄♑ ☍ n.☉♋ (1/3) t.♄♑ Rx ☍ n.☉♋ (2/3) t.♄♑ ☍ n.☉♋ (3/3)	FEB 25, 2020 AUG 1, 2020 NOV 24, 2020
Transiting Saturn in Aquarius oppose Natal Mercury in Leo	t.♄♒ ☍ n.☿♌	FEB 7, 2022
Transiting Saturn in Aquarius square Natal Mars in Taurus	t.♄♒ □ n.♂♉	FEB 2, 2021
Transiting Saturn in Aquarius square Natal Pluto in Scorpio	t.♄♒ □ n.♇♏	JAN 27, 2022

♅

EVENT	GLYPH	DATE
Transiting Uranus Station Retrograde in Taurus sextile Natal Moon in Cancer (1/5) Transiting Uranus in Taurus sextile Natal Moon in Cancer (2/5) Transiting Uranus Retrograde in Taurus sextile Natal Moon in Cancer (3/5) Transiting Uranus Station Direct sextile Natal Moon in Cancer (4/5) Transiting Uranus sextile in Taurus sextile Natal Moon in Cancer (5/5)	t.♅♉ SR ✶ n.☽♋ (1/5) t.♅♉ ✶ n.☽♋ (2/5) t.♅♉ Rx ✶ n.☽♋ (3/5) t.♅♉ SD ✶ n.☽♋ (4/5) t.♅♉ ✶ n.☽♋ (5/5)	AUG 14, 2020 MAY 5, 2021 JAN 3, 2022 JAN 17, 2022 FEB 2, 2022
Transiting Uranus in Taurus conjoin Natal Mars in Taurus	t.♅♉ ☌ n.♂♉	APR 5, 2020
Transiting Uranus Station Retrograde in Taurus oppose Natal Pluto in Scorpio	t.♅♉ SR ☍ n.♇♏	AUG 19, 2020

♆		
EVENT	**GLYPH**	**DATE**
Transiting Neptune Station Retrograde in Pisces trine Natal Jupiter in Cancer	t.♆♓ SR △ n.♃♋	JUN 25, 2021
Transiting Neptune in Pisces sextile Natal Saturn in Capricorn (1/3) Transiting Neptune Retrograde in Pisces sextile Natal Saturn in Capricorn (2/3) Transiting Neptune in Pisces sextile Natal Saturn in Capricorn (3/3)	t.♆♓ ⚹ n.♄♑ (1/3) t.♆♓ Rx ⚹ n.♄♑ (2/3) t.♆♓ ⚹ n.♄♑ (3/3)	APR 4, 2021 SEP 22, 2021 FEB 4, 2022

♇		
EVENT	**GLYPH**	**DATE**
Transiting Pluto in Capricorn oppose Natal Jupiter in Cancer (1/3) Transiting Pluto Retrograde in Capricorn oppose Natal Jupiter in Cancer (2/3) Transiting Pluto in Capricorn oppose Natal Jupiter in Cancer (3/3)	t.♇♑ ☍ n.♃♋ (1/3) t.♇♑ Rx ☍ n.♃♋ (2/3) t.♇♑ ☍ n.♃♋ (3/3)	FEB 11, 2020 JUL 15, 2020 DEC 18, 2020

4		Place all events from Steps 2A-3E in chronological order.	Information as to when these events will occur and if they occur simultaneously.

2020							
JAN		**FEB**		**MAR**		**APR**	
EVENT	**DAY**	**EVENT**	**DAY**	**EVENT**	**DAY**	**EVENT**	**DAY**
		t.♃♑ ⚹ n.♇♏ t.♇♑ ☍ n.♃♋ (1/3) t.♄♑ ☍ n.☉♋ (1/3)	6 11 25	t. ♆ → 11th (1/3) t.♃♑ ☌ n.♄♑ (1/3) t. ♄ → 9th (1/3) t.♃♑ ☍ n.♃♋ (1/3)	17 12 23 27	t.♅♉ ☌ n.♂♉	5
MAY		**JUN**		**JUL**		**AUG**	
EVENT	**DAY**	**EVENT**	**DAY**	**EVENT**	**DAY**	**EVENT**	**DAY**
t.♃♑ SR ☍ n.☉♋ (1/2) t. ♅ → 12th (1/3)	14 28			t. ♄ → 8th (2/3) t.♃♑ Rx ☍ n.♃♋ (2/3) t.♇♑ ☍ n.♃♋ (2/3) t.♃♑ Rx ☌ n.♄♑ (2/3)	1 4 15 21	t.♄♑ Rx ☍ n.☉♋ (2/3) t.♅♉ SR ⚹ n.☽♋ (1/5) t.♅♉ SR ☍ n.♇♏	1 14 19

SEP		OCT		NOV		DEC	
EVENT	DAY	EVENT	DAY	EVENT	DAY	EVENT	DAY
		t. ♆ → 10th (2/3)	14	t.♃♑ ♂ n.♄♑ (3/3)	4	t. ♄ → 9th (3/3)	17
				t. ♅ → 11th (2/3)	8	t.♆♑ ☍ n.♃♋ (3/3)	18
				t.♃♑ ☍ n.♃♋ (3/3)	19	t. ♃ → 9th	20
				t.♄♑ ☍ n.☉♋ (3/3)	24		

2021							

JAN		FEB		MAR		APR	
EVENT	DAY	EVENT	DAY	EVENT	DAY	EVENT	DAY
t.♃♓ △ n.♀♋	3	t. t.♄♒ □ n.♂♉	2	t. ♃ → 10th	13	t.♆♓ ⚹ n.♄♑ (1/3)	4
t.♃♒ □ n.♂♉	12	t.♃♒ □ n.♆♏	21	t.♃♑ ☍ n.☉♋ (2/2)	13		
t. ♆ → 11th (3/3)	14	t.♃♒ ☍ n.♇♌	28	t.♃♒ ♂ n.MC♒	19		
t.♃♓ ⚹ n.♅♑	30			t. ♅ → 12th (3/3)	19		

MAY		JUN		JUL		AUG	
EVENT	DAY	EVENT	DAY	EVENT	DAY	EVENT	DAY
t.♅♉ ⚹ n.☽♋ (2/5)	5	t.♆♓ SR △ n.♃♋	25	t.♃♓ Rx △ n.ASC♋ (2/3)	28		
t.♃♓ △ n.ASC♋ (1/3)	14						

SEP		OCT		NOV		DEC	
EVENT	DAY	EVENT	DAY	EVENT	DAY	EVENT	DAY
t.♆♓ Rx ⚹ n.♄♑ (2/3)	22					t.♃♓ △ n.ASC♋ (3/3)	29

2022			

JAN		FEB	
EVENT	DAY	EVENT	DAY
t.♅♉ Rx ⚹ n.☽♋ (3/5)	3	t.♅♉ ⚹ n.☽♋ (5/5)	2
t.♅♉ SD ⚹ n.☽♋ (4/5)	17	t.♆♓ ⚹ n.♄♑ (3/3)	4
t.♃♓ ⚹ n.♂♉	24	t.♄♒ ☍ n.♇♌	7
t.♄♒ □ n.♆♏	27	t.♃♓ ⚹ n.♆♑	24

5		Determine the most inauspicious and auspicious months for the individual.	Determine the most inauspicious and auspicious months for the individual.

AUSPICIOUS	INAUSPICIOUS
MAY 2021	JUL 2020
JUN 2021	FEB 2021
JUL 2021	

6	IV-4	Create transit formulas for every event listed in steps 3A-3E.	Various realms within the person's life that will be influenced by the event.

EVENT	FORMULA
t.♃♑ ☍ n.☉♋	t.♃♑ in 8th (R. 11th) ☍ n.☉♋ in 2nd (R. 3rd & 4th)
t.♃♒ ☍ n.☿♌	t.♃♒ in 9th (R. 11th) ☍ n.☿♌ in 3rd (R. 4th)
t.♃♓ △ n.♀♋	t.♃♓ in 10th (R. 11th) △ n.♀♋ in 1st (R. 12th)
t.♃♒ □ n.♂♉	t.♃♒ in 10th (R. 11th) ⚹ n.♂♉ in 11th (R. 6th)
t.♃♓ ⚹ n.♂♉	t.♃♓ in 10th (R. 11th) ⚹ n.♂♉ in 11th (R. 6th)
t.♃♑ ☍ n.♃♋	t.♃♑ in 8th (R. 11th) ☍ n.♃♋ 2nd (R.11th)
t.♃♑ ☌ n.♄♑	t.♃♑ in 8th (R. 11th) ☌ n.♄♑ in 8th (R.7th, 8th, 9th, & 10th)
t.♃♓ ⚹ n.♅♑	t.♃♓ in 9th (R. 11th) ⚹ n.♅♑ in 7th (R. 10th)
t.♃♓ ⚹ n.♆♑	t.♃♓ in 10th (R. 11th) ⚹ n.♆♑ in 7th (R. 11th)
t.♃♑ ⚹ n.♇♏	t.♃♑ in 8th (R. 11th) ⚹ n.♇♏ in 6th (R. 6th)
t.♃♒ □ n.♇♏	t.♃♒ in 9th (R. 11th) □ n.♇♏ in 6th (R.6th)
t.♃♓ ⚹ n.♆♑	t.♃♓ in 10th (R.11th) ⚹ n.♆♑ in 7th (R. 11th)
t.♃♓ △ n.ASC♋	t.♃♓ in 10th (R. 11th) △ n.ASC♋
t.♃♒ ☌ n.MC♒	t.♃♒ in 9th (R. 11th) ☌ n.MC♒
t.♄♑ ☍ n.☉♋	t.♄♑ in 8th (R.7th, 8th, 9th, & 10th) ☍ n.☉♋ in 2nd (R. 3rd & 4th)
t.♄♒ ☍ n.☿♌	t.♄♒ in 9th (R.7th, 8th, 9th, & 10th) ☍ n.☿♌ in 3rd (R. 4th)
t.♄♒ □ n.♂♉	t.♄♒ in 9th (R.7th, 8th, 9th, & 10th) □ n.♂♉ in in 11th (R. 6th)
t.♄♒ □ n.♇♏	t.♄♒ in 8th (R. 8th, 9th, & 10th) □ n.♇♏ in 6th (R. 6th)
t.♅♉ ⚹ n.☽♋	t.♅♉ in 12th (R. 10th) ⚹ n.☽♋ in 1st (R. 1st & 2nd)
t.♅♉ ☌ n.♂♉	t.♅♉ in 11th (R. 10th) ☌ n.♂♉ in 11th (R. 6th)
t.♅♉ ☍ n.♇♏	t.♅♉ in 12th (R. 10th) ☍ n.♇♏ in 6th (R. 6th)

t.♆♓ △ n.♃♋	t.♆♓ in 10th (R.11th) △ n.♃♋ in 2nd (R. 11th)
t.♆♓ ✶ n.♄♑	t.♆♓ in 10th (R.11th) ✶ n.♄♑ in 8th (R.7th, 8th, 9th, & 10th)
t.♀♑ ☍ n.♃♋	t.♀♑ in 8th (R. 6th) ☍ n.♃♋ in 2nd (R. 11th)

7		Compose a summary of your findings from step 4-6.	Summary of Analysis.

Five-Hit Event

One occurrence you might have noticed that has yet to be seen has to do with transiting Uranus in Taurus sextile natal Moon in Cancer (t.♅♉ ✶ n.☽♋). Instead of experiencing three hits, which is normal for any retrograde event in astrology, this transit encounters five hits instead. This is because when transiting Uranus goes station direct and station retrograde, it does so at the same degree point that causes a sextile with the Moon. For example, when transiting Uranus went station retrograde on August 14, 2020, it did so at 10° ♉ 41' with the Moon sextile point being 10° ♉ 54'. Although this station retrograde does not establish an exact hit up to the minute with the Moon, it is still within one degree or less which makes it valid, nevertheless.

When this occurs, it not only prolongs aspect events for the individual, it makes it so they encounter and feel these energies on five separate occasions. Additionally, these occurrences can be even more intense at the stationary periods given that the transiting planet has slowed down to a temporary halt. It is important to catch and consider these factors when you discover a five-hit retrograde event. The good news for Client A is that this event is a sextile, which gives them an opportunity to fix and adjust their outward persona and inward emotional realms in relation to their career as evidenced by the planets and houses involved according to the transit formula:

t.♅♉ in 12th (R. 10th) ✶ n.☽♋ in 1st (R. 1st & 2nd)

The only difference is that instead of experiencing this transit three times over the course of 11 months according to Table V-4, they will now encounter this transit five times within a span of approximately 1.5 years.

Multiples Ingresses

The next interesting factor with Client A's transits has to do with the multitude of ingresses that are occurring from 2020-2021. During this time, Client A's transit Jupiter ingresses into the 9th and 10th, Saturn into the 9th, Uranus into the 12th, and Neptune into the 11th. Ingresses indicate major shifts in energy where the focus of the transiting planet leaves the energies of the old house and ignites the energies of the new house it enters. This occurrence is highly significant for Client A because four out of the five outer planets shift their energies in this way within the span of approximately one year.

This means that Client A can witness a substantial purge of sorts where situations are concluding, and new ones are beginning. For example, Saturn enters the 9th house and Jupiter also enters the 9th house and eventually into the 10th house. This tells me that Client A's philosophical outlook will be tested and reformed during this time, but these new ideals will help them to refocus their career goals along with their outlook towards their fellow human beings and the society Client A is placed within.

With Uranus and Neptune, there is an interesting mixture of harmony here because Uranus is entering the 12th house, the house of Pisces typically ruled by Neptune, and Neptune is entering the 11th house, the house of Aquarius typically ruled by Uranus. (NOTE: Notice that I am referring to the general principles of house rulerships here. In Client A's chart, their 11th house is housed in Pisces, which means it ruled by Neptune, and their 12th house is housed in Taurus, which is ruled by Venus. In my example, I am referring to what was mentioned in Part II-Section 6 in that in their "natural state," the 11th house is the house of Aquarius, and the 12th house is the house of Pisces. This means, in this natural state, the 11th house is ruled by Uranus/Saturn and the 12th house is ruled by Pisces even though in the natal chart this is not the case.)

Since Neptune is entering the 11th house, which is naturally ruled by Uranus, and Uranus is entering the 12th house, the house naturally ruled by Neptune, some sort of mutual harmony is occurring. This tells me that Client A's philosophical explorations brought on by Saturn and Jupiter's journey into the 9th house also causes Client A to reevaluate their spiritual practices and ideologies along with the friends and social groups that they associate with in order to accommodate their newly developed spiritual and ideological outlooks. This stems from Client A concluding and looking back at their experiences from the recent past where these planets were before they entered their new houses. Now, with these new energies, Client A moves on to the next stage of their development where they take what they have learned and implement it into new ways of thinking, associating, accomplishing, and connecting with spiritual realms and with society at large.

Oppositions with Saturn and Jupiter

The next intense correlation that occurs within Client A's transits involves the multiple oppositions created by transiting Jupiter and Saturn along with the opposition from transiting Pluto to natal Jupiter. More specifically, transiting Jupiter opposes natal Sun, Mercury, and Jupiter (t.♃♑ ☍ n.☉♋, t.♃♒ ☍ n.☿♌, t.♃♑ ☍ n.♃♋), transiting Saturn opposes natal Sun and Mercury (t.♄♑ ☍ n.☉♋, t.♄♒ ☍ n.☿♌), and transiting Pluto opposes natal Jupiter (t.♇♑ ☍ n.♃♋).

Similar to the multiple ingresses that Client A experiences, these numerous oppositions indicate an important time of culmination and climax of situations before they begin to settle down and conclude. In other words, the ingresses cause Client A to change their motives, spiritual and mental outlook, and social groups, but the oppositions involve the events that have caused them to reach these conclusions and subsequent shifts in energies and focus. To get a better idea as to which energies are involved in these oppositions, let us observe the various transit formulas (Table V-6).

TABLE V-6. Various Oppositions for Client A.

EVENT	FORMULA
t.♃♑ ☍ n.☉♋	t.♃♑ in 8th (R. 11th) ☍ n.☉♋ in 2nd (R. 3rd & 4th)
t.♃♒ ☍ n.☿♌	t.♃♒ in 9th (R. 11th) ☍ n.☿♌ in 3rd (R. 4th)
t.♃♑ ☍ n.♃♋	t.♃♑ in 8th (R. 11th) ☍ n.♃♋ 2nd (R.11th)
t.♄♑ ☍ n.☉♋	t.♄♑ in 8th (R.7th, 8th, 9th, & 10th) ☍ n.☉♋ in 2nd (R. 3rd & 4th)
t.♄♒ ☍ n.☿♌	t.♄♒ in 9th (R.7th, 8th, 9th, & 10th) ☍ n.☿♌ in 3rd (R. 4th)
t.♇♑ ☍ n.♃♋	t.♇♑ in 8th (R. 6th) ☍ n.♃♋ in 2nd (R. 11th)

397

From these formulas, I notice a lot of 8th, 9th, 10th, 11th, 4th, and 3rd house energies, which is interesting because this correlates to the ingresses of the outer planets that were previous discussed that are ingressing into the 9th, 10th, 11th, and 12th houses. Similarly, the transiting planets involved in these oppositions are mostly Jupiter and Saturn, and it is Jupiter and Saturn that are likewise ingressing into the various houses. When correlations like this occur, this helps to place confidence in your analysis because you are finding more than one data point leading to the same outcome/conclusion. Another correlation is that with these oppositions, the natal planets Sun, Mercury, and Jupiter are all involved more than once.

Client A has been trying to reinvent themself over the past few years. How they communicate, how they express who they are, and how this reflects towards their overall sense of pessimism and/or optimism are all coming into play here. Through these experiences, Client A has probably come to learn that the old way of acting and of doing things no longer serves them any purpose. They are therefore beginning to see where the pitfalls are, and this in turn has caused them to reflect and adjust their individual personality and outlook based upon these observations. These changes simply translate over to the ingresses because now that Client A wants to change certain parts of who they are, the energies of life similarly change and adjust with them.

Auspicious Moments

Client A has a string of auspicious activity within the three consecutive months of May, June, and July 2021. During this time, transiting Uranus sextiles natal Moon, transiting Jupiter trines the Ascendant, and transiting Neptune trines natal Jupiter (t.♅♉ ✶ n.☽♋, t.♃♓ △ n.ASC♋, t.♆♓ △ n.♃♋) (Table V-7).

TABLE V-7. Formulas for Client A's Auspicious Moments.

EVENT	FORMULA
t.♅♉ ✶ n.☽♋	t.♅♉ in 12th (R. 10th) ✶ n.☽♋ in 1st (R. 1st & 2nd)
t.♃♓ △ n.ASC♋	t.♃♓ in 10th (R. 11th) △ n.ASC♋
t.♆♓ △ n.♃♋	t.♆♓ in 10th (R.11th) △ n.♃♋ in 2nd (R. 11th)

As already mentioned, Client A has been experiencing events that have caused them to reevaluate their approach towards individuals and situations that stem from their personal and spiritual outlook. These evaluations have consequently caused Client A to evaluate their outward persona, inward emotional stability, and how these two can change and adjust due to the new information they have gathered.

During these three months in 2021, there will be a moment where Client A can begin to take their new approaches and personality out into the world with great success. The trines and sextiles indicate that Client A will have much ease at implementing these new ideals and personalities. With the 11th, 10th, 2nd, and 1st houses being activated tells me this is going to greatly affect their career and career goals, their social groups and humanitarian efforts, their own personality and physical self, and lastly, what they hold valuable to them. During these three months, Client A should take advantage of these harmonious forces and begin to integrate and establish confidence into their new personality and outlook.

INAUSPICIOUS MOMENTS

The first inauspicious month, July 2020, mostly involves transiting Jupiter opposing natal Jupiter, transiting Pluto opposing natal Jupiter, and transiting Jupiter conjoin natal Saturn (t.♃♑ ☍ n.♃♋, t.♇♑ ☍ n.♃♋, t.♃♑ ☌ n.♄♑). The second month, February 2021, involves transiting Saturn square natal Mars, transiting Jupiter square natal Pluto, and transiting Jupiter opposes natal Mercury (t.♄♒ ◻ n.♂♉, t.♃♑ ✳ n.♇♏, t.♃♒ ☍ n.☿♌) (Table V-8).

TABLE V-8. Formulas for Client A's Inauspicious moments.

EVENT	FORMULA
t.♇♑ ☍ n.♃♋	t.♇♑ in 8th (R. 6th) ☍ n.♃♋ in 2nd (R. 11th)
t.♃♑ ☌ n.♄♑	t.♃♑ in 8th (R. 11th) ☌ n.♄♑ in 8th (R.7th, 8th, 9th, & 10th)
t.♃♑ ☍ n.♃♋	t.♃♑ in 8th (R. 11th) ☍ n.♃♋ 2nd (R.11th)
t.♄♒ ◻ n.♂♉	t.♄♒ in 9th (R.7th, 8th, 9th, & 10th) ◻ n.♂♉ in in 11th (R. 6th)
t.♃♒ ◻ n.♇♏	t.♃♒ in 9th (R. 11th) ◻ n.♇♏ in 6th (R.6th)
t.♃♒ ☍ n.☿♌	t.♃♒ in 9th (R. 11th) ☍ n.☿♌ in 3rd (R. 4th)

What makes July 2020 difficult is that the oppositions of this month cause Client A to experience certain events that will lead them to realize that they need to change their ways due to conflict with others. This could have involved an ending of some kind, either an ending of a friendship, a relationship, or a death of someone close (8th and 11th houses involved). Whatever the event may be, it caused Client A to reevaluate what they hold important to themself personally, and how this translates into their life goals and personal portrayal. What makes these matters more difficult is Jupiter conjoining Saturn. Resources and speculation towards a happier ending are quashed. Client A feels stuck with having to deal with the various issues at hand, with nowhere to go to seek solace in order to catch their breath. Thankfully, as you will find with all transits, energies eventually wind down and once this month has concluded, so do these intense energies.

In February 2021, these new outlooks, personalities, emotional stability, friends, and goals will experience their first conflict with the outside world. There could be some authoritative power that tries to suppress Client A's newfound confidence which can greatly cause them to go back to square one. Furthermore, the Jupiter square to Mercury makes it hard for Client A to voice what they are feeling, or it can cause some miscommunications to occur with what they are trying to say, which becomes misinterpreted the wrong way.

Client A should not completely give up after this happens. Instead, they should think of it as a sort of checkpoint where their new approaches are simply being tested by the outside world. Instead of reacting how they normally would, I would encourage them to try to take the situation with their new outlook and see if that changes how they would address the various situations. It might be difficult as they feel less confident now, but if they can push through and try it differently, their confidence could easily come back to them because they are showing themself that their new way of doing things is ultimately beneficial to them in the long run.

| 1 | IV-3 | Obtain a transit chart for the present day as a reference. | Preliminary data. |

CLIENT B: TRANSIT CHART

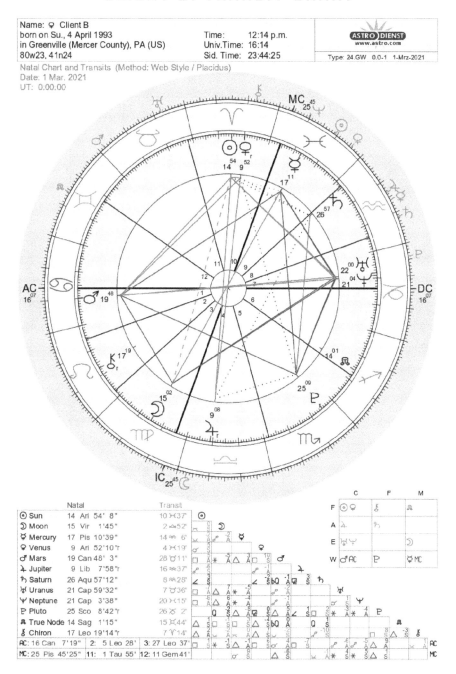

	Natal	Transit
☉ Sun	14 Ari 54' 8"	10 ♓ 37'
☽ Moon	15 Vir 1'45"	2 ♏ 52'
☿ Mercury	17 Pis 10'39"	14 ♒ 6'
♀ Venus	9 Ari 52'10"r	4 ♓ 19'
♂ Mars	19 Can 48' 3"	28 ♉ 11'
♃ Jupiter	9 Lib 7'58"r	16 ♒ 37'
♄ Saturn	26 Aqu 57'12"	8 ♒ 28'
♅ Uranus	21 Cap 59'32"	7 ♉ 36'
♆ Neptune	21 Cap 3'38"	20 ♓ 15'
♇ Pluto	25 Sco 8'42"r	26 ♑ 2'
♌ True Node	14 Sag 1'15"	15 ♊ 44'
⚷ Chiron	17 Leo 19'14"r	7 ♈ 14'
AC: 16 Can 7'19"	2: 5 Leo 28'	3: 27 Leo 37'
MC: 25 Pis 45'25"	11: 1 Tau 55'	12: 11 Gem 41'

2A	IV-3	Trace the Ephemeris one year before and after from the day of the reading and observe if transiting Jupiter has ingresses or regressed into a house.	Preliminary data.
2B	IV-3	Repeat for transiting Saturn.	Preliminary data.
2C	IV-3	Repeat for transiting Uranus.	Preliminary data.
2D	IV-3	Repeat for transiting Neptune.	Preliminary data.
2E	IV-3	Repeat for transiting Pluto.	Preliminary data.

♃		
EVENT	**GLYPH**	**DATE**
Transiting Jupiter ingresses into the 7th House	t. ♃ → 7th	FEB 12, 2020
Transiting Jupiter ingresses into the 8th House	t. ♃ → 8th	JAN 13, 2021
Transiting Jupiter ingresses into the 9th House (1/3)	t. ♃ → 9th (1/3)	APR 26, 2021
Transiting Jupiter regresses into the 8th House (2/3)	t. ♃ → 8th (2/3)	AUG 17, 2021
Transiting Jupiter ingresses into the 9th House (3/3)	t. ♃ → 9th (3/3)	DEC 15, 2021

♄		
EVENT	**GLYPH**	**DATE**
Transiting Saturn ingresses into the 8th House	t. ♄ → 8th	FEB 3, 2021

♅		
EVENT	**GLYPH**	**DATE**
NONE		

♆		
EVENT	**GLYPH**	**DATE**
NONE		

♇		
EVENT	**GLYPH**	**DATE**
NONE		

3A	IV-3	Trace the Ephemeris one year before and after from the day of the reading and observe if Jupiter makes an aspect to any of the 12 natal points.	Preliminary data.
3B	IV-3	Repeat for transiting Saturn.	Preliminary data.
3C	IV-3	Repeat for transiting Uranus.	Preliminary data.

3D	IV-3	Repeat for transiting Neptune.	Preliminary data.
3E	IV-3	Repeat for transiting Pluto.	Preliminary data.

♃

EVENT	GLYPH	DATE
Transiting Jupiter in Capricorn square Natal Sun in Aries	t.♃♑ □ n.☉♈	FEB 5, 2020
Transiting Jupiter in Aquarius sextile Natal Sun in Aries	t.♃♒ ✶ n.☉♈	FEB 21, 2021
Transiting Jupiter in Capricorn trine Natal Moon in Virgo	t.♃♑ △ n.☽♍	FEB 7, 2020
Transiting Jupiter in Capricorn sextile Natal Mercury in Pisces (1/2) Transiting Jupiter Station Direct in Capricorn sextile Natal Mercury in Pisces (2/2)	t.♃♑ ✶ n.☿♓ (1/2) t.♃♑ SD ✶ n.☿♓ (2/2)	FEB 17, 2020 SEP 13, 2020
Transiting Jupiter in Aquarius sextile Natal Venus in Aries	t.♃♒ ✶ n.♀♈	JAN 27, 2021
Transiting Jupiter in Capricorn oppose Natal Mars in Cancer (1/3) Transiting Jupiter Retrograde in Capricorn oppose Natal Mars in Cancer (2/3) Transiting Jupiter in Capricorn oppose Natal Mars in Cancer (3/3)	t.♃♑ ☍ n.♂♋ (1/3) t.♃♑ Rx ☍ n.♂♋ (2/3) t.♃♑ ☍ n.♂♋ (3/3)	MAR 2, 2020 AUG 3, 2020 OCT 22, 2020
Transiting Jupiter in Aquarius trine Natal Jupiter in Libra	t.♃♒ △ n.♃♎	JAN 28, 2021
Transiting Jupiter in Aquarius conjoin Natal Saturn in Aquarius (1/3) Transiting Jupiter Retrograde in Aquarius conjoin Natal Saturn in Aquarius (2/3) Transiting Jupiter in Aquarius conjoin Natal Saturn in Aquarius (3/3)	t.♃♒ ☌ n.♄♒ (1/3) t.♃♒ Rx ☌ n.♄♒ (2/3) t.♃♒ ☌ n.♄♒ (3/3)	APR 14, 2021 AUG 23, 2021 DEC 11, 2021
Transiting Jupiter in Capricorn conjoin Natal Uranus in Capricorn (1/3) Transiting Jupiter Retrograde in Capricorn conjoin Natal Uranus in Capricorn (2/3) Transiting Jupiter in Capricorn conjoin Natal Uranus in Capricorn (3/3)	t.♃♑ ☌ n.♅♑ (1/3) t.♃♑ Rx ☌ n.♅♑ (2/3) t.♃♑ ☌ n.♅♑ (3/3)	MAR 15, 2020 JUL 18, 2020 NOV 7, 2020
Transiting Jupiter in Capricorn conjoin Natal Neptune in Capricorn (1/3) Transiting Jupiter Retrograde in Capricorn conjoin Natal Neptune in Capricorn (2/3) Transiting Jupiter in Capricorn conjoin Natal Neptune in Capricorn (3/3)	t.♃♑ ☌ n.♆♑ (1/3) t.♃♑ Rx ☌ n.♆♑ (2/3) t.♃♑ ☌ n.♆♑ (3/3)	MAR 9, 2020 JUL 25, 2020 NOV 1, 2020

Event	Glyph	Date
Transiting Jupiter in Capricorn sextile Natal Pluto in Scorpio (1/3) Transiting Jupiter Retrograde in Capricorn sextile Natal Pluto in Scorpio (2/3) Transiting Jupiter in Capricorn sextile Natal Pluto in Scorpio (3/3)	t.♃♑ ⚹ n.♇♏ (1/3) t.♃♑ Rx ⚹ n.♇♏ (2/3) t.♃♑ ⚹ n.♇♏ (3/3)	APR 5, 2020 JUN 21, 2020 NOV 25, 2020
Transiting Jupiter in Aquarius square Natal Pluto in Scorpio (1/3) Transiting Jupiter Retrograde in Aquarius square Natal Pluto in Scorpio (2/3) Transiting Jupiter in Aquarius square Natal Pluto in Scorpio (3/3)	t.♃♒ □ n.♇♏ (1/3) t.♃♒ Rx □ n.♇♏ (2/3) t.♃♒ □ n.♇♏ (3/3)	APR 10, 2021 SEP 6, 2021 NOV 28, 2021
Transiting Jupiter in Capricorn oppose Cancer Ascendant	t.♃♑ ☍ n.ASC♋	FEB 13, 2020
Transiting Jupiter in Capricorn sextile Pisces Midheaven (1/3) Transiting Jupiter Retrograde in Capricorn sextile Pisces Midheaven (2/3) Transiting Jupiter in Capricorn sextile Pisces Midheaven (3/3)	t.♃♑ ⚹ n.MC♓ (1/3) t.♃♑ Rx ⚹ n.MC♓ (2/3) t.♃♑ ⚹ n.MC♓ (3/3)	APR 13, 2020 JUN 15, 2020 NOV 28, 2020
♄		
EVENT	GLYPH	DATE
Transiting Saturn in Aquarius sextile Natal Sun in Aries	t.♄♒ ⚹ n.☉♈	JAN 28, 2022
Transiting Saturn in Aquarius sextile Natal Venus in Aries (1/3) Transiting Saturn Retrograde in Aquarius sextile Natal Venus in Aries (2/3) Transiting Saturn in Aquarius sextile Natal Venus in Aries (3/3)	t.♄♒ ⚹ n.♀♈ (1/3) t.♄♒ Rx ⚹ n.♀♈ (2/3) t.♄♒ ⚹ n.♀♈ (3/3)	MAR 14, 2021 AUG 7, 2021 DEC 11, 2021
Transiting Saturn in Aquarius tine Natal Jupiter in Libra (1/3) Transiting Saturn Retrograde in Aquarius tine Natal Jupiter in Libra (2/3) Transiting Saturn in Aquarius tine Natal Jupiter in Libra (3/3)	t.♄♒ △ n.♃♎ (1/3) t.♄♒ Rx △ n.♃♎ (2/3) t.♄♒ △ n.♃♎ (3/3)	MAR 7, 2021 AUG 16, 2021 DEC 2, 2021
Transiting Saturn in Capricorn sextile Natal Pluto in Scorpio (1/2) Transiting Saturn Station Direct in Capricorn sextile Natal Pluto in Scorpio (2/2)	t.♄♑ ⚹ n.♇♏ (1/2) t.♄♑ SD ⚹ n.♇♏ (2/2)	FEB 1, 2020 SEP 13, 2020

404

EVENT	GLYPH	DATE
Transiting Saturn in Capricorn sextile Pisces Midheaven (1/4) Transiting Saturn Retrograde in Capricorn sextile Pisces Midheaven (2/4) Transiting Saturn Station Direct in Capricorn sextile Pisces Midheaven (3/4) Transiting Saturn in Capricorn sextile Pisces Midheaven (4/4)	t.♄♑ ⚹ n.MC♓ (1/4) t.♄♑ Rx ⚹ n.MC♓ (2/4) t.♄♑ SD ⚹ n.MC♓ (3/4) t.♄♑ ⚹ n.MC♓ (4/4)	FEB 7, 2020 SEP 6, 2020 SEP 13, 2020 OCT 23, 2020

♅

EVENT	GLYPH	DATE
NONE		

♆

EVENT	GLYPH	DATE
Transiting Neptune in Pisces conjoin Natal Mercury in Pisces	t.♆♓ ☌ n.☿♓	FEB 4, 2020
Transiting Neptune in Pisces trine Natal Mars in Cancer (1/3) Transiting Neptune Retrograde in Pisces trine Natal Mars in Cancer (2/3) Transiting Neptune in Pisces trine Natal Mars in Cancer (3/3)	t.♆♓ △ n.♂♋(1/3) t.♆♓ Rx △ n.♂♋ (2/3) t.♆♓ △ n.♂♋ (3/3)	APR 15, 2020 SEP 2, 2020 FEB 17, 2021
Transiting Neptune in Pisces sextile Natal Uranus in Capricorn (1/3) Transiting Neptune Retrograde in Pisces sextile Natal Uranus in Capricorn (2/3) Transiting Neptune in Pisces sextile Natal Uranus in Capricorn (3/3)	t. ♆♓ ⚹ n.♅♑ (1/3) t. ♆♓ Rx ⚹ n.♅♑ (2/3) t. ♆♓ ⚹ n.♅♑ (3/3)	APR 17, 2021 SEP 8, 2021 FEB 17, 2022
Transiting Neptune in Pisces sextile Natal Neptune in Capricorn (1/3) Transiting Neptune Retrograde in Pisces Retrograde sextile Natal Neptune in Capricorn (2/3) Transiting Neptune in Pisces sextile Natal Neptune in Capricorn (3/3)	t. ♆♓ ⚹ n.♆♑ (1/3) t. ♆♓ Rx ⚹ n.♆♑ (2/3) t. ♆♓ ⚹ n.♆♑ (3/3)	MAR 22, 2021 OCT 12, 2021 JAN 20, 2022

♇		
EVENT	**GLYPH**	**DATE**
Transiting Pluto in Capricorn sextile Natal Pluto in Scorpio (1/3) Transiting Pluto Retrograde in Capricorn sextile Natal Pluto in Scorpio (2/3) Transiting Pluto in Capricorn sextile Natal Pluto in Scorpio (3/3)	t.♇♑ ⚹ n.♇♏ (1/3) t.♇♑ Rx ⚹ n.♇♏ (2/3) t. ♇♑ ⚹ n.♇♏ (3/3)	JAN 20, 2021 AUG 7, 2021 DEC 3, 2021
Transiting Pluto in Capricorn sextile Pisces Midheaven (1/3) Transiting Pluto Retrograde in Capricorn sextile Pisces Midheaven (2/3) Transiting Pluto in Capricorn sextile Pisces Midheaven (3/3)	t. ♇♑ ⚹ n.MC♓ (1/3) t. ♇♑ Rx ⚹ n.MC♓ (2/3) t. ♇♑ ⚹ n.MC♓ (3/3)	FEB 19, 2021 AUG 23, 2021 DEC 26, 2021

4		Place all events from Steps 2A-3E in chronological order.	Information as to when these events will occur and if they occur simultaneously.

2020							
JAN		**FEB**		**MAR**		**APR**	
EVENT	**DAY**	**EVENT**	**DAY**	**EVENT**	**DAY**	**EVENT**	**DAY**
		t.♄♑ ⚹ n.♇♏ (1/2) t.♆♓ ☌ n.♆♓ t.♃♑ □ n.☉♈ t.♃♑ △ n.☽♍ t.♄♑ ⚹ n.MC♓ (1/4) t. ♃ → 7th t.♃♑ ☍ n.ASC♋ t.♃♑ ⚹ n.♆♓ (1/2)	1 4 5 7 7 12 13 17	t.♃♑ ☍ n.♂♋ (1/3) t.♃♑ ☌ n.♆♑ (1/3) t.♃♑ ☌ n.♅♑ (1/3)	2 9 15	t.♃♑ ⚹ n.♇♏ (1/3) t.♃♑ ⚹ n.MC♓ (1/3) t.♆♓ △ n.♂♋(1/3)	5 13 15
MAY		**JUN**		**JUL**		**AUG**	
EVENT	**DAY**	**EVENT**	**DAY**	**EVENT**	**DAY**	**EVENT**	**DAY**
		t.♃♑ Rx ⚹ n.MC♓ (2/3) t.♃♑ Rx ⚹ n.♇♏ (2/3)	15 21	t.♃♑ Rx ☌ n.♅♑ (2/3) t.♃♑ Rx ☌ n.♆♑ (2/3)	18 25	t.♃♑ Rx ☍ n.♂♋ (2/3)	3

SEP		OCT		NOV		DEC	
EVENT	DAY	EVENT	DAY	EVENT	DAY	EVENT	DAY
t.♆♓ Rx △ n.♂♋ (2/3) t.♄♑ Rx ⚹ n.MC♓ (2/4) t.♃♑ SD ⚹ n.♇♓ (2/2) t. t.♄♑ SD ⚹ n.♇♏ (2/2) t.♄♑ SD ⚹ n.MC♓ (3/4)	2 6 13 13 13	t.♃♑ ☍ n.♂♋ (3/3) t.♄♑ ⚹ n.MC♓ (4/4)	22 23	t.♃♑ ☌ n.♆♑ (3/3) t.♃♑ ☌ n.♅♑ (3/3) t.♃♑ ⚹ n.♇♏ (3/3) t.♃♑ ⚹ n.MC♓ (3/3)	1 7 25 28		

2021

JAN		FEB		MAR		APR	
EVENT	DAY	EVENT	DAY	EVENT	DAY	EVENT	DAY
t. ♃ → 8th t.♇♑ ⚹ n.♇♏ (1/3) t.♃♒ ⚹ n.♀♈ t.♃♒ △ n.♃♎	13 20 27 28		3 17 19 21	t.♄♒ △ n.♃♎ (1/3) t.♄♒ ⚹ n.♀♈ (1/3) t. ♆♓ ⚹ n.♆♑ (1/3)	7 14 22	t.♃♒ □ n.♇♏ (1/3) t.♃♒ ☌ n.♄♒ (1/3) t. ♆♓ ⚹ n.♅♑ (1/3) t. ♃ → 9th (1/3)	10 14 17 26

MAY		JUN		JUL		AUG	
EVENT	DAY	EVENT	DAY	EVENT	DAY	EVENT	DAY
						t.♄♒ Rx ⚹ n.♀♈ (2/3) t.♇♑ Rx ⚹ n.♇♏ (2/3) t.♄♒ Rx △ n.♃♎ (2/3) t. ♃ → 8th (2/3) t. ♇♑ Rx ⚹ n.MC♓ (2/3) t.♃♒ Rx ☌ n.♄♒ (2/3)	7 7 16 17 23 23

SEP		OCT		NOV		DEC	
EVENT	DAY	EVENT	DAY	EVENT	DAY	EVENT	DAY
t.♃♒ Rx □ n.♆♏ (2/3) t. ♆♓ Rx ⚹ n.♅♑ (2/3)	6 8		12	t.♃♒ □ n.♆♏ (3/3)	28	t.♄♒ △ n.♃♎ (3/3) t. ♆♑ ⚹ n.♆♏(3/3) t.♃♒ ☌ n.♄♒ (3/3) t.♄♒ ⚹ n.♀♈ (3/3) t. ♃ → 9th (3/3) t. ♆♑ ⚹ n.MC♓ (3/3)	2 3 11 11 15 26

2022			
JAN		FEB	
EVENT	DAY	EVENT	DAY
t. ♆♓ ⚹ n.♆♑ (3/3) t.♄♒ ⚹ n.☉♈	20 28	t. ♆♓ ⚹ n.♅♑ (3/3)	17

5		Determine the most inauspicious and auspicious months for the individual.	This will let the individual know when there are times of immense struggle or benefit which they can either prepare for the harder times and/or utilize the better times to their fullest potential.

AUSPICIOUS	INAUSPICIOUS
SEP 2020	FEB 2020
JAN 2021	NOV 2021
FEB 2021	
MAR 2021	
AUG 2021	
DEC 2021	

6	IV-4	Create transit formulas for every event listed in steps 3A-3E.	Various realms within the person's life that will be influenced by the event.

EVENT	FORMULA
t.♃♑ □ n.☉a	t.♃♑ in 6th (R. 6th & 10th) □ n.☉♈ in 10th (R. 2nd & 3rd)
t.♃♒ ⚹ n.☉♈	t.♃♒ in 7th (R. 6th & 10th) ⚹ n.☉♈ in 10th (R. 2nd & 3rd)
t.♃♑ △ n.☽♍℞	t.♃♑ in 6th (R. 6th & 10th) △ n.☽♍℞ in 3rd (R.1st)
t.♃♑ ⚹ n.⚷♓	t.♃♑ in 7th (R. 6th & 10th) ⚹ n.⚷♓ in 9th (R. 4th & 12th)
t.♃♒ ⚹ n.♀♈	t.♃♒ in 8th (R. 6th & 10th) ⚹ n.♀♈ in 10th (R. 11th)
t.♃♑ ☍ n.♂♋	t.♃♑ in 7th (R. 6th & 10th) ☍ n.♂♋ in 1st (R. 5th)
t.♃♒ △ n.♃♎	t.♃♒ in 8th (R. 6th & 10th) △ n.♃♎ in 4th (R. 6th & 10th)
t.♃♒ ☌ n.♄♒	t.♃♒ in 8th (R. 6th & 10th) ☌ n.♄♒ in 8th (R. 7th, 8th, & 9th)
t.♃♑ ☌ n.♅♑	t.♃♑ in 7th (R. 6th & 10th) ☌ n.♅♑ in 7th (R. 8th & 9th)
t.♃♑ ☌ n.♆♑	t.♃♑ in 7th (R. 6th & 10th) ☌ n.♆♑ in 7th (R. 10th)
t.♃♑ ⚹ n.♇♏	t.♃♑ in 7th (R. 6th & 10th) ⚹ n.♇♏ in 5th (R. 5th)
t.♃♒ □ n.♇♏	t.♃♒ in 8th (R. 6th & 10th) □ n.♇♏ in 5th (R. 5th)
t.♃♑ ☍ n.ASC♋	t.♃♑ in 7th (R. 6th & 10th) ☍ n.ASC♋
t.♃♑ ⚹ n.MC♓	t.♃♑ in 7th (R. 6th & 10th) ⚹ n.MC♓
t.♄♒ ⚹ n.☉♈	t.♄♒ in 7th (R. 7th, 8th, & 9th) ⚹ n.☉♈ in 10th (R. 2nd & 3rd)
t.♄♒ ⚹ n.♀♈	t.♄♒ in 7th (R. 7th, 8th, & 9th) ⚹ n.♀♈ in 10th (R. 11th)
t.♄♒ △ n.♃♎	t.♄♒ in 8th (R. 7th, 8th, & 9th) △ n.♃♎ in 4st (R. 6th & 10th)
t.♄♑ ⚹ n.♇♏	t.♄♑ in 8th (R. 7th, 8th, & 9th) ⚹ n.♇♏ in 5th (R. 5th)
t.♄♑ ⚹ n.MC♓	t.♄♑ in 7th (R. 7th & 9th) ⚹ n.MC♓
t.♆♓ ☌ n.⚷♓	t.♆♓ in 7th (R. 10th) ☌ n.⚷♓ in 9th (R.4th & 12th)
t.♆♓ △ n.♂♋	t.♆♓ in 9th (R. 10th) △ n.♂♋ in 1st (R. 5th)
t.♆♓ ⚹ n.♅♑	t.♆♓ in 9th (R. 10th) ⚹ n. ♅♑ in 7th (R. 8th & 9th)
t.♆♓ ⚹ n.♆♑	t.♆♓ in 9th (R. 10th) ⚹ n.♆♑ in 7th (R. 10th)
t.♇♑ ⚹ n.♇♏	t.♇♑ in 7th (R. 5th) ⚹ n.♇♏ in 5th (R. 5th)
t.♇♑ ⚹ n.MC♓	t.♇♑ in 7th (R. 5th) ⚹ n.MC♓

7		Compose a summary of your findings from step 4-6.	Summary of Analysis.

New Beginnings with Jupiter and Neptune

Throughout 2020-2021, Client B experiences four conjunctions, which include transiting Jupiter conjunct natal Saturn, Uranus, and Neptune, and transiting Neptune conjunct natal Mercury (t.♃♒ ☌ n.♄♒, t.♃♑ ☌ n.♅♑, t.♃♑ ☌ n.♆♑, t.♆♓ ☌ n.☿♓) (Table V-9).

As we have learned with conjunctions, they indicate a blending of the two planets, but they also indicate a new beginning of a larger cycle. For transiting Jupiter, these larger cycles are 12 years long and therefore Client B is starting to witness the themes involved within these new cycles during this time. With natal Saturn being placed within the 8th house, it is already difficult for Client B to become vulnerable around others, which causes them to have their guard up constantly. These Jupiter conjunctions soften up this natal insecurity and allow for Client B to try to take themself out of their comfort zone in order to process and discuss important issues surrounding their close relationships with their significant other, and possibly with their father or work superior as evidenced by the houses involved (7th, 8th, and 10th). Additionally, with the 6th and 9th houses, Client B will be able to have a more critical lens into these matters and look back at how their childhood experiences attributed to their present-day outlook. This probably comes out of the fact that Neptune conjoins Mercury, which causes confusion and difficulty in communicating thoughts and emotions. This signals to Client B that something is off and needs to be addressed.

These outworn outlooks will be reexamined during this time especially if Client B gives themself permission to be honest and open to others with whom they have needed to clear the air out for a while. For example, Client B might realize that the reason why they are so reserved stems from their past experiences with their father. This causes them to finally

TABLE V-9. Client B's Jupiter and Neptune Conjunctions

EVENT	FORMULA
t.♃♒ ☌ n.♄♒	t.♃♒ in 8th (R. 6th & 10th) ☌ n.♄♒ in 8th (R. 7th, 8th, & 9th)
t.♃♑ ☌ n.♅♑	t.♃♑ in 7th (R. 6th & 10th) ☌ n.♅♑ in 7th (R. 8th & 9th)
t.♃♑ ☌ n.♆♑	t.♃♑ in 7th (R. 6th & 10th) ☌ n.♆♑ in 7th (R. 10th)
t.♆♓ ☌ n.☿♓	t.♆♓ in 7th (R. 10th) ☌ n.☿♓ in 9th (R.4th & 12th)

talk to their father about these issues, which causes even further analysis and adjustments onto Client B's psychology and outlook. The good news is that this gives Client B the ability to change these patterns of behavior based upon their new discoveries. Again, this is not necessarily how it will precisely manifest; this is simply a hypothesis based upon the houses and planets involved. Nevertheless, the overarching themes and undercurrents from these various lessons will become manifest and experienced regardless of how the outcome comes about.

Opportunities with Pluto

Additionally, during this time, Pluto makes sextiles to the Midheaven and natal Pluto (♇♑ ✶ n.MC♓, t.♇♑ ✶ n.♇♏) (Table V-10).

Observing the houses involved (5th and 7th) we observe correlations to the various themes we have already been discussing. Mainly, that Client B will be facing childhood issues that have stemmed from their parental upbringing and is now starting to conflate how they communicate with others. Particularly with those in authority and those that are closest to them. With these sextiles, it gives Client B the chance to address these issues with those from their past in the appropriate way. As a consequence, they will gain a lot of understanding and healing from these interactions.

However, as it is with all sextiles, Client B needs to make an honest and intentional effort in achieving these aims as it will not just happen out of the blue. Client B needs to take initiation and confront those from their past, which will take a lot of courage and strength, but if they are able to do this the outcome will be heavily to their benefit as they will seek answers to life-long questions in regards to the person that they have become in their adult life.

TABLE V-10. Formulas for Client B's Pluto Transits.

EVENT	FORMULA
t.♇♑ ✶ n.♇♏	t.♇♑ in 7th (R. 5th) ✶ n.♇♏ in 5th (R. 5th)
t. ♇♑ ✶ n.MC♓	t.♇♑ in 7th (R. 5th) ✶ n.MC♓

Auspicious Moments

The year 2021 for Client B is incredibly auspicious for most of the year. Even the months that are less favorable still contain beneficial buffers that help to counterbalance the more difficult transits. There are numerous sextiles and trines that can be found in the table below (Table V-11).

We are seeing house themes primarily with the 8th, 5th, 6th, and 10th, with occasional occurrences with the 4th, 3rd, 2nd, and 9th. This tells me that through the issues already discussed above, Client B is going to find the motivation and courage to face these issues once and for all. Furthermore, with beneficial aspects to the Sun and Moon, these intimate discussions and observations will change Client B on an internal and external level for the better and in a profound way.

All of these auspicious aspects tell me that when Client B discusses these issues with those close to them and with those from their past, it will not be as painful or traumatic as Client B

TABLE V-11. Client B's Most Auspicious Moments

EVENT	FORMULA
t.♃♒ ✶ n.☉♈	t.♃♒ in 7th (R. 6th & 10th) ✶ n.☉♈ in 10th (R. 2nd & 3rd)
t.♃♑ △ n.☽♍	t.♃♑ in 6th (R. 6th & 10th) △ n.☽♍ in 3rd (R.1st)
t.♃♑ ✶ n.☿♓	t.♃♑ in 7th (R. 6th & 10th) ✶ n.☿♓ in 9th (R. 4th & 12th)
t.♃♒ ✶ n.♀♈	t.♃♒ in 8th (R. 6th & 10th) ✶ n.♀♈ in 10th (R. 11th)
t.♃♒ △ n.♃♎	t.♃♒ in 8th (R. 6th & 10th) △ n.♃♎ in 4th (R. 6th & 10th)
t.♃♒ ☌ n.♄♒	t.♃♒ in 8th (R. 6th & 10th) ☌ n.♄♒ in 8th (R. 7th, 8th, & 9th)
t.♃♑ ✶ n.♆♏	t.♃♑ in 7th (R. 6th & 10th) ✶ n.♆♏ in 5th (R. 5th)
t.♄♒ ✶ n.☉♈	t.♄♒ in 7th (R. 7th, 8th, & 9th) ✶ n.☉♈ in 10th (R. 2nd & 3rd)
t.♄♒ ✶ n.♀♈	t.♄♒ in 7th (R. 7th, 8th, & 9th) ✶ n.♀♈ in 10th (R. 11th)
t.♄♒ △ n.♃♎	t.♄♒ in 8th (R. 7th, 8th, & 9th) △ n.♃♎ in 4st (R. 6th & 10th)
t.♄♑ ✶ n.♆♏	t.♄♑ in 8th (R. 7th, 8th, & 9th) ✶ n.♆♏ in 5th (R. 5th)
t.♆♓ △ n.♂♋	t.♆♓ in 9th (R. 10th) △ n.♂♋ in 1st (R. 5th)
t.♆♓ ✶ n.♅♑	t.♆♓ in 9th (R. 10th) ✶ n. ♅♑ in 7th (R. 8th & 9th)
t.♆♓ ✶ n.♆♑	t.♆♓ in 9th (R. 10th) ✶ n.♆♑ in 7th (R. 10th)
t.♇♑ ✶ n.♆♏	t.♇♑ in 7th (R. 5th) ✶ n.♆♏ in 5th (R. 5th)
t.♇♑ ✶ n.MC♓	t.♇♑ in 7th (R. 5th) ✶ n.MC♓

might have expected. Instead, their fears could be mostly due to misunderstandings, which can be remedied by expressing their feelings on the matter, which helps to overcome latent and deeply rooted trauma. Either way, 2021 is a very transformative time for Client B where they can let go of issues from the past, and this will have a direct effect into their present and future dealings with others. Particularly with those that they have established a close connection such as a romantic partner, close friends, colleagues, and/or superiors.

INAUSPICIOUS MOMENTS

As already mentioned, even the inauspicious moments for Client B are not as bad as they could be. Transiting Jupiter will be squaring their natal Sun and Pluto, but we must remember that Jupiter transits are firstly, not long-lasting relative to the other outer planets and secondly, do not cause major distresses but more of a minor setback and irritation if functioning inharmoniously. The biggest inauspicious moment involves transiting Neptune conjoining natal Mercury (Table V-12).

As already mentioned, the Neptune conjunction to Mercury is indicative of Client B's inability to properly communicate, causing misunderstandings and cloudy logic along with increased subjectivity. As frustrating as this is, this acts as Client B's cue to work on these issues by addressing their previous experiences with those from their past that have shaped their adult outlook. However, this transit can have some benefits in that it encourages Client B to quiet the mind altogether through mediation and other spiritual disciplines. This is how Client B can counteract the more negative side of this transit by acknowledging that their logical and deductive functions are currently compromised. Therefore, the best way to approach this issue is to shut them down altogether. Again, the answer lies with those from their past with whom Client B should engage with and strive to understand their reasoning for behavior which shaped Client B when they were younger.

TABLE V-12. Client B's Most Inauspicious Moments

EVENT	FORMULA
t.♃♑ □ n.☉♈	t.♃♑ in 6th (R. 6th & 10th) □ n.☉♈ in 10th (R. 2nd & 3rd)
t.♃♒ □ n.☿♏	t.♃♒ in 8th (R. 6th & 10th) □ n.☿♏ in 5th (R. 5th)
t.♆♓ ☌ n.☿♓	t.♆♓ in 7th (R. 10th) ☌ n.☿♓ in 9th (R.4th & 12th)

413

CLIENT C: TRANSIT CHART

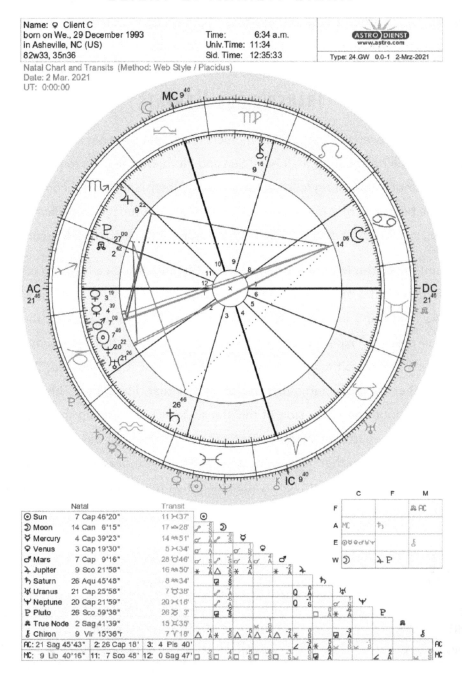

Name: ♀ Client C
born on We., 29 December 1993
in Asheville, NC (US)
82w33, 35n36

Time: 6:34 a.m.
Univ. Time: 11:34
Sid. Time: 12:35:33

ASTRO DIENST
www.astro.com
Type: 24.GW 0.0-1 2-Mrz-2021

Natal Chart and Transits (Method: Web Style / Placidus)
Date: 2 Mar. 2021
UT: 0:00:00

	Natal	Transit
☉ Sun	7 Cap 46'20"	11 ⋈ 37'
☽ Moon	14 Can 6'15"	17 ≈ 28'
☿ Mercury	4 Cap 39'23"	14 ≈ 51'
♀ Venus	3 Cap 19'30"	5 ⋈ 34'
♂ Mars	7 Cap 9'16"	28 ♉ 46'
♃ Jupiter	9 Sco 21'58"	16 ≈ 50'
♄ Saturn	26 Aqu 45'48"	8 ≈ 34'
♅ Uranus	21 Cap 25'58"	7 ♉ 38'
♆ Neptune	20 Cap 21'59"	20 ⋈ 18'
♇ Pluto	26 Sco 59'38"	26 ♑ 3'
☊ True Node	2 Sag 41'39"	15 ⋈ 35'
⚷ Chiron	9 Vir 15'36"r	7 ♈ 18'

AC: 21 Sag 45'43"	2: 26 Cap 18'	3: 4 Pis 40'
MC: 9 Lib 40'16"	11: 7 Sco 48'	12: 0 Sag 47'

2A	IV-3	Trace the Ephemeris one year before and after from the day of the reading and observe if transiting Jupiter has ingresses or regressed into a house.	Preliminary data.
2B	IV-3	Repeat for transiting Saturn.	Preliminary data.
2C	IV-3	Repeat for transiting Uranus.	Preliminary data.
2D	IV-3	Repeat for transiting Neptune.	Preliminary data.
2E	IV-3	Repeat for transiting Pluto.	Preliminary data.

♃

EVENT	GLYPH	DATE
Transiting Jupiter ingresses into the 2nd House (1/3)	t. ♃ → 2nd (1/3)	APR 20, 2020
Transiting Jupiter regresses into the 1st House (2/3)	t. ♃ → 1st (2/3)	JUN 8, 2020
Transiting Jupiter ingresses into the 2nd House (3/3)	t. ♃ → 2nd (3/3)	DEC 1, 2020
Transiting Jupiter ingresses into the 3rd House	t. ♃ → 3rd	JAN 19, 2022

♄

EVENT	GLYPH	DATE
Transiting Saturn ingresses into the 2nd House (1/3)	t. ♄ → 2nd (1/3)	FEB 13, 2020
Transiting Saturn regresses into the 1st House (2/3)	t. ♄ → 1st (2/3)	AUG 25, 2020
Transiting Saturn ingresses into the 2nd House (3/3)	t. ♄ → 2nd (3/3)	NOV 2, 2020

♅

EVENT	GLYPH	DATE
Transiting Uranus ingresses into the 5th House (1/3)	t. ♅ → 5TH (1/3)	MAY 18, 2020
Transiting Uranus regresses into the 4th House (2/3)	t. ♅ → 4th (2/3)	NOV 22, 2020
Transiting Uranus ingresses into the 5th House (3/3)	t. ♅ → 5th (3/3)	MAR 6, 2021

♆

EVENT	GLYPH	DATE
NONE		

♇

EVENT	GLYPH	DATE
Transiting Pluto ingresses into the 2nd House (1/3)	t. ♇ → 2nd (1/3)	MAR 13, 2021
Transiting Pluto regresses into the 1st House (2/3)	t. ♇ → 1st (2/3)	JUN 15, 2021
Transiting Pluto ingresses into the 2nd House (3/3)	t. ♇ → 2nd (3/3)	JAN 13, 2022

3A	IV-3	Trace the Ephemeris one year before and after from the day of the reading and observe if Jupiter makes an aspect to any of the 12 natal points.	Preliminary data.
3B	IV-3	Repeat for transiting Saturn.	Preliminary data.
3C	IV-3	Repeat for transiting Uranus.	Preliminary data.
3D	IV-3	Repeat for transiting Neptune.	Preliminary data.
3E	IV-3	Repeat for transiting Pluto.	Preliminary data.

♃

EVENT	GLYPH	DATE
Transiting Jupiter in Pisces sextile Natal Sun in Capricorn	t.♃♓ ⚹ n.☉♑	FEB 3, 2022
Transiting Jupiter in Capricorn oppose Natal Moon in Cancer	t.♃♑ ☍ n.☽♋	FEB 2, 2020
Transiting Jupiter in Pisces sextile Natal Mercury in Capricorn	t.♃♓ ⚹ n.☿♑	JAN 21, 2022
Transiting Jupiter in Pisces sextile Natal Venus in Capricorn	t.♃♓ ⚹ n.♀♑	JAN 14, 2022
Transiting Jupiter in Pisces sextile Natal Mars in Capricorn	t.♃♓ ⚹ n.♂♑	JAN 31, 2022
Transiting Jupiter in Aquarius square Natal Jupiter in Scorpio	t.♃♒ □ n.♃♏	JAN 29, 2021
Transiting Jupiter in Pisces trine Natal Jupiter in Scorpio	t.♃♓ Δ n.♃♏	FEB 10, 2021
Transiting Jupiter in Aquarius conjoin Natal Saturn in Aquarius (1/3) Transiting Jupiter Retrograde in Aquarius conjoin Natal Saturn in Aquarius (2/3) Transiting Jupiter in Aquarius conjoin Natal Saturn in Aquarius (3/3)	t.♃♒ ☌ n.♄♒ (1/3) t.♃♒ Rx ☌ n.♄♒ (2/3) t.♃♒ ☌ n.♄♒ (3/3)	APR 18, 2021 AUG 22, 2021 DEC 10, 2021
Transiting Jupiter in Capricorn conjoin Natal Uranus in Capricorn (1/3) Transiting Jupiter Retrograde in Capricorn conjoin Natal Uranus in Capricorn (2/3) Transiting Jupiter in Capricorn conjoin Natal Uranus in Capricorn (3/3)	t.♃♑ ☌ n.♅♑ (1/3) t.♃♑ Rx ☌ n.♅♑ (2/3) t.♃♑ ☌ n.♅♑ (3/3)	MAR 11, 2020 JUL 22, 2020 NOV 3, 2020

Event	Glyph	Date
Transiting Jupiter in Capricorn conjoin Natal Neptune in Capricorn (1/3) Transiting Jupiter Retrograde in Capricorn conjoin Natal Neptune in Capricorn (2/3) Transiting Jupiter in Capricorn conjoin Natal Neptune in Capricorn (3/3)	t.♃♑ ☌ n.♆♑ (1/3) t.♃♑ Rx ☌ n.♆♑ (2/3) t.♃♑ ☌ n.♆♑ (3/3)	MAR 4, 2020 JUL 31, 2020 OCT 26, 2020
Transiting Jupiter in Capricorn sextile Natal Pluto in Scorpio (1/3) Transiting Jupiter Retrograde in Capricorn sextile Natal Pluto in Scorpio (2/3) Transiting Jupiter in Capricorn sextile Natal Pluto in Scorpio (3/3)	t.♃♑ ✶ n.♇♏ (1/3) t.♃♑ Rx ✶ n.♇♏ (2/3) t.♃♑ ✶ n.♇♏ (3/3)	MAY 1, 2020 MAY 28, 2020 DEC 5, 2020
Transiting Jupiter in Aquarius square Natal Pluto in Scorpio (1/3) Transiting Jupiter in Aquarius Retrograde square Natal Pluto in Scorpio (2/3) Transiting Jupiter in Aquarius square Natal Pluto in Scorpio (3/3)	t.♃♒ □ n.♇♏ (1/3) t.♃♒ Rx □ n.♇♏ (2/3) t.♃♒ □ n.♇♏ (3/3)	APR 24, 2021 AUG 22, 2021 DEC 12, 2021
Transiting Jupiter in Aquarius sextile Sagittarius Ascendant	t.♃♒ ✶ n.ASC♐	MAR 24, 2021
Transiting Jupiter in Aquarius trine Libra Midheaven	t.♃♒ △ n.MC♎	JAN 30, 2021
♄		
EVENT	GLYPH	DATE
Transiting Saturn in Aquarius square Natal Pluto in Scorpio (1/3) Transiting Saturn Retrograde in Aquarius square Natal Pluto in Scorpio (2/3) Transiting Saturn in Aquarius square Natal Pluto in Scorpio (3/3)	t.♄♒ □ n.♇♏ (1/3) t.♄♒ Rx □ n.♇♏ (2/3) t.♄♒ □ n.♇♏ (3/3)	MAR 10, 2021 AUG 14, 2021 DEC 5, 2021
Transiting Saturn in Aquarius trine Libra Midheaven (1/3) Transiting Saturn Retrograde in Aquarius trine Libra Midheaven (2/3) Transiting Saturn in Aquarius trine Libra Midheaven (3/3)	t.♄♒ △ n.MC♎ (1/3) t.♄♒ Rx △ n.MC♎ (2/3) t.♄♒ △ n.MC♎ (3/3)	MAR 12, 2021 AUG 10, 2021 DEC 9, 2021

♅		
EVENT	**GLYPH**	**DATE**
Transiting Uranus in Taurus trine Natal Sun in Capricorn (1/3) Transiting Uranus Retrograde in Taurus trine Natal Sun in Capricorn (2/3) Transiting Uranus in Taurus trine Natal Sun in Capricorn (3/3)	t.♅♉ △ n.☉♑ (1/3) t.♅♉ Rx △ n.☉♑ (2/3) t.♅♉ △ n.☉♑ (3/3)	MAY 17, 2020 NOV 24, 2020 MAR 5, 2021
Transiting Uranus in Taurus sextile Natal Moon in Cancer (1/3) Transiting Uranus Retrograde in Taurus sextile Natal Moon in Cancer (2/3) Transiting Uranus in Taurus sextile Natal Moon in Cancer (3/3)	t.♅♉ ✶ n.☽♋ (1/3) t.♅♉ Rx ✶ n.☽♋ (2/3) t.♅♉ ✶ n.☽♋ (3/3)	JUL 9, 2021 AUG 19, 2021 OCT 1, 2021
Transiting Uranus in Taurus trine Natal Mercury in Capricorn	t.♅♉ △ n.☿♑	MAR 22, 2020
Transiting Uranus in Taurus trine Natal Venus in Capricorn	t.♅♉ △ n.♀♑	FEB 17, 2020
Transiting Uranus in Taurus trine Natal Mars in Capricorn (1/3) Transiting Uranus Retrograde in Taurus trine Natal Mars in Capricorn (2/3) Transiting Uranus in Taurus trine Natal Mars in Capricorn (3/3)	t.♅♉ △ n.♂♑ (1/3) t.♅♉ Rx △ n.♂♑ (2/3) t.♅♉ △ n.♂♑ (3/3)	MAY 5, 2020 DEC 14, 2020 FEB 14, 2021
Transiting Uranus in Taurus oppose Natal Jupiter in Scorpio (1/3) Transiting Uranus Retrograde in Taurus oppose Natal Jupiter in Scorpio (2/3) Transiting Uranus in Taurus oppose Natal Jupiter in Scorpio (3/3)	t.♅♉ ☍ n.♃♏ (1/3) t.♅♉ Rx ☍ n.♃♏ (2/3) t.♅♉ ☍ n.♃♏ (3/3)	JAN 16, 2020 OCT 16, 2020 APR 8, 2021
♆		
EVENT	**GLYPH**	**DATE**
Transiting Neptune in Pisces sextile Natal Uranus in Capricorn (1/3) Transiting Neptune Retrograde in Pisces sextile Natal Uranus in Capricorn (2/3) Transiting Neptune in Pisces sextile Natal Uranus in Capricorn (3/3)	t.♆♓ ✶ n.♅♑ (1/3) t.♆♓ Rx ✶ n.♅♑ (2/3) t.♆♓ ✶ n.♅♑ (3/3)	APR 10, 2021 SEP 29, 2021 JAN 30, 2022

418

EVENT	GLYPH	DATE
Transiting Neptune in Pisces sextile Natal Neptune in Capricorn (1/5)	t.ΨӾ ⚹ n.ΨVꙅ (1/5)	MAY 6, 2020
Transiting Neptune Station Retrograde in Pisces sextile Natal Neptune in Capricorn (2/5)	t.ΨӾ SR ⚹ n.ΨVꙅ (2/5)	JUN 22, 2020
Transiting Neptune Retrograde in Pisces sextile Natal Neptune in Capricorn (3/5)	t.ΨӾ Rx ⚹ n.ΨVꙅ (3/5)	AUG 11, 2020
Transiting Neptune in Pisces sextile Natal Neptune in Capricorn (4/5)	t.ΨӾ ⚹ n.ΨVꙅ (4/5)	MAR 3, 2021
Transiting Neptune Station Direct in Pisces sextile Natal Neptune in Capricorn (5/5)	t.ΨӾ SD ⚹ n.ΨVꙅ (5/5)	DEC 2, 2021
Transiting Neptune in Pisces square Sagittarius Ascendant (1/3)	t.ΨӾ □ n.ASC♐ (1/3)	APR 10, 2021
Transiting Neptune Retrograde in Pisces square Sagittarius Ascendant (2/3)	t.ΨӾ Rx □ n.ASC♐ (2/3)	SEP 15, 2021
Transiting Neptune in Pisces square Sagittarius Ascendant (3/3)	t.ΨӾ □ n.ASC♐ (3/3)	FEB 9, 2022

♆

EVENT	GLYPH	DATE
NONE		

4		Place all events from Steps 2A-3E in chronological order.	Information as to when these events will occur and if they occur simultaneously.

2020

JAN		FEB		MAR		APR	
EVENT	DAY	EVENT	DAY	EVENT	DAY	EVENT	DAY
t.♅♉ ☍ n.♃♏ (1/3)	16	t.♃Vꙅ ☍ n.☽♋	2	t.♃Vꙅ ♂ n.ΨVꙅ (1/3)	4	t. ♃ → 2nd (1/3)	20
		t. ♄ → 2nd (1/3)	13		11		
		t.♅♉ △ n.♀Vꙅ	17	t.♃Vꙅ ♂ n.♅Vꙅ (1/3)	22		
				t.♅♉ △ n.♀Vꙅ			

MAY		JUN		JUL		AUG	
EVENT	DAY	EVENT	DAY	EVENT	DAY	EVENT	DAY
t.♃♑ ⚹ n.♇♏ (1/3)	1	t. ♃ → 1ˢᵗ (2/3)	8	t.♃♑ Rx ♂ n.♅♑ (2/3)	22	t.♇♓ Rx ⚹ n.♇♑ (3/5)	11
t.♅♉ △ n.♂♑ (1/3)	5	t.♇♓ SR ⚹ n.♇♑ (2/5)	22	t.♃♑ Rx ♂ n.♇♑ (2/3)	31	t. ♄ → 1ˢᵗ (2/3)	25
t.♇♓ ⚹ n.♇♑ (1/5)	6						
t.♅♉ △ n.☉♑ (1/3)	17						
t. ♅ → 5ᵀᴴ (1/3)	18						
t.♃♑ Rx ⚹ n.♇♏ (2/3)	28						

SEP		OCT		NOV		DEC	
EVENT	DAY	EVENT	DAY	EVENT	DAY	EVENT	DAY
		t.♅♉ Rx ☍ n.♃♏ (2/3)	16	t. ♄ → 2ⁿᵈ (3/3)	2	t. ♃ → 2ⁿᵈ (3/3)	1
		t.♃♑ ♂ n.♇♑ (3/3)	26	t.♃♑ ♂ n.♅♑ (3/3)	3	t.♃♑ ⚹ n.♇♏ (3/3)	5
				t. ♅ → 4ᵗʰ (2/3)	22	t.♅♉ Rx △ n.♂♑ (2/3)	14
				t.♅♉ Rx △ n.☉♑ (2/3)	24		

2021							
JAN		FEB		MAR		APR	
EVENT	DAY	EVENT	DAY	EVENT	DAY	EVENT	DAY
t.♃♒ □ n.♃♏	29	t.♃♓ △ n.♃♏	10	t.♇♓ ⚹ n.♇♑ (4/5)	3	t.♅♉ ☍ n.♃♏ (3/3)	8
t.♃♒ △ n.MC♎	30	t.♅♉ △ n.♂♑ (3/3)	14	t.♅♉ △ n.☉♑ (3/3)	5	t.♇♓ ⚹ n.♅♑ (1/3)	10
				t. ♅ → 5ᵗʰ (3/3)	6	t.♇♓ □ n.ASC♐ (1/3)	10
				t.♄♒ □ n.♇♏ (1/3)	10	t.♃♒ ♂ n.♄♒ (1/3)	18
				t.♄♒ △ n.MC♎ (1/3)	12	t.♃♒ □ n.♇♏ (1/3)	24
				t. ♇ → 2ⁿᵈ (1/3)	13	t.♃♒ ⚹ n.ASC♐	24
				t.♃♒ ⚹ n.ASC♐	24		

420

MAY		JUN		JUL		AUG	
EVENT	DAY	EVENT	DAY	EVENT	DAY	EVENT	DAY
		t. ♆ → 1st (2/3)	15	t.♅♉ ✶ n.☽♋ (1/3)	9	t.♄♒ Rx △ n.MC♎ (2/3)	10
						t.♄♒ Rx □ n.♀♏ (2/3)	14
						t.♅♉ Rx ✶ n.☽♋ (2/3)	19
						t.♃♒ Rx ☌ n.♄♒ (2/3)	22
						t.♃♒ Rx □ n.♀♏ (2/3)	22

SEP		OCT		NOV		DEC	
EVENT	DAY	EVENT	DAY	EVENT	DAY	EVENT	DAY
t.♆♓ Rx □ n.ASC♐ (2/3)	15	t.♅♉ ✶ n.☽♋ (3/3)	1			t.♆♓ SD ✶ n.♆♑ (5/5)	2
t.♆♓ Rx ✶ n.♅♑ (2/3)	29					t.♄♒ □ n.♀♏ (3/3)	5
						t.♄♒ △ n.MC♎ (3/3)	9
						t.♃♒ ☌ n.♄♒ (3/3)	10
						t.♃♒ □ n.♀♏ (3/3)	12

2022			
JAN		FEB	
EVENT	DAY	EVENT	DAY
t. ♆ → 2nd (3/3)	13	tt.♃♓ ✶ n.☉♑	3
t.♃♓ ✶ n.♀♑	14	t.♆♓ □ n.ASC♐ (3/3)	9
t. ♃ → 3rd	19		
t.♃♓ ✶ n.☿♑	21		
t.♆♓ ✶ n.♅♑ (3/3)	30		
t.♃♓ ✶ n.♂♑	31		

421

5		Determine the most inauspicious and auspicious months for the individual.	This will let the individual know when there are times of immense struggle or benefit which they can either prepare for the harder times and/or utilize the better times to their fullest potential.

AUSPICIOUS	INAUSPICIOUS
MAR 2020	APR 2021
MAY 2020	DEC 2021
DEC 2020	
FEB 2021	

6	IV-4	Create transit formulas for every event listed in steps 3A-3E.	Various realms within the person's life that will be influenced by the event.

EVENT	FORMULA
t.♃♓ ⚹ n.☉j	t.♃♓ in 3rd (R. 1st, 3rd, & 12th) ⚹ n.☉♑ in 1st (R. Nothing)
t.♃♑ ☍ n.☽♋	t.♃♑ in 1st (R. 1st, 3rd, & 12th) ☍ n.☽♋ in 7th (R. 8th)
t.♃♓ ⚹ n.☿♑	t.♃♓ in 2nd (R. 1st, 3rd, & 12th) ⚹ n.☿♑ in 1st (R. 6th, 7th, & 9th)
t.♃♓ ⚹ n.♀♑	t.♃♓ in 2nd (R. 1st, 3rd, & 12th) ⚹ n.♀♑ in 1st (R. 10th & 5th)
t.♃♓ ⚹ n.♂♑	t.♃♓ in 3rd (R. 1st, 3rd, & 12th) ⚹ n.♂♑ in 1st (R. 4th & 11th)
t.♃♒ □ n.♃♏	t.♃♒ in 2nd (R. 1st, 3rd, & 12th) □ n.♃♏ in 11th (R. 1st, 3rd, & 12th)
t.♃♓ △ n.♃♏	t.♃♓ in 2nd (R. 1st, 3rd, & 12th) △ n.♃♏ in 11th (R. 1st, 3rd, & 12th)
t.♃♒ ☌ n.♄♒	t.♃♒ in 2nd (R. 1st, 3rd, & 12th) ☌ n.♄♒ in 2nd (R. 2nd)
t.♃♑ ☌ n.♅♑	t.♃♑ in 1st (R. 1st, 3rd, & 12th) ☌ n.♅♑ in 1st (R. Nothing)
t.♃♑ ☌ n.♆♑	t.♃♑ in 1st (R. 1st, 3rd, & 12th) ☌ n.♆♑ in 1st (R. 3rd)
t.♃♑ ⚹ n.♇♏	t.♃♑ in 2nd (R. 1st, 3rd, & 12th) ⚹ n.♇♏ in 1th (R. 11th)
t.♃♒ □ n.♇♏	t.♃♒ in 2nd (R. 1st, 3rd, & 12th) □ n.♇♏ in 1th (R. 11th)
t.♃♒ ⚹ n.ASC♐	t.♃♒ in 2nd (R. 1st, 3rd, & 12th) ⚹ n.ASC♐
t.♃♒ △ n.MC♎	t.♃♒ in 2nd (R. 1st, 3rd, & 12th) △ n.MC♎
t.♄♒ □ n.♇♏	t.♄♒ in 2nd (R. 2nd) □ n.♇♏ in 1th (R. 11th)
t.♄♒ △ n.MC♎	t.♄♒ in 2nd (R. 2nd) △ n.MC♎
t.♅♉ △ n.☉♑	t.♅♉ in 4th (R. Nothing) △ n.☉♑ in 1st (R. Nothing)
t.♅♉ ⚹ n.☽♋	t.♅♉ in 5th (R. Nothing) ⚹ n.☽♋ in 7th (R. 8th)

t.♅♉ △ n.☿♑	t.♅♉ in 4th (R. Nothing) △ n.☿♑ in 1st (R. 6th, 7th, & 9th)
t.♅♉ △ n.♀♑	t.♅♉ in 4th (R. Nothing) △ n.♀♑ in 1st (R. 10th & 5th)
t.♅♉ △ n.♂♑	t.♅♉ in 4th (R. Nothing) △ n.♂♑ in 1st (R. 4th & 11th)
t.♅♉ ☍ n.♃♏	t.♅♉ in 5th (R. Nothing) ☍ n.♃♏ in 11th (R. 1st, 3rd, & 12th)
t.♆♓ ⚹ n.♅♑	t.♆♓ in 3rd (R. 3rd) ⚹ n.♅♑ in 1st (R. Nothing)
t.♆♓ ⚹ n.♆♑	t.♆♓ in 3rd (R. 3rd) ⚹ n.♆♑ in 1st (R. 3rd)
t.♆♓ □ n.ASC♐	t.♆♓ in 3rd (R. 3rd) □ n.ASC♐

7		Compose a summary of your findings from step 4-6.	Summary of Analysis.

Multiple Hits due to Stellium

Client C has six planets in Capricorn with four of these planets within a tight range of 4° apart. When planets are in close quarters in this way, you will notice that transits hit them all at once for better or for worse. This makes sense because a transiting planet that hits one of the natal planets will subsequently make another transit hit to the other natal planets within a short period of time due to the tight orb that the natal planets share. This occurs in Client C's chart with transiting Uranus in Taurus, which trines four of their natal planets in Capricorn one right after the other. This will be further discussed below, but for now I wanted to point out the intensity of such interactions when planets are in close proximity within the birth chart.

Multiple Ingresses

Similar to Client A, Client C is also experiencing numerous ingresses between this time frame which will also indicate a wave of new energies as older ones fade away into the past. In the case of Client C, these involve Jupiter ingressing into the 2nd and 3rd houses, Saturn ingressing into the 2nd house, Uranus into the 5th, and Pluto into the 2nd. During this time, I would advise that Client C be mindful of their personal finances, possessions, and property due to the multiple planets entering the 2nd house. They might begin to learn what they can do without and how to limit what they own. Due to these limiting factors that could cause issues with material possessions, they can learn during this time what is truly valuable to them and how they can live more modestly. There could also be disputes and a redistribution of ownership on some items or property. Client C should not be too attached to a certain outcome or item and be flexible as to what they might lose. Indeed, this is a time of financial frugality and conservation.

Uranus ingressing into the 5th house can bring sparks of originality into their individual expression and creativity. They might find new interests and hobbies or become more engaged with outlets that help them to express their own talents. However, Client C should be mindful of rebellious children if they have any children, or rebellious younger people in general that might question and counter the way in which they do things. The more Client C takes on a rebellious childlike approach themself, the easier this energy will manifest itself.

Saturn Return

At this time, I would like to slightly digress from Client C's analysis and discuss the incredibly important Saturn return. Although Client C is not expecting their first Saturn return to officially begin until 2023, it is important to note that they are on the verge of their Saturn return. Therefore, the energies involved in 2020-2022 become relevant because they act as the precursor to this highly significant event in Client C's life, and indeed all lives.

The Saturn return occurs when transiting Saturn conjoins natal Saturn, and usually happens to individuals between the ages of 28-31 for their first return and 56-62 for their second return. The first Saturn return is incredibly important because it not only concludes the first 30 years of their life, it paves the way for the next 30 years that they will encounter.

Essentially, at the first Saturn return, it is as though your childhood officially ends and your entry into adulthood becomes solidified and pointed towards a certain direction. As such, people tend to make very adult decisions during their Saturn returns like getting married, having children, or advancing themselves into a career.

This is all fine, but there is a catch. That catch is: you need to be 1,000% sure that what you are committing to is something that you are willing to commit to for the next 30 years of your life.

424

If you get married, be sure that you are completely serious when you say, "for better or worse, 'till death do you part." If you are having a child, be sure that you can and will devote your life to that child by removing all personal ambitions for the sake of that child's development. Lastly, if you are entering a career, be sure that it is a career that you can see yourself participating in for the next 30 years of your life. If people only knew the gravity of such decisions and how they impact their experiences until they are 60, then I would predict a lot more people would take these commitments more seriously. Instead, individuals tend to simply do as they are told either by society, tradition, or their parents and do all the things that are expected of them instead of asking themselves what they want out of life.

I like to say that at your Saturn return, it is as though the father head of Saturn comes knocking at your door for a little check-in. He asks, "Where is your life headed and where should it be headed? What have you learned, and what do you still need to learn? What do you want to accomplish and how do you plan to get there? Where are your insecurities and pitfalls, and have you been addressing them?" The answers to these questions become known to you during your Saturn return but remember, Saturn only informs; he does not direct.

Saturn will show you what is and is not working, but it is always up to you to take his advice and adjust your life plan, or to stubbornly ignore his warnings only to be made a fool when he comes back around knocking at your door at your second Saturn return when you are 60. At that time, if you did not take his warnings and advice during your first Saturn return, then there is no choice but to sleep in the bed you have made. Saturn loves to say, "I hate to say I told you so, but I did tell you so." Do not give Saturn that chance to prove you wrong and him right. Before you or anyone makes any major any life commitments around the time of the Saturn return, I would heavily advice caution, hesitation, and serious introspection towards these matters.

Regarding Client C, I would also echo these same sentiments and tell them that what is happening to them now is extremely important. They should be mindful of what the universe is telling them to let go of because it does not serve their long-term interests. This is very hard to do at the Saturn return because we always feel as though as are wasting time or that time is fleeting, only to realize after the fact that 30 is still a very young age when you compare it to the normal lifespan of an individual. There are plenty more years thereafter to experience and accomplish life pursuits. This is the secret to unlocking a Saturn return: time and accomplishments are only relative.

Jupiter Troubles

As already mentioned, the effects of Jupiter are milder and more expedient when compared to other outer planetary transits. In a way, Jupiter can either give you a boost when you are experiencing harder transits, or he can make those experiences more difficult by his own transiting aspects. The reverse can also be true for auspicious moments as well. In the case of Client C, transiting Jupiter's square to natal Jupiter and conjunctions to natal Saturn, Uranus, and Neptune can prove to be a little frustrating at times (t.♃♒ □ n.♃♏, t.♃♒ ♂ n.♄♒, t.♃♑ ♂ n.♅♑, t.♃♑ ♂ n.♆♑) (Table V-12).

With the 2nd house appearing again, it tells me that Client C can experience some moments of low self-esteem with the 1st house interacting with the 2nd house issues that the ingresses of Saturn and Pluto also bring about during this time. This bleeds into their abilities to communicate with others, along with their connections to the spiritual realms, evidenced by the 3rd and 12th house interactions. Client C should not attach too much of their self-worth to their bank accounts or property at this time. They should also try to not curse nature for their current predicament. Again, it is important to note that these instances are only temporary, and that Client C has more auspicious moments than inauspicious ones. Nevertheless, Jupiter is not helping much with the aspects mentioned above, which can cause the more difficult moments to seem more insurmountable at the time. Once these Jupiter influences disappear, it will be easier for Client C to obtain some clarity and personal strength to deal with the matters at hand.

TABLE V-12. Client C's Difficult Jupiter Transits

EVENT	FORMULA
t.♃♓ △ n.♃♏	t.♃♓ in 2nd (R. 1st, 3rd, & 12th) △ n.♃♏ in 11th (R. 1st, 3rd, & 12th)
t.♃♒ ♂ n.♄♒	t.♃♒ in 2nd (R. 1st, 3rd, & 12th) ♂ n.♄♒ in 2nd (R. 2nd)
t.♃♑ ♂ n.♅♑	t.♃♑ in 1st (R. 1st, 3rd, & 12th) ♂ n.♅♑ in 1st (R. Nothing)
t.♃♑ ♂ n.♆♑	t.♃♑ in 1st (R. 1st, 3rd, & 12th) ♂ n.♆♑ in 1st (R. 3rd)

Saturn trine the Midheaven/Neptune square the Ascendant

Client C has two significant interactions to their cardinal points during 2021-2022 with transiting Saturn trine the Midheaven and transiting Neptune square the Ascendant (t.♄♒ Δ n.MC♎ , t.♆♓ □ n.ASC♐). On one hand, the Saturn trine to the Midheaven makes this a fruitful time for Client C's career and life goals. They will find it easier to obtain accomplishments and promotions, and their work will be recognized and acknowledged by their superiors. On the other hand, with Neptune square to Ascendant, this brings substantially low confidence and loss of self-identity during this time as well. This could either be due to the new advancements within their career which makes them hesitant and intimidated by their new role and responsibilities. Or the issues mentioned above, with Client C having to approach and deal with their values and limited possessions, can have a direct effect towards their overall confidence and sense of self-worth. Client C should address these issues when they arise because it can obscure the benefits of the Saturn trine to the Midheaven. Whatever kinks within their armor they are finding within their emotional and personal sense of self-worth needs to be addressed so that they are prepared for the advancements they will experience within their career life.

Multiple Trines with Transiting Uranus

As previously mentioned, natal charts with planets that are located close to one another will cause the individual to experience events in bigger bulks since transiting planets will interact with multiple natal planets within the same time span. To this point, Client C will experience transiting Uranus trine to their natal Sun, Mercury, Venus, and Mars one right after the other (t.♅♉ Δ n.☉♑, t.♅♉ Δ n.☿♑, t.♅♉ Δ n.♀♑, t.♅♉ Δ n.♂♑) (Table V-13).

TABLE V-13. Client C's Multiple Uranus Transits

EVENT	FORMULA
t.♅♉ Δ n.☉♑	t.♅♉ in 4th (R. Nothing) Δ n.☉♑ in 1st (R. Nothing)
t.♅♉ Δ n.☿♑	t.♅♉ 4th (R. Nothing) Δ n.☿♑ in 1st (R. 6th, 7th, & 9th)
t.♅♉ Δ n.♀♑	t.♅♉ 4th (R. Nothing) Δ n.♀♑ in 1st (R. 10th & 5th)
t.♅♉ Δ n.♂♑	t.♅♉ 4th (R. Nothing) Δ n.♂♑ in 1st (R. 4th & 11th)

These four trines with transiting Uranus to their natal planets indicate a time of immense change and personal revolution. With the 1st and 4th houses heavily involved, this tells me that their relationship to their family and towards their mother will drastically change during this time. It could be that Client C is going to rely on these individuals more than usual, probably due to their limited resources as indicated by the ingresses into the 2nd house. Through these new interactions, Client C can receive a new perspective, respect, and appreciation for their family members, which not only changes their dynamic with these individuals, it also helps Client C to regain their personal strength that they have lost from the 2nd house ingresses and from Neptune squaring their Ascendant.

The home life and family are where Client C is going to be able to recharge and ground themself during the times that are more difficult. This is because their family and home life make it easy for them to be themself, assert themself, communicate themself, and most importantly, simply be themself. These interactions will have a profound affect on Client C through the encouragement they bring about, which will stay with them for some time. This allows for them to welcome new attitudes and perceptions due to the safe space that the 4th house is providing.

Auspicious Moments

During the auspicious months of March 2020, May 2020, December 2020, and February 2021 some of the Uranus trines that were previously mentioned above occur. Additionally, positive Jupiter transits, like transiting Jupiter trine to natal Jupiter and sextile natal Pluto, help to give Uranus some additional backing during these months (Table V-14).

TABLE V-14. Client C's Auspicious Transits During MAR/MAY/DEC 2020 and FEB 2021

EVENT	FORMULA
t.♃♒ □ n.♃♏	t.♃♒ in 2nd (R. 1st, 3rd, & 12th) □ n.♃♏ in 11th (R. 1st, 3rd, & 12th)
t.♃♓ △ n.♃♏	t.♃♓ in 2nd (R. 1st, 3rd, & 12th) △ n.♃♏ in 11th (R. 1st, 3rd, & 12th)
t.♃♑ ☌ n.♅♑	t.♃♑ in 1st (R. 1st, 3rd, & 12th) ☌ n.♅♑ in 1st (R. Nothing)
t.♃♑ ✶ n.♇♏	t.♃♑ in 2nd (R. 1st, 3rd, & 12th) ✶ n.♇♏ in 1th (R. 11th)
t.♅♉ △ n.☉♑	t.♅♉ in 4th (R. Nothing) △ n.☉♑ in 1st (R. Nothing)
t.♅♉ △ n.☿♑	t.♅♉ 4th (R. Nothing) △ n.☿♑ in 1st (R. 6th, 7th, & 9th)
t.♅♉ △ n.♂♑	t.♅♉ 4th (R. Nothing) △ n.♂♑ in 1st (R. 4th & 11th)

This makes these months a time where Client C can recharge their batteries and once again feel a sense of optimism in their lives with a mindset that everything will work out for the better. Client C should take full advantage of these months so that when the more difficult months come around, they are solid within their foundation.

Inauspicious Moments

April 2021 is quite difficult for Client C because they will experience transiting Neptune square the Ascendant in addition to transiting Jupiter square natal Pluto and conjunct natal Saturn (Table V-15).

This will make it difficult for Client C to work through the identity crises that Neptune brings about with the square to the Ascendant. They can therefore become so downtrodden that they find it hard to see how they can improve upon the situation because of the Jupiter conjoin Saturn along with the square to Pluto perturbs Client C's thinking and access to usual resources.

These sorts of feelings and themes will resurface on December 2021 when transiting Saturn square to natal Pluto along with natal Jupiter square to natal Pluto (t.♄♒ □ n.♇♏, t.♃♑ ⚹ n.♇♏). Again, Client C can feel helpless and have trouble seeing if and when there is an end in sight. It is therefore important for Client C to utilize what they have learned during their beneficial Uranus trines towards their personal planets throughout 2020.

During these harder months, it will be too easy for Client C to fall back into their older habits that they have worked on fixing during 2020. Therefore, Client C should see these moments

TABLE V-15. Client C's Inauspicious Transits during APR/DEC 2021

EVENT	FORMULA
t.♃♒ ☌ n.♄♒	t.♃♒ in 2nd (R. 1st, 3rd, & 12th) ☌ n.♄♒ in 2nd (R. 2nd)
t.♃♒ □ n.♇♏	t.♃♒ in 2nd (R. 1st, 3rd, & 12th) □ n.♇♏ in 1th (R. 11th)
t.♄♒ □ n.♇♏	t.♄♒ in 2nd (R. 2nd) □ n.♇♏ in 1th (R. 11th)
t.♅♉ ☍ n.♃♏	t.♅♉ 5th (R. Nothing) ☍ n.♃♏ in 11th (R. 1st, 3rd, & 12th)
t.♆♓ □ n.ASC♐	t.♆♓ in 3rd (R. 3rd) □ n.ASC♐

as a test to their abilities to cope with obstacles using the new approaches that they have gathered. When things get dark, pessimistic, and gloomy, Client C can rely on their family once again and remember the inner strength that their family and home life has given to them in the recent past. In other words, Client C already has the answers; they just need to ignore the intensity of the ordeals that befall them in order to remember that they are more than capable of tackling any issue.

1	IV-3	Obtain a transit chart for the present day as a reference.	Preliminary data.

CLIENT D: TRANSIT CHART

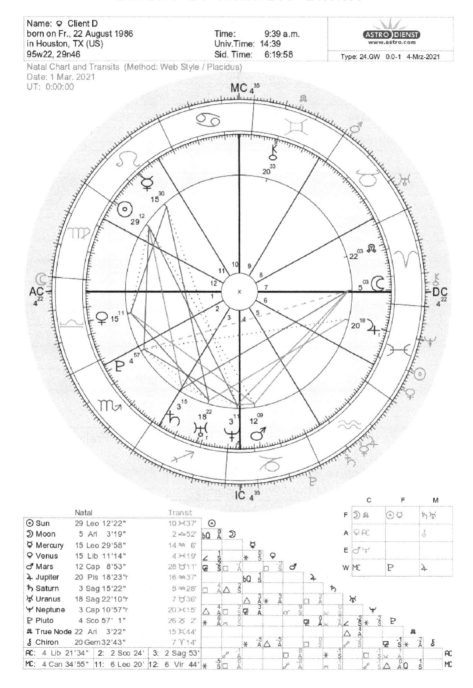

Name: ♀ Client D
born on Fr., 22 August 1986
in Houston, TX (US)
95w22, 29n46

Time: 9:39 a.m.
Univ.Time: 14:39
Sid. Time: 6:19:58

ASTRO DIENST
www.astro.com

Type: 24.GW 0.0-1 4-Mrz-2021

Natal Chart and Transits (Method: Web Style / Placidus)
Date: 1 Mar. 2021
UT: 0:00:00

	Natal	Transit
☉ Sun	29 Leo 12'22"	10 ✕ 37'
☽ Moon	5 Ari 3'19"	2 ♎ 52'
☿ Mercury	15 Leo 29'58"	14 ♒ 6'
♀ Venus	15 Lib 11'14"	4 ✕ 19'
♂ Mars	12 Cap 8'53"	28 ♉ 11'
♃ Jupiter	20 Pis 18'23"r	16 ♒ 37'
♄ Saturn	3 Sag 15'22"	8 ♒ 28'
♅ Uranus	18 Sag 22'10"r	7 ♉ 36'
♆ Neptune	3 Cap 10'57"r	20 ✕ 15'
♇ Pluto	4 Sco 57' 1"	26 ♑ 2'
⚷ True Node	22 Ari 3'22"	15 ✕ 44'
⚸ Chiron	20 Gem 32'43"	7 ♈ 14'

AC:	4 Lib 21'34"	2:	2 Sco 24'	3:	2 Sag 53'
MC:	4 Can 34'55"	11:	6 Leo 20'	12:	6 Vir 44'

431

2A	IV-3	Trace the Ephemeris one year before and after from the day of the reading and observe if transiting Jupiter has ingresses or regressed into a house.	Preliminary data.
2B	IV-3	Repeat for transiting Saturn.	Preliminary data.
2C	IV-3	Repeat for transiting Uranus.	Preliminary data.
2D	IV-3	Repeat for transiting Neptune.	Preliminary data.
2E	IV-3	Repeat for transiting Pluto.	Preliminary data.

♃		
EVENT	**GLYPH**	**DATE**
Transiting Jupiter ingresses into the 5th House	t. ♃ → 5th	Jan 16, 2021
Transiting Jupiter ingresses into the 6th House	t. ♃ → 6th	Jan 29, 2022

♄		
EVENT	**GLYPH**	**DATE**
Transiting Saturn ingresses into the 5th House	t. ♄ → 5th	FEB 10, 2021

♅		
EVENT	**GLYPH**	**DATE**
NONE		

♆		
EVENT	**GLYPH**	**DATE**
NONE		

♇		
EVENT	**GLYPH**	**DATE**
NONE		

3A	IV-3	Trace the Ephemeris one year before and after from the day of the reading and observe if Jupiter makes an aspect to any of the 12 natal points.	Preliminary data.
3B	IV-3	Repeat for transiting Saturn.	Preliminary data.
3C	IV-3	Repeat for transiting Uranus.	Preliminary data.
3D	IV-3	Repeat for transiting Neptune.	Preliminary data.
3E	IV-3	Repeat for transiting Pluto.	Preliminary data.

♃		
EVENT	**GLYPH**	**DATE**
Transiting Jupiter in Capricorn square Natal Venus in Libra	t.♃♑ □ n.♀♎	FEB 8, 2020
Transiting Jupiter in Aquarius trine Natal Venus in Libra	t.♃♒ △ n.♀♎	FEB 22, 2021
Transiting Jupiter in Pisces sextile Natal Mars in Capricorn	t.♃♓ ✶ n.♂♑	FEB 21, 2022
Transiting Jupiter in Capricorn sextile Natal Jupiter in Pisces (1/3) Transiting Jupiter Retrograde in Capricorn sextile Natal Jupiter in Pisces (2/3) Transiting Jupiter in Capricorn sextile Natal Jupiter in Pisces (3/3)	t.♃♑ ✶ n.♃♓ (1/3) t.♃♑ Rx ✶ n.♃♓ (2/3) t.♃♑ ✶ n.♃♓ (3/3)	MAR 5, 2020 JUL 30, 2020 OCT 26, 2020
Transiting Jupiter in Aquarius sextile Natal Saturn in Sagittarius	t.♃♒ ✶ n.♄♐	JAN 14, 2021
Transiting Jupiter in Pisces square Natal Saturn in Sagittarius	t.♃♓ □ n.♄♐	JAN 14, 2022
Transiting Jupiter in Aquarius sextile Natal Uranus in Sagittarius	t.♃♒ ✶ n.♅♐	MAR 8, 2021
Transiting Jupiter in Pisces sextile Natal Neptune in Capricorn	t.♃♓ ✶ n.♆♑	JAN 13, 2022
Transiting Jupiter in Aquarius square Natal Pluto in Scorpio	t.♃♒ □ n.♇♏	JAN 10, 2021
Transiting Jupiter in Pisces trine Natal Pluto in Scorpio	t.♃♓ △ n.♇♏	JAN 21, 2022
Transiting Jupiter in Aquarius trine Libra Ascendant	t.♃♒ △ n.ASC♎	JAN 7, 2021
Transiting Jupiter in Pisces trine Cancer Midheaven	t.♃♓ △ n.MC♋	JAN 20, 2022
♄		
EVENT	**GLYPH**	**DATE**
Transiting Saturn in Aquarius sextile Natal Moon in Aries	t.♄♒ ✶ n.☽♈	JAN 30, 2021
Transiting Saturn in Aquarius oppose Natal Mercury in Leo	t.♄♒ ☍ n.☿♌	FEB 1, 2022
Transiting Saturn in Aquarius trine Natal Venus in Libra	t.♄♒ △ n.♀♎	JAN 30, 2022
Transiting Saturn in Aquarius sextile Natal Saturn in Sagittarius	t.♄♒ ✶ n.♄♐	JAN 14, 2021
Transiting Saturn in Aquarius sextile Natal Uranus in Sagittarius	t.♄♒ ✶ n.♅♐	FEB 25, 2022
Transiting Saturn in Aquarius square Natal Pluto in Scorpio	t.♄♒ □ n.♇♏	JAN 29, 2021
Transiting Saturn in Aquarius trine Libra Ascendant	t.♄♒ △ n.ASC♎	JAN 24, 2021

♅		
EVENT	**GLYPH**	**DATE**
Transiting Uranus in Taurus trine Natal Mars in Capricorn (1/3) Transiting Uranus Retrograde in Taurus trine Natal Mars in Capricorn (2/3) (Transiting Uranus in Taurus trine Natal Mars in Capricorn (3/3)	t.♅♉ △ n.♂♑ (1/3) t.♅♉ Rx △ n.♂♑ (2/3) t.♅♉ △ n.♂♑ (3/3)	MAY 26, 2021 NOV 21, 2021 (PAST FEB 2022)

♆		
EVENT	**GLYPH**	**DATE**
Transiting Neptune in Pisces conjoin Natal Jupiter in Pisces (1/5) Transiting Neptune Station Retrograde in Pisces conjoin Natal Jupiter in Pisces (2/5) Transiting Neptune Retrograde in Pisces conjoin Natal Jupiter in Pisces (3/5) Transiting Neptune in Pisces conjoin Natal Jupiter in Pisces (4/5) Transiting Neptune Station Direct in Pisces conjoin Natal Jupiter in Pisces (5/5)	t.♆♓ ☌ n.♃♓ (1/5) t.♆♓ SR ☌ n.♃♓ (2/5) t.♆♓ Rx ☌ n.♃♓ (3/5) t.♆♓ ☌ n.♃♓ (4/5) t.♆♓ SD ☌ n.♃♓ (5/5)	MAY 3, 2020 JUN 22, 2020 AUG 14, 2020 MAR 2, 2021 DEC 2, 2021
Transiting Neptune in Pisces square Natal Uranus in Sagittarius (1/3) Transiting Neptune Retrograde in Pisces square Natal Uranus in Sagittarius (2/3) Transiting Neptune in Pisces square Natal Uranus in Sagittarius (3/3)	t.♆♓ □ n.♅♐ (1/3) t.♆♓ Rx □ n.♅♐ (2/3) t.♆♓ □ n.♅♐ (3/3)	MAR 7, 2020 NOV 1, 2020 DEC 23, 2020

♇		
EVENT	**GLYPH**	**DATE**
NONE		

4		Place all events from Steps 1A-2E in chronological order.	Information as to when these events will occur and if they occur simultaneously.

2020							
JAN		FEB		MAR		APR	
EVENT	DAY	EVENT	DAY	EVENT	DAY	EVENT	DAY
		t.♃♑ □ n.♀♎	8	t.♃♑ ⚹ n.♃♓ (1/3) t.♆♓ □ n.♅♐ (1/3)	5 7		
MAY		JUN		JUL		AUG	
EVENT	DAY	EVENT	DAY	EVENT	DAY	EVENT	DAY
t.♆♓ ☌ n.♃♓ (1/5)	3	t.♆♓ SR ☌ n.♃♓ (2/5)	22	t.♃♑ Rx ⚹ n.♃♓ (2/3)	30	t.♆♓ Rx ☌ n.♃♓ (3/5)	14
SEP		OCT		NOV		DEC	
EVENT	DAY	EVENT	DAY	EVENT	DAY	EVENT	DAY
		t.♃♑ ⚹ n.♃♓ (3/3)	26	t.♆♓ Rx □ n.♅♐ (2/3)	1	t.♆♓ □ n.♅♐ (3/3)	23

2021							
JAN		FEB		MAR		APR	
EVENT	DAY	EVENT	DAY	EVENT	DAY	EVENT	DAY
t.♃♒ Δ n.ASC♎ t.♃♒ □ n.♇♏ t.♃♒ ⚹ n.♄♐ t.♄♒ ⚹ n.♄♐ t. ♃ → 5th t.♄♒ Δ n.ASC♎ t.♄♒ □ n.♇♏ t.♄♒ ⚹ n.☽♈	7 10 14 14 16 24 29 30	t. ♄ → 5th t.♃♒ Δ n.♀♎	10 22	t.♆♓ ☌ n.♃♓ (4/5) t.♃♒ ⚹ n.♅♐	2 8		
MAY		JUN		JUL		AUG	
EVENT	DAY	EVENT	DAY	EVENT	DAY	EVENT	DAY
t.♅♉ Δ n.♂♑ (1/3) t.♅♉ Δ n.♂♑ (1/3)	16 26						

SEP		OCT		NOV		DEC	
EVENT	DAY	EVENT	DAY	EVENT	DAY	EVENT	DAY
				t.♅♉ Rx △ n.♂♑ (2/3)	21	t.♆♓ SD ☌ n.♃♓ (5/5)	2

2022			
JAN		FEB	
EVENT	DAY	EVENT	DAY
t.♃♓ ⚹ n.♆♑ t.♃♓ □ n.♄♐ t.♃♓ △ n.MC♋ t.♃♓ △ n.♇♏ t. ♃ → 6th t.♄♒ △ n.♀♎	13 14 20 21 29 30	t.♄♒ ☍ n.☿♌ t.♃♓ ⚹ n.♂♑ t.♄♒ ⚹ n.♅♐	1 21 25

5		Determine the most inauspicious and auspicious months for the individual.	This will let the individual know when there are times of immense struggle or benefit which they can either prepare for the harder times and/or utilize the better times to their fullest potential.

AUSPICIOUS	INAUSPICIOUS
MAY 2021	NOV 2020
JAN 2022	DEC 2020
JAN 2021	

6	IV-4	Create transit formulas for every event listed in steps 2A-3E.	Various realms within the person's life that will be influenced by events.

EVENT	FORMULA
t.♃♑ □ n.♀♎	t.♃♑ in 4th (R. 6th & 3rd) □ n.♀♎ in 1st (R. 1st & 8th)
t.♃♒ △ n.♀♎	t.♃♒ in 5th (R. 6th & 3rd) △ n.♀♎ in 1st (R. 1st & 8th)
t.♃♓ ⚹ n.♂♑	t.♃♓ in 6th (R. 6th & 3rd) ⚹ n.♂♑ in 4th (R. 7th & 2nd)
t.♃♑ ⚹ n.♃♓	t.♃♑ in 4th (R. 6th & 3rd) ⚹ n.♃♓ in 6th (R. 6th & 3rd)
t.♃♒ ⚹ n.♄♐	t.♃♒ in 4th (R. 6th & 3rd) ⚹ n.♄♐ in 3rd (R. 4th & 5th)
t.♃♓ □ n.♄♐	t.♃♓ in 5th (R. 6th & 3rd) □ n.♄♐ in 3rd (R. 4th & 5th)
t.♃♒ ⚹ n.♅♐	t.♃♒ in 5th (R. 6th & 3rd) ⚹ n.♅♐ in 3rd (R. 5th)
t.♃♓ ⚹ n.♆♑	t.♃♓ in 5th (R. 6th & 3rd) ⚹ n.♆♑ in 3rd (R. 6th)
t.♃♒ □ n.♇♏	t.♃♒ in 4th (R. 6th & 3rd) □ n.♆♑ in 2nd (R. 2nd)

t.♃♓ △ n.♆♏	t.♃♓ in 5th (R. 6th & 3rd) △ n.♆♑ in 2nd (R. 2nd)
t.♃♒ △ n.ASC♎	t.♃♒ in 4th (R. 6th & 3rd) △ n.ASC♎
t.♃♓ △ n.MC♋	t.♃♓ in 5th (R. 6th & 3rd) △ n.MC♋
t.♄♒ ⚹ n.☽♈	t.♄♒ in 4th (R. 4th & 5th) ⚹ n.☽♈ in 7th (R. 10th)
t.♄♒ ☍ n.☿♌	t.♄♒ in 4th (R. 4th & 5th) ☍ n.☿♌ in 11th (R. 9th & 12th)
t.♄♒ △ n.♀♎	t.♄♒ in 4th (R. 4th & 5th) △ n.♀♎ in 1st (R. 1st & 8th)
t.♄♒ ⚹ n.♄♐	t.♄♒ in 4th (R. 4th & 5th) ⚹ n.♄♐ in 3rd (R. 4th & 5th)
t.♄♒ ⚹ n.♅♐	t.♄♒ in 5th (R. 4th & 5th) ⚹ n.♅♐ in 3rd (R. 5th)
t.♄♒ □ n.♆♏	t.♄♒ in 4th (R. 4th & 5th) □ n.♆♏ in 2nd (R. 2nd)
t.♄♒ △ n.ASC♎	t.♄♒ in 4th (R. 4th & 5th) △ n.ASC♎
t.♅♉ △ n.♂♑	t.♅♉ in 8th (R. 5th)△ n.♂♑ in 4th (R. 7th & 2nd)
t.♆♓ ☌ n.♃♓	t.♆♓ in 6th (R. 6th) ☌ n.♃♓ in 6th (R. 6th & 3rd)
t.♆♓ □ n.♅♐	t.♆♓ in 6th (R. 6th) □ n.♅♐ in 3rd (R. 5th)

7		Compose a summary of your findings from step 4-6.	Summary of Analysis.

Jupiter trines Ascendant and Midheaven/Saturn trine Ascendant

Client D has remarkably beneficial transits to their Ascendant and Midheaven with transiting Jupiter and Saturn on January 2021/2022 (t.♃♒ △ n.ASC♎, t.♃♓ △ n.MC♋, t.♄♒ △ n.ASC♎). This gives Client D great confidence and an ability to reinvent themself similar to Client C who also has beneficial Midheaven and Ascendant transits. The difference is, Client C will have more internal conflicts and will have to tackle low self-confidence and through that struggle, Client C will emerge stronger with a newfound sense of what they want to accomplish and the type of person they want to be out in the world. For Client D, the journey is a little easier for them because, not only does the trine to the Ascendant with Jupiter and Saturn happen simultaneously, it also occurs with other beneficial transits at the same time.

This is certainly a time for Client D to take advantage of this moment because their self-confidence will be at an all-time high. This buoyancy and positive attitude allows for them to go out into the world and accomplish a great deal.

It seems that Client D will shed their skin, portray a new positive outlook and personality. As a consequence, they will attract benefits for their career, not only due to their hard work and focus, but also due to their newly found charisma. This charismatic nature is simply born out of the fact that Client D now has a newness about them which people, especially their superiors, admire and are attracted to at this time. With this newness, they are willing to place confidence in themself because they are portraying so much assuredness in their abilities.

Neptune conjoin Jupiter

Throughout 2020-2021, Client D will experience a five-hit event with transiting Neptune conjoin natal Jupiter with the formula for that event below:

$$t.\Psi\text{Ӿ in 6}^{th} (\text{R. 6}^{th}) \, \sigma \, n.\text{ꝟӾ in 6}^{th} (\text{R. 6}^{th} \, \& \, 3^{rd})$$

This event is substantial for Client D for a few reasons. Firstly, because this is a five-hit event, it will take a while for Client D to experience the transit event fully. Secondly, with the traditional and modern ruler of Pisces conjoin together in this way, it doubles the power of the event.

Client D can expect to have a spiritual awakening of some kind during this time. Due to the houses involved, 3rd and 6th, it will most likely come about through books, the internet, or some other form of literature that invigorates Client D to explore these new spiritual philosophies and prospects further. Or, it is possible that Client D can become inspired to work with the downtrodden and health profession due to the nature of the two planets involved along with the nature of the 6th house. Either way, Client D is going to experience a profound wave of sympathy and empathy for humanity which encourages them to explore this further, either through their own religious observations or through the work that they do. Client D becomes heavily inspired to let go of their petty ego attachments for the sake of something greater, whether that be a greater spiritual calling, a greater humanitarian cause, or both.

Uranus trine Mars

Relating back to the themes of the reinvention of their personality, Client D also experiences transiting Uranus trine natal Mars with the formula as follows:

$$t.\text{ⵋ}\text{ŏ in 8}^{th} (\text{R. 5}^{th}) \Delta \, n.\sigma\text{Ⅴ}\text{Ꞵ in 4}^{th} (\text{R. 7}^{th} \, \& \, 2^{nd})$$

This ties back to Client D's opportunity to break free from old habits, thought processes, and even a worn-out personality in general. This transit event only aids more in this process because it allows for Client D to meet new people who encourage them to work on their own unique self-expression. This is due to the 5th and 7th houses being involved.

This would also be a good time for Client D to take on new physical regiments because their ability to work on their bodies and health through new methods are also apparent with natal Mars being involved. In other words, this is a time where Client D can feel good inside and out, on the physical as well as the mental and spiritual. The more they can revolutionize themself in all of these various ways, the more they will sense that they have indeed shed their old skin and have entered into a new world of possibilities due to their new outlook, physique, and personal portrayal towards others.

SATURN TRINE VENUS AND OPPOSE MERCURY

On January and February 2022, literally a day apart, Client D will experience transiting Saturn oppose their natal Mercury and trine their natal Venus (t.♄♒ ☍ n.☿♌, t.♄♒ △ n.♀♎) (Table V-16).

With the revitalization that Client D is experiencing through all the transits mentioned above, it appears that it will have a direct effect towards their romantic life and how they communicate with their more intimate partners. Assuming Client D takes advantage of the Uranus/Mars energy, they can expect to have more intense and meaningful sexual experiences with Venus ruling the 1st and 8th houses. They will also be able to establish more of a home life and root themself within their relationships with Saturn ruling and being placed in the 4th house. Marriage or committing further into a relationship might happen at this time.

The Saturn opposition to Mercury also ties back to Client D's experience with transiting Uranus trine natal Mars. Through this transit, they were able to meet new people which gave them the ability to express themselves in new ways. This Saturn opposition to Mercury furthers their

TABLE V-16. Client D's Saturn transits to Natal Venus and Mercury

t.♄♒ ☍ n.☿♌	t.♄♒ in 4th (R. 4th & 5th) ☍ n.☿♌ in 11th (R. 9th & 12th)
t.♄♒ △ n.♀♎	t.♄♒ in 4th (R. 4th & 5th) △ n.♀♎ in 1st (R. 1st & 8th)

experiences by expanding their social networks through the 11th and 5th houses. Only this time, it seems that Client D will also begin to translate their spiritual awakening found with the Neptune/Jupiter conjunction as evidenced by the 12th and 9th houses within the Saturn/Mercury opposition.

In other words, through these new contacts, friendships, and persona, they can begin to voice what they think about the world in new ways towards new people. Their renewed philosophy comes in handy because during the Saturn/Mercury opposition they may meet people who disagree with them at first. Client D does not back away from these experiences but instead relishes in them because it gives them an opportunity to share their thoughts and opinions through these new contacts.

In a way, this is where the hard work of 2020-2021 begins to be put to the test as it will now come to a head with other people's thoughts and opinions. If Client D can keep their cool during these interactions, then everyone will benefit from them in different ways. Client D will benefit because they feel they can voice their opinions well and share their insights, and others that hear these insights will benefit from learning about new perspectives on life. Client D only needs to remember to hear others as fully and they expect others to hear them.

5ᵀᴴ House Energy

When Client D experiences the changes to their outward personality in early 2021, Saturn and Jupiter both ingress into the 5th house. Again, this ties back to Client D's opportunity to work on new ways of expressing themself. If they have creative outlets or hobbies, this is a good time to explore those further and to see how these explorations can benefit their career. Either way, these ingresses help Client D to find their new voice out into the world through their artistic and individualized expression.

Remember, although this is starting to sound redundant, this is truly a good thing because we are finding different transit events that are indicative of similar energies and outcomes. From a scientific perspective, this is simply a way to make data driven correlations that produce the same conclusions, which gives us confidence in predicting said events. In the case of Client D, the same themes of reinvention, improved self-confidence and self-expression, meeting new people, establishing new spiritual ideas, adjusting their career goals for the sake of helping others, an improved romantic life, physicality, and sexuality are all intertwined through these various transit events.

Auspicious Moments

May 2021 begins the Uranus/Mars trine which has already been previously discussed. Additionally, on January 2022, Client D receives an abundance of beneficial transits with transiting Jupiter sextile natal Neptune and trine Midheaven (t.♃♓ ⚹ n.♆♑, t.♃♓ Δ n.MC♋), and transiting Saturn trine natal Venus and Ascendant (t.♄♒ Δ n.♀♎, t.♄♒ Δ n.ASC♎) (Table V-17).

January 2022 is when Client D will be able to utilize their beneficial transits to their Midheaven, Ascendant, and Venus. Essentially, this is the key month where Client D will reap all of the benefits of the past two years. I would therefore recommend that Client D make the most out of this month and to remind them that all events that occurred throughout 2020-2021 all lead up to January 2022.

If a client is expecting a month like this in the future after a more trying period, it is best to bring this up to the client for a few reasons. Firstly, it gives the client a "light at the end of the tunnel" feeling where they can remind themself that the harder moments before this event are simply leading up to this more auspicious event. Secondly, it reminds the client to be proactive in the months before so that they can utilize this beneficial month to their fullest capacity. This is what I would relate to Client D in their reading which will take place in 2021. I would inform them that this is a time to be introspectively aware of what is going on around them, and that all conflicts and concerns that occur from 2020-2021 will be addressed and resolved on January 2022.

TABLE V-17. Client D's Transits during Auspicious Months

EVENT	FORMULA
t.♃♓ ⚹ n.♆♑	t.♃♓ in 5th (R. 6th & 3rd) ⚹ n.♆♑ in 3rd (R. 6th)
t.♃♓ Δ n.MC♋	t.♃♓ in 5th (R. 6th & 3rd) Δ n.MC♋
t.♄♒ Δ n.♀♎	t.♄♒ in 4th (R. 4th & 5th) Δ n.♀♎ in 1st (R. 1st & 8th)
t.♄♒ Δ n.ASC♎	t.♄♒ in 4th (R. 4th & 5th) Δ n.ASC♎
t.♅♉ Δ n.♂♑	t.♅♉ in 8th (R. 5th)Δ n.♂♑ in 4th (R. 7th & 2nd)

Inauspicious Moments

On November and December 2020, Client D will experience transiting Neptune square natal Uranus the formula of which is as follows:

$$\text{t.}\Psi\mathcal{H} \text{ in } 6^{th} \text{ (R. } 6^{th}\text{) } \square \text{ n.}\mathcal{H}\nearrow \text{ in } 3^{rd} \text{ (R. } 5^{th}\text{)}$$

One thing to mention is that because this transit involves the natal planet Uranus, this transit is more global and less personal because a lot of individuals born several years before and after Client D will also experience this transit at around the same time. Still, this transit is relevant because it seems to act as a catalyst that encourages Client D to begin their spiritual awakening and the shedding of their skin through establishing new personas and individual expressions. With this transit, however, Client D begins to feel confusion in these matters and cannot rely on their usual resources to portray themself properly out into the world. Therefore, after this event happens, it encourages Client D to introspect more into these matters and see where improvement is needed.

January 2021

January 2021 is an interesting month for Client D because they are experiencing a mixture of auspicious and inauspicious events (Table V-18).

TABLE V-18. Client D's Transits in January 2021

EVENT	FORMULA
t.♃⋙ ✶ n.♄♐	t.♃⋙ in 4ᵗʰ (R. 6ᵗʰ & 3ʳᵈ) ✶ n.♄♐ in 3ʳᵈ (R. 4ᵗʰ & 5ᵗʰ)
t.♃⋙ □ n.♀♏	t.♃⋙ in 4ᵗʰ (R. 6ᵗʰ & 3ʳᵈ) □ n.♀♑ in 2ⁿᵈ (R. 2ⁿᵈ)
t.♃⋙ △ n.ASC♎	t.♃⋙ in 4ᵗʰ (R. 6ᵗʰ & 3ʳᵈ) △ n.ASC♎
t.♄⋙ ✶ n.☽♈	t.♄⋙ in 4ᵗʰ (R. 4ᵗʰ & 5ᵗʰ) ✶ n.☽♈ in 7ᵗʰ (R. 10ᵗʰ)
t.♄⋙ ✶ n.♄♐	t.♄⋙ in 4ᵗʰ (R. 4ᵗʰ & 5ᵗʰ) ✶ n.♄♐ in 3ʳᵈ (R. 4ᵗʰ & 5ᵗʰ)
t.♄⋙ □ n.♀♏	t.♄⋙ in 4ᵗʰ (R. 4ᵗʰ & 5ᵗʰ) □ n.♀♏ in 2ⁿᵈ (R. 2ⁿᵈ)
t.♄⋙ △ n.ASC♎	t.♄⋙ in 4ᵗʰ (R. 4ᵗʰ & 5ᵗʰ) △ n.ASC♎

For the most part, Client D is experiencing auspicious moments during this month. However, they need to be aware of some pitfalls with their natal Pluto who is experiencing a square with transiting Jupiter and Saturn.

With natal Pluto ruling and residing in the 2nd house, this could mean that they could experience some issues with their property, resources, and/or finances. With the indications of the 4th house, this could relate to their physical home or familial property and finances. Either way, they need to be aware that this month might be a little tight money wise, and they might need to learn how to conserve more. Nevertheless, Client D is simultaneously experiencing numerous beneficial transits which will help to dilute the more frustrating energies of these two squares to natal Pluto. The sextiles during this month can bring stability to Client D if they act upon them by intrinsically desiring to establish that stability through discipline and emotional security.

| 1 | IV-3 | Obtain a transit chart for the present day as a reference. | Preliminary data. |

CLIENT E: TRANSIT CHART

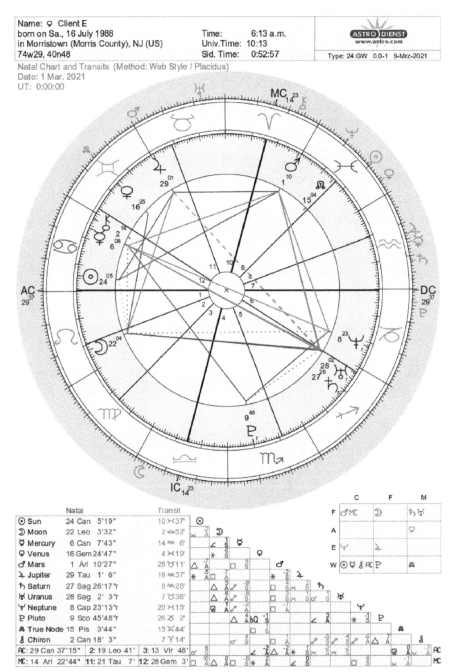

Name: ♀ Client E
born on Sa., 16 July 1988
in Morristown (Morris County), NJ (US)
74w29, 40n48

Time: 6:13 a.m.
Univ.Time: 10:13
Sid. Time: 0:52:57

ASTRO ⟩ DIENST
www.astro.com

Type: 24.GW 0.0-1 9-Mrz-2021

Natal Chart and Transits (Method: Web Style / Placidus)
Date: 1 Mar. 2021
UT: 0:00:00

	Natal	Transit
☉ Sun	24 Can 5'19"	10 ♓ 37'
☽ Moon	22 Leo 3'32"	2 ♒ 52'
☿ Mercury	6 Can 7'43"	14 ♒ 6'
♀ Venus	16 Gem 24'47"	4 ♓ 19'
♂ Mars	1 Ari 10'27"	28 ♉ 11'
♃ Jupiter	29 Tau 1' 6"	16 ♒ 37'
♄ Saturn	27 Sag 26'17"r	8 ♒ 28'
♅ Uranus	28 Sag 2' 3"r	7 ♉ 36'
♆ Neptune	8 Cap 23'13"r	20 ♓ 15'
♇ Pluto	9 Sco 45'48"r	26 ♑ 2'
⚷ True Node	15 Pis 3'44"	15 ♊ 44'
⚷ Chiron	2 Can 18' 3"	7 ♈ 14'
AC: 29 Can 37'15"	2: 19 Leo 41'	3: 13 Vir 48'
MC: 14 Ari 22'44"	11: 21 Tau 7'	12: 28 Gem 3'

	C	F	M
F	♂ MC	☽	♄ ♅
A			♀
E	♆	♃	
W	☉ ☿ ⚷ AC ♇		♌

2A	IV-3	Trace the Ephemeris one year before and after from the day of the reading and observe if transiting Jupiter has ingresses or regressed into a house.	Preliminary data.
2B	IV-3	Repeat for transiting Saturn.	Preliminary data.
2C	IV-3	Repeat for transiting Uranus.	Preliminary data.
2D	IV-3	Repeat for transiting Neptune.	Preliminary data.
2E	IV-3	Repeat for transiting Pluto.	Preliminary data.

♃		
EVENT	**GLYPH**	**DATE**
Transiting Jupiter ingresses into the 7th House	t. ♃ → 7th	DEC 17, 2020
Transiting Jupiter ingresses into the 8th House	t. ♃ → 8th	MAR 14, 2021
Transiting Jupiter ingresses into the 9th House	t. ♃ → 9th	FEB 28, 2022

♄		
EVENT	**GLYPH**	**DATE**
Transiting Saturn ingresses into the 7th House (1/3)	t. ♄ → 7th (1/3)	MAR 18, 2020
Transiting Saturn regresses into the 6th House (2/3)	t. ♄ → 6th (2/3)	JUL 8, 2020
Transiting Saturn ingresses into the 7th House (3/3)	t. ♄ → 7th (3/3)	DEC 13, 2020

♅		
EVENT	**GLYPH**	**DATE**
NONE		

♆		
EVENT	**GLYPH**	**DATE**
NONE		

♇		
EVENT	**GLYPH**	**DATE**
NONE		

3A	IV-3	Trace the Ephemeris one year before and after from the day of the reading and observe if Jupiter makes an aspect to any of the 12 natal points.	Preliminary data.
3B	IV-3	Repeat for transiting Saturn.	Preliminary data.
3C	IV-3	Repeat for transiting Uranus.	Preliminary data.
3D	IV-3	Repeat for transiting Neptune.	Preliminary data.
3E	IV-3	Repeat for transiting Pluto.	Preliminary data.

2		
EVENT	**GLYPH**	**DATE**
Transiting Jupiter in Capricorn opposes Natal Sun in Cancer (1/3) Transiting Jupiter Retrograde in Capricorn opposes Natal Sun in Cancer (2/3) Transiting Jupiter in Capricorn opposes Natal Sun in Cancer (3/3)	t.♃♑ ☍ n.☉♋ (1/3) t.♃♑ Rx ☍ n.☉♋ (2/3) t.♃♑ ☍ n.☉♋ (3/3)	MAR 29, 2020 JUL 1, 2020 NOV 19, 2020
Transiting Jupiter in Aquarius oppose Natal Moon in Leo (1/2) Transiting Jupiter Station Direct in Aquarius oppose Natal Moon in Leo (2/2)	t.♃♒ ☍ n.☽♌ (1/2) t.♃♒ SD ☍ n.☽♌ (2/2)	MAR 26, 2021 OCT 10, 2021
Transiting Jupiter in Pisces trine Natal Mercury in Cancer	t.♃♓ △ n.☿♋	JAN 27, 2022
Transiting Jupiter in Aquarius trine Natal Venus in Gemini	t.♃♒ △ n.♀♊	FEB 28, 2021
Transiting Jupiter in Aquarius sextile Natal Mars in Aries	t.♃♒ ✶ n.♂♈	DEC 24, 2020
Transiting Jupiter in Capricorn trine Natal Jupiter in Taurus	t.♃♑ △ n.♃♉	DEC 13, 2020
Transiting Jupiter in Aquarius square Natal Jupiter in Taurus (1/3) Transiting Jupiter Retrograde in Aquarius square Natal Jupiter in Taurus (2/3) Transiting Jupiter in Aquarius square Natal Jupiter in Taurus (3/3)	t.♃♒ □ n.♃♉ (1/3) t.♃♒ Rx □ n.♃♉ (2/3) t.♃♒ □ n.♃♉ (3/3)	MAY 6, 2021 AUG 5, 2021 DEC 23, 2021
Transiting Jupiter in Aquarius sextile Natal Saturn in Sagittarius (1/3) Transiting Jupiter Retrograde in Aquarius sextile Natal Saturn in Sagittarius (2/3) Transiting Jupiter in Aquarius sextile Natal Saturn in Sagittarius (3/3)	t.♃♒ ✶ n.♄♐ (1/3) t.♃♒ Rx ✶ n.♄♐ (2/3) t.♃♒ ✶ n.♄♐ (3/3)	APR 24, 2021 AUG 19, 2021 DEC 14, 2021
Transiting Jupiter in Aquarius sextile Natal Uranus in Sagittarius (1/3) Transiting Jupiter Retrograde in Aquarius sextile Natal Uranus in Sagittarius (2/3) Transiting Jupiter in Aquarius sextile Natal Uranus in Sagittarius (3/3)	t.♃♒ ✶ n.♅♐ (1/3) t.♃♒ Rx ✶ n.♅♐ (2/3) t.♃♒ ✶ n.♅♐ (3/3)	APR 28, 2021 AUG 14, 2021 DEC 18, 2021
Transiting Jupiter in Pisces sextile Natal Neptune in Capricorn	t.♃♓ ✶ n.♆♑	FEB 6, 2021
Transiting Jupiter in Aquarius square Natal Pluto in Scorpio	t.♃♒ □ n.♇♏	JAN 30, 2021

Transiting Jupiter in Pisces trine Natal Pluto in Scorpio	t.♃♓ △ n.♇♏	FEB 10, 2022
Transiting Jupiter in Capricorn oppose Cancer Ascendant	t.♃♑ ☍ n.ASC♋	DEC 17, 2020
Transiting Jupiter in Capricorn square Aries Midheaven	t.♃♑ □ n.MC♈	FEB 4, 2020
Transiting Jupiter in Aquarius sextile Aries Midheaven	t.♃♒ ✶ n.MC♈	FEB 18, 2021

♄		
EVENT	**GLYPH**	**DATE**
Saturn in Aquarius trine Natal Venus in Gemini	t.♄♒ △ n.♀♊	FEB 8, 2022
Transiting Saturn in Aquarius sextile Natal Mars in Aries (1/4) Transiting Saturn Station Retrograde in Aquarius sextile Natal Mars in Aries (2/4) Transiting Saturn Retrograde in Aquarius sextile Natal Mars in Aries (3/4) Transiting Saturn in Aquarius sextile Natal Mars in Aries (4/4)	t. ♄♒ ✶ n.♂♈ (1/4) t.♄♒ SR ✶ n.♂♈ (2/4) t.♄♒ Rx ✶ n.♂♈ (3/4) t.♄♒ ✶ n.♂♈ (4/4)	APR 8, 2020 MAY 10, 2020 JUN 12, 2020 DEC 28, 2020
Transiting Saturn in Capricorn trine Natal Jupiter in Taurus (1/3) Transiting Saturn Retrograde in Capricorn trine Natal Jupiter in Taurus (2/3) Transiting Saturn in Capricorn trine Natal Jupiter in Taurus (3/3)	t.♄♑ △ n.♃♉ (1/3) t.♄♑ Rx △ n.♃♉ (2/3) t.♄♑ △ n.♃♉ (3/3)	MAR 10, 2020 JUL 14, 2020 DEC 8, 2020
Transiting Saturn in Aquarius square Natal Pluto in Scorpio (1/3) Transiting Saturn Retrograde in Aquarius square Natal Pluto in Scorpio (2/3) Transiting Saturn in Aquarius square Natal Pluto in Scorpio (3/3)	t.♄♒ □ n.♇♏ (1/3) t.♄♒ Rx □ n.♇♏ (2/3) t.♄♒ □ n.♇♏ (3/3)	MAR 13, 2021 AUG 8, 2021 DEC 10, 2021
Transiting Saturn in Capricorn oppose Cancer Ascendant (1/3) Transiting Saturn Retrograde in Capricorn oppose Cancer Ascendant (2/3) Transiting Saturn in Capricorn oppose Cancer Ascendant (3/3)	t.♄♑ ☍ n.ASC♋ (1/3) t.♄♑ Rx ☍ n.ASC♋ (2/3) t.♄♑ ☍ n.ASC♋ (3/3)	MAR 18, 2020 JUL 8, 2020 DEC 13, 2020
Transiting Saturn in Aquarius sextile Aries Midheaven	t.♄♒ ✶ n.MC♈	JAN 22, 2022

447

♅		
EVENT	**GLYPH**	**DATE**
Transiting Uranus in Taurus sextile Natal Mercury in Cancer (1/2) Transiting Uranus Station Direct in Taurus sextile Natal Mercury in Cancer (2/2)	t.♅♉ ✶ n.☿♋ (1/2) t.♅♉ SD ✶ n.☿♋ (2/2)	APR 19, 2020 JAN 13, 2021
Transiting Uranus in Taurus trine Natal Neptune in Capricorn (1/3) Transiting Uranus Retrograde in Taurus trine Natal Neptune in Capricorn (2/3) Transiting Uranus in Taurus trine Natal Neptune in Capricorn (3/3)	t.♅♉ △ n.♆♑ (1/3) t.♅♉ Rx △ n.♆♑ (2/3) t.♅♉ △ n.♆♑ (3/3)	MAY 28, 2020 NOV 8, 2020 MAR 20, 2021
Transiting Uranus in Taurus oppose Natal Pluto in Scorpio (1/3) Transiting Uranus Retrograde in Taurus oppose Natal Pluto in Scorpio (2/3) Transiting Uranus in Taurus oppose Natal Pluto in Scorpio (3/3)	t.♅♉ ☍ n.♇♏ (1/3) t.♅♉ Rx ☍ n.♇♏ (2/3) t.♅♉ ☍ n.♇♏ (3/3)	JUN 27, 2020 OCT 4, 2020 APR 14, 2021
♆		
EVENT	**GLYPH**	**DATE**
NONE		
♇		
EVENT	**GLYPH**	**DATE**
Transiting Pluto in Capricorn oppose Natal Sun in Cancer (1/4) Transiting Pluto Retrograde in Capricorn oppose Natal Sun in Cancer (2/4) Transiting Pluto in Capricorn oppose Natal Sun in Cancer (3/4) Transiting Pluto Station Direct in Capricorn oppose Natal Sun in Cancer (4/4)	t.♇♑ ☍ n.☉♋ (1/4) t.♇♑ Rx ☍ n.☉♋ (2/4) t.♇♑ ☍ n.☉♋ (3/4) t.♇♑ SD ☍ n.☉♋ (4/4)	FEB 23, 2020 JUL 2, 2020 DEC 28, 2020 OCT 3, 2021

4		Place all events from Steps 1A-2E in chronological order.	Information as to when these events will occur and if they occur simultaneously.

2020							
JAN		**FEB**		**MAR**		**APR**	
EVENT	**DAY**	**EVENT**	**DAY**	**EVENT**	**DAY**	**EVENT**	**DAY**
		t.♃♑ □ n.MC♈ t.♇♑ ☍ n.☉♋ (1/4)	4 23	t.♄♑ △ n.♃♉ (1/3) t. ♄ → 7th (1/3) t.♄♑ ☍ n.ASC♋ (1/3) t.♃♑ ☍ n.☉♋ (1/3)	10 18 18 29	t.♄♒ ⚹ n.♂♈ (1/4) t.♅♉ ⚹ n.☿♋ (1/2)	8 19
MAY		**JUN**		**JUL**		**AUG**	
EVENT	**DAY**	**EVENT**	**DAY**	**EVENT**	**DAY**	**EVENT**	**DAY**
t.♄♒ SR ⚹ n.♂♈ (2/4) t.♅♉ △ n.♆♑ (1/3)	10 28	t.♄♒ Rx ⚹ n.♂♈ (3/4) t.♅♉ ☍ n.♇♏ (1/3)	12 27	t.♃♑ Rx ☍ n.☉♋ (2/3) t.♇♑ Rx ☍ n.☉♋ (2/4) t. ♄ → 6th (2/3) t.♄♑ Rx ☍ n.ASC♋ (2/3) t.♄♑ Rx △ n.♃♉ (2/3)	1 2 8 8 14		
SEP		**OCT**		**NOV**		**DEC**	
EVENT	**DAY**	**EVENT**	**DAY**	**EVENT**	**DAY**	**EVENT**	**DAY**
		t.♅♉ Rx ☍ n.♇♏ (2/3)	4	t.♅♉ Rx △ n.♆♑ (2/3) t.♃♑ ☍ n.☉♋ (3/3)	8 19	t.♄♑ △ n.♃♉ (3/3) t. ♄ → 7th (3/3 t.♃♑ △ n.♃♉ t.♄♑ ☍ n.ASC♋ (3/3) t. ♃ → 7th t.♃♑ ☍ n.ASC♋ t.♃♒ ⚹ n.♂♈ t.♄♒ ⚹ n.♂♈ (4/4) t.♇♑ ☍ n.☉♋ (3/4)	8 13 13 13 17 17 24 28 28

2021							
JAN		FEB		MAR		APR	
EVENT	DAY	EVENT	DAY	EVENT	DAY	EVENT	DAY
t.♅♉ SD ⚹ n.☿♋ (2/2) t.♃♒ □ n.♇♏	13 30	t.♃♓ ⚹ N.♆♑ t.♃♒ ⚹ N.☋☿♈ t.♃♒ Δ N.♀♊	6 18 28	t.♄♒ □ n.♇♏ (1/3) t. ♃ → 8th t.♅♉ Δ n.♆♑ (3/3) t.♃♒ ☍ n.☽♌ (1/2)	13 14 20 26	t.♅♉ ☍ n.♇♏ (3/3) t.♃♒ ⚹ n.♄♐ (1/3) t.♃♒ ⚹ n.♅♐ (1/3)	14 24 28
MAY		JUN		JUL		AUG	
EVENT	DAY	EVENT	DAY	EVENT	DAY	EVENT	DAY
t.♃♒ □ n.♃♉ (1/3)	6					t.♃♒ Rx □ n.♃♉ (2/3) t.♄♒ Rx □ n.♇♏ (2/3) t.♃♒ Rx ⚹ n.♅♐ (2/3) t.♃♒ Rx ⚹ n.♄♐ (2/3)	5 8 14 19
SEP		OCT		NOV		DEC	
EVENT	DAY	EVENT	DAY	EVENT	DAY	EVENT	DAY
		t.♇♑ SD ☍ n.☉♋ (4/4) t.♃♒ S♀ ☍ N.☽♌ (2/2)	3 10			t.♄♒ □ n.♇♏ (3/3) t.♃♒ ⚹ n.♄♐ (3/3) t.♃♒ ⚹ n.♅♐ (3/3) t.♃♒ □ n.♃♉ (3/3)	10 14 18 23

2022			
JAN		FEB	
EVENT	DAY	EVENT	DAY
t.♄♒ ⚹ n.MC♈ t.♃♓ Δ n.☿♋	22 27	t.♄♒ Δ n.♀♊ t.♃♓ Δ n.♇♏ t. ♃ → 9th	8 10 28

5		Determine the most inauspicious and auspicious months for the individual.	This will let the individual know when there are times of immense struggle or benefit which they can either prepare for the harder times and/or utilize the better times to their fullest potential.

AUSPICIOUS	INAUSPICIOUS
DEC 2020	AUG 2021
FEB 2021	DEC 2021
FEB 2022	

6	IV-4	Create transit formulas for every event listed in steps 3A-3E.	Various realms within the person's life that will be influenced by the event.

EVENT	FORMULA
t.♃♑ ☍ n.☉d	t.♃♑ in 6th (R. 6th & 9th) ☍ n.☉♋ in 12th (R. 2nd)
t.♃♒ ☍ n.☽♌	t.♃♒ in 8th (R. 6th & 9th) ☍ n.☽♌ in 2nd (R. 1st)
t.♃♓ △ n.☿♋	t.♃♓ in 8th (R. 6th & 9th) △ n.☿♋ in 12th (R. 12th & 3rd)
t.♃♒ △ n.♀♊	t.♃♒ in 7th (R. 6th & 9th) △ n.♀♊ in 11th (R. 11th & 4th)
t.♃♒ ✶ n.♂♈	t.♃♒ in 7th (R. 6th & 9th) ✶ n.♂♈ in 9th (R. 10th & 5th)
t.♃♑ △ n.♃♉	t.♃♑ in 6th (R. 6th & 9th) △ n.♃♉ in 11th (R. 6th & 9th)
t.♃♒ □ n.♃♉	t.♃♒ in 8th (R. 6th & 9th) □ n.♃♉ in 11th (R. 6th & 9th)
t.♃♒ ✶ n.♄♐	t.♃♒ in 8th (R. 6th & 9th) ✶ n.♄♐ in 5th (R. 7th & 8th)
t.♃♒ ✶ n.♅♐	t.♃♒ in 8th (R. 6th & 9th) ✶ n.♅♐ in 5th (R. 8th)
t.♃♓ ✶ n.♆♑	t.♃♓ in 7th (R. 6th & 9th) ✶ n.♆♑ in 6th (R. 9th)
t.♃♒ □ n.♇♏	t.♃♒ in 7th (R. 6th & 9th) □ n.♇♏ in 4th (R. 5th)
t.♃♓ △ n.♇♏	t.♃♓ in 8th (R. 6th & 9th) △ n.♇♏ in 4th (R. 5th)
t.♃♑ ☍ n.ASC♋	t.♃♑ in 7th (R. 6th & 9th) ☍ n.ASC♋
t.♃♑ □ n.MC♈	t.♃♑ in 6th (R. 6th & 9th) □ n.MC♈
t.♃♒ ✶ n.MC♈	t.♃♒ in 7th (R. 6th & 9th) ✶ n.MC♈
t.♄♒ △ n.♀♊	t.♄♒ in 7th (R. 7th & 8th) △ n.♀♊ in 11th (R. 11th & 4th)
t.♄♒ ✶ n.♂♈	t.♄♒ in 7th (R. 7th & 8th) ✶ n.♂♈ in 9th (R. 10th & 5th)
t.♄♑ △ n.♃♉	t.♄♑ in 7th (R. 7th & 8th) △ n.♃♉ in 11th (R. 6th & 9th)
t.♄♒ □ n.♇♏	t.♄♒ in 7th (R. 7th & 8th) □ n.♇♏ in 4th (R. 5th)
t.♄♑ ☍ n.ASC♋	t.♄♑ in 7th (R. 7th & 8th) ☍ n.ASC♋

451

t.♄♒ ⚹ n.MC♈	t.♄♒ in 7th (R. 7th & 8th) ⚹ n.MC♈
t.♅♉ ⚹ n.☿♋	t.♅♉ in 10th (R. 8th) ⚹ n.☿♋ in 12th (R. 12th & 3rd)
t.♅♉ Δ n.♆♑	t.♅♉ in 10th (R. 8th) Δ n.♆♑ in 6th (R. 9th)
t.♅♉ ☍ n.♇♏	t.♅♉ in 10th (R. 8th) ☍ n.♇♏ in 4th (R. 5th)
t.♇♑ ☍ n.☉♋	t.♇♑ in 6th (R. 5th) ☍ n.☉♋ in 12th (R. 2nd)

7		Compose a summary of your findings from step 4-6.	Summary of Analysis.

Multiple Oppositions

Client E is experiencing six oppositions during this time frame: transiting Jupiter oppose natal Sun, Moon, and Ascendant, transiting Saturn oppose Ascendant, transiting Uranus oppose natal Pluto, and transiting Pluto oppose natal Sun (t.♃♑ ☍ n.☉♋, t.♃♒ ☍ n.☽♌, t.♃♑ ☍ n.ASC♋, t.♄♑ ☍ n.ASC♋, t.♅♉ ☍ n.♇♏, t.♇♑ ☍ n.☉♋) (Table V-16).

It is significant that five out of these six oppositions deal with the deeply personal planets of the Sun, Moon, and the Ascendant primarily within the realms of the 2nd, 6th, 9th, 12th, and 8th houses. This means that Client E will encounter opposing views and forces that cause them to compromise and sacrifice parts of their ego in order to cohabitate with various individuals and circumstances. It could be that some event causes new unforeseen details or previously unknown facts to resurface causing Client E to review decisions and opinions they have previously held in the recent past. With the new information that has been given, they will need to realize

TABLE V-16. Oppositions Experienced by Client E

EVENT	FORMULA
t.♃♑ ☍ n.☉♋	t.♃♑ in 6th (R. 6th & 9th) ☍ n.☉♋ in 12th (R. 2nd)
t.♃♒ ☍ n.☽♌	t.♃♒ in 8th (R. 6th & 9th) ☍ n.☽♌ in 2nd (R. 1st)
t.♃♑ ☍ n.ASC♋	t.♃♑ in 7th (R. 6th & 9th) ☍ n.ASC♋
t.♄♑ ☍ n.ASC♋	t.♄♑ in 7th (R. 7th & 8th) ☍ n.ASC♋
t.♅♉ ☍ n.♇♏	t.♅♉ in 10th (R. 8th) ☍ n.♇♏ in 4th (R. 5th)
t.♇♑ ☍ n.☉♋	t.♇♑ in 6th (R. 5th) ☍ n.☉♋ in 12th (R. 2nd)

where they were right and where they were wrong and accommodate appropriately. This entire situation acts as a litmus test for Client E to consider what parts of their personality need to be eliminated for the sake of better cooperation with others.

This is a good time for Client E to learn to swallow their pride and if they cannot, they need to realize where those insecurities come from that make them incapable of backing down. The thing is, with transiting Saturn and Pluto involved, there is no getting away from previous inappropriate actions and thinking. The more Client E can relate and collaborate with the people on the opposite side of the circumstance, the better they can remedy the situation and grow from the experience.

Saturn Trines

Client E will encounter two beneficial trines with transiting Saturn during this time with natal Venus and Jupiter (t.♄♒ Δ n.♀♊, t.♄♑ Δ n.♃♉) (Table V-17).

During these transits, Client E will experience extreme closeness with those that they are intimately tied to. With transiting Saturn trine natal Venus, it is possible that someone close could divulge a personal secret to Client E or vice versa. Either way, Client E will be able to strengthen the bonds between these individuals due to the sensitive subject matter being discussed. Additionally, due to this transit, Client E could dedicate themself further with their romantic partners and/or find more stability within these relationships.

With transiting Saturn trine Jupiter, Client E will have a perfect opportunity to accomplish certain goals. Or Client E could decide to go back to school or partake in a learning program that will advance their career and qualifications. Whatever and however they choose to advance their career, the trine to natal Jupiter indicates that they do not have to worry about it being a struggle because Jupiter will make sure that everything works out in their favor. As such, this is a good time for Client E to ask for a raise or a promotion.

TABLE V-17. Formulas for Client E's Saturn Trines

EVENT	FORMULA
t.♄♒ Δ n.♀♊	t.♄♒ in 7th (R. 7th & 8th) Δ n.♀♊ in 11th (R. 11th & 4th)
t.♄♑ Δ n.♃♉	t.♄♑ in 7th (R. 7th & 8th) Δ n.♃♉ in 11th (R. 6th & 9th)

Auspicious Moments

Client E has three months of highly beneficial activity in December 2020, February 2021, and February 2022. In December 2020, transiting Jupiter will trine natal Jupiter and sextile natal Mars and transiting Saturn will trine natal Jupiter and sextile natal Mars (t.♃♑ Δ n.♃♉, t.♃♒ ✶ n.♂♈, t.♄♑ Δ n.♃♉, t.♄♒ ✶ n.♂♈). In February 2021, transiting Jupiter sextiles natal Neptune and Midheaven and trines natal Venus (t.♃♓ ✶ n.♆♑, t.♃♒ ✶ n.MC♈, t.♃♒ Δ n.♀♊). Finally, in February 2022, transiting Saturn will trine natal Venus and transiting Jupiter will trine natal Pluto (t.♄♒ Δ n.♀♊, t.♃♓ Δ n.♇♏) (Table V-18).

These transits give Client E great ease in their activities along with a positive outlook that helps them to attract desirable circumstances and people. With natal Venus, they will be able to relate to others more easily and will find it effortless to meet in the middle. This is probably due to the fact that, after all of those oppositions that they have encountered, they are able to use that knowledge to mend and establish more sound connections with others in their daily life.

With natal Mars, Client E can properly assert themself without others feeling too threatened. This not only boosts Client E's confidence, it allows for others to put their confidence in them. Similarly, Client E is able to establish beneficial exercise regiments and benefits well from hard physical outputs such as outdoor excursions, sports, and weightlifting.

TABLE V-18. Transit formulas for Client E's Most Auspicious Months

t.♃♒ Δ n.♀♊	t.♃♒ in 7th (R. 6th & 9th) Δ n.♀♊ in 11th (R. 11th & 4th)
t.♃♒ ✶ n.♂♈	t.♃♒ in 7th (R. 6th & 9th) ✶ n.♂♈ in 9th (R. 10th & 5th)
t.♃♑ Δ n.♃♉	t.♃♑ in 6th (R. 6th & 9th) Δ n.♃♉ in 11th (R. 6th & 9th)
t.♃♒ ✶ n.MC♈	t.♃♒ in 7th (R. 6th & 9th) ✶ n.MC♈
t.♃♓ ✶ n.♆♑	t.♃♓ in 7th (R. 6th & 9th) ✶ n.♆♑ in 6th (R. 9th)
t.♃♓ Δ n.♇♏	t.♃♓ in 8th (R. 6th & 9th) Δ n.♇♏ in 4th (R. 5th)
t.♄♒ Δ n.♀♊	t.♄♒ in 7th (R. 7th & 8th) Δ n.♀♊ in 11th (R. 11th & 4th)
t.♄♒ ✶ n.♂♈	t.♄♒ in 7th (R. 7th & 8th) ✶ n.♂♈ in 9th (R. 10th & 5th)
t.♄♑ Δ n.♃♉	t.♄♑ in 7th (R. 7th & 8th) Δ n.♃♉ in 11th (R. 6th & 9th)

Transits made to natal Neptune and Pluto help Client E to put their guard down when it is needed. Remember, all those oppositions caused Client E to reevaluate their stubbornness and ability to compromise. Neptune and Pluto helps them to admit fault more readily. This works out in their favor because it establishes immense respect from the other individuals involved. These transits will also improve their family life and their relationships with children due to the 4th and 5th house influences.

With the trines to natal Jupiter, Client E simply develops an undercurrent feeling that everything will work out in the end. There is no more uncertainty and confusion, and Jupiter adds a general hope for the future which aids in their courage to take calculated risks which work out in their favor. In other words, things begin to work out for Client E because Jupiter gives them the positive mentality to be open to such outcomes.

INAUSPICIOUS MOMENTS

Client E has two difficult months in August and December 2021 when transiting Jupiter squares natal Jupiter and transiting Saturn squares natal Pluto (t.♃☵ □ n.♃♉, t.♄☵ □ n.♇♏) (Table V-19).

As mentioned above, when trines are established with transiting Jupiter, it gives the client an open head and heart so that opportunities can come their way with great ease. When squares are established with transiting Jupiter, however, the opposite occurs, and the client begins to feel that they cannot overcome certain roadblocks that come their way during the time of the transit. I would advise Client E that firstly, these feelings are temporary and not long lasting because they involve transiting Jupiter whose energies do not last for too long compared to the other outer planets. Secondly, Jupiter is only asking them to be a bit more resourceful and scale back their plans for the time being to make sure that they are headed in the appropriate direction. Once transiting Jupiter leaves the square point with natal Jupiter, they will once again have the chance to proceed on their course.

TABLE V-19. Client E's Transit Formulas during Most Inauspicious Months

t.♃☵ □ n.♃♉	t.♃☵ in 8th (R. 6th & 9th) □ n.♃♉ in 11th (R. 6th & 9th)
t.♄☵ □ n.♇♏	t.♄☵ in 7th (R. 7th & 8th) □ n.♇♏ in 4th (R. 5th)

Transiting Saturn square natal Pluto might look incredibly daunting at first but there are a few things to remember. For one, due to the slow-moving nature of Pluto, we must remember that this planet is more generational than personal. This is evidenced by the fact that practically every case study encounters this transit at some point during 2020-2022 due to their proximity in age. Therefore, the energies that come out of this transit are more global than individualized. However, it is significant for Client E because other inauspicious aspects occur simultaneously which exacerbate the energies of transiting Saturn square natal Pluto.

It could be that Client E is more influenced by the global issues involving their country or community more than others. I would also warn Client E to not fall into any form of addiction during this time along with the possibility of witnessing some friction between certain familial ties. With the combination of a square to natal Jupiter and Pluto, Client E needs to be mindful of too much negative thinking because it can cause them to act irrationally and self-destructively. I would advise them to wait it out and, for the moment, do not act or react but instead fall more into the background until these unfavorable months conclude.

* * *

Before we continue to the next part of the book, I want to mention an interesting correlation that caught my eye while I was computing the transits of these various case studies. When I announced the need for case studies on Reddit on February 26, 2021, I selected the individuals mostly on a first come, first serve basis without looking at any of the charts up front. I did this to not only eliminate any bias, but to also ensure a random sample. Weeks later, once I began to compute their various transits, I noticed that everyone had a significant transit occur around this date (Table V-20).

TABLE V-20. Case Study Transits Around February 26ⁱ 2021

CLIENT	TRANSIT DATE	TRANSIT	TRANSIT FORMULA
A	FEB 28, 2021	t.♃♒ ☍ n.♅♌	t.♃♒ in 9th (R. 11th) ☍ n.♅♌ in 3rd (R. 4th)
B	FEB 21, 2021	t.♃♒ ✶ n.☉♈	t. ♃♒ in 7th (R. 6th & 10th) ✶ n.☉♈ in 10th (R. 2nd & 3rd)
C	FEB 14, 2021	t.♅♉ △ n.♂♑	t. ♅♉ in 4th (R. Nothing) △ n.♂♑ in 1st (R. 4th & 11th)
D	FEB 22, 2021	t.♃♒ △ n.♀♎	t.♃♒ in 5th (R. 6th & 3rd) △ n.♀♎ in 1st (R. 1st & 8th)
E	FEB 28, 2021	t.♃♒ △ n.♀♊	t.♃♒ in 7th (R. 6th & 9th) △ n.♀♊ in 11th (R. 11th & 4th)

Notice the various correlations around these events. For one, all events occurred close to the date Feb 26, 2021 with the average being 5 days and the standard deviation being 3.7 days. Three aspects out of the five involve trines, one involves a sextile, and the other involves an opposition. Furthermore, four of the five transits involve transiting Jupiter in Aquarius and one involves transiting Uranus in Taurus. Either way, both are relevant because astrology is ruled by Aquarius and its planetary ruler, Uranus.

These alignments cannot be dismissed as coincidence and I personally had no idea that they occurred until weeks after I chose the participants. This begs the question: did I really pick them out of my own autonomy, or were they already fatalistically planned to be the participants within this book? This is a great example of how astrology tows the line between free will and fate and our place within these two extremes. Why were these five chosen at random and not the others who applied? Perhaps they were already destined to be chosen, or at least by participating, this is how these various transits became manifest within their lives. Either way, it is substantially important to note that astrological phenomena can be quantified in this way in order to satisfy statistical and scientific parameters.

Now that we have examined various methods that will function as your primary source of chart interpretation for yourself and for your clients, we can move forward into more advanced techniques. The first of these being planetary progressions.

PART VI: THE PROGRESSED CHART

"Character is destiny…Every person we meet in life is endowed with a character, strong or weak, good or evil, pronounced or indifferent; and we are all of us affected, consciously or unconsciously by the character of everyone with whom we come into contact. Bad characters will corrupt weaker ones, and good characters will raise the standards of others. Character will make itself manifest, and it will either control, modify or stir into greater activity passing events; in fact, on close investigation 'character' is found to be at the root of every difference that we remark between one human and another."- Alan Leo from The Progressed Horoscope p. 4

THIS SECTION IS DEDICATED TO MY TEACHER JOHN MARCHESELLA WHO INSTILLED WITHIN ME THE IMPORTANCE OF THE PROGRESSED HOROSCOPE

The progressed chart works on the metaphysical principle of "higher octaves." This is the same concept we see among geometrical and numeric proportions. For example, if I have Square A that is 2x2 and Square B that is 4x4, this means that both squares are in proportion to one another at a ratio of 1:2. Astrology simply utilizes this concept of proportions within the progressed chart by having 1 day of time equating to 1 year of time (1 day = 1 year).

For example, if I was born on June 1, 1978, then the planetary locations found on June 11, 1978, 10 days after my birthdate, equate to how my birth chart is "progressing" at 10 years of age. Similarly, if I was born on March 4, 2004 then the planetary locations found on March 24, 2004 tells me how my chart is progressing at 20 years of age because March 24 is 20 days after March 4.

When you experience progressed events within your life, they are akin to outer planetary transits in a couple of ways. For one, due to the slower rate of movement found within both, these events are more personalized and significant for the individual. Secondly, specialized events that emerge out of progressions can take years or so to experience and conclude. As you will see further in this section, the progressed chart is the ultimate "time clock" and tells us if we are in a 14-year period of rest or a 14-year period of production. Therefore, a lot of valuable information can be lost by ignoring the progressed chart.

The transiting planets indicate how the present-day moment is interacting with our birth chart, but the progressed chart shows how the individual psychology is evolving through time. In other words, transiting planets indicate the how and what when it comes to events within our life, but the progressed chart tells us why they are occurring to us. The progressed chart also shows what is primarily available to us in terms of resources towards our life predicaments. But before we can further discuss analysis, we must first learn how to calculate our progressions.

SECTION 1-CALCULATING PROGRESSIONS

Progression calculations are incredibly similar to transit calculations you experienced in Part IV. Most of the methodology and mathematics are the same; all that differs are the proportions. Just as it was with transits, the first step is to gather the data.

Recall in Part IV-Section 3, dates within an ephemeris tell you where the planet was located from Point A to Point B, midnight to midnight. We are going to take this same concept but instead, our Points A and B will indicate Jan 1 of a certain year so that the distance between Point A to Point B is 1 year or 365 days (Fig VI-1).

We will be completing a slightly different reference sheet in order to make sure we have the appropriate data organized in one location. The first information we need to gather is the data for Year X (Point A) and Year Y (Point B). We do this by obtaining our progressed chart on astro. com for the year you want to analyze (Year X/Point A) and the subsequent year (Year Y/Point B) (Table VI-1).

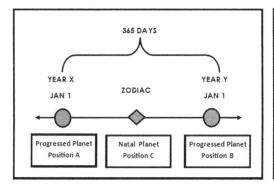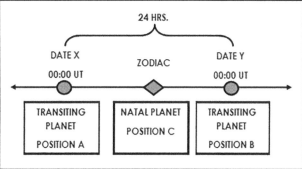

FIGURE VI-1. Visual Representation of Proportional Changes from Transits to Progressions

TABLE VI-1. How to Obtain your Progressed Horoscope on ASTRO.COM

(1) On the ASTRO.COM main page, under the HOROSCOPES tab, chose EXTENDED CHART SELECTION under DRAWINGS, CALCULATIONS, DATA.

(2) Confirm that the appropriate individual is selected under HOROSCOPE FOR.

(3) Under CHART TYPE, select NATAL AND PROGRESSED CHART.

(4) Under START DATE choose JAN 1 for the Year you want to explore. In our example, we will be using the year 2026 with the same chart we used in Part IV. This will be your Point A

(5) Click CLICK HERE TO SHOW CHART.

(6) Fill in data within the reference sheet including house placements and natal points.

(7) Repeat the process for Point B by putting Jan 1 for the following year.

YEAR X: 2026

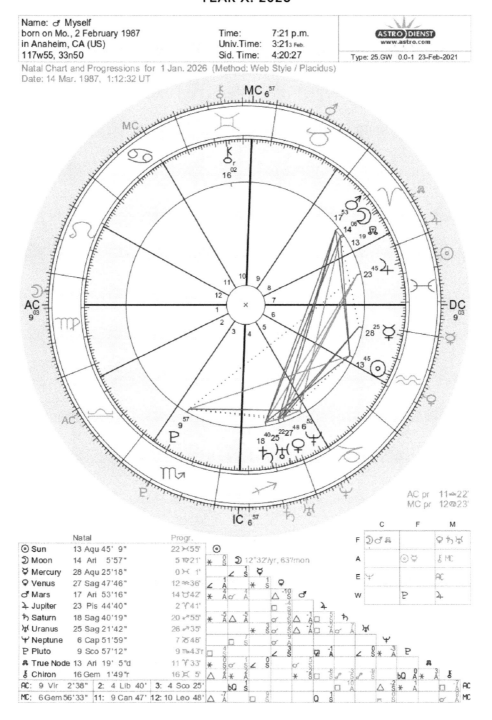

AC pr 11≏22'
MC pr 12♋23'

	Natal	Progr.
☉ Sun	13 Aqu 45' 9"	22 ⨯55'
☽ Moon	14 Ari 5'57"	5 ♏21'
☿ Mercury	28 Aqu 25'18"	0 ⨯ 1'
♀ Venus	27 Sag 47'46"	12 ≈36'
♂ Mars	17 Ari 53'16"	14 ♉42'
♃ Jupiter	23 Pis 44'40"	2 ♈41'
♄ Saturn	18 Sag 40'19"	20 ♐55'
♅ Uranus	25 Sag 21'42"	26 ♐35'
♆ Neptune	6 Cap 51'59"	7 ♑48'
♇ Pluto	9 Sco 57'12"	9 ♏43'r
☊ True Node	13 Ari 19' 5"d	11 ♈33'
⚷ Chiron	16 Gem 1'49"r	16 ⨯ 5'
AC: 9 Vir 2'38"	2: 4 Lib 40'	3: 4 Sco 25'
MC: 6 Gem 56'33"	11: 9 Can 47'	12: 10 Leo 48'

463

YEAR Y: 2027

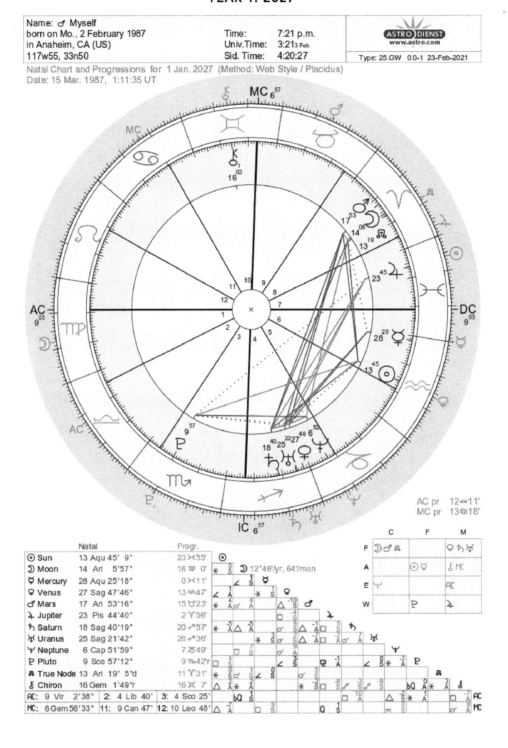

Name: ♂ Myself
born on Mo., 2 February 1987
in Anaheim, CA (US)
117w55, 33n50

Time: 7:21 p.m.
Univ.Time: 3:21 3 Feb.
Sid. Time: 4:20:27

ASTRO DIENST
www.astro.com

Type: 25.GW 0.0-1 23-Feb-2021

Natal Chart and Progressions for 1 Jan. 2027 (Method: Web Style / Placidus)
Date: 15 Mar. 1987, 1:11:35 UT

AC pr   12≈11'
MC pr   13♋18'

	Natal	Progr.
☉ Sun	13 Aqu 45' 9"	23 ♓ 55'
☽ Moon	14 Ari 5'57"	18 ♍ 0'
☿ Mercury	28 Aqu 25'18"	0 ♓ 11'
♀ Venus	27 Sag 47'46"	13 ≈ 47'
♂ Mars	17 Ari 53'16"	15 ♉ 23'
♃ Jupiter	23 Pis 44'40"	2 ♈ 56'
♄ Saturn	18 Sag 40'19"	20 ♐ 57'
♅ Uranus	25 Sag 21'42"	26 ♐ 36'
♆ Neptune	6 Cap 51'59"	7 ♑ 49'
♇ Pluto	9 Sco 57'12"	9 ♏ 42'r
☊ True Node	13 Ari 19' 5"d	11 ♈ 31'
⚷ Chiron	16 Gem 1'49"r	16 ♓ 7'
AC: 9 Vir 2'38"	2: 4 Lib 40'	3: 4 Sco 25'
MC: 6 Gem 56'33"	11: 9 Can 47'	12: 10 Leo 48'

464

PROGRESSED POINTS REFERENCE SHEET

PLANET/CARDINAL POINT	YEAR X HOUSE	YEAR X ZODIAC	NATAL POINT	YEAR Y ZODIAC	YEAR Y HOUSE
☉					
☽					
☿					
♀					
♂					
♃					
♄					
♅					
♆					
♇					
ASC					
MC					

PROGRESSED POINTS REFERENCE SHEET

PLANET/CARDINAL POINT	YEAR X HOUSE	YEAR X ZODIAC	NATAL POINT	YEAR Y ZODIAC	YEAR Y HOUSE
☉	7	22° ♓ 55′	13° ♒ 45′	23° ♓ 55′	7
☽	12	5° ♍ 21′	14° ♈ 5′	18° ♍ 0′	1
☿	6	0° ♓ 1′	28° ♒ 25′	0° ♓ 11′	6
♀	6	12° ♒ 36′	27° ♐ 47′	13° ♒ 47′	6
♂	9	14° ♉ 42′	17° ♈ 53′	15° ♉ 23′	9
♃	7	2° ♈ 41′	23° ♓ 44′	2° ♈ 56′	7
♄	4	20° ♐ 55′	18° ♐ 40′	20° ♐ 57′	4
♅	4	26° ♐ 35′	25° ♐ 21′	26° ♐ 36′	4
♆	4	7° ♑ 48′	6° ♑ 51′	7° ♑ 49′	4
♇	3	9° ♏ 43′	9° ♏ 57′	9° ♏ 42′	3
ASC	2	11° ♎ 22′	9° ♍ 2′	12° ♎ 11′	2
MC	11	12° ♋ 23′	6° ♊ 56′	13° ♋ 18′	11

TABLE VI-2. How to Calculate Progressed Events

STEP #	DESCRIPTION	EQUATIONS/MATERIALS USED
1	Determine the event and which natal point will cause the event (Point C).	Compare the Natal Points (Point C) to the Progressed Points within the reference sheet (Points A and B).
2	Write down the progressed point's location from Year to Year (Points A and B).	Progressed Point Reference Sheet
3	Set up the Transit Constant Equation and solve being mindful of converting when necessary.	$Transit\ Constant = \dfrac{(C - A)}{(B - A)}$
4A	Multiply the Transit Constant by 365 days to determine how many days have passed from the starting point.	Transit Constant x 365 days = 00.00 where 00.= days and .00=hours
4B	Round up the whole number found in Step 4A	00.= Days that have passed since starting point
5	Determine which month of the year by subtracting from the monthly conversion table (TABLE VI-3).	MONTH 00

Now that we have our data points A, B, and C on the reference sheet, it is time to compare the traveling movements of the progressed planets to the fixed natal points. This Is how we will get our practice in with progressions, but before we begin, let us review the steps that will be required to calculate the time of progressed events by examining the various steps it takes, and then discussing the differences between transit math and progressed math (TABLE VI-2).

The first thing you will notice is that the transit constant and concepts behind what points are points A, B, and C to be exactly the same. The first difference comes in step 4A where we multiply by 365 days instead of 24 hours for transits. Because we are dealing with larger time frames, it is okay to round up to the nearest whole number. This tells us how many days have passed since Jan 1 of the starting year, but we need to put that into terms of actual months. We do this by subtracting this whole number from the table below (TABLE VI-3).

466

TABLE VI-3. Monthly Conversion Table

MONTH	DAY	MONTH	DAY
JAN	0	JUL	180
FEB	30	AUG	211
MAR	58	SEP	242
APR	89	OCT	272
MAY	119	NOV	303
JUN	150	DEC	333

This is how the conversion table works. Let us say that the number we get from Step 4B is 246. This means that 246 days have passed starting from Jan 1, the starting point. To convert this into a month, we look at the conversion table above and find the number closest to our number without going over. In our example, this number would be 242 which is the number for Sep. This means that the event will occur in Sep, and to find out the day we take the difference.

246 DAYS – 242 DAYS (SEP) = SEP 4

This will make more sense once we get into some examples, so let us begin and treat the progressed chart the same way we treated transits by first observing any ingresses, and then aspects.

PART I: Progressed Ingresses

For reference, the next two parts will be using the filled out Progressed Points Reference Sheet found above. Furthermore, for this section, we need to be in mindful of the natal chart house doorways which have been copied below.

HOUSES (INGRESSES)			
ASC/1	9° ♍ 2'	DSC/7	9° ♓ 2'
2	4° ♎ 40'	8	4° ♈ 40'
3	4° ♏ 25'	9	4° ♉ 25'
IC/4	6° ♐ 56'	MC/10	6° ♊ 56'
5	9° ♑ 47'	11	9° ♋ 47'
6	10° ♒ 48'	12	10° ♌ 48'

467

Now we compare these doorways to the progressed points' travels from year to year and see if any planets ingress or regress into a house. Thankfully, we already have this information because we filled out the columns "Year X House and Year Y House" which makes for an easy comparison. From that, we notice that the only ingress that occurs with the progressed planets is the Progressed Moon from the 12th house to the 1st house. Recall, this also means that the Progressed Moon will conjoin the Natal Ascendant at the same time.

STEP #	DESCRIPTION	EQUATIONS/MATERIALS USED
1	Determine the event and which natal point will cause the event (Point C).	**EVENT:** Progressed Moon ingresses into the 1st house (p.☽ → 1ST)/Progressed Moon in Virgo conjoins the Natal Virgo Ascendant (p. ☽♍ ☌ n. Asc ♍) **POINT C:** 9° ♍ 2' (1st House Doorway)
2	Write down the progressed point's location from Year to Year (Points A and B).	**POINT B:** p. ☽ 18° ♍ 0' **POINT A:** p. ☽ 5° ♍ 21'
3	Set up the Transit Constant Equation and solve being mindful of converting when necessary.	$Transit\ Constant = \dfrac{(C-A)}{(B-A)} = \dfrac{(9°2' - 5°21')}{(18°0' - 5°21')}$ $= \dfrac{(8°62' - 5°21')}{(17°60' - 5°21')}$ $= \dfrac{221'}{759'} = 0.291$
4A	Multiply the Transit Constant by 365 days to determine how many days have passed from the starting point.	0.291 x 365 days = 106.2 DAYS
4B	Round up the whole number found in Step 4A	106 DAYS
5	Determine which month of the year by subtracting from the monthly conversion table (TABLE VI-3).	106 DAYS – 89 (APRIL) = 17 **APRIL 17, 2026**

Notice in Step 3, the conversion contained larger values that we have not seen before. This is because we are dealing with the Moon, which is the fastest moving planet within Astrology. This means we can expect large distances of travel when dealing with the progressed Moon.

According to our reference sheet, this was the only progressed ingress for 2026. That means we can now continue to see if any aspects occur between the progressed points and the natal points.

PART II: Progressed Aspects

We will now have to once again use the various aspects within the Transit Points Reference sheet in Part IV-Section 3, but for the sake of efficiency, it would be helpful to have the various aspect patters memorized by now. Starting with the fixed Natal Sun point, compare this fixed point to the traveling progressed points by simply going down the Progressed Point Reference Sheet. Going down as such, we notice that the Progressed Venus in Aquarius conjoins the Natal Sun in Aquarius.

STEP #	DESCRIPTION	EQUATIONS/MATERIALS USED
1	Determine the event and which natal point will cause the event (Point C).	**EVENT:** Progressed Venus in Aquarius conjoin Natal Sun in Aquarius (p. ♀♒ ☌ n. ☉♒) **POINT C:** 13° ♒ 45′ (Aquarius conjunction Point)
2	Write down the progressed point's location from Year to Year (Points A and B).	**POINT B:** p. ♀ 13° ♒ 47′ **POINT A:** p. ♀ 12° ♒ 36′
3	Set up the Transit Constant Equation and solve being mindful of converting when necessary.	$Transit\ Constant = \dfrac{(C-A)}{(B-A)} = \dfrac{(13°45' - 12°36')}{(13°47' - 12°36')}$ $= \dfrac{69'}{71'} = 0.972$
4A	Multiply the Transit Constant by 365 days to determine how many days have passed from the starting point.	0.972 x 365 days = 354.8 DAYS
4B	Round up the whole number found in Step 4A	355 DAYS
5	Determine which month of the year by subtracting from the monthly conversion table (TABLE VI-3).	355 DAYS – 333 (DEC) = 22 **DEC 22, 2026**

The other progressed points make no aspects to the Natal Sun, so let us continue to the Natal Moon point. After reviewing all of the progressed travel ranges, there are no aspects made to the Natal Moon. Moving on to Natal Mercury, Venus, and Mars, there are similarly no aspect points made to the progressed points. However, when I observe Natal Jupiter, I see that the Progressed Sun in Pisces will conjoin Natal Jupiter in Pisces.

STEP #	DESCRIPTION	EQUATIONS/MATERIALS USED
1	Determine the event and which natal point will cause the event (Point C).	**EVENT:** Progressed Sun in Pisces conjoins Natal Jupiter in Pisces (p. ☉♓ ☌ n. ♃♓) **POINT C:** 23° ♓ 44′ (Pisces conjunction Point)
2	Write down the progressed point's location from Year to Year (Points A and B).	**POINT B:** p. ☉ 23° ♓ 55′ **POINT A:** p. ☉ 22° ♓ 55′
3	Set up the Transit Constant Equation and solve being mindful of converting when necessary.	$Transit\ Constant = \dfrac{(C-A)}{(B-A)} = \dfrac{(23°44' - 22°55')}{(23°55' - 22°55')}$ $= \dfrac{(22°104' - 22°55')}{(22°115' - 22°55')}$ $= \dfrac{49'}{60'} = 0.817$
4A	Multiply the Transit Constant by 365 days to determine how many days have passed from the starting point.	0.817 x 365 days = 298.2 DAYS
4B	Round up the whole number found in Step 4A	298 DAYS
5	Determine which month of the year by subtracting from the monthly conversion table (TABLE VI-3).	298 DAYS – 272 (OCT) = 26 **OCT 26, 2026**

That is the only progressed event for Natal Jupiter. Moving on, Natal Saturn and Uranus do not yield any progressed events, but Natal Neptune experiences a trine with the Progressed Moon.

STEP #	DESCRIPTION	EQUATIONS/MATERIALS USED
1	Determine the event and which natal point will cause the event (Point C).	**EVENT:** Progressed Moon in Virgo trine Natal Neptune in Capricorn (p. ☽♍ △ n. ♆♑) **POINT C:** 6° ♍ 52′(Virgo Trine Point)
2	Write down the progressed point's location from Year to Year (Points A and B).	**POINT B:** p. ☽ 18° ♍ 0′ **POINT A:** p. ☽ 5° ♍ 21′
3	Set up the Transit Constant Equation and solve being mindful of converting when necessary.	$Transit\ Constant = \dfrac{(C-A)}{(B-A)} = \dfrac{(6°52' - 5°21')}{(18°0' - 5°21')}$ $= \dfrac{(6°52' - 5°21')}{(17°60' - 5°21')}$ $= \dfrac{91'}{759'} = 0.120$

STEP #	DESCRIPTION	EQUATIONS/MATERIALS USED
4A	Multiply the Transit Constant by 365 days to determine how many days have passed from the starting point.	0.120 x 365 days = 43.8 DAYS
4B	Round up the whole number found in Step 4A	44 DAYS
5	Determine which month of the year by subtracting from the monthly conversion table (TABLE VI-3).	44 DAYS – 30 (FEB) = 14 **FEB 14, 2026**

Now moving on to natal Pluto in Capricorn, the Progressed Moon once again makes an aspect (sextile).

STEP #	DESCRIPTION	EQUATIONS/MATERIALS USED
1	Determine the event and which natal point will cause the event (Point C).	**EVENT:** Progressed Moon in Virgo sextile Natal Pluto in Scorpio (p. ☽♍ ⚹ n. ♇♏) **POINT C:** 9° ♍ 57′ (Virgo sextile Point)
2	Write down the progressed point's location from Year to Year (Points A and B).	**POINT B:** p. ☽ 18° ♍ 0′ **POINT A:** p. ☽ 5° ♍ 21′
3	Set up the Transit Constant Equation and solve being mindful of converting when necessary.	$Transit\ Constant = \dfrac{(C-A)}{(B-A)} = \dfrac{(9°57'-5°21')}{(18°0'-5°21')}$ $= \dfrac{(9°57'-5°21')}{(17°60'-5°21')}$ $= \dfrac{276'}{759'} = 0.364$
4A	Multiply the Transit Constant by 365 days to determine how many days have passed from the starting point.	0.364 x 365 days = 132.9 DAYS
4B	Round up the whole number found in Step 4A	133 DAYS
5	Determine which month of the year by subtracting from the monthly conversion table (TABLE VI-3).	133 DAYS – 119 (MAY) = 14 **MAY 14, 2026**

471

Lastly, the Progressed Moon makes one more aspect to the Natal Midheaven.

STEP #	DESCRIPTION	EQUATIONS/MATERIALS USED
1	Determine the event and which natal point will cause the event (Point C).	**EVENT:** Progressed Moon in Virgo square Natal Midheaven in Gemini (p. ☽♍ □ n. MC♊) **POINT C:** 6° ♍ 56′(Virgo square Point)
2	Write down the progressed point's location from Year to Year (Points A and B).	**POINT B:** p. ☽ 18° ♍ 0′ **POINT A:** p. ☽ 5° ♍ 21′
3	Set up the Transit Constant Equation and solve being mindful of converting when necessary.	$$\text{Transit Constant} = \frac{(C-A)}{(B-A)} = \frac{(6°56′ - 5°21′)}{(18°0′ - 5°21′)}$$ $$= \frac{(6°56′ - 5°21′)}{(17°60′ - 5°21′)}$$ $$= \frac{95′}{759′} = 0.125$$
4A	Multiply the Transit Constant by 365 days to determine how many days have passed from the starting point.	0.125 x 365 days = 45.6 DAYS
4B	Round up the whole number found in Step 4A	46 DAYS
5	Determine which month of the year by subtracting from the monthly conversion table (TABLE VI-3).	46 DAYS – 30 (FEB) = 16 **FEB 16, 2026**

Finally, we can put in all of our information into one location to see the various progressed events for the year (TABLE VI-4).

Again, these events during the year will be felt just as heavily as an outer planetary transit. They likewise indicate major events and shifts of energy that are important to understand and identify. The next section will introduce a technique where progressed events can be analyzed similar to birth chart and transit chart interpretation in Part V.

TABLE VI-4. Summary of Progressed Events for 2026

PROGRESSED EVENT	GLYPH	DATE
Progressed Moon ingresses into the 1st House	p. ☽ → 1st	APR 17, 2026
Progressed Moon in Virgo conjoin Natal Ascendant in Virgo	p. ☽♍ ☌ n. Asc♍	APR 17, 2026
Progressed Venus in Aquarius conjoin Natal Sun in Aquarius	p. ♀♒ ☌ n. ☉♒	DEC 22, 2026
Progressed Sun in Pisces conjoin Natal Jupiter in Pisces	p. ☉♓ ☌ n. ♃♓	OCT 26, 2026
Progressed Moon in Virgo trine Natal Neptune in Capricorn	p. ☽♍ △ n. ♆♑	FEB 14, 2026
Progressed Moon in Virgo sextile Natal Pluto in Scorpio	p. ☽♍ ✶ n. ♇♏	MAY 14, 2026
Progressed Moon in Virgo square Natal Midheaven in Gemini	p. ☽♍ □ n. MC♊	FEB 16, 2026

473

SECTION 2-INTERPRETING PROGRESSIONS WITH CASE STUDIES

Just as we have been analyzing various charts within astrology step by step and determining important events and energies, it is now time to do the same with the progressed chart. Once again, we will analyze each of the client's progressed charts for the year of their reading (2021), and I once again encourage you to attempt to fill out the steps yourself first, and then compare your answers to mine. The table below plans out the various steps required to properly analyze a progressed chart along with a blank reference sheet if you want to fill out on your own (TABLE VI-7A-B). Notice that when I calculate when the dates will occur, the math will not be shown for the sake of efficiency.

TABLE VI-7A. Steps on how to Comprehensively Analyze a Progressed Chart

STEP #	SECTION IN BOOK	DESCRIPTION	INFORMATION IT PROVIDES
1	VI-1	Obtain the progressed chart for Jan 1 of Year X and Jan 1 of Year Y	Preliminary data for the year you want to observe.
2	VI-1	Determine the moon phase for that year.	The person's overall energy level and whether this is a time for expansion or recuperation.
3A	VI-1	Determine progressed planetary and cardinal points house and zodiac locations for Jan 1 of Year X.	This will be your Point A when it comes to determining progressed events.
3B	VI-1	Repeat the process but determine the information for Jan 1 of the following year (Year Y).	This will be your Point B when it comes to determining progressed events.

STEP #	SECTION IN BOOK	DESCRIPTION	INFORMATION IT PROVIDES
4A	VI-1	Compare the data range from steps 3A-3B and determine if any of the progressed planets, Asc, or Dc ingress or regress into a house.	Indicates a progressed event.
4B	VI-1	Compare the data range from steps 3A-3B and determine if any of the progressed planets, Ascendant or Descendant makes an aspect to a fixed Natal point.	Indicates a progressed event.
5A	VI-1	Take the data from steps 4A-4B and calculate when they will occur.	Exact moment of event.
5B		Put the events into chronological order.	Determines if the events occur simultaneously.
6	IV-4	Create transit formulas for every event listed in step 4B.	Various realms within the person's life that will be influenced by events.
7		Compose a summary of your findings from steps 2, 5, & 6	Summary of Analysis.

TABLE VI-7B. Blank Progressed Point Reference Sheet

PLANET/CARDINAL POINT	YEAR X HOUSE	YEAR X ZODIAC	NATAL POINT	YEAR Y ZODIAC	YEAR Y HOUSE
☉					
☽					
☿					
♀					
♂					
♃					
♄					
♅					
♆					
♇					
ASC					
MC					

1	VI-1	Obtain the progressed chart for Jan 1 of Year X and Jan 1 of Year Y	Preliminary data for the year you want to observe.

CLIENT A: PROGRESSED CHART YEAR X (2021)

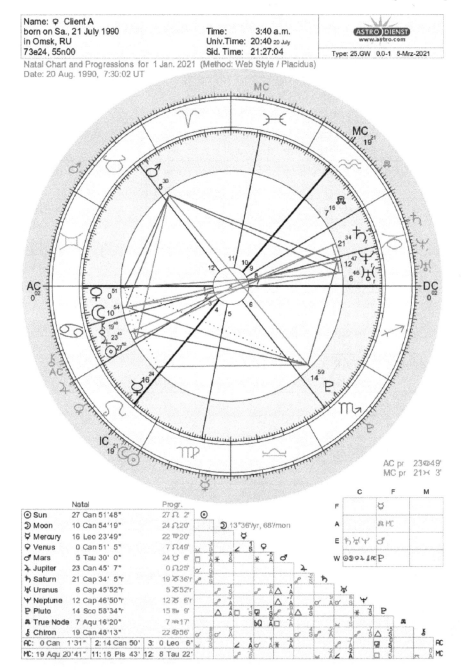

Name: ♀ Client A
born on Sa., 21 July 1990
in Omsk, RU
73e24, 55n00

Time: 3:40 a.m.
Univ.Time: 20:40 20 July
Sid. Time: 21:27:04

ASTRO DIENST
www.astro.com
Type: 25.GW 0.0-1 5-Mrz-2021

Natal Chart and Progressions for 1 Jan. 2021 (Method: Web Style / Placidus)
Date: 20 Aug. 1990, 7:30:02 UT

AC pr 23♋49'
MC pr 21♓ 3'

	Natal	Progr.
☉ Sun	27 Can 51'48"	27 ♌ 2'
☽ Moon	10 Can 54'19"	24 ♌20'
☿ Mercury	16 Leo 23'49"	22 ♍20'
♀ Venus	0 Can 51' 5"	7 ♌49'
♂ Mars	5 Tau 30' 0"	24 ♉ 6'
♃ Jupiter	23 Can 45' 7"	0 ♌25'
♄ Saturn	21 Cap 34' 5"r	19 ♑36'r
♅ Uranus	6 Cap 45'52"r	5 ♑52'r
♆ Neptune	12 Cap 46'50"r	12 ♑ 6'r
♇ Pluto	14 Sco 58'34"r	15 ♏ 9'
☊ True Node	7 Aqu 16'20"	7 ♒17'
⚷ Chiron	19 Can 48'13"	22 ♋56'
AC: 0 Can 1'31"	2: 14 Can 50'	3: 0 Leo 6'
MC: 19 Aqu 20'41"	11: 18 Pis 43'	12: 8 Tau 22'

☽ 13°36'/yr, 68'/mon

CLIENT A: PROGRESSED CHART YEAR Y (2022)

Name: ♀ Client A	Time: 3:40 a.m.	**ASTRO DIENST**
born on Sa., 21 July 1990	Univ.Time: 20:40 20 July	www.astro.com
in Omsk, RU	Sid. Time: 21:27:04	
73e24, 55n00		Type: 25.GW 0.0-1 5-Mrz-2021

Natal Chart and Progressions for 1 Jan. 2022 (Method: Web Style / Placidus)
Date: 21 Aug. 1990, 7:29:04 UT

AC pr 24♋31'
MC pr 22♓ 7'

	Natal	Progr.		C	F	M
⊙ Sun	27 Can 51'48"	28 ♌ 0' ⊙		F		☿	
☽ Moon	10 Can 54'19"	7 ♍47' ☽ 13°19'/yr, 67'/mon	A		♏ MC	
☿ Mercury	16 Leo 23'49"	22 ♍45' ☿	E	♄♅♀	♂	
♀ Venus	0 Can 51' 5"	9 ♌ 2'	W	⊙☽☿♃♂♀ ♇	
♂ Mars	5 Tau 30' 0"	24 ♉40'			
♃ Jupiter	23 Can 45' 7"	0 ♌35'			
♄ Saturn	21 Cap 34' 5"r	19 ♑33'r			
♅ Uranus	6 Cap 45'52"r	5 ♑51'r			
♆ Neptune	12 Cap 46'50"r	12 ♑ 5'r			
♇ Pluto	14 Sco 58'34"r	15 ♏10'			
☊ True Node	7 Aqu 16'20"	7 ♒15'			
⚷ Chiron	19 Can 48'13"	23 ♋ 2'			
AC: 0 Can 1'31"	2: 14 Can 50'	3: 0 Leo 6'			
MC: 19 Aqu 20'41"	11: 18 Pis 43'	12: 8 Tau 22'			

2	VI-1	Determine the moon phase for that year.	The person's overall energy level and whether this is a time for expansion or recuperation.

Client A is experiencing a progressed new moon phase during 2021 which is highly significant. This means that they are beginning the start of a new 29-year cycle where whatever projects they start now will act as the primary themes for the next 29 years of their life. Until that time, I would recommend that they take it easy, save their energy, and take stock of what they have in preparation for their new launching platform that they will have once this new moon phase occurs.

3A	VI-1	Determine progressed planetary and cardinal points house and zodiac locations for Jan 1 of Year X.	This will be your Point A when it comes to determining progressed events.
3B	VI-1	Repeat the process but determine the information for Jan 1 of the following year (Year Y).	This will be your Point B when it comes to determining progressed events.

PLANET/CARDINAL POINT	YEAR X HOUSE	YEAR X ZODIAC	NATAL POINT	YEAR Y ZODIAC	YEAR Y HOUSE
☉	4	27° ♌ 2′	27° ♋ 51′	28° ♌ 0′	4
☽	4	24° ♌ 20′	10° ♋ 54′	7° ♍ 47′	4
☿	5	22° ♍ 20′	16° ♌ 23′	22° ♍ 45′	5
♀	3	7° ♌ 49′	0° ♋ 51′	9° ♌ 2′	3
♂	12	24° ♉ 6′	5° ♉ 30′	24° ♉ 40′	12
♃	3	0° ♌ 25′	23° ♋ 45′	0° ♌ 38′	3
♄	8	19° ♑ 36′	21° ♑ 34′	19° ♑ 33′	8
♅	7	5° ♑ 52′	6° ♑ 45′	5° ♑ 51′	7
♆	7	12° ♑ 6′	12° ♑ 46′	12° ♑ 5′	7
♇	6	15° ♏ 9′	14° ♏ 58′	15° ♏ 10′	6
ASC	2	23° ♋ 49′	0° ♋ 1′	24° ♋ 31′	2
MC	11	21° ♓ 3′	19° ♒ 20′	22° ♓ 7′	11

4A	VI-1	Compare the data range from steps 3A-3B and determine if any of the progressed planets, Asc, or Dc ingress or regress into a house.	Indicates a progressed event.
		NONE	

4B	VI-1	Compare the data range from steps 3A-3B and determine if any of the progressed planets, Ascendant or Descendant makes an aspect to a fixed Natal point.	Indicates a progressed event.

NATAL ☉	
EVENT	GLYPH
NONE	

NATAL ☽	
EVENT	GLYPH
NONE	

NATAL ☿	
EVENT	GLYPH
NONE	

NATAL ♀	
EVENT	GLYPH
Progressed Moon in Virgo sextile Natal Venus in Cancer	p.☽♍ ⚹ n.♀♋

NATAL ♂	
EVENT	GLYPH
Progressed Moon in Virgo trine Natal Mars in Taurus	p.☽♍ △ n.♂♉

NATAL ♃	
EVENT	GLYPH
NONE	

NATAL ♄	
EVENT	GLYPH
Progressed Midheaven in Pisces sextile Natal Saturn in Capricorn	p.MC♓ ⚹ n.♄♑

NATAL ♅	
EVENT	GLYPH
Progressed Moon in Virgo trine Natal Uranus in Capricorn	p.☽♍ △ n.♅♑

NATAL ♆	
EVENT	GLYPH
NONE	

NATAL ♇	
EVENT	GLYPH
NONE	

NATAL ASCENDANT	
EVENT	GLYPH
Progressed Moon in Virgo sextile Natal Cancer Ascendant	p.☽♍ ✶ n.ASC♋
NATAL DESCENDANT	
EVENT	GLYPH
NONE	

5A	VI-1	Take the data from steps 4A-4B and calculate when they will occur.	Exact moment of event.	
5B		Put the events into chronological order.	Determines if the events occur simultaneously.	

EVENT	GLYPH	DATE
Progressed Moon in Virgo sextile Natal Venus in Cancer	p.☽♍ ✶ n.♀♋	JUN 27
Progressed Moon in Virgo trine Natal Mars in Taurus	p.☽♍ △ n.♂♉	NOV 1
Progressed Midheaven in Pisces sextile Natal Saturn in Capricorn	p.MC♓ ✶ n.♄♑	NOV 29
Progressed Moon in Virgo trine Natal Uranus in Capricorn	p.☽♍ △ n.♅♑	DEC 3
Progressed Moon in Virgo sextile Natal Cancer Ascendant	p.☽♍ ✶ n.ASC♋	JUN 4

2021

JAN		FEB		MAR		APR	
EVENT	DAY	EVENT	DAY	EVENT	DAY	EVENT	DAY

MAY		JUN		JUL		AUG	
EVENT	DAY	EVENT	DAY	EVENT	DAY	EVENT	DAY
		p.☽♍ ✶ n.ASC♋ p.☽♍ ✶ n.♀♋	4 27				

SEP		OCT		NOV		DEC	
EVENT	DAY	EVENT	DAY	EVENT	DAY	EVENT	DAY
				p.☽♍ △ n.♂♉ p.MC♓ ✶ n.♄♑	1 29	p.☽♍ △ n.♅♑	3

6	IV-4	Create transit formulas for every event listed in step 4B.	Various realms within the person's life that will be influenced by events.

EVENT	FORMULA
p.☽♍ ✶ n.♀♋	p.☽♍ in 4th (R. 1st, 2nd, & 3rd) ✶ n.♀♋ in 1st (R. 12th)

p.☽♍ △ n.♂♉	p.☽♍ in 4th (R. 1st, 2nd, & 3rd) △ n.♂♉ in 11th (R. 6th)
p.MC♓ ✶ n.♄♑	p.MC♓ ✶ n.♄♑ in 8th (R. 8th, 9th, & 10th)
p.☽♍ △ n.♅♑	p.☽♍ in 4th (R. 1st, 2nd, & 3rd) △ n.♅♑ in 7th (R. 9th & 10th)
p.☽♍ ✶ n.ASC♋	p.☽♍ in 4th (R. 1st, 2nd, & 3rd) ✶ n.ASC♋

7		Compose a summary of your findings from steps 2, 5, & 6	Summary of Analysis.

If you recall from our discussion in Part V-Section 3 with regards to transits, you will come across redundancy with certain data. Again, this shows that when different astrological events allude to the same conclusion, this only strengthens your analysis because these various and unique events are all pointing to the same outcome. Similarly, when you begin to compare progression events to transit events, you will once again come across different sources of information that tell the same story only from a different angle.

Looking back at the transit analysis for Client A, the key theme I continue to bring up is "reinvention." The progressed chart confirms this again in different ways. For one, the progressed new moon phase is an ultimate astrological marker for a new beginning after experiencing a 29-year cycle of events. As such, Client A has the ability to truly step forward onto a new path in life taking the wisdom that they have gathered and leave the unneeded personality traits that no longer serve them behind. The progressed new moon gives the individual a sense of autonomy and self-assurance that they may have been lacking prior to the event.

Similarly, with the progressed Moon's trine to natal Uranus and Mars (p.☽♍ △ n.♅♑, p.☽♍ △ n.♂♉), this gives Client A the courage and open mind to shed their old skin and work on a new persona based upon new perspectives and ideologies due to the 6th and 9th houses. In turn, their social groups and close relationships change and evolve at the same time due to the 7th and 11th houses being involved. Furthermore, with Uranus ruling the 10th house, this could also translate over to their career by either deciding to work in more progressive minded fields or by bringing fresh ideas into their current career. This is also due to the progressed Midheaven's sextile to natal Saturn (p.MC♓ ✶ n.♄♑) which helps in these endeavors if Client A takes the appropriate risks. The good news is, due to the progressed Moon's trine to natal Mars, finding the strength to take chances will come more readily than at other times.

481

The progressed Moon also establishes sextiles to natal Venus and the Ascendant (p.☽♍ ✶ n.♀♌, p.☽♍ ✶ n.ASC♌). With natal Venus residing in the 1st house and the Ascendant being the 1st house cusp, this all ties back to Client A's moment of personal reinvention. Additionally, just as these new attitudes and persona begins to bloom, so will their romantic encounters. Or, Client A will simply find it easier to get along with others as other people do not see them as a threat but as a gentle presence.

Overall, Client A has tremendously beneficial progressions during 2021 and should make the most out of the situation. This echoes Client A's transit analysis as their auspicious months occur within the same year (2021). Both of these outcomes indicate a very buoyant and beneficial year that paves the way for Client A for the next 29 years.

CLIENT B: PROGRESSED CHART YEAR X (2021)

Name: ♀ Client B
born on Su., 4 April 1993
in Greenville (Mercer County), PA (US)
80w23, 41n24

Time: 12:14 p.m.
Univ.Time: 16:14
Sid. Time: 23:44:25

ASTRO DIENST
www.astro.com

Type: 25.GW 0.0-1 6-Mrz-2021

Natal Chart and Progressions for 1 Jan. 2021 (Method: Web Style / Placidus)
Date: 2 May 1993, 10:05:32 UT

AC pr   7♌58'
MC pr 25♈18'

	Natal	Progr.
☉ Sun	14 Ari 54' 8"	12 ♉ 1'
☽ Moon	15 Vir 1'45"	20 ♍38'
☿ Mercury	17 Pis 10'39"	27 ♈11'
♀ Venus	9 Ari 52'10"r	5 ♉30'
♂ Mars	19 Can 48' 3"	2 ♌ 8'
♃ Jupiter	9 Lib 7'58"r	6 ♎ 3'r
♄ Saturn	26 Aqu 57'12"	29 ♒ 7'
♅ Uranus	21 Cap 59'32"	22 ♑11'r
♆ Neptune	21 Cap 3'38"	21 ♑ 6'r
♇ Pluto	25 Sco 8'42"r	24 ♏29'
☊ True Node	14 Sag 1'15"	12 ♐32'
⚷ Chiron	17 Leo 19'14"r	17 ♌24'
AC: 16 Can 7'19"	2: 5 Leo 28'	3: 27 Leo 37'
MC: 25 Pis 45'25"	11: 1 Tau 55'	12: 11 Gem 41'

☽ 14°41'/yr, 73'/mon

	C	F	M
F	☉♀	⚷	☊
A	♃	♄	
E	♅♆		☽
W	♂AC	♇	☿MC

CLIENT B: PROGRESSED CHART YEAR Y (2022)

Name: ♀ Client B
born on Su., 4 April 1993
in Greenville (Mercer County), PA (US)
80w23, 41n24

Time: 12:14 p.m.
Univ.Time: 16:14
Sid. Time: 23:44:25

ASTRO DIENST
www.astro.com
Type: 25.GW 0.0-1 6-Mrz-2021

Natal Chart and Progressions for 1 Jan. 2022 (Method: Web Style / Placidus)
Date: 3 May 1993, 10:04:35 UT

AC pr   8♌44'
MC pr 26♈21'

	Natal	Progr.
☉ Sun	14 Ari 54' 8"	12 ♉ 59'
☽ Moon	15 Vir 1'45"	5 ♎ 23'
☿ Mercury	17 Pis 10'39"	29 ♈ 4'
♀ Venus	9 Ari 52'10"r	5 ♈ 52'
♂ Mars	19 Can 48' 3"	2 ♌ 37'
♃ Jupiter	9 Lib 7'58"r	5 ♏ 58'r
♄ Saturn	26 Aqu 57'12"	29 ♒ 11'
♅ Uranus	21 Cap 59'32"	22 ♑ 10'r
♆ Neptune	21 Cap 3'38"	21 ♑ 7'r
♇ Pluto	25 Sco 8'42"r	24 ♏ 28'r
☊ True Node	14 Sag 1'15"	12 ♐ 28'
⚷ Chiron	17 Leo 19'14"r	17 ♌ 26'
AC: 16 Can 7'19"	2: 5 Leo 28'	3: 27 Leo 37'
MC: 25 Pis 45'25"	11: 1 Tau 55'	12: 11 Gem 41'

484

2	VI-1	Determine the moon phase for that year.	The person's overall energy level and whether this is a time for expansion or recuperation.

Client B is in a developing progressed moon phase that is about to reach the full moon in a few years from now. I would therefore recommend that Client B continue in investing time and energy into their personal projects and goals because they have the energy to back up whatever they are trying to accomplish. Furthermore, they should expect to witness the culmination of these efforts in a few years from now.

3A	VI-1	Determine progressed planetary and cardinal points house and zodiac locations for Jan 1 of Year X.	This will be your Point A when it comes to determining progressed events.
3B	VI-1	Repeat the process but determine the information for Jan 1 of the following year (Year Y).	This will be your Point B when it comes to determining progressed events.

PLANET/CARDINAL POINT	YEAR X HOUSE	YEAR X ZODIAC	NATAL POINT	YEAR Y ZODIAC	YEAR Y HOUSE
☉	11	12° ♉ 1'	14° ♈ 54'	12° ♉ 59'	11
☽	3	20° ♍ 38'	15° ♍ 1'	5° ♎ 23'	4
☿	10	27° ♈ 11'	17° ♓ 10'	29° ♈ 4'	10
♀	10	5° ♈ 30'	9° ♈ 52'	5° ♈ 52'	10
♂	1	2° ♌ 8'	19° ♋ 48'	2° ♌ 37'	1
♃	4	6° ♎ 3'	9° ♎ 7'	5° ♎ 58'	4
♄	9	29° ♒ 7'	26° ♒ 57'	29° ♒ 11'	9
♅	7	22° ♑ 11'	21° ♑ 59'	22° ♑ 10'	7
♆	7	21° ♑ 8'	21° ♑ 3'	21° ♑ 7'	7
♇	5	24° ♏ 29'	25° ♏ 8'	24° ♏ 28'	5
ASC	2	7° ♌ 58'	16° ♋ 7'	8° ♌ 44'	2
MC	10	25° ♈ 18'	25° ♈ 45'	26° ♈ 21'	10

4A	VI-1	Compare the data range from steps 3A-3B and determine if any of the progressed planets, Asc, or Dc ingress or regress into a house.	Indicates a progressed event.

EVENT		GLYPH
Progressed Moon ingresses into the 4th House		p. ☽ → 4th

4B	VI-1	Compare the data range from steps 3A-3B and determine if any of the progressed planets, Ascendant or Descendant makes an aspect to a fixed Natal point.	Indicates a progressed event.
NATAL ☉			
	EVENT		GLYPH
	NONE		
NATAL ☽			
	EVENT		GLYPH
	NONE		
NATAL ☿			
	EVENT		GLYPH
	NONE		
NATAL ♀			
	EVENT		GLYPH
	NONE		
NATAL ♂			
	EVENT		GLYPH
	NONE		
NATAL ♃			
	EVENT		GLYPH
	NONE		
NATAL ♄			
	EVENT		GLYPH
	NONE		
NATAL ♅			
	EVENT		GLYPH
	Progressed Moon in Virgo trine Natal Uranus in Capricorn		p.☽♍ △ n.♅♑
NATAL ♆			
	EVENT		GLYPH
	Progressed Moon in Virgo trine Natal Uranus in Capricorn		p.☽♍ △ n.♆♑
NATAL ♇			
	EVENT		GLYPH
	Progressed Moon in Virgo sextile Natal Pluto in Scorpio		p.☽♍ ✳ n.♇♏

486

NATAL ASCENDANT	
EVENT	GLYPH
NONE	
NATAL DESCENDANT	
EVENT	GLYPH
Progressed Moon in Virgo oppose Pisces Midheaven	p.☽♍ ☍ n.MC♓

5A	VI-1	Take the data from steps 4A-4B and calculate when they will occur.	Exact moment of event.	
5B		Put the events into chronological order.	Determines if the events occur simultaneously.	
EVENT			**GLYPH**	**DATE**
Progressed Moon ingresses into the 4th House			p. ☽ → 4th	MAY 7
Progressed Moon in Virgo trine Natal Uranus in Capricorn			p.☽♍ △ n.♅♑	FEB 3
Progressed Moon in Virgo trine Natal Uranus in Capricorn			p.☽♍ △ n.♆♑	JAN 10
Progressed Moon in Virgo sextile Natal Pluto in Scorpio			p.☽♍ ✶ n.♇♏	MAY 8
Progressed Moon in Virgo oppose Pisces Midheaven			p.☽♍ ☍ n.MC♓	MAY 7

2021

JAN		FEB		MAR		APR	
EVENT	DAY	EVENT	DAY	EVENT	DAY	EVENT	DAY
p.☽♍ △ n.♆♑	10	p.☽♍ △ n.♅♑	3				

MAY		JUN		JUL		AUG	
EVENT	DAY	EVENT	DAY	EVENT	DAY	EVENT	DAY
p. ☽ → 4th p.☽♍ ☍ n.MC♓ p.☽♍ ✶ n.♇♏	7 7 8						

SEP		OCT		NOV		DEC	
EVENT	DAY	EVENT	DAY	EVENT	DAY	EVENT	DAY

6	IV-4	Create transit formulas for every event listed in step 4B.	Various realms within the person's life that will be influenced by events.
EVENT		**FORMULA**	
p.☽♍ △ n.♅♑		p.☽♍ in 3rd (R. 1st) △ n.♅♑ in 7th (R. 8th & 9th)	
p.☽♍ △ n.♆♑		p.☽♍ in 3rd (R. 1st) △ n.♆♑ in 7th (R. 10th)	

6	IV-4	Create transit formulas for every event listed in step 4B.	Various realms within the person's life that will be influenced by events.
p.☽♍ ✶ n.♇♏		p.☽♍ in 3rd (R. 1st) ✶ n.♇♏ in 5th (R. 5th)	
p.☽♍ ☍ n.MC♓		p.☽♍ in 3rd (R. 1st) ☍ n.MC♓	

7		Compose a summary of your findings from steps 2, 5, & 6	Summary of Analysis.

Looking back at the transit analysis of Client B, it appears that this time in their life involves identifying and overcoming personal insecurities and determining where they stem from through unconscious motivations. In fact, the exact words that were used were "[observe how] childhood experiences attribute to present day outlook." These themes are confirmed by the progressed Moon ingressing into the 4th house. From this ingress, Client B can now focus on home and family matters and will be doing so for the next two years approximately. The good news is that these introspective and investigative endeavors are somewhat easy to handle due to the beneficial transits to their natal Pluto and other natal planets. The same can be said for their progressed events, which help Client B to come to these necessary realizations.

It should be noted that each progressed event involves the outer planets Uranus, Neptune, and Pluto (p.☽♍ △ n.♅♑, p.☽♍ △ n.♆♑, p.☽♍ ✶ n.♇♏). Recall, when it comes to planetary transits, when a transiting planet aspects a natal outer planet such as these, an entire generation of individuals also experiences those transits. This is because people born years before and after the individual in question most likely have the same natal outer planet located at the same point along the zodiac due to their slow movement. However, when it comes to progressions, this is not necessarily the case because progressed planetary locations along the zodiac are solely determined by the birth data of the individual. For example, if an individual was born 10 days after Client B, that means their progressed moon is 10 years off from that of Client B. This makes progressed events, even those that involve outer natal planets, just as individualized and personal, as if it were a progressed event with a natal inner planet.

For Client B, the progressed Moon events to their natal Uranus, Neptune, and Pluto involve sextiles and trines which greatly aid in their search of self-discovery during this time. With the 8th and 5th houses involved, Client D will be able to dig deep into their unconsciousness and

488

weed out their childhood patterns of behavior. Similarly, with the 7th house, they will be able to discuss these personal matters with those involved, their romantic partners, close friends, or with a psychologist. In fact, psychological counseling would do Client B a great service at this time as they can act as a good objective observer for Client B to work through their personal issues.

The sextile to natal Pluto allows for Client B to not only get to the bottom of the situation, but to also reveal their innermost feelings with others. The trine to Neptune helps Client B to release any ego tensions that have prevented them from having these experiences in the past. Consequently, Client B receives substantial healing energies at this time. Lastly, with a trine to natal Uranus, Client B will be able to break free out of their mold effortlessly with an excitement for what the future holds. I would therefore conclude that, similar to Client A, Client B has incredibly beneficial progressions during 2021 and should therefore make the most out of these events. Once their progressed moon phase reaches the full moon in a few years from now, all of the work put in today will reach its fullest expression.

CLIENT C: PROGRESSED CHART YEAR X (2021)

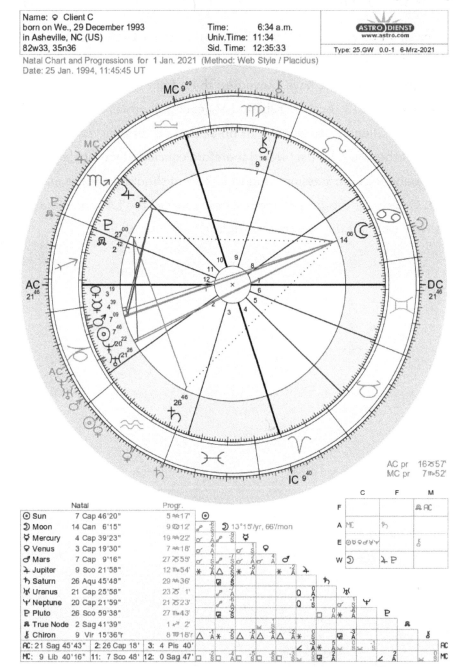

Name: ♀ Client C
born on We., 29 December 1993
in Asheville, NC (US)
82w33, 35n36

Time: 6:34 a.m.
Univ.Time: 11:34
Sid. Time: 12:35:33

ASTRO)DIENST
www.astro.com

Type: 25.GW 0.0-1 6-Mrz-2021

Natal Chart and Progressions for 1 Jan. 2021 (Method: Web Style / Placidus)
Date: 25 Jan. 1994, 11:45:45 UT

AC pr 16♒57'
MC pr 7♏52'

	Natal	Progr.
☉ Sun	7 Cap 46'20"	5 ♒17'
☽ Moon	14 Can 6'15"	9 ♋12' 13°15'/yr, 66'/mon
☿ Mercury	4 Cap 39'23"	19 ♒22'
♀ Venus	3 Cap 19'30"	7 ♒18'
♂ Mars	7 Cap 9'16"	27 ♑55'
♃ Jupiter	9 Sco 21'58"	12 ♏54'
♄ Saturn	26 Aqu 45'48"	29 ♒36'
♅ Uranus	21 Cap 25'58"	23 ♑1'
♆ Neptune	20 Cap 21'59"	21 ♑23'
♇ Pluto	26 Sco 59'38"	27 ♏43'
☊ True Node	2 Sag 41'39"	1 ♐2'
⚷ Chiron	9 Vir 15'36"r	8 ♍18'r
AC: 21 Sag 45'43"	2: 26 Cap 18'	3: 4 Pis 40'
MC: 9 Lib 40'16"	11: 7 Sco 48'	12: 0 Sag 47'

CLIENT C: PROGRESSED CHART YEAR Y (2022)

Name: ♀ Client C
born on We., 29 December 1993
in Asheville, NC (US)
82w33, 35n36

Time: 6:34 a.m.
Univ.Time: 11:34
Sid. Time: 12:35:33

ASTRO·DIENST
www.astro.com

Type: 25.GW 0.0-1 6-Mrz-2021

Natal Chart and Progressions for 1 Jan. 2022 (Method: Web Style / Placidus)
Date: 26 Jan. 1994, 11:44:47 UT

AC pr 17♑59'
MC pr 8♏53'

	Natal	Progr.
☉ Sun	7 Cap 46'20"	6 ♒18'
☽ Moon	14 Can 6'15"	22 ♋38'
☿ Mercury	4 Cap 39'23"	21 ♒ 0'
♀ Venus	3 Cap 19'30"	8 ♒33'
♂ Mars	7 Cap 9'16"	28 ♑42'
♃ Jupiter	9 Sco 21'58"	13 ♏ 0'
♄ Saturn	26 Aqu 45'48"	29 ♒43'
♅ Uranus	21 Cap 25'58"	23 ♑ 5'
♆ Neptune	20 Cap 21'59"	21 ♑25'
♇ Pluto	26 Sco 59'38"	27 ♏44'
☊ True Node	2 Sag 41'39"	0 ♐54'
⚷ Chiron	9 Vir 15'36"r	8 ♍15'r
AC: 21 Sag 45'43"	2: 26 Cap 18'	3: 4 Pis 40'
MC: 9 Lib 40'16"	11: 7 Sco 48'	12: 0 Sag 47'

☽ 13°37'/yr, 68'/mon

2	VI-1	Determine the moon phase for that year.	The person's overall energy level and whether this is a time for expansion or recuperation.

Similar to Client B, Client C is in a developing progressed moon phase that is about to reach the full moon in a matter of years. I would therefore recommend Client C to continue investing time and energy into their personal projects and goals because they have the energy to back up whatever it is they are trying to accomplish. Furthermore, they should expect to witness the culmination of these efforts in a few years from now.

3A	VI-1	Determine progressed planetary and cardinal points house and zodiac locations for Jan 1 of Year X.	This will be your Point A when it comes to determining progressed events.
3B	VI-1	Repeat the process but determine the information for Jan 1 of the following year (Year Y).	This will be your Point B when it comes to determining progressed events.

PLANET/CARDINAL POINT	YEAR X HOUSE	YEAR X ZODIAC	NATAL POINT	YEAR Y ZODIAC	YEAR Y HOUSE
☉	2	5° ♒ 17'	7° ♑ 46'	6° ♒ 18'	2
☽	7	9° ♋ 12'	14° ♋ 6'	22° ♋ 38'	7
☿	2	19° ♒ 22'	4° ♑ 39'	21° ♒ 0'	2
♀	2	7° ♒ 18'	3° ♑ 19'	8° ♒ 33'	2
♂	2	27° ♑ 55'	7° ♑ 9'	28° ♑ 42'	2
♃	11	12° ♏ 54'	9° ♏ 21'	13° ♏ 0'	11
♄	2	29° ♒ 36'	26° ♒ 45'	29° ♒ 43'	2
♅	1	23° ♑ 1'	21° ♑ 25'	23° ♑ 5'	1
♆	1	21° ♑ 23'	20° ♑ 21'	21° ♑ 25'	1
♇	11	27° ♏ 43'	26° ♏ 59'	27° ♏ 44'	11
ASC	1	16° ♑ 57'	21° ♐ 45'	17° ♑ 59'	1
MC	11	7° ♏ 52'	9° ♎ 40'	8° ♏ 53'	11

4A	VI-1	Compare the data range from steps 3A-3B and determine if any of the progressed planets, Asc, or DC ingress or regress into a house.	Indicates a progressed event.
		NONE	

4B	VI-1	Compare the data range from steps 3A-3B and determine if any of the progressed planets, Ascendant or Descendant makes an aspect to a fixed Natal point.	Indicates a progressed event.

NATAL ☉	
EVENT	GLYPH
NONE	

NATAL ☽	
EVENT	GLYPH
Progressed Moon in Cancer conjoin Natal Moon in Cancer	p.☽♋ ☌ n.☽♋
NONE	

NATAL ☿	
EVENT	GLYPH
NONE	

NATAL ♀	
EVENT	GLYPH
NONE	

NATAL ♂	
EVENT	GLYPH
NONE	

NATAL ♃	
EVENT	GLYPH
Progressed Moon in Cancer trine Natal Jupiter in Scorpio	p.☽♋ △ n.♃♏

NATAL ♄	
EVENT	GLYPH
NONE	

NATAL ♅	
EVENT	GLYPH
Progressed Moon in Cancer oppose Natal Uranus in Capricorn	p.☽♋ ☍ n.♅♑
Progressed Neptune in Capricorn conjoin Natal Uranus in Capricorn	p.♆♑ ☌ n.♅♑

NATAL ♆	
EVENT	GLYPH
Progressed Moon in Cancer oppose Natal Neptune in Capricorn	p.☽♋ ☍ n.♆♑

NATAL ♇	
EVENT	**GLYPH**
NONE	
NATAL ASCENDANT	
EVENT	**GLYPH**
NONE	
NATAL DESCENDANT	
EVENT	**GLYPH**
NONE	

5A	VI-1	Take the data from steps 4A-4B and calculate when they will occur.	Exact moment of event.
5B		Put the events into chronological order.	Determines if the events occur simultaneously.

EVENT	GLYPH	DATE
Progressed Moon in Cancer conjoin Natal Moon in Cancer	p.☽♋ ☌ n.☽♋	MAY 14
Progressed Moon in Cancer trine Natal Jupiter in Scorpio	p.☽♋ △ n.♃♏	JAN 4
Progressed Moon in Cancer oppose Natal Uranus in Capricorn	p.☽♋ ☍ n.♅♑	NOV 28
Progressed Neptune in Capricorn conjoin Natal Uranus in Capricorn	p.♆♑ ☌ n.♅♑	DEC 31
Progressed Moon in Cancer oppose Natal Neptune in Capricorn	p.☽♋ ☍ n.♆♑	OCT 30

2021							
JAN		**FEB**		**MAR**		**APR**	
EVENT	**DAY**	**EVENT**	**DAY**	**EVENT**	**DAY**	**EVENT**	**DAY**
p.☽♋ △ n.♃♏	4						
MAY		**JUN**		**JUL**		**AUG**	
EVENT	**DAY**	**EVENT**	**DAY**	**EVENT**	**DAY**	**EVENT**	**DAY**
p.☽♋ ☌ n.☽♋	14						
SEP		**OCT**		**NOV**		**DEC**	
EVENT	**DAY**	**EVENT**	**DAY**	**EVENT**	**DAY**	**EVENT**	**DAY**
		p.☽♋ ☍ n.♆♑	30	p.☽♋ ☍ n.♅♑	28	p.♆♑ ☌ n.♅♑	31

6	IV-4	Create transit formulas for every event listed in step 4B.	Various realms within the person's life that will be influenced by events.
EVENT		**FORMULA**	
p.☽℗ ♂ n.☽d		p.☽℗ in 7th (R. 8TH) ♂ n.☽℗ in 7th (R. 8TH)	
p.☽℗ △ n.♃♏		p.☽℗ in 7th (R. 8TH) △ n.♃♏ in 11th (R. 1st & 3rd)	
p.☽℗ ☍ n.♅♑		p.☽℗ in 7th (R. 8TH) ☍ n.♅♑ in 1st (R. Nothing)	
p.♆♑ ♂ n.♅♑		p.♆♑ in 1st (R. 3rd) ♂ n.♅♑ in 1st (R. Nothing)	
p.☽℗ ☍ n.♆♑		p.☽℗ in 7th (R. 8TH) ☍ n.♆♑ in 1st (R. 3rd)	

7		Compose a summary of your findings from steps 2, 5, & 6	Summary of Analysis.

Client C is very close to approaching the progressed full moon phase which they will experience around 2022. At this time, the life experiences and developments of the past 14 years reaches its climax, which Client C will begin to slowly integrate into some form of permanence for the next 14 years as the progressed moon phase begins to disseminate. This is also confirmed by the two oppositions the progressed Moon makes to natal Uranus and Neptune (p.☽℗ ☍ n.♅♑, p.☽℗ ☍ n.♆♑) which also involve some sort of reaching a climactic endpoint in their lives. The problem is for Client C, it might not be the end goal they have wanted.

Referring back to Client C's transits, they are having to deal with limited resources and finances due to multiple outer planetary ingresses to their 2nd house. Furthermore, with transiting Neptune squaring their natal Ascendant, this brings about moments of low self-esteem and self-confidence. With all of this occurring at the same time of culmination within the progressed chart, it can have Client C think to themself, "I've worked so hard at this and this is all I have to show for my efforts?"

The good news is that some of their progressed events help to counter these more negative viewpoints and mindsets. For one, with the progressed Moon trine natal Jupiter (p.☽℗ △ n.♃♏) this helps to dilute the Jupiter issues seen within their transit events. With the 11th house involved, Client C should heavily rely on their friends at this time for comfort and support. Furthermore, with the progressed Moon conjoin natal Moon (p.☽℗ ♂ n.☽℗) Client C is starting to rely on their close partnerships and counseling as well, which helps them to get back on their feet because the 7th and 8th houses are involved.

Essentially, Client C is starting to experience the natural feelings and circumstances that surround the first Saturn return. They are having to pick themselves up and dust themselves off by not worrying about any previous failures they might have recently encountered. The progressed and transit events indicate that Client C is starting to learn about what really matters in life: close connections with people who love them unconditionally, and that all other forms of success are not real indicators of one's true value. It is a hard lesson to learn, but truly helps in the evolution of the soul.

I would advise Client C to take it easy during this time and to discover what drives them and to make sure that their drives and goals are realistic and are not a requirement for their self-esteem. If Client C works through these issues at this time and relies on their emotional support network, then after their Saturn return, they will be able to start fresh with a new mindset and with even closer bonds to those that are important to them.

CLIENT D: PROGRESSED CHART YEAR X (2021)

Name: ♀ Client D
born on Fr., 22 August 1986
in Houston, TX (US)
95w22, 29n46

Time: 9:39 a.m.
Univ.Time: 14:39
Sid. Time: 6:19:58

ASTRO DIENST
www.astro.com

Type: 25.GW 0.0-1 6-Mrz-2021

Natal Chart and Progressions for 1 Jan. 2021 (Method: Web Style / Placidus)
Date: 25 Sept. 1986, 23:20:02 UT

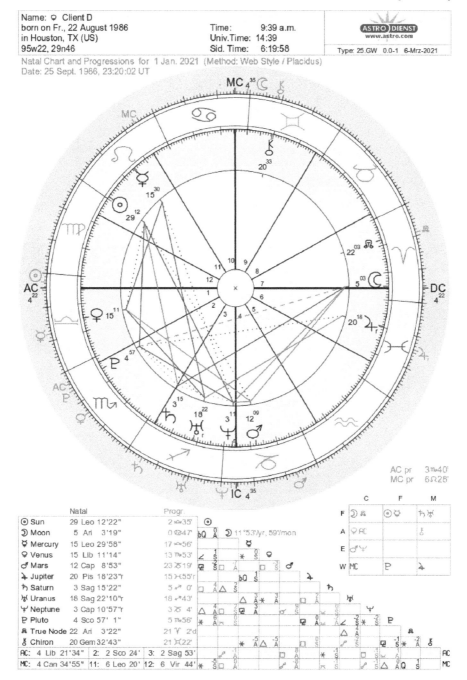

AC pr 3♏40'
MC pr 6♌28'

	Natal	Progr.
☉ Sun	29 Leo 12'22"	2 ♎35'
☽ Moon	5 Ari 3'19"	0 ♋47'
☿ Mercury	15 Leo 29'58"	17 ♎56'
♀ Venus	15 Lib 11'14"	13 ♏53'
♂ Mars	12 Cap 8'53"	23 ♑19'
♃ Jupiter	20 Pis 18'23"r	15 ♓55'r
♄ Saturn	3 Sag 15'22"	5 ♐0'
♅ Uranus	18 Sag 22'10"r	18 ♐43'
♆ Neptune	3 Cap 10'57"r	3 ♑4'
♇ Pluto	4 Sco 57' 1"	5 ♏56'
♇ True Node	22 Ari 3'22"	21 ♈2'd
⚷ Chiron	20 Gem 32'43"	21 ♓22'
AC: 4 Lib 21'34"	2: 2 Sco 24'	3: 2 Sag 53'
MC: 4 Can 34'55"	11: 6 Leo 20'	12: 6 Vir 44'

Name: ♀ Client D
born on Fr., 22 August 1986
in Houston, TX (US)
95w22, 29n46

Time: 9:39 a.m.
Univ.Time: 14:39
Sid. Time: 6:19:58

ASTRO DIENST
www.astro.com
Type: 25.GW 0.0-1 6-Mrz-2021

Natal Chart and Progressions for 1 Jan. 2022 (Method: Web Style / Placidus)
Date: 26 Sept. 1986, 23:19:05 UT

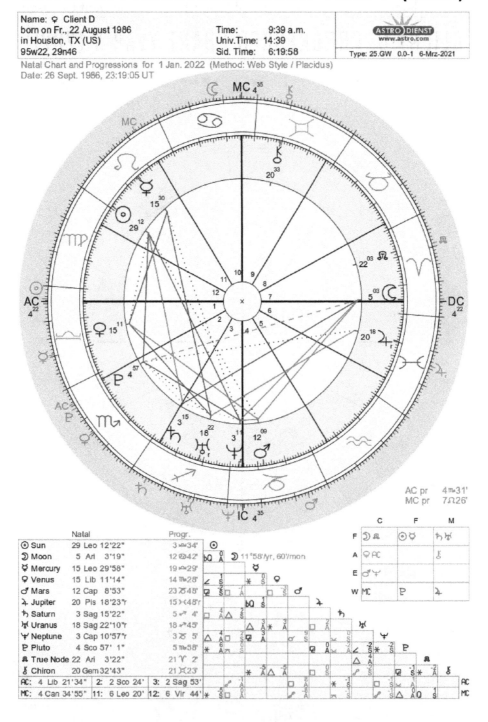

AC pr 4♏31'
MC pr 7♌26'

	Natal	Progr.
☉ Sun	29 Leo 12'22"	3 ♒34'
☽ Moon	5 Ari 3'19"	12 ♋42'
☿ Mercury	15 Leo 29'58"	19 ♒29'
♀ Venus	15 Lib 11'14"	14 ♏28'
♂ Mars	12 Cap 8'53"	23 ♉48'
♃ Jupiter	20 Pis 18'23"r	15 ♓48'r
♄ Saturn	3 Sag 15'22"	5 ♐ 4'
♅ Uranus	18 Sag 22'10"r	18 ♐45'
♆ Neptune	3 Cap 10'57"r	3 ♉ 5'
♇ Pluto	4 Sco 57' 1"	5 ♏58'
☊ True Node	22 Ari 3'22"	21 ♈ 2'
⚷ Chiron	20 Gem 32'43"	21 ♓23'
AC: 4 Lib 21'34"	2: 2 Sco 24'	3: 2 Sag 53'
MC: 4 Can 34'55"	11: 6 Leo 20'	12: 6 Vir 44'

☽ 11°58'/yr, 60'/mon

2	VI-1	Determine the moon phase for that year.	The person's overall energy level and whether this is a time for expansion or recuperation.

Client D is approaching the last quarter of their progressed Moon phase. This tells me that their energies are starting to diminish, and they need to begin to conclude their various projects and goals in order to rest and save their energy for when the Moon phase begins to increase in energy in about five years from now.

3A	VI-1	Determine progressed planetary and cardinal points house and zodiac locations for Jan 1 of Year X.	This will be your Point A when it comes to determining progressed events.
3B	VI-1	Repeat the process but determine the information for Jan 1 of the following year (Year Y).	This will be your Point B when it comes to determining progressed events.

PLANET/CARDINAL POINT	YEAR X HOUSE	YEAR X ZODIAC	NATAL POINT	YEAR Y ZODIAC	YEAR Y HOUSE
☉	12	2° ♎ 35'	29° ♌ 12'	3° ♎ 34'	12
☽	9	0° ♋ 47'	5° ♈ 3'	12° ♋ 42'	10
☿	1	17° ♎ 56'	15° ♌ 29'	19° ♎ 29'	1
♀	2	13° ♏ 53'	15 ♎ 11'	14° ♏ 28'	2
♂	4	23° ♑ 19'	12° ♑ 8'	23° ♑ 48'	4
♃	6	15° ♓ 55'	20° ♓ 18'	15° ♓ 48'	6
♄	3	5° ♐ 0'	3° ♐ 15'	5° ♐ 4'	3
♅	3	18° ♐ 43'	18° ♐ 22'	18° ♐ 45'	3
♆	3	3° ♑ 4'	3° ♑ 10'	3° ♑ 5'	3
♇	2	5° ♏ 56'	4° ♏ 57'	5° ♏ 58'	2
ASC	2	3° ♏ 40'	4° ♎ 21'	4° ♏ 31'	2
MC	11	6° ♌ 28'	4° ♋ 34'	7° ♌ 26'	11

4A	VI-1	Compare the data range from steps 3A-3B and determine if any of the progressed planets, Asc, or DC ingress or regress into a house.	Indicates a progressed event.

EVENT	GLYPH
Progressed Moon ingresses into the 10th House	p. ☽ → 10th

4B	VI-1	Compare the data range from steps 3A-3B and determine if any of the progressed planets, Ascendant or Descendant makes an aspect to a fixed Natal point.	Indicates a progressed event.

NATAL ☉	
EVENT	GLYPH
NONE	

NATAL ☽	
EVENT	GLYPH
Progressed Moon in Cancer square Natal Moon in Aries	p.☽♋ ☐ n.☽♈
Progressed Saturn in Sagittarius trine Natal Moon in Aries	p.♄♐ Δ n.☽♈

NATAL ☿	
EVENT	GLYPH
NONE	

NATAL ♀	
EVENT	GLYPH
NONE	

NATAL ♂	
EVENT	GLYPH
Progressed Moon in Cancer oppose Natal Mars in Capricorn	p.☽♋ ☍ n.♂♑

NATAL ♃	
EVENT	GLYPH
NONE	

NATAL ♄	
EVENT	GLYPH
NONE	

NATAL ♅	
EVENT	GLYPH
Progressed Mercury in Libra sextile Natal Uranus in Sagittarius	p.☿♎ ✳ n.♅♐

NATAL ♆	
EVENT	GLYPH
Progressed Moon in Cancer oppose Natal Neptune in Capricorn	p.☽♋ ☍ n.♆♑

NATAL ♇	
EVENT	GLYPH
Progressed Moon in Cancer trine Natal Pluto in Scorpio	p.☽♋ Δ n.♇♏

500

NATAL ASCENDANT	
EVENT	**GLYPH**
Progressed Moon in Cancer square Libra Ascendant	p.☽♋ □ n.ASC♎
NATAL DESCENDANT	
EVENT	**GLYPH**
Progressed Moon in Cancer conjoin Cancer Midheaven	p.☽♋ ☌ n.MC♋

5A	VI-1	Take the data from steps 4A-4B and calculate when they will occur.	Exact moment of event.
5B		Put the events into chronological order.	Determines if the events occur simultaneously.

EVENT	GLYPH	DATE
Progressed Moon ingresses into the 9th House	p. ☽ → 10th	MAY 3
Progressed Moon in Cancer square Natal Moon in Aries	p.☽♋ □ n.☽♈	MAY 11
Progressed Saturn in Sagittarius trine Natal Moon in Aries	p.♄♐ △ n.☽♈	OCT 1
Progressed Moon in Cancer oppose Natal Mars in Capricorn	p.☽♋ ☍ n.♂♑	DEC 14
Progressed Mercury in Libra sextile Natal Uranus in Sagittarius	p.☿♎ ⚹ n.♅♐	JUL 20
Progressed Moon in Cancer oppose Natal Neptune in Capricorn	p.☽♋ ☍ n.♆♑	MAR 15
MAR 15Progressed Moon in Cancer trine Natal Pluto in Scorpio	p.☽♋ △ n.♇♏	MAY 8
Progressed Moon in Cancer square Libra Ascendant	p.☽♋ □ n.ASC♎	MAY 14
Progressed Moon in Cancer conjoin Cancer Midheaven	p.☽♋ ☌ n.MC♋	MAY 3

2021							
JAN		**FEB**		**MAR**		**APR**	
EVENT	**DAY**	**EVENT**	**DAY**	**EVENT**	**DAY**	**EVENT**	**DAY**
				p.☽♋ ☍ n.♆♑	15		
MAY		**JUN**		**JUL**		**AUG**	
EVENT	**DAY**	**EVENT**	**DAY**	**EVENT**	**DAY**	**EVENT**	**DAY**
p. ☽ → 10th p.☽♋ ☌ n.MC♋ p.☽♋ △ n.♇♏ p.☽♋ □ n.☽♈ p.☽♋ □ n.ASC♎	3 3 8 11 14			p.☿♎ ⚹ n.♅♐	20		
SEP		**OCT**		**NOV**		**DEC**	
EVENT	**DAY**	**EVENT**	**DAY**	**EVENT**	**DAY**	**EVENT**	**DAY**
		p.♄♐ △ n.☽♈	1			p.☽♋ ☍ n.♂♑	14

6	IV-4	Create transit formulas for every event listed in step 4B.	Various realms within the person's life that will be influenced by events.

EVENT	FORMULA
p.☽♋ □ n.☽a	p.☽♋ 9th (R. 10th) □ n.☽♈ in 7th (R. 10th)
p.♄♐ Δ n.☽♈	p.♄♐ in 3rd (R. 4th & 5th) Δ n.☽♈ in 7th (R. 10th)
p.☽♋ ☍ n.♂♑	p.☽♋ in 9th (R. 10th) ☍ n.♂♑ in 4th (R. 7th & 12th)
p.☿♎ ⚹ n.♅♐	p.☿♎ in 1st (R. 9th & 12th) ⚹ n.♅♐ in 3rd (R. 5th)
p.☽♋ ☍ n.♆♑	p.☽♋ in 8th (R. 10th) ☍ n.♆♑ in 3rd (R. 6th)
p.☽♋ Δ n.♇♏	p.☽♋ in 9th (R. 10th) Δ n.♇♏ in 2nd (R. 2nd)
p.☽♋ □ n.ASC♎	p.☽♋ in 9th (R. 10th) □ n.ASC♎
p.☽♋ ☌ n.MC♋	p.☽♋ in 9th (R. 10th) ☌ n.MC♋

7		Compose a summary of your findings from step 2, 5, & 6	Summary of Analysis.

Again, a key factor I would want to reiterate to Client D is that their overall energy is dwindling and will continue to do so for the next 4-6 years approximately. Therefore, this is not a time for expansion but for conservation of resources and energy. As such, this could be a time where Client D is finding themself more irritable or prone to illness due to the progressed Moon in a square to the natal Ascendant and Moon, and opposition to natal Mars (p.☽♋ □ n.ASC♎, p.☽♋ □ n.☽♈, p.☽♋ ☍ n.♂♑). Client D should make sure that when they are a bit more on the grumpy side, they can instigate conflict with others as an outlet to these emotional frustrations.

However, Client D can rely on wise individuals at this time due to progressed Saturn trine to natal Moon, and progressed Mercury sextile to natal Uranus (p. ♄♐ Δ n.☽♈, p. ☿♎ ⚹ n.♅♐). Working out problems through therapy and modern therapeutic techniques can help Client D to work through their emotional frustrations that they are feeling during this time. Or, if there is a confidant that Client D usually seeks advice from, they should utilize them more during these progressed events.

It appears the catalyst for these events has to do with the progressed Moon opposition to natal Neptune (p.☽♋ ☍ n.♆♑). With the 6th and 3rd house being involved, things are getting lost in the details, as Client D tries to understand what is making them feel the way they are feeling, but they have a hard time with discernment and therefore cannot come to any logical and cohesive conclusions. This is why an objective and wise individual is useful at this time.

Similarly, with the 8th and 10th house involved, Client D has a hard time flying under the radar and might find their coworkers and bosses to be overly critical, which does not help. Client D should try to work on themself a bit for now instead of pushing for any type of promotion or more work. Their body and mind are telling them they have enough to handle and need to work on personal issues first before they can move on toward their personal goals. The opportunity to do so will be at their progressed new moon 4-6 years from now.

Nevertheless, it needs to be accounted that the progressed Moon ingresses into the 10th house during this time. This could indicate Client D is reaching some goal post in their life, and the next step of advancement into these endeavors will be on Client D's mind. However, I would recommend that Client D take stock of where they have come but try to focus their energy elsewhere because they probably will not find the same fulfillment if they try to push through on the same path.

This is due to the fact that Client D is also experiencing transiting Neptune conjoin their natal Jupiter at the same time. This means that Client D will probably want to move their goals towards more humanitarian or spiritual goals, which could alter their current life path. I would recommend that they enjoy the fruits of their labors, but also recharge and revitalize until their new moon which is not going to come until a couple of years from now. Instead, look back at their success and take a step back so that, when they figure out where they want to focus their energies next, they will have more than enough emotional and physical vigor and strength within them to do so.

CLIENT E: PROGRESSED CHART YEAR X (2021)

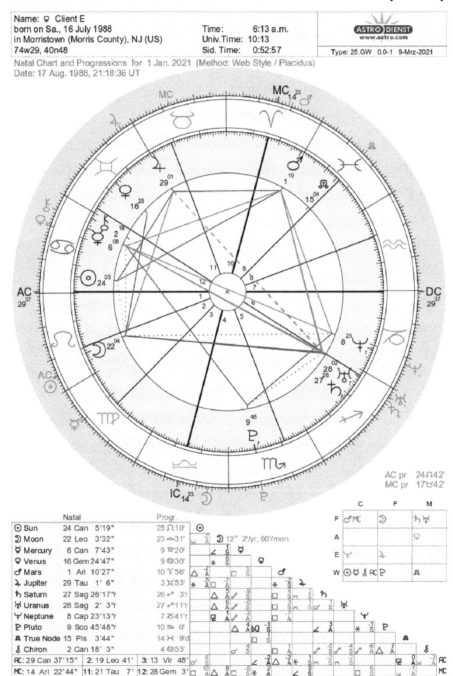

Name: ♀ Client E
born on Sa., 16 July 1988
in Morristown (Morris County), NJ (US)
74w29, 40n48

Time: 6:13 a.m.
Univ.Time: 10:13
Sid. Time: 0:52:57

ASTRO DIENST
www.astro.com

Type: 25.GW 0.0-1 9-Mrz-2021

Natal Chart and Progressions for 1 Jan. 2021 (Method: Web Style / Placidus)
Date: 17 Aug. 1988, 21:18:36 UT

AC pr 24 ♌ 42'
MC pr 17 ♉ 42'

	Natal	Progr.
☉ Sun	24 Can 5'19"	25 ♌ 10'
☽ Moon	22 Leo 3'32"	23 ♎ 31'
☿ Mercury	6 Can 7'43"	9 ♍ 20'
♀ Venus	16 Gem 24'47"	9 ♋ 30'
♂ Mars	1 Ari 10'27"	10 ♈ 56'
♃ Jupiter	29 Tau 1' 6"	3 ♓ 53'
♄ Saturn	27 Sag 26'17"r	26 ♐ 3'r
♅ Uranus	28 Sag 2' 3"r	27 ♐ 11'r
♆ Neptune	8 Cap 23'13"r	7 ♑ 41'r
♇ Pluto	9 Sco 45'48"r	10 ♏ 0'
⚷ True Node	15 Pis 3'44"	14 ♓ 9'd
⚷ Chiron	2 Can 18' 3"	4 ♋ 55'
AC: 29 Can 37'15"	2: 13 Vir 48'	
MC: 14 Ari 22'44"	11: 21 Tau 7'	12: 28 Gem 3'

☽ 12° 2'/yr, 60'/mon

CLIENT E: PROGRESSED CHART YEAR Y (2022)

Name: ♀ Client E
born on Sa., 16 July 1988
in Morristown (Morris County), NJ (US)
74w29, 40n48

Time: 6:13 a.m.
Univ.Time: 10:13
Sid. Time: 0:52:57

ASTRO DIENST
www.astro.com

Type: 25.GW 0.0-1 9-Mrz-2021

Natal Chart and Progressions for 1 Jan. 2022 (Method: Web Style / Placidus)
Date: 18 Aug. 1988, 21:17:39 UT

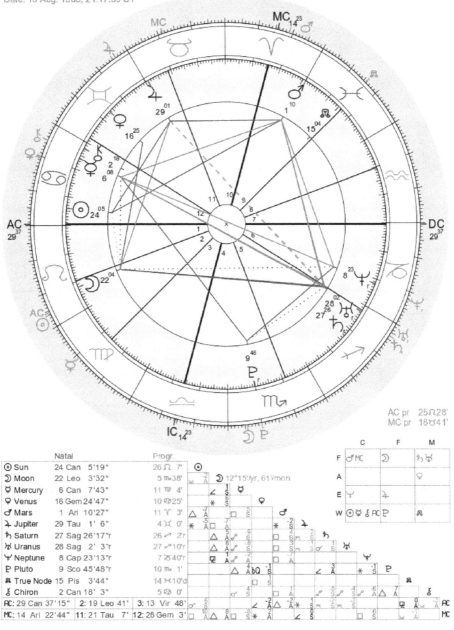

AC pr 25♌28'
MC pr 18♉41'

	Natal	Progr.
☉ Sun	24 Can 5'19"	26 ♌ 7'
☽ Moon	22 Leo 3'32"	5 ♏ 38'
☿ Mercury	6 Can 7'43"	11 ♍ 4'
♀ Venus	16 Gem 24'47"	10 ♋ 25'
♂ Mars	1 Ari 10'27"	11 ♈ 3'
♃ Jupiter	29 Tau 1' 6"	4 ♊ 0'
♄ Saturn	27 Sag 26'17"r	26 ♐ 2'r
♅ Uranus	28 Sag 2' 3"r	27 ♐ 10'r
♆ Neptune	8 Cap 23'13"r	7 ♑ 40'r
♇ Pluto	9 Sco 45'48"r	10 ♏ 1'
☊ True Node	15 Pis 3'44"	14 ♓ 10'd
⚷ Chiron	2 Can 18' 3"	5 ♋ 0'
AC: 29 Can 37'15"	2: 19 Leo 41'	3: 13 Vir 48'
MC: 14 Ari 22'44"	11: 21 Tau 7'	12: 26 Gem 3'

☽ 12°15'/yr, 61'/mon

505

2	VI-1	Determine the moon phase direction for that year.	The person's overall energy level and whether this is a time for expansion or recuperation.

Client E is approaching the first quarter of the developing progressed moon phase. This tells me that Client E should continue to invest time and energy into their various goals and projects because they are at a position where these various realms are still growing and will eventually climax at the progressed full moon which does not happen until approximately eight years from now. Additionally, some form of testing towards their ambitions will occur sooner than that at the first quarter progressed Moon phase.

3A	VI-1	Determine progressed planetary and cardinal points house and zodiac locations for Jan 1 of Year X.	This will be your Point A when it comes to determining progressed events.
3B	VI-1	Repeat the process but determine the information for Jan 1 of the following year (Year Y).	This will be your Point B when it comes to determining progressed events.

PLANET/CARDINAL POINT	YEAR X HOUSE	YEAR X ZODIAC	NATAL POINT	YEAR Y ZODIAC	YEAR Y HOUSE
☉	2	25° ♌ 10′	24° ♋ 5′	26° ♌ 7′	2
☽	4	23° ♎ 31′	22° ♌ 3′	5° ♍ 38′	4
☿	2	9° ♍ 20′	6° ♋ 7′	11° ♍ 4′	2
♀	12	9° ♋ 30′	16° ♊ 24′	10° ♋ 25′	12
♂	9	10° ♈ 56′	1° ♈ 10′	11° ♈ 3′	9
♃	11	3° ♊ 53′	29° ♉ 1′	4° ♊ 0′	11
♄	5	26° ♐ 3′	27° ♐ 26′	26° ♐ 2′	5
♅	5	27° ♐ 11′	28° ♐ 2′	27° ♐ 10′	5
♆	6	7° ♍ 41′	8° ♑ 23′	7° ♑ 40′	6
♇	4	10° ♏ 0′	9° ♏ 45′	10° ♏ 1′	4
ASC	2	24° ♌ 42′	29° ♋ 37′	25° ♌ 28′	2
MC	10	17° ♉ 42′	14° ♈ 22′	18° ♉ 41′	10

4A	VI-1	Compare the data range from steps 3A-3B and determine if any of the progressed planets, Asc, or DC ingress or regress into a house.	Indicates a progressed event.
		NONE	

4B	VI-1	Compare the data range from steps 3A-3B and determine if any of the progressed planets, Ascendant or Descendant makes an aspect to a fixed Natal point.	Indicates a progressed event.

NATAL ☉	
EVENT	**GLYPH**
Progressed Moon in Libra square Natal Sun in Cancer	p.☽♎ □ n.☉♋

NATAL ☽	
EVENT	**GLYPH**
NONE	

NATAL ☿	
EVENT	**GLYPH**
NONE	

NATAL ♀	
EVENT	**GLYPH**
NONE	

NATAL ♂	
EVENT	**GLYPH**
NONE	

NATAL ♃	
EVENT	**GLYPH**
NONE	

NATAL ♄	
EVENT	**GLYPH**
Progressed Moon in Libra sextile Natal Saturn in Sagittarius	p.☽♎ ✶ n.♄♐

NATAL ♅	
EVENT	**GLYPH**
Progressed Moon in Libra sextile Natal Uranus in Sagittarius	p.☽♎ ✶ n.♅♐

NATAL ♆	
EVENT	**GLYPH**
NONE	

NATAL ♇	
EVENT	**GLYPH**
Progressed Mercury in Virgo sextile Natal Pluto in Scorpio	p.☿♍ ✶ n.♇♏
Progressed Venus in Cancer trine Natal Pluto in Scorpio	p.♀♋ △ n.♇♏

NATAL ASCENDANT	
EVENT	**GLYPH**
Progressed Moon in Libra square Cancer Ascendant	p.☽♎ □ n.ASC♋
NATAL DESCENDANT	
EVENT	**GLYPH**
NONE	

5A	VI-1	Take the data from steps 4A-4B and calculate when they will occur.	Exact moment of event.
5B		Put the events into chronological order.	Determines if the events occur simultaneously.

EVENT	GLYPH	DATE
Progressed Moon in Libra square Natal Sun in Cancer	p.☽♎ □ n.☉♋	JAN 17
Progressed Moon in Libra sextile Natal Saturn in Sagittarius	p.☽♎ ⚹ n.♄♐	MAY 2
Progressed Moon in Libra sextile Natal Uranus in Sagittarius	p.☽♎ ⚹ n.♅♐	MAY 17
Progressed Mercury in Virgo sextile Natal Pluto in Scorpio	p.☿♍℞ ⚹ n.♇♏	APR 2
Progressed Venus in Cancer trine Natal Pluto in Scorpio	p.♀♋ Δ n.♇♏	APR 10
Progressed Moon in Libra square Cancer Ascendant	p.☽♎ □ n.ASC♋	JUL 3

2021							
JAN		**FEB**		**MAR**		**APR**	
EVENT	**DAY**	**EVENT**	**DAY**	**EVENT**	**DAY**	**EVENT**	**DAY**
p.☽♎ □ n.☉♋	17					p.☿♍℞ ⚹ n.♇♏ p.♀♋ Δ n.♇♏	2 10
MAY		**JUN**		**JUL**		**AUG**	
EVENT	**DAY**	**EVENT**	**DAY**	**EVENT**	**DAY**	**EVENT**	**DAY**
p.☽♎ ⚹ n.♄♐ p.☽♎ ⚹ n.♅♐	2 17			p.☽♎ □ n.ASC♋	3		
SEP		**OCT**		**NOV**		**DEC**	
EVENT	**DAY**	**EVENT**	**DAY**	**EVENT**	**DAY**	**EVENT**	**DAY**

6	IV-1	Create transit formulas for every event listed in step 4B.	Various realms within the person's life that will be influenced by events.
EVENT			**FORMULA**
p.☽♎ □ n.☉♋			p.☽♎ in 4th (R. 1st) □ n.☉♋ in 12th (R. 2nd)
p.☽♎ ⚹ n.♄♐			p.☽♎ in 4th (R. 1st) ⚹ n.♄♐ in 5th (R. 7th & 8th)
p.☽♎ ⚹ n.♅♐			p.☽♎ in 4th (R. 1st) ⚹ n.♅♐ in 5th (R. 8th)
p.☿♍ ⚹ n.♇♏			p.☿♍ in 2nd (R. 3rd & 12th) ⚹ n.♇♏ in 4th (R. 5th)
p.♀♋ Δ n.♇♏			p.♀♋ in 12th (R. 11th & 4th) Δ n.♇♏ in 4th (R. 5th)
p.☽♎ □ n.ASC♋			p.☽♎ in 4th (R. 1st) □ n.ASC♋

7		Compose a summary of your findings from step 2, 5, & 6	Summary of Analysis.

Client E has a mixture of beneficial and detrimental progressions. If you recall from the transit analysis, Client E's multiple oppositions are causing them to not only be on guard for frequent conflicts with others, these various conflicts could humble them and inform them of new insights that they have to be willing to accept and incorporate into their personal perception. This involves the way in which they have perceived other individuals and circumstances. Therefore, Client E can expect an ego death of some form where they might have to take a step back and admit wrongdoing.

These themes are confirmed by the progressed Moon in a square to natal Sun and Ascendant (p.☽♎ □ n.☉♋, p.☽♎ □ n.ASC♋). From these progressions, Client E can be caught off guard in some circumstance, causing them to react inappropriately. From these ego conflict, they need to reexamine how the situation deteriorated as it did, and to try to mend the wounds. Client E needs to remember that they simply reacted out of a fight or flight response, and that their reaction is in no way a true reflection of their real personality and perspective. Thankfully, progressed aspects to the natal outer plants will give Client E a lifeline to handle these matters.

For one, natal Pluto is aspected by sextile to progressed Mercury and a trine to progressed Venus (p.☿♍ ⚹ n.♇♏, p.♀♋ Δ n.♇♏). This allows for Client E to rely on people close to them that can help them through the ego death and rebirth that needs to occur and does so in a loving and supportive environment. With the 4th and 5th house involved, the family unit will be of great service to Client E during this time, especially children within the family. They can help Client E to remember to possess a child-like attitude and heart towards adult matters. This will help Client E to release some of the intense feelings they might currently be harboring. Additionally, Client E finds welcoming and healing spaces with those they trust and find that their support unit is just one way they are blessed in this world.

Furthermore, progressed Moon's sextiles to natal Saturn and Uranus (p.☽︎♎︎ ✶ n.♄♐︎, p.☽︎♎︎ ✶ n.♅♐︎) helps Client E to approach old issues with new perspectives and maturity. The catch is that Client E needs to be willing to divulge their issues with those close to them as evidenced by the 7th and 8th houses at play. The support structure being there for Client E is not the problem, the problem is the willingness to become vulnerable so that support system can properly help them through this process. Client E simply needs to be strong and if they cannot, they must admit that they need strength from others, then they will find the process to not only be easier, but incredibly healing.

* * *

In a nutshell, progressions might seem supplemental, but they are nevertheless substantial. There is so much information that you can be accidently withholding from your client or from yourself if you do not properly look at the progressed chart in addition to the transit chart. For example, what if you recommend to your client that they should expand their energy into projects without knowing their progressed moon phase is disseminating? This could be a critical and damaging recommendation that could hurt your client. Additionally, when you observe progressed events, they help to confirm the analysis of your transit events and give your client more information not only towards how they will manifest, but how they can approach those events.

In a way, transits and progressions are two halves of a whole that paint the entire picture as to what life circumstances are surrounding the individual during a certain point in time. Utilizing both gives you a great advantage because you are not cutting any corners by considering all of the information that is available. Now, in Part VII, we will examine other techniques that are valuable to yourself and to your client because they deal with common questions that clients have for their astrological analysis. Namely, the astrology of relationships, relocations, and birthdays.

PART VII: ADDITIONAL TECHNIQUES WITH CASE STUDIES

"The question is thus not 'how can we avoid pain, crisis or change?' but rather 'how can we understand and use these periods in our lives most creatively?'-Howard Sasportas from Gods of Change, p. 4

All of the information and techniques found in Parts V and VI constitute the bulk of astrological analysis. Namely, the natal chart, transit chart, and the progressed chart. However, as an individual student or practitioner, you will always have more questions that can be further answered using specific techniques. The most common inquiries that I find clients have in this regard involve relationships, relocating to a different part of the world, and a summary of the year ahead. Respectively, these realms can be observed by studying the composite and bi-wheel charts, relocation and astrocartography charts, and the solar return chart.

If you are able to work with these various charts using the techniques within this part of the book, you will be able to deliver the most thorough and comprehensive reading you possibly can. However, recall from the ethics discussion in Part V-Section 1, if you do not feel comfortable in providing more information, feel free to tell your client the truth. This is why it is my hope that after you have learned the skills in this final part, you will never leave your client or yourself in the dark with any possible realm of inquiry that astrology helps to answer.

As you have already witnessed throughout this book, astrological techniques have a wonderous way of taking the same fixed data within your birth chart and then rearranging the information in various ways, whether that be by progressing the chart, observing the transiting planets, or simply by observing the original natal chart itself. The various charts in this part of the book similarly take the natal data and manipulate its information into various logically mathematical ways that paint a different, yet related, picture. The charts discussed in Parts V, VI, and VII are the most common astrological inquiries and by witnessing all of these variations to the same theme, you are beginning to see the depth and versatility within astrology and the subsequent utility that comes out of these multiple variations.

We will discuss how each method in Part VII is mathematically composed, although we will not be having to compute any more math ourselves thanks to modern technology. Also, note that in this section, not all five case studies will be used for relocation and relationship analysis as only Clients A, B, and D had relocation questions and Clients C, D, and E had relationship questions. With that, let us begin our discussion with relationship charts.

SECTION 1-RELATIONSHIP BI-WHEEL AND COMPOSITE CHARTS

After the personal analysis provided in Parts V and VI, the next most common question you get as a practitioner is to look over intimate partnerships and how they interact with the client. This typically is meant to mean their romantic partner but know that the skills in this section can be applied towards any sort of partnerships, whether it be romantic, professional, platonic, or familial in nature. The composite and bi-wheel charts show you how the two people in question are interacting with one another along with their strengths and weakness, and how these varying strengths and weaknesses manifest into their personal relationship as a cohesive unit.

The bi-wheel is named as such because all that is occurring is that one natal chart is placed outside of the person in question. This way, you have two birth charts (bi-wheel) on the same page and can therefore see how they are interacting with each other.

The composite chart is a little more involved in its calculation. This chart essentially takes the midpoints of both individuals in question and creates a new chart based upon these midpoints. In other words, you would take Person A's and Person B's planetary location, and simply divide by 2 in order to find out what point along the zodiac is in the middle of these two points. Doing this to all cardinal points and planets creates a new chart altogether which we call the composite chart.

With this in mind, it is important to note that if you do not have the exact birth time of the partner, you have to ignore house placements and cardinal points placements because they are not accurate. When you do not know the birth time of the partner, this only gives you half of the picture but there is still enough information to obtain.

513

The best way to summarize the difference between the bi-wheel and composite chart is that the bi-wheel tells you how the individuals interact with one another as autonomous units, and the composite chart tells you how they interact as a coupled unit. For example, the bi-wheel chart could show that they are both very compatible to one another, but the composite chart can show that as a couple, most of their friends do not understand how they could possibly be dating, or perhaps their families are not approving of the relationship. This is why it is important to utilize both in order to see both the personal relationships between the two and then how the two engage with the world hand in hand.

When it comes to analyzing both chart types, the main areas of focus are the inner planets (Sun, Moon, Mercury, Venus, and Mars) and the cardinal points. This is because the outer planets are generational due to their slower movements, which will still have an effect towards the two individuals in question, but when it comes to their core relationship and compatibility, this is found within the inner planetary alignments. To this point, use the table below to understand further what the inner planets indicate within a relationship chart (Table VII-1).

Observing these five inner planets and how they interact with the cardinal points and outer planets of the partner's chart and the composite chart gives us the core understanding of the overall compatibility and relationship dynamics of the two individuals in question. The outer planets simply add more depth to this core understanding.

TABLE VII-1. Inner Planetary Representations within a Relationship Chart

PLANET	GLYPH	WHAT IT REPRESENTS
SUN	☉	Self-confidence and the ability to be fully expressive around the partner and vice versa.
MOON	☽	Ability to feel comfortable and inwardly/emotionally supportive around the partner and vice versa.
MERCURY	☿	How well we can share our thoughts and communicate our opinions around our partner and vice versa.
VENUS	♀	How romantic we are and our general passion/ love towards our partner and vice versa.
MARS	♂	Our ability to be sexually expressive and how prone to conflict we are towards our partner and vice versa.

Below you will find a step-by-step guide on how to obtain these charts and how to analyze them. We will once again show these various steps through the case studies we have already been using within Parts V and VI (Table VII-2A-B and VII-3A-B).

TABLE VII-2A. How to obtain a Bi-Wheel Chart on ASTRO.COM

(1) On the ASTRO.COM main page, under the HOROSCOPES tab, chose EXTENDED CHART SELECTION under DRAWINGS, CALCULATIONS, DATA.
(2) Under CHART TYPE, select SYNASTRY CHART.
(3) Confirm that the appropriate individual is selected under HOROSCOPE FOR, and that their partner's chart is chosen under the PARTNER selection.
(4) Click CLICK HERE TO SHOW CHART.

TABLE VII-2B. Steps on how to Comprehensively Analyze a Bi-Wheel Chart

STEP #	SECTION IN BOOK	DESCRIPTION	INFORMATION IT PROVIDES
1		Obtain the partner's birth data and create a bi-wheel chart with both birth charts.	This way ASTRO.COM knows which two charts to work with.
2	II-5	Determine if there are any aspects between their Suns and Moons along with the orb.	This is the ultimate glue that binds and will determine deep connectivity.
3	II-5 II-7	Determine if any of the individual's Sun or Moon is connected to their partner's cardinal points with an orb range of 0°-8°.	This similarly indicates strong ties between the individuals.
4	II-5 II-3	Determine aspect connections between the individual's inner planets to their partners with an orb range of 0°-8°.	Various elements into how they interact with one another depending on the planets involved and the aspects made.
5		Categorize the most beneficial and least beneficial aspects with their orbs.	Determine the couple's biggest strengths and weaknesses.
6		Compose a summary of your findings from step 2-5.	Summary of Analysis.

TABLE VII-3A. How to obtain a Composite Chart on ASTRO.COM

(1) On the ASTRO.COM main page, under the HOROSCOPES tab, chose EXTENDED CHART SELECTION under DRAWINGS, CALCULATIONS, DATA.
(3) Under CHART TYPE, select COMPOSITE CHART, MIDPOINT METHOD.
(2) Confirm that the appropriate individual is selected under HOROSCOPE FOR, and that their partner's chart is chosen under the PARTNER selection.
(4) Click CLICK HERE TO SHOW CHART.

TABLE VII-3B. Steps on how to Comprehensively Analyze a Composite Chart

STEP #	SECTION IN BOOK	DESCRIPTION	INFORMATION IT PROVIDES
1		Obtain the partner's birth data and create a composite chart with both birth charts along with the orb.	This way ASTRO.COM knows which two charts to work with.
2A	II-5	Determine if there are any aspects between the composite Sun and Moon.	Again, this demonstrates how strong the relationship is foundationally.
2B	II-5 II-6	**If both birth times are accurate,** determine the house placements of the composite Sun and Moon.	How these fundamental energies are manifested.
2C	II-5 II-3	Determine any aspect connections to the composite Sun and Moon with an orb range of 0°-5°.	Further details the quality of these fundamental energies within the relationship.
3	II-5 II-3	**If both times are accurate,** determine any aspect connections to composite Ascendant and Midheaven with an orb range of 0°-8°.	Just like the Sun and Moon, composite Midheaven and Ascendant indicate substantial overall quality of the relationship.
4A	II-5 II-3	Determine any aspect connections to composite Mercury, Venus, and Mars with an orb range of 0°-5°.	This completes the picture with the varying inner planets.
4B	IV-4	**If both times are accurate,** determine the house placements for composite Mercury, Venus, and Mars	Highlights the realms of influence the planets emphasize depending on house placement and aspect type.
5		Categorize the most beneficial and least beneficial aspects with their orbs.	Determine the couple's biggest strengths and weaknesses.
6		Compose a summary of your findings from Steps 2A-5.	Summary of Analysis.

CLIENT C: BI-WHEEL CHART

STEP #	SECTION IN BOOK	DESCRIPTION	INFORMATION IT PROVIDES
1		Obtain the partner's birth data and create a bi-wheel chart with both birth charts.	This way ASTRO.COM knows which two charts to work with.

Name: ♀ Client C
born on We., 29 December 1993
in Asheville, NC (US)
82w33, 35n36

Time: 6:34 a.m.
Univ.Time: 11:34
Sid. Time: 12:35:33

ASTRO DIENST
www.astro.com
Type: 61.GW 0.0-1+2 18-Mrz-2021

Comparison with: ♂ Client C'S Partner (outside) (Method: Web Style / Placidus)

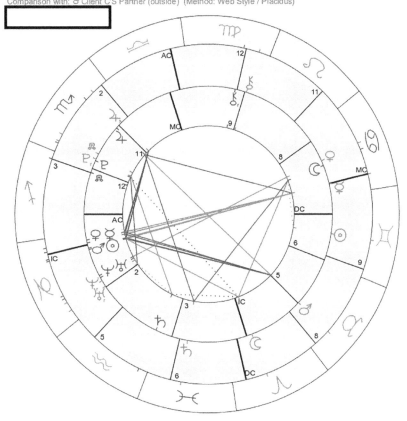

☉ Sun	7 Cap 46'20"	12 ♓58'
☽ Moon	14 Can 6'15"	12 ♈13'
☿ Mercury	4 Cap 39'23"	5 ♋24'
♀ Venus	3 Cap 19'30"	16 ♋24'
♂ Mars	7 Cap 9'16"	8 ♉ 6'
♃ Jupiter	9 Sco 21'58"	5 ♏57'r
♄ Saturn	26 Aqu 45'48"	12 ♓ 6'
♅ Uranus	21 Cap 25'58"	25 ♑53'r
♆ Neptune	20 Cap 21'59"	22 ♑57'r
♇ Pluto	26 Sco 59'38"	26 ♏14'r
☊ True Node	2 Sag 41'39"	23 ♏44'd
⚷ Chiron	9 Vir 15'36"r	3 ♍51'

AC: 21 Sag 45'43"	2: 26 Cap 18'	3: 4 Pis 40'	4♒57'
MC: 9 Lib 40'16"	11: 7 Sco 48'	12: 0 Sag 47'	5♑28'

517

2	II-5	Determine if there are any aspects between their Suns and Moons along with the orb.	This is the ultimate glue that binds and will determine deep connectivity.		

ASPECT		GLYPH*	ORB
Inner partner's Moon in Cancer square Outer partner's Moon in Aries		i.☽♋ □ o.☽♈	2
Inner partner's Sun in Capricorn square Outer partner's Moon in Aries		i.☉♑ □ o.☽♈	5

*KEY: i.=Natal Planet located in the inner circle. **o**=Natal Planet located in the outer circle.

3	II-5 II-7	Determine if any of the individual's Sun or Moon is connected to their partner's cardinal points with an orb range of 0°-8°.	This similarly indicates strong ties between the individuals.

ASPECT		GLYPH	ORB
Inner partner's Sun in Capricorn oppose Outer partner's Cancer Midheaven		i.☉♑ ☍ o.MC♋	2
Inner partner's Libra Midheaven trine Outer partner's Sun in Gemini		i.MC♎ △ o.☉♊	3
Inner partner's Sun in Capricorn square Outer partner's Libra Ascendant		i.☉♑ □ o.ASC♎	3
Inner partner's Libra Midheaven oppose Outer partner's Moon in Aries		i.MC♎ ☍ o.☽♈	3
Inner partner's Libra Midheaven conjoin Outer partner's Libra Ascendant		i.MC♎ ☌ o.ASC♎	5

4	II-5 II-3	Determine aspect connections between the individual's inner planets to their partners with an orb range of 0°-8°.	Various elements into how they interact with one another depending on the planets involved and the aspects made.

ASPECT		GLYPH	ORB
Inner partner's Sun in Capricorn trine Outer partner's Mars in Taurus		i.☉♑ △ o.♂♉	1
Inner partner's Mercury in Capricorn oppose Outer partner's Mercury in Cancer		i.☿♑ ☍ o.☿♋	1
Inner partner's Mars in Capricorn trine Outer partner's Mars in Taurus		i.♂♑ △ o.♂♉	1

Inner partner's Sun in Capricorn oppose Outer partner's Mercury in Cancer	i.☉♑ ☍ o.☿♋	2
Inner partner's Moon in Cancer conjoin Outer partner's Venus in Cancer	i.☽♋ ☌ o.♀♋	2
Inner partner's Venus in Capricorn oppose Outer partner's Mercury in Cancer	i.♀♑ ☍ o.☿♋	2
Inner partner's Mars in Capricorn oppose Outer partner's Mercury in Cancer	i.♂♑ ☍ o.☿♋	2
Inner partner's Mercury in Capricorn trine Outer partner's Mars in Taurus	i.☿♑ △ o.♂♉	4
Inner partner's Venus in Capricorn trine Outer partner's Mars in Taurus	i.♀♑ △ o.♂♉	5
Inner partner's Mars in Capricorn square Outer partner's Moon in Aries	i.♂♑ □ o.☽♈	5
Inner partner's Moon in Cancer sextile Outer partner's Mars in Taurus	i.☽♋ ✶ o.♂♉	7
Inner partner's Mercury in Capricorn square Outer partner's Moon in Aries	i.☿♑ □ o.☽♈	8

5		Categorize the most beneficial and least beneficial aspects with their orbs.	Determine the couple's biggest strengths and weaknesses.

MOST BENEFICIAL		LEAST BENEFICIAL	
ASPECT	ORB	ASPECT	ORB
i.☉♑ △ o.♂♉	1	i.☿♑ ☍ o.☿♋	1
i.♂♑ △ o.♂♉	1	i.☽♋ □ o.☽♈	2
i.☽♋ ☌ o.♀♋	2	i.☉♑ ☍ o.☿♋	2
i.☉♑ ☍ o.MC♋	2	i.♀♑ ☍ o.☿♋	2
i.MC♎ △ o.☉♊	3	ii.♂♑ ☍ o.☿♋	2
i.☿♑ △ o.♂♉	4	i.☉♑ □ o.MC♎	3
i.MC♎ ☌ o.ASC♎	5	i.☉♑ □ o.☽♈	5
i.♀♑ △ o.♂♉	5	i.♂♑ □ o.☽♈	5
i.☽♋ ✶ o.♂♉	7	i.☿♑ □ o.☽♈	8

6		Compose a summary of your findings from step 2-5.	Summary of Analysis.

Before getting too ahead of ourselves, we should quickly point out that Client C's composite chart below tells a very different story compared to their bi-wheel chart in that the bi-wheel chart shows a more difficult interaction, and the composite chart indicates a well-balanced arrangement. When this happens, it simply means that when the couple works cohesively as a unit, then the relationship works out very well. However, if the two individuals act at cross purposes, it can become very frustrating and self-destructive.

The biggest issue involves Client C's Sun and Moon squaring their partner's Moon (i.☉♑ □ o.☽♈, i.☽♋ □ o.☽♈). The partner deals with and expresses their emotions in a completely different way than Client C. This brings frustrations because the partner is unable to voice themselves readily, and Client C does not know how to help them because the way they would approach the same issue cannot translate into their partner's way of approaching inward emotional states and their expression.

Consequently, with the numerous oppositions to the partner's Mercury in Cancer (i.☿♑ ☍ o.☿♋, i.☉♑ ☍ o.☿♋, i.♀♑ ☍ o.☿♋, i.♂♑ ☍ o.☿♋), there is a lot of back and forth and subsequent frustrations because the partner has a hard time becoming vulnerable enough to share their personal insights. This is mostly due to the fact that the partner's Moon and Mercury square one another. With the Mercury in Cancer, their partner's usual way of communicating is though their feelings. However, the Moon in Aries makes it hard for them to connect and establish feelings because they can feel them quickly albeit intensely. In other words, if Client C were to ask their partner what was wrong, the issue is that the partner has a hard time discerning what truly is wrong even though they know something is off internally, but they cannot put it into words. Instead, it becomes expressed as an intense feeling which can lead to conflict.

The resolution to this problem involves the multiple trines to the partner's Mars (i.☉♑ △ o.♂♉, i.♂♑ △ o.♂♉). This indicates that the two individuals have a lot in common and enjoy playful competition. There is also a lot of passion between them although it may not be the most flamboyant. If Client C can encourage their partner to engage in activities in which they both enjoy (preferably physical activities like dancing or hiking) then this will help their partner to realize that Client C is trustworthy and easily identifiable. In time, this will soften up the partner a bit more and they will be able to slowly open up as they should.

There certainly is a lot of love between the two indicated by Client C's Moon conjoin their partner's Venus (i.☽♋ ☌ o.♀♋). This shows that they both care for one another and the spark of romantic love does exist. These two individuals enjoy making memories together and discussing long-term plans like owning a home and raising a family. Although there can be conflict at times, this creates a strong bond that makes them supportive to one another in the long run.

The issue comes in running into frustrations when the relationship is not working out. In addition to the partner's Moon being squared by Client C's Sun and Moon, their Mars and Mercury also squares their partners Moon (i.♂♑ □ o.☽♈, i.☿♑ □ o.☽♈). Frustrations, conflict, and the inability to resolve issues are problematic with these multiple squares to the partner's Moon. The key point to remember is whatever personal issues the partner may have, Client C is not able and should not be expected to resolve all of them. They need someone in the middle, like a counselor for their partner, where they can communicate with someone that is not as emotionally involved as Client C. This would greatly help their relationship because Client C will feel less pressured to resolve their partner's irrationality and instead act as a support and as someone who simply wants to enjoy life with them.

1		Obtain the partner's birth data and create a composite chart with both birth charts.	This way ASTRO.COM knows which two charts to work with.

Name: ♀ Client C
born on We., 29 December 1993
in Asheville, NC (US)
82w33, 35n36

Time: 6:34 a.m.
Univ.Time: 11:34
Sid. Time: 12:35:33

ASTRO DIENST
www.astro.com

Type: 621.GW 0.0-1+2 18-Mrz-2021

Composite Chart with: ♂ Client C'S Partner (Method: Web Style / Placidus)

⊙ Sun	25 Pis 22' 8"	
☽ Moon	28 Tau 9'45"	
☿ Mercury	5 Lib 1'29"	+opp.house
♀ Venus	9 Lib 51'44"	
♂ Mars	7 Pis 37'41"	
♃ Jupiter	7 Sco 39'25"	
♄ Saturn	4 Pis 25'44"	
♅ Uranus	23 Cap 39'39"	
♆ Neptune	21 Cap 39'39"	
♇ Pluto	26 Sco 36'46"	
♋ True Node	28 Sco 12'41"	
⚷ Chiron	6 Vir 33'12"	

AC: 13 Sco 21'28"	2: 14 Sag 15'	3: 18 Cap 43'
MC: 22 Leo 34'10"	11: 22 Vir 56'	12: 19 Lib 35'

2A	II-5	Determine if there are any aspects between the composite Sun and Moon along with the orb.	Again, this demonstrates how strong the relationship is foundationally.	

ASPECT			GLYPH	ORB
Composite Sun in Pisces sextile Composite Moon in Taurus			c. ☉♓ ✶ c. ☽♉	3

2B	II-5 II-6	**If both birth times are accurate**, determine the house placements of the composite Sun and Moon.	How these fundamental energies are manifested.

PLANET	GLYPH	HOUSE
SUN	☉	5
MOON	☽	7

2C	II-5 II-3	Determine any aspect connections to the composite Sun and Moon with an orb range of 0°-5°.	Further details the quality of these fundamental energies within the relationship.

ASPECT	GLYPH	ORB
Composite Sun in Pisces trine Composite Pluto in Scorpio	c.☉♓ △ c.♇♏	1
Composite Sun in Pisces sextile Composite Uranus in Capricorn	c.☉♓ ✶ c.♅♑	2
Composite Moon in Taurus oppose Composite Pluto in Scorpio	c.☽♉ ☍ c.♇♏	2
Composite Sun in Pisces sextile Composite Neptune in Capricorn	c.☉♓ ✶ c.♆♑	4
Composite Moon in Taurus trine Uranus in Capricorn	c.☽♉ △ c.♅♑	5

3	II-5 II-3	**If both times are accurate**, determine any aspect connections to composite Ascendant and Midheaven with an orb range of 0°-8°.	Just like the Sun and Moon, composite Midheaven and Ascendant indicate substantial overall quality of the relationship.

ASPECT	GLYPH	ORB
Composite Pluto in Scorpio square Composite Leo Midheaven	c.♇♏ ☐ c.MC♌	4
Composite Moon in Taurus square Composite Leo Midheaven	c.☽♉ ☐ c.MC♌	6
Composite Mars in Pisces trine Composite Scorpio Ascendant	c.♂♓ △ c.ASC♏	6
Composite Jupiter in Scorpio conjoin Composite Scorpio Ascendant	c.♃♏ ☌ c.ASC♏	6

523

4A	II-5 II-3	Determine any aspect connections to composite Mercury, Venus, and Mars with an orb range of 0°-5°.	This completes the picture with the varying inner planets.	

ASPECT			GLYPH	ORB
Composite Mars in Pisces trine Composite Jupiter in Scorpio			c.♂♓ △ c.♃♏	0
Composite Mars in Pisces conjoin Composite Saturn in Pisces			c.♂♓ ☌ c.♄♓	3
Composite Mercury in Libra conjoin Composite Venus in Libra			c.☿♎ ☌ c.♀♎	5

4B	IV-4	**If both times are accurate**, determine the house placements for composite Mercury, Venus, and Mars	Highlights the realms of influence the planets emphasize depending on house placement and aspect type.

PLANET	GLYPH	HOUSE
MERCURY	☿	11
VENUS	♀	11
MARS	♂	4

5		Categorize the most beneficial and least beneficial aspects with their orbs.	Determine the couple's biggest strengths and weaknesses.

MOST BENEFICIAL		LEAST BENEFICIAL	
ASPECT	ORB	ASPECT	ORB
c.♂♓ △ c.♃♏	0	c.☽♉ ☍ c.♆♏	2
c.☉♓ △ c.♆♏	1	c.♆♏ □ c.MC♌	4
c.☉♓ ✶ c.♅♑	2	c.☽♉ □ c.MC♌	6
c. ☉♓ ✶ c. ☽♉	3		
c.♂♓ ☌ c.♄♓	3		
c.☉♓ ✶ c.♆♑	4		
c.☽♉ △ c.♅♑	5		
c.☿♎ ☌ c.♀♎	5		
c.♂♓ △ c.ASC♏	6		
c.♃♏ ☌ c.ASC♏	6		

6		Compose a summary of your findings from Steps 2A-5.	Summary of Analysis.

The composite chart for Client C and their partner paints a completely different picture from their bi-wheel chart. As previously mentioned, this means that when they both act together as a cohesive unit with similar goals and open communication, they work out very well together. To this point, the main downside within this composite chart appears to be the Pluto and Moon square to the Midheaven (c.♇♏ □ c.MC♌, c.☽♉ □ c.MC♌). This shows that there can be a lot of sacrifice required when it comes to reaching their fullest potential. There is a balancing act required where both parties need independence to pursue what they want to pursue. This requires an acceptance with each other's goals so that they can co-exist in harmony. The good news is that the rest of the composite chart indicates that this is very possible.

Similar to the bi-wheel chart, the couple's composite chart also has a strong Mars due to the trine to composite Jupiter and Ascendant (c.♂♓ △ c.♃♏, c.♂♓ △ c.ASC♏). Again, this shows a passionate relationship and the ability to be great company as a unit towards others with the Ascendant involved. Similarly, Mars' conjunction to Saturn (c.♂♓ ☌ c.♄♓) gives the couple discipline and focus in order to reach their long-term relationship goals, like obtaining property, and a marriage.

The Sun and Moon within the composite chart have great aspect alignments not only to themselves but towards other planets as well. The sextile with the Sun and Moon (c. ☉♓ ✳ c. ☽♉) gives the relationship a general sense of optimism and happiness because the Sun and Moon are working together in harmony. However, as with all sextiles, effort is required to bring about these beneficial manifestations, but this has been a main theme for the couple in that when the relationship works, it works tremendously well and when it does not, there are intense hardships between the two.

Nevertheless, the Sun's trine to Pluto and sextile to Uranus (c.☉♓ △ c.♇♏, c.☉♓ ✳ c.♅♑) makes the relationship incredibly intimate where both individuals feel safe to be vulnerable and therefore divulge deeply rooted secrets and feelings that they might not have shared with others. Uranus helps in the process because it gives them both an open mind to not judge the other person when they bring up more serious topics. Additionally, as a couple, they have a good network of friends and others are generally supportive of the relationship.

The Moon and Sun aspects simply confirm these conclusions with a trine to Uranus and sextile to Neptune (c.☽☌ △ c.♅♑, c.☉♓ ✶ c.♆♑). This helps both partners to release their egos and hear the other person out when there is conflict. The couple is open to new possibilities and desires a sort of freshness to be included within the relationship at times and both individuals properly deliver. As mentioned in the bi-wheel section, the problem only occurs when the issues at hand are beyond their control or expertise. When this arises, they simply need bring in professional help that can aid in psychological analysis and catharsis that way the couple can continue to enjoy each other's company in harmony.

In the bi-wheel chat, we noticed a beneficial conjunction with Client C's Moon to their partner's Venus. Again, we witness another beneficial Venus aspect with a conjunction to Mercury (c.☿♎ ☌ c.♀♎). This makes communication between the two to be very easy along with romance because both speak the same romantic language. For example, Client C might enjoy being surprised by a spontaneous gift or a planned-out date. Their partner also agrees in these forms of romantic expression, so they are able to voice their love for one another and the partner receives it willingly. This ties back to the strong support structure that surrounds these two as they both feel they can be completely honest and open. Indeed, this is the glue that binds the two when it comes to their rougher patches. When these harder moments come about, they need to remember that there is a connection there and they both do want nothing but the best for the other. This couple experiences very high highs and very low lows, but if they are willing to stick it out, their lows make them closer and stronger as a couple and as individuals.

CLIENT D: BI-WHEEL CHART

STEP #	SECTION IN BOOK	DESCRIPTION	INFORMATION IT PROVIDES
1		Obtain the partner's birth data and create a bi-wheel chart with both birth charts.	This way ASTRO.COM knows which two charts to work with.

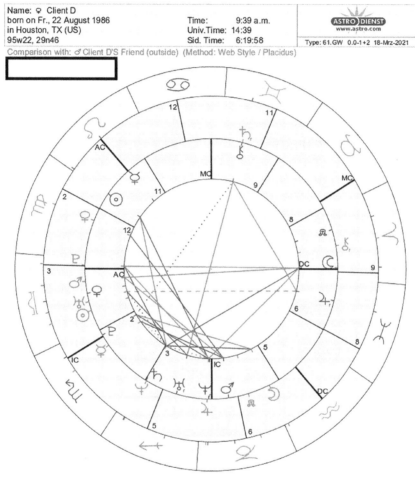

Name: ♀ Client D
born on Fr., 22 August 1986
in Houston, TX (US)
95w22, 29n46

Time: 9:39 a.m.
Univ.Time: 14:39
Sid. Time: 6:19:58

ASTRO DIENST
www.astro.com

Type: 61.GW 0.0-1+2 18-Mrz-2021

Comparison with: ♂ Client D'S Friend (outside) (Method: Web Style / Placidus)

☉ Sun	29 Leo 12'22"	22 ≏ 59'
☽ Moon	5 Ari 3'19"	1 ≈ 20'
☿ Mercury	15 Leo 29'58"	10 ♏ 15'
♀ Venus	15 Lib 11'14"	12 ♍ 38'
♂ Mars	12 Cap 8'53"	9 ≏ 54'
♃ Jupiter	20 Pis 18'23"r	2 ♉ 27'
♄ Saturn	3 Sag 15'22"	20 ♓ 26'r
♅ Uranus	18 Sag 22'10"r	18 ≏ 59'
♆ Neptune	3 Cap 10'57"r	3 ♐ 31'
♇ Pluto	4 Sco 57' 1"	2 ≈ 42'
♫ True Node	22 Ari 3'22"	21 ♉ 16'
⚷ Chiron	20 Gem 32'43"	14 ♈ 43'r

AC:	4 Lib 21'34"	2:	2 Sco 24'	3:	2 Sag 53'	15 ♌ 45'
MC:	4 Can 34'55"	11:	6 Leo 20'	12:	6 Vir 44'	5 ♉ 31'

527

2	II-5	Determine if there are any aspects between their Suns and Moons along with the orb.	This is the ultimate glue that binds and will determine deep connectivity.

ASPECT		GLYPH*	ORB
Inner partner's Moon in Aries sextile Outer partner's Moon in Aquarius		i. ☽♈ ⚹ o. ☽♒	4
Inner partner's Sun in Leo sextile Outer partner's Sun in Libra		i. ☉♌ ⚹ o. ☉♎	7

*KEY: **i.**=Natal Planet located in the inner circle. **o**=Natal Planet located in the outer circle.

3	II-5 II-7	Determine if any of the individual's Sun or Moon is connected to their partner's cardinal points with an orb range of 0°-8°.	This similarly indicates strong ties between the individuals.

ASPECT	GLYPH	ORB
Inner partner's Libra Ascendant trine Outer partner's Moon in Aquarius	i.ASC♎ △ o.☽♒	3

4	II-5 II-3	Determine aspect connections between the individual's inner planets to their partners with an orb range of 0°-8°.	Various elements into how they interact with one another depending on the planets involved and the aspects made.

ASPECT	GLYPH	ORB
Inner partner's Mars in Capricorn trine Outer partner's Venus in Virgo	i.♂♑ △ o.♀♍	0
Inner partner's Mars in Capricorn sextile Outer partner's Mercury in Scorpio	i.♂♑ ⚹ o.☿♏	2
Inner partner's Mars in Capricorn square Outer partner's Mars in Libra	i.♂♑ □ o.♂♎	3
Inner partner's Moon in Aries oppose Outer partner's Mars in Libra	i.☽♈ ☍ o.♂♎	4
Inner Partner's Mercury in Leo square Outer partner's Mercury in Scorpio	i.☿♌ □ o.☿♏	5
Inner partner's Mercury in Leo sextile Outer partner's Mars in Libra	i.☿♌ ⚹ o.♂♎	6
Inner partner's Venus in Libra conjoin Outer partner's Mars in Libra	i.♀♎ ☌ o.♂♎	6
Inner partner's Venus in Libra conjoin Outer partner's Sun in Libra	i.♀♎ ☌ o.☉♎	7
Inner partner's Mercury in Leo sextile Outer partner's Sun in Libra	i.☿♌ ⚹ o.☉♎	7

5		Categorize the most beneficial and least beneficial aspects with their orbs.		Determine the couple's biggest strengths and weaknesses.	
MOST BENEFICIAL			LEAST BENEFICIAL		
ASPECT		ORB	ASPECT		ORB
i.♂♑ △ o.♀♍		0	i.♂♑ □ o.♂♎		3
i.♂♑ ✶ o.☿♏		2	i.☽♈ ☍ o.♂♎		4
i.ASC♎ △ o.☽♒		3	i.☿♌ □ o.☿♏		5
i. ☽♈ ✶ o. ☽♒		4			
i.☿♌ ✶ o.♂♎		6			
i.♀♎ ☌ o.♂♎		6			
i.♀♎ ☌ o.☉♎		7			
i.☿♌ ✶ o.☉♎		7			
i. ☉♌ ✶ o. ☉♎		7			

6		Compose a summary of your findings from step 2-5.	Summary of Analysis.

From the outset, one of the factors that make Client D and their friend immensely compatible involves the sextiles to their Suns and Moons (i. ☉♌ ✶ o. ☉♎, i. ☽♈ ✶ o. ☽♒). This creates substantial harmony between the two because they both have a great flow of synchronistic energy where they are able to be open and honest, which allows for both of them to be true to themself which is a great benefit for both. This is a person where Client D does not have to put up a front and can ground themselves in this way; the same goes for their friend.

However, this harmony can be lost when there is conflict between the two. Indeed, I would say this is their biggest weakness due to their Mars being in a square to one another in addition to their Mercuries (i.♂♑ □ o.♂♎, i.☿♌ □ o.☿♏). Not only do these alignments make it easy for the two to come into conflict with Mars, it makes it hard to resolve due to Mercury. Additionally, conflicts can simply arise out of misunderstandings which instigate a trigger within the other that causes egos to be inflamed. When these situations flair up, Client D should try to take a step back and give their friend space to cool down and vice versa. Then, approach the situation once everything has calmed down. That way the beneficial sextiles to their Suns and Moons can work their magic and resolve any frustrations that came about.

The biggest irony to the above problem is that both Client D and their friend rely on one another to vent their frustrations a lot of the time due to their Mars in sextile to the other individual's Mercury (i.♂♑ ⚹ o.☿♏, i.☿♌ ⚹ o.♂♎). What I suspect happens is that when Client D or their friend have a frustration and want to talk it out, they do so with each other. However, it could be possible that while they hear the other person, they might not take their side and in fact disagree with their friend's assessment. In turn, this causes frustration to now happen between the two. They were trying to utilize the other for support but because they are not complying, they tell them what they might not necessarily want to hear. Still, these two individuals are still helpful to one another in this regard if they both agree with the same conclusion. When they do, then they can properly vent and work through the issue as a team.

Additionally, although these two individuals are friends, there could be some romantic and sexual tension between the two because Client D's Mars is in a trine to their friend's Venus, and the friend's Mars in in a conjunction to Client D's Venus (i.♂♑ △ o.♀♍℞, i.♀♎ ☌ o.♂♎). This is not necessarily a bad thing. It simply means that they both find each other sexually and physically attractive which only adds to their adoration for one another as friends. However, a "friends with benefits" situation might not be the best outcome due to the Mars and Mercury squares which can cause issues in this regard. In other words, there are indicators that make the two attracted to one another physically and mentally, but due to how easy it is to raise conflict and how hard it is to resolve conflict, I would not recommend taking it any further than friends because it would be hard to jump those hurdles the more complicated the relationship becomes.

Either way, both Client D and their friend see a lot of themself within the other due to Client D's Ascendant in a trine to their friend's Moon, and their Venus in conjunction to their friend's Sun (i.ASC♎ △ o.☽♒, i.♀♎ ☌ o.☉♎). This is how they are both able to be honest in who they are around one another. They see aspects of themself through the other. This allows for this honesty because they empathize towards each other very well. The bonds between the two certainly run deep, which cause both to intensely care for the other. Although this is indicative of qualities you would want to find in a romantic partner, I would again advice caution in complicating the relationship unless both are very cognizant towards their moments of conflict.

CLIENT D: COMPOSITE CHART

1		Obtain the partner's birth data and create a composite chart with both birth charts.	This way ASTRO.COM knows which two charts to work with.

Name: ♀ Client D
born on Fr., 22 August 1986
in Houston, TX (US)
95w22, 29n46

Time: 9:39 a.m.
Univ.Time: 14:39
Sid. Time: 6:19:58

ASTRO)DIENST
www.astro.com

Type: 621.GW 0.0-1+2 18-Mrz-2021

Composite Chart with: ♂ Client D'S Friend (Method: Web Style / Placidus)

⊙ Sun	26 Vir 5'53"
☽ Moon	3 Pis 11'38"
☿ Mercury	27 Vir 52'19"
♀ Venus	28 Vir 54'43"
♂ Mars	26 Sco 1'30"
♃ Jupiter	11 Aqu 22'42"
♄ Saturn	11 Vir 50'32"r
♅ Uranus	18 Sco 40'24"
♆ Neptune	18 Sag 20'47"
♇ Pluto	18 Lib 49'36"
☊ True Node	6 Pis 39'50"
⚷ Chiron	17 Tau 37'57"r
AC: 10 Vir 3'31"	2: 4 Lib 40'	3: 3 Sco 0'
MC: 5 Gem 3' 4"	11: 9 Can 6'	12: 11 Leo 32'

531

2A	II-5	Determine if there are any aspects between the composite Sun and Moon along with the orb.	Again, this demonstrates how strong the relationship is foundationally.	
		ASPECT	**GLYPH**	**ORB**
		NONE		
2B	II-5 II-6	**If both birth times are accurate,** determine the house placements of the composite Sun and Moon.	How these fundamental energies are manifested.	

PLANET	GLYPH	HOUSE
SUN	☉	1
MOON	☽	6

2C	II-5 II-3	Determine any aspect connections to the composite Sun and Moon with an orb range of 0°-5°.	Further details the quality of these fundamental energies within the relationship.	
		ASPECT	**GLYPH**	**ORB**
		Composite Sun in Virgo sextile Composite Mars in Scorpio	c.☉♍ ✶ c.♂♏	0
		Composite Sun in Virgo conjoin Composite Mercury in Virgo	c.☉♍ ☌ c.☿♍	2
		Composite Sun in Virgo conjoin Composite Venus in Virgo	c.☉♍ ☌ c.♀♍	3

3	II-5 II-3	**If both times are accurate,** determine any aspect connections to composite Ascendant and Midheaven with an orb range of 0°-8°.	Just like the Sun and Moon, composite Midheaven and Ascendant indicate substantial overall quality of the relationship.	
		ASPECT	**GLYPH**	**ORB**
		Composite Moon in Pisces square Composite Gemini Midheaven	c.☽♓ □ c.MC♊	2
		Composite Saturn in Virgo conjoin Virgo Ascendant	c.♄♍ ☌ c.ASC♍	2
		Composite Venus in Virgo trine Gemini Midheaven	c.♀♍ △ c.MC♊	6
		Composite Jupiter in Aquarius trine Gemini Midheaven	c.♃♒ △ c.MC♊	6
		Composite Moon in Pisces oppose Virgo Ascendant	c.☽♓ ☍ c.ASC♍	7
		Composite Mercury in Virgo trine Gemini Midheaven	c.☿♍ △ c.MC♊	7
		Composite Saturn in Virgo square Gemini Midheaven	c.♄♍ □ c.MC♊	7
		Composite Neptune in Sagittarius square Virgo Ascendant	c.♆♐ □ c.ASC♍	8

4A	II-5 / II-3	Determine any aspect connections to composite Mercury, Venus, and Mars with an orb range of 0°-5°.		This completes the picture with the varying inner planets.

ASPECT	GLYPH	ORB
Composite Mercury in Virgo conjoin Composite Venus in Virgo	c.☿♍ ☌ c.♀♍	1
Composite Mercury in Virgo sextile Composite Mars in Scorpio	c.☿♍ ✶ c.♂♏	2
Composite Venus in Virgo sextile Composite Mars in Scorpio	c.♀♍ ✶ c.♂♏	3

4B	IV-4	**If both times are accurate,** determine the house placements for composite Mercury, Venus, and Mars	Highlights the realms of influence the planets emphasize depending on house placement and aspect type.

PLANET	GLYPH	HOUSE
MERCURY	☿	1
VENUS	♀	1
MARS	♂	3

5		Categorize the most beneficial and least beneficial aspects with their orbs.	Determine the couple's biggest strengths and weaknesses.

MOST BENEFICIAL		LEAST BENEFICIAL	
ASPECT	ORB	ASPECT	ORB
c.☉♍ ✶ c.♂♏	0	c.☽♓ □ c.MC♊	2
c.☿♍ ☌ c.♀♍	1	c.♄♍ ☌ c.ASC♍	2
c.☿♍ ✶ c.♂♏	2	c.♄♍ □ c.MC♊	7
c.☉♍ ☌ c.☿♍	2	c.♆♐ □ c.ASC♍	8
c.♀♍ ✶ c.♂♏	3		
c.☉♍ ☌ c.♀♍	3		
c.♀♍ △ c.MC♊	6		
c.♃♒ △ c.MC♊	6		
c.☽♓ ☍ c.ASC♍	7		
c.☿♍ △ c.MC♊	7		

6		Compose a summary of your findings from Steps 2A-5.	Summary of Analysis.

It is significant to point out that the least beneficial aspects that occur in Client D and their friend's composite chart involve the Midheaven or Ascendant (c.☽♓ □ c.MC♊, cc.♄♍ □ c.MC♊, c.♄♍ ☌ c.ASC♍, c.♆♐ □ c.ASC♍). If you recall, the composite chart shows more how the two individuals act together as one cohesive unit. These aspects tell me the same conclusion as their bi-wheel chart in that they both should probably stay good friends and nothing more. There is something that prevents them from working well together and do better when they are two autonomous individuals co-experiencing life instead. These are two independent individuals that enjoy being able to share their individuality with one another. However, the Neptune square and Saturn conjunction to the Ascendant tells me that there are too many limiting factors that breed confusion and possibly a victim/savor complex that can arise if they were to become a romantic couple. The two squares to the Midheaven by the Moon and Saturn tell me that they should not try to achieve things together, but instead act as the support network for the other when it comes to their individualized goals.

Other than that, just how it was with the bi-wheel chart, the composite chart carries multiple beneficial aspects that make this friendship solid in its foundation and profound in the effect it gives to both parties involved. For one, the Sun, Mercury, and Venus are in a tight conjunction in the 1st house (c.☿♍ ☌ c.♀♍, c.☉♍ ☌ c.☿♍, c.☉♍ ☌ c.♀♍). Other friends that are involved with these two, or any boyfriends/girlfriends that are welcomed into the circle can tell right away that these two have a tight bond and they are not afraid to show their relationship to others. It would be wise if Client D or their friend does not bring jealous partners into the mix because there is no hiding the closeness they share. This closeness comes from these three planets in conjunction, which cause them to be open, trustworthy, and appreciative of the other. A partner with low self-esteem might project that towards them and accuse them of cheating or of not being that open with them. They need to understand that Client D and their friend have established these bonds over a long period of time through many struggles and happy moments and they are not going to simply choose them over their friendship.

To further this point, these three conjunctions all form a sextile to Mars located in the 3rd house (c.☉♍ ⚹ c.♂♏, c.☿♍ ⚹ c.♂♏, c.♀♍ ⚹ c.♂♏). This ties back to the potentially physical and sexual attraction that exists between the two with Mars being involved. With Mars in the 3rd house, this slightly contradicts the bi-wheel chart that shows that the two can be prone to conflicts due to misunderstandings or not being on the same side of an argument. Here, in the composite chart, it shows that if the two are indeed in agreement, then not only do they communicate well with one another, they invigorate the passion of their stance and seek to work cooperatively. For example, if Client D and their friend both agree on a form of social injustice, they might encourage one another to both participate in a protest, or some form of community service together in order to put their ideologies into practice.

Although the Ascendant and Midheaven both have uncomplimentary aspects within the composite chart, there also exists a multitude of beneficial aspects as well particularly with the Midheaven (c.♀♍ Δ c.MC♊, c.♃♒ Δ c.MC♊, c.☿♍ Δ c.MC♊). Again, this ties back that both can work very well together as long as they both are in complete agreement. For example, both would do well starting a business together because they are able to be objective enough to not make it personal and because the end goal is the same for both, to make a profit, this is something they both can agree to and get behind. If they both work towards the same goal, there is a lot of good fortune behind their efforts with Jupiter involved.

CLIENT E: BI-WHEEL CHART

STEP #	SECTION IN BOOK	DESCRIPTION	INFORMATION IT PROVIDES
1		Obtain the partner's birth data and create a bi-wheel chart with both birth charts.	This way ASTRO.COM knows which two charts to work with.

Name: ♀ Client E
born on Sa., 16 July 1988
in Morristown (Morris County), NJ (US)
74w29, 40n48

Time: 6:13 a.m.
Univ.Time: 10:13
Sid. Time: 0:52:57

ASTRO DIENST
www.astro.com
Type: 61.GW 0.0-1+2 18-Mrz-2021

Comparison with: ♂ Client E'S Fiance (outside) (Method: Web Style / Placidus)

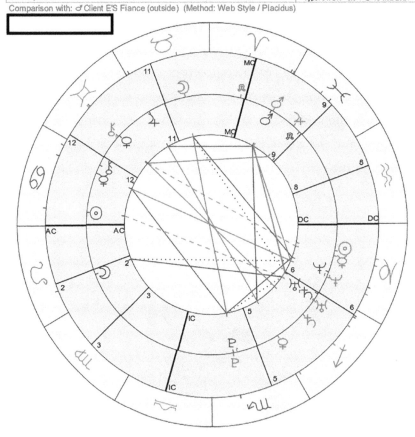

⊙ Sun	24 Can 5'19"	18 ♑ 9'
☽ Moon	22 Leo 3'32"	11 ♉ 23'
☿ Mercury	6 Can 7'43"	15 ♑ 52'
♀ Venus	16 Gem 24'47"	1 ♐ 29'
♂ Mars	1 Ari 10'27"	0 ♈ 20'
♃ Jupiter	29 Tau 1' 6"	18 ♓ 50'
♄ Saturn	27 Sag 26'17"r	16 ♐ 15'
♅ Uranus	28 Sag 2' 3"r	24 ♐ 4'
♆ Neptune	8 Cap 23'13"r	5 ♑ 59'
♇ Pluto	9 Sco 45'48"r	9 ♏ 38'
☊ True Node	15 Pis 3'44"	16 ♈ 17'
⚷ Chiron	2 Can 18' 3"	16 ♓ 56'r

| AC: 29 Can 37'15" | 2: 19 Leo 41' | 3: 13 Vir 48' | 29 ♌ 52' |
| MC: 14 Ari 22'44" | 11: 21 Tau 7' | 12: 28 Gem 3' | 13 ♈ 56' |

536

2	II-5	Determine if there are any aspects between their Suns and Moons along with the orb.	This is the ultimate glue that binds and will determine deep connectivity.

ASPECT		GLYPH*	ORB
Inner partner's Sun in Cancer oppose Outer partner's Sun in Capricorn		i. ☉♋ ☍ o. ☉♑	6

KEY: i.=Natal Planet located in the inner circle. o=Natal Planet located in the outer circle.

3	II-5 II-7	Determine if any of the individual's Sun or Moon is connected to their partner's cardinal points with an orb range of 0°-8°.	This similarly indicates strong ties between the individuals.

ASPECT	GLYPH	ORB
Inner partner's Aries Midheaven square Outer partner's Sun in Capricorn	i.MC♈ □ o.☉♑	4
Inner Partner's Sun in Cancer conjoin Outer Partner's Cancer Ascendant	i.☉♋ ☌ o.ASC♋	5

4	II-5 II-3	Determine aspect connections between the individual's inner planets to their partners with an orb range of 0°-8°.	Various elements into how they interact with one another depending on the planets involved and the aspects made.

ASPECT	GLYPH	ORB
Inner partner's Mars in Aries trine Outer partner's Venus in Sagittarius	i.♂♈ △ o.♀♐	0
Inner partner's Mars in Aries conjoin Outer partner's Mars in Aries	i.♂♈ ☌ o.♂♈	1
Inner partner's Mercury in Cancer sextile Outer partner's Moon in Taurus	i.☿♋ ✶ o.☽♉	5
Inner partner's Mercury in Cancer square Outer partner's Mars in Aries	i.☿♋ □ o.♂♈	6

5		Categorize the most beneficial and least beneficial aspects with their orbs.	Determine the couple's biggest strengths and weaknesses.

MOST BENEFICIAL		LEAST BENEFICIAL	
ASPECT	ORB	ASPECT	ORB
i.♂♈ △ o.♀♐	0	i.MC♈ □ o.☉♑	4
i.♂♈ ☌ o.♂♈	1	i. ☉♋ ☍ o. ☉♑	6

i.☉♋ ☌ o.ASC♋	5	i.☿♋ □ o.♂♈	6
i.☿♋ ✶ o.☽♉	5		

6		Compose a summary of your findings from step 2-5.	Summary of Analysis.

Client E and their fiancé's Suns are in opposition to one another (i. ☉♋ ☍ o. ☉♑). Additionally, although the orb is very wide, their Moons are in a square with Client E's Moon in Leo and their fiancé's Moon in Taurus. Although both approach life somewhat similarly, there can be ego clashes at times. When these occur, it is difficult to diffuse them because both operate on a different emotional level. Due to this, confrontational exchanges take a while to resolve because, as with all oppositions, the necessity to sacrifice part of the ego in order to meet in the middle is essential. With these two individuals, when emotions are high, that mental state where you can admit some fault on both parties is impossible until individual feelings cool off after a while.

The answer is Mercury, but even then, both parties need to tread lightly because it seems that their fiancé is only open to talking it out when, and if, they are ready to do so. Client E is able to connect to their fiancé through their Mercury which is in sextile to their Moon (i.☿♋ ✶ o.☽♉). When those windows of opportunity exist, Client E takes advantage of them and tries to connect back to their fiancé internally by asking them to express their feelings more. Similarly, their fiancé finds it easy to relate what they are feeling back to Client E. The trick is to make sure Client E does not attempt to make amends at the wrong time due to their Mercury in a square to their fiancé's Mars (i.☿♋ □ o.♂♈).

If Client E tries to resolve the issue when their fiancé is not ready, it can only reignite frustrations and put them in a one step forward, two steps back situation. Client E simply needs to be patient and wait for when it feels right. If they can do this, then they will have an easier time fixing the problems between the two.

There certainly is romantic and sexual passion between the two with Client E's Mars in trine to their fiancé's Venus, and both of their Mars in conjunction (i.♂♈ △ o.♀♐, i.♂♈ ☌ o.♂♈). This passion is what drives them both, which gives them a lot of motivation to work together and encourage the other. They are very much the other person's support group, and both can find inspiration through their union. This is a solution to their above-mentioned issues because it indicates that when egos do engage in conflict, it is due to inflamed passions that manifest into frustrations and irritability. They need to remind each other that, paradoxically, they are only angry at one another because they care so much about one another. Once the intensity winds down, these two can reground and center themselves through this intense passion.

Similar to other Ascendant combinations we have witnessed above, Client E sees a lot of themself within their fiancé and vice versa due to their Sun/Ascendant conjunction (i.☉ ♂ o.ASC☉). This connects them in a deep way and gives them both understanding and empathy for the other. Again, this helps in their romantic connection because there is an empathy that only the two can give to each other. They understand and relate primarily through this commonality.

CLIENT E: COMPOSITE CHART

1		Obtain the partner's birth data and create a composite chart with both birth charts.	This way ASTRO.COM knows which two charts to work with.

Name: ♀ Client E
born on Sa., 16 July 1988
in Morristown (Morris County), NJ (US)
74w29, 40n48

Time: 6:13 a.m.
Univ.Time: 10:13
Sid. Time: 0:52:57

ASTRO DIENST
www.astro.com

Type: 621.GW 0.0-1+2 18-Mrz-2021

Composite Chart with: ♂ Client E'S Fiance (Method: Web Style / Placidus)

	⊙ Sun	21 Lib 7'18"	+opp.house
	☽ Moon	1 Can 43'11"	
	☿ Mercury	11 Ari 0' 4"	+opp.house
	♀ Venus	8 Vir 56'53"	
	♂ Mars	0 Ari 44'59"	
	♃ Jupiter	23 Ari 55'35"	
	♄ Saturn	21 Sag 50'45"	
	♅ Uranus	26 Sag 2'53"	
	♆ Neptune	7 Cap 11'13"	
	♇ Pluto	9 Sco 41'56"	
	☊ True Node	0 Ari 40'19"	
	⚷ Chiron	24 Gem 37'55"	

AC: 29 Can 44'46" | 2: 19 Leo 39' | 3: 13 Vir 39'
MC: 14 Ari 9'31" | 11: 21 Tau 0' | 12: 28 Gem 8'

540

2A	II-5	Determine if there are any aspects between the composite Sun and Moon along with the orb.	Again, this demonstrates how strong the relationship is foundationally.	

ASPECT			GLYPH	ORB
NONE				

2B	II-5 II-6	**If both birth times are accurate,** determine the house placements of the composite Sun and Moon.	How these fundamental energies are manifested.	

PLANET	GLYPH	HOUSE
SUN	☉	4
MOON	☽	12

2C	II-5 II-3	Determine any aspect connections to the composite Sun and Moon with an orb range of 0°-5°.	Further details the quality of these fundamental energies within the relationship.

ASPECT	GLYPH	ORB
Composite Sun in Libra sextile Composite Saturn in Sagittarius	c.☉♎ ✶ c.♄♐	1
Composite Moon in Cancer square Composite Mars in Aries	c.☽♋ □ c.♂♈	1
Composite Sun in Libra oppose Composite Jupiter in Aries	c.☉♎ ☍ c.♃♈	3
Composite Sun in Libra sextile Composite Uranus in Sagittarius	c.☉♎ ✶ c.♅♐	5
Composite Moon in Cancer oppose Composite Neptune in Capricorn	c.☽♋ ☍ c.♆♑	5

3	II-5 II-3	**If both times are accurate,** determine any aspect connections to composite Ascendant and Midheaven with an orb range of 0°-8°.	Just like the Sun and Moon, composite Midheaven and Ascendant indicate substantial overall quality of the relationship.

ASPECT	GLYPH	ORB
Composite Mars in Aries trine Composite Cancer Ascendant	c.♂♈ △ c.ASC♋	1
Composite Mercury in Aries conjoin Composite Aries Midheaven	c.☿♈ ☌ c.MC♈	3
Composite Jupiter in Aries square Composite Cancer Ascendant	c.♃♈ □ c.ASC♋	6
Composite Sun in Libra oppose Composite Aries Midheaven	c.☉♎ ☍ c.MC♈	7
Composite Neptune in Capricorn square Composite Aries Midheaven	c.♆♑ □ c.MC♈	7
Composite Saturn in Sagittarius trine Composite Aries Midheaven	c.♄♐ △ c.MC♈	8

541

| 4A | II-5 | Determine any aspect connections to composite Mercury, Venus, and Mars with an orb range of 0°-5°. | | This completes the picture with the varying inner planets. |
| | II-3 | | | |

ASPECT			GLYPH	ORB
Composite Venus in Virgo sextile Composite Pluto in Scorpio			c.♀℠ ✶ c.♇♏	1
Composite Venus in Virgo trine Composite Neptune in Capricorn			c.♀℠ △ c.♆♑	2
Composite Mercury in Aries square Composite Neptune in Capricorn			c.☿♈ □ c.♆♑	4
Composite Mars in Aries square Composite Uranus in Sagittarius			c.♂♈ □ c.♅♐	5

4B	IV-4	**If both times are accurate**, determine the house placements for composite Mercury, Venus, and Mars	Highlights the realms of influence the planets emphasize depending on house placement and aspect type.

PLANET	GLYPH	HOUSE
MERCURY	☿	9
VENUS	♀	2
MARS	♂	9

5		Categorize the most beneficial and least beneficial aspects with their orbs.	Determine the couple's biggest strengths and weaknesses.

MOST BENEFICIAL		LEAST BENEFICIAL	
ASPECT	ORB	ASPECT	ORB
c.☉♎ ✶ c.♄♐	1	c.☽♋ □ c.♂♈	1
c.♂♈ △ c.ASC♋	1	c.☿♈ □ c.♆♑	4
c.♀℠ ✶ c.♇♏	1	c.♂♈ □ c.♅♐	5
c.♀℠ △ c.♆♑	2	c.♃♈ □ c.ASC♋	6
c.☉♎ ☍ c.♃♈	3	c.☉♎ ☍ c.MC♈	7
c.☿♈ ☌ c.MC♈	3	c.♆♑ □ c.MC♈	7
c.☉♎ ✶ c.♅♐	5		
c.☽♋ ☍ c.♆♑	5		
c.♄♐ △ c.MC♈	8		

6		Compose a summary of your findings from Steps 2A-5.	Summary of Analysis.

The composite Venus in sextile to composite Pluto and trine to Neptune (c.♀♍ ✶ c.♇♏, c.♀♍ Δ c.♆♑) shows a transcendental connection between Client E and their fiancé. The connection that they share is almost indescribable as it comes from a deeply spiritual perspective. This establishes a strong connection where both feel secure, and therefore grow, because this allows for both of them to process things that they might not be able to process with others. This is further confirmed with the composite Moon in the 12th house and composite Sun in the 4th house. There is a general feeling of non-judgement between them which provides a certain acceptance that they may not have received from their past.

Composite Mars seems to be a double-edged sword of sorts with a trine to the Ascendant and a square to the Moon and Uranus (c.♂♈ Δ c.ASC♋, c.☽♋ □ c.♂♈, c.♂♈ □ c.♅♐). On one hand, Mars gives them both the ability to show a good face with others and the world seems to approve of their relationship, which allows for them to work towards common interests because they are not purposely deterred by the self-doubts of others. On the other hand, the squares to Uranus and the Moon indicates possible emotional volatility and unpredictability. This ties back to the ego-clashes we saw in the bi-wheel chart. Similarly, to this point, the square between composite Mercury and Neptune (c.☿♈ □ c.♆♑) also indicates how hard it can be to mend the gap between these conflicts as communication can sometimes become diluted in confusion and emotional responses.

The secret to keep these in balance is twofold. For one, with the composite Sun sextile to Saturn and Uranus (c.☉♎ ✶ c.♄♐, c.☉♎ ✶ c.♅♐), grounding themselves in facts and other objective parties like trustworthy friends or counselors will help to get rid of the subjective emotional stances that get in the way of resolution. Secondly, with composite Mercury conjoin the Midheaven (c.☿♈ ☌ c.MC♈), the couple should remind themselves of what they have going for them along with shared goals they are trying to achieve. Reminding themselves of these various achievements will remind both that they are on the same team, and therefore working at cross purposes is ultimately self-destructive and counterproductive.

When it comes to their future plans and goals, these two are able to achieve them readily through hard work as indicated by the composite Saturn trine the Midheaven (c.♄♐ Δ c.MC♈). This tells me that these two can create a firm foundation and would make great parents together with

Saturn residing in the 5th house. Similarly, any sort of creative outlet that the two might share could create some impressive outputs if both put their brainstorming minds together. Either way, the Saturn trine is indicative of hard work and discipline paying off in the end.

The issue is determining what the two individuals ultimately want out of the relationship with Neptune in opposition to the Moon and square the Midheaven (c.☽♋ ☍ c.♆♑, c.♆♑ □ c.MC♈). This tells me that when things between the two become tense, they can sometimes be a little too pessimistic and start to think "what are we really trying to do here?" Again, the answer is to bring in an objective third party that can help to set any record straight and help the two realign themselves to where they work cooperatively once again. Similar to Client C, this couple experiences very high highs, and very low lows. In order for the pendulum to swing from down to up once again, they both need to not get lost in the fog of negative thinking. Instead, focus on the ways in which their relationship does work.

Indeed, this is not a relationship where everything comes easy due to Jupiter squaring the Ascendant and opposing the Sun (II.♃♈ □ II.☉s☿♋, II.☉♎ ☍ II.♃♈). However, it is a relationship where both gain a great deal of therapy and focus when they channel their love towards a positive direction. The issue is that they sometimes cannot put this love into words because it is incredibly ethereal and mystical. They do not know why they love one another; they just do. This inexplicable connection is a strength, not a weakness, and both should remember this very important concept. Instead of focusing on the "why" of it all, they should focus on the "what." What can we accomplish? What are we supposed to learn from one another? What do we want out of this relationship and what are the means to obtain these various ambitions? Many things in life are inexplainable at times, and feelings of love are no exception. All they need to do is focus on what works, capitalize off this, and take time and patience to fix what does not work with others when conflict arises.

* * *

Applying relationship analysis for yourself and for your client is incredibly beneficial because these questions inevitably arise. People are always interested in knowing more about their partners and why they do or do not work out. Similarly, it is a good idea to observe your own potential romantic and business interests to see if harmony does exist between the two. The most significant benefit this gives you is that you can see why things do not work and what you can do to remedy those situations. Composite and bi-wheel charts eventually become indispensable once you learn how to interpret them. Now, we will continue to the next specialized astrological technique involving relocation and astrocartography charts, which help you to determine where there are good places to live, have a vacation, retire, find a career, and even yourself.

SECTION 2- RELOCATION AND ASTROCARTOGRAPHY CHARTS

❧

As you have witnessed in Parts V and VI, planetary powers, whether harmonious or inharmonious, drastically affect the individual depending on the various statuses of the natal planets. Therefore, it is recommended that the individual emphasize or deemphasize certain planets in order to work with the various energies that are found within the birth chart. This is the core idea behind astrocartography and relocation. Mainly, that one can emphasize or deemphasize planetary powers by relocating to parts of the globe that have natal planets located along the various cardinal points.

Remember from Part II-Section 7, the cardinal points act as anchors for the birth chart and any planets that are aspected to them heavily influence the way the cardinal points are manifested. With astrocartography, the goal is to place planetary energies that are desired along themes of the cardinal points by shifting the chart to different latitudes and longitudes.

The reason as to why this works is because the planets are still moving even after the "snapshot" was taken at the time of birth. Because of this, planetary travels continue around the globe and as they do, they make these invisible lines that astrocartography traces. These lines show where the planet in question is conjoined to the Ascendant, Midheaven, Descendant, or IC superimposed on a map of the planet (Fig. VII-1).

These lines show where an individual can emphasize or deemphasize certain planetary energies depending on which planet is involved and which cardinal point is also involved. Then, all we have to do is determine if the planet is harmonious or inharmonious, which will help to determine if we want to move to an area where those energies are highlighted or avoid them at all cost. The following tables below show you how to obtain an astrocartography and relocation chart in addition to their analysis (Table VII-4A-C).

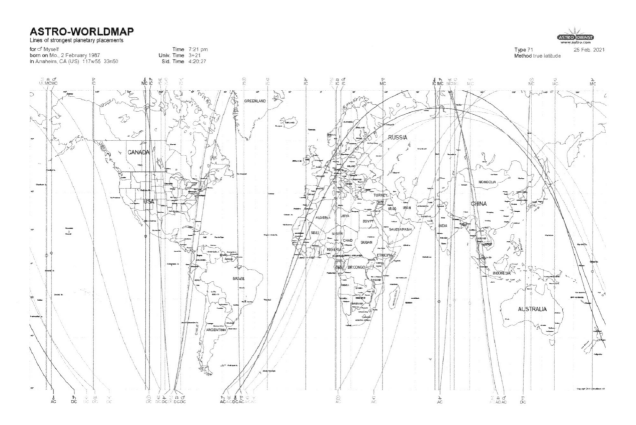

FIGURE VII-1. Example of an Astrocartography Map

TABLE VII-4A. How to obtain an Astrocartography Map on ASTRO.COM

---

(1) On the ASTRO.COM main page, under the HOROSCOPES tab, chose EXTENDED CHART SELECTION under DRAWINGS, CALCULATIONS, DATA.
(2) Confirm that the appropriate individual is selected under HOROSCOPE FOR.
(3) Select the SPEICAL tab.
(4) Under CHART TYPE, select ASTROMAP WORLD, or choose a continent that you want to further observe.
(5) Click CLICK HERE TO SHOW CHART.

TABLE VII-4B. Steps on how to Comprehensively Analyze an Astrocartography Chart

STEP #	SECTION IN BOOK	DESCRIPTION	INFORMATION IT PROVIDES
1	II-6 II-7	Determine what areas of life the individual wants to emphasize or deemphasize and determine the house and cardinal point whose themes best align with that intention. **OR** Determine where the individual wants you to observe if they already have a location in mind AND SKIP TO STEP 5.	What area of life they want to explore (house placement) and how they want to explore it (cardinal point).
2	II-2 II-3	Determine the planet(s) within the birth chart that rules that house.	Planetary house ruler.
3	II-4 II-5 II-6 V-2	Determine the overall nature of that planetary ruler using dignities, debilities, house, and aspect placement.	If that planet is functioning harmoniously or inharmoniously.
4A	V-2	If planetary ruler is functioning harmoniously, recommend emphasizing that planet and determine best Planet/ Line combination.	Places that will strengthen the Planet's already powerful nature.
4B	V-2	If planetary ruler is functioning inharmoniously, recommend deemphasizing that planet and determine best Planet/ Line combination.	Further weakens malefic Planets within the birth chart.
5		Using the astrocartography map, determine where these planetary lines are located.	This tells you where in the world the various planetary energies can be emphasized.
6		Relocate the birth chart to the desired location and confirm that the overall condition of the chart is to your liking. (See table VII-4C).	Confirms the astrocatrography map.
7		Compose a summary of your findings from Steps 1-6.	Summary of Analysis.

TABLE VII-4C. How to obtain a Relocation Chart on ASTRO.COM

(1) On the ASTRO.COM main page, under the HOROSCOPES tab, chose EXTENDED CHART SELECTION under DRAWINGS, CALCULATIONS, DATA.
(2) Confirm that the appropriate individual is selected under HOROSCOPE FOR.
(3) Under CHART TYPE, select RELOCATION CHART.
(4) Under DEFAULT SETTINGS click MODIFY DATA.
(5) Select location in question and click CONTINUE.
(6) Confirm that this new location is present next to REFERENCE POINT under DEFAULT SETTINGS.
(7) Click CLICK HERE TO SHOW CHART.

CLIENT A: ASTROCARTOGRAPHY

1	II-6 II-7	Determine what areas of life the individual wants to emphasize or deemphasize and determine the house and cardinal point whose themes best align with that intention. **OR** Determine where the individual wants you to observe if they already have a location in mind AND SKIP TO STEP 5.	What area of life they want to explore (house placement) and how they want to explore it (cardinal point).

Client A wants to know if Toronto, Ontario, Canada is the best place for them. Because Client A has a place already in mind, we will continue and skip down to Step 5.

5		Using the astrocartography map, determine where these planetary lines are located.	This tells you where in the world the various planetary energies can be emphasized.

Astromap North America

for ♀ Client A
born on Sa., 21 July 1990
at 3:40 am   Univ. Time 20-40   Sid. Time 21:27:04
in Omsk, RU   73e24   55n00

Type 732   18 Mar. 2021
Method true latitude

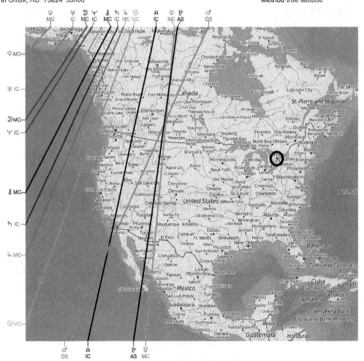

6		Relocate the birth chart to the desired location and confirm that the overall condition of the chart is to your liking. (See table VII-4C).	Confirms the astrocatrography map.

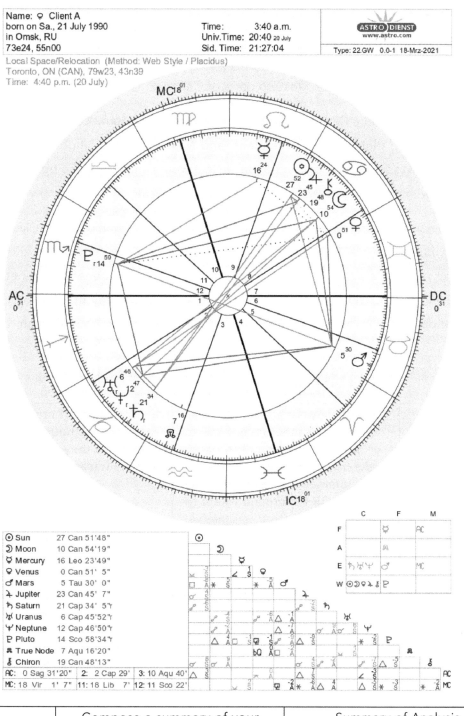

☉ Sun	27 Can 51'48"	
☽ Moon	10 Can 54'19"	
☿ Mercury	16 Leo 23'49"	
♀ Venus	0 Can 51' 5"	
♂ Mars	5 Tau 30' 0"	
♃ Jupiter	23 Can 45' 7"	
♄ Saturn	21 Cap 34' 5"r	
♅ Uranus	6 Cap 45'52"r	
♆ Neptune	12 Cap 46'50"r	
♇ Pluto	14 Sco 58'34"r	
☊ True Node	7 Aqu 16'20"	
⚷ Chiron	19 Can 48'13"	
AC: 0 Sag 31'20"	2: 2 Cap 29'	3: 10 Aqu 40'
MC: 18 Vir 1' 7"	11: 18 Lib 7'	12: 11 Sco 22'

7		Compose a summary of your findings from Steps 1-6.	Summary of Analysis.

According to the astrocartography map and the relocation chart, no natal planets are touching a cardinal point line within Toronto, Canada, which probably explains why Client A is not really feeling any advantages or disadvantages towards living there. However, Client A has various influential lines in the middle and western parts of Canada.

Slightly west of Saskatoon, Canada, Client A has an incredible intersection of three lines: Mars on the Descendant, Pluto on the Ascendant, and Mercury on the Midheaven. I would not recommend moving to this part of Canada because it would emphasize the tight Mercury/Pluto square found within the natal chart.

However, the northwestern coastline of Canada near Prince Rupert would benefit Client A because it would put Jupiter on the Midheaven. This is beneficial for Client A because, referring to our natal analysis in Part V-Section 2, Jupiter is one of Client A's most beneficial planets and rules the 2nd and 11th houses within the natal chart. Therefore, I would say that this part of Canada is a place where Client A can make friendships, obtain property, and benefit from their career.

CLIENT B: ASTROCARTOGRAPHY

1	II-6 II-7	Determine what areas of life the individual wants to emphasize or deemphasize and determine the house and cardinal point whose themes best align with that intention. **OR** Determine where the individual wants you to observe if they already have a location in mind AND SKIP TO STEP 5.	What area of life they want to explore (house placement) and how they want to explore it (cardinal point).

Client B wants to relocate to Grand Junction, CO, USA and wants to know if this is a good idea. Because they already have a location in mind, we can skip over to Step 5.

5		Using the astrocartography map, determine where these planetary lines are located.	This tells you where in the world the various planetary energies can be emphasized.

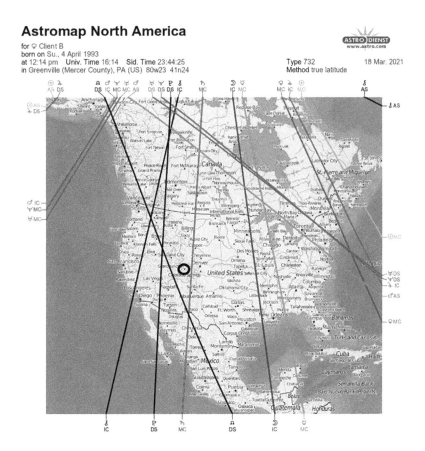

Astromap North America

for ♀ Client B
born on Su., 4 April 1993
at 12:14 pm   Univ. Time 16:14   Sid. Time 23:44:25
in Greenville (Mercer County), PA (US) 80w23 41n24

Type 732   18 Mar. 2021
Method true latitude

6		Relocate the birth chart to the desired location and confirm that the overall condition of the chart is to your liking. (See table XC).	Confirms the astrocatrography map.

553

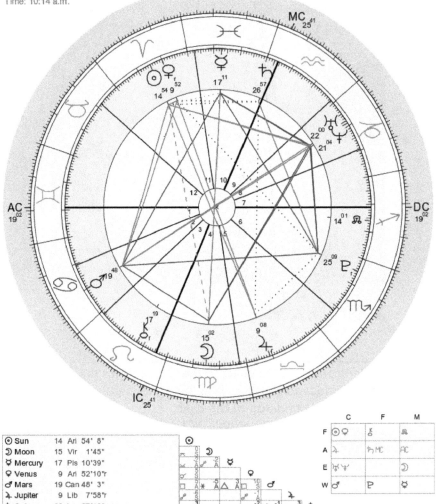

Name: ♀ Client B
born on Su., 4 April 1993
in Greenville (Mercer County), PA (US)
80w23, 41n24

Time: 12:14 p.m.
Univ.Time: 16:14
Sid. Time: 23:44:25

ASTRO DIENST
www.astro.com

Type: 22.GW 0.0-1 18-Mrz-2021

Local Space/Relocation (Method: Web Style / Placidus)
Grand Junction, CO (US), 108w33, 39n04
Time: 10:14 a.m.

☉ Sun	14 Ari 54' 8"	
☽ Moon	15 Vir 1'45"	
☿ Mercury	17 Pis 10'39"	
♀ Venus	9 Ari 52'10"r	
♂ Mars	19 Can 48' 3"	
♃ Jupiter	9 Lib 7'58"r	
♄ Saturn	26 Aqu 57'12"	
♅ Uranus	21 Cap 59'32"	
♆ Neptune	21 Cap 3'38"	
♇ Pluto	25 Sco 8'42"r	
☊ True Node	14 Sag 1'15"	
⚷ Chiron	17 Leo 19'14"r	

AC: 19 Gem 2'22" 2: 10 Can 28' 3: 1 Leo 23'
MC: 25 Aqu 40'46" 11: 27 Pis 27' 12: 8 Tau 15'

	C	F	M
F	☉ ♀	⚷	♺
A	♃	♄ MC	AC
E	♅ ♆		☽
W	♂	♇	☿

7		Compose a summary of your findings from Steps 1-6.	Summary of Analysis.

As determined by the map and confirmed by the relocation chart, Client B's Saturn touches the Midheaven line close to Grand Junction, CO, USA. In fact, this line is located from the norther border of Colorado all the way to the southern border. This means that the entire state will have this energy, especially if Client B moves towards the middle part of the state, closer to Denver for example. For the most part this is a beneficial location for Client B, but I would also point out some pitfalls.

Saturn on the Midheaven is a great placement for career advancement. Furthermore, because Saturn rules the 7th, 8th, and 9th houses within Client B's birth chart, this is also a good place to dedicate themself to a marriage where joint property and finances are involved. This is also a good place for Client B to go to college. Although it might not be the most relaxing places to live or visit, this location certainly is a place where Client B can invest in their education, long-term goals, and intimate relationships.

However, there is a pitfall. Looking back at the birth chart, it should be noted that Saturn only makes one aspect to another planet and that is a tight square to Pluto. This means that Client B will definitely face some challenges along the way like going against authority, run-ins with institutions of power, and an overall more difficult time in reaching their goals. The good news is that Pluto is in fact very well aspected within their birth chart, which dilutes these issues a bit. Pluto rules the 5th house within Client B's chart so I would remind them in order to counter the Saturn difficulties, they need to remember to take it easy and incorporate recreation into their lives as best as they can. Also, I would say that if Client B wanted to raise children in this location, they will also find fulfillment in this regard. If Client B can incorporate their beneficial Pluto by communicating with honesty, establishing authority of their own when it is warranted, and an overall open and conscious mind, then this placement and all of Colorado will be beneficial for Client B.

CLIENT D: ASTROCARTOGRAPHY

1	II-6 II-7	Determine what areas of life the individual wants to emphasize or deemphasize and determine the house and cardinal point whose themes best align with that intention. **OR** Determine where the individual wants you to observe if they already have a location in mind AND SKIP TO STEP 5.	What area of life they want to explore (house placement) and how they want to explore it (cardinal point).

Client D wants to know where a good place to live would be for their career specifically looking at Los Angeles, CA, USA.

2	II-2 II-3	Determine the planet(s) within the birth chart that rules that house.	Planetary house ruler.

We are looking at career success, which means we are looking at the planetary rulers of the 10th house, which are Jupiter and Neptune because Pisces is the sign on the 10th house cusp.

3	II-4 II-5 II-6 V-2	Determine the overall nature of that planetary ruler using dignities, debilities, house, and aspect placement.	If that planet is functioning harmoniously or inharmoniously.

For the most part, Jupiter and Neptune are decently aspected within the birth chart but there are some caveats to mention. Jupiter opposes Venus and the Sun within the birth chart, which means that, although Jupiter is a good planet to have on the Midheaven, Client D will also unearth some personal issues that might not have been on their radar prior to moving to that location. This is because if Jupiter is touching the Midheaven, then the Sun and Venus will be touching the IC at the same time. Additionally, Neptune squares the Sun in the birth chart, which means that Client D can either be more prone to addiction or an overall ego-confusion if they are to live on a Jupiter or Neptune Midheaven line. For example, when it gets difficult, Client D could highly doubt their abilities and worry about the choice they have made. I would also warn against accidents and physical confrontations because Neptune opposes Mars.

What helps these anxieties are the beneficial aspects to Neptune, which include a trine to their Moon and a sextile to Mercury. If Client D can work through their internal struggles that are unearthed by living on this line, they will be able prevent mishaps because they are no longer bottling up their emotions.

4A	V-2	If planetary ruler is functioning harmoniously, recommend emphasizing that planet and determine best Planet/Line combination.	Places that will strengthen the Planet's already powerful nature.
4B	V-2	If planetary ruler is functioning inharmoniously, recommend deemphasizing that planet and determine best Planet/Line combination.	Further weakens malefic Planets within the birth chart.

In general, I would tell Client D that a Jupiter or Neptune on the Midheaven line would be somewhat beneficial, but I would proceed with extreme caution. It seems that it would be good for their career in some ways, but not without intense internal struggle. For a better manifestation of what Client D desires, I would recommend locating somewhere where their natal Mercury or Moon would be touching the Midheaven simply because these planets are beneficially stronger within the birth chart even though they do not rule the 10th house within the birth chart.

5		Using the astrocartography map, determine where these planetary lines are located.	This tells you where in the world the various planetary energies can be emphasized.

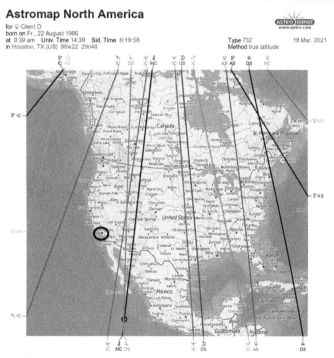

Astromap North America

557

6		Relocate the birth chart to the desired location and confirm that the overall condition of the chart is to your liking. (See table XC).	Confirms the astrocatrography map.

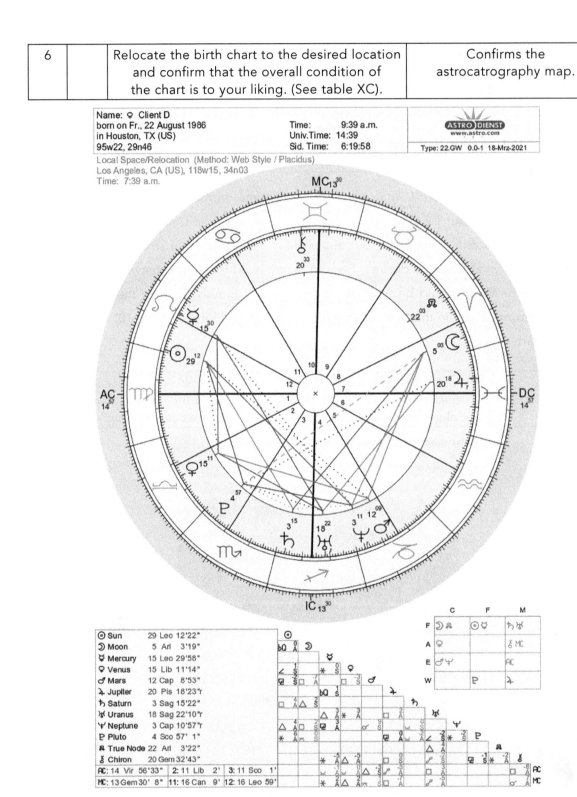

Name: ♀ Client D
born on Fr., 22 August 1986
in Houston, TX (US)
95w22, 29n46

Time: 9:39 a.m.
Univ.Time: 14:39
Sid. Time: 6:19:58

ASTRO⟩DIENST
www.astro.com

Type: 22.GW 0.0-1 18-Mrz-2021

Local Space/Relocation (Method: Web Style / Placidus)
Los Angeles, CA (US), 118w15, 34n03
Time: 7:39 a.m.

⊙ Sun	29 Leo 12'22"
☽ Moon	5 Ari 3'19"
☿ Mercury	15 Leo 29'58"
♀ Venus	15 Lib 11'14"
♂ Mars	12 Cap 8'53"
♃ Jupiter	20 Pis 18'23"r
♄ Saturn	3 Sag 15'22"
♅ Uranus	18 Sag 22'10"r
♆ Neptune	3 Cap 10'57"r
♇ Pluto	4 Sco 57' 1"
♌ True Node	22 Ari 3'22"
⚷ Chiron	20 Gem 32'43"

| AC: 14 Vir 56'33" | 2: 11 Lib 2' | 3: 11 Sco 1' |
| MC: 13 Gem 30' 8" | 11: 16 Can 9' | 12: 16 Leo 59' |

	C	F	M
F	☽ ♌	⊙ ☿	♄ ♓
A	♀		⚷ MC
E	♂ ♆		AC
W		♇	♃

7		Compose a summary of your findings from Steps 1-6.	Summary of Analysis.

According to the astrocartography map, Client D has no Midheaven lines within North America and the west coast is void of lines. This means that this location will not harm nor aid the client in any way. However, it is important to note that Jupiter is slightly close to the Descendant line, which means all of the issues that Jupiter can bring about mentioned above can manifest though their relationships. Particularly if they were to move to places like Arizona where the line is adjacent. I would therefore not recommend this location for a vacation with their partner.

* * *

A great way to test the functionality of asstrocatrpgraphy is to look at places you have lived or traveled to and see if your experiences match with planetary lines that might lie adjacent to those various locations. Similar to the astro-twins search discussed in the introduction of this book, this is a sure and efficient way to test the validity of astrology in addition to your skills. This also helps you to understand more of your chart because if a certain location emphasized any planet within your birth chart, you were given a greater glimpse into the functionality of that planet. The next section involves interpretation of the annual birthday chart, which helps to discern energies that will be of importance throughout an individual's year.

SECTION 3-THE SOLAR RETURN CHART

Although it is less common within the United States to hear the phrase "many happy returns," it is a common, albeit old-fashioned, way of wishing someone a happy birthday. The phrase stems from the fact that the Earth has reached the same place during its annual rotation as it was located at the time you were born. Hence, the Sun has "returned" to the moment of your birth. This is what we mean when we say solar return, and essentially a solar return chart is a chart that is erected at the moment the Sun has reached the exact degree and minute location along the zodiac found within your birth chart.

There are some contradicting theories as to where one should locate their solar return chart. Some camps believe you should locate the chart at your original place of birth, but others claim that you should locate the chart at the place where you are celebrating your birthday for that year. In fact, some astrologers hypothesize that you can use astrocartography along with your solar return chart to properly emphasize or deemphasize certain planets within your solar return chart, which will subsequently alter the energies you will experience during that entire year. Personally, I have experimented with both and have found validity in both methods, but I find the standard practice is a chart that is located at your place of birth. However, I urge you to experiment with both methods and see what you experience.

The solar return chart tells you the various themes, struggles, and benefits you can expect for that year. It is very similar to the birth chart in terms of analysis. The only difference is the degree of importance some factors receive when analyzing both. Below is a step-by-step guide on how to obtain your solar return chart in addition to what you need to observe within your analysis (Tables VII-5A-B).

560

TABLE VII-5A. How to Obtain your Solar Return Chart on ASTRO.COM

(1) On the ASTRO.COM main page, under the HOROSCOPES tab, chose EXTENDED CHART SELECTION under DRAWINGS, CALCULATIONS, DATA.
(2) Confirm that the appropriate individual is selected under HOROSCOPE FOR.
(3) Under CHART TYPE, select SOLAR RETURN CHART.
(4) Under START DATE choose the day after birthdate with the corresponding year you want to analyze. [NOTE: The reason why you want to choose the date after your birthday is because sometimes your UT time will accidently procure a chart for the previous year. This is just a sure way to be safe to make sure this does not happen.]
(5) Click CLICK HERE TO SHOW CHART.

TABLE VII-5B. Steps on how to Comprehensively Analyze a Solar Return Chart

STEP #	SECTION IN BOOK	DESCRIPTION	INFORMATION IT PROVIDES
1A	V-2	Determine the chart ruler by observing the ruler of the Ascendant	The main Planet of the chart.
1B	V-2	Determine the chart ruler's overall condition by using dignities and debilities, house, and aspect placements with an orb range of 0°-8°.	If the Chart Ruler is functioning harmoniously or inharmoniously.
2A	II-6	Determine the Sun's house location.	Major themes that are activated for that year.
2B	II-5	Determine any aspects made to the Sun with an orb range of 0°-8°.	Overall condition of the year ahead.
3A	II-6	Determine the Moon's house location.	Inner themes for that year.
3B	II-5	Determine any aspects made to the Moon with an orb range of 0°-8°.	Overall condition of these explorations.
4	V-2	Determine the condition of all other planets using dignities and debilities, sign and house placements, and aspects with an orb range of 0°-5°.	Various strengths and weaknesses for the year based on the planetary condition within.
5	V-2	Determine the house ruler for each of the 12 houses.	Areas that will similarly manifest strongly or weakly depending on the condition of the planetary house ruler(s).
6		Compose a summary of your findings from Steps 1A-5.	Summary of Analysis.

CLIENT A: SOLAR RETURN CHART

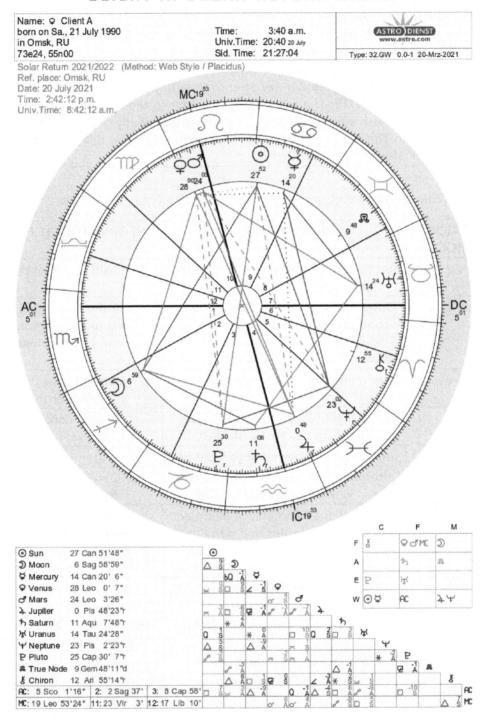

Name: ♀ Client A
born on Sa., 21 July 1990
in Omsk, RU
73e24, 55n00

Time: 3:40 a.m.
Univ.Time: 20:40 20 July
Sid. Time: 21:27:04

ASTRO DIENST
www.astro.com
Type: 32.GW 0.0-1 20-Mrz-2021

Solar Return 2021/2022 (Method: Web Style / Placidus)
Ref. place: Omsk, RU
Date: 20 July 2021
Time: 2:42:12 p.m.
Univ.Time: 8:42:12 a.m.

☉ Sun	27 Can 51'48"
☽ Moon	6 Sag 58'59"
☿ Mercury	14 Can 20' 6"
♀ Venus	28 Leo 0' 7"
♂ Mars	24 Leo 3'26"
♃ Jupiter	0 Pis 48'23"r
♄ Saturn	11 Aqu 7'48"r
♅ Uranus	14 Tau 24'28"
♆ Neptune	23 Pis 2'23"r
♇ Pluto	25 Cap 30' 7"r
☊ True Node	9 Gem 48'11"d
⚷ Chiron	12 Ari 55'14"r
AC: 5 Sco 1'16"	2: 2 Sag 37'	3: 8 Cap 58'
MC: 19 Leo 53'24"	11: 23 Vir 3'	12: 17 Lib 10'

562

CLIENT A: SOLAR RETURN CHART ANALYSIS

1A	V-2	Determine the chart ruler by observing the ruler of the Ascendant	The main Planet of the chart.
1B	V-2	Determine the chart ruler's overall condition by using dignities and debilities, house, and aspect placements with an orb range of 0°-8°.	If the Chart Ruler is functioning harmoniously or inharmoniously.

ASCENDANT	CHART RULER(S)	HOUSE PLACEMENT	SIGN PLACEMENT	E/R/D/F
♏	♂ & ♇	10 & 3	♌ & ♑	NONE

♂

ASPECT	GLPYPH	ORB
Solar return Mars in Leo conjoin Solar return Venus in Leo	sr. ♂♌ ☌ sr. ♀♌	4
Solar return Mars in Leo conjoin Solar return Leo Midheaven	sr. ♂♌ ☌ sr. MC♌	4
Solar return Mars in Leo oppose Solar return Jupiter in Pisces	sr. ♂♌ ☍ sr. ♃♓	7

♇

ASPECT	GLPYPH	ORB
Solar return Pluto in Capricorn oppose Solar return Sun in Cancer	sr.♇♑ ☍ sr.☉♋	2
Solar return Pluto in Capricorn sextile Solar return Neptune in Pisces	sr.♇♑ ✶ sr.♆♓	2

2A	II-6	Determine the Sun's house location.	Major themes that are activated for that year.
2B	II-5	Determine any aspects made to the Sun with an orb range of 0°-8°.	Overall condition of the year ahead.

HOUSE	ASPECTS	
9	GLYPH	ORB
	sr. ☉♋ ☍ sr. ♆♑	2
	sr. ☉♋ △ sr.♆♓	5
	sr. ☉♋ □ sr. ASC♏	7

3A	II-6	Determine the Moon's house location.	Inner themes for that year.
3B	II-5	Determine any aspects made to the Moon with an orb range of 0°-8°.	Overall condition of these explorations.

HOUSE	ASPECTS	
2	**GLYPH**	**ORB**
	sr. ☽♐ ⚹ sr. ♄♒	4
	sr. ☽♐ □ sr. ♃♓	6

4	V-2	Determine the condition of all other planets using dignities and debilities, sign and house placements, and aspects with an orb range of 0°-5°.		Various strengths and weaknesses for the year based on the planetary condition within.

PLANET	SIGN PLACEMENT	HOUSE PLACEMENT	E/R/D/F	ASPECTS	
☿	♋	9	NONE	**GLYPH**	**ORB**
				sr. ☿♋ ⚹ sr. ♅♉	0
♀	♌	10	NONE	**GLYPH**	**ORB**
				sr. ♀♌ ☍ sr. ♃♓	3
♃	♓	4	RULER	**GLYPH**	**ORB**
				sr. ♃♓ △ sr. ASC♏	4
♄	♒	3	RULER	**GLYPH**	**ORB**
				sr. ♄♒ □ sr. ♅♉	3
♅	♉	7	N/A	**GLYPH**	**ORB**
				sr. ♅♉ □ sr. MC♌	5
♆	♓	4	N/A	ALREADY MENTIONED ABOVE	

5	V-2	Determine the house ruler for each of the 12 houses.	Areas that will similarly manifest strongly or weakly depending on the condition of the planetary house ruler(s).

HOUSE	RULER	HOUSE	RULER
ASC/1	♂ & ♆	DC/7	♀
2	♃	8	☿
3	♄	9	☽
IC/4	♄ & ♅	MC/10	☉
5	♃ & ♆	11	☿
6	♂	12	♀

6		Compose a summary of your findings from Steps 1A-5.	Summary of Analysis.

Client A's solar return chart shows that it is a good time for career and romance. As far as career is concerned, this is shown by the chart ruler Mars in conjunction to the Midheaven (sr. ♂♌ ☌ sr. MC♌) and residing in the 10th house while ruling the 6th house. This tells me that if Client A works hard, especially on tasks that might seem redundant or repetitive, they will nevertheless achieve a great deal in the long run. Mars ruling the 6th also tells me this is a good year for Client A to focus on health issues and general routines that are beneficial, like daily walks or eating meals at the appropriate time. For romance, this is shown with the chart ruler Mars in conjunction to Venus (sr. ♂♌ ☌ sr. ♀♌), which also rules the 7th house in this chart. This not only adds passion to relationships, it helps give Client A courage in meeting new people because others respect their candor. However, it should be noted that these achievements and newly developed confidence does not come easy with chart ruler Mars in opposition to Jupiter, and chart ruler Pluto in opposition to the Sun (sr. ♂♌ ☍ sr. ♃♓, sr.♇♑ ☍ sr.☉♋). This tells me that Client A will have to shed their skin a bit and overcome previous insecurities in order to reap the benefits of Mars this year. They can do this by taking chances, admitting what needs to be released in terms of psychological baggage and thinking, and incorporate an overall confidence that might not have been there in the past.

Indeed, the biggest hurdle to overcome involves some sort of psychological transformation that is brought on by the solar return Sun in a square to the Ascendant and solar return Moon in a square to Jupiter (sr. ☉♋ □ sr. ASC♏, sr. ☽♐ □ sr. ♃♓). Again, nothing is going to come easy for Client A, but if they work hard and try to function in a detail-oriented way, they can overcome past insecurities that have been haunting them for a while now.

The solution lies with the solar return Sun's trine to Neptune and the solar return Moon's sextile to Saturn (sr. ☉♋ △ sr.♆♓, sr. ☽♐ ✶ sr. ♄♒). With Saturn ruling the 3rd and 4th house in the chart, Client A simply needs to talk it out, especially with people in their family. Additionally, with Neptune ruling the 5th house, Client A needs to take a step back and enjoy life more instead of being overcome by the harshness that life can sometimes bring. This is a time where they need to not sweat the small stuff, enjoy some of life's pleasures, and clear the air by discussing what has been on their mind. Again, this is a slow process that only brings just as much benefits as

Client A puts into their efforts. Nevertheless, this is a great year to work on goals, rely on those that they can rely upon, increase their romantic and sexual encounters, and take chances using newly developed confidence.

The way to get there is to have faith that it will all work out in the end even though they may not know the outcome themself. This is because Jupiter is in a trine to the Ascendant, and Mercury is in a sextile to Uranus (sr. ♃ △ sr. ASC♏, sr. ☿ ✶ sr. ♅). With Jupiter ruling the 2nd and Uranus ruling the 4th, again, Client A can ground themselves through familiar and familial sources, which help them to create a solid base within. This allows them to tackle new challenges of which they are more than capable. The harder they try, the better the outcome.

CLIENT B: SOLAR RETURN CHART

Name: ♀ Client B
born on Su., 4 April 1993
in Greenville (Mercer County), PA (US)
80w23, 41n24

Time: 12:14 p.m.
Univ.Time: 16:14
Sid. Time: 23:44:25

Type: 32.GW 0.0-1 20-Mrz-2021

Solar Return 2021/2022 (Method: Web Style / Placidus)
Ref. place: Greenville (Mercer County), PA (US)
Date: 4 Apr. 2021
Time: 7:12:02 a.m.
Univ.Time: 11:12:02 a.m.

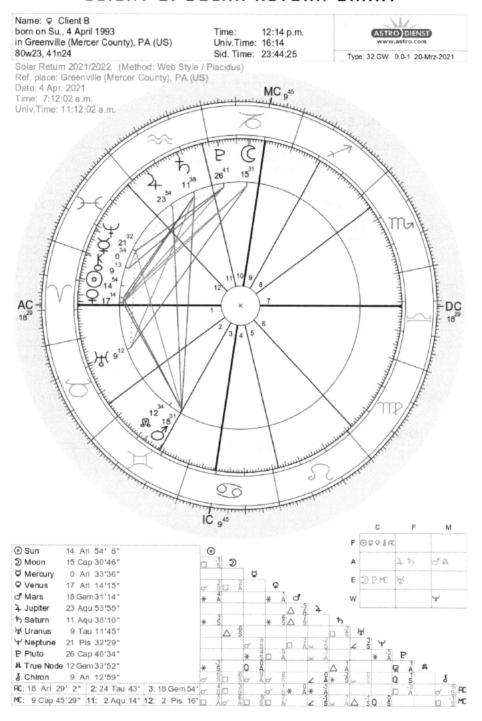

☉ Sun	14 Ari 54' 8"
☽ Moon	15 Cap 30'46"
☿ Mercury	0 Ari 33'36"
♀ Venus	17 Ari 14'15"
♂ Mars	18 Gem 31'14"
♃ Jupiter	23 Aqu 53'55"
♄ Saturn	11 Aqu 36'10"
♅ Uranus	9 Tau 11'45"
♆ Neptune	21 Pis 32'29"
♇ Pluto	26 Cap 40'34"
☊ True Node	12 Gem 33'52"
⚷ Chiron	9 Ari 12'59"

| AC: 18 Ari 29' 2" | 2: 24 Tau 43' | 3: 18 Gem 54' |
| MC: 9 Cap 45'29" | 11: 2 Aqu 14' | 12: 2 Pis 16' |

CLIENT B: SOLAR RETURN CHART ANALYSIS

1A	V-2	Determine the chart ruler by observing the ruler of the Ascendant			The main Planet of the chart.
1B	V-2	Determine the chart ruler's overall condition by using dignities and debilities, house, and aspect placements with an orb range of 0°-8°.			If the Chart Ruler is functioning harmoniously or inharmoniously.

ASCENDANT	CHART RULER(S)	HOUSE PLACEMENT	SIGN PLACEMENT	E/R/D/F
♈	♂	2	♊	NONE

♂		
ASPECT	**GLPYPH**	**ORB**
Solar return Mars in Gemini sextile Aries Ascendant	sr. ♂♊ ⚹ sr. ASC♈	0
Solar return Mars in Gemini sextile Solar return Sun in Aries	sr. ♂♊ ⚹ sr. ☉♈	1
Solar return Mars in Gemini sextile Solar return Venus in Aries	sr. ♂♊ ⚹ sr. ♀♈	1
Solar return Mars in Gemini square Solar Return Neptune in Pisces	sr. ♂♊ □ sr. ♆♓	3
Solar return Mars in Gemini trine Solar return Saturn in Aquarius	sr. ♂♊ △ sr. ♄♒	5

2A	II-6	Determine the Sun's house location.	Major themes that are activated for that year.
2B	II-5	Determine any aspects made to the Sun with an orb range of 0°-8°.	Overall condition of the year ahead.

HOUSE	ASPECTS	
12	**GLYPH**	**ORB**
	sr. ☉♈ □ sr. ☽♑	1
	sr. ☉♈ ☌ sr. ♀♈	2
	sr. ☉♈ ⚹ sr. ♄♒	3
	sr. ☉♈ ☌ sr. ASC♈	4
	sr. ☉♈ □ sr. MC♑	5

3A	II-6	Determine the Moon's house location.	Inner themes for that year.
3B	II-5	Determine any aspects made to the Moon with an orb range of 0°-8°.	Overall condition of these explorations.

<table>
<tr><th>HOUSE</th><th>ASPECTS</th></tr>
<tr><td>10</td><td><table>
<tr><th>GLYPH</th><th>ORB</th></tr>
<tr><td>sr. ☽♑ □ sr. ♀♈</td><td>2</td></tr>
<tr><td>sr. ☽♑ □ sr. ASC♈</td><td>3</td></tr>
<tr><td>sr. ☽♑ △ sr. ♅♉</td><td>6</td></tr>
<tr><td>sr. ☽♑ ☌ sr. MC♑</td><td>6</td></tr>
</table></td></tr>
</table>

<table>
<tr><td>4</td><td>V-2</td><td colspan="2">Determine the condition of all other planets using dignities and debilities, sign and house placements, and aspects with an orb range of 0°-5°.</td><td>Various strengths and weaknesses for the year based on the planetary condition within.</td></tr>
<tr><th>PLANET</th><th>SIGN PLACEMENT</th><th>HOUSE PLACEMENT</th><th>E/R/D/F</th><th>ASPECTS</th></tr>
<tr><td>☿</td><td>♈</td><td>12</td><td>NONE</td><td><table><tr><th>GLYPH</th><th>ORB</th></tr><tr><td>sr. ☿♈ ⚹ sr. ♇♑</td><td>4</td></tr></table></td></tr>
<tr><td>♀</td><td>♈</td><td>12</td><td>DETRIMENT</td><td><table><tr><th>GLYPH</th><th>ORB</th></tr><tr><td>sr. ♀♈ ☌ sr. ASC♈</td><td>1</td></tr></table></td></tr>
<tr><td>♃</td><td>♒</td><td>11</td><td>NONE</td><td><table><tr><th>GLYPH</th><th>ORB</th></tr><tr><td>sr. ♃♒ ⚹ sr. ASC♈</td><td>5</td></tr></table></td></tr>
<tr><td>♄</td><td>♒</td><td>11</td><td>RULER</td><td><table><tr><th>GLYPH</th><th>ORB</th></tr><tr><td>sr. ♄♒ □ sr. ♅♉</td><td>2</td></tr></table></td></tr>
<tr><td>♅</td><td>♉</td><td>1</td><td>N/A</td><td><table><tr><th>GLYPH</th><th>ORB</th></tr><tr><td>sr. ♅♉ △ sr. MC♑</td><td>1</td></tr></table></td></tr>
<tr><td>♆</td><td>♓</td><td>12</td><td>N/A</td><td><table><tr><th>GLYPH</th><th>ORB</th></tr><tr><td>sr. ♆♓ ⚹ sr. ♇♑</td><td>5</td></tr></table></td></tr>
<tr><td>♇</td><td>♑</td><td>10</td><td>N/A</td><td>ALREADY MENTIONED ABOVE</td></tr>
</table>

5	V-2	Determine the house ruler for each of the 12 houses.		Areas that will similarly manifest strongly or weakly depending on the condition of the planetary house ruler(s).	
		HOUSE	**RULER**	**HOUSE**	**RULER**
		ASC/1	♂	DC/7	♀
		2	♀	8	♂ & ♇
		3	☿	9	♃
		IC/4	☽	MC/10	♄
		5	☉	11	♄ & ♅
		6	☿	12	♃ & ♆

6		Compose a summary of your findings from Steps 1A-5.	Summary of Analysis.

For Client B, their solar return is a chart of personal transformation that works in their favor if they are willing to accept certain truths. The good news is that the chart ruler Mars establishes multiple beneficial aspects between other planets (sr. ♂Ⅱ ⚹ sr. ASC♈, sr. ♂Ⅱ ⚹ sr. ☉♈, sr. ♂Ⅱ ⚹ sr. ♀♈, sr. ♂Ⅱ △ sr. ♄♒). For one, with Mars ruling the 8th house and Venus ruling the 2nd house, Client B might experience a promotion of some kind this year or some sort of financial upwind that allows for them to update their surroundings, which in turn breeds inner confidence. Additionally, with Saturn ruling the 10th and 11th houses, this is a great time to firm up friendships into some sort of permeance and to also work on long-term goals. The sextile to the Sun, which rules the 5th house, gives Client B an entirely new outlook on life, which allows for them to act more giddy and less rigid as they might have been in the recent past. The only exception to these auspicious placements involves the square between Mars and Neptune (sr. ♂Ⅱ □ sr. ♆♓). With Neptune ruling the 12th house, Client B needs to be mindful of individuals that might be offering the world to them all to realize later that they are being swindled. Similarly, it could be too easy for Client B to feel slightly cynical that things are working out a little too well for them right now. Because the chart ruler Mars is indicative of so many positive changes, it could cause Client B to think, "Ok, when is the other shoe going to drop?" This can breed anxiety and negative thinking, which could counter all of the positive energy coming their way if they are not too careful.

Client B needs to not worry about why the sudden windfall is occurring and should simply enjoy the benefits as they come and be thankful that the universe is providing even if it defies logic and reasoning.

Essentially, Client B needs to make sure that they are not their worst enemy during this year as evidenced by the Sun square to the Moon and Midheaven, and the Moon in a square to the Venus and Ascendant (sr. ☉♈ □ sr. ☽♑, sr. ☉♈ □ sr. MC♑ sr. ☽♑ □ sr. ♀♈, sr. ☽♑ □ sr. ASC♈). Unlike Client A, whose benefits seem to come out of hard work and personal output, for Client B at times they seem to come out of thin air. This makes Client B uncomfortable and doubt their own abilities and worthiness. This can seep into personal relationships with the square to Venus and internal struggles with the Sun square to the Moon. This is not a time for Client B to push forward because they are not in the right mindset. Instead, they need to work on personal issues and understand that while they do this, the universe will provide for them. Family and children can become a burden at this time with the 4th and 5th houses involved, and instead of running away from these issues, Client B should face them head-on and determine how they affect them on a personal level. This will make Client B more productive and lucid in the future because they are working out the internal struggles this year.

Client B should not fret because, in addition to the less ideal aspects listed above, their solar return Sun and Moon also make multiple beneficial aspects to other planets (sr. ☉♈ ☌ sr. ♀♈, sr. ☉♈ ✶ sr. ♄♒, sr. ☉♈ ☌ sr. ASC♈, sr. ☽♑ △ sr. ♅♉, sr. ☽♑ ☌ sr. MC♑). These aspects tell me that Client B will be surrounded by supportive friends, partners, and family. It is only themself that can close off all of this love and support if they allow to be consumed by their personal struggles and conflicts. It seems as though there is no more hiding these issues with others anymore and intimate ties are willing to help them process through these problems. It is up to Client B to allow for their help and support.

The good news is that this is more than possible with the solar return Mercury in sextile to Pluto (sr. ☿♈ ✶ sr. ♇♑). With Pluto ruling the 8th house and Mercury ruling the 3rd house, I would say this is a great time to seek counselors or put trust in their close connections enough to divulge their true feelings and conflicts. If they do, they will be able to let go of what is holding them down and will find open arms ready to hold them during the therapeutic process. Additionally, with solar return Venus in conjunction with the Ascendant and Jupiter in sextile to the Ascendant (sr. ♀♈ ☌ sr. ASC♈, sr. ♃♒ ✶ sr. ASC♈), makes this process easier than Client B might realize because they are being aided by these beneficial planets and aspects. With Jupiter ruling the 9th and 12th houses, it makes it easy for Client B to let go of their ego and to also find optimism when it might be hard at times. Regardless of how it manifests, their network of support becomes a safety net of sorts where Client B can vent, process, and release.

CLIENT C: SOLAR RETURN CHART

Name: ♀ Client C
born on We., 29 December 1993
in Asheville, NC (US)
82w33, 35n36

Time: 6:34 a.m.
Univ.Time: 11:34
Sid. Time: 12:35:33

ASTRO)DIENST
www.astro.com

Type: 32.GW 0.0-1 20-Mrz-2021

Solar Return 2021/2022 (Method: Web Style / Placidus)
Ref. place: Asheville, NC (US)
Date: 29 Dec. 2021
Time: 2:06:13 a.m.
Univ.Time: 7:06:13 a.m.

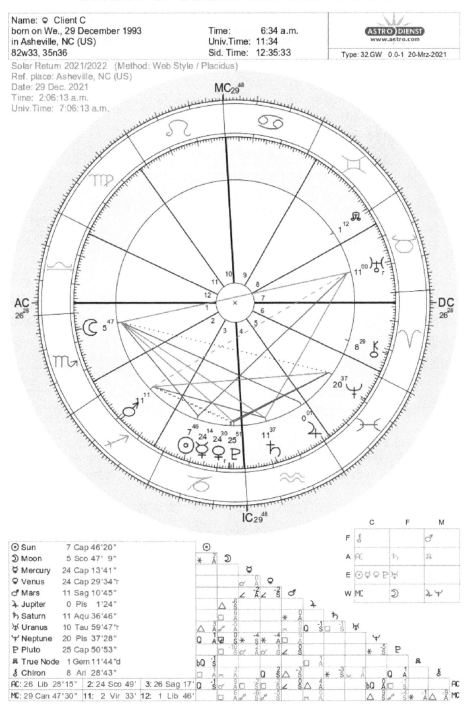

⊙ Sun	7 Cap 46'20"	
☽ Moon	5 Sco 47' 9"	
☿ Mercury	24 Cap 13'41"	
♀ Venus	24 Cap 29'34"r	
♂ Mars	11 Sag 10'45"	
♃ Jupiter	0 Pis 1'24"	
♄ Saturn	11 Aqu 36'46"	
♅ Uranus	10 Tau 59'47"r	
♆ Neptune	20 Pis 37'28"	
♇ Pluto	25 Cap 50'53"	
☊ True Node	1 Gem 11'44"d	
⚷ Chiron	8 Ari 28'43"	
AC: 26 Lib 28'15"	2: 24 Sco 49'	3: 26 Sag 17'
MC: 29 Can 47'30"	11: 2 Vir 33'	12: 1 Lib 46'

CLIENT C: SOLAR RETURN CHART ANALYSIS

1A	V-2	Determine the chart ruler by observing the ruler of the Ascendant	The main Planet of the chart.
1B	V-2	Determine the chart ruler's overall condition by using dignities and debilities, house, and aspect placements with an orb range of 0°-8°.	If the Chart Ruler is functioning harmoniously or inharmoniously.

ASCENDANT	CHART RULER(S)	HOUSE PLACEMENT	SIGN PLACEMENT	E/R/D/F
♎	♀	3	♑	NONE

♀		
ASPECT	**GLPYPH**	**ORB**
Solar return Venus in Capricorn conjoin Solar return Mercury in Capricorn	sr. ♀♑ ☌ sr. ☿♑	0
Solar return Venus in Capricorn conjoin Solar return Pluto in Capricorn	sr. ♀♑ ☌ sr. ♇♑	2
Solar return Venus in Capricorn square Libra Ascendant	sr. ♀♑ □ sr. ASC♎	2
Solar return Venus in Capricorn sextile Solar return Neptune in Pisces	sr. ♀♑ ⚹ sr. ♆♓	4
Solar return Venus in Capricorn oppose Cancer Midheaven	sr. ♀♑ ☍ sr. MC♋	5

2A	II-6	Determine the Sun's house location.	Major themes that are activated for that year.
2B	II-5	Determine any aspects made to the Sun with an orb range of 0°-8°.	Overall condition of the year ahead.

HOUSE	ASPECTS	
3	**GLYPH**	**ORB**
	sr. ☉♑ ⚹ sr. ☽♏	2
	sr. ☉♑ △ sr. ♅♉	3

3A	II-6	Determine the Moon's house location.	Inner themes for that year.
3B	II-5	Determine any aspects made to the Moon with an orb range of 0°-8°.	Overall condition of these explorations.

HOUSE	ASPECTS	
1	**GLYPH**	**ORB**
	sr. ☽♏ ☍ sr. ♅♉	5
	sr. ☽♏ □ sr. ♄♒	6
	sr. ☽♏ △ sr. ♃♓	6
	sr. ☽♏ □ sr. MC♋	6

4	V-2	Determine the condition of all other planets using dignities and debilities, sign and house placements, and aspects with an orb range of 0°-5°.			Various strengths and weaknesses for the year based on the planetary condition within.

PLANET	SIGN PLACEMENT	HOUSE PLACEMENT	E/R/D/F	ASPECTS	
☿	♑	3	NONE	**GLYPH**	**ORB**
				sr. ☿♑ ☌ sr. ♇♑	1
				sr. ☿♑ □ sr. ASC♎	2
				sr. ☿♑ ✶ sr. ♆♓	4
				sr. ☿♑ ☍ sr. MC♋	5
♂	♐	2	NONE	**GLYPH**	**ORB**
				sr. ♂♐ ✶ sr. ♄♒	0
♃	♓	4	RULER	**GLYPH**	**ORB**
				sr. ♃♒ △ sr. ASC♎	4
♄	♒	4	RULER	**GLYPH**	**ORB**
				sr. ♄♒ □ sr. ♅♉	1
♅	♉	7	N/A	ALREADY MENTIONED ABOVE	
♆	♓	5	N/A	**GLYPH**	**ORB**
				sr. ♆♓ ✶ sr. ♇♑	5
♇	♑	3	N/A	**GLYPH**	**ORB**
				sr. ♇♑ □ sr. ASC♎	1
				sr. ♇♑ ☍ sr. MC♋	4

5	V-2	Determine the house ruler for each of the 12 houses.		Areas that will similarly manifest strongly or weakly depending on the condition of the planetary house ruler(s).	
		HOUSE	**RULER**	**HOUSE**	**RULER**
		ASC/1	♀	DC/7	♂
		2	♂ & ♇	8	♀
		3	♃	9	☿
		IC/4	♄	MC/10	☽
		5	♃ & ♇	11	☿
		6	♂	12	♀

6		Compose a summary of your findings from Steps 1A-5.	Summary of Analysis.

Client C's chart ruler, Venus, is in retrograde while their solar return takes place for this year. This tells me that the majority of their year will revolve around processing feelings and events from previous partners. This is confirmed by the chart ruler Venus in conjunction to Mercury and Pluto (sr. ♀♑ ☌ sr. ☿♑, sr. ♀♑ ☌ sr. ♇♑). It could be possible that an old acquaintance reaches Client C out of the blue to wish them a happy birthday. From that encounter, it brings up a lot of unprocessed feelings that Client C might have felt they have processed a while ago only to have them come back up again, which brings frustration, unwanted feelings, and irritability that is hard to hide with Venus in square to the Ascendant (sr. ♀♑ □ sr. ASC♎). The solution is simply forgiveness instead of dwelling on feelings and people from the past due to the sextile between Venus and Neptune (sr. ♀♑ ✶ sr. ♆♓). Some sort of unfinished business can be brought up this year, but Client C should try to not ponder too much about whose fault it was or who did what to whom. They should capitalize off of the Neptune energy and try hard to let it go. The reason why it these issues are coming up now is to show them that it still needs to be processed and they are able to do just that.

With so much 3rd house energy involved, open communication is key. The good news is with solar return Sun in sextile to Moon and trine to Uranus (sr. ☉♑ ✶ sr. ☽♏, sr. ☉♑ △ sr. ♅♉), they can approach their feelings and opinions with a clear head and an objective viewpoint. This might have differed from the past when they were still emotionally involved and therefore subjective in their thoughts. Now that some time has passed, there is a fresh perspective that helps Client C to approach the issues at hand with a more level head.

This not a time for Client C to work on career or long-term goals because their unwanted and unneeded baggage is preventing them from being able to focus on anything else at this time as evidenced by the solar return Moon in square to the Midheaven and Saturn (sr. ☽♏ □ sr. MC♋, sr. ☽♏ □ sr. ♄♒). They should also be aware that although their friends are there to support them, they are not going to tolerate any victim mentality or venting just for the sake of venting due to the solar return Moon opposition to Uranus (sr. ☽♏ ☍ sr. ♅♉). This could inadvertently cause conflict between those that are trying to help them. However, with the solar return Moon trine to Jupiter, which rules the 3rd house (sr. ☽♏ △ sr. ♃♓), this is less common because Jupiter is helping Client C to voice themself more directly than in the past when they were more emotionally charged. If Client C can be truthful and trustworthy to talk directly to the issues that arise now with those that are willing to listen, then this is the year when they will finally be able to leave their emotional ties to their exes for good.

With solar return Mercury in conjunction to Pluto and square to the Ascendant, and Pluto in square to the Ascendant (sr. ☿♑ ☌ sr. ♇♑, sr. ☿♑ □ sr. ASC♎, sr. ♇♑ □ sr. ASC♎) there is no getting around what needs to be addressed. Furthermore, the more they fight the process of letting go, the more foolish they look to others for their illogical behavior. This can also hinder any first-impressions Client C could be trying to make at this time because they can come off as immature.

Nevertheless, with solar return Mars' sextile to Saturn, Mercury's sextile to Neptune and Jupiter's trine to the Ascendant (sr. ♂♐ ✶ sr. ♄♒, sr. ☿♑ ✶ sr. ♆♓, sr. ♃♒ △ sr. ASC♎), the more they can let go of their ego and work on what needs to be worked on, then they will appear incredibly mature and inspirational towards others. In other words, this process is easy and doable if Client C allows it to be so. The more they can forgive and forget, the more the universe rewards them with a clear head and heart which they can utilize in the future.

CLIENT D: SOLAR RETURN CHART

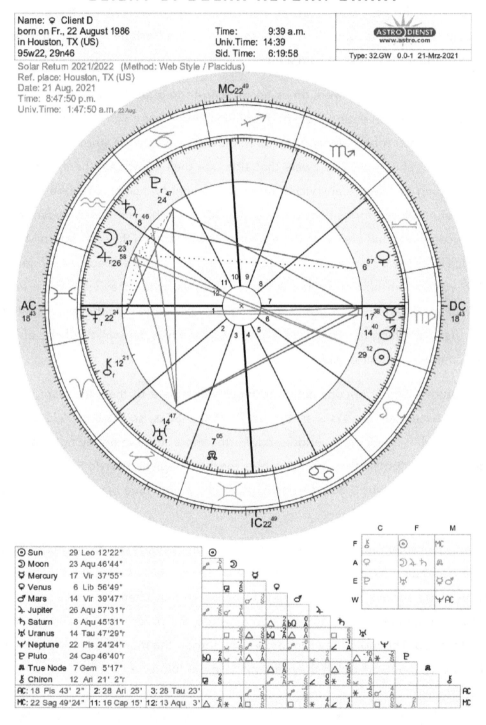

Name: ♀ Client D
born on Fr., 22 August 1986
in Houston, TX (US)
95w22, 29n46

Time: 9:39 a.m.
Univ. Time: 14:39
Sid. Time: 6:19:58

ASTRO DIENST
www.astro.com

Type: 32.GW 0.0-1 21-Mrz-2021

Solar Return 2021/2022 (Method: Web Style / Placidus)
Ref. place: Houston, TX (US)
Date: 21 Aug. 2021
Time: 8:47:50 p.m.
Univ.Time: 1:47:50 a.m. 22 Aug.

		C	F	M
F	☿	☉	MC
A	♀	☽♃♄	☊
E	♇	♅	☿♂
W			♆ AC

☉ Sun	29 Leo 12'22"
☽ Moon	23 Aqu 46'44"
☿ Mercury	17 Vir 37'55"
♀ Venus	6 Lib 56'49"
♂ Mars	14 Vir 39'47"
♃ Jupiter	26 Aqu 57'31"r
♄ Saturn	8 Aqu 45'31"r
♅ Uranus	14 Tau 47'29"r
♆ Neptune	22 Pis 24'24"r
♇ Pluto	24 Cap 46'40"r
☊ True Node	7 Gem 5'17"
⚷ Chiron	12 Ari 21' 2"r

AC: 18 Pis 43' 2" 2: 28 Ari 25' 3: 28 Tau 23'
MC: 22 Sag 49'24" 11: 16 Cap 15' 12: 13 Aqu 3'

CLIENT D: SOLAR RETURN CHART ANALYSIS

1A	V-2	Determine the chart ruler by observing the ruler of the Ascendant	The main Planet of the chart.
1B	V-2	Determine the chart ruler's overall condition by using dignities and debilities, house, and aspect placements with an orb range of 0°-8°.	If the Chart Ruler is functioning harmoniously or inharmoniously.

ASCENDANT	CHART RULER(S)	HOUSE PLACEMENT	SIGN PLACEMENT	E/R/D/F
♓	♃ & ♆	12 & 1	♒ & ♓	NONE

♃

ASPECT	GLPYPH	ORB
Solar return Jupiter in Aquarius oppose Solar return Sun in Leo	sr. ♃♒ ☍ sr. ☉♌	2
Solar return Jupiter in Aquarius conjoin Solar return Moon in Aquarius	sr. ♃♒ ☌ sr. ☽♒	3
Solar return Jupiter in Aquarius sextile Solar return Sagittarius Midheaven	sr. ♃♒ ✶ sr. MC♐	4

♆

ASPECT	GLPYPH	ORB
Solar return Neptune in Pisces square Solar return Sagittarius Midheaven	sr. ♆♓ □ sr. MC♐	0
Solar return Neptune in Pisces sextile Solar return Pluto in Capricorn	sr. ♆♓ ✶ sr. ♇♑	2
Solar return Neptune in Pisces conjoin Solar return Pisces Ascendant	sr. ♆♓ ☌ sr. ASC♓	4
Solar return Neptune in Pisces oppose Solar return Mercury in Virgo	sr. ♆♓ ☍ sr. ☿♍	5
Solar return Neptune in Pisces oppose Solar return Mars in Virgo	sr. ♆♓ ☍ sr. ♂♍	8

2A	II-6	Determine the Sun's house location.	Major themes that are activated for that year.
2B	II-5	Determine any aspects made to the Sun with an orb range of 0°-8°.	Overall condition of the year ahead.

HOUSE	ASPECTS	
6	**GLYPH**	**ORB**
	sr. ☉♌ ☍ sr. ☽♒	5
	sr. ☉♌ △ sr. MC♐	6

3A	II-6	Determine the Moon's house location.	Inner themes for that year.
3B	II-5	Determine any aspects made to the Moon with an orb range of 0°-8°.	Overall condition of these explorations.

HOUSE	ASPECTS	
12	**GLYPH**	**ORB**
	sr. ☽♒ ✶ sr. MC♐	1

4	V-2	Determine the condition of all other planets using dignities and debilities, sign and house placements, and aspects with an orb range of 0°-5°.	Various strengths and weaknesses for the year based on the planetary condition within.

PLANET	SIGN PLACEMENT	HOUSE PLACEMENT	E/R/D/F	ASPECTS	
☿	♍	6	RULER EXALTATION	**GLYPH**	**ORB**
				sr. ☿♍ ☍ sr. ASC♓	1
				sr. ☿♍ ☌ sr. ♂♍	3
				sr. ☿♍ △ sr. ♅♉	3
				sr. ☿♍ ☍ sr. ♆♓	5
				sr. ☿♍ □ sr. MC♐	5
♀	♎	7	RULER	**GLYPH**	**ORB**
				sr. ♀♎ △ sr. ♄♒	2
♂	♍	6	RULER	**GLYPH**	**ORB**
				sr. ♂♍ △ sr. ♅♉	0
				sr. ♂♍ ☍ sr. ASC♓	4
♄	♒	11	RULER	ALREADY MENTIONED ABOVE	

♅	♉	2	N/A	GLYPH		ORB
				sr. ♅♉ ✶ sr. ASC♓		4
♆	♑	11	N/A	ALREADY MENTIONED ABOVE		

5	V-2	Determine the house ruler for each of the 12 houses.		Areas that will similarly manifest strongly or weakly depending on the condition of the planetary house ruler(s).	
		HOUSE	**RULER**	**HOUSE**	**RULER**
		ASC/1	♃ & ♆	DC/7	☿
		2	♂	8	♀
		3	♀	9	♂ & ♆
		IC/4	☿	MC/10	♃
		5	☽	11	♄
		6	☉	12	♄ & ♅

6		Compose a summary of your findings from Steps 1A-5.	Summary of Analysis.

The chart ruler Jupiter within Client D's solar return chart is indicative of a very beneficial year with a conjunction to the Moon, opposition to the Sun, and sextile to the Midheaven (sr. ♃♒ ♂ sr. ☽♒, sr. ♃♒ ☍ sr. ☉♌, sr. ♃♒ ✶ sr. MC♐). This is a very mystical time for Client D and there could be some form of spiritual awakening that occurs. This is also a good time for Client D to brush up on their spiritual philosophy and incorporate meditative and other techniques where they can connect to the heavenly realm. Indeed, with the other chart ruler, Neptune, in conjunction to the Ascendant (sr. ♆♓ ♂ sr. ASC♓), Client D can become quite consumed by the process, which could adversely become an Achille's heel if they are not too careful.

This is due to the chart ruler Neptune in square to the Midheaven and opposition to Mercury and Mars (sr. ♆♓ □ sr. MC♐, sr. ♆♓ ☍ sr. ☿♍, sr. ♆♓ ☍ sr. ♂♍). It could be that Client D's newfound pursuits can engulf them to a point where all other matters disappear in the pursuit of higher spiritual knowledge. Client D should remember moderation and maintain one foot in the ethereal realm and another foot in the practical realm. Even if practical matters do not interest them at this time. Otherwise, it is possible that misunderstandings and conflict arise out of their perceived disinterest in others and towards their occupation. It could be that their spiritual exploration makes everything else seem meaningless in comparison, but unless they continue to put just as much effort towards the real world, then their spiritual world will likewise suffer because they are not staying grounded.

The other reason why this is not a good time to lose this sort of self-interest is because this is a good year to get noticed due to solar return Sun's trine to the Midheaven and the Moon's sextile to the Midheaven (sr. ☉♌ △ sr. MC♐, sr. ☽♒ ✶ sr. MC♐). This does wonders for their reputation and superiors begin to notice their hard work, dedication, and emotional investment. Being noticed by their superiors is also due to the solar return Venus in trine Saturn (sr. ♀♎ △ sr. ♄♒). It would be a shame for Client D to waste this opportunity by having their head too much in the clouds. As such, there could be added responsibilities and an increased workload because they are being expected to deal with more obligations. Instead of shutting down and exploring more of the otherworldly as they would like, they need to equally buckle down and show that they are capable of the trust that has been placed upon them at this time.

Due to Client D's exploration into the unexplainable, their Mercury during the solar return reflects the difficulty of coming back down into the world where words, facts, and figures become important once again. This is because Mercury squares the Midheaven and opposes the Ascendant and Neptune (sr. ☿♍ □ sr. MC♐, sr. ☿♍ ☍ sr. ASC♓, sr. ☿♍ ☍ sr. ♆♓). This explains why Client D would rather avoid that kind of work altogether; it is unusually difficult to find the right words and explanations for things. It consumes more time and energy than it normally would at other times. Client D needs to fight through these frustrations and budget the extra time it will take to get their thoughts on paper.

Solar return Uranus is helping out Client D a lot this year with a trine to Mercury and Mars, and a sextile to the Ascendant (sr. ☿♍ △ sr. ♅♉, sr. ♂♍ △ sr. ♅♉, sr. ♅♉ ✶ sr. ASC♓). Again, with Uranus ruling the 12th house, this gives Client D an open mind and new perspective to welcome in new paradigms of looking at the universe and their place within. This motivates Client D to explore these realms in the first place, and they will certainly witness a transformation in how they respond to the world around them due to these explorations for the better. They will learn to not sweat the small stuff or to not get so caught up in conflicts because their view of the world and the universe is expanding during this time. This improves their relationships with others because it makes them more amicable and approachable. In a way, this is the key to balance Client D's desire to explore spiritual goals and the need to be grounded in reality. If they take the lessons they learn from their metaphysical explorations and apply them towards how they approach the world, then they are integrating higher ideals and philosophies into daily encounters. This is how Client D can reap the benefits of their mystical journeys.

CLIENT E SOLAR RETURN CHART

Name: ♀ Client E
born on Sa., 16 July 1988
in Morristown (Morris County), NJ (US)
74w29, 40n48

Time: 6:13 a.m.
Univ.Time: 10:13
Sid. Time: 0:52:57

ASTRO·DIENST
www.astro.com
Type: 32.GW 0.0-1 22-Mrz-2021

Solar Return 2021/2022 (Method: Web Style / Placidus)
Ref. place: Morristown (Morris County), NJ (US)
Date: 16 July 2021
Time: 5:45:23 a.m.
Univ.Time: 9:45:23 a.m.

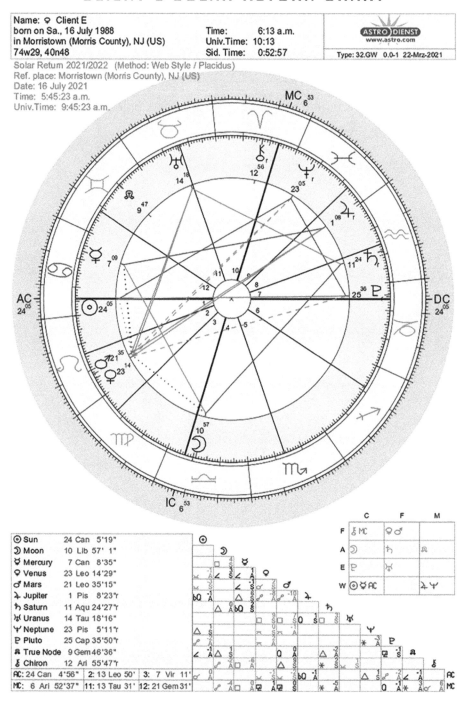

☉ Sun	24 Can	5'19"
☽ Moon	10 Lib	57' 1"
☿ Mercury	7 Can	8'35"
♀ Venus	23 Leo	14'29"
♂ Mars	21 Leo	35'15"
♃ Jupiter	1 Pis	8'23"r
♄ Saturn	11 Aqu	24'27"r
♅ Uranus	14 Tau	18'16"
♆ Neptune	23 Pis	5'11"r
♇ Pluto	25 Cap	35'50"r
☊ True Node	9 Gem	46'36"
⚷ Chiron	12 Ari	55'47"r

AC: 24 Can 4'56"	2: 13 Leo 50'	3: 7 Vir 11'
MC: 6 Ari 52'37"	11: 13 Tau 31'	12: 21 Gem 31'

CLIENT E: SOLAR RETURN CHART ANALYSIS

1A	V-2	Determine the chart ruler by observing the ruler of the Ascendant	The main Planet of the chart.
1B	V-2	Determine the chart ruler's overall condition by using dignities and debilities, house, and aspect placements with an orb range of 0°-8°.	If the Chart Ruler is functioning harmoniously or inharmoniously.

ASCENDANT	CHART RULER(S)	HOUSE PLACEMENT	SIGN PLACEMENT	E/R/D/F
♋	☽	4	♎	NONE

☽		

ASPECT	GLPYPH	ORB
Composite Moon in Libra trine Composite Saturn in Aquarius	sr. ☽♎ △ sr. ♄♒	0
Composite Moon in Libra square Composite Mercury in Cancer	sr. ☽♎ □ sr. ☿♋	4
Composite Moon in Libra oppose Aries Midheaven	sr. ☽♎ ☍ sr. MC♈	4

2A	II-6	Determine the Sun's house location.	Major themes that are activated for that year.
2B	II-5	Determine any aspects made to the Sun with an orb range of 0°-8°.	Overall condition of the year ahead.

HOUSE	ASPECTS	
1	GLYPH	ORB
	sr. ☉♋ ☌ sr. ASC♋	0
	sr. ☉♋ △ sr. ♆♓	1
	sr. ☉♋ ☍ sr. ♆♑	2

3A	II-6	Determine the Moon's house location.	Inner themes for that year.
3B	II-5	Determine any aspects made to the Moon with an orb range of 0°-8°.	Overall condition of these explorations.
HOUSE		ASPECTS	
SEE ABOVE			

4	V-2	Determine the condition of all other planets using dignities and debilities, sign and house placements, and aspects with an orb range of 0°-5°.		Various strengths and weaknesses for the year based on the planetary condition within.

PLANET	SIGN PLACEMENT	HOUSE PLACEMENT	E/R/D/F	ASPECTS	
☿	♋	12	NONE	**GLYPH**	**ORB**
				sr. ☿♋ □ sr. ASC♈	0
♀	♌	2	NONE	**GLYPH**	**ORB**
				sr. ♀♌ ☌ sr. ♂♌	2
♂	♌	2	NONE	ALREADY MENTIONED ABOVE	
♃	♓	8	RULER	NONE	
♄	♒	7	RULER	**GLYPH**	**ORB**
				sr. ♄♒ □ sr. ♅♉	3
				sr. ♄♒ ✶ MC♈	5
♅	♉	11	N/A	ALREADY MENTIONED ABOVE	
♆	♓	9	N/A	**GLYPH**	**ORB**
				sr. ♆♓ △ sr. ASC♋	1
				sr. ♆♓ ✶ sr. ♇♑	3
♇	♑	7	N/A	**GLYPH**	**ORB**
				sr. ♇♑ ☍ sr. ASC♋	2

5	V-2	Determine the house ruler for each of the 12 houses.		Areas that will similarly manifest strongly or weakly depending on the condition of the planetary house ruler(s).

HOUSE	RULER	HOUSE	RULER
ASC/1	☽	DC/7	♄
2	☉	8	♄ & ♅
3	☿	9	♃ & ♆
IC/4	♀	MC/10	♂
5	♂ & ♇	11	♀
6	♃	12	☿

6		Compose a summary of your findings from Steps 1A-5.	Summary of Analysis.

Client E will spend a lot of their solar return focused on improving their reputation and how they portray themself out into the world due to the chart ruler Moon trine Saturn and oppose the Midheaven, and the Sun conjoin the Ascendant (sr. ☽♎ △ sr. ♄♒, sr. ☽♎ ☍ sr. MC♈, sr. ☉♋ ☌ sr. ASC♋). With Saturn ruling the 7th and 8th houses, this is great year for Client E to network with people that can help them to get ahead in career maters or with people that have resources they can use to achieve similar goals. Client E is putting on a positive and friendly face, which others gravitate towards which cause them to trust Client E and be willing to work cooperatively. What helps with this is the solar return Sun trine to Neptune (sr. ☉♋ △ sr. ♆♓). This makes it so Client E does not seem intimidating and a team player which others enjoy witnessing. Indeed, Client E understands the need for cooperation and is able to release any ego drives to where they can work well with others towards the same goal.

However, Client E needs to make sure to not overstep any bounds due to the solar return Moon in a square to Mercury (sr. ☽♎ □ sr. ☿♋). With Mercury ruling the 3rd and 12th houses, Client E might have a hard time communicating what they are trying to explain or want from the team. Instead, they should let others do the talking and Client E should do more of the directing and support. The issue is, due to the solar return's opposition to Pluto (sr. ☉♋ ☍ sr. ♇♑), power struggles can occur even though, ironically, people in power are greatly helping Client E at this time. The trick is to show appreciation by not pushing too much in taking the reins and micromanage all prospects of a job. The more egalitarian Client E approaches this year, the more the benefits will come their way.

With solar return Sun trine Neptune (sr. ☉♋ △ sr. ♆♓), others might come to them during this year for their advice. With Neptune ruling the 9th house, Client E's spiritual philosophy works well during these encounters as they can give sound wisdom to those who seek it. Similarly, this helps Client E to remove any ego drives that can cause conflict with others as mentioned above. Client E inherently trusts others and the universe that it will all work out in their favor. The more they can rely on this trust, the more things will unfold in this way, and rather effortlessly on their part.

Mercury does seem to be a troublemaker by squaring the Ascendant in the solar return chart (sr. ☿♋ □ sr. ASC♈). Again, this can cause others to misunderstand Client E, and Client E can also have a hard time explaining what they mean. This confirms that Client E should let others do more of the talking, and they should act more in the background, adjusting situations and outcomes as needed.

Client E's romantic life receives a nice spark of passion with solar return Venus conjoin Mars (sr. ♀♌ ☌ sr. ♂♌). Client E can expect to explore newly found desires with their partner, which will help with their emotional connection in the long-term. This aspect also helps them to utilize their leadership abilities with Mars ruling the 10th. With Venus ruling the 4th, Client E connects with people on an emotional level which encourages them to work cooperatively with Client E. In other words, the more Client E relates to others with emotions instead of words is the answer to how they can bring in their skillset to whatever befalls them during this year.

Many outer planets establish aspects to the Ascendant and Midheaven (sr. ♄♒ ✶ MC♈, sr. ♆♓ △ sr. ASC♋, sr. ♇♑ ☍ sr. ASC♋). For the most part, these connections help Client E in multiple ways. With Saturn's sextile to the Midheaven, this reiterates Client E's ability to network and be part of a team that reaches some sort of goal. This helps their career both in the short-term and long-term. Neptune's trine to the Ascendant makes it easy for others to approach Client E because they are showing a calm and collective demeanor that tells others that they are not their enemy but their friend who can empathize. Therefore, Client E can expect to play the counselor and go-to friend for others who are experiencing moments of crises. The Pluto opposition to the Ascendant again confirms that the more Client E uses their skills to establish power, but does not abuse that power, the more others will be willing to work with them and under their leadership. Overall, Client E can expect a year where they are able to utilize their leadership potential at work, and their healing skills with close friends who will rely on them during this time. They will also experience a nice romantic connection with their partner, which will reignite their passions and love.

* * *

From an economic point of view, one of the benefits of offering solar return charts is that it encourages your clients to visit you on a yearly basis. At these yearly sessions, you can inform them of their year ahead not only through the solar return chart, but through their transits and progressions as well. The solar return chart is simply a good marketing tool you can use to obtain loyal and dedicated clients.

Either way, the solar return chart helps to lay out major themes that the individual will encounter and will process during that year. This gives individuals short-term goals and expectations that might not otherwise be there with transits and progressions. In general, the solar return encompasses those same events by creating a better context for the year in which the progressions and transits occur within.

* * *

Now having learned all the methods found within Parts V, VI, and now VII, you are well equipped to handle any sort of difficult question that yourself or your client might have. Truly, no stone will be left unturned now that you understand how to view a birth chart from all these various perspectives. All that is left is practice, patience, and perseverance. I wish you the best of luck when it comes to establishing your own astrological skills, and I hope that your methods and practice go beyond the scope of this book as you learn to personalize your theories and procedures. With your continued exploration, astrology can and will indeed flourish well into the 21st century and beyond. You should feel a great sense of accomplishment and honor for being a part of this ancient and incredibly important human science.

THE FOOL'S JOURNEY, POEM BY DOSAJNA

Who is the god we worship now?
Where is our dying savior?
I've come to seek the meaning
Behind my trials and my labors

* * *

I've searched and sought
And then I thought
What is that primal force?

We cannot see
But there it be
Guiding us on its course

Who is the one that sees it all?
Who makes this world so dense?
It's hard to grasp when there's just me
And they are omniscient

Is there a hand that guides the tide?
Who creates stillness out of the chaotic?
And while the world lays back and simply abides
I must comprehend the cosmic and its logic

I see the fine
Invisible lines
That have caused us such great distress

The countless wars
That I do abhor
Where only the victors are considered blessed

You are my brother
And yet, you suffer
Are we under the right persuasion?

Like night to the dawn
Children are now forgone
'Tis the consequences of causation?

I need to know what it's all for
The meaning behind my birth
Out of all of the galaxies and planets
I could possibly explore
Why, god, planet Earth?

Prepared and packed,
I grabbed my sack
I have but one simple plea:

That when I return
I'll no longer yearn
For my inquiry

I kissed farewell
And then I yelled,
"Will no one come with me?"

The silence only grew
And that's when I knew
This was but my journey

I took my map and
I plotted the points
Of whom I planned to meet

The wisest, the brightest who
have proven themselves
Amongst the chaff, they are the wheat

590

I walk through the pine
With my trusty canine
I have her as my only companion

No longer afraid
Of the rugged terrain
I pass over hills, and valleys, and canyons

Every step must be pondered
Every trail must be crossed
I am following the footsteps of many
And many have become lost

Days have passed
But then, at last!
I have reached the first one on my list
Chivalrous in his robes
He stood next to his globe
The noble scientist

"Who is the god we worship now?
Where is our dying savior?
I've come to seek the meaning
Behind my trials and my labors."

"Since long before,"
He said with a roar,
"To the times of Emperor Nero

Man knew his life was a paradox, you see,
And that's why god is the number zero."

"I think I understand," I said,
"But something is still amiss
For before nothing can become nothing,
Does not something have to exist?"

"Get out! Get out! You blasphemous child!
I'll have none of that nonsense here!"
I replied,
"I don't understand, I'm just trying to understand
But you shroud yourself in darkness, in fear."

He did not take that well
I was out in a spell
From him, I have learned all that I can

Still, I press forth
Adherent to my course
To the house of the rich businessman

I was greeted there by sixty servants
In front of a mansion made of solid gold
I explained to them my journey's purpose
And they took me in from out of the cold

After many halls and many doors
Into the library I was led
Countless books had covered the walls
But how many were actually read?

Behind his desk
His eyes did express
A piercing penetrative prophet

Slightly snide
He stood there with pride
Gazing over the quarterly profits

"Who is the god we worship now?
Where is our dying savior?
I've come to seek the meaning
Behind my trials and my labors."

He grabbed his graphs
And said with a laugh,
"God has no real power

It's loans to lend
And dividends
Is how I built my tower!

It's gold, and silver, and yens, and euros,
That is what's placed upon the altar
Don't you see, my boy, there is nothing
in this world more sacred
Then that of the all-mighty dollar!

This is the god we worship now!
This is our only savior!"

I replied,
"But you are flesh, and breath,
and brains, and blood
And money is only paper.

You say that money makes the world go 'round
And that is thanks to our economy
But at what cost is everything lost
Including our autonomy?"

"My boy," he said
"You've been misled
Where you see people, I see mice

It's quite naïve
To think you're a son of Eve
Even a human body has its price.

Now leave! Get lost! I want you gone!
And don't even think about touching my décor!"
Ever since I started this journey, I thought,
I'm even more confused than I ever was before

Why can't I discover what it's all for?
What is this mischievous scheme?
I'm seeking answers, they are preaching lore
Those men of such high esteem!

That's it! I'm gone!
I will not press on!
And I wept started to grieve

I feel jolted and whirled
By this cruel world
Whose evils I cannot conceive

Then in an alarm
I felt on my arm
The wet nose of my trusty companion

No longer afraid
Of the mess I have made
I pass over hills, and valleys, and canyons

I take a deep breath
Feeling so close to death
As I navigate along with my compass

There is still one force
Who can put me on the right course
And her name is aptly, Justice

She lived on top of the highest mountain
Over the wilted and the wise
And although the whole world was under her feet
She could not see it with her eyes

I was over swept
With merriment
With her I could not fail

No troubled youth
Could mend the truth
Which lay upon her scales

"Who is the god we worship now?
Where is our dying savior?
I've come to seek the meaning
Behind my trials and my labors."

She said,
"Have no doubts
There is only one route
For fairness is seen in my courts

But lines can blur
As humans err
And judges can easily become coerced

Yes, it is true
I do protect you
And I can save the poor, the petty, and the weak
But all it takes is some weight on my scales
And I cannot help but to take a peek

The system is flawed
There is no god
I ignite the entropy

Along with my gavel
I have seen lives unravel
And adhere to my destiny

Just try and change the rules
You fool
But the world still lays in apathy

You cannot contend
With the judicial web
That harnesses my faculty!

The questions stop here
I am the puppeteer
And by now as you probably have guessed

An influential one
Has placed a heave sum
And I am now placing you under arrest!"

She grabbed her sword
And headed towards me
I was ready to put up a fight!

But then in a beat
My dog took a leap
And bit her with all of her might

The instant flickered
Yet I couldn't help but snicker
"For a woman who is so attuned

You may be smart
But when it comes to a dog's bark
It appears you aren't immune!"

Then I ran, and ran, and ran down the hill
Attempting not to fall or skid
And as night crept over the mountains near by
Into the forest I went and hid

That's it! No more!
I have been scalped to my core!
There is no answer! I have tried!

Then up in the clouds
A mysterious voice said aloud
"Have you ever bothered to look inside?

Have you ever dared to quiet your mind?
And calm your conscious streak?
How do you expect god to voice themself
If you do not make room for them to speak?

Look past the fine
Invisible lines
Reach out and feel the affection

Since time began
Your fellow man
Has always been nothing but an honest reflection

Where is humanity's integrity?
Lost in the hostility?
Peace is god's only cannon

And though demons do exist
Out from the abyss
God is not war, nor anger, nor famine

Have you ever taken the time to
see the beauty of it all?
From the dolphin to the flower to the hare?
Like a string of pearls, we are all one
And god is always there

Humankind is sick
Humankind is trapped
Always clenching the other one's fist

Abundance for all
We can have it all
And this is god's only wish

When it is all said and done
The answer always equals one
One planet, one peoples, one om
Distractions only go so far
And it is time to fix your home

So, the answer that you so seek, my boy,
Is so simple,
Don't you see?

You are the dying savor
And your labor
Is to set the Earth
And your heart
Free"